# REA's Test Prep Books Are The Best!
## (a sample of the <u>hundreds of letters</u> REA receives each year)

" I did well because of your wonderful prep books... I just wanted to thank you for helping me prepare for these tests. "
*Student, San Diego, CA*

" My students report your chapters of review as the most valuable single resource they used for review and preparation. "
*Teacher, American Fork, UT*

" Your book was such a better value and was so much more complete than anything your competition has produced—and I have them all! "
*Teacher, Virginia Beach, VA*

" Compared to the other books that my fellow students had, your book was the most useful in helping me get a great score. "
*Student, North Hollywood, CA*

" Your book was responsible for my success on the exam, which helped me get into the college of my choice... I will look for REA the next time I need help. "
*Student, Chesterfield, MO*

" Just a short note to say thanks for the great support your book gave me in helping me pass the test... I'm on my way to a B.S. degree because of you! "
*Student, Orlando, FL*

*(more on next page)*

*(continued from front page)*

" I just wanted to thank you for helping me get a great score on the AP U.S. History exam... Thank you for making great test preps! "
*Student, Los Angeles, CA*

" Your *Fundamentals of Engineering Exam* book was the absolute best preparation I could have had for the exam, and it is one of the major reasons I did so well and passed the FE on my first try. "
*Student, Sweetwater, TN*

" I used your book to prepare for the test and found that the advice and the sample tests were highly relevant... Without using any other material, I earned very high scores and will be going to the graduate school of my choice. "
*Student, New Orleans, LA*

" What I found in your book was a wealth of information sufficient to shore up my basic skills in math and verbal... The section on analytical ability was excellent. The practice tests were challenging and the answer explanations most helpful. It certainly is the *Best Test Prep for the GRE*! "
*Student, Pullman, WA*

" I really appreciate the help from your excellent book. Please keep up the great work. "
*Student, Albuquerque, NM*

" I am writing to thank you for your test preparation... your book helped me immeasurably and I have nothing but praise for your *GRE* preparation. "
*Student, Benton Harbor, MI*

*(more on back page)*

# The Best Test Preparation for the

# AP Latin
## Vergil Exam
## Literature Exam

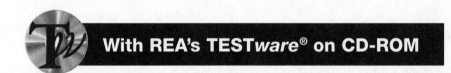 With REA's TEST*ware*® on CD-ROM

**Ronald B. Palma, M.A.**
Holland Hall School
Tulsa, OK

 **Research & Education Association**
*Visit our website at*
**www.rea.com**

**Research & Education Association**
61 Ethel Road West
Piscataway, New Jersey 08854
E-mail: info@rea.com

**The Best Test Preparation for the
AP LATIN: VERGIL EXAM &
LATIN LITERATURE EXAM**
With TEST*ware*® on CD-ROM

Printed in the United States of America

Library of Congress Control Number 2006933744

International Standard Book Number 0-7386-0293-0

Windows® is a registered trademark of Microsoft Corporation.

REA® and TEST*ware*® are registered trademarks of
Research & Education Association, Inc.

# CONTENTS

## About Our Author

**Ronald B. Palma** has been teaching Latin and other classics courses at Holland Hall School in Tulsa, Oklahoma, for the past 32 years. He holds an A.B. in Classics from Cornell University and an M.A. in Classics from the University of Cincinnati, where he did doctoral work funded by a Louise Taft Semple Fellowship. He has co-authored *Ecce Romani: A Latin Reading Program* (Prentice-Hall, 2005), now in its third edition, and is also the author of REA's *Best Test Preparation for the SAT Subject Test: Latin.* Palma has received numerous fellowships and awards for both teaching and scholarship, including Rockefeller and Fulbright grants, the Summer Fellowship of the Classical Society of the American Academy in Rome, a Presidential Scholar Award from the U.S. Department of Education, a Special Recognition Award from the College Board, and the Excellence in Pre-Collegiate Teaching Award from the American Philological Association.

The author, who invites comments on this book, may be reached by e-mail at *rpalma@hollandhall.org.*

## Author Acknowledgments

I would like to acknowledge and thank several individuals for their invaluable personal and professional support in the production of this book. Mille grazie to Diane Goldschmidt, Senior Editor, Research & Education Association, for her guidance and patience; to Tom Benediktson, Professor of Classics and Dean of the School of Arts and Sciences at the University of Tulsa, for his careful eye and his friendship; and lastly and most importantly, to Fay, my wife of 39 years, whose continual support throughout my career has given me both the opportunity and the confidence to share with others my love of the past.

## Dedication

This book is dedicated to my high school Latin teacher (1960–64), Marion Harvey, of Bernards High School in Bernardsville, New Jersey, where she taught Latin for thirty-four years. I hope to have inspired my students as she inspired me.

Ronald B. Palma
Holland Hall School
Tulsa, Oklahoma

## About Research & Education Association

Founded in 1959, Research & Education Association (REA) is dedicated to publishing the finest and most effective educational materials—including software, study guides, and test preps—for students in middle school, high school, college, graduate school, and beyond.

REA's test preparation series includes books and software for all academic levels in almost all disciplines. REA publishes test preps for students who have not yet entered high school, as well as high school students preparing to enter college. Students from countries around the world seeking to attend college in the United States will find the assistance they need in REA's publications. For college students seeking advanced degrees, REA publishes test preps for many major graduate school admission examinations in a wide variety of disciplines, including engineering, law, and medicine. Students at every level, in every field, with every ambition can find what they are looking for among REA's publications.

REA's publications and educational materials are highly regarded and continually receive an unprecedented amount of praise from professionals, instructors, librarians, parents, and students. Our authors are as diverse as the subject matter represented in the books we publish. They are well known in their respective disciplines and serve on the faculties of prestigious colleges and universities throughout the United States and Canada.

Today REA's wide-ranging catalog is a leading resource for teachers, students, and professionals.

We invite you to visit us at *www.rea.com* to find out how "REA is making the world smarter."

## Staff Acknowledgments

In addition to our author, we would like to thank Larry B. Kling, Vice President, Editorial, for supervising development; Pam Weston, Vice President, Publishing, for production integrity and managing the publication to completion; John Cording, Vice President, Technology, for coordinating the design and development of REA's TEST*ware*®; Diane Goldschmidt, Senior Editor, for coordinating revisions and quality assurance; Anne Winthrop Esposito, Senior Editor and Molly Solanki, Associate Editor, for editorial contributions; Heena Patel and Michelle Boykins-Smith, Technology Project Managers, for their design contributions and software testing efforts; Jeff LoBalbo, Senior Graphic Artist, for his graphic arts contributions and post-production file mapping, and Christine Saul, Senior Graphic Artist, for designing our cover.

We also gratefully acknowledge Dr. Tom Benediktson for technically reviewing the manuscript and Kathy Caratozzolo of Caragraphics for typesetting this edition.

# STUDY SCHEDULE
## AP Latin

Here is REA's suggested six-week study schedule to guide your prep for the AP Latin Exam. Depending on how soon you will be taking the exam, you can expand or condense this timetable. The key to gaining a firm command of the subject matter and the test itself is to set aside time each day for study. Once you commit to an activity, stick with it to the end. This will help ensure that you cover everything you need to be completely in control of the material—and the exam—come test day.

| Week | Activity |
|---|---|
| **1** | Read and study Chapter 1, General Content and Format of the AP Latin Exam for Vergil or Literature, which will introduce you to the AP Latin Examination. Depending on which exam you will be taking, read and study Chapter 2 or Chapter 3, which will give you specific information regarding the format and content of the AP Latin: Vergil or AP Latin Literature exam. |
| **2 and 3** | Use these weeks to read and study Chapters 4 through 11 to learn more specific information about the AP Latin exams. These chapters will tell you what you need to know for the exams as well as give you reliable on-line resources to explore to increase your knowledge of Latin. Answer all the practice questions included in the chapters and be sure to read and understand thoroughly the explanations of the answers. |
| **4** | Read Chapter 12 to understand how to do your best when taking the AP Latin Exam and how the exam is scored. Then take Practice Exam 1 on CD-ROM for the appropriate AP Latin exam (Vergil or Literature) to pinpoint your strengths and weaknesses. After comparing your answers against the answer key and reading the detailed explanations, flag any test items that were difficult for you. Use the index to delve further into those problem areas. |
| **5** | Take the time this week to read through Part III of this book, Review of Grammar and Syntax. By so doing, you will foster your understanding of Latin grammar and syntax, which in turn will help improve your performance on the exam. Also, take some time to re-study areas that gave you difficulty on the practice exam. |
| **6** | Take Practice Exam 2 of the appropriate AP Latin exam (Vergil or Literature) in this book. If you are not satisfied with your performance, take the time to backtrack from the answer explanations to the specific chapter mentioned to improve your understanding of the subject matter. If time allows, retake either of the appropriate practice tests, paying special attention to the questions with which you had difficulty the first time. |

# A Note from the Author

Congratulations on reaching the pinnacle of your high school Latin career! You are preparing to join more than 7,500 of the nation's best Latin students who take the Advanced Placement Latin Exam annually. This book is designed to assist you in reaching the goal of doing your best on what may either be the end or the beginning of your career in Latin. Because of an increase of interest in the study of Latin in recent years and because of the growing availability of the opportunity to take college classes in high school, the number of students taking the AP Latin Exam has been rising in recent years. A slight edge in numbers goes to those who study Vergil, as opposed to any one of the three Latin Literature courses. You have become a member of a proud fraternity!

This book provides you with a focused review and an abundance of practice questions and answers that are aligned with the AP Latin Exam in both subject matter and difficulty level to help you evaluate your preparation There are also plenty of tips on how you might strengthen not only your test-readiness, but your overall skills in Latin. The organization of this book, review, practice questions and the approaches that it offers are products of my career-long participation in numerous conference and in-service presentations and workshops on AP Latin, experience as an Exam Reader (grader), service on National Latin Exam committees of the American Classical League, and formal analysis of the AP Latin Exam in preparation for writing this book. Most importantly, this book is the product of 30 years of teaching AP Latin in an independent high school. I hope that this book will also be useful to teachers, both to those who are beginning an AP Latin program in their schools and to veterans who may be seeking approaches that are new or who hope to reinforce those long held.

It is my wish that this book will help you make the most out of your experience with the AP Latin Exam. You are to be congratulated for challenging yourself by taking a college-equivalent Latin course in high school and for taking the risk of showing what you know on the AP Latin Exam.

**Fortes fortuna adiuvat! Bona fortuna!**

Ronald B. Palma
Holland Hall School

# PREPARE WITH CONFIDENCE
## Excelling on the AP Latin Exam

If you're looking for a true edge on Test Day . . .

And if you're not willing to settle for second best . . .

*. . .then REA's AP Latin test prep is for you.*

REA gives you **all the tools** you'll need to master the Advanced Placement Examinations in Latin for both Literature and Vergil, to wit:

- Unrivaled exam-centered review in a context that will sharpen classroom discussion and help you get more out of your textbook.

- Tips and strategies to bolster your test-readiness.

- A systematic, AP curriculum-based approach to mastering grammar and syntax.

- Four full-length, true-to-format practice exams—two that emulate the AP Latin Literature Exam, two modeled after the AP Latin: Vergil Exam—that will prepare you for the actual AP exam like no other book.

- Full explanations of every practice-exam answer.

- Comprehensive index that speeds specific referencing.

In preparing this book, REA has thoroughly aligned our thinking with that of the AP Latin Development Committee. In fact, we expect that many AP instructors will want to use this book to supplement their classroom text and lectures precisely because it so comprehensively supports specific curriculum objectives for the AP course and exam.

## ABOUT REA's TEST*ware*®

One practice test for both the AP Latin: Vergil and the AP Latin Literature is included in two formats: in printed format in this book, and in TEST*ware*® format on the enclosed CD. We strongly recommend that you begin your preparation with the TEST*ware*® practice exams. The software provides the added benefits of automatic, accurate scoring and enforced time conditions. The content and format of the actual AP Latin exams are faithfully mirrored.

# INSTALLING REA's TESTware®

## SYSTEM REQUIREMENTS

Pentium 75 MHz (300 MHz recommended) or a higher or compatible processor; Microsoft Windows 98 or later; 64 MB available RAM; Internet Explorer 5.5 or higher

## INSTALLATION

1.  Insert the AP Latin TEST*ware*® CD-ROM into the CD-ROM drive.
2.  If the installation doesn't begin automatically, from the Start Menu choose the RUN command. When the RUN dialog box appears, type *d*:\setup (where *d* is the letter of your CD-ROM drive) at the prompt and click OK.
3.  The installation process will begin. A dialog box proposing the directory "Program Files\REA\AP_Latin" will appear. If the name and location are suitable, click OK. If you wish to specify a different name or location, type it in and click OK.
4.  Start the AP Latin TEST*ware*® application by double-clicking on the icon.

REA's AP Latin TEST*ware*® is **EASY** to **LEARN AND USE**. To achieve maximum benefits, we recommend that you take a few minutes to go through the on-screen tutorial on your computer.

## SSD ACCOMMODATIONS FOR STUDENTS WITH DISABILITIES

Many students qualify for extra time to take the AP Latin exam, and our TEST*ware*® can be adapted to accommodate your time extension. This allows you to practice under the same extended-time accommodations that you will receive on the actual test day. To customize your TEST*ware*® to suit the most common extensions, visit our website at *www.rea.com.ssd*.

## TECHNICAL SUPPORT

REA's TEST*ware*® is backed by customer and technical support. For questions about **installation or operation of your software**, contact us at:

**Research & Education Association**
**Phone: (732) 819-8880 (9 a.m. to 5 p.m. ET, Monday–Friday)**
**Fax: (732) 819-8808**
**Website: http://www.rea.com**
**E-mail: info@rea.com**

**Note to Windows XP Users:** In order for the TEST*ware*® to function properly, please install and run the application under the same computer administrator-level user account. Installing the TEST*ware*® as one user and running it as another could cause file-access path conflicts.

# PART I

## The AP Latin Course and Exam

# Chapter 1

# General Content and Format of the AP Latin Exam

## Content of the AP Latin Exam

For at least the past four years (2002–2005), the number of students taking the AP Latin Exam has increased and now averages well over 7,000 per year.[1] Whether or not this statistic indicates that more students are studying Latin, it does indicate that more students are studying Latin at the college level while in high school. AP Latin Exams test the proficiency of high school Latin students when compared to college students who have taken a fourth- to sixth-semester Latin course. (Traditionally, one semester of college study has been approximately equivalent to one year of high school study.) If you are reading this book, it is likely that you are among the high-achieving students who either want to demonstrate their facility with the Latin language at the end of their study or who intend to continue studying Latin in college. The focus of this book is to help you to prepare for the AP Latin Exam: to assess and expand not only your general skills of comprehending, translating, and analyzing Latin, but also to help you to understand and appreciate the importance of the ability to write coherently and persuasively in English.

Since 1994, there have been two different AP Latin exams available, one that evaluates your knowledge of Vergil's *Aeneid* and the other, Latin Literature, that assesses your preparation of one of three combinations of authors. Each of the latter exams includes the poems of Catullus, i.e., Catullus-Cicero, Catullus-Horace, and Catullus-Ovid. Both the AP Vergil and the AP Latin Literature exams may be taken in the same year; however, special arrangements need to be made with your school to schedule the second exam.[2] The specific content and format of both the Vergil and Latin Literature Exams are described in greater detail in succeeding chapters of this book. The scoring of the exam is explained at the end.

---

[1] Enrollment data for 2002–2005 are available at College Board Online. In 2005, there were 4,362 Vergil students and 3,530 Latin Literature students who took the AP Latin Exam.

[2] Be sure to let your high school office know which specific AP course or exam you are taking, i.e., Vergil or one of the three Latin Literature exams: Catullus-Cicero, Catullus-Horace, or Catullus-Ovid. This information will be helpful in representing your background in Latin to the colleges and universities to which you send your scores. The scores they receive designate only that you took the Vergil Exam or the Latin Literature Exam.

## Format of the AP Latin Exam

The AP Latin Exam, the format of which was changed in 1999, now consists of two parts: a multiple-choice section (40 percent) and a free-response section (60 percent). The multiple-choice section, which is administered first, consists of 50 multiple-choice questions over three sight passages of prose and poetry and one syllabus-based passage, that is, one passage from the lines or poems that you have prepared in Latin. The sight readings of the multiple-choice section are common to the two exams, and the syllabus-based passage comes from either Vergil or Catullus, as appropriate. You have 60 minutes for this part. The free-response section consists of five questions for Vergil and six for Latin Literature, the latter consisting of three on Catullus and three on the choice author Cicero, Horace, or Ovid. These questions, which consist of translations, long and short essays, and discussions of background or short identifications, evaluate your preparation of the assigned syllabus. Those portions of the *Aeneid* and of Cicero's *De Amicitia* not prepared in Latin must be read in English. You are given one hour and 45 minutes for the free-response section, plus a 15-minute "reading period," during which you may organize your thinking and plan your answers. The total time for the AP Latin Exam is three hours, plus about one-half hour of administrative and break time.

Be aware that, periodically, changes are made to the content or format of the AP Latin Exam. **For instance, in the Cicero syllabus the *Pro Caelio* has been replaced for the 2007 exam with the *Pro Archia Poeta* and selections from the *De Amicitia*** (for specific information, see Chapter 3). Every five years or so, the entire AP Latin Exam, both Vergil and Latin Literature, is released and published for reference by students and teachers.

## Terms Used in AP Latin

- **Acorn Book:** see **syllabus**.

- **background question:** the final question on the free-response section of the Vergil Exam. This question tests knowledge of those portions of the *Aeneid* read in English. It requires 20 minutes and counts 15 percent of your free-response score.

- **choice author:** Cicero, Horace, or Ovid. These authors supplement Catullus, which is required for all three Latin Literature Exams.

- **chunk:** see **segment**.

- ***The Classical Outlook*:** the official journal of the American Classical League, published quarterly. Contact *The Classical Outlook*, Department of Classics, Montclair State University, Upper Montclair, NJ 07043 (ISSN: 0009–8361), e-mail englishm@mail.montclair.edu, or go to http://www.aclclassics.org. Annual reports on the AP Latin Exam, prepared by the Chief Reader, appear in this journal, usually in the fall and winter. There are usually separate reports for each Exam.

- **free response:** the larger part of the AP Latin Exam in time (1 hour, 45 minutes) and weight (60 percent), the free-response consists of five or six questions that call for you to translate, compose essays in English, and demonstrate your knowledge of the *Aeneid* in its entirety or answer short questions on a passage of Latin (choice authors only).

- **gloss:** annotations at the foot of a Latin text, in either the multiple-choice or free-response sections. Glosses occur rarely, but when they do, they provide assistance with a particularly difficult or uncommon word or form, especially the names of unfamiliar people and places. Glosses no longer include variations in the spelling of the Latin.

- **item:** College Board terminology for an AP Exam question. The word "question" will be used in this book.

- **"literal":** the rendering of Latin in English with attention to the precise and accurate expression of all vocabulary and forms.

- **long essay:** a (30 or 45-minute) written discussion and analysis of a given passage or passages of Latin on the free-response section. Long essays are required for Vergil and Catullus only. The suggested time for the long essay for Vergil, which is worth 35 percent of your score on the free-response section, is 45 minutes. The suggested time for the long essay on Catullus is 30 minutes, and this long essay counts 20 percent, the same as the other short essays on the Latin Literature Exam. See also **short essay**.

- **multiple choice:** the smaller part of the AP Latin Exam in time (one hour) and weight (40 percent). There are 50 questions on three sight passages, each 10–15 lines long, from Latin poets and at least one prose author. One additional passage comes from the prepared syllabus of either Vergil or Catullus, depending upon the exam selected. Each multiple-choice question consists of four answers, one of which is correct.

- **prompt:** a term used mostly by those who produce or grade the exam. It refers to the essential question being asked within the wording of an essay question on the free-response section.

- **Reader:** a volunteer high school or college teacher who grades the AP Latin Exam in mid-June. Readers are organized into groups, each of which is guided by a Table Leader, or more experienced grader. Readers spend their grading time evaluating one specific question on the exam. Questions are frequently re-graded at random to ensure consistency.

- **reading period:** the 15-minute preface to actually writing answers in the pink answer booklet. This time is provided to encourage you to think through and organize your answers before actually writing. You may make notes anywhere on your green test sheets.

- **released exams:** every five years or so, the entire AP Latin Vergil and AP Latin Literature Exams are published by the College Board for use by students and teachers.

- **scoring guidelines:** these are the rubrics, or criteria, used by the Readers in scoring your exam. They are published by the Chief Reader sometime after the exams have been graded and include sample student responses, along with their scores. You might find these guidelines useful in determining how the exams are graded and therefore how you might improve your preparation. In addition to finding information about the scoring of the AP Latin Exam in this book, you may consult the College Board Web pages for AP Latin or the annual reports published by the Chief Reader in *The Classical Outlook* (for which, see above).

- **segment:** a small combination of syntactically related words, used in determining units of sense within a Latin sentence. Segments are used as the criteria in evaluating a literal translation. For examples other than those provided in this book, see the Scoring Guidelines online or the appropriate articles in *The Classical Outlook*.

- **short essay:** all short essays consist of a suggested time of 20 minutes, although the point-value of these questions varies from 15 percent to 20 percent (see Chapter 7 for details). The length of your writing, i.e., the number of pages it takes you to answer the question, is of little consequence. The difference between short and long essays, in addition to the suggested time and point value, concerns the length of the passage under consideration and the corresponding expectation of increased breadth and depth in your analysis on the long essay. See also **long essay**.

- **sight reading:** a passage that has not been previously seen, i.e., unfamiliar, unprepared.

- **spot question:** another name for the short-answer or identification question for choice authors on the free-response section.

- **"suggested time":** the College Board provides a "suggested time" for each free-response question, in order to help you to plan your time. It is assumed that you have practiced taking timed tests during your preparation for the AP Latin Exam and that you have some idea about how you perform under the pressure of time. The simplest advice for you to remember is that you should not use substantially more or less time than that suggested. You are not penalized if you do not stay within the suggested time.

- **syllabus-based:** this phrase refers to the passages from the Latin syllabi of Vergil or Catullus (as appropriate) given in the multiple-choice section of the exam.

- **syllabus:** refers to an outline or summary of the Latin reading required for the AP Latin Exam. This is published semi-annually by the College Board in the *AP Latin Course Description* or so-called Acorn Book (the acorn is the logo of the College Board).

- **". . . throughout the passage/s or poem/s":** this phrase appears in the instructions for the essay questions on the free-response section of the exam. It is designed to remind you to consider the poem *as a whole* in your answer and to draw support for your discussion from the entirety of the Latin text. Failure to do this is a common shortcoming and often leads to a reduced score on the question.

- **"well-developed"**: this phrase is found in the directions for the long essay. A well-developed essay is not necessarily a long essay. A well-developed essay includes organization, coherence, completeness, and sound analysis, which makes liberal use of specific and relevant references to the entire Latin text. When references are made to figures of speech, attention should be paid to how the figure affects the meaning of the Latin.

## AP Latin Resources of the College Board[3]

### Bibliography of Publications Useful for Exam Preparation

- *Latest edition of the AP Latin Course Description* (published annually or biennially, last published for the 2006 and 2007 exams) (Item # 727247)

- *2005 AP Latin Literature and Latin: Vergil Released Exams*, complete multiple-choice and free-response sections of both the Vergil and Literature exams (Item #05008172)

- *1999 AP Latin Literature and Latin: Vergil Released Exams* (Item #255180)

- *1994 AP Latin Free-Response Guide with Multiple-Choice Section* (Item #255154)

- *Teacher's Guide (for AP Latin)*, by Jeff S. Greenberger, n.d. (Item #989390)

- Relevant issues of *The Classical Outlook* (The Journal of the American Classical League).

Note:

> Each year in *The Classical Outlook (CO)*, an analytical report on each of the two AP Latin Exams is given by the Chief Reader. This report provides valuable feedback on how the expectations of the teachers who designed the exams were met by the students who took the exams. This report, which also includes scoring guidelines, and sample student and Reader responses, is especially useful because it provides insight into the grading of literal translations required on the free-response sections. See, for example, John Sarkissian, "The Grading of the 2005 Advanced Placement Examinations in Latin: Vergil," *CO*, Fall 2005, Vol. 83, No. 1, pp. 1–12.

The materials listed above are available from the CBO (College Board Online) website http://apcentral.collegeboard.com (click on "The Exams," then "Exam Questions Index" then "Latin Literature" or "Latin: Vergil"). Additional resources are available from

> College Board Publications
> Dept. CBO
> PO Box 869010
> Plano, TX 75074
> (212) 713–8165

---

[3] As of this writing, scoring information and data about the 2006 AP Latin Exam were unavailable.

## Webliography of Online Sites Useful for Exam Preparation

- The Official College Board AP Latin website: http://apcentral.college-board.com

  For the AP Latin: Vergil Course Home Page, go to
  http://apcentral.collegeboard.com/latinvergil

  For the AP Latin Literature Course Home Page, go to
  http://apcentral.collegeboard.com/latinlit

  Note:

  > Within these Web pages, you may may download the *AP Latin Course Description* "Acorn Book" and gain access to specific course and exam information, e.g., sample teacher-made multiple-choice questions. These pages provide much information about the exams, including the complete free-response sections for 2001–2006 and the scoring rubrics for each, plus sample student and Reader responses.

- An Unofficial Website for AP Latin (Ginny Lindzey and the Texas Classical Association) http://txclassics.org/aplatin.htm

- "Useful Internet Links for AP Latin" (Barbara McManus and Marianthe Colakis, VRoma = Virtual Rome, Miami University, Oxford, OH) http://www.vroma.org/~bmcmanus/aplinks.html

# Online Latin Texts of all AP Latin Authors

For additional electronic resources, see Chapters 2 and 3.

- Bibliotheca Augustana (Ulrich Harsch, Augsburg University, Germany)
  http://www.fh-augsburg.de/~harsch/Chronologia/Lsante01/Vergilius/ver_intr.html
  Unannotated texts, plus additional resources in Latin.

- The Latin Library at Ad Fontes Academy
  http://thelatinlibrary.com
  Unannotated texts.

- The Perseus Digital Library (click on Classics, then scroll down to "P. Vergilius Maro")
  http://www.perseus.tufts.edu
  Latin hypertexts and online parsers.

# Chapter 2

# Content and Format: Vergil

## Content of the AP Vergil Exam

The Latin reading content for the Vergil exam consists of the following lines of the *Aeneid*. The remainder of the *Aeneid* is to be prepared in English.

| | | |
|---|---|---|
| Book 1: | lines 1-519 | 519 lines |
| Book 2: | lines 1-56, 199-297, 469-566, and 735-804 | 323 lines |
| Book 4: | lines 1-448, 642-705 | 512 lines |
| Book 6: | lines 1-211, 450-76, and 847-901 | 293 lines |
| Book 10: | lines 420-509 | 90 lines |
| Book 12: | lines 791-842, 887-952 | 118 lines |
| | | Total: 1,855 lines |

In 1999, selections in Latin from Books 10 and 12 were added to the syllabus because there was concern among college teachers that AP Vergil students were not acquainting themselves with the entire work of the *Aeneid*. Keep this in mind as you prepare for the AP Latin: Vergil Exam. Your preparation of the Latin of the *Aeneid* is evaluated in the syllabus-based question on the multiple-choice section and in four of the five questions on the free-response section. Your familiarity with the characters and situations of the epic as a whole in English is tested on the second of the 20-minute short essay questions found in the free-response section. Several questions on background may also appear in the syllabus-based passage in the multiple-choice section.

## Format of the Vergil Exam

### Multiple-Choice Section

The multiple-choice section of the Vergil exam consists of 50 multiple-choice questions over three sight readings/passages of poetry and prose, plus one syllabus-based passage covering the required lines of the *Aeneid* in Latin. You have 60 minutes in which to answer all questions. For the specific skills tested on the multiple-choice section, see Chapter 4.

## Free-Response Section

The free-response section of the Vergil exam consists of five questions, for which you have 1 hour and 45 minutes, plus a 15-minute "reading period" for preparation.

| | | |
|---|---|---|
| Question V1: | 10-minute translation (15 percent) | |
| Question V2: | 10-minute translation (15 percent) | |
| Question V3: | 45-minute long essay (35 percent) | |
| Question V4: | 20-minute short essay (20 percent) | |
| Question V5: | 20-minute short essay based on the parts of the *Aeneid* read in English. You will be given a list of characters and/or events from which to choose the subject of this essay (15 percent) | |

# Webliography for Vergil

The Web sites provided in this book have been chosen for their utility and "user-friendliness" in helping you to prepare for the AP Latin Exam. All sites are active as of 2006. For the best current textbooks and translations, consult your teacher, and see also the following book, which has been well-received by AP Latin students: Christine G. Perkell, ed., *Reading Vergil's* Aeneid: *An Interpretive Guide*, Oklahoma Series in Classical Culture, University of Oklahoma Press, 1999. See also the resources listed in Chapters 8 and 12.

## The Life and Works of Vergil

- Aelius Donatus, Life of Vergil (David Wilson-Okamura, virgil.org)
  http://virgil.org/vitae/
  Fourth-century CE biographer of Vergil, translated by Wilson-Okamura.

- The Secret Life of a Very Private Poet (William Harris, Middlebury College)
  http://community.middlebury.edu/~harris/Classics/Vergil-TheSecretLife.html

- Suetonius, Life of Vergil (Fordham University)
  http://www.fordham.edu/halsall/pwh/suet-vergil.html
  Loeb translation, 1913.

- Wikipedia hypertext article on Vergil
  http://en.wikipedia.org/wiki/Virgil

## Useful General Resources for Vergil and the *Aeneid* (Online)

- AP Vergil site (Tim Abney, Marquette High School)
  http://abney.homestead.com/aeneid.html
  Teacher website chock full o' goodies for AP Latin, including helpful writing tips and grammar review materials; updated regularly.

- Article on the *Aeneid* (Classics Technology Center, Ablemedia)
  http://ablemedia.com/ctcweb/netshots/vergil.htm
  Hypertext discussion of literary epic, historical background for Vergil; reading the *Aeneid*; questions on comprehension and interpretation.

- Electronic Resources for the *Aeneid* (The Evolution of the Female Image in the Epic Tradition, Zina B. Lewis, Monmouth College) http://personal.monm.edu/lewis_zinab/webpages/epicpoetlinks/vergil-websites.htm
Links to current websites on Vergil and the *Aeneid.* See also Jim O'Hara, UNC-Chapel Hill,
http://www.unc.edu/~oharaj/VergilLinks.html.

- Mr. J's Vergil Page (Bruce M. Johnson, Park View High School) http://www.hoocher.com/vergil.htm
Includes useful teacher-produced articles on the Augustan Age, the epic hero, and the mythological background of the Trojan War.

- The Story of Aeneas (Instructor Resources, The Nature of Roman Mythology, support website for Mark P.O. Morford and Robert J. Lenardon, *Classical Mythology*, 7th edition, Oxford Univ. Press) http://www.us.oupcom/us/companionwebsites/0195153448/instructorresources/?view=usa
Outline of book content: legends of the founding of Rome, the tradition before Vergil, Vergil's *Aeneid*, Aeneas as a new epic hero, etc.

- The Vergil Project (The Legend of Aeneas and the Foundation of Rome, Vergil's *Aeneid*: Commentary, Univ. Pennsylvania) http://vergil.classics.upenn.edu/comm2/legend/legend.html
Hypertext article bridging the time of Trojan Aeneas with that of the Alban Kings and Romulus and Remus.

- The Virgil Home Page (Steven Hale, DeKalb College) http://www.gpc.edu/~shale/humanities/literature/world_literature/virgil.html
Links to online texts and translations, background readings, Internet resources on the *Aeneid,* Vergil websites.

- Virgil.org (David Scott Wilson-Okamura) http://virgil.org
Thorough collection of information about Vergil's life and works, including information about the commentator Servius, the Latin text of "The Thirteenth Book of the *Aeneid*," etc., plus a search engine for the *Aeneid.*

For a sample description of a college course on Vergil's *Aeneid* (David Cramer, Univ. Texas), go to http://ccwf.cc.utexas.edu/~dcramer/312k/. See also, "The Epic Tradition" (Rob S. Rice, Univ. Pennsylvania), http://ccat.sas.upenn.edu/rrice/clas160.html.

## Translations of the *Aeneid* (Online)

- Romans Online
  http://www.romansonline.com/sources/vrg/Indx01.asp
  Hypertext English translation by Theodore H. White (1910) with facing Latin text.

- Anthony (Tony) S. Kline (2002)
  http://www.tkline.freeserve.co.uk/Virgilhome.htm

- Andrew Wilson (The Classics Pages, 2003)
  http://www.users.globalnet.co.uk/%7Eloxias/oldindex.htm
  Translations of Books 1 (2005), 2, 4, and 6; Books 2 and 6 are hypertexts, with or without frames. Book 6 is incomplete.

# Chapter 3

# Content and Format: Latin Literature

## Content of the AP Latin Literature Exam

The syllabi for Catullus, Cicero, Horace, and Ovid are as follows:

**Catullus:** Poems 1, 2, 3, 4, 5, 7, 8, 10, 11, 12, 13, 14a, 22, 30, 31, 35, 36, 40, 43, 44, 45, 46, 49, 50, 51, 60, 64 (lines 50–253), 65, 68 (lines 1–40), 69, 70, 72, 76, 77, 84, 85, 86, 87, 96, 101, 109, 116.

Total: 804 lines

plus either

**Cicero:** *Pro Archia Poeta* (entire 32 sections)

*De Amicitia*, Sections 17 (*ego vos hortari . . .* ) –23 ( *. . . iudicari potest*) Sections 100 (*Virtus, virtus . . .* ) –104 (end)

Note:

That part of the *De Amicitia* not prepared in Latin is to be read in English. Also, be aware that **this is a new syllabus for Cicero, beginning with the 2007 exam.**

or

| **Horace:** | *Odes,* Book 1. 1, 5, 9, 11, 13, 22, 23, 24, 25, 37, 38 | 220 lines |
|---|---|---|
| | Book 2. 3, 7, 10, 14 | 108 lines |
| | Book 3. 1, 9, 13, 30 | 104 lines |
| | Book 4. 7 | 132 lines |
| *Satires,* 1.9 | | 78 lines |

Total: 642 lines

or

| **Ovid:** | *Metamorphoses*, Book 1—Daphne and Apollo (lines 452–567) | 115 lines |
|---|---|---|
| | Book 4—Pyramus and Thisbe (lines 55–166) | 111 lines |
| | Book 8—Daedalus and Icarus (lines 183–235) | 52 lines |
| | Baucis and Philemon (lines 616–724) | 108 lines |
| | Book 10—Pygmalion (lines 238–297) | 59 lines |
| *Amores,* Book 1, Poems 1, 3, 9, 11, 12; Book 3, Poem 15 | | 180 lines |

Total: 625 lines

# Format of the Latin Literature Exam

## Multiple-Choice Section

As with the Vergil Exam, the Latin Literature Exam contains a multiple-choice section of 50 questions to be answered in 60 minutes. This section consists of three sight passages of prose or poetry and one-syllabus-based passage on the poems required for Catullus. (For the specific skills tested on the multiple-choice section, see Chapter 4.)

## Free-Response Section

The free-response section of the Literature Exam consists of six questions, for which you have 1 hour and 45 minutes, plus a 15–minute "reading period" for preparation. There are three questions on Catullus and three covering the choice author. The questions for both authors include translation and essay writing. The sequence of the questions for the choice author was changed in 2005 to allow you more time to answer the short essay question, which has the greatest weight of the three choice-author questions.

> **Catullus (required)**
>
> > Question 1: 10–minute translation (15 percent)
> >
> > Question 2: 30–minute long essay (20 percent)
> >
> > Question 3: 20–minute short essay (15 percent)
>
> > plus
>
> **Choice Author: Cicero (4, 5, 6), Horace (7, 8, 9), or Ovid (10, 11, 12)**
>
> > Question 4, 7, or 10: 20–minute short essay (20 percent)
> >
> > Question 5, 8, or 11: 15–minute translation (15 percent)
> >
> > Question 6, 9, or 12: 10–minute short identification (or "spot" question) (15 percent)

# Webliography for Latin Literature

The Web sites provided in this book have been chosen for their utility and "user-friendliness" in helping you to prepare for the AP Latin Exam. All sites are active as of 2006. For the best current textbooks and translations, consult your teacher. A book useful for its simple but cogent analyses of the poems but, alas, now out of print, is Stuart G.P. Small's, *Catullus, a Reader's Guide to the Poems,* Roman and Littlefield, 1983. See also the resources listed in Chapter 8.

## Catullus

### Useful General Resources for Catullus (Online)

- AP Catullus Page (Tim Abney, Marquette High School)
  http://abney.homestead.com/catullus.html
  See activities for scansion and figures of speech under "Working with Individual Poems."

- C. Valerius Catullus (John Porter, Univ. Saskatchewan)
  http://duke.usask.ca/~porterj/CourseNotes/CatullusNotes.html
  The poems and life of Catullus: Catullus as Eques; Catullus as Neoteric
  Poet; Catullus and Lesbia (cross-linked with English translations of relevant Catullan poems).

- Catullus' Social Set: His Friends, Lovers, Rivals (Henry Walker, Bates College, VRoma)
  http://www.vroma.org/~hwalker/VRomaCatullus/Friends.html

- Catullus Web Sites (Useful Internet Links for AP Latin, Barbara McManus and Marianthe Colakis, VRoma), http://www.vroma.org/~bmcmanus/
  aplinks.html
  Three useful sites on background, and five on texts, all annotated.

- The Life of Catullus (Derek Adams, Sol Magazine)
  http://www.solpubs.freeserve.co.uk/catullus.htm
  Reconstruction of the life of Catullus, using translated excerpts from his
  poems as resources.

- Mr. J's Catullus Page (Bruce M. Johnson, Park View High School), http://
  www.hoocher.com/catullus.htm
  Links to teacher-produced biography of Catullus, many links to other
  common-used Catullan web sites

- Links for the Study of Catullus (Alison W. Barker, VRoma)
  http://www.vroma.org/~abarker/catulluslinks.html
  Eighteen links to texts, history and culture, and language and meter.

- The Modern Student's Guide to Catullus (Raymond M. Koehler, Brunswick School, Ablemedia, Classics Technology Center), http://ablemedia.
  com/ctcweb/consortium/catullusguideintro.html
  Fictional scenario in the Catullan Room of The Museum of Lyric; Latin
  texts of Poems 1, 51, 8, 85, 7; 2, 85, 4, 8 read/sung aloud. Cross-linked to
  Walker's VRoma texts and translations.

### Latin Texts and Translations of Catullus (Online)

- The Gaius Valerius Catullus Society [**Latin texts**]
  http://www.informalmusic.com/Catullus/
  Includes Latin texts of all poems, numbered every five lines, and links useful for Catullan meters.

- Anthony (Tony) S.Kline (2001) [**translations**]
  http://www.adkline.freeuk.com/Catullus.htm
  Best translations online; with titles.

- Rudy Negenborn (Utrecht, Netherlands) [**with Latin texts**]
  http://www.negenborn.net/catullus/
  Translations in many languages, Latin texts, sample scansions.

- Shocked Catullus (Robert Larson, Kent State University) [**Latin hyper-texts**]
  http://www.personal.kent.edu/~rlarson/catullus/
  Needs Shockwave plug-in. Does not include syllabus poems added in 2005, but excellent for reading practice.

- VRoma Catullus web site (Henry Walker, Bates College) [**Latin texts with translations**]
  http://www.vroma.org/~hwalker/VRomaCatullus/
  Latin text with side-by-side/facing line-by-line translation. Linked to Merrill's Perseus text. Includes many support resources.

- Wikipedia hypertext article on Catullus [**select Latin texts and translations**]
  http://en.wikipedia.org/wiki/Catullus
  Latin texts of 24 poems, with translations of the 18 that appear on the AP syllabus. Poem 1 is scanned in hendecasyllabic meter. Cross-linked with Walker's VRoma site.

For a sample AP Catullus-Ovid high school reading schedule (Tim Abney, Marquette High School), see http://www.tabney.com/files/catullus/ap-catullus-ovid-syllabus.htm (Term 1– Catullus, Term 2– Ovid; Catullus read in sequence of corpus numbers). See also Tom Sears, Univ. North Carolina, AP Catullus-Horace course online at http://www.learnnc.org/courses/AP_Latin_Literature.

# The Choice Authors

## Cicero

### *Useful General Resources for Cicero (Online)*

- AP Cicero Web site (Bruce M. Johnson, Park View High School)
  http://www.hoocher.com/cicero.htm
  Good source of links.

- The Cicero Homepage (Andrew M. Riggsby, Univ. Texas-Austin)
  http://www.utexas.edu/depts/classics/documents/Cic.html
  Links to major Latin texts of Cicero, chronology of life, bibliography.

- Cicero Web Sites (Useful Internet Links for AP Latin, Barbara McManus and Marianthe Colakis, VRoma)
  http://www.vroma.org/~bmcmanus/aplinks.html
  Six sites usful for background (not updated for *Pro Archia Poeta* and *De Amicitia*).

- Home and Forum: Cicero between "Public" and Private" (Susan Treggiari, Stanford Univ.)
  http://www.apaclassics.org/Publications/PresTalks/TREGGIARI97.html
  Cicero's personal values in his public life.

- Wikipedia hypertext article on Cicero
  http://en.wikipedia.org/wiki/Cicero

### Texts and Translations of Pro Archia Poeta *(Online)*

- Cicero's Orations (Southwest Missouri State Univ.) [**Latin texts with translations**]
  http://cicero.missouristate.edu/~cicero/Orationes/default.htm
  Latin text, plus English translation.

- J.B. Greenough (via Nicholas Koenig, Univ. Texas) [**Latin text**]
  http://www.utexas.edu/depts/classics/documents/archia.html

- Claude Pavur (Saint Louis Univ.) [**Latin text**]
  http://www.slu.edu/colleges/AS/languages/classical/latin/tchmat/readers/
  accreaders/cicero/archia.htm
  The Latin text is laid out in what the College Board would consider sense units or "segments."

- Joseph T. Richardson (The Society for Ancient Languages) [**Latin text with translation**]
  http://www.uah.edu/student_life/organizations/SAL/texts/latin/classical/
  cicero/proarchia.html
  With introduction, Latin text, English translation, translation notes

- Wikipedia: Marcus Tullius Cicero—*Orationes- Pro A. Licinio Archia poeta* [**Latin texts**]
  http://la.wikisource.org/wiki/Marcus_Tullius_Cicero
  This site includes the Latin texts of all orations.

### Texts and Translations of De Amicitia *(Online)*

- Andrew P. Peabody [**translation**]
  http://ancienthistory.about.com/library/bl/bl_text_cic_friendship.htm
  Includes introduction and a one-sentence synopsis of the complete work, section-by-section.

- Joseph T. Richardson (The Society for Ancient Languages) [**Latin text with translation**]
  http://www.uah.edu/student_life/organizations/SAL/texts/latin/classical/
  cicero/deamicitia.html
  Latin text, English translation, and text with facing translation.

- Wikipedia: Marcus Tullius Cicero—Operae Philosophae—*Laelius De Amicitia* [**Latin text**]
  http://la.wikisource.org/wiki/Laelius_de_Amicitia

For a typical syllabus of a college course on Cicero (Ann R. Raia, College of New Rochelle), see http://www.cnr.edu/home/araia/cicero2.htm.

## Horace

### Useful General Resources for Horace (Online)

- Analysis of the Roman Odes (P. Balmforth, ancienthistory.about.com)
  http://ancienthistory.about.com/gi/dynamic/offsite.htm?zi=1/XJ&sdn=anc
  ienthistory&zu=http%3A%2F%2Fwww.angelfire.com%2Fart%2Farchict
  ecture%2Farticles%2F046.htm
  Book 3, *Odes* 1–6 (Ode 3.1 on syllabus).

- Horace (Joan Jahnige, Kentucky Educational Television)
  http://www.dl.ket.org/latinlit/carmina/index.htm
  Biography (life, works, philosophy), people of Horace, mythical references
  in Ode 2.14, hypertext of *Satires* 1.9.

- Horace Web Sites (Useful Internet Links for AP Latin, Barbara McManus
  and Marianthe Colakis, VRoma)
  http://www.vroma.org/-bmcmanus/aplinks.html
  Five useful sites on background, and four on texts, all annotated.

- Links for the Study of Horace's *Odes* (Alison Barker, VRoma)
  http://www.vroma.org/-abarker/horaceodes.html
  Twelve links to texts and translations, mythology, archaeology, meter, et
  al., including Stoicism and Epicureanism.

- Quotations from Horace http://www.brainyquote.com/quotes/authors/h/
  horace.html (BrainyQuote.com)
  A convenient quick study of Horace's view of the world. See also  http://
  www.quotationspage.com/quotes/Horace (The Quotations Page)

- Wikipedia hypertext article on Horace
  http://en.wikipedia.org/wiki/Horace
  Horace's life, works, later influence, English translators, links.

### Latin Texts and Translations of Horace (Online)

### Odes

- A New Interpretation of the Pyrrha Ode (1.5) (Shirley Werner's Rutgers
  students, VRoma)
  http://www.vroma.org/-bmcmanus/werner_pyrrha.html
  Contrasts *Ode* 1.5 with Catullus 8.

- Anthony (Tony) S. Kline (2005) [**translations**]
  http://www.tkline.freeserve.co.uk/Horacehome.htm

- Diotima site (Steven Willett, stoa.org) [**select translations**]
  http://www.stoa.org/diotima/anthology/horawill.shtml
  Translations of *Odes* 1.5, 1.11, 1.13, 1.23, 1,25, 1.37; linked to Perseus Latin
  text of Horace.

- Project Gutenberg (C. Smart, Pembroke College, Cambridge, 2004)
  [**translations**] http://www.gutenberg.org/catalog/world/readfile?fk_files=
  106758&pageno=2

- Horace's Villa Page (Bernard Frischer) [**select Latin texts with translations**]
  http://www.humnet.ucla.edu/horaces-villa/poetry/Ode1.22.html
  Fourteen Latin texts and facing translations of poems (only two from syllabus, 3.1 and 3.3), some read aloud. Good for sight reading practice.

- Intratext [**Latin texts**]
  http://www.intratext.com/Catalogo/Autori/Aut186.HTM
  *Odes* and *Satires* 1.9. Linked to concordance.

- *Odes* (Joseph Richardson, The Society for Ancient Languages) [**Latin texts**]
  http://www.uah.edu/student_life/organizations/SAL/texts/latin/classical/horace/carmina.html
  Includes an introduction to the *Odes*.

- *Odes* of Horace (Michael Gilleland) [**select Latin texts with translations**]
  http://www.merriampark.com/horace.htm
  Latin text, translation, notes for syllabus poems 1.9, 1.11, 1.22, 1.38; 2.3, 2.14; 3.13; 4.7; includes Latin prose paraphrases of the above poems and other resources.

- Poet Seers [**select translations**]
  http://www.poetseers.org/the_great_poets/the_classics/horace/poems_horace
  Seven translated poems from the syllabus: 1.9, 1.11, 1.38, 2.3, 2.10, 2.14, 4.7.

- Shocked Horace (Robert Larson, Kent State University) [**Latin hypertexts**]
  http://www.personal.kent.edu/-rlarson/horace/
  All AP Horace poems, save *Satires* 1.9. Excellent for reading practice!

## Satires 1.9

- Kentucy Educational Television (Joan Jahnige) [**Latin hypertext**]
  http://www.dl.ket.org/latinlit/carmina/index.htm
  Wonderful color-coded Latin hypertext of *Satires* 1.9, with pop-up windows.

- The Society for Ancient Languages (Joseph J. Richardson) [**Latin hypertexts and translations**]
  http://www.uah.edu/student_life/organizations/SAL/texts/latin/classical/horace/sermones.html
  Includes introduction, hypertext, and translation notes available as a frame below the Latin text.

- Wikipedia, *Satires* 1.9 [**Latin text**]
  http://la.wikisource.org/wiki/Sermones_%28Horatius%29_-_Liber_prior_-_Sermo_IX_-_Ibam_forte_via_sacra%2C_sicut_meus_est_mos
  Numbered every five lines.

# Ovid

## *Useful General Resources for Ovid (Online)*

- AP Ovid (Tim Abney, Marquette High School)
  http://abney.homestead.com/ovid1.html
  Valuable site for interactive exercises on scansion and figures of speech for
  both *Metamorphoses* and *Amores*.
- Ovid Web Sites (Useful Internet Links for AP Latin, Barbara McManus
  and Marianthe Colakis, VRoma)
  http://www.vroma.org/~bmcmanus/aplinks.html
  Four useful links to background Web sites, and four to those on texts, all
  annotated.
- FAQs about Ovid (Sean Redmond)
  http://www.jiffycomp.com/smr/rob/faq/ovid_faq.php3
  Who was Ovid? What did Ovid write? Why was Ovid exiled?, etc. Answers to questions include links to other resources.
- Wikipedia hypertext article on Ovid
  http://en.wikipedia.org/wiki/Ovid
  Works and artists inspired by Ovid, links, et al.

## *Texts and Translations of the* Metamorphoses *(Online)*

- Intratext [**Latin text**] http://www.intratext.com/IXT/LAT0537/_P48.
  HTM
- The Ovid Collection (Electronic Text Center, Univ. Virginia Library)
  [**Latin text**]
  http://etext.lib.virginia.edu/toc/modeng/public/OviLMet.html
- Anthony (Tony) S. Kline [**translation**]
  http://www.tkline.freeserve.co.uk/Ovhome.htm
  Recent (2000) prose paragraph translation, hyper-linked to the mythology
  index. Also available at
  http://etext.lib.virginia.edu/latin/ovid/trans/Ovhome.htm (Electronic Text
  Center, Univ. Virginia) and http://www.mythology.us/ovid_metamorphoses
  _book_1.htm
- *Metamorphoses* by Ovid [**translation**]
  http://www.mythology.us

## *Texts and Translations of the* Amores *(Online)*

- Intratext [**Latin texts**]
  http://www.intratext.com/X/LAT0086.htm
- Anthony (Tony) S. Kline (2001) [**translations**]
  http://www.adkline.freeuk.com/Amoreshome.htm

For a description of a typical college course on Ovid (Timothy Moore, Univ. Texas), see http://www.utexas.edu/depts/classics/faculty/Moore.

### Content and Analysis of the Metamorphoses *(Online)*

- Bookrags: *Metamorphoses*
  http://www.bookrags.com/notes/met/
  Bio, one-page plot summary, character descriptions, object/place descriptions, theme tracker (revenge, violence, women), book-by-book summaries of the mythological stories.

- Ovid's *Metamorphoses* (Larry A. Brown)
  http://larryavisbrown.homestead.com/files/xeno.ovid1.htm
  An intro and commentary, with discussion of myths and links to sources and influences in art and literature. Some analysis and thematic cross-linked summaries.

- The Structure of the *Metamorphoses* (Joseph Farrell, Univ. Pennsylvania)
  http://ccat.sas.upenn.edu/~jfarrell/courses/spring96/myth/metstruc.html
  A detailed outline of the entire work.

- Wikipedia: *Metamorphoses*
  http://en.wikipedia.org/wiki/Metamorphoses_%28poem%29

### Content and Analysis of the Amores *(Online)*

- Diotima article on the *Amores* (John Svarlien and Diane Arnson Svarlien, stoa.org)
  http://www.stoa.org/diotima/anthology/amores_index.shtml
  Good background information by William W. Batstone.

- Wikipedia: *Amores*
  http://en.wikipedia.org/wiki/Amores

## Chapter 4

# The Multiple-Choice Section

The multiple-choice section is the first of two sections on the AP Latin Exam. The other is the free-response section. As indicated in Chapter 1 of this book, these two sections differ in length, content, and format. The multiple-choice section consists of 50 multiple-choice questions on three sight reading passages and one syllabus-based passage, the latter of which comes from the prepared lines of either Vergil or Catullus. Each question has four possibile answers, from which you are to select the one that is correct. At the end of this chapter, you will find several examples of the types of passages and questions (with answers) that you will meet on this section of the Exam. On the actual AP Latin Exam, you are given 60 minutes for completion of this section, which counts 40 percent of your total score.

## Content of the Multiple-Choice Section

The questions on this section of the exam approximate those on the Reading Comprehension Section of the SAT Subject Test in Latin. That is, they require demonstration of your ability to read, i.e., translate or interpret, a phrase or sentence, to identify in context grammatical forms and syntactical uses, and to explicate references, allusions, and words understood. The remaining questions focus on the mechanics of literary analysis, e.g., figures of speech and metrics. The seven different types of questions found on the multiple-choice section are translation, comprehension, grammar, reference, figures of speech, metrics, and background.

## Sight Reading Passages

Authors selected for sight readings are equivalent in difficulty to the following intermediate authors. For prose, Caesar, Cicero, Gellius, Livy, Nepos, Pliny the Younger, and Sallust; for poetry, Lucan, Lucretius, Martial, Ovid,[1] Propertius, and Tibullus. The authors covered in the multiple-choice section for the released 1994 exam were Martial, Pliny, Vergil, and Catullus. Those covered on the released 1999 multiple-choice sections included syllabus-based passages from Catullus (Poem 35.1-15) and Vergil, (*Aeneid*, 6.162-174), plus sight passages from Cicero, Ovid, and Tibullus. For the released 2005 exam, the syllabus-based passages were Vergil, (*Aeneid*, 3.90-104) and Catullus (Poem 64.177-87), plus sight readings from Juvenal, Livy, and Statius.

Below, you will find a more specific description of the skills tested on this section, plus sample types of questions. The sample multiple-choice passages given for prac-

---

[1] Sight passages for these authors will be taken from works other than those covered on the syllabus.

tice below include syllabus-based passages from Vergil and Catullus and sight passages from Pliny the Younger and Tibullus.

## Skills Tested on the Multiple-Choice Section

| 35–45 percent (17–23 questions) | Translation or comprehension of a phrase or sentence |
|---|---|
| 20-30 percent (10–15 questions) | Grammar: contextual questions on grammar, syntax, and word meaning |
| 20–30 percent (10–15 questions) | Reference: identification of the person or thing to which a pronoun or adjective refers; inference of meaning from words that are assumed or understood; recognition of references or allusions to a specific person, place, or event mentioned in the text |
| 2–5 percent (1–3 questions) | Figures of speech |
| 2–5 percent (1–3 questions) | Metrics<br><br>Vergil: hexameter line<br><br>Literature: hendecasyllabic line; either line of the elegaic couplet |
| 2–5 percent (1–3 questions) | Literary and cultural background questions (syllabus-based passages only) |

## The Format of Latin Passages on the Multiple-Choice Section

**Here is a sample to illustrate the format of the Latin text in the multiple-choice section:**

| | |
|---|---|
| Brief title | **Mourning for Phaethon** |
| Sentences with initial caps<br>No macrons | Naides Hesperiae trifida¹ fumantia flamma<br>corpora dant tumulo, signant quoque carmine saxum:<br>"Hic situs est Phaethon, currus auriga paterni; |
| Lines numbered every five lines | *Line* quem si non tenuit, magnis tamen excidit ausis."<br>5 Nam pater obductos, luctu miserabilis aegro,<br>condiderat vulnus: et si modo credimus, unum<br>isse diem sine sole ferunt. Incendia lumen<br>praebebant, aliquisque malo fuit usus in illo. |
| Glossing of unfamiliar words | ¹ trifidus, -a, -um, adj.: three-forked |

**Notes:**

1. Titles are not provided for Latin passages in the free-response section; however, all Latin passages on the latter section are attributed.
2. Accusative plurals of third declension **i**-stems appear as **–es**, rather than **–is**, e.g., **cives** rather than **civis**; consonantal **i** is used instead of **j**, i.e., **iam** rather than **jam**.

## e Multiple-Choice Section

hich students found to be the most difficult on the
005 AP Latin Exam provides insight into what
n.[2]

which students found the most challeng-

ion: "Line 1 tells us that . . . ," or "In lines 1–2 we learn

ing the form of a noun or adjective: "The case and number of **corpora** is . . . ," or "The case of **corpora** is determined by . . . ."

3. Pronoun reference: "In line 3, **se** refers to . . . ."

4. (tie) Adjective-noun agreement: "In line 4, **omnes** modifies . . . ."

   Translation of a phrase, clause, sentence, or line: "Line 5 is translated. . . ."

5. (tie) Identifying the subject of a verb: "The subject of **sacravit** is . . . ."

   Identifying the mood and tense of a verb: "The tense and mood of **possim** are . . . ."

   Translation of an individual word in context: "In line 6, the word **cum** is translated . . . ."

   Identifying a figure of speech: "A figure of speech that appears in line 7 is . . . ."

Later chapters of this book are devoted to review of grammar and syntax, in order to help you prepare for grammar and translation questions as they appear in this section of the Exam.

## FAQs About the Multiple-Choice Section

- **How can I best prepare for this part of the exam?**

  Here are some general tips for the long term:

  1. Master the fundamentals of Latin: spend extra time during class grammar review and review regularly on your own. Ask your teacher for suggestions on how to strengthen your weak areas. (Don't do this on the eve of the exam!)

  2. Approach your daily reading assignment as a sight reading. Attempt to do as much of the decision-making as possible without recourse to references. When translating, pay particular attention to noun/pronoun-adjective agreement, identification of the references of pronouns, and

---

[2] This frequency study was done for the 2005 Latin Lit multiple-choice section only. It is assumed that the result for the Vergil section would be approximately the same. For the actual questions appearing on the 2005 multiple-choice section, consult the College Board AP Latin Web site or the publication of the released 2005 AP Latin Exams, for which, see Chapter 1 of this book.

the proper rendering of verb forms, as well as to the words that define phrases and clauses.

3. Become familiar with the types of questions asked on the multiple-choice section, and with their degree of difficulty, by practicing with the sample materials found in this book and those provided by The College Board.

4. For short-term strategies on preparing for the AP Latin Exam, see Chapter 12.

- **Should I guess on this section if I'm not sure of the answer?**

It is best not to "random guess." There is a penalty of 1/3 pt. for each wrong answer, as opposed to 1/4 pt. on the SAT. Random guessing will likely lower your score because of penalty-grading and because it wastes time. If you can narrow your choices to two, then go for it! This constitutes an "educated guess." In making an educated guess, use all the language skills at your disposal, such as recall, analogy and deduction, and reference to English and other languages. You have 60 minutes to answer 50 questions, which means you have 15 minutes to spend on each of the four passages. This averages out to about one question per minute. You need not answer every question correctly in order to achieve a solid score on this section of the test, nor do you even need to answer every question. If you are stumped and cannot eliminate one or two answers as incorrect, move on.

- **How will my performance on the multiple-choice section influence my overall score?**

The multiple-choice section counts for 40 percent of your total exam score. For further information, see Chapter 12, "Taking and Scoring the AP Latin Exam." It is important to remember that the multiple-choice section is tested first during the exam period and is considered by many students to be the more difficult of the two sections of the exam, so don't become discouraged.

## Types of Questions Asked on the Multiple-Choice Section

### Translation and Comprehension

**Romae** (line 2) is best translated . . .

In line 3, **occurri** is translated . . .

In lines 6–7, **ad urbem defendendam** is best translated . . .

Which of the following is a literal translation of the sentence **Es germana . . . fluctus** (lines 7–8)?

From the words **Sed . . . affugerat** (lines 8–9), we learn that . . .

From the clause **cum . . . vidisset** (lines 9–10), we learn that . . .

The sentence **Occidit . . . Troia** (line 11) states that . . .

From lines 10–12 (**Si voluit . . . est resistendum**), we learn that . . .

## Grammar and Syntax

The case of **gaudio** (line 1) is dependent upon . . .

The case and number of **templa** (line 2) are . . .

The case of the words **dolori, irae,** and **gaudio** (lines 2–3) is . . .

The case and number of **haec** (line 4) are . . .

In line 5, **tantas** modifies . . .

The main verb in **Cum . . . vocari** (lines 4-5) is . . .

The gender of **posita** (line 6) is determined by . . .

The subject of **spectavisse** (line 7) is . . .

The direct object of **dedit** (line 11) is . . .

What part of speech is **munere** (line 8)?

In line 9, both **vive** and **ama** are . . .

The tense of **tradiderint** (line 10) is . . .

## Reference

In line 1, **eos** refers to . . .

The word **illo** (line 2) refers to the same person as . . .

In line 4, the word **quae** refers to . . .

In line 5, **se** refers to . . .

In line 6, the word **suos** in the phrase **suos viros** refers to . . .

**-que** (line 7) joins **optimis** to . . .

In line 8, **advocati** refers to . . .

The implied subject of **conspicit** (line 9) is . . .

**Festinate** (line 10) is addressed to . . .

## Figures of Speech

The words **non . . . ignara** (line 1) are an example of . . .

What figure of speech occurs in **minis aut blandimentis corrupta** (line 3)?

## Metrics

How many elisions occur in line 4?

The metrical pattern of the first four feet of line 3 is . . .

Note:
　　Answers will be given in the form "dactyl-spondee-spondee-dactyl."

## Background Questions (syllabus-based passage only!)

Which of the following poems is most closely linked thematically with this poem?

In lines 6–8 (**Vos . . . charta**), Catullus voices his disapproval of the work of a fellow poet. Which of the following is another writer who prompts a negative opinion from Catullus?

From lines 10–11 (**Remitte . . . indulgentiae tuae**), we can infer that . . .

The speaker in this passage is . . .

## How to Prepare for the Syllabus-Based Passage

- The syllabus-based passages are usually selected from the less familiar portions of the required readings from Vergil or Catullus. Be sure to prepare the required Latin thoroughly!

- Glance over the passage quickly in Latin to see if you can recognize a familiar word, phrase, sentence, or proper name, which will help to orient you. If you do not recognize the passage, attempt to sight read it, using your knowledge of the context.

## How to Read Latin at Sight

- Read quickly through the entire passage in the order in which the Latin is given. Try to follow the main ideas and the general drift of the meaning without translating. Do not translate the reading passage word-for-word unless instructed to do so in answer to a specific question.

- Pay attention to the clues given in the English title and glossed vocabulary and incorporate their hints into your understanding of the passage.

- Scan the passage a second time, noting the main constructions, idiomatic expressions, and transition points in the writer's thinking. Remember that Latin prefers to use subordinate clauses and participles whose meaning is equivalent to subordinate clauses. As you read, focus on groups of words that go together. Pay particular attention to:

     noun-adjective agreement

     antecedents and references of pronouns

     tense, voice, and mood of verbs

     boundaries of phrases and clauses

  Try to anticipate the forms by observing the guide words that usually introduce constructions such as indirect statements, subordinate clauses, etc.

- Work from each question back to the text, trying to locate the specific answer. Note that the questions are asked in the sequence of the sentences in the passage and that there is usually at least one question for each sentence. Line numbers and Latin citations are always provided in the question, to assist you in locating the relevant Latin quickly. Remember, if you are stumped and cannot eliminate one or two answers as incorrect, move on.

- Practice sight reading. Ask your teacher for passages with which to practice, or go online for the reading comprehension passages from previous National Latin Exams (answers provided!): http://www.nle.org/exams. html#exams_previous).

# Practice Questions

Note that a few more questions are provided here than the 50 that are usually found on the actual multiple-choice section. This section includes syllabus-based passages from both Vergil and Catullus and sight passages from Pliny (prose) and Tibullus (poetry). The answers to these questions are provided at the end of the chapter, along with translations of all passages, for your convenience.

## 1. Syllabus-Based Passage: Vergil

### The destiny of the Romans is assured

"Et nunc cedo equidem pugnasque exosa relinquo.
Illud te, nulla fati quod lege tenetur,
pro Latio obtestor, pro maiestate tuorum:
*Line*    cum iam conubiis pacem felicibus (esto)
   5   component, cum iam leges et foedera iungent,
ne vetus indigenas nomen mutare Latinos
neu Troas fieri iubeas Teucrosque vocari
aut vocem mutare viros aut vertere vestem.
Sit Latium, sint Albani per saecula reges,
  10  sit Romana potens Itala virtute propago:
occidit, occideritque sinas cum nomine Troia."

1.   The emotion expressed by the speaker in line 1 is

   (A)  confusion        (C)  resignation

   (B)  joy              (D)  contemplation

2.   Based upon your knowledge of this passage, who is speaking to whom?

   (A)  Juno to Aeneas     (C)  Aeneas to Jupiter

   (B)  Latinus to Aeneas   (D)  Juno to Jupiter

3.   <u>Illud</u> (lines 2) refers to

   (A)  what is said in the previous line

   (B)  fate

   (C)  what is said in lines 4–8

   (D)  Latium

4. The metrical pattern of the first four feet of line 3 is

    (A) dactyl-dactyl-spondee-spondee

    (B) dactyl-spondee-spondee-spondee

    (C) spondee-spondee-dactyl-spondee

    (D) spondee-dactyl-spondee-dactyl

5. In line 4, <u>cum</u> is best translated

    (A) when         (C) with

    (B) since        (D) although

6. What figure of speech occurs in lines 4–5?

    (A) hyperbole     (C) simile

    (B) anaphora     (D) apostrophe

7. According to lines 4–5 (<u>cum</u> . . . <u>iungent</u>), what two things will join the Trojans and the Latins?

    (A) peace and happiness

    (B) pressure from others and conscience

    (C) intermarriage and laws

    (D) language and culture

8. The figure of speech occurring in line 6 is

    (A) chiasmus     (C) aposiopesis

    (B) asyndeton     (D) interlocked word order (synchysis)

9. In lines 6–7, <u>ne</u>...<u>iubeas</u> is translated

    (A) may you not command

    (B) you are not commanding

    (C) do not command

    (D) you will not command

10. As it appears in line 7, -que joins

    (A) <u>iubeas</u> and <u>Teucros</u>

    (B) <u>ne</u> (line 6) and <u>neu</u>

    (C) <u>Troas fieri</u> and <u>Teucros vocari</u>

    (D) <u>Latinos</u> (line 6) and <u>Teucros</u>

11. In lines 6–8, we learn that all but which of the following will remain unchanged?

    (A) clothing          (C) name

    (B) language          (D) religion

12. In line 10, <u>Itala</u> modifies

    (A) <u>Romana</u>          (C) <u>propago</u>

    (B) <u>virtute</u>          (D) a noun that is understood

13. The technique of anaphora found in 9–10 is used to

    (A) confuse          (C) emphasize

    (B) explain          (D) understate

14. In line 11, the speaker wishes that

    (A) the Roman people should adopt the identity of Trojans

    (B) Troy should avenge her destruction

    (C) anyone with the name Trojan should die

    (D) even the name Troy should disappear

## 2. Syllabus-Based Passage: Catullus

### A woman scorned

"Certe ego te in medio versantem turbine leti
eripui, et potius germanum amittere crevi
quam tibi fallaci supremo in tempore dessem.
*Line* Pro quo dilaceranda feris dabor alitibusque[1]
5 praeda, neque iniecta tumulabor mortua terra.
Quaenam te genuit[2] sola sub rupe leaena,
quod mare conceptum spumantibus exspuit undis,
quae Syrtis, quae Scylla rapax, quae vasta Charybdis,
talia qui reddis pro dulci praemia vita?"

1. <u>ales</u>, <u>alitis</u>, m./f.: large bird
2. <u>gigno, gignere, genui, genitum</u>: give birth to, produce

15. Who is addressing whom, in this speech?

    (A) Aegeus to Theseus

    (B) Ariadne to Theseus

    (C) Theseus to Minotaur

    (D) Ariadne to Aegeus

16. The words <u>potius</u> . . . <u>quam</u> (lines 2–3) are an example of
    (A) tmesis
    (B) hendiadys
    (C) ellipsis
    (D) assonance

17. The word <u>dessem</u> (line 3) is
    (A) an infinitive
    (B) a noun
    (C) a participle
    (D) a subjunctive

18. What do we learn from lines 1–3?
    (A) The speaker had killed his/her brother
    (B) The speaker had rescued the addressee from death
    (C) The addressee had died as a result of deceit
    (D) The addressee had saved the speaker from a storm

19. <u>Dilaceranda</u> (line 4) is translated
    (A) about to be torn apart
    (B) tearing apart
    (C) having been torn apart
    (D) about to tear apart

20. Lines 4–5 (<u>Pro quo</u> . . . <u>praeda</u>) tells us that the speaker
    (A) wishes to die
    (B) awaits a terrible death
    (C) will bring death to another person
    (D) will make a sacrifice

21. The case and number of <u>iniecta</u> . . . <u>terra</u> (line 5) are
    (A) nominative singular
    (B) accusative plural
    (C) ablative singular
    (D) nominative plural

22. What figure of speech occurs in line 7 (<u>quae</u> . . . <u>Charybdis</u>)?
    (A) litotes
    (B) simile
    (C) chiasmus
    (D) onomatopoeia

23. From lines 6–8 (<u>Quaenam</u> . . . <u>Charybdis</u>), we learn that
    (A) the speaker thinks the addressee was born from a monster
    (B) the addressee has had a dangerous journey
    (C) the speaker is calling upon creatures associated with the sea
    (D) a life lived well will protect anyone from danger

24. In line 9, <u>qui</u> refers to

    (A) Charybdis       (C) the addressee

    (B) the speaker       (D) the reader

# Passages for Sight Reading

## 3. Sight Reading: Prose

### Pliny misses his wife

C. Plinius Calpurniae Suae S.[1]
Incredibile est quanto desiderio tui tenear. In causa amor
primum, deinde quod non consuevimus abesse. Inde est quod
*Line*    magnam noctium partem in imagine tuā vigil exigo; inde
5    quod interdiu, quibus horis te visere solebam, ad diaetam[2]
tuam ipsi me, ut verissime dicitur, pedes ducunt; quod
denique aeger et maestus ac similis excluso a vacuo limine
recedo. Unum tempus his tormentis caret, quo in foro et
amicorum litibus[3] conteror.[4] Aestima tu, quae vita mea sit,
10    cui requies in labore, in miseria curisque solacium. Vale.

1. <u>S.</u> = <u>Salutem Dicit</u>: sends greetings
2. <u>diaeta, diaeta</u>, f.: room
3. <u>lis, litis</u>, f.: lawsuit, court
4. <u>contero, contere, contrivi, contritum</u>: wear out

25. In line 2, <u>quanto</u> introduces

    (A) a characteristic clause

    (B) a relative descriptive clause

    (C) a purpose clause

    (D) an indirect question clause

26. In lines 2–3, Pliny says he misses his wife because he loves her and because

    (A) they are always apart, but have never gotten used to it

    (B) they are unaccustomed to being apart

    (C) most Romans are not accustomed to traveling

    (D) they have only recently been married

27. In lines 3–4, we learn that Pliny

    (A) stays awake thinking of his wife

    (B) sleeps the night through

    (C) has nightmares

    (D) tries not to think of his wife

28. The case and number of <u>noctium</u> (line 4) are

    (A) accusative singular     (C) genitive plural

    (B) accusative plural       (D) nominative singular

29. The adjective <u>vigil</u> (line 4) modifies

    (A) <u>partem</u> (4)

    (B) <u>imagine</u> (4)

    (C) the subject of <u>exigo</u> (4)

    (D) Calpurnia, understood

30. In line 6, <u>ut</u> is best translated

    (A) that             (C) in order to

    (B) as              (D) when

31. Lines 4–6 (<u>inde</u> . . . <u>ducunt</u>) tell us that Pliny

    (A) continues to visit his wife's room at the usual times

    (B) sleeps in his wife's room out of loneliness

    (C) avoids his wife's room, which reminds him of her absence

    (D) cleans his wife's room during the day

32. The words <u>aeger et maestus</u> (line 7) describe Pliny's mood as

    (A) gloomy       (C) apathetic

    (B) angry        (D) puzzled

33. The phrase <u>similis excluso</u> (line 7) suggests a

    (A) trusted confidante     (C) condemned criminal

    (B) freed slave          (D) spurned lover

34. In line 8, <u>his tormentis</u> is ablative because it

    (A) is in a prepositional phrase

    (B) expresses time

    (C) completes the meaning of the verb <u>caret</u>

    (D) indicates location

35. From lines 8–9 (<u>Unum</u> . . . <u>conteror</u>), we learn that Pliny

    (A) is never at ease in his wife's absence

    (B) feels the loneliest when he has to be in public

    (C) finds sole consolation in his work in the courts

    (D) is exhausted by his daily routine

36. <u>Requies in labore</u> (line 10) is an example of

    (A) anaphora                (C) hyperbole

    (B) oxymoron                (D) apostrophe

37. The clauses <u>cui</u> . . . <u>labore</u> and (cui) <u>in</u> . . . <u>solacium</u> (line 10) lack a

    (A) subject                 (C) noun

    (B) verb                    (D) prepositional phrase

## 4. Sight Reading: Poetry

### The First Weapon

Quis fuit, horrendos primus qui protulit enses?[1]
Quam ferus et vere ferreus ille fuit!
Tum caedes hominum generi, tum proelia nata,
*Line*    tum brevior dirae mortis aperta via est.
  5  An nihil ille miser meruit, nos ad mala nostra
vertimus, in saevas quod dedit ille feras?
Divitis hoc vitium est auri, nec bella fuerunt,
faginus[2] astabat cum scyphus[3] ante dapes.[4]
Non arces, non vallus erat, somnumque petebat
  10  securus varias dux gregis inter oves.
Tum mihi vita foret, Valgi,[5] nec tristia nossem
arma nec audissem corde micante[6] tubam.
Nunc ad bella trahor, et iam quis forsitan hostis
haesura in nostro tela gerit latere.

1. <u>ensis, ensis</u>, m.: sword
2. <u>faginus</u>, -a, -um, adj.: of beechwood
3. <u>scyphus</u>, -i, m.: drinking cup
4. <u>daps, dapis</u>, f., meal
5. <u>Valgi</u>: vocative
6. <u>mico, micare, micui</u>: flutter, beat

38. Line 1 (<u>Quis</u> . . . <u>enses?</u>) is translated

    (A) Was he terrible who first produced the sword?

    (B) Who was he who first brought forth the terrible sword?

    (C) Who was the terrible one who produced the first sword?

    (D) Weren't swords terrible when they were first produced?

39. The word <u>Quam</u> (line 2) is translated

    (A) Which                   (C) How

    (B) Whom                    (D) Than

40. <u>Vere ferreus ille fuit</u> (line 2) is an example of what figure of speech?

    (A)  transferred epithet   (C)  zeugma

    (B)  alliteration          (D)  metaphor

41. The form missing from the verb <u>nata</u> (line 3) is

    (A)  <u>est</u>            (C)  <u>sunt</u>

    (B)  <u>sit</u>            (D)  <u>esse</u>

42. The word <u>brevior</u> (line 4) modifies

    (A)  <u>mortis</u> (line 4)    (C)  <u>via</u> (line 4)

    (B)  <u>aperta est</u> (line 4)  (D)  an understood noun

43. According to what the writer says in lines 5–6, the first sword was most likely intended for

    (A)  self-destruction     (C)  religious ritual

    (B)  protection           (D)  status symbol

44. Lines 7–8 (<u>Divitis</u> . . . <u>dapes</u>) suggest that man's aggressiveness results from

    (A)  a natural inclination to fight

    (B)  blood feuds

    (C)  controversy over land

    (D)  material possessions

45. The case of the adjective <u>Divitis</u> (line 7) is

    (A)  ablative             (C)  genitive

    (B)  nominative           (D)  dative

46. In lines 9–10 (<u>Non arces</u> . . . <u>oves</u>), which of the following is considered by the writer to be a product of the simple life?

    (A)  food on the table    (C)  shelter

    (B)  safety and security  (D)  a loving family

47. In line 11, <u>Tum mihi vita foret</u> is best translated

    (A)  I would have lived then

    (B)  I was living then

    (C)  If I had been alive then

    (D)  While I was still alive

48. In line 12, <u>nec audissem</u> is translated

    (A) I had not heard

    (B) not to have heard

    (C) not having been heard

    (D) I would not have heard

49. The verbal form <u>micante</u> (line 12) is a

    (A) main verb               (C) present participle

    (B) gerundive               (D) perfect participle

50. Regarding the writer's personal feelings about going to war, the word <u>trahor</u> (line 13) suggests that he is

    (A) eager                   (C) reluctant

    (B) apathetic               (D) obsessive

51. The verbal form <u>haesura</u> (line 14) is translated

    (A) about to stick          (C) about to be stuck

    (B) having been stuck       (D) sticking

52. In the last line (line 14), the meaning is reinforced by use of the figure of speech

    (A) enjambment

    (B) interlocking word order (synchysis)

    (C) personification

    (D) anaphora

53. The word <u>nostro</u> (line 14) refers to

    (A) the Romans              (C) Valgius

    (B) the enemy               (D) the writer

## Answers

| 1. Vergil | 2. Catullus | 3. Sight Prose | 4. Sight Poetry |
|-----------|-------------|----------------|-----------------|
| 1. C | 15. B | 25. D | 38. B |
| 2. D | 16. A | 36. B | 39. C |
| 3. C | 17. D | 27. A | 40. D |
| 4. B | 18. B | 28. C | 41. A |
| 5. A | 19. A | 29. C | 42. C |
| 6. B | 20. B | 30. B | 43. B |
| 7. C | 21. C | 31. A | 44. D |
| 8. D | 22. D | 32. A | 45. C |
| 9. A | 23. A | 33. D | 46. B |
| 10. C | 24. C | 34. C | 47. C |
| 11. D | | 35. C | 48. D |
| 12. C | | 36. B | 49. C |
| 13. C | | 37. B | 50. C |
| 14. D | | | 51. A |
| | | | 52. B |
| | | | 53. D |

## Translations:

### 1. Syllabus-based: Vergil

"And now I yield, yes, and hating the fighting, I abandon it. To the following, which is held by (under the control of) no law of fate, for the sake of Latium and for the sake of the greatness of your own (descendants), I call upon you as a witness: when now they will make peace with happy bridal rites — so be it! — when now they will join in laws and agreements, may you not command the native Latins to change their ancient name nor to become Trojans and be called Teucrians, nor to change their language or alter their clothing. Let Latium be, let Alban kings last through the generations, let there be Roman offspring mighty in Italic valor: may you allow Troy to fall, and with it the (very) name of Troy." (Vergil, *Aeneid* 12.818–28)

### 2. Syllabus-based: Catullus

"Surely I rescued you, tossing amid the whirlwind of death, and I decided to lose my brother rather than fail treacherous you at the final moment (of death). For which I will be given to wild beasts and birds to be torn as prey, nor will I, now dead, be buried, having been sprinkled with earth. What lioness bore you beneath a lonely cliff? What sea conceived and spit you out into the foaming waves, what (African) sandbanks, what greedy Scylla, what monstrous Charybdis (bore you), who for sweet life return such payment?" (Catullus, Poem 64.149–57)

### 3. Sight Prose

Gaius Pliny sends greetings to his Calpurnia

It is unbelievable with how much longing for you I am held (prisoner). (My) love (for you) is the first reason, then the fact that we have not grown accustomed to being apart. As a result, I spend a great part of (my) nights staying awake thinking of you; and, too, throughout the day, during the hours when I was in the habit of visiting you, my feet lead me (I speak the truth) to your room; and finally, sick and sorrowful like a spurned lover, I withdraw from (your) empty doorway. The one time that I am free from these torments is when I wear myself out in the Forum and with the lawsuits of my friends. Imagine what life there is for me, for whom there is rest in work and distraction in unhappiness and anxiety. Farewell. (Pliny, *Epistulae* 7.5)

### 4. Sight Poetry

Who was the first who brought forth the terrible sword? How fierce and truly made-of-iron he was! Then slaughter, then battles were born to the world of men, then there was opened a shorter path for frightful death. Or perhaps that poor wretch deserved no (blame), but we have turned to our wicked (purposes) that which he gave (us) against the wild beasts. This is the curse of costly gold, nor were there wars when the cup of beechwood stood before the meal. Neither citadels nor stockades were there (then), and the shepherd without care sought sleep among his diverse sheep. At that time I (wish I) would have lived, Valgius, neither would I have known grim war nor, with fluttering heart, would I have heard the war horn. Now I am pulled into war, and perhaps already some enemy is bearing the weapon (that he is) about to stick in my side. (Tibullus, *Elegies* 1.10.1–14)

## Chapter 5

# The Free-Response Section

The free-response section is the second of the two sections of the AP Latin Exam. (Remember that you will be given a short break between the two sections.) As indicated in Chapter 1 of this book, the multiple-choice and free-response sections differ in content, format, length, and value. The free-response section on the *Aeneid* consists of five questions. The free-response section on Latin Literature consists of three questions covering the required syllabus for Catullus—this section is common to all Latin Literature exams, regardless of choice author—plus three additional questions on the syllabus for Cicero, Horace, or Ovid (see Chapters 2 and 3 for syllabi). The free-response section requires two hours: a 15–minute reading period and 1 hour and 45 minutes for writing. This section counts 60 percent of your total score.

## Content of the Free-Response Section

You are called upon to demonstrate your command of the prepared Latin by answering translation, essay, and short answer questions that assess your ability both to give a close reading of the Latin text and to express your understanding of that text with regard to a specific question.

As mentioned, there are five free-response questions on the Vergil Exam and six for Latin Literature. The free-response section of the Vergil Exam contains two translation questions, a long essay, and two short essays. One short essay calls for you to be able to produce a comparative analysis of characters or situations in the context of those portions of the *Aeneid* read in English. The free-response section of the Latin Literature Exam consists of three questions on Catullus and three on the choice author. The questions on Catullus consist of a translation, a long essay, and a short essay. Those on the choice author consist of a translation, one short essay, and short identification questions that may require you to identify a figure of speech or scan a line of poetry in the appropriate meter. For specific information about each type of question that appears on the free-response section of the AP Latin Exam, see the chapters that follow.

## Abilities Tested on the Free-Response Section

The free-response section anticipates that you can:

- give a literal English translation of a prepared Latin passage;
- analyze excerpts from the required reading and compare and contrast parts of the same poem or different sets of lines, poems, or passages and

draw generalized conclusions about keynote themes and motifs expressed in these excerpts as they relate to the entire poem or work;

- examine and interpret the writing style of the author, including characteristic features such as word choice, organization and structure, mood and tone, figures of speech, and sound and rhythm;

- demonstrate knowledge of the *Aeneid* as a whole or answer specific spot questions on the content, figures of speech, and meter of a passage of Latin from the appropriate choice author.

## Format of The Free-Response Section

### Vergil (these questions on the Exam are designated as V1, V2, etc.)

**Question V1:** 10–minute translation (15 percent)

**Question V2:** 10–minute translation (15 percent)

**Question V3:** 45–minute long essay (35 percent)

**Question V4:** 20–minute short essay (20 percent)

**Question V5:** 20–minute short essay (15 percent)

### Latin Literature (Lit questions are labeled on the Exam as LL1, LL2, etc.)

**Catullus** (all Latin Literature students answer these questions; 50 percent of this section)

> **Question LL1:** 10–minute translation (15 percent)
>
> **Question LL2:** 30–minute long essay (20 percent)
>
> **Question LL3:** 20–minute short essay (15 percent)
>
> plus

**Choice Author** (Cicero, Horace, or Ovid only; 50 percent of this section)

> **Question LL4, 7, 10:** 20–minute essay (20 percent)
>
> **Question LL5, 8, 11:** 15–minute translation (15 percent)
>
> **Question LL6, 9, 12:** 10–minute short identification (15 percent)

## FAQs About the Free-Response Section

- **What is the free-response section like?**

  This section tests the specific reading syllabus that you've prepared, whether this preparation occurred in a course specifically designated as Advanced Placement, in an advanced Latin course not labelled as AP, or in a self-taught or tutorial setting. This section measures your ability to read and understand the Latin that you have prepared, as well as your ability to express your understanding in organized and coherent English. You will write your answers longhand in a booklet roughly equivalent to the blue book used in colleges (except that it's pink!) For AP-style free-response questions, see the Practice Exams at the end of this book.

- **What is the "15-minute reading period"?**

   This time is provided at the beginning of the free-response section. You are allowed to read through all the free-response questions in the green test booklet. You may plan your answers by writing marginal or intertextual notes and by assessing the time that you will require for each question, based upon your recognition of the passages. During the reading period, circle or otherwise highlight the key words in each question, then think about how you will approach your answer and underline or otherwise highlight words, phrases, clauses, lines/sentences of the Latin text that are relevant to your answer. Jot down notes in the margin that will help you to remember and organize points that you wish to make later in your formal answer. Use the reading period productively in order to organize your thinking (this is called prewriting or brainstorming). The reading period will be discussed further in Chapter 12.

- **How can I best prepare for the free-response section?**

   Your success on this section is directly proportional to the amount of the syllabus that you have prepared and to the thoroughness of that preparation.

   1. Prepare your daily assignments thoroughly and consistently. Don't fall behind, which will leave gaps in your preparation and therefore in your recognition and comprehension of the Latin. Prior to the exam, it is best not to rush through uncompleted portions of the syllabus at the last minute, as this will only create confusion and anxiety. Concentrate on preparing thoroughly what you have done and use your sight-reading skills and ability as a writer to address that question or those questions on passages that you do not recognize. Not every student can answer every question!

   2. Minimize your reliance on reference materials (reading or class notes, published translations, dictionaries, online resources, friends, tutors) when you are preparing your reading.

   3. Ask questions of your teacher or classmates when you don't know or aren't sure.

   4. Become familiar with the format and level of difficulty of free-response questions by using old exams. Practice understanding the intent and implications of a free-response question. Use the resources provided in this book and in Chapter 1.

   5. Pretend that each unit test you take during your preparation is an AP Exam and adjust your test-taking style to deal with the challenges of thinking and writing under the pressure of time.

   6. Leave time for review before the AP Latin Exam (for which, see Chapter 12).

## A Catalogue of Passages and Poems Tested on the Free-Response Section of Recent AP Latin Exams (2006–2001)

The passages and poems listed below are given in the order in which they appeared on each exam. Remember that there are two translation passages for Vergil and that the sequence of questions for the choice authors differs from that of the required authors. These readings, which illustrate the length and degree of difficulty of Latin passages appearing on the free-response section, are provided as samples. Note that the long essays often contain two passages. Also note that a different book of the *Aeneid* is represented by each question. It is not customary for the same passage or poem to be tested in consecutive years. For the actual exams, see The College Board AP Latin Web site.

## Vergil

| 2006 | 2003 |
|---|---|
| Translation: *Aeneid* 1.378–85 | Translation: *Aeneid* 4.160–66 |
| Translation: *Aeneid* 2.560–66 | Translation: *Aeneid* 12.803–809 |
| Long Essay: *Aeneid* 6.868–86 | Long Essay: *Aeneid* 2.768–93 |
| Short Essay: *Aeneid* 10.491–96, 500–505 | Short Essay: *Aeneid* 1.450–65 |
| Background: function in plot: Helenus, Iarbas, Lausus/Allecto, Camilla, Juturna | Background: deception: Cupid, Sinon/Allecto, Iris, Juturna |

| 2005 | 2002 |
|---|---|
| Translation: *Aeneid* 2.201–207 | Translation: *Aeneid* 12.908–14 |
| Translation: *Aeneid* 12.930–36 | Translation: *Aeneid* 2.289–94 |
| Long Essay: *Aeneid* 1.92–101, 1.198–209 | Long Essay: *Aeneid* 4.20–29, 4.320–30 |
| Short Essay: *Aeneid* 6.83–94 | Short Essay: *Aeneid* 1.291–96 |
| Background: **pietas**: Anchises, Dares or Entellus, Helenus/Amata, Camilla, Juturna | Background: unfair events: Camilla, Palinurus, Lausus, games in Book 5, Amata |

| 2004 | 2001 |
|---|---|
| Translation: *Aeneid* 2.10–16 | Translation: *Aeneid* 10.450, 453–56 |
| Translation: *Aeneid* 6.893–99 | Translation: *Aeneid* 2.237–43 |
| Long Essay: *Aeneid* 1.124–41, 4.84–89 | Long Essay: *Aeneid* 1.37–49, 12.818–28 |
| Short Essay: *Aeneid* 10.467–75 | Short Essay: *Aeneid* 4.675–85 |
| Background: reasonable vs. rash: Aeneas and Helen, Trojan women, burn ships, Dares and Entellus boxing/Amata's behavior after Lavinia's engagement, Hercules and Cacus, midnight foray of Nisus and Euryalus | Background: revealing the future |

## Catullus

| 2006 | 2003 |
|---|---|
| Translation: Poem 35.1–10 | Translation: Poem 44.6–12 |
| Long Essay: Poems 40 and 116 | Long Essay: Poem 10.1–7, 14–34 |
| Short Essay: Poem 69 | Short Essay: Poem 5 |
| **2005** | **2002** |
| Translation: Poem 31.7–14 | Translation: Poem 9.1–8 (now omitted) |
| Long Essay: Poems 14.12–23 and 30 | Long Essay: Poem 3 |
| Short Essay: Poem 51.1–12 | Short Essay: Poem 83 |
| **2004** | **2001** |
| Translations: Poem 70 and 87 | Translation: Poem 46 |
| Long Essay: Poems 1 and 95a and b (now omitted) | Long Essay: Poems 77 and 84 |
| Short Essay: Poems 72.5–8 and 85 | Short Essay: Poem 86 |

## Cicero

As indicated, the syllabus for Cicero has been changed, beginning with the exam in 2007. For information on recent Cicero exams, see the College Board AP Latin Literature Web site.

## Horace

In the choice authors, the sequence of questions was changed in 2005. From 2001–2004, the order was identification, translation, and short essay. From 2005 to the present, the order is short essay, translation, and identification.

| 2006 | 2003 |
|---|---|
| Short Essay: *Satires* 1.9.60–68 | Identification: *Satires* 1.9.35–41 |
| Translation: *Odes* 3.1.37–46 | Translation: *Odes* 1.22.17–24 |
| Identification: *Odes* 1.1.3–10 | Short Essay: *Odes* 3.9.9–24 |
| **2005** | **2002** |
| Short Essay: *Odes* 3.1.5–16 | Identification: *Odes* 1.24.3–10 |
| Translation: *Odes* 1.9.1–9 | Translation: *Odes* 3.13.9–16 |
| Identification: *Odes* 1.23 | Short Essay: *Odes* 2.10.1–8 and 21–24 |
| **2004** | **2001** |
| Identification: *Odes* 2.7.1–12 | Identification: *Odes* 4.7.17–28 |
| Translation: *Odes* 1.13.1–8 | Translation: *Odes* 2.3.13–20 |
| Short Essay: *Satires* 1.9.48–60 | Short Essay: *Odes* 1.11 |

## Ovid

P & T = Pyramus and Thisbe, D & I = Daedalus and Icarus, etc.

| 2006 | 2003 |
|------|------|
| Short Essay: *Metamorphoses* 4.147–57 (P & T) | Identification: *Metamorphoses* 10.238–46 (P) |
| Translation: *Amores* 1.9.25–32 | Translation: *Metamorphoses* 8.183–89 (D & I) |
| Identification: *Amores* 1.12.1–7 | Short Essay: *Amores* 1.1.5–6, 19–27 |

| 2005 | 2002 |
|------|------|
| Short Essay: *Metamorphoses* 8.203–13 (D & I) | Identification: *Amores* 1.9.17–24 |
| Translation: *Metamorphoses* 4.55–62 (P & T) | Translation: *Metamorphoses* 8.223–28 (D & I) |
| Identification: *Amores* 3.15.1–7 | Short Essay: *Metamorphoses* 4.71–80 (P & T) |

| 2004 | 2001 |
|------|------|
| Identification: *Metamorphoses* 1.481–89 (D & A) | Identification: *Amores* 1.3.5–12 |
| Translation: *Metamorphoses* 8.681–86 (B & P) | Translation: *Amores* 1.11.11–15 |
| Short Essay: *Metamorphoses* 1.553–67 (D & A) | Short Essay: *Metamorphoses* 8.631–36, 712–30 (B & P) |

# A Catalogue of Free-Response Passages and Poems Tested on AP Latin Exams (2006–2001)

| Vergil | | Catullus | Horace | | Ovid | |
|---|---|---|---|---|---|---|
| *Aeneid* | | *Carmina* | *Odes* | | *Metamorphoses* | |
| Book 1 | 37–49 | Poem 1 | Book 1 | Ode 1.3–10 | Book 1 | 481–89 |
| | 92–101 | 3 | | Ode 2.17–24 | | 553–67 |
| | 124–41 | 5 | | Ode 9.1–9 | Book 4 | 55–62 |
| | 198–209 | 10.1–7, 14–34 | | Ode 13.1–8 | | 71–80 |
| | 291–96 | 14a.12–23 | | Ode 11 | | 147–57 |
| | 378–85 | 30 | | Ode 23 | Book 8 | 183–89 |
| | 450–65 | 31.7–14 | | Ode 24.3–10 | | 203–13 |
| Book 2 | 10–16 | 35.1–10 | Book 2 | Ode 3.13–20 | | 223–28 |
| | 201–207 | 40 | | Ode 7.1–12 | | 631–36 |
| | 237–43 | 44.6–12 | | Ode 10.1–8 | | 681–86 |
| | 289–94 | 46 | | Ode 10.21–24 | | 712–30 |
| | 560–66 | 51.1–12 | Book 3 | Ode 1.5–16 | Book 10 | 238–46 |
| | 768–93 | 69 | | Ode 1.37–46 | *Amores* | |
| Book 4 | 20–29 | 70 | | Ode 9.9–24 | Book 1 | 1.5–6 |
| | 84–89 | 72.5–8 | | Ode 13.9–16 | | 1.19–27 |
| | 160–66 | 77 | Book 4 | Ode 7.17–28 | | 3.5–12 |
| | 237–43 | 83 | *Satires* 1.9 | | | 9.17–24 |
| | 320–30 | 84 | | Lines 35–41 | | 9.25–32 |
| | 675–85 | 85 | | Lines 48–60 | | 11.11–15 |
| Book 6 | 83–94 | 86 | | Lines 60–68 | Book 3 | 15.1–7 |
| | 868–86 | 87 | | | | |
| | 893–99 | 116 | | | | |
| Book 10 | 450, 453–56 | | | | | |
| | 467–75 | | | | | |
| | 491–96 | | | | | |
| | 500–505 | | | | | |
| Book 12 | 803–809 | | | | | |
| | 818–28 | | | | | |
| | 908–14 | | | | | |
| | 930–36 | | | | | |

# Chapter 6

# Translation

The free-response section of the AP Latin Exam requires a "literal translation" from Latin into English. This means that you must account in English for every word and every form in the passage. Stated more succinctly, you should "stay as close to the Latin forms and structure as good English allows."[1] Nouns should be translated as nouns, adjectives as adjectives, and so on. Nouns that are singular should be rendered as singular, etc.[2] You must demonstrate your ability to translate the Latin rather than present an English translation from memory. All Latin students know that it is difficult to render one language in another, especially in poetry. (Robert Frost said that poetry is what is lost in translation.) The fact remains that your ability to translate Latin literally is considered important by those who teach Latin at the college level, as indicated by the fact that translation counts as 30 percent of your score on the free-response section. Remember, however, that translation is only a part of comprehension, which is the ultimate goal of reading Latin. Comprehension is understanding the meaning of the Latin, i.e., "wrapping your head around it." Comprehension is a three-step process: reading, translation, and analysis. The Latin should always be read as Latin first, followed by a "carrying over" of the Latin into English. It has been said that words are only the flesh and bones of language. One classicist has written, "A good translation must carry over the very soul and spirit, the feelings and the emotions, that are concealed between the lines but pervade the whole text."[3] With respect to translating Latin, most would agree on two main principles: 1] that you read and render the Latin in sense units or word-groupings, such as noun-adjective combinations, phrases, and clauses, and avoid translating individual words, and 2] that you make accuracy your goal and avoid simply giving a general impression of what the Latin says. Although close paraphrasing is allowed on most questions of the free-response section, "translationese" and loose paraphrasing do not substitute for precision on the translation question of the AP Latin Exam. One teacher has written, "The College Board never penalizes for being too literal, but may

---

[1] Quoted from page 4 of 2005 *AP Latin Literature and AP Latin: Vergil Released Exams*.

[2] The mistake of translating singular for plural and plural for singular is often addressed in the published general comments and recommendations on the Exams. This, however, is apparently discretionary. For instance, the scoring guidelines for the first translation of the 2005 Vergil exam accept the translation of **aras** in **sollemnes taurum ingentem mactabat ad aras** as either singular or plural. These may, of course, be justified as poetic plurals, e.g., **Tantae animis caelestibus irae**, *Can anger so fierce (exist) in the heavenly heart?* (Vergil, *Aeneid* 1.11).

[3] Charles W. Siedler, *Guide to Cicero*, Oxford Book Co., NY, 1935, p. 87.

very well penalize for not being literal enough."[4] For more on literal translation, see below and Chapter 4.

On the AP Latin Exam, passages for translation are usually six to eight lines in length for poetry and two to four sentences for prose. Remember that there are two translation questions for Vergil and one each for Catullus and the choice author on the Latin Lit Exam. The passage to be translated may consist of a connected series of lines or sentences or an entire poem. Note: variations in spelling due to assimilation, e.g., **summovere/submovere**, are no longer glossed. Latin passages containing sexual content or numerous proper names, especially difficult place names, such as Catullus Poem 36.11–25, are avoided.

## Some FAQs About Translation

- **How can I prepare for the translation questions on the free-response section?**

  Don't just "get the gist" of what is happening when you are preparing your daily assignments. Work through the Latin carefully. Struggle with the challenges of discovering the meaning and of articulating it by finding the appropriate English to express the Latin. Avoid the temptation to incorporate someone else's translation into your own. If your teacher does not insist on or expect a "word-for-word" translation, practice doing this on your own. When translating, pay close attention to the items of grammar and syntax listed below as "hot spots" (see also Chapter 4):

  - Noun-adjective agreement:

    Example:

    > **Celsae graviore casu / cecidunt turres feriuntque summos / fulgura montes.** (Horace, *Odes* 2.10.10–12)

    Note:

    > Do not take **summos** with **turres**, which is feminine, but with **montes**.

  - Pronoun reference:

    Example 1:

    > **Dabisne mihi tabellam? Ego volo eam legere.**

    Note:

    > The pronoun **eam** refers to **tabellam**: *I wish to read it (the tablet)*, not *her.*

---

[4] David Perry, in a discussion about translation on The College Board Electronic Discussion Group (online), Saturday, July 22, 2006.

50

Example 2:

> In **Hoc, iucunde, tibi poema feci, / ex quo perspice-**
> **res meum dolorem** (Catullus, Poem 50.16–17) the word
> **quo** refers to
>
> (A) **iucunde**
>
> (B) **poema**
>
> (C) **dolorem**
>
> (D) Catullus (understood)

Answer:

> (B)   The antecedent of **quo** is **poema**, which is a neuter
> singular Greek form, cued by the modifying demonstra-
> tive **Hoc**.

- Subject-verb agreement:

  Example:

  > Hunc video mihi nunc frustra sumptum esse laborem,
  >
  > Gelli, nec nostras hinc valuisse preces.
  >
  > Contra nos tela ista tua <u>evitabimus</u> acta,
  >
  > at fixus nostris tu dabis supplicium.
  >
  > **Catullus 116.5–8**

  Question:

  > The subject of **evitabimus** (line 3) is
  >
  > (A) Gellius
  >
  > (B) Catullus
  >
  > (C) **preces**
  >
  > (D) **tela**

  Answer:

  > (B)   The first person plural of this verb reflects the
  > poetic plural found previous in **nostras** and **nos**. **Video**
  > **. . . mihi** in line 1 informs us that  Catullus is writing the
  > poem.

- Tense, voice, person, number, and mood of verbs:

  Example:

  > **Multa . . . statuunt, ut nocte silenti / fallere custodes**
  > **. . . temptent** (Ovid, *Metamorphoses* 4.84–85)

  Note:

  > It is tempting to confuse **temptent**, which is subjunctive
  > in the present tense in an **ut** purpose clause, with a form
  > of the future tense indicative.

- The time relationships between participles and other verbs, infinitives in indirect statement and their introductory verbs, and sequence of tenses in subjunctive clauses.

    Examples:

    **Caesare in Gallia <u>pugnante</u>, Pompeius Romae manebat.**

    *While Caesar <u>was fighting</u> in Gaul, Pompey <u>stayed</u> in Rome* (not *is fighting*).

    **<u>Dixit</u> laborem <u>confectum esse</u>.**

    *He <u>said</u> that the work <u>had been finished</u>* (not *is* or *has been finished*).

    **Si Colosseum <u>deletum esset</u>, Roma non <u>deleta esset</u>.**

    *If the Colosseum <u>had been destroyed</u>, Rome <u>would</u> not <u>have been destroyed</u>* (not *was destroyed*).

- Acceptable variations in the expression of ablatives absolute:

    Example:

    **Tabulas . . . publicas, quas Italico bello <u>incenso tabulario</u> interisse scimus omnes.** (Cicero, *Pro Archia Poeta* 8)

    Translated literally: *The (Heraclean) records office having been burned.*

    Translated as a clause: *When the (Heraclean) records office had been burned.*

- **How are translated passages evaluated by exam readers?**

    For details about the mechanics of this process, which will be illustrated below, see Chapter 12 and the Answers to the Practice Exams. For the purpose of evaluation, the Latin passage is divided into small sense units called "chunks" or "segments." Each segment consists of a prepositional phrase, an infinitive phrase, a noun-adjective or subject-verb combination, and so forth. In other words, a segment is a coherent combination of words that fit together grammatically or syntactically. Alternative meanings and renderings, within a range of acceptability, are provided to the Reader for each word or phrase in the segment. When scored, translations are divided into 18 segments, each of which counts as one-half point, totalling nine points. Here is an example of how the accuracy of a translation question on the free-response section is assessed. (Note that the example here is abbreviated, that is, it contains only 12 segments and six points.)

    > Fracti bello fatisque repulsi
    > ductores Danaum tot iam labentibus annis
    > instar montis equum divina Palladis arte
    > aedificant, sectaque intexunt abiete costas;
    > votum pro reditu simulant; ea fama vagatur.

    ***Aeneid*** 2.13–17

**Sample Literal Translation:**

Broken in war and driven back by the fates, the Greek leaders, with so many years already passing by, build a horse, huge as a mountain, with the divine skill of Pallas Athena, and weave together its ribs with cut fir; they pretend (that it is) an offering for (their) return; that rumor spreads far and wide.

### 1/2 pt. alloted for each of the following segments or sense units

1. fracti bello
2. fatisque repulsi
3. ductores Danaum
4. tot iam labentibus annis
5. instar montis
6. equum . . . aedificant
7. divina arte Palladis
8. sectaque . . . abiete
9. intexunt . . . costas
10. votum . . . simulant
11. pro reditu
12. ea fama vagatur

### Acceptable meanings:

1. **fracti:** (having been) broken/shattered/destroyed [perfect passive participle]

   **bello:** in/by/by means of war [ablative of means]

2. **fatisque:** by/by means of fate/the fates [ablative of means; may be singular]

   **-que:** [connects **fracti** and **repulsi**]

   **repulsi:** (having been) driven back/repelled/spurned [perfect passive participle]

3. **ductores:** leaders/commanders/captains/rulers [subject of the main verbs in this passage]

   **Danaum:** = **Danaorum**, Danai/Danaans/Greeks/Achaeans [genitive plural]

4. **tot:** so many/so much

   **iam:** already/now

   **labentibus:** (while) sliding/gliding/slipping/passing/flowing [take with **annis** in ablative absolute]

   **annis:** years/time/season

5. **instar:** likeness of/image of [indeclinable neuter noun]

   **montis:** mountain [genitive; must be taken with **instar; instar montis** is in apposition to **equum**]

6. **equum:** horse

   **aedificant:** they build/are building/do build/construct/fashion/craft/erect/establish [may be past tense]

7. **divina:** divine/godly [take with **arte,** or with **Palladis** as transferred epithet]

   **arte:** art/skill/craftsmanship/technique

   **Palladis:** Pallas Athena/Athena/Minerva/Pallas

8. **sectaque:** (having been) cut/cleaved/sliced/hewn [past participle taken with **abiete**]

   **-que:** [connects **aedificant** and **intexunt**]

   **abiete:** (by means of or with) silver fir/fir/wood [ablative of means]

9. **intexunt:** they weave/twine together/interweave/plait/put together [may be past tense]

   **costas:** rib/side

10. **votum:** vow/pledge/promise/(votive) offering/prayer

    **simulant:** they pretend/feign/imitate/simulate/give the appearance of [may be past tense]

11. **pro:** for/on behalf of  **reditu:** return/homecoming/going or coming back

12. **ea:** this/that

    **fama:** rumor/report/gossip/word of mouth

    **vagatur:** is spread abroad or far and wide/wander/rove/drift/meander [deponent verb; may have a passive meaning and may be past tense]

**Here are some hypothetical sample student responses and their scores:**

**Student Response A:**

> Having been broken in war and repelled by fate, the leaders of the Greeks, as so much time is already passing, build a big-as-a-mountain horse with divine Athena's skill, and they interweave the ribs with fir wood that has been cut. They pretend that it (the horse) is a vow for their return. That rumor spreads abroad.

This student receives full credit of six points, as all twelve segments have been rendered correctly.

**Student Response B:**

> In war and in fate, I drove back and broke the Greek leaders, after so many years had passed, so that they build a mountain-sized horse with the divine help of Athena and weave the cut wood together into ribs. Having made a vow, they pretend to return; that gossip is passed around.

No credit for segments 1 and 2, as the student incorrectly assumes that **fracti** and **repulsi** are forms of the first person singular of the perfect tense active; and "in war and in fate" expresses time/place, rather than means. Segment 3 is expressed as an object, rather than a subject, although the forms **ductores Danaum** could be taken as objective. (If **ductores** is taken as an object, there is no other noun that could serve as the subject of **aedificant . . . intexunt . . .** and **simulant**.) Segment 4 does not receive credit because the present participle **labentibus** is rendered as a past participle, "after . . . had passed." Segments 5, 6, and 7 receive full credit, although "help" does not fully express the meaning of **arte**. Segments 8 and 9 are acceptable, as are 10, 11, and 12.

Thus, the score is four points.

**Student Response C:**

> With war broken (discontinued) and the fates driven away, the leaders build a Greek horse, working for years, ___ (standing?) mountain with Pallas' divine skill they cut and weave ___. (?) They pretend to vote for the return (home). The news gets out.

This effort is intermittently a translation and a paraphrase, with words missing or misidentified. There is only a general sense of what is happening. Segments 1 and 2 don't work because **fracti** is taken as modifying **bello** and **repulsi** as modifying **fatis**. Segment 3 is unacceptable because **Danaum** does not modify **equum**, despite the common ending. The student mistranslates the verb **labor (labentibus)** for **laboro (laborantibus)** and omits **tot** and **iam** (also **annis** cannot express extent of time). Segments 6 and 7 are acceptable, but 8 and 9 are only partially correct ("cut and weave" is satisfactory for **sectaque intexunt**). "Vote" is not an acceptable meaning for **votum** in Segment 10. Segment 11 is acceptable, but Segment 12, although close, omits **ea** and gives an imprecise meaning of **vagatur**, which means that the news is not just broadcast, but broadcast far and wide. This student receives a score of two points.

- **What is meant by "translate as literally as possible?"**

The directions for the translation question ask for you to "translate as literally as possible." As noted earlier, a "literal" translation accounts for every word and every form in the original Latin. This is different from a "literary" translation, which perhaps preserves more of the poetic essence or spirit of the original. Literal translation is, essentially, an exercise in grammar and syntax. One teacher has defined literal translation as, "the process by which the exact thought of a Latin sentence is transferred to an English one, identical insofar as English idiom, word-order, emphasis, and style will permit."[5] What makes for a literal translation that is acceptable to the College Board Readers? This is determined only through practice over time, with guidance from your teacher. As you have been advised previously, practice reading the phrases, clauses, and sense units of Latin, rather than individual words at random and in isolation. <u>You are better served by staying true to the Latin, regardless of the requirements of English, than by producing a "free" translation or paraphrase for the sake of better English expression</u>. To achieve better accuracy and precision in translating, pay attention to the "hot-spot" areas listed earlier in this chapter and remember that translation is a part of the process of comprehension: read first, and then "carry over" the Latin into English. Here are some examples of literal and non-literal translations of the final lines of Catullus, Poem 51:

**gemina teguntur / lumina nocte**.

Literal translations:

> *(My) eyes are covered with a twofold night*. (Translated by the author)

Note:

> You have the option of recognizing **gemina** as a transferred epithet with **lumina**, resulting in the meaning *My twin eyes are covered with night*.

> *At once my eyes are covered in darkness*. (Charles Martin, The Johns Hopkins University Press, 1990. Points off for omitting **gemina**!)

> *Twin darkness covers the light of my eyes*. (Guy Lee, Oxford World's Classics, 1990. Points off for changing the passive verb to active!)

Non-literal translations:

> *Eyes gaze on stars that fall forever into deep midnight*. (Horace Gregory, Grove Press, Inc., 1956)

> *And, as for my eyes, dense darkness blindfolds them both*. (James Mitchie, The Folio Society, 1981)

> *My eyes are covered by veils of night*. (Roy Arthur Swanson, Bobbs-Merrill Library of Liberal Arts, 1982)

---

[5] Dorrance Stinchfield White, *The Teaching of Latin*, Scott-Foresman, Chicago, 1941, pp. 142–43.

*My eyes veiled in a double darkness.* (Rudy Negenborn, http://www.negenborn.net/catullus/, 1997)

*My eyes are quenched in twofold night.* (Harry Walker, http://www.vroma.org/-hwalker/VRomaCatullus/, 1998)

*My eyes are covered with the dark of night.* (Anthony Kline, http://www.adkline.freeuk.com/Catullus.htm, 2001)

*My lights immersed in a double night.* (David Mulroy, The University of Wisconsin Press, 2002)

*While night curtains both my eyes into darkness.* (Peter Green, Univ. California Press, 2005)

## Translation Passages Tested on Recent AP Latin Exams (2006–2001)

This information is provided to give you a sense of the length and degree of difficulty of the passages found in this part of the free-response section. See the College Board AP Latin Literature Web site for sample translation questions on Cicero's *Pro Caelio*, which will give you an idea of what to expect on the translation question for *Pro Archia Poeta*.

| Vergil | | Catullus | Horace | Ovid | |
|---|---|---|---|---|---|
| *Aeneid* | | *Carmina* | *Odes* | *Metamorphoses* | |
| Book 1 | 378–85 | Poem 31.7–14 | Book 1 *Ode* 24.3–10 | Book 1 | 481–49 |
| Book 2 | 10–16 | 35.1–10 | Book 2 *Ode* 7.3–12 | Book 4 | 147–57 |
| | 201–207 | 44.6–12 | Book 3 *Ode* 1.5–16 | Book 8 | 203–13 |
| | 237–43 | 46 | Book 4 *Ode* 7.17–28 | Book 10 | 238–46 |
| | 289–94 | 70 | | | |
| | 560–66 | 87 | *Satires* 1.9 | *Amores* | |
| | | lines 25–41 | | Book 1 | 3.5–12 |
| Book 4 | 160–66 | lines 60–68 | | | 9.17–24 |
| Book 6 | 893–99 | | | | |
| Book 10 | 450 and 453–56 | | | | |
| Book 12 | 803–809 | | | | |
| | 908–14 | | | | |
| | 930–36 | | | | |

## Passages for Practice

The author's annotated versions of literal translations of these passages may be found below. Note that traditional renderings of verbs in the perfect tense are equally acceptable, i.e., **amavit**, *he loved* or *he has loved,* as long as the action expressed is both past and completed. **Amabat** may be translated as *he was loving* or *he loved* (but not *he did love*), i.e., rendered as imperfect or simple past. Note, too, that translation of some present tenses may be acceptable as past and that some plural nouns or pronouns, and their accompanying verbs, may be translated as singular.

### Vergil

#### Passage A

> Talia flammato secum dea corde volutans
> nimborum in patriam, loca feta furentibus Austris,
> Aeoliam venit. Hic vasto rex Aeolus antro
>
> *Line*   luctantes ventos tempestatesque sonoras
>     5   imperio premit ac vinclis et carcere frenat.
> Illi indignantes magno cum murmure montis
> circum claustra fremunt; celsa sedet Aeolus arce
> sceptra tenens mollitque animos et temperat iras.

***Aeneid*** 1. 50–57

#### Passage B

> "I, sequere Italiam ventis, pete regna per undas.
> Spero equidem mediis, si quid pia numina possunt,
> supplicia hausurum scopulis et nomine Dido
>
> *Line*   saepe vocaturum. Sequar atris ignibus absens
>     5   et, cum frigida mors anima seduxerit artus,
> omnibus umbra locis adero. Dabis, improbe, poenas.
> Audiam et haec manes veniet mihi fama sub imos."

***Aeneid*** 4. 381–87

#### Passage C

> Nescia mens hominum fati sortisque futurae
> et servare modum rebus sublata secundis!
> Turno tempus erit magno cum optaverit emptum
>
> *Line*   intactum Pallanta, et cum spolia ista diemque
>     5   oderit. . . .
> O dolor atque decus magnum rediture parenti,
> haec te prima dies bello dedit, haec eadem aufert,
> cum tamen ingentes Rutulorum linquis acervos!

***Aeneid*** 10. 501–509

# Catullus
## *Passage D*

Fui libenter in tua suburbana
villa, malamque pectore expuli tussim,
non immerenti quam mihi meus venter,
*Line* dum sumptuosas appeto, dedit, cenas.
5 Nam, Sestianus dum volo esse conviva,
orationem in Antium petitorem
plenam veneni et pestilentiae legi.
Hic me gravedo frigida et frequens tussis
quassavit usque dum in tuum sinum fugi
10 et me recuravi otioque et urtica.

**Catullus, Poem 44**

## *Passage E1*

Nulli se dicit mulier mea nubere malle
quam mihi, non si se Iuppiter ipse petat.
Dicit: sed mulier cupido quod dicit amanti
in vento et rapida scribere oportet aqua.

**Catullus, Poem 70**

## *Passage E2*

Iucundum, mea vita, mihi proponis amorem,
hunc nostrum inter nos perpetuumque fore.
Di magni, facite ut vere promittere possit,
*Line* atque id sincere dicat et ex animo,
5 ut liceat nobis tota perducere vita
aeternum hoc sanctae foedus amicitiae.

**Catullus, Poem 109**

## *Passage F*

O di, si vestrum est misereri, aut si quibus umquam
extremam iam ipsa in morte tulistis opem.
me miserum aspicite et, si vitam puriter egi,
*Line* eripite hanc pestem perniciemque mihi.
5 Heu, mihi surrepens imos ut torpor in artus
expulit ex omni pectore laetitias!
Ipse valere opto et taetrum hunc deponere morbum.
O di, reddite mi hoc pro pietate mea.

**Catullus, Poem 76.17–22, 25–26**

## Cicero
### Passage G

Nam quoad longissime potest mens mea respicere spatium praeteriti
temporis et pueritiae memoriam recordari ultimam, inde usque repetens
hunc video mihi principem et ad suscipiendam et ad ingrediendam
*Line* rationem horum studiorum exstitisse. Quod si haec vox, huius hortatu
5 praeceptisque confirmata, non nullis aliquando saluti fuit, a quo id
accepimus quo cetermis opitulari et alios servare possemus, huic profecto
ipsi, quantum est situm in nobis, et opem et salutem ferre debemus.

**Cicero, *Pro Archia Poeta* 1**

### Passage H

Quaeres a nobis, Grati, cur tanto opere hoc homine delectemur. Quia
suppeditat nobis ubi et animus ex hoc forensi strepitu reficiatur et aures
convitio defessae conquiescant. An tu existimas aut suppetere nobis
*Line* posse quod cotidie dicamus in tanta varietate rerum, nisi animos nostros
5 doctrina excolamus, aut ferre animos tantam posse contentionem, nisi
eos doctrina eadem relaxemus?

**Cicero, *Pro Archia Poeta* 12**

### Passage I

Sed quoniam res humanae fragiles caducaeque sunt, semper aliqui
anquirendi sunt quos diligamus et a quibus diligamur; caritate enim
benevolentiaque sublata omnis est e vita sublata iucunditas. Mihi
quidem Scipio, quamquam est subito ereptus, vivit tamen semperque
vivet; virtutem enim amavi illius viri, quae exstincta non est.

**Cicero, *De Amicitia* 102**

## Horace
### Passage J

Divesne, prisco natus ab Inacho,
nil interest an pauper et infima
   de gente sub divo moreris;
      victima nil miserantis Orci.
*Line*
5 Omnes eodem cogimur, omnium
versatur urna serius ocius
   sors exitura et nos in aeternum
      exsilium impositura cumbae.

**Horace, Odes 2.3.21–28**

### Passage K

Exegi monumentum aere perennius
regalique situ pyramidum altius,
quod non imber edax, non Aquilo impotens
*Line* possit diruere aut innumerabilis
5 annorum series et fuga temporum.
Non omnis moriar, multaque pars mei
vitabit Libitinam.

**Horace, Odes 3. 30.1–7**

### Passage L

Haec dum agit, ecce
Fuscus Aristius occurrit, mihi carus et illum
qui pulchre nosset. Consistimus. "Unde venis?" et,
*Line* "Quo tendis?" rogat et respondet. Vellere coepi,
5 et prensare manu lentissima bracchia, nutans,
distorquens oculos, ut me eriperet. Male salsus
ridens dissimulare: meum iecur urere bilis.

**Horace, *Satires* 1. 9. 60–66**

## Ovid

### Passage M

Protinus alter amat, fugit altera nomen amantis,
silvarum latebris captivarumque ferarum
exuviis gaudens, innuptaeque aemula Phoebes;
*Line* vitta coercebat positos sine lege capillos.
5 Multi illam petiere; illa, aversata petentes
impatiens expersque viri, nemora avia lustrat,
nec, quid Hymen, quid Amor, quid sint conubia, curat.

**Ovid, *Metamorphoses* 1. 474–480**

### Passage N

Sunt tamen obscenae Venerem Propoetides ausae
esse negare deam; pro quo sua, numinis ira,
corpora cum forma primae vulgasse feruntur,
*Line* utque pudor cessit sanguisque induruit oris,
5 in rigidum parvo silicem discrimine versae.
Quae quia Pygmalion aevum per crimen agentes
viderat, offensus vitiis, quae plurima menti
femineae natura dedit, sine coniuge caelebs
vivebat thalamique diu consorte carebat.

**Ovid, *Metamorphoses* 10. 238–46**

### Passage O

Ite hinc, difficiles, funebria ligna, tabellae,
   tuque, negaturis cera referta notis,
quam, puto, de longae collectam flore cicutae[1]

*Line*   melle sub infimi, Corsica misit apis.

5  At, tamquam minio[2] penitus medicata, rubebas –
   ille color vere sanguinulentus erat!
Proiectae triviis iaceatis, inutile lignum,
   vosque rotae frangat praetereuntis onus.

1. cicuta, -ae, f: the hemlock plant
2. minium, -i, n: cinnabar, source of red pigment

**Ovid, *Amores* 1. 12.7–14**

## Suggested Passages for Translation Practice

### Vergil (8- to 10-Line Passages of Particular Relevance to the Storyline)

Book 1:   Lines 1–11; 26–32; 50–57; 65–70; 81–87; 88–96; 94–101; 104–12; 113–19; 124-30; 132–39; 148–56; 187–94; 198–206; 229–37; 272–79; 286–94; 297–304; 327-34; 348–56; 378–85; 402–10; 430–36; 459–65; 479–87, and 513–19

Book 2:   Lines 1–13; 13–20; 25–32; 42–48; 50–56; 203–12; 220–27; 234–40; 241–49; 254- 59 and 265–67; 281–86; 289–95; 486–94; 512–20; 526–32; 547–50 and 554–58; 559–66; 735–40; 745–51; 776–84, and 790–95

Book 4:   Lines 1–8; 20–29; 45–53; 68–73; 107–14; 160–72; 173–77 and 181–88; 211–18; 296–303; 305–11; 314–23; 333–39; 351–58; 365–71; 393–400; 441–49; 651–58; 663–71; 675–83; 685–92, and 700–705

Book 6:   Lines 42–51; 65–70; 86–94; 125–31; 456–66; 847–53; 860–66

Book 10:   Lines 433–38; 445–51; 464–72; 491–97, and 501–509

Book 12:   Lines 800–806; 819–28; 829–37; 930–38, and 938–44

### Catullus (Passages from Poems Over 12 Lines; Shorter Poems May Be Tested in Their Entirety)

Polymetrics:   Poem 3, lines 1–10 and 11–18; Poem 4, lines 1–8, 13–19, and 2–27; Poem 5, lines 1–6 and 7–13; Poem 8, lines 1–8 and 12–19; Poem 10, lines 1–8, 14–20, and 28–34; Poem 11, stanzas 1, 2, 4 or 1, 3, 4; Poem 12, lines 1–9 and 10–17; Poem 13, lines 1–8; Poem 14a, lines 8-16; Poem 22, lines 9–17; Poem 31, lines 7-14; Poem 35, lines 1–10; Poem 36, lines 1–8 and

11 and 16–20; Poem 44, lines 1–9 and 13–21; Poem 45, lines 19–26, and Poem 50, lines 14–21

Epyllion: Poem 64, lines 50–59; 76–85; 105–111; 116–23; 132–38; 139–48; 149–57; 171–78; 184–91; 192–201, and 238–48

Elegiacs: Poem 65, lines 1–8 and 10–18; Poem 68, lines 1–10, 11–20, and 33–40; and Poem 76, lines 1–8, 9–16, 17–26

## Cicero

*Pro Archia Poeta*

| | |
|---|---|
| Chapter 1: | Si qui . . . exstitisse. |
| Chapter 3: | quaeso . . . dicendi. |
| Chapter 5: | Erat Italia . . . Catulo. |
| Chapter 8: | Est ridiculum . . . collocavit. |
| Chapter 14: | Nam nisi . . . conformabam. |
| Chapter 16: | Quod si . . . rusticantur. |
| Chapter 23: | Nam si quis . . . laborum. |
| Chapter 26: | Neque . . . volunt. |
| Chapter 27: | Qua re . . . abhorrere. |
| Chapter 28: | Atque . . . exerceamus. |
| Chapter 30: | An statuas . . . delector. |

*De Amicitia*

| | |
|---|---|
| Chapter 18: | Sed . . . debemus. |
| Chapter 19: | Qui . . . ducem; Sic . . . manet. |
| Chapter 22: | Talis . . . molesta est. |
| Chapter 23: | Verum . . . possit everti. |
| Chapter 100: | Virtus . . . quaesita. |
| Chapter 104: | Nam quid . . . memoria mea. |

## Horace (Exam Passages Are Usually Two Strophes in Length)

*Odes*

| | | |
|---|---|---|
| Book 1 | Ode 1 | Lines 1–10;19–28; 29–36 |
| | Ode 5 | Lines 1–8 or 12; 5–13 or 16 |
| | Ode 9 | Lines 1–8 or 12; 13–18; 18–24 or 13–24 |
| | Ode 13 | Lines 1–8; 12–20 |
| | Ode 22 | Lines 1–8; 9–16; 17–24 |
| | Ode 24 | Lines 1–8; 5–12; 13–20 |
| | Ode 25 | Lines 1–8 |

Ode 37  Lines 1–8; 12–21; 25–32

Book 2  Ode 3  Lines 1–8; 9–16

Ode 7  Lines 1–8; 13–20; 21–28

Ode 10  Lines 1–8 or 4–12; 13–22

Ode 14  Lines 1–9; 5–12; 13–20; 21–28

Book 3  Ode 1  Lines 1–8; 9–16; 17–24; 25–32; 33–40; 41–48

Ode 9  Lines 1–8; 9–16; 17–24

Ode 13  Lines 1–8; 9–16

Ode 30  Lines 10–16

Book 4  Ode 7  Lines 1–8; 5–12; 13–20; 21–28

*Satires* 1.9

Lines  1–8:  Ibam. . . eris.

8–16:  Misere. . . est tibi.

13–21:  Ut . . . onus.

35–43:  Ventum erat . . . sequor.

43–54:  Maecenas . . . proximus esse.

70–78:  Nulla . . . Apollo.

## Ovid (Passages Are 7 to 10 Lines in Length)

*Metamorphoses*

Book 1  452–567 (Apollo and Daphne)

Lines 452–62; 466–73; 481–87; 490–96; 504–11; 514–24; 533–39; 543–52; 553–59, and 557–67

Book 4  55–166 (Pyramus and Thisbe)

Lines 55–62 or 64; 71–77 or 73–80; 83–90; 96–104; 108–15; 128–36; 140–46; 147–53; 154–61 or 158–66

Book 8  183–235 (Daedalus and Icarus)

Lines 188–95; 195–202; 225–35

616–724 (Baucis and Philemon)

Lines 626–34 or 629–36; 637–47; 651–63; 684–93; 703–10; 711–19

Book 10  238–97 (Pygmalion)

Lines 247–53; 270–79; 280–89; 290–97

# Annotated Translations of Practice Passages

## Vergil

### Passage A

The goddess, turning over such things (**Talia . . . volutans**) in her inflamed heart (**flammato . . . corde**) came to Aeolia, fatherland of storm-clouds (**nimborum in patriam . . . Aeoliam**), a place teeming (**loca feta**) with raging winds (**furentibus; Austris** can mean winds in general). Here in his vast cave Aeolus rules with authority (**imperio premit**) over the wrestling winds and roaring storms (**luctantes ventos tempestatesque sonoras**) and controls (or bridles, **frenat**) them with chains and a prison (**vinclis et carcere**). They, in their impatience (**indignantes**), roar around the enclosure (**circum claustra fremunt; claustra** may be singular), with the mountain's mighty reverberation (**magno cum murmure montis**); on his high throne sits Aeolus (**celsa sedet Aeolus arce**), holding his scepter (**sceptra tenens; sceptra** may be singular) and calms their spirits (**molitque animos**) and eases their anger (**et temperat iras; iras** may be singular).

### Passage B

"Go, follow Italy with the winds (**sequere Italiam ventis**), seek a kingdom over the waves (**pete regna per undas; regna** may be singular). Truly I hope that, if in any way (**si quid**) divinities can be just (**pia numina [esse] possunt**), that you (**te** is understood as the subject of **hausurum [esse]** in indirect statement) will swallow down your punishment (**hausurum supplicia; supplicia** may be singular) in the midst of rock-cliffs (**mediis . . . scopulis**) and repeatedly call Dido by name (**et nomine Dido saepe vocaturum [esse]**). Apart (from you), I will follow you (**Sequar . . . absens**) with dark firebrands (**atris ignibus**) and, when cold death (**cum frigida mors**) will have separated limb from soul (**anima seduxerit artus; cum . . . seduxerit** may be translated as present tense; **artus** may be singular), I will be everywhere (**omnibus . . . locis adero**) as a ghost (**umbra**). You will pay the price (**dabis . . . poenas; poenas** may be singular), cruel one. I will listen and this story (**haec . . . fama**) will reach my shade (in the world) below (**manes veniet . . . sub imos**)."

### Passage C

Mind of man (**hominum** may be singular), ignorant of fate and future destiny (**nescia fati sortisque futurae**) and (how) to preserve moderation (**servare modum**) when elevated by favorable circumstances (= "high on success," **rebus sublata secundis; sublata** modifies **mens**)! To Turnus will come the time when he will have wished (**cum . . . optaverit**; may be translated as present tense) that Pallas has been (or was) redeemed (**emptum [esse]**) uninjured (**intactum Pallanta**) at a great (price) (**magno**; ablative of price) and when he (Turnus) will have hated (**cum . . . oderit; oderit** may be translated as present tense) those spoils (**spolia ista**) and (that) day (**diemque**). O (Turnus) about to return (**rediture**) to your father (**parenti**) as a great grief and also a great glory (**dolor atque decus magnum**), this day first gave you to war (**haec . . . dedit**), this same (day) (**haec eadem**) takes you away (from it, **aufert**; may be translated as past), (the day) when yet you leave behind (**linquis**; may be translated as past) enormous heaps (**ingentes . . . acervos**) of (dead) Rutulians (**Rutulorum**).

## Catullus

### Passage D

Gladly (**libenter**) was I (present) in your villa (or retreat, country home) out-of-town (where I) drove from my chest (**pectore expuli**) a wicked cough (**malamque . . . tussim**), which my belly (or greediness, via metonymy) gave to me not undeservedly (**quam non immerenti . . . mihi meus venter dedit**), while I seek out (**dum . . . appeto**; may be translated as past) a lavish feast (**sumptuosas . . . cenas**; may be singular). For, since I wanted (**volo** may be translated as past) to be a dinner guest of Sestius (**Sestianus . . . conviva**), I read (his) speech (**orationem . . . legi**) against the candidate Antius (**in Antium petitorem**), (a speech which (**quam** is feminine and therefore cannot modify **petitorem**) was full of poison and plague (**plenam veneni et pestilentiae**). This shivering cold (**gravedo frigida**) and persistent cough (**frequens tussis**) shook me (**quassavit**) until I fled to your embrace (**dum in tuum sinum fugi**) and cured myself (**me recuravi**) with rest and nettle tea (**otioque et urtica**).

### Passage E1

*Note that the translation question may consist of two short poems or passages, as in Passages E1 and E2.*

My woman (**mulier mea**) says that she prefers to marry (**se dicit . . . nubere malle**) no one (other) than me (**Nulli . . . quam mihi**), not (even) if Jove himself should ask her (**non si se Iuppiter ipse petat**). She says (this): but what a woman says (**quod dicit**) to a desirous lover (**cupido . . . amanti**) should be (**oportet**) written (**scribere** may be taken as passive) on the wind and running water (**in vento et rapida . . . aqua**).

### Passage E2

Joyful, my life, is the love (**Iucundum . . . amorem**) you promise to me (**mihi proponis**), and that this love of ours (**hunc [amorem] nostrum**) will be (**foret**

= **futurum esse**; future infinitive in indirect statement after **proponis**) mutual (**inter nos**) and ever-lasting (**perpetuumque**). Almighty gods, see to it (**facite**) that she can promise (this) truly (**ut . . . vere promittere possit**; substantive result clause after **facite**) and says it sincerely and from the heart (**atque . . . ex animo**), so that we may be allowed (**ut liceat nobis**; more literally, "so that it may be allowed to us"; **ut** purpose clause) to lead throughout (our) whole life (**tota perducere vita**; note that the ablative, instead of the accusative, is used here to express extent of time; check the quantity via scansion), this eternal bond (**aeternum . . . foedus**) of blessed friendship (**sanctae . . . amicitiae**).

## Passage F

O gods, if it is your (place) (**vestrum est**; partitive genitive) to have pity (**misereri**; deponent infinitive), or if you have ever brought final aid (**umquam / extremam . . . tulistis opem**; **extremam** may be transferred to **morte**) to anyone (**quibus**) at the very moment of death (**ipsa in morte**), look upon me in my unhappiness (**aspicite me miserum**) and, if I have lived life virtuously (**et si vitam puriter egi**), remove this plague and pestilence (**eripite hanc pestem perniciemque**) from me (**mihi**, dative of reference). Alas, like a numbness (or "sluggishness;" **ut torpor**, simile) while slithering (its way) (**surrepens**; must be expressed as a participle, but may be rendered as "was slithering," because the main verb **expulit** is in the past tense) into my innermost limbs ( or "deep into my limbs," **imos . . . in artus**), it has driven happiness (**omni** may be transferred from **pectore** to **laetitias**; **laetitias** may be singular) from my whole heart (**ex omni pectore**)! I wish for myself to be well again (**Ipse valere opto**) and to put aside this horrible disease (**et taetrum hunc deponere morbum**). O gods, grant (to) me this (**reddite mi hoc**) in return for my devotion (**pro pietate mea**).

## Cicero

### Passage G

*Note that verbs and pronouns appearing in the first person plural may be rendered as singular.*

For as far as (**Quoad longissime**) my mind is able to look back (**potest mens mea respicere**) at (that) period of past time (**spatium praeteriti temporis**) and (is able to) recall the remote memory of my boyhood (**pueritiae memoriam recordari ultimam**), looking back as far as that (**inde usque repetens**), I see that this (man Archias) stood out (**hunc video . . . exstitisse**) as the architect (**principem**) with regard to my undertaking (**ad suscipiendam**) and pursuing (**ad ingrediendam**) the curriculum of these liberal studies (**rationem horum studiorum**). But if this voice of mine, trained (**conformata**) by his encouragement and principles (**huius hortatu praeceptisque**), was at anytime (**aliquando**) the source of salvation for someone (**non nullis . . . saluti fuit**; double dative), I received that from him (**a quo id accepimus**) by which I could give help to and perhaps save others (**quo ceteris opitulari et alios servare possemus**), then I surely (**profecto**) should bring aid and assistance (**et opem et salutem ferre debemus**) to this man (or situation), as much as it lies in my control (to do so) (**quantum est situm in nobis**).

### Passage H

*Note that verbs and pronouns appearing in the first person plural may be rendered as singular.*

You will ask me (**Quaeres a nobis**), Gratius, why I take delight in this man (**hoc homine delectemur**) in such a significant way (**tanto opere**). Since he is at hand for me (**Quia suppeditat nobis**; causal clauses with the subjunctive after **quia** here and following, i.e., (**quia**) . . . **reficiatur** and (**quia**) . . . **conquiescant**) when both my spirit should be refreshed (**animus . . . reficiatur**) from this noisy court (**ex hoc forensi strepitu**) and my ears, worn out from the insults (**convitio defessae**), should get some rest (**conquiescant**). But do you think (**An existimas**) either that I could provide myself (**aut suppetere nobis**; **suppetere** may be translated as a historical present, i.e., in the past) with what I say each day (**quod cotidie dicamus**) on such a variety of topics (**in tanta varietate rerum**), if I did not cultivate (**nisi . . . excolamus**, may be translated as past) my mind (**animos nostros**, may be singular) with learning (**doctrina**, ablative of means), or (do you think that) I could endure (**[me] ferre . . . posse**, may be translated as past) such squabbling (**tantam . . . contentionem**) if I did not relax my mind (**nisi . . . eos [= animos] . . . relaxemus**; both **eos** and **relaxemus** may be singular) with the same learning (**doctrina eadem**)?

### Passage I

But since human affairs (**res humanae**) are frail and perishable (**fragiles caducaeque sunt**), we must always be searching for someone (**semper aliqui anquirendi sunt**; passive periphrastic) whom we may love (**quos diligamus**; subjunctive, relative clause of characteristic) and by whom we may be loved (**et a quibus diligamur**); for affection and goodwill having been removed (**caritate . . . sublata**; ablative absolute), all pleasure (**omnis . . . iucunditas**) has been taken out of life (**est e vita sublata;** note the reversal of the more usual word order of **sublata est**). Indeed, for me (**mihi quidem**), Scipio, although he was taken suddenly (**quamquam est subito ereptus**), nevertheless is living and always will live (**vivit tamen semperque vivet**); for I cherished the virtue (moral excellence, courage, etc.) of that man (**illius viri**), which has not been extinguished (**quae exstincta non est**).

## Horace

### Passage J

It matters not (**nil interest**) whether (**-ne**, introducing an indirect question is balanced by **an** in the next line, "whether . . . or") you spend time (or stay, dwell; **moreris** is present subjunctive) under the open sky (**sub divo**) rich (**Divesne**) (and) born (**natus**) from (the line of) ancient Inachus (**prisco . . . Inacho**), or (are) poor and of lowly birth (**an pauper et infima de gente**); (you are) the victim (**victima**; understand **es**) of Orcus, who pities nothing (**nil miserantis**). We are all gathered in the same (place) (**omnes eodem cogimur**), and, sooner (or) later (**serius ocius**), the lot of all is turned in the urn (**omnium versatur urna . . . sors**; **urna** is ablative; check via scansion) (the lot) about to come out (**exitura;**

along with **impositura**, active periphrastic with **est**, understood) and place (**impositura**) us in eternal exile (**in aeternum exsilium**) in the small boat (**cumbae**; dative after **impositura**).

## Passage K

I have completed (**Exegi**) a monument more lasting than bronze (**aere perennius**; **perennius**, and **altius** below, modify **monumentum**) and more towering than the royal edifice of the pyramids (**regalique situ pyramidum altius**), which neither the greedy rain (**quod non imber edax**) nor the violent wind (**non Aquilo impotens**; a named wind can stand for the wind, by metonymy), or the countless succession of years (**aut innumerabilis annorum series**) and the advance of time (**et fuga temporum**), can tear down (**possit diruere**; a relative clause of characteristic following **quod**). I will not die completely (**Non omnis moriar**) and a great part of me (**multaque pars mei**) will avoid (the funeral goddess) Libitina.

### Passage L

While he is doing these things (**Haec dum agit**), look, Aristius Fuscus meets up (with us) (**occurrit**; understand **nobis**), dear to me and a person of the type who would know him (the pest; **qui . . . nosset** is a relative clause of characteristic) well (**pulchre**). We stop. "Where are you coming from?" (**Unde venis?**) and "Where are you headed?" (**Quo tendis?**), he asks and answers. I began to tug at (his toga) (**Vellere**, not **velle**!) and to grab with my hand (**et prensare manu**) his completely uncooperative arms (**levissima bracchia**), nodding (**nutans**), twisting my eyes (**distorquens oculos**), so that he might rescue me (**ut me eriperet**; purpose clause). Smiling (**ridens**) with a sense of humor (idiom, **male salsus**), he pretended (**dissimulare**; historical infinitive; understand something like "not to understand" after **dissimulare** here): bile burned (**urere** is an historical infinitive = "it burned") my liver (**meum iecur**).

## Ovid

### Passage M

Immediately one (**alter**) is in love (**amat**) and the other (**altera**) flees (even) the name of lover (**fugit . . . nomen amantis**), delighting in (**gaudens**) the dark woods (**silvarum latebris**) and the hides of captured animals (i.e., as clothes; **captivarumque ferarum exuviis**), imitating unmarried Diana (**innuptaeque aemula Phoebes**; genitive with **aemula**); a headband held back her hair (**vitta coercebat . . . capillos**) arranged carelessly (**positos sine lege**). Many (**Multi** is a substantive) courted her (**petiere** = **petiverunt**); she, having turned away (**aversata**; deponent verb) those seeking her (**petentes**) and intolerant of and inexperienced with men (**impatiens expersque viri**; **viri**, genitive after the preceding adjectives, may be translated as plural) she roams the trackless groves (**nemora avia lustrat**), and cares not (**nec. . . . curat**) what Hymen (god of marriage), Love (Venus or Cupid are also acceptable), or wedding rites are (**sint** accompanies a series of indirect questions after **quid** and **quae**).

## Passage N

Moreover, the loathsome Propoetides (**obscenae Propoetides**) dared (**Sunt . . . ausae**; deponent) to deny that Venus was a goddess (**Venerem . . . esse . . . deam**; indirect statement after **negare**); for which (**pro quo**), because of the anger of the goddess (**numinis ira; ira** is ablative of cause), are said (**feruntur**) (to have been) the first to have prostituted (**primae vulgasse**) their beautiful bodies (**sua . . . corpora cum forma**; = hendiadys), and as their chastity departed (**utque pudor cessit**; indicative **ut**-clause) and their blood grew hard (**sanguisque induruit**) in their faces (**in oris**), with little change (**parvo . . . discrimine**) they were turned (**versae [sunt]**) into hardened stone (**rigidum . . . silicem**). Since Pygmalion had seen these (**quae**) spending their lives (**aevum . . . agentes**) in wickedness (**per crimen**), offended by their faults (**offensus vitiis**), very many of (which) nature gave to the female disposition (**quae plurima menti femineae natura dedit**), he lived celibate (**caelebs**), without a partner (**sine coniuge**), and lacked a partner for his bed (**thalamique . . . consorte carebat; consorte** is ablative after **carebat**) for some time.

## Passage O

Get out of here, troublesome tablets (**difficiles tabellae; tabellae** may be translated as a diminutive, "little tablets"), wood fit for the funeral pyre, and you, wax (**cera**) filled with words that say No (**negaturis . . . referta notis**), (wax) which, I think, the Corsican bee (**Corsica . . . apis**) gathered (**collectam**; modifies (**cera**) **quam . . .** ) from the flower of the long hemlock (**de longae flore cicutae**; may be rendered "from the long flower of the hemlock") and sent (to us in Rome) at the bottom of its ill-famed honey (**melle sub infami**). But, as if (**tamquam**) thoroughly dyed (**penitus medicata**) with red cinnabar (**minio**), you turned red (i.e., "blushed," in personification; **rubebas**) – that hue was really blood-colored! May you lie (**iaceatis**; jussive subjunctive), flung away (**proiectae**, past participle with **tabellae**) at the crossroads (**triviis**), useless wood, and may the load of a passing wheel-cart crush you (**vosque rotae frangat praetereuntis onus**; note the synecdoche of **rotae**).

# Chapter 7

# The Long and Short Essays

## The Long and the Short of It

The free-response section of the AP Latin Exam requires that you produce both "long" and "short" essays in answer to questions that ask you to analyze a given poem or poems, sections of a poem or poems, or a multi-sentence passage of prose. A long essay question appears on both exams over the required authors, i.e., Vergil and Catullus, and it follows the translation question/s on both of those exams. The long essay is the single most important question on the free-response section, as it requires the most working time (45 and 30 minutes for the Vergil and Catullus exams, respectively) and carries the most weight (35 percent and 20 percent, respectively, although the short essay on the choice author is equal in weight to the long essay on Catullus). The short essay question immediately follows the long essay on the exams for the required authors; however, it precedes the translation question on the exams for the choice authors (for the format of the free-response section, see Chapter 5). The suggested time for all short essays is 20 minutes and the weight varies from 15 to 20 percent of your score on the free-response section. The so-called "background question" on the Vergil Exam is essentially a short essay question. Be aware that the length of your answer is of little or no consequence to its quality. How much is enough is whatever it takes to answer the specific question asked in a manner that is "well-developed." Well-developed means that your writing is coherent, concise, focused, organized, substantive, and copiously and properly documented from the Latin text. More on this in a bit.

## The Essay Questions

| | Long Essay | | Short Essay 1 | | Short Essay 2 | |
|---|---|---|---|---|---|---|
| | Minutes | Percentage | Minutes | Percentage | Minutes | Percentage |
| **Vergil** | 45 | 35 | 20 | 20 | 20 | 15 |
| **Catullus** | 30 | 20 | 20 | 20 | | |
| **Choice Author** | | 20 | 20 | | | |

## The Long Essay

The word most commonly found in an AP Latin Exam essay question is "discuss." In your discussion, you may be asked to analyze a single passage or to compare and contrast two passages. A question that asks you to compare and contrast two parts of the same passage or poem, or two different passages or poems by the same author, is a favorite on the exam. Of the 12 long essay questions over the years 2006–2001 (one each year for Vergil and Catullus), eight asked for you to compare and contrast two passages from the same author/work.[1] You are never asked to compare Horace with Catullus, for example, although this was the case some years ago. Compare and contrast means that you are to find both similarities and differences between the passages provided. In answering such questions, state the points of comparison and contrast as explicitly as you are able and strive for balance. There are two effective ways to answer a compare-and-contrast question:

1] create two separate paragraphs, each devoted to an analysis of one of the two passages, and then summarize the similarities and differences in a concluding paragraph;

2] outline the main points of similarity and difference before writing, and then cover each point by interweaving your analysis of both poems together, so that you are comparing or contrasting the two passages directly and immediately as you proceed through the Latin. Discuss both passages at the same time, back and forth.

Choose the approach that best suits your writing style or the one that is most effective in communicating your understanding of the passages. For examples of this type of question, see Practice Vergil Exam 1, Questions 3 and 4; Practice Vergil Exam 2, Question 4; and Practice Latin Lit Exam 2, Catullus Question 2, all found at the end of this book.

## Topics Covered on Recent Long Essay Questions

### Vergil

2006: Anchises grieves for the death of Marcellus (*Aeneid* 6.868–86)

2005: the character of Aeneas in action, via his speeches (*Aeneid* 1.92–101 and 198–209)

2004: the behavior of sovereigns in their realms (*Aeneid* 1.124–41 and 4.74–89)

2003: how the Trojan war disrupts the lives of Aeneas and Creusa (*Aeneid* 2.768–93)

---

[1] Compare-and-contrast questions may be found on AP Latin Exams for the years 2001, 2002, 2004, and 2005 for Vergil and the years 2001, 2004, 2005, and 2006 for Catullus. See The College Board AP Latin Web site.

2002: Dido's feelings at the beginning and end of her relationship with Aeneas (*Aeneid* 4.20–29 and 320–30)

2001: Juno's positions on the Trojan mission (*Aeneid* 1.37–49 and 12.818–28)

### Catullus

2006: confrontation with two acquaintances (Poems 40 and 116)

2005: the behavior of two friends (Poems 14a.12–23 and 30)

2004: the literary merits of two writers (Poems 1 and 95 a and b, now omitted)

2003: descriptions of the poet as **neglegentem** and a female friend as **insulsa** (Poem 10.1–7, 14–34)

2002: on the death of Lesbia's pet sparrow: serious or playful? (Poem 3)

2001: observations about two people (Poems 77 and 84)

# The Short Essay

The short essay topic is usually confined to a single poem or passage, or to a portion of a single poem or passage. Unlike the long essay, short essay questions appear on the exams for both the required authors and the choice authors. Note that the suggested time for all short essays is 20 minutes, although the point value differs from 15 to 20 percent. No topics for Cicero are provided, because of the change in syllabus. For the background question on the Vergil Exam, which also is defined as a short essay, see the next chapter.

## Topics Covered on Recent Short Essay Questions

### Vergil

2006: Jupiter characterizes Rome's future (*Aeneid* 1.291–96)

2005: Aeneas' emotions in witnessing mural of the Trojan War (*Aeneid* 1.450–65)

2004: the effect of Dido's suicide on Anna (*Aeneid* 4.675–85)

2003: Sibyl's prophecy (*Aeneid* 6.83–94)

2002: Pallas fights Turnus: hope vs. reality (*Aeneid* 10.457–65)

2001: Turnus as hero (*Aeneid* 10.491–96, 500–505)

### Catullus

2006: personal advice to a friend (Poem 69)

2005: the poet sees Lesbia for the first time (Poem 51.1–12)

2004: the poet's feelings about Lesbia (Poems 72.5–8 and 85)

2003: let us live and love (Poem 5)

2001: the poet compares Quintia and Lesbia (Poem 86)

### Horace

2006: a friend arrives while the poet is pursued by the Pest (*Satires* 1.9.60–68)

2005: the poet's political philosophy (*Odes* 3.1.5–16)

2004: conversation with the Pest about Maecenas (*Satires* 1.9.48–60)

2003: verbal competition between Lydia and her lover (*Odes* 3.9.9–24)

2002: the poet's personal philosophy (The Golden Mean) (*Odes* 2.10.1–8 and 21–24)

2001: advice to seize the day (*Odes* 1.11)

### Ovid

2006: Thisbe reacts to Pyramus' dying (*Metamorphoses* 4.147–57)

2005: Daedalus instructs Icarus on flying (*Metamorphoses* 8. 203–13)

2004: Baucis and Philemon before and after their encounter with the gods (*Metamorphoses* 8.631–36 and 8.712–20)

2003: Cupid responds to the poet's complaint (*Amores* 1.1.5–6 and 19–27)

2002: Pyramus and Thisbe at the wall (*Metamorphoses* 4.71–80)

2001: Daphne's metamorphosis, after Apollo overtakes her (*Metamorphoses* 1.553–67)

## Analysis of Latin Poetry

"How can I do my best on the essay questions in the free-response section?" The following attempt to answer this request is limited to poetic analysis because the vast majority of AP Latin students read poetry. You can find success on the essay questions in the same way that you can reach Carnegie Hall: practice, practice, practice! Write as often as you can, both within the context of your AP Latin course and in the context of your other courses. Ask your Latin teacher, your English teacher, your Mom and Dad, your friends, and anyone else who is willing, to read and comment on your writing. (Hint: never say, in the presence of your teacher, "But this is Latin, not English"!) Practice thinking and writing under the pressure of time. Hopefully, your teacher will have prepared you for what you will find on the AP Latin Exam by challenging you with AP-style Latin tests throughout the year. If not, practice on your own. The resources provided in this book should help you to improve your analytical writing for the AP Latin Exam, especially if you study the answers to the sample Practice Exam essays which are provided at the end of this book.

# How Latin Poetry Differs from Prose

- An adjective and its noun may be widely separated:

  **Tu face nescio quos esto contentus amores/irritare tua.** (*Metamorphoses* 1.461–62)

  > You (Cupid) be content to light <u>with your torch</u> some love affair or other.

  **Nam color in pomo est, ubi permaturuit, ater.** (*Metamorphoses* 4.165)

  > For the <u>color</u> of the mulberry fruit is <u>dark</u> when it matures.

- Antecedents sometimes follow their relative clauses and are even pulled inside the clause:

  **Nec prosunt domino, quae prosunt omnibus, artes!** (*Metamorphoses* 1.524)

  > Nor are the <u>skills</u>, <u>which</u> are useful for all (others), useful for their lord!

  **Quas vaga moverat aura,/captabat plumas.** (*Metamorphoses* 8.197–98)

  > He was catching <u>feathers that</u> the passing breeze had moved.

  **At tu, quae ramis arbor miserabile corpus/nunc tegis unius.** (*Metamorphoses* 4.158)

  > But you, <u>tree</u>, <u>that</u> with (your) branches now shade the poor body of one.

- Words that introduce clauses are postponed, often to second position, sometimes later:

  **Sagitta/. . . , in vacuo quae vulnera pectore fecit!** (*Metamorphoses* 1.520)

  > An arrow . . . <u>which</u> has made wounds in (my) empty heart!

  **Exigua cum summum stringitur aura.** (*Metamorphoses* 4.136)

  > <u>When</u> its surface is touched with a slight breeze.

  **Hos aliquis tremula dum captat harundine pisces . . . vidit.** (*Metamorphoses* 8.217–19)

  > These someone (saw) <u>while</u> catching fish with his quivering rod.

- The first and last word of a line or phrase can often "frame" the inner words, creating a chiastic or interlocking effect, e.g., **eque sagittifera prompsit duo tela pharetra** (the quiver actually encloses the two arrows; *Metamorphoses* 1.468) or

  **ab alto/quae teneram prolem produxit in aera nido,** where the young bird, **teneram prolem**, is protected in the middle of the high nest (*Metamorphoses* 8.213–14)

- A word common to two parallel expressions is often expressed in the last one only (condensation):

  **Qui dare certa (vulnera) (possumus) ferae, dare (certa) vulnera possumus hosti.** (Note the use of poetic plural. *Metamorphoses* 1.458)

> (*I*) *who* (*can*) *give inescapable* (*wounds*) *to the wild beast, who can give* (*inescapable*) *wounds to my enemy.*

**Fugat hoc (amorem), facit illud amorem.** (*Metamorphoses* 1.469)

> *This* (*arrow*) *puts* (*love*) *to flight, that one creates love.*

# SWIMTAG

There are several ways to improve your success in writing critical essays. Before writing, outline or list the points you wish to make in your discussion during the reading period of the exam (for the reading period, see Chapters 5 and 12). Or, learn one of the several formulaic approaches to poetic analysis that have been developed by experienced AP Latin teachers. The most well-known is designated as SWIMTAG.[2] The acronym SWIMTAG, actually S W (x 2) I M (x 2) T (x 2) A G, when expanded means **S**ounds, **W**ord order, **W**ord choice, **I**mages, **M**eter, **M**ood, **T**one, **T**heme, **A**llusions, and **G**rammar. These categories sum up the poetic qualities worthy of consideration when you analyze and discuss a Latin poem or passage of verse. However, remember to use SWIMTAG or other such methods <u>as a means to the end of producing a well-developed critical essay rather than as an end in itself</u>. When you write a critical essay, avoid the temptation to substitute a collection of stylistic devices for a well-developed and well-supported critical analysis. You will find here below further information about SWIMTAG.

## 1. Sounds

What sounds do you hear when you say the words? How do these affect the meaning? What sounds create what effects? What evidence is there of alliteration, assonance, onomatopoeia, rhyme, or sound play?

- The consonants B, C, D, G, P, and T give an abrupt, harsh, rigid sound:

    **Taurus et incertam excussit cervice securim.** (*Aeneid* 2.224).

    **Conciderant ictae nivea cervice iuvencae.** (Ovid, *Metamorphoses* 10.272)

- F, H, S, and Z are soft, soothing sounds, as in wind, the sea, whispers, or sleep; sibilation can also indicate evil, as in the hissing of a snake:

    **Praecipitat suadentque cadentia sidera somnos.** (*Aeneid* 2.9).

    **Ardentesque oculos suffecti sanguine et igni.** (*Aeneid* 2.210)

    **Quod mare conceptum spumantibus exspuit undis.** (Catullus, Poem 64.155)

- L and R are liquid sounds, used with laughing, singing, or flowing water:

    **Unde loquaces lymphae desiliunt tuae.** (Horace, *Odes* 3.13.15–16)

---

[2] SWIMTAG was created by Sally Davis. The author is also indebted to Linda Montross for her workshop presentations on poetic analysis. For these and other references, see the resources at the end of this chapter.

- M and N are longer, heavy sounds, suggesting humming, moaning, or rumbling, often expressing through alliteration, consonance, or assonance the solemnity of sadness or death:

    **Si quicquam mutis gratum acceptumve sepulcris.** (Catullus, Poem 96.1)

    **O multum miseri meus illiusque parentes.** (Ovid, *Metamorphoses* 4.155)

- O and U are impressive, round, or substantial; the interjection **O!** is often used in high-sounding apostrophes:

    **O patria, O divum domus Ilium et incluta bello.** (*Aeneid* 2.241)

    **O fons Bandusiae splendidior vitro.** (Horace, *Odes* 3.13.1)

## 2. Word order

Look for the following figures of speech that reveal manipulated word order: chiasmus and synchysis, anastrophe and hyperbaton, asyndeton and polysyndeton, hysteron-proteron and prolepsis, hendiadys and zeugma, tmesis, and word picture. (For more on these and other figures of speech, see Chapter 10.)

## 3. Word choice (also known as diction)

What specific words suggest or reinforce the context? Are there exotic or unusual words?

## 4. Images

What pictures does your mind create? What figurative language appears? Figurative language includes the use of antithesis, hyperbole, irony, metaphor, metonymy, oxymoron, personification, simile, and synecdoche. (Again, see Chapter 10 for further information about imagery.)

## 5. Meter

Are there any obvious features of rhythm or cadence within the passage? (For meter, see Chapter 11.)

## 6. Mood

What emotions are expressed in the passage, explicitly or implicitly? How do the descriptive words reveal the feelings conveyed? Do words such as angry, anxious, apathetic, fearful, humorous, joyful, optimistic, or sad apply to the passage?

## 7. Tone

How does the writer feel about the characters or situations he is creating? Does he give any insight into his own feelings, either through direct commentary or suggestive diction?

## 8. Theme

What is the essential topic about which the author is writing? What is his message? Does the author have "an agenda"? How does the selected passage fit into the larger context in which it is found?

## 9. Allusions

What proper nouns occur? What does the use of these reveal about the poet's intentions? What does their appearance imply about the cultural literacy of the audience?

## 10. Grammar

Do unusual forms appear? Is the sentence structure simple or complex? Are imperatives, interjections, etc., used for dramatic effect?

# Using SWIMTAG to Write a Good Critical Essay

In the following section, you will find a poetic analysis of the passage provided below, based on the criteria supplied by SWIMTAG:

> Saepe pater dixit, "Generum mihi, filia, debes";
> saepe pater dixit, "Debes mihi, nata, nepotes."
> Illa, velut crimen taedas exosa iugales,
> *Line*    pulchra verecundo suffunditur ora rubore,
> 5    inque patris blandis haerens cervice lacertis,
> "Da mihi perpetua, genitor carissime," dixit,
> "virginitate frui: dedit hoc pater Dianae."

> **Ovid, *Metamorphoses* 1.481–87**

## 1. Sounds

Note the rhyming of the end-words in lines 1–3: **debes**, **nepotes**, and **iugales**. Note, too, how the redundancy of internal vowel sounds (assonance) in lines 6–7 contributes to Daphne's insistence.

## 2. Word order

Words, phrases, clauses, or sentences in a series can suggest intensity of power and momentum, or can reduce the speed of a line or thought. The repetition and balance of the words in lines 1–2 emphasizes father Peneus' insistence that he have grandsons. Certain figures of speech, those required on the syllabus as well as those not required, designate word order that is deliberately manipulated by the poet.

- As mentioned, the <u>anaphora</u> of **Saepe pater dixit** and of **debes**, found in lines 1–2, draws attention to these important lines.

- The <u>chiasmus</u> of "**Generum mihi, filia, debes**"/and "**Debes mihi, nata, nepotes**" and the resulting prime position of the important words **Generum** and its correspondent, **nepotes**, express Peneus' insistence.

- Note the placement of **exosa**, *hating*, between **taedas . . . iugales**, *marriage torches*.

- Close study of line 4, **pulchra verecundo suffunditur ora rubore**, reveals the so-called <u>golden line</u>, which is found regularly in Ovid. The words in this line are interlocked, bringing together Daphne's facial beauty (**pulchra ora**) with the blush (**verecundo rubore**) resulting from her father's statement in lines 1–2. The word order is contrived for effect: Adj. A, Adj. B, Verb, Noun A, Noun B.

- The embracing of her father's neck by Daphne's arms is suggested by the near-<u>synchysis</u> **in patris . . . cervice** intertwined with **blandis . . . lacertis**. The <u>juxtaposition</u> of **cervice** and **lacertis** is also notable.

- Furthermore, since it is not really her arms that are doing the coaxing, **blandis** may be considered a <u>transferred epithet</u>, modifying both **lacertis** and Daphne herself.

- The words **virginitate frui** are postponed from line 6 to the next line, creating an <u>enjambment</u>, or surprise. Note the suggestive distancing of the adjective **perpetua** from its noun **virginitate**.

## 3. Word choice

Note Peneus' variation in the words for daughter (**filia** and **nata**) and Daphne's designation of her father as **genitor**, a word usually reserved for Jupiter. Peneus also distinguishes between a son-in-law (**gener**) and grandsons (**nepotes**), which clarify his appeal to Daphne. Note, too, the use of the powerful and unusual word **exosa** (line 3).

## 4. Images

There is little imagery here, because the passage consists mostly of dialogue. Note the use of **taedas . . . iugales**, *marriage torches*, as a metonymy for marriage itself.

## 5. Meter

The rhythm of several lines reinforce the context in which they are found, e.g., the highly emotive line 1 shows dactyls alternating with spondees:

$$- \; u \; u \; - \quad - \; - \quad u \; u \; - \quad \quad u \; u \; \text{-uu} \quad - \; -$$
Saepe pater dixit generum mihi filia debes

and line 3, in which Daphne attempts to calm and soothe her father, consists mainly of slower spondees:

$$- \quad u \; u \; - \quad - \quad - \quad - \; - \quad \quad - \; - \; u \; u \; - \; -$$
inque patris blandis haerens cervice lacertis

## 6. Mood

The mood here is one of dramatic tension: Daphne is caught between her sense of duty to her father and her personal wishes for herself. Ovid's choice and repetition of the words **saepe . . . dixit** and **debes** (lines 1–2) indicates Peneus' expectation that Daphne has a duty to perform, i.e., to marry and bear him grandsons. The words **crimen** and **exosa** in line 3 help to convey Daphne's negative attitude toward marriage.

## 7. Tone

Despite her use of the respectful word **genitor** (line 6), Daphne is challenging her father's wishes and authority. This situation runs counter to the gender norms of Roman society.

## 8. Theme

The theme of the story of Daphne and Apollo is allegorical, that is, the "victory" of Cupid over Apollo represents the triumph of passion over reason. This passage contributes to the theme by setting the stage for the fact that Daphne, unlike Diana, will not remain "her own woman" and that passion (Cupid) will triumph over reason (Apollo).

## 9. Allusion

In line 7, Daphne refers to the goddess Diana and reminds her father that the goddess Diana's father, Jupiter, granted her request to remain unmarried.

## 10. Grammar

The only grammar worthy of note here is the use of the accusative of respect or specification: **suffunditur <u>ora</u>** means *suffused or covered <u>with respect to her face</u>* (**ora** is a plural neuter noun and cannot serve as the subject of **suffunditur**).

# Some Points to Consider in Writing a Good Critical Essay

1. First and foremost, <u>answer the specific question asked</u>! This continues to be a concern voiced in the Chief Reader's annual report on student performance on the AP Latin Exam and should therefore be addressed by future candidates, such as yourself. To help you maintain your focus when writing, consider the following:

   a. During the reading period, do as much prewriting or brainstorming as you can. Underline or otherwise highlight the specific words in the question that prompt your thinking.

   b. Begin your lead or topic sentence by quoting or reproducing keywords in English from the wording of the question.

    c. Organize your thinking. Avoid making vague generalizations and "free-writing," that is, writing everything you know about the subject as soon as it occurs to you. And avoid making casual reference to other poems or works by the same author (unless specifically directed to do so), as this is distracting and rarely contributes to the topic under discussion. You need not produce a formal three- or five-paragraph essay, but your discussion should have a beginning, a middle, and an end.

2. Avoid being descriptive or narrative in your discussion, that is, don't simply give a line-by-line paraphrase (or translation!) of the passage. <u>Be focused and critical in your writing, explaining how the evidence drawn from the Latin text supports each observation.</u>

3. Thoroughness is a third consideration, and one which has prompted very specific wording on each free-response essay question. The directions read "Be sure to refer specifically to the Latin <u>throughout</u> the passages to support your essay."[3] This is an area where unnecessary points are often lost. The word "throughout" means that you are to <u>include documented reference to the entire passage – beginning, middle, and end – in your discussion</u>. It is helpful to determine during the reading period how the Latin passages are organized, i.e. where the sense units are or the breaks in the thought occur. Bracket or otherwise designate these on your test paper for future reference.

4. Essays that receive full credit <u>make frequent reference to the Latin text in the correct format</u> (for the latter, see below). You must collect and present the "evidence" that will solve the "mystery" that is the exam question. The College Board states, "The responsibility rests with the student to convince the Reader that the student is drawing conclusions from the Latin text and not from a general recall of the passage."[4]

5. Here are several pieces of personal advice with regard to your writing: write legibly (speed sometimes reduces even the finest calligraphy to scribble!), use good English, and avoid slang or "bad language."

## Guidelines for Citing Latin Correctly in an Essay

1. Select only the Latin that is <u>relevant</u> to your discussion. Don't write out several lines or an entire sentence of Latin text in the hope that the evidence is contained somewhere therein. This is time-consuming and will rarely be considered acceptable evidence for the point you are making.

2. <u>Translate or give a close paraphrase</u> of the specific Latin that you have cited. Be sure to include all the Latin. When translating, use parentheses

---

[3] 2005 *AP Latin Literature and AP Latin: Vergil, Released Exams*, p. 28.

[4] *AP Latin Course Description*, May 2006 and May 2007, p. 30.

or quotation marks to distinguish the English from the Latin, e.g., for the line **agnosco veteris vestigia flammae** (*Aeneid* 4.23):

> Translation: "I recognize traces of the old flame."

> Close paraphrase: Dido recognizes feelings that she once had for her (now-deceased) husband. Avoid loose paraphrases, such as "Dido is in love."

3. <u>Write out the Latin and/or cite line numbers</u>. When referring to a specific word or short phrase, you should write out the Latin. It is a good idea to underline the Latin cited, as this is correct format in quoting a foreign language in English and it also brings the Reader's attention to your evidence. You may use ellipsis points for longer citations, that is, quote the first word, indicate the intervening and assumed words by three ellipsis points (. . .), and then close the citation with the final relevant word. Thus, if you were using the first two lines of the *Aeneid* to support a point in your discussion, you would write **Arma . . . venit** or **Arma . . . venit** (lines 1–2 or, simply, 1–2). Remember that, although ellipsis points may be used in citing longer clauses or sentences, it is a good idea to <u>limit the length of your citations to a few relevant words</u>. Use single words or phrases whenever possible. And avoid giving vague citations, such as "in lines 1–10."

## Sample Short Essay Question

This sample essay is provided to illustrate the three points discussed above. For additional short essay questions, see the Practice Exams and Answers at the end of this book.

### Essay question:

In Poem 49, Catullus thanks Cicero for some unknown reason. In a short essay, discuss the possible appearance of irony in this poem, that is, whether Catullus actually means what he says.

### Sample answer:

In this poem, it is apparent at first glance that Catullus feels gratitude for something that Cicero has said or done: <u>gratias tibi maximas</u> . . . <u>agit</u>, "he (Catullus) gives you (Cicero) greatest thanks." After a second look, however, Catullus seems to overdo or exaggerate this gratitude. He makes extensive use of superlative adjectives (<u>disertissime, pessimus, pessimus, optimus</u>), which contributes to the tone of exaggeration. Catullus uses hyperbole in lines 2–3: <u>quot</u> . . . <u>annis</u>, "as many (of Romulus' ancestors, i.e., Romans) as there are, as there were, and as there will be in other years hereafter." The last, and perhaps most compelling, piece of evidence that Catullus is being facetious here appears in the final two lines in the correlation between Catullus as the worst poet (<u>pessimus</u> . . . <u>poeta</u>) and Cicero as the best defender (<u>optimus</u> . . . <u>patronus</u>). The comparison is heightened by the equality of position in the words <u>pessimus omnium poeta</u> and <u>optimus omnium patronus</u>

at the end of their respective lines. The pattern makes it difficult not to observe that Catullus is using the genitive phrase <u>omnium patronus</u>, meaning "everyone's patron," to suggest a conflict of interest on the part of Cicero. Familiarity with Catullus' literary persona through his other writings suggests that Catullus has more than a high opinion of himself as a poet. This suggests that he is not being honest in calling himself the "worst poet" and that therefore Cicero is, in the poet's unstated opinion, far from being the "best defender."

## Some Topics for Practice in Essay Writing

These suggestions for essay topics are intended to supplement those questions that appear on previous AP Latin Exams for the years 2006–2001 (the Latin passages for which are listed by author below). Some liberties have been taken with what might be considered standard AP Latin Exam wording, for the sake of broadening the scope of some questions.

### Vergil

*Passages from the* Aeneid *tested on recent AP Vergil Exams:*

| **Long Essay** | **Short Essay** |
| --- | --- |
| Book 1, lines 37–49 and 12.818–28 | Book 1, lines 291–96 |
| 92–101 and 198–209 | 1, lines 450–65 |
| 124–41 and 4.84–89 | Book 4, lines 675–85 |
| Book 2, lines 768–93 | Book 6, lines 83–94 |
| Book 4, lines 20–29 and 320–30 | Book 10, lines 457–65 |
| Book 6, lines 868–86 | 491–96 and 500–505 |

*Additional topics for essays:*

- What are the themes of the *Aeneid* as they are introduced in lines 1–11? In what ways does the poet express these themes?

- The simile in Book 1, lines 148–52, describes a scene from public life in the Rome of Vergil's time. In a short essay, discuss the picture of Rome that is presented in this simile, identify the historical reason for it, and comment on the appropriateness of this comparison to the poetic context in which it is found.

- In each of these two passages (Books 1.286–96 and 6.860–76), Vergil makes reference to events that happened during his lifetime and within the context in which he wrote. Discuss the historical significance of each event and the writer's purpose in introducing these events in the poetic context in which they appear.

- In each of these two passages (Book 2.281–95 and 776–89), a phantom has appeared to Aeneas. Compare and contrast the speeches given to the hero by these phantoms. Include in your discussion their respective identities and their purpose in addressing Aeneas.

- Analyze the following speech of Dido (Book 4.305–330), exploring the various ways in which the queen attempts to appeal to Aeneas upon his departure. What are the different arguments that she uses? Does she change her strategy during the speech? If so, how?

- In these passages (Books 4.296–303 and 6.46–51), two women have become possessed by forces that cause in them a dramatic change. In a short essay, compare and contrast how the poet portrays each transformation, paying special attention to the imagery used and to the reason why each character finds herself in this state.

- In these two passages (Books 4.365–70 and 6.469–76), reference is made to someone being "hard as flint." In a short essay, identify both individuals, then describe the circumstances that account for this characterization and how these circumstances relate to one another psychologically.

- These two speeches (Books 1.65–70 and 12.818–28) portray two different attitudes held by the same character. Compare and contrast these two attitudes and account for the change.

## Thought questions:

- Explore the conflict between **pietas** (rational judgment) and **furor** (mindless emotion) as an essential theme of the *Aeneid*.

- The word **fatum** in its various forms appears many times in the early books of the *Aeneid*. Argue from the poem the place of fate in the workings of the gods and in the lives of men.

- The noble Roman understood his duty to the gods, his homeland, his friends and followers, and most importantly, his family, in the person of the father. Explore the subject of patriarchal responsibility and filial duty as a major theme of the *Aeneid*.

- One scholar has written about the dominant imagery of Book 2: the serpent and the flame.[5] Write an essay in which you discuss the relevance of these images to each other and to the context in which they are found.

- Compare Dido's curses (Book 4.380–91 and 607–29) with Jupiter's prophecy (Book 1.257–96), that of Anchises in the "Parade of Heroes" (Book 6.756–886), or the Shield of Aeneas (8.626–728).

- In Books 1 and 4, discuss the specific points of comparison in the orator simile (1.148–53), bee simile (1.430–36), Dido the huntress simile (4.68–73), the ant simile (4.402–407), and the oak tree in a high wind simile (4.441–46). In Books 10 and 12, discuss these similes: lion and the bull (10.454–56), the boar (10.707–15), wounded African lion (12.4–9), bull charging a tree (12.101–106), the hailstorm (12. 451–58), the mountain

---

[5] Bernard Knox, "The Serpent and the Flame: The Imagery of the Second Book of the *Aeneid*," *Virgil: A Collection of Critical Essays*, Steelle Commager, ed., Englewood Cliffs, NJ, Prentice-Hall, 1966.

rockfall (12.684–90), the dream-state (12.908–14), and the shot from a catapult (12.921–23).

- Compare and contrast these two speeches made by women who have been scorned: Dido (Book 4.376–87; cf. 4.607–20, in English) and Ariadne (Catullus, Poem 64.192–201). Another good pair for comparison is Catullus, Poem 64.132–44, and *Aeneid* 4.305–19.

- T.S. Eliot called Aeneas' meeting with Dido in the Underworld (Book 6.450–76) "the most civilized passage in all of Western literature." Comment on the reason/s why you think Eliot felt this way.

- Write a character study of Turnus as the anti-hero who displays the passion that is the counter- point to the self-control of Aeneas. Support your observations with examples from the second half of the *Aeneid*.

## Catullus

| **Long Essay** | **Short Essay** |
| --- | --- |
| Poems 1 and 95 a and b (now omitted) | Poem 5 |
| Poem 3 | Poem 51.1–12 |
| Poem 10.1–7 and 14–34 | Poem 69 |
| Poems 14a.12–23 and 30 | Poems 72.5–8 and 85 |
| Poems 40 and 116 | Poem 83 |
| Poems 77 and 84 | Poem 86 |

> **Note:** Catullus provides ample opportunity for practice with compare-and-contrast essays, e.g., 5 and 7, 43 and 86, and 96 and 101.

- In Poem 8, the poet has a conversation with himself about his feelings toward Lesbia. Discuss the ways in which the poet portrays his mixed feelings throughout the poem. Comment on whether or not the poet resolves his confusion by the end and justify your point of view using the Latin text.

- If the name Catullus were not mentioned in line 7, what characteristics of Poem 13 would lead you to believe that it was written by Catullus? Consider word choice, imagery, figures of speech, tone, and meter.

- Poems 14a.1–7 and 50.1–8 present two scenarios in which Catullus addresses his friend Licinius Calvus about writing. Determine the mood of the poet in each case by carefully examining the language of both passages.

- These two poems (30.1–6 and 77; see also 76) express feelings of betrayal on the part of the poet. Compare and contrast the ways in which the poet expresses these feelings. What elements do the poems have in common? What elements are different?

- In Poem 46, the poet strives to convey an atmosphere suitable to its context. In a short essay, describe this atmosphere and discuss the ways in which the poet evokes it.

- The poet attempts to create sympathy for himself in this single-sentence poem (Poem 60). In a short essay, discuss how he does this and whether or not he is successful.

- Compare and contrast the ways in which Catullus speaks about his brother's death in Poems 65 (lines 5–14) and 68 (lines 20–26) and the effect that this event had on Catullus' relationship with the friends addressed in each poem.

- In Poem 72, Catullus attempts to define his relationship with Lesbia, as it was in the past and as it is in the present. In a short essay, discuss how the poet contrasts how he once felt with how he now feels.

- In Poems 76 (lines 17–20) and 109 (lines 3–6), Catullus prays to the gods. In a short essay, discuss the reason for each prayer and how the themes of the poems relate to one another.

### Thought questions:

- What do the causes of the deaths of King Aegeus of Athens (Catullus, Poem 64.2–7ff.) and Queen Amata of Laurentum (*Aeneid*, Book 12.554ff.) have in common?

- In Catullus, Poem 5 and Horace, *Odes* 1.9.5–16, the poets advise their addressees to live life according to certain criteria. Write an essay in which you compare and contrast the line of reasoning used by both poets and the way in which they convey their advice.

- In Catullus, Poem 44 (lines 6–15) and Horace, *Odes* 2.7 (lines 9–16), each poet admits to an error in personal judgment. Discuss the circumstances of each and indicate how the poet feels about what he has done. (Cf. Poem 10.27–34.)

- In Catullus, Poem 51 and Horace, *Odes* 1.23, each poet wishes to meet a woman. Compare and contrast each poet's impression of this woman and the effect that this impression has on the writer.

- Identify the instances of colloquial language found in Catullus, Poem 10 and Horace, *Satires* 1.9.1–21 or 60–78.

- How do Catullus, Poem 11 and Ovid, *Amores* 1.11, compare, other than their corpus numbers?

- In the poems of Catullus, Ovid, and Horace, locate a poem or passage that presents the poet's feelings about homecoming. Discuss the similarities and differences in treatment.

## Cicero

### *Pro Archia Poeta*

- Discuss the two pieces of evidence to which Cicero refers in his attempt to disprove the prosecution's case. (*Pro Archia Poeta* 8 to ... **Heracliensium dicunt**.)

- In his speech in defense of Archias, in what specific ways does Cicero claim that his own study of literature has served him during his professional career? Make specific reference to the Latin that you use to answer this question. (*Pro Archia Poeta* 14)

- What ultimate benefit comes to a man who has devoted his life to the liberal arts? In your answer, comment on the insight we receive into Cicero's perception of himself in this regard. (*Pro Archia, Poeta* 30)

- In his summation, Cicero completes his account of Archias' achievements. What specific points does Cicero make on the defendant's behalf? (*Pro Archia Poeta* 31)

### *De Amicitia*

- How does Cicero define friendship in *De Amicitia*? (17–18, **Ego vos hortari ... est consecutus**)

- What are the particular advantages of friendship, as presented in *De Amicitia*? (22 to ... **numquam molesta est**)

## Thought question

- Compare what Cicero says about friendship in *De Amicitia* to the description of his friendship with Archias in *Pro Archia Poeta*, 1, 5–6, 12–14, 28–30, and 31.

## Horace

**Short Essay**

*Odes* 1.11

*Odes* 2.10.1–8, 21–24

*Odes* 3.1.5–16

*Odes* 3.9.9–24

*Satires* 1.9.48–60

*Satires* 1.9.60–68

### *Odes*

- Horace likes to give examples in his poems. With reference to *Odes* 1.1.19–28, discuss the content and relevance of the examples given to the message of the poem as a whole.

- How does the poet contrast Pyrrha's current lover with himself in *Odes* 1.5?

- In what ways does the poet express his personal philosophy of life in the Soracte Ode (1.9.9–24)?

- What do you learn about Horace's personal philosophy of life from *Odes* 1.11.3–7 and 1.24.13–20? Comment on the effectiveness of the imagery used.

- Discuss how the poet uses nature in *Odes* 1.23 to express to the reader his feelings about Chloe.

- In *Odes* 1.24.9–20, how does the poet attempt to console Vergil for the death of Quintilius? What imagery does he use and what point does he attempt to make by using this imagery?

- Discuss the various ways employed by the poet in *Odes* 1.25 to convince Lydia that her days as a lover are over.

- Horace enjoys using the element of surprise in his poetry. In *Odes* 1.37 (lines 21–32), he reveals his personal attitude towards an enemy of Rome. Describe this attitude and tell why it surprises the reader, given the context of the entire poem.

- In *Odes* 2.3.21–28, Horace reflects on the subject of mortality. Discuss how the poet emphasizes here that death is both inevitable and universal. (Cf. *Odes* 2.14.5–12)

## Satires 1.9

- With reference to lines 1–13, discuss the various attempts, both behavioral and verbal, used by the Pest to maintain contact with Horace. Include the way in which the poet responds to each.

- In lines 26–34, Horace contrives a masterful "hint" to the Pest. Discuss the content of this hint and comment on the insight it gives into Roman daily life.

## Thought questions

- Explain the imagery used in each of the following passages and discuss how it contributes to the reader's appreciation of the inevitability of death.

  | | |
  |---|---|
  | *Odes* 1.9.13–24 | *Odes* 2.3.15–16, 21–28 |
  | *Odes* 1.11.3–8 | *Odes* 2.14.5–20 |
  | *Odes* 1.24.13–20 | *Odes* 4.7.14–28 |

- Write an essay in which you compare and contrast these dialogues between two lovers: Horace, *Odes* 3.9 and Catullus 45.

- Compare and contrast Horace's attitude toward Lydia as expressed in *Odes* 2.13.13–20 and 2.25.1–8.

### Ovid

#### Short Essay

*Metamorphoses* 1.553–67 (Daphne and Apollo)

*Metamorphoses* 4.71–80 (Pyramus and Thisbe)

*Metamorphoses* 4.147–57 (Pyramus and Thisbe)

*Metamorphoses* 8.203–13 (Daedalus and Icarus)

*Metamorphoses* 8.631–36, 712–30 (Baucis and Philemon)

*Amores* 1.1.5–6, 19–27

## Metamorphoses

- Discuss the ways in which the poet uses his poetic skill in *Metamorphoses* 1.466–73 to describe Cupid's victory over Apollo. In what way can this scene be regarded as allegorical?

- What arguments in *Metamorphoses* 1.514–24 does Apollo present to convince Daphne that he means her no harm? How does he undercut his boasting at the end of his speech?

- In this passage (*Metamorphoses* 4.105–15), Pyramus has discovered Thisbe's scarf and imagines the worst. Describe how his fears are portrayed and how he reacts to the possibility that his fears will be realized.

- Compare Ovid's account of the story of Daedalus (*Metamorphoses* 8.203–13) with that provided by Vergil (Book 6, lines 14–33). See also Catullus, Poem 64, lines 76ff.

- In *Metamorphoses* 8.628–36, an aged couple receives two visitors who are unknown to them. Discuss the ways in which the poet creates the feeling in the reader that the elderly man and his wife are equal partners in their marriage.

- As described in these two passages (*Metamorphoses* 10.243–46 and 290–97), Pygmalion has experienced a "metamorphosis" of his own. With reference to these passages, explain the nature of this transformation and the reason or reasons for it.

## Amores

- Compare and contrast Ovid's characterization of Cupid in the story of Daphne and Apollo (*Metamorphoses* 1.452 ff.) with that found in *Amores* 1.1.

- In *Amores* 1.9.33–40, Ovid describes some famous love-relationships. Identify each of these allusions and what they contribute to the poet's theme.

- Compare the allusion in Horace, *Odes* 1.5.13–16, with that found in *Amores* 1.11.27–28.

- Make a case for considering the poems *Amores* 1.11 and 12 together as the two leaves in a **tabella.**

- Compare and contrast how Horace and Ovid feel about their own writing (*Odes* 3.30.8–16 and *Amores* 3.15.7–14, respectively).

## Thought questions

- Compare and contrast the two passages alluding to the goddess Diana (*Metamorphoses*, 1.474–77 and *Aeneid* 1.498–502). Why, in each case, has the poet chosen this particular deity?

- Compare Apollo's appreciation for Daphne's beauty (*Metamorphoses*, 1.498–502) with that of Pygmalion for his creation (*Metamorphoses*, 10.254–58).

- In a discussion of Ovid, *Metamorphoses* 1.504–509 and Horace, *Odes* 1.23, compare and contrast the god and the poet as beasts on the prowl.

- In the *Metamorphoses*, mortals are transformed into objects, and objects into mortals. Compare and contrast the transformations described in these two passages: *Metamorphoses* 1.548–56 and 10.280–89.

- Using the transformations into trees described in the stories of Daphne and Apollo (1.548–56), Pyramus and Thisbe (4.158–66), and Baucis and Philemon (8.712–24), comment on the metaphorical similarity between trees and people. Illustrate from the Latin how the poet exploits this comparison.

## How Essays Are Scored

All essays on the free-response section, long and short, are graded on a six-point scale, which provides Readers with both latitude and boundaries (remember that the assessment of writing is necessarily subjective). Scores of 6 and 5 are excellent, 4 and 3 good, and 2 and 1 minimal. A zero is assigned if the answer is random, irrelevant, or totally disconnected from the question. No score is given if there is no attempt at answering the question, or if the answer is off-task, such as doodling or a "personal anecdote." For your information, the average score on the two long essay questions for 2005 was 3.34 out of 6 (56 percent) on the Vergil exam and 2.26 out of six (38 percent) on the Literature exam.[6] After you have written your essays for the Practice Exams found at the end of this book, be sure to read carefully the author-produced essays found in the Answer section following each Exam. These practice essay questions will help you to know what to expect on the AP Latin Exam. Below you will find sample scoring guidelines for essays to give you an idea of the range and scope of expectations on essay questions.

---

[6] 2005 *AP Latin Literature and AP Latin: Vergil Released Exams*, pp. 149 and 68, respectively. For sample student answers on essay questions, with scores and helpful commentary provided by the Chief Reader, see the resources listed in Chapter 1. For further information about scoring the essay questions and the AP Latin Exam in general, see Chapter 12.

## Six

A six is awarded to an effective essay that completely answers the question and is supported by relevant and copious documentation from the Latin. The writing is characterized by sound argument and discussion that is coherent and persuasive. Minor mistakes in interpretation or translation are acceptable and usually do not compromise an overall impression of competence.

## Five

This essay is solid and competent, but perhaps lacking in effective development (depth), textual references, or sophistication. The student understands the question asked and is acquainted with the Latin text, but falls short of the top mark in one or more areas.

## Four

The essay that earns a four is adequate or satisfactory. It may fall somewhat short of a six or five in the quality and/or quantity of its citations, in failing to address the question completely, e.g., addressing only one of two passages substantively, or in presenting a narrative or paraphrase without adequate analysis of the text.

## Three

This score arises from failing to cite any of the Latin text, continually citing Latin that is immaterial, giving inadequate attention to one of the two passages, or answering the question in a manner that is superficial or inaccurate. Sometimes only a translation is given.

## Two

This essay is unsatisfactory because it does not answer the question asked or completely ignores one of the two passages; presents statements that are vague, incorrect, or unsubstantiated; or ignores the Latin text or includes citations that do not indicate comprehension.

## One

This essay answers the question in a minimal way. It is apparent that the student recognizes the passage but is unable to respond to the question in any coherent way, either because the question is not understood or because the student's command of the text is faulty or based on memorization. There is no substantive discussion and little or no relevant support.

# Quick-Studies of the Literary Styles of AP Latin Authors

## Vergil

- The *Aeneid* is a literary epic, whose story is modeled upon the *Iliad* and *Odyssey* of Homer. The motivation for the story of the settlement of Aeneas in Italy and the founding of Rome was Augustus' interest in giving divine sanction and the weight of antiquity to his establishment of empire. This, of course, had personal consequences for Augustus too, seeing that his family, the **gens Iulia**, could therefore derive its origins from Aeneas' son, Iulus/Ascanius. In the context of the civil wars of the first century BCE, a return to the stability and traditions of the good old days, on which Augustus' rule was predicated, required formal and public acknowledgment and celebration of the role of both the gods and the family in the development of Rome.

- Vergil's sense of national pride in the glory of Rome and in the patronage of the Emperor, as well as his personal commitment to the Sisyphean task of composing the *Aeneid* itself, are summed up in Book 1, line 33: **tantae molis erat Romanam condere gentem**.

- The fact that the *Aeneid* is filled with Greek forms and cadences, with references and allusions to things Greek, is a product of Vergil's education in Athens. However, Vergil reshapes the Homeric epic to Roman purposes by creating a story of personal sacrifice made in pursuit of the common good. In a sense, Vergil, who was physically weak, shy, and a "sentimental idealist," experienced life vicariously through his character Aeneas.[7]

- The story of the *Aeneid* reveals that Vergil believed that men's lives were controlled by the gods. For Vergil, whether the gods and fate were the same or whether the gods themselves were under the control of fate are questions that continue to be argued.

- Vergil's literary style is epic with respect to his use of the dactylic hexameter, the appearance of the gods, the elaborate and allusive language, focus on a heroic character whose actions are noble, lengthy speeches, and a long but unified story of events of national significance.

- "Homer is a world; Vergil, a style."[8] Vergil's style is characterized by narrative skill. As an epic poet, Vergil

    — produces strongly-drawn main characters

    — skillfully weaves long speeches into the action

    — makes the action more vivid by using imagery, such as the simile

---

[7] For Vergil as a "sentimental idealist," see Clyde Pharr, *Vergil's Aeneid, Books I-VI*, Wauconda, IL, Bolchazy-Carducci Publishers, Inc., 1997, p.3.

[8] Mark Van Doren.

— is effective in suggesting sound

— is pictorial in his descriptions

— uses verbal and situational reminiscence and foreshadowing.

## Catullus

- Catullus' style is colloquial and, at the same time, artful and skilled (he is referred to as **doctus poeta**). His poems give the appearance of spontaneity and sincerity, but are carefully-crafted. Catullus writes short, personal lyrics (published in a **libellus**), full of diction favored by the **novi poetae.** He is preoccupied with **urbanitas** (sophistication). Wit and brevity are the focal points of his poetic circle. The first two lines of Poem 1 nicely illustrate his style:

  > Cui dono lepidum novum libellum
  > arida modo pumice expolitum?

- The language of the **novi poetae** includes a number of "fashionable" adjectives and nouns: adjectives include **beatus, bellus, delicatus, doctus, elegans, illepidus, ineptus, infacetus, insapiens, invenustus, iucundus, lepidus, misellus/miser, otiosus, salsus, suavis, tener,** and **venustus.** Nouns include **deliciae, facetiae, infacetiae, lepor** (not **lepus!**), **libellus, otium, sal,** and **venustas.**

- His writing reveals a character that is independent, sarcastic, witty, self-absorbed, passionate/ emotional, social, playful, and ironical.

- His poems can contain more than a single addressee, rhetorical questions, self-address, epigrammatic "punch-lines," and ring-composition (organization of thought in which poems begin and end with the same point).

- Catullus' poems are often "psychological" in that they explore male and female relationships, examine social mores, and mock human pretensions.

- Secondary criticism has been pre-occupied with the thorny question of the order of the poems. Most agree that Catullus' corpus can be divided into three parts: Poems 1–60 are polymetric (written in a variety of meters, many hendecasyllabic), Poems 61–64 (some say 68) are the longer poems (averaging nearly 200 lines each), and 65–116 the elegiac poems (a common meter for writing love poetry).

- Catullus writes in dactylic hexameter, elegiac couplet, and the hendecasyllable.

## Cicero

- Eloquence: Cicero was a master of the art of self-expression and persuasion by means of speech, although seemingly insecure and indecisive in his personal and political life.

- His strengths as a speaker and writer include presentation of facts in an argument, arrangement in an effective order, and choice of words suitable to the thought and emotions of the audience.

- Cicero's oratorical style is dramatic and vivid.

- His use of Latin features clarity (effective presentation of ideas), force (stimulation of emotions), and beauty (musical cadence and rhythm, "poetic prose").

- In the *Pro Archia Poeta*, Cicero combines judicial/forensic and demonstrative styles of oratory. This speech was given the year after Cicero's consulship and contains allusions to it.

- According to Cicero's *De Oratore*, there are five qualities considered essential in a successful orator: **inventio** (accumulation of facts=discovery), **dispositio** (clear and skillful arrangement of arguments), **elocutio** (delivery in a polished rhetorical style), **memoria** (accurate retention of facts and a delivery that is without lapses), and **actio** (effective vocal intonation, use of melody, rhythm, and harmony, facial expression, gesture, movement, etc.)

- Favorite stylistic features: repetition (especially, anaphora and tricolon), proportion and balance, subtlety and elegance of expression, melody and euphony, and periodic and highly complex sentences.

## Horace

- Horace is best known for what has been called **callida iunctura**, skillful joining or artful juncture, which refers to the poet's unique ability to get the most out of the words he uses, e.g., **virenti canities** (*Odes* 1.9.17), which contrasts **virenti**, having meanings of youth/green/spring, with **canities**, with meanings of old age/white/winter. Friedrich Nietzsche describes the effect of Horace's verse as "a mosaic of words, in which every unit spreads its power to the left and to the right over the whole, by its sound, by its place in the sentence, and by its meaning."[9] Alfred Lord Tennyson hailed the verses of the *Odes* as "Jewels five-words-long/That on the stretch'd forefinger of all Time/Sparkle for ever."[10]

- The *Odes* are **simplex munditiis** (*Odes* 1.5.5), simple in their elegance or, as the British poet John Milton expressed it, "plain in their neatness." The poems are dense and compact and lack the intensity of Catullus. Embedded within are many pithy aphorisms, of which **Carpe diem** (*Odes* 1.11.8) is the most familiar.

- Horace encourages the reader to adopt the Epicurean world view of gathering rosebuds and living for the moment, but he also preaches the Golden Mean (Nothing in Excess). He is preoccupied with the passage of time and

---

[9] *Twilight of the Idols.*

[10] *The Princess, II.*

the inevitability and universality of death. In his writing, wine and foliage are life symbols.

- As an imperial spokesman, he is respectful of his patrons, Maecenas and Augustus, and of the traditions and values of the Roman state (see the Roman Odes, which are Book 3, *Odes* 1–6).

- He loves the countryside and uses images from nature often.

- He enjoys using learned (often pedantic, at least to us) allusions to the Greek and Roman past.

- Assessment of his character and personality might include the words tolerant, humane, realistic, detached/meditative, self-aware, affectionate (but not passionate), loyal, and humorous (*Satires* 1.9). Horace possesses an astute sense of situation, but is more an observer than a participant in the human comedy.

- His writing expresses qualities of economy, control, and harmony. Horace likes to give examples to illustrate his point and frequently uses the negative. Much in his lyric poetry is allegorical, metaphorical, or otherwise symbolic.

- Horace uses a number of different Greek meters in his poems.

## Ovid

- Ovid's literary style is rhetorical (he was trained as a lawyer), especially in speeches given by characters. His poetic art may be summed up in his own words: **ars adeo latet arte sua** (*Metamorphoses* 10.252).

- He is "psychological": explores young and old (Daedalus and Icarus), male and female (Pygmalion, Daphne and Apollo), mortal and divine (Baucis and Philemon), love (Pyramus and Thisbe), etc.

- His poems express variation in dramatic tone, from the nearly Falstaff-like characterization of Apollo in the story of Daphne to the suspenseful foreshadowing of Icarus' fall and the tragic death-scenes of Pyramus and Thisbe.

- His poetry is musical. He creates imaginative sound effects through frequent use of alliteration, assonance, onomatopoeia, and sound play.

- Ovid favors a highly visual style, with much figurative language and imagery. He produces "cinematic" word pictures and word play via chiasmus, synchysis, and the golden line.

- He frequently attaches the enclitic **–que** to the first word of a quotation rather than to the main verb in the speech. An example of this is found in *Metamorphoses* 1.456, **"Quid"que, "tibi, lascive puer, cum fortibus armis?"/dixerat**.

- Ovid writes in both dactylic hexameter and elegiac meters.

# Resources for Essay Writing

## Recommended In-Print Resources for Poetic Analysis in General

- Edward Hirsch, *How to Read a Poem and Fall in Love with Poetry*, San Diego, CA, A Harvest Book, Harcourt, Inc., 1999.

- Laurence Perrine and Thomas R. Arp, *Sound and Sense: An Introduction to Poetry*, 8th edition, Fort Worth, TX, Harcourt Brace College Publishers, 1992.

- John R. Trimble, *Writing with Style: Conversations on the Art of Writing*, 2nd edition, Prentice Hall, 2000.

## Analysis of Latin Poetry (Online)

- How to Write a Critical Essay on Latin Poetry (Linda Montross; Joan Jahnige, Kentucky Educational Television) http://www.dl.ket.org/latinlit/carmina/terminology/howtowrite.htm

- Questions to Ask of Any Poem (George Mason University Writing Center) http://www.gmu.edu/departments/writingcenter/handouts/poetry.html

- SWIMTAG (Sally Davis; Joan Jahnige, Kentucky Educational Television) http://www.dl.ket.org/latinlit/carmina/terminology/swimtag.htm.

## Writing an Effective Essay in English (Online)

- The Writing Center Guide to Taking Essay Tests (George Mason University Writing Center) http://www.gmu.edu/departments/writingcenter/handouts/essaytes.html

- Writing Tips: In-Class Essay Exams (Univ. Illinois at Champaign-Urbana) http://www.english.uiuc.edu/cws/wworkshop/writer_resources/writing_tips/in-class_essay_exams.html

# Chapter 8

# The Background and Spot Questions

The final free-response question that we will discuss is different for the two exams. For the AP Vergil Exam, the so-called "background" question evaluates your familiarity with the *Aeneid* as a whole, especially those parts read in English (for the Vergil syllabus, see Chapter 2). More generally, your familiarity with the life and times of Vergil and with the "literary" and mythological backgrounds of Homer, the *Iliad* and *Odyssey*, and the story of Troy are anticipated, although not tested directly. This question is the last of the five free-response questions on the Vergil Exam and is designed for 15 minutes of writing time and counts as 20 percent of your score on that section. Although there is no background question on the Catullus section of the Latin Literature Exam, there is a short identification question, also called a short-answer or "spot" question, on each of the exams for the choice authors. Its position in the rotation of questions has recently been changed from first to last among the questions on the choice authors, to allow you to spend more time and energy on the short essay question (for which, see the previous chapter). The spot question is designed for a writing time of approximately 10 minutes and counts as 15 percent of your free-response score. (For comparison, the short essay on the choice author is 20 minutes and 20 percent.)

## The Background Question on the *Aeneid*

The background question is not based on a Latin passage, nor does it ask you to cite or translate Latin. This question asks you to discuss one specific set of characters or events in the story to illustrate your familiarity with the *Aeneid* as an entire work of literature. The characters and events typically appear in those lines and books not read in Latin. For those Books of which only a portion is required in English, see the reading syllabus for Vergil in Chapter 2; for a complete outline of the entire *Aeneid*, see the next chapter. The background question is equivalent to a short essay. It consists of two sets of three or four characters or events, from each set of which you are to choose one item for your essay. A sample is given below. Again, the format and wording of the simulated background questions provided throughout this chapter may be slightly altered from that found on the exam itself, but hopefully you will gain a sense of the range and scope of the actual exam questions.

## Sample background question:

A major theme of the *Aeneid* is the relationship of father and son, which is an element of the Roman concept of **pietas,** meaning duty or loyalty. Choose one father-son combination from the list below and discuss whether their particular relationship illustrates this concept.

Aeneas and Ascanius

Anchises and Aeneas

Evander and Pallas

Mezentius and Lausus

# Background Questions on the AP Vergil Exam

Here are some characters and events in the *Aeneid* that have been selected for attention in the background question on AP Vergil Exams, 2006–2001. Characters are now given a short tag to help you begin, e.g., Latinus, king of the Latins, or Pallas, son of Evander. Questions generally seem to focus on supporting actors, both mortal and divine, in these background questions. See below for a glossary of characters and events appearing in the *Aeneid*.

| Characters | Events |
|---|---|
| Allecto (twice) | Aeneas' encounter with Helen while Troy sacked (Book 2) |
| Amata | Anchises during the fall of Troy (Book 2) |
| Camilla (twice) | One of the funeral games (Book 5) |
| Cupid | Boxing match, Dares and Entellus (Book 5) (twice) |
| Helenus | Trojan women attempt to burn ships in Sicily (Book 5) |
| Iarbas | How Amata behaves after Lavinia's engagement to Aeneas (Books 7 and 12) |
| Iris | |
| Juturna (twice) | Hercules and Cacus (Book 8) Lausus (twice) |
| Palinurus | |
| Sinon | |

### Here are some themes covered on previous background questions:

"How does the character..."

- affect the plot?
- reveal tension between rash and rational behavior?
- misrepresent him/herself, and for what purpose?
- illustrate that life can be unfair?

## A Glossary of Proper Names in the *Aeneid*

You might review these names by designing a crossword puzzle or by creating and playing "20 Questions," "Concentration," or "Jeopardy" with your classmates. Remember what Quintilian said about learning: **Lusus sit**!

### Characters

Note: locations in the *Aeneid* that are indicated below reflect the greatest frequency of appearance. Those bearing an asterisk have appeared on a background question of the Vergil Exam.

#### *The Greeks:*

Achivi (Achaeans), Argives, Danai (Danaans), Graii (Greeks), Pelasgae (Pelasgians).

**Achaemenides**: companion of Ulysses who was left behind on Sicily, land of the Cyclopes. Rescued by Aeneas, he helped the Trojans sail along the island's coast (Book 3).

**Achilles**: protagonist of the *Iliad* and slayer of Trojan Hector (Book 2).

**The Atridae** (sons of Atreus = **Agamemnon** and **Menelaus**): Agamemnon of Mycenae was leader of the Greek armies at Troy; his brother Menelaus was the husband of Helen (both are mentioned occasionally.)

**Pyrrhus (also Neoptolemus)**: son of Achilles, and the Greek who slew Priam (Book 2).

**Sinon\***: Greek spy who allows himself to be captured by the Trojans in order to convince them to bring the wooden horse into Troy (beginning Book 2).

**Tydides (Diomedes)**: son of Tydeus, one of the greatest Greek warriors at Troy; refused to join the Latins when asked by Turnus to help him against the Trojans (Books 8 and 11).

**Ulixes** (also Ithacus, Odysseus, Ulysses): "many-sided" hero of the *Odyssey* who had the idea of the wooden horse (Book 2).

### The Trojans

Aeneadae (men of Aeneas), Dardanidae (Dardanians), Phrygii (Phrygians), Teucri (Teucrians), Troes (Trojans).

### The Trojan Royal Family

**Andromache**: wife of Hector; she later married the surviving Trojan Helenus.

**Cassandra**: daughter of Priam and Hecuba who was cursed by Apollo with the gift of prophecy (but no one would believe her). She foretold the fall of Troy (Book 2).

**Hector**: the son of Priam and Hecuba and husband of Andromache. The greatest of the Trojan warriors, he is slain by Achilles in a duel and his body is dragged around the walls of the city. He later appears to Aeneas in a vision with a warning to abandon Troy (Book 2).

**Hecuba**: wife of Priam and mother of Cassandra, Hector, and Paris (Book 2).

**Polites**: young son of Priam and Hecuba who is killed by Pyrrhus as Priam watches (Book 2).

**Priam**: noble king of Troy, husband of Hecuba, slain by Pyrrhus during the sack of Troy (Book 2).

### Other Trojans playing a role

**Acestes**: king of Sicily who is friendly to the Trojans and helps them during the time of indecision about the future. The Trojans who remain behind in Sicily after the torching of the ships name a city in his honor (Book 5).

**Dares and Entellus\***: Trojan boxers at the funeral games for Anchises. Dares was the favorite, but Entellus won (Book 5).

**Helenus\***: son of Priam, and a prophet, who becomes the second husband of Andromache. After the Trojan War, he settled in Epirus, where he helps Aeneas with directions and prophecies, including that of the white sow with thirty piglets (Book 3).

**Laocoon**: Trojan priest of Neptune whose actions precipitate the bringing of the wooden horse into the city after he and his two sons are strangled by serpents in response to defiling the horse as a gift to Athena/Minerva (Book 2).

**Nisus and Euryalus\***: young Trojans and best friends who help each other during a foot race at the games in Sicily (Book 5) and who later break out to summon Aeneas from Pallanteum. They pass through the Rutulian camp, killing many, but then they themselves are killed (Book 9).

**Polydorus**: son of Priam, slain in Thrace by Polymnestor; he speaks to Aeneas from his burial mound and tells him to leave Thrace (Book 3).

### Aeneas' Family

**Aeneas** (also Anchisiades, son of Anchises): son of Venus and Anchises, prince of Troy who settles in Italy. He is characterized as *pius* (god-fearing, dutiful) throughout the *Aeneid*.

**Anchises**: Trojan father of Aeneas, who as an old man is carried on his son's shoulders from the burning city of Troy. He dies in Sicily before the Trojans are driven by a storm to Africa. He appears to Aeneas in the Underworld and narrates the "Parade of Heroes" that foretells the future of Rome (Books 2, 3, 5, and 6).

**Creusa**: Trojan wife of Aeneas and mother of Ascanius. She appears to Aeneas in a vision while they are escaping from the city and advises him to leave without her, as a new bride awaits him in Italy (end of Book 2).

**Iulus/Ascanius**: Trojan son of Aeneas and Creusa, called Iulus after the fall of Troy (Ilion/Ilium). He assists in the action and is given military responsibilities when on Italian soil. Ascanius later founds Alba Longa (as the son of Aeneas and Lavinia?) Vergil uses the name Iulus for Ascanius in tribute to his literary patron Augustus, who belonged to the **gens Iulia (Julia)**.

### Aeneadae

**Achates**: faithful (*fidus*) companion of Aeneas; his most important appearance occurs in Book 1 when he accompanies Aeneas on a hunt and both are enveloped in a mist by Venus.

**Cloanthus, Nisus and Euryalus, Entellus and Dares, Eurytion**: Trojan participants in the funeral games on Sicily (Book 5).

**Ilioneus**: Trojan who leads the surviving Trojans after they are separated from Aeneas by the storm; he introduces the Trojans to Dido (Book 1) and he also addresses Latinus on behalf of the Trojans (Book 7).

**Misenus**: Trojan bugler who dies at the hands of an envious Triton. He is found dead on the shore and is buried by Aeneas after consulting the Sibyl (Book 6). The location in Italy is still known as *Capo Miseno*.

**Nautes**: elderly Trojan who advises that the Trojans who are unhappy should be left behind on Sicily (Book 5).

**Palinurus***: skillful helmsman of Aeneas' ship who, on the journey from Sicily to Italy, drifts into sleep, falls overboard, and dies (Book 5). He meets Aeneas in the Underworld and describes what had happened (Book 6).

### Carthaginians

Poeni (Phoenicians), Tyrii (people of Tyre)

**Anna**: Dido's sister, who encourages Dido's love for Aeneas but is then duped into assisting in her suicide (Book 4).

**Barce**: the nurse whom Dido sends to summon Anna on the eve of her suicide (Book 4).

**Dido** (also Elissa, Phoenissa, Sidonia): queen and foundress of Carthage, a colony of Phoenician Tyre, husband of the deceased Sychaeus, and sister of Pygmalion. She falls in love with Aeneas and then, abandoned by him, kills herself (Book 4).

**Iarbas***: an African prince from whom Dido obtains the land for Carthage and whom she later rejects as a suitor. His prayer to Jupiter leads to Mercury's warning to Aeneas that he leave Troy (Book 4).

**Pygmalion**: brother of Dido; he murders her husband Sychaeus, as Dido herself describes in Book 1.

**Sychaeus**: husband of Dido, murdered by her greedy brother Pygmalion (Book 1).

## Turnus' Allies

**Amata***: queen of the Latins, wife of Latinus, and mother of Lavinia, who believes that Turnus is the appropriate and rightful husband for her daughter. She hangs herself when she hears (mistakenly) that Turnus has been killed (Books 7 and 12).

**Camilla** (of the Volsci)*: heroic ally of Turnus, leader of the cavalry, and devotee of the goddess Diana, she is slain in battle by the Etruscan Arruns (Book 11).

**Latinus** (Latini/Laurentes; city Laurentum): king of the Latins, husband of Amata, and father of Lavinia. He believes that Aeneas is the "foreigner" whom Lavinia is prophesied to marry (Book 7).

**Lausus**: son of Mezentius, who faces Pallas in battle and eventually dies defending his father (Book 10).

**Lavinia**: Latin daughter of Latinus and Amata and pawn in the marriage-brokering of the latter half of the *Aeneid*. She is the "foreign bride" alluded to in the prophetic speeches of Creusa (Book 2) and the Sibyl (Book 6) and plays Helen to Aeneas' Paris. She eventually marries Aeneas, who founds Lavinium in her name.

**Mezentius*** (also called Tyrrhenus = the Tuscan): renegade Etruscan king who becomes the ally of Turnus. He is slain by Aeneas after being gallantly defended by his son Lausus (Book 10).

**Silvia**: it was her pet deer that Allecto causes Anchises to slay and thus advance hostilities (Book 7).

**Turnus***: leader of the Rutulians who desires marriage with Lavinia and pursues war with the newly-arrived Trojans. His sister is Juturna, the water nymph. Turnus first appears in Book 7. The *Aeneid* ends with his death at the hands of Aeneas in a duel (Book 12).

## Aeneas' Allies

**Evander** (Arcades/Arcadians; city Pallanteum): Arcadian king of Pallanteum who sends his son Pallas with an armed force to assist Aeneas against the Latins (Books 8, 10, and 11).

**Pallas**: young son of Evander, who puts him in the service of Aeneas. Pallas is killed in a pathetic duel with Turnus, who takes from him the swordbelt that eventually leads to Turnus' own death at the hands of Aeneas. (See Book 10 for Pallas).

**Tarchon**: an Etruscan ally of Aeneas who offers to make him chief of the Etruscans. Tarchon is instrumental in the battle at the ships and in the field (Book 10).

## Places

### *Italy*

Italia; also Ausonia, Hesperia, Lavinian shores, Oenotrian land, Saturnian land.

**Alba Longa**: town, southeast of Rome, founded by Ascanius.

**Cumae**: site of the Sibyl, oracle of Apollo, upcoast from the Bay of Naples.

**Latium**: the region of west-central Italy in which the Latins ruled and, ultimately, Rome was founded.

**Laurent(i)um**: city of Latinus and the Latins; famous later as the location of Pliny's seaside villa.

**Lavinium**: settlement founded by Aeneas and named after his wife, Lavinia.

**Mt. Aetna**: still-active volcano on the northeastcoast of Sicily, thought to be the home of Vulcan and his forge.

**Pallanteum**: home-city of Evander and the Arcadians and future site of Rome.

**Sicily** (or Trinacria): the island to the southeast of the boot of Italy that figures heavily into the journey of Aeneas to Italy (Books 3 and 5).

**Thybris** (Tiber River): the river that runs northeast to southwest through Rome, ending at Ostia. The waterway much travelled by the Trojans and Arcadians during the hostilities.

### *Asia Minor*

**Mt. Ida**: also the name of a mountain in Crete, this mountain near Troy was a refuge for the fleeing Trojans after Troy was sacked.

**Phrygia**: area east of Troy in the west-central or Anatolian highland of Asia Minor (Turkey).

**Tenedos**: the island off the northwest coast of Turkey behind which the Greek ships hid.

**Troia** (Greek Ilion, Latin Ilium or Pergamum): city-state in western Anatolia, a seaport and gateway to the Black Sea in ancient times. Famous for its walls, horses, and windy location. Site of the legendary conflict between the Greeks and the Trojans during the Bronze Age (12th century BCE), later celebrated in the *Iliad* and the *Odyssey* by Homer.

**Xanthus and Simois Rivers**: rivers near Troy that served as battle sites. Equated to the Tiber in Sibyl's speech to Aeneas in Book 6.

### *Greece*

**Argos**: second-oldest city of Greece, close to Mycenae in the Peloponnesus. Greeks in the *Aeneid* were generically referred to as "Argives."

**Mycenae**: walled city of the "Lion Gate" in the northeast portion of the Peloponnese, which was ruled by Agamemnon, commander-in-chief of the Greek forces at Troy. This city was the dominant Greek city-state during the Late Bronze Age and produced both an entire culture (the Mycenaean = My-sin-ee-an) and the first language considered Greek. Mycenae is mentioned periodically in the *Aeneid*, but is often confused with Argos.

**Strophades Islands**: small islands off the northwest coast of the Greek Peloponnese and home of the Harpies.

### Africa

(also known as Libya)

**Carthage** (Karthago, also Byrsa): north African colony of the Phoenician cities of Tyre and Sidon founded by Dido (Elissa) in the 9th century BCE. Antagonist of Rome during the historical Punic Wars.

### Phoenicia

**Tyre and Sidon**: major coastal Phoenician cities of what is now Lebanon. Often substituted for each other by Vergil.

### The Underworld

(also referred to as Avernus, Dis, Elysium, Erebus, or Tartarus)

**Rivers**: Acheron (river of lamentation), Cocytus (river of woe), Lethe (river of forgetfulness), Phlegethon (river of fire), Styx (river of unbroken divine oaths). The Acheron and Styx are interchangeable in the *Aeneid*.

**Cerberus**: three-headed dog who guarded the portals of the Underworld (Book 6, lines 417–25).

**Charon**: ferryman of souls across the river Styx (or Acheron) (Book 6, lines 298–330).

## Deities

### Main Players

**Juno** (also Saturnia): wife and brother of Jupiter and queen of the gods. She is Aeneas' nemesis throughout the *Aeneid* for reasons outlined in the early lines of Book 1.

**Jupiter/Jove** (also Saturnius): often addressed as father (**genitor**), king of the gods and husband/brother of Juno. He appears periodically in the *Aeneid*: in Book 1, he gives a long speech to Venus about the future history of the Trojans; in Book 4, he intervenes in the events at Carthage; and in Book 12, he finally brings Juno under control.

**Phoebus** (Apollo): with respect to the events of the *Aeneid*, Apollo is most important as god of prophecy, via the Sibyl Deiphobe. In Book 6, Aeneas' promise to build what is to become the Augustan Temple of Apollo enables him to secure the cooperation of the god with regard to fulfilling his father Anchises' request to meet him in the Underworld.

**Venus** (also Cytherea): goddess of love and beauty, mother of Aeneas, and, with Mars, parent of Rome. Venus protects the interests of her son and the Trojans throughout the *Aeneid*, in disguise (as a huntress), through her son Cupid (who substitutes for Ascanius), and as a means to thwart Juno's attempts to destroy Aeneas.

### Supporting Actors

**Aeolus**: ruler of the winds who, at Juno's insistence, allows them to escape in order to create the storm which causes the detour of Aeneas into Dido's kingdom in north Africa.

**Allecto**\*: "she who does not rest" is one of the Furies (for which, see below). Juno sends Allecto to stir up trouble in a final attempt to control or influence Aeneas' destiny by instigating Turnus' anger at the prospect of losing Lavinia to him (Book 7).

**Mercury** (son of Maia; Cyllenius): In Book 4, Mercury serves several times as Jupiter's emissary to Aeneas, prompted first by Venus and then by Iarbas. On Jove's behalf, Mercury warns Aeneas to leave Carthage.

**Neptune**: god of the sea, Neptune calms the winds (see the famous orator simile in Book 1) so that Aeneas can continue his journey.

**Pallas Athena** (Minerva, Tritonia): Minerva's main scene in the *Aeneid* is her association with the wooden horse (she is said to have inspired Ulysses with the whole idea). Vergil indicates that Diomedes and Ulysses had stolen the Palladium, an ancient sacred image of Pallas (Athena/Minerva), which had the city of Troy under its protection (see Sinon's speech in Book 2). More common tradition held that Aeneas rescued the statue from Troy and brought it to Italy, where it was known as the Penates.

**Vulcan**: the god of fire is spotlighted in Book 8, where he is asked by his wife Venus to make armor and weapons for her son Aeneas in anticipation of his confrontation with Turnus. Vulcan complies, designing a wonderful shield upon which are engraved high-points of Roman history, including Augustus' victory over Antony and Cleopatra at the Battle of Actium.

### Bit Parts

**Aquilo, Auster, Eurus, Zephyrus**: personifications of various winds (north, south, east, west). **Notus** is another name for the south wind.

**Atlas**: Titan turned into a mountain by Perseus and mentioned in a wonderfully descriptive passage in Book 4 (lines 246–53) while Mercury is flying to Carthage.

**Aurora**: goddess of the dawn; Greek Eos.

**Cacus**: fire-breathing giant and son of Vulcan. He lived in a cave on the Aventine Hill, on the future site of Rome, and consumed human flesh. He was overcome by Hercules, in whose honor a feast is given by King Evander. The story is told in Book 8 (lines 184–279) after Aeneas has arrived in Pallanteum.

**Celaeno**: a Harpy, encountered on the Strophades Islands. She gave Aeneas prophecies to assist him on his journey.

**Cupid***: son of Venus, Cupid was asked by his mother to impersonate Ascanius with the purpose of making Dido fall in love with Aeneas (end of Book 2).

**Cybele**: the great Mother of the Gods (*Magna Mater*) or Earth Mother, Cybele was worshipped by Eastern cultures. In Book 2, Cybele kept Creusa in Troy. As the first to teach men how to fortify cities, she is depicted as Rome personified, wearing a crown of turrets as she rides in a chariot pulled by lions (Book 6, lines 784–87).

**Diana**: the goddess of nature and sister of Apollo, Diana appears several times in the *Aeneid*. In a simile in Book 1, Dido is compared to Diana in stately array. She also appears in Book 11, when she tries to protect Camilla during the fighting.

**Faunus**: father of Latinus and grandson of Saturn, associated with the Greek Pan, and patron god of agriculture and livestock. He appears throughout Book 7, when Aeneas is being introduced to the legends and traditions of Latium.

**The Furies** (also known as The Dirae, "The Terrible Ones" or, in Greek, Erinyes, "The Angry Ones"): three goddesses of justice (or vengeance), who are Allecto, Megaera, and Tisiphone. They are mentioned generically in Books 4, 8, and 12. See also **Allecto**.

**Hercules**: cult-hero of Evander's city of Pallanteum, because he slew Cacus, the flesh-eating giant (see **Cacus**). The presence of Hercules in Latium was extensive (cf. the early round temple still standing near the Tiber). In Book 10, Evander's son Pallas calls upon Hercules to assist him in his confrontation with Turnus, but the hero is "warned off" by Jupiter.

**Iris***: messenger goddess, who mostly assists Juno in the *Aeneid*: she cuts a lock of Dido's hair to release her soul (Book 4) and later rouses the Trojan women to burn the ships in Sicily (Book 5) and Turnus to attempt to burn the Trojan ships in Italy (Book 9).

**The Parcae** (The Fates): three sisters, Clotho (who spun the thread of life), Lachesis (who measured the thread), and Atropos (who cut the thread at the allotted end of one's life). (See Book 1, line 22.)

**Tiberinus**: god of the Tiber River who assisted Aeneas several times. including appearing to him in a vision in which he encourages Aeneas that he is, indeed, in the promised land because the white sow and thirty piglets are close by (Book 8).

## Themes in the *Aeneid*

The main themes of the *Aeneid* are skillfully introduced by Vergil in the first eleven lines of the poem.

Study these lines thoroughly. Better yet, memorize them, and in meter. Stated simply, the two main themes of the *Aeneid* are "nothing in excess" and be **pius** or "true" to the gods, homeland, family, and friends.

- The triumph of Order over Disorder: the rational control of passion and the acceptance of fate. The storm scene in Book 1 represents the time of the civil wars, which were ended by Augustus (represented by Neptune), who closed the Gates of War and established the **Pax Romana**, which was a time of peace, order, and stability. The struggle of order (reason) versus disorder (passion) is personified by Dido. For many, the killing of Turnus by Aeneas at the very end of Book 12 violates the idea that **pietas** is transcendant over **furor**.

- The primacy of Fate (the word **fatum** in its various forms appears forty times in the first three Books of the *Aeneid*), which is a divine, religious principle that governs the course of history and thus the Roman Empire. Here are some additional points regarding fate:

    The direction and destination of Aeneas' mission are preordained: Aeneas, motivated by **pietas**, follows the dictates of fate.

    Juno, Dido, and Turnus resist fate.

    The Romans believed that the Fates were the guiding principle in man's life. Consider the role of omens, oracles, prodigies, and prophecies in the epic.

- The significance of the Gods

    Fate is often associated with the will of Jupiter.

    The gods, e.g., the Penates that Aeneas carries (**inferretque deos Latio**), are the transubstantiation of the identity of the Roman people.

    It is unclear whether the gods themselves are subject to fate.

    A return to the old-time religion is necessary to establish and maintain the stability of the new Augustan order.

    The importance of Home: the wanderings of the Trojans at sea, as were those of Odysseus, are a metaphor for the uncertainty of life.

    The founding of a city (Troy, Carthage, Rome) is the ultimate expression of civilization, for it serves as the refuge from the unpredictable and irrational.

- The glory of Rome

    The Romans were chosen by the gods, specifically Jupiter, to rule (Book 6.847–53), and since the lineage of Emperor Augustus is divine (Venus – Aeneas – Iulus/Ascanius – **gens Iulia**), he has the divine right to rule. The *Aeneid* is Augustan propaganda.

- Nobility

    The interests of the commonwealth (finding a new Troy) are transcendant over those of the individual (Aeneas). The heroic warrior (Achilles) has been replaced by the heroic citizen (Aeneas); war is a means to an end, rather than an end in itself ("arms and a man").

    Achievement requires suffering; the Stoic ideal of forebearance was the traditional expression of what was Roman.

- Acknowledgment of patriarchal primacy

   Women ultimately have subordinate roles in the *Aeneid*, e.g., Amata, Dido, and Juno.

   Women are seen as victims or as a threat to the male. The identity of a family derives from and is dependent upon the father or father-figure, e.g., Aeneas, Anchises, Evander, Latinus, Priam, and Turnus.

## Practice Background Questions

Unlike the format of the actual background question on the AP Latin Exam, several of the questions below do not ask for a comparison, but they achieve the same goal, that is, they prompt you to think about the *Aeneid* as a whole.

1. Within the action of the *Aeneid*, there are various turning points that occur in which the action is redirected. Select <u>two</u> of the following events and discuss how each represents a turning point in the story.

   — Cupid substitutes for Ascanius (Book 1)

   — Sinon is captured by the Trojans (Book 2)

   — The Trojan women attempt to burn the ships in Sicily (Book 5)

   — Allecto comes to Turnus as an old woman (Book 7)

   — Tiberinus, god of the Tiber River, visits Aeneas in a dream (Book 8)

   — The ghost of Aeneas appears to Turnus (Book 10)

2. The concept of **fides,** trustworthiness or honesty, is essential to all personal relationships in Roman culture. Select <u>one</u> of the relationships listed below and, in a short essay, discuss whether the relationship <u>does</u> or <u>does not</u> possess this quality. Be sure to support what you say with specific details.

   — Aeneas and Achates

   — Aeneas and Evander, king of the Arcadians

   — Latinus and Amata, king and queen of the Latins

   — Nisus and Euryalus, Trojan comrades

3. Omens, oracles, prophecies, and prodigies abound in the *Aeneid*. Among these are dream-visions, in which a mortal or an immortal appears to Aeneas with some direct or indirect information about what is to happen next. An oracle is an oral prediction by a god or a god's representative, usually in a temple or shrine. Choose <u>one</u> character from Group A, each of which appears to Aeneas in a dream-vision and <u>one</u> from Group B, each of which serves as giver of an oracle. In a short essay, discuss the effect that one dream-vision and one oracle has on Aeneas' future.

| Dream-Vision | Oracle |
|---|---|
| Anchises | at Delos |
| Penates | Faunus |
| Tiberinus | Helenus |

4. Because of the roles of Juno and Dido, it has been observed that women are portrayed in the *Aeneid* as subordinates and that they are continually subject to the authority of men. Do you agree or disagree? Argue this point by choosing <u>two</u> of the following women and discussing their roles in the *Aeneid*.

| Amata | Creusa |
|---|---|
| Camilla | Hecuba |
| Cassandra | Juturna |

5. Strictly speaking, ecphrasis is a rhetorical device used to describe one work of art by means of another, e.g., poetry. Select one of the following examples of ecphrasis from the *Aeneid* and discuss the significance of the artwork in its context.

—Temple mural in Carthage (Book 2)

—Bronze doors of the Temple of Apollo at Cumae (Book 6)

—Shield of Aeneas (Book 8)

## Preparation for the Background Question on the *Aeneid*

- As you review the entire *Aeneid* in preparation for this question, see also "Outlines and Summaries," Chapter 9. By the time of the exam, your paperback translation of the *Aeneid* should be well-thumbed! Focus your review for this question on those Books of the *Aeneid* not required in Latin.

- Review this question on previous exams and look over the accompanying commentary by the Chief Reader, published on the College Board AP Latin Web site.

- Assuming that you have read the entire *Aeneid* in English, there is no shame in consulting one of the quick-study Web sites (see the end of Chapter 12). These are useful in helping you to "see the full picture."

- Buddy-up with a classmate and try to stump each other in a game of "20 Questions" about the *Aeneid*.

- You might consider designing (and sharing!) your own background questions as good practice for the exam.

# The Spot Question on the AP Latin Literature Exam

Unlike the background question on the Vergil Exam, the short identification or "spot" question on the Latin Literature Exam does not call for you to write an essay (yay!) This sixth question on the Latin Literature Exam asks that you give brief answers to four to six questions (some may contain several parts) on a single passage of Latin selected from one of the choice authors, Cicero, Horace, or Ovid. The length of the passage varies from seven to about twelve lines. The questions within this question ask you to apply your skills in critical analysis, such as writing out and scanning a line of poetry or naming a figure of speech in the passage and writing out its corresponding Latin. The majority of the questions ask you to interpret a portion of, or extract information from, the passage, e.g., "What activity is described. . .?" or "According to lines . . ?" or "What do we learn . . . ?" You may be asked to answer in English (usually no more than a single sentence is necessary) or to cite the Latin and include a translation or paraphrase. Citing Latin using ellipsis points (. . .) is not acceptable on this question! Questions here include the specific Latin addressed and its location in the text, e.g., "What is the poet suggesting that Dellius do in lines 1–2 (Aequam . . . mentem)?" Also note that the short identification questions are asked in the order that the answers appear in the passage. You may also be asked to identify or comment on the historical, literary, or socio-cultural context of someone or something mentioned or alluded to in the passage.

## Practice Spot Questions

### Spot Question 1 (Cicero)

> Quae cum ita sint, petimus a vobis, iudices, si qua non modo
> humana, verum etiam divina in tantis ingeniis commendatio debet esse,
> ut eum, qui vos, qui vestros imperatores, qui populi Romani res gestas
> *Line* semper ornavit, qui etiam his recentibus nostris vestrisque domesticis
> 5 periculis aeternum se testimonium laudis daturum esse profitetur, estque
> ex eo numero, qui semper apud omnes sancti sunt habiti itaque dicti, sic
> in vestram accipiatis fidem, ut humanitate vestra levatus potius quam
> acerbitate violatus esse videatur.

***Pro Archia Poeta* 31**

1.  Translate Quae cum ita sint (line 1).

2.  This passage consists of a long, complex sentence that contains an indirect command clause prompted by the verb petimus (line 1). Cite the two Latin words, including line numbers, that introduce and end this dependent clause.

3.  (a) In lines 3–4 (<u>ut</u>. . . <u>ornavit</u>), for what particular reason does Cicero claim that the jury should acquit Archias?

    (b) According to lines 4–5 (<u>qui</u> <u>etiam</u> . . . <u>profitetur</u>), what is Cicero's second reason?

    (c) What do lines 5–6 (<u>estque</u> . . . <u>dicti</u>) tell us is Cicero's third reason?

4.  Name a figure of speech that occurs in lines 3–6 (<u>ut</u> . . . <u>dicti</u>) and indicate how this figure contributes to the effectiveness of the passage.

5.  What do we learn about Archias' profession from lines 5–7 (<u>estque</u> . . . <u>fidem</u>)?

6.  What is Cicero asking the judges to do in lines 6–8 (<u>sic</u> . . . <u>videatur</u>)?

## Spot Question 2 (Cicero)

Si nihil aliud nisi de civitate ac lege dicimus, nihil dico amplius: causa dicta est. Quid enim horum infirmari, Grati, potest? Heracleaene esse tum ascriptum negabis? Adest vir summa auctoritate et religione et fide,

*Line*
    5

M. Lucullus, qui se non opinari sed scire, non audisse sed vidisse, non interfuisse sed egisse dicit. Adsunt Heraclienses legati, nobilissimi homines, huius iudici causa cum mandatis et cum publico testimonio venerunt, qui hunc ascriptum Heracleae esse dicunt.

***Pro Archia Poeta* 8**

1.  In lines 1–2 (<u>Si</u> . . . <u>dicta est</u>), what attitude toward the case against Archias does Cicero seem to express?

2.  To what, specifically, does the pronoun <u>horum</u> (line 2) refer?

3.  According to lines 2–3 (<u>Heracleaene</u> . . . <u>negabis</u>), what evidence has Cicero brought against the charge referred to as <u>civitas</u> (line 1)?

4.  (a) In lines 3–5 (<u>Adest</u> . . . <u>dicit</u>), what supporting evidence does Cicero present on the charge of <u>civitas</u>?

    (b) Why does Cicero feel that his witness is incorruptible?

5.  What is the more common form of <u>audisse</u> (line 4)? Write out the Latin form and translate.

6.  (a) In lines 5–7 (<u>Adsunt</u> . . . <u>dicunt</u>), we learn that what other witnesses are supporting Cicero's defense?

    (b) What is the specific nature of the evidence that they have provided?

### Spot Question 3 (Cicero)

Virtus, inquam, C. Fanni, et tu, Q. Muci, et conciliat amicitias et
conservat. In ea est enim convenientia rerum, in ea stabilitas, in ea
constantia; quae cum se extulit et ostendit suum lumen et idem aspexit
*Line*    agnovitque in alio, ad id se admovet vicissimque accipit illud, quod in altero
5    est, ex quo exardescit sive amor sive amicitia; utrumque enim dictum est
ab amando. Amare autem nihil est aliud nisi eum ipsum diligere quem
ames, nulla indigentia, nulla utilitate quaesita.

*De Amicitia* **100**

1. In lines 1–2 (<u>Virtus</u> . . . <u>conservat</u>), we learn that virtue has **two** characteristics. What are they?

2. (a) According to lines 2–3 (<u>In ea</u> . . . <u>constantia</u>), what are the **three** ingredients found in virtue? Cite the Latin and give the meaning of each.

   (b) Name the figure of speech found in this sentence, cite the Latin, and comment on its effectiveness in context.

3. In lines 3–5 (<u>quae</u> . . . <u>amicitia</u>), Cicero creates a metaphor:

   (a) How is this image used to describe virtue?

   (b) How is this image then used to explain the affection of one person for another?

4. With reference to lines 5–6 (<u>ex quo</u> . . . <u>ab amando</u>), why does Cicero seem to feel that love and friendship are related?

5. According to lines 6–7 (<u>Amare</u> . . . <u>quaesita</u>), what **two** things should **not** be sought from a relationship of love or friendship?

# Horace

## Spot passages from Horace found in previous AP Latin Literature Exams

*Odes* 1.1.3–10 (we all have our different roles to play)

*Odes* 1.23 (don't be afraid, Chloe)

*Odes* 1.24.3–10 (Quintilius was a solid citizen, Vergil)

*Odes* 2.7.1–12 (war-buddy Pompeius receives amnesty)

*Odes* 4.7.17–28 (you can't escape the Underworld, Torquatus)

*Satires* 1.9.35–41 (the busy-body meets the plaintiff in his case)

## Spot Question 4 (Horace)

Sed minuit furorem
vix una sospes navis ab ignibus,
mentemque lymphatam Mareotico
*Line*    redegit in veros timores
5        Caesar ab Italia volantem

remis adurgens, accipiter velut
molles columbas aut leporem citus
venator in campis nivalis
Haemoniae, daret ut catenis

*10*   fatale monstrum.

***Odes* 1. 37.12–21**

1.  What is the historical significance of the event alluded to in lines 1–2 (Sed . . . ab ignibus)?

2.  In what meter was this poem written?

3.  How is the person about whom this poem is written described in lines 3–4 (mentemque . . . timores)?

4.  Name a figure of speech that occurs in line 5–6 (Caesar . . . adurgens) and write out the Latin that illustrates it.

5.  In lines 6–9 (accipiter . . . Haemoniae), the poet makes two comparisons. How are the two individuals compared? In your answer, cite and translate or accurately paraphrase the Latin, making clear the specific points of comparison.

6.  With regard to word order in prose, what is unusual about the placement of the word accipiter (line 6), relative to velut?

7.  According to lines 9–10 (daret ut . . . monstrum), what was the purpose of the activity described in lines 5–6 (Caesar . . . adurgens)?

## Spot Question 5 (Horace)

> "Quid si prisca redit Venus
> diductosque iugo cogit aeneo,
> si flava excutitur Chloe
> *Line*   reiectaeque patet ianua Lydiae?"
> 5   "Quamquam sidere pulchrior
> ille est, tu levior cortice et improbo
> iracundior Hadria,
> tecum vivere amem, tecum obeam libens."

**Odes 3. 9.17–24**

1.   (a) In what **two** ways does the male lover in lines 1 (Quid . . . Venus) and 3 (si . . . Chloe) suggest that he and Lydia might get back together?

(b) Explain the meaning of the imagery found in line 2 (diductosque . . . aeneo).

2.   Name a figure of speech that occurs in line 1 (Quid . . . Venus) and write out the Latin that illustrates it.

3.   What **two** comparisons does the female lover make in lines 6–7 (tu . . . Hadria)?

4.   (a) Demonstrate how the words on either side of ille est (line 6) form a chiasmus.

(b) What effect does this chiasmus have on the point being made?

5.   Translate the final line (tecum . . . libens).

6.   Identify in the final line a poetic way in which the female lover emphasizes her new commitment.

## Spot Question 6 (Horace)

> "Ignosces: alias loquar." Huncine solem
> tam nigrum surrexe mihi! Fugit improbus ac me
> sub cultro linquit. Casu venit obvius illi
> adversarius et, "Quo te turpissime?" magna
> inclamat voce, et, "Licet antestari?" Ego vero
> oppono auriculam. Rapit in ius: clamor utrimque:
> undique concursus. Sic me servavit Apollo.

*Line* is marked at line 4, and *5* at line 5.

*Satires* **1. 9.72–78**

1. What does the poet mean by his exclamation <u>Huncine . . . mihi!</u> (lines 1–2)? Translate or closely paraphrase.

2. Identify the poetic technique illustrated by the form <u>surrexe</u> (line 2), give its prose equivalent, and then translate the resulting form.

3. <u>Fugit improbus</u> refers to the poet's abandonment by his friend Fuscus. Given the predicament that he has been in, what does Horace mean by the phrase me / sub cultro <u>linquit</u> (lines 3–4)?

4. According to lines 3–4 (<u>Casu . . . adversarius</u>):

   (a) Who says "<u>Quo te turpissime?</u>" and to whom?

   (b) To whom are the words "<u>Licet antestari?</u>" (line 5) addressed? What is he being asked?

5. (a) In lines 6–7 (<u>Rapit . . . concursus</u>), cite and translate or accurately paraphrase **two** Latin words or phrases that describe the general situation that unfolds.

   (b) What figure of speech does the poet use to accelerate the action in lines 6–7?

6. What is ironic about the poet's declaration <u>Sic me servavit Apollo</u> (line 7)?

# Ovid

## Spot passages from Ovid found in previous AP Latin Literature Exams

*Metamorphoses* 1.481–89 (Daphne wants to remain unmarried)

*Metamorphoses* 10.238–46 (the Propoetides disillusion Pygmalion)

*Amores* 1.3.5–12 (what the poet does and doesn't have to offer a lover)

*Amores* 1.9.17–24 (some of things the soldier does)

*Amores* 1.12.1–7 (the poet complains about Nape being bad luck)

*Amores* 3.15.1–7 (Ovid brags about his reputation back home)

## Spot Question 7 (Ovid)

Unicus anser erat, minimae custodia villae,
quem dis hospitibus domini mactare parabant;
ille celer penna tardos aetate fatigat
*Line*    eluditque diu tandemque est visus ad ipsos
5    confugisse deos. Superi vetuere necari,
"Di"que, "sumus, meritasque luet vicinia poenas
impia," dixerunt; "vobis immunibus huius
esse mali dabitur."

**Metamorphoses 8.684–91**

1.    With reference to lines 1–2 (Unicus . . . parabant):

(a) What is happening?

(b) Write out and give the meaning of one Latin word that expresses or suggest the generosity apparent here.

2.    Tell how the situation described in line 3 reveals the poet's sense of humor.

3.    To what word does the enclitic –que join eluditque (line 4)?

4.    How was the fugitive eventually saved?

5.    Name a figure of speech used in lines 6–7 ("Di"que . . . dixerunt) and write out the Latin that illustrates it.

6.    In lines 6–8 ("Di"que . . . "dabitur"), the gods promise two things. Translate or accurately paraphrase both.

## Spot Question 8 (Ovid)

"Invide," dicebant, "paries, quid amantibus obstas?
Quantum erat, ut sineres toto nos corpore iungi
aut, hoc si nimium est, vel ad oscula danda pateres?
*Line*   Nec sumus ingrati: tibi nos debere fatemur,
5   quod datus est verbis ad amicas transitus aures."
Talia diversa nequiquam sede locuti,
sub noctem dixere, "Vale," partique dedere
oscula quisque suae non pervenientia contra.

**Metamorphoses 4.73–80**

1.    What question is being asked in line 1 (Invide . . . obstas?)

2.    Name a figure of speech found in line 1 (Invide . . . obstas) and write out the Latin that illustrates it.

3.    In lines 2–3 (Quantum . . . pateres?) what **two** things do the lovers suggest that they be allowed to do?

4.    Is danda in line 3 a gerund or gerundive? Explain your answer.

5.    Name one figure of speech found in line 4 (Nec . . . fatemur) and write out the Latin that illustrates it.

6.    According to lines 4–5 (Nec . . . aures), for what reason are the lovers grateful?

7.    To what circumstance or situation, specifically, do the words diversa . . . sede (line 6) refer?

8.    Lines 7–8 (partique . . . contra) reveal a sad fact about the lovers' situation. What is this fact?

## Spot Question 9 (Ovid)

Arma gravi numero violentaque bella parabam
edere, materia conveniente modis.
Par erat inferior versus; risisse Cupido
*Line*   dicitur atque unum surripuisse pedem,
5   "Quis tibi, saeve puer, dedit hoc in carmina iuris!
Pieridum vates, non tua, turba sumus!

**Amores 1.1.1–6**

1.  With reference to lines 1–2 (<u>Arma</u> . . . <u>modis</u>), identify and translate **two** Latin words that reveal or suggest the subject of Ovid's current literary interest.

2.  (a) What, specifically, is the <u>gravi numero</u> (line 1) to which the poet refers?

    (b) What does the poet mean by <u>Par erat inferior versus</u> (lines 3)?

    (c) Write out and scan line 1.

3.  According to lines 3–4 (<u>risisse</u> . . . <u>pedem</u>), Cupid plays a trick on the poet. Cite and translate or accurately paraphrase the relevant Latin and explain the trick.

4.  (a) What do the words **saeve puer** (line 5) suggest about the tone of this poem?

    (b) How do the sounds and syllables of line 6 (<u>Pieridum</u> . . . <u>sumus</u>) reflect this tone?

5.  To whom or what, in general, does the reference **Pieridum** (line 6) apply?

## Answers to Spot Questions

Each question is worth one point, unless designated otherwise, for a total of eight points. (For more on the scoring of spot questions, see Chapter 12.) Latin citations are included in some answers below for instructional purposes. Citations are not required for the spot question on the actual AP Latin Exam unless so specified.

### Answer: Spot Question 1 (Cicero)

1.  "Since these things are so" (or "Since this is so").

2.  The clause begins with <u>ut</u> (line 2) and ends with <u>accipiatis</u> (line 6). (The other subjunctive verb, <u>videatur</u> in line 7, completes a purpose clause introduced by <u>ut</u> in the previous line.)

3.  Throughout Archias' career, his writing has been most complimentary to the jurors, the generals, and the entire history of Rome.

4.  Archias has begun a poetic work that will celebrate recent "public perils" (<u>domesticis periculis</u>), referring to the conspiracy of Catiline.

5.  Such talent (for writing) deserves serious consideration by the jurors and, indeed, a verdict of acquittal.

6.  Anaphora appears in the five-time use of <u>qui</u>. This redundancy emphasizes the various points Cicero is making.

7.  We learn that Archias' profession (i.e., poet), is considered sacrosanct (or inviolable or holy; <u>sancti</u>, line 6) both in word and deed.

8.  Cicero is asking the judges to accept Archias into their protection (or confidence or trust) "so that he might seem to have been supported by their humanity" (<u>ut humanitate. . . levatus [esse]</u> . . . <u>videatur</u>) rather than "to have been penalized by their displeasure" (<u>acerbitate</u> . . . <u>violatus esse</u>).

## Answer: Spot Question 2 (Cicero)

1.  That the case is closed (<u>causa dicta est</u>). The prosecution has not made its case because Cicero has successfully refuted the charges.

2.  <u>De civitate</u> . . . <u>dicimus</u> and <u>ac lege dicimus</u> (line 1), citizenship and (compliance with) the law, which are the two charges against Archias. (The Latin or the English translation, or both, are acceptable as an answer.)

3.  Archias was enrolled as a citizen in Heraclea during the time in question ("citizen of Heraclea" is also acceptable.)

4.  (a) Because he says that Lucullus was present to witness the enrollment of Archias as a citizen and will testify to that.

    (b) That Lucullus will state what he knows and not what he thinks (<u>qui se non opinari, sed scire</u>), not what he heard, but what he saw (<u>non audisse, sed vidisse</u>), and that he was not merely present at the event but had precipitated it (<u>non interfuisse, sed egisse</u>).

5.  <u>Audivisse</u>, to have heard.

6.  (a) Distinguished representatives from Heraclea (<u>Heraclienses legati, nobilissimi homines</u>).

    (b) They have brought the actual citizenship records (<u>qui hunc ascriptum Heracleae dicunt</u>).

## Answer: Spot Question 3 (Cicero)

1.  Virtue both establishes (<u>conciliat</u>) friendship and preserves (<u>conservat</u>) it.

2.  (a) <u>Convenientia rerum</u> (compatibility); <u>stabilitas</u> (immutability); and <u>constantia</u> (fidelity).

    (b) Anaphora (<u>in ea</u>), which emphasizes each characteristic of virtue, OR asyndeton, which is also cumulative and emphatic.

3.    (a) Virtue is depicted as a light (<u>suum lumen</u>) that shines from someone who has virtue and is recognized by another who also possesses it.

     (b) Love or friendship bursts or leaps into flame (glows, grows hot).

4.    Cicero says that love (<u>amor</u>) and friendship (<u>amicitia</u>) are related because both words derive from the verb <u>amare</u>.

5.    Love (or friendship) is not sought out of need (<u>indigentia</u>), i.e., pity, compassion, etc., or benefit (<u>utilitate</u>), i.e., a material benefit that one might receive from the relationship.

## Answer: Spot Question 4 (Horace)

1.    The Battle of Actium. (Also acceptable: the naval defeat of Antony and Cleopatra by Octavian.)

2.    Alcaic strophe, reserved for more "patriotic" themes.

3.    Drunken (<u>mentemque lymphatam Mareotico</u>) and afraid (<u>in veros timores</u>).

4.    Metaphor: (<u>eam</u>) <u>volantem</u>, Cleopatra is "flying" from Italy.

5.    <u>Accipiter velut molles columbas</u>, "like a hawk (= Caesar) chases the gentle doves (= Cleopatra)" or <u>leporem citus venator in campis nivalis Haemoniae</u>, "(like) a swift hunter (= Caesar) tracks the hare (= Cleopatra) in the fields of snowy Haemonia (or Thessaly). (<u>Columbas</u> may be singular; <u>nivalis</u> may be transferred to <u>campis</u>, "snowy fields." The answer should reflect the fact that a verb such as <u>adurget</u> (line 6) needs to be understood in both similes.) (**This question is worth two points.**)

6.    Since <u>accipiter</u> is the subject of the first simile, it should be found after <u>velut</u>, which is the word that introduces the simile.

7.    To put Cleopatra, the <u>fatale monstrum</u>, in chains.

## Answer: Spot Question 5 (Horace)

1.    (a) If the former love (Venus) returns (<u>si prisca venit Venus</u>) and if golden-haired Chloe is spurned (<u>si flava excutitur Chloe</u>).

     (b) To force those led apart (<u>diductosque</u>) "under the bronze yoke" (<u>iugo cogit aeneo</u>). Reference to the <u>iugum</u> here is a military metaphor, as the "yoke" was a goalpost-like set of spears under which the conquered foe was required to pass. The symbolism here refers to the authority of Venus bringing the lovers back together.

2.	Metonymy: <u>Venus</u> = love.

3.	That her lover is "lighter than a cork" (<u>levior cortice</u>) and that he is "more tempestuous than the unpredictable Adriatic" (<u>improbo iracundior Hadria</u>). ("Fickle" is also acceptable for <u>levior</u>, and for <u>iracundior</u>, "headstrong, willful, stormy.")

4.	(a) <u>Sidere pulchrior</u> . . . <u>levior cortice</u>, ABBA, noun-adjective-adjective noun or ablative-nominative- nominative-ablative.

	(b) The chiasmus allows the poet to compare Lydia's former lover (<u>ille</u>) with the present one (<u>tu</u>).

5.	"I would gladly live with you, I would gladly die with you."

6.	Emphasis is provided by anaphora (<u>tecum</u>), asyndeton (<u>amem tecum</u>), and the condensed and parallel structure: <u>tecum vivere amem (libens), tecum obeam libens</u>. (Any one of these observations is acceptable.)

## Answer: Spot Question 6 (Horace)

1.	"To think that this sun (day) has risen so black for me!" means "I can't believe what a bad day I'm having!"

2.	<u>Surrexe</u> = syncope of <u>surrexit</u>, "(it) rose or has arisen." <u>Solem</u>, the subject, is exclamatory accusative.

3.	"He left me under the knife" means the same as "He left me in hot water," i.e., in danger.

4.	(a) The litigant/plaintiff (<u>adversarius</u>) in the Pest's case or lawsuit. <u>Quo te turpissime</u> is addressed to the Pest.

	(b) Horace; the plaintiff is asking him to serve as a witness (<u>antestari</u>).

5.	(a) <u>Rapit in ius</u>, "he snatches (him) into court"; <u>clamor utrimque</u>, "(there is) shouting on both sides"; <u>undique concursus</u>, "(there is) running every-where." (Any two of these three for full credit.)

	(b) Ellipsis (no verb with <u>clamor utrimque</u> and <u>undique concursus</u>) OR asyn-deton (no conjunctions throughout the sentence (<u>Rapit</u> . . . <u>concursus</u>, 6–7).

6.	Horace might mean, "Whew, Apollo has saved me" (<u>sic</u> = the plaintiff has res-cued him from the Pest), or, ironically, "Rats, is <u>this</u> the way Apollo has saved me?" (<u>sic</u> = having to go to court).

## Answer: Spot Question 7 (Ovid)

1.  (a) Baucis and Philemon are attempting to catch their only goose for dinner.

    (b) <u>Unicus</u>, "one and only" (or sole, single) OR <u>minimae</u> (<u>villae</u>), "tiny (household)."

2.  The stubborn goose is wearing out the poor old folks. (Note the contrast of <u>celer</u> with <u>tardos</u>.)

3.  <u>Eluditque</u> is joined by –<u>que</u> with <u>fatigat</u> in the previous line.

4.  The gods (Jupiter and Mercury) intervened (<u>superi vetuere necari</u>).

5.  Synchysis/Interlocked word order: <u>meritasque</u> ... <u>vicinia poenas impia</u>, ABAB, OR enjambment of <u>impia</u> in line 7.

6.  "And this godless neighborhood will pay the price (that it) deserves"; "it will be given to you to be exempted from this punishment." (A reasonably accurate paraphrase is also acceptable. **This question is worth two points**.)

## Answer: Spot Question 8 (Ovid)

1.  "Why do you stand in the way of lovers, hateful wall?" OR, as a paraphrase, "why does the wall separate the lovers (Pyramus and Thisbe)"?

2.  Apostrophe; an address to the wall, <u>paries</u>.

3.  To be allowed to embrace each other (<u>toto nos corpore iungi</u>), or to be allowed to kiss (<u>ad oscula danda</u>).

4.  <u>Danda</u> is a gerundive in a gerundive of purpose construction after <u>ad</u>. The word <u>danda</u> modifies the noun <u>oscula</u>, therefore it is an adjective.

5.  Litotes: <u>nec</u> ... <u>ingrati</u> ("we are not ungrateful").

6.  That they are given a crack or passageway (<u>transitus</u>) through which they can communicate.

7.  That the two lovers are separated by the wall.

8.  Their goodbye kisses cannot be returned.

## Answer: Spot Question 9 (Ovid)

1.  <u>Arma</u>, arms or weapons; <u>violentaque</u>, violent, destructive, brutal; <u>bella</u>, wars (may be singular). (Any two of these three is acceptable for full credit.)

2.  (a) The "heavy rhythm" of hexameter, used for epic themes such as war.

    (b) The second verse was equal (in length) to the first, i.e., every line of dactylic hexameter has six feet.

    $$- \ u \ u \ - \ u \ u \ - \ uu \ - \ u \ u \ \ - \ u \ u \ - \ -$$
    (c) Arma gravi numero violentaque bella parabam

3.  "Cupid is said to have stolen away one foot." This refers to the loss of a foot in the second line of the elegaic couplet, which is a pentameter line. The elegaic couplet is frequently used in love poetry.

4.  (a) That it is mock-serious, or in fun (<u>risisse</u>).

    (b) The sounds are short and choppy, betraying emotion, with emphatic consonance of the letter -<u>t</u>- (<u>vates</u> . . . <u>tua turba</u>).

5.  The Pierides were daughters of Pierus, i.e., the Muses. (Either answer is acceptable.)

# Online Resources for Background Questions

## Vergil

- Homer's *Iliad and Odyssey*, and the Story of Troy The Aftermath: post-Iliad through the Odyssey (Donna Patrick, et al., Ablemedia, Classics Technology Center)

  http://ablemedia.com/ctcweb/consortium/aftermathpath.html

  Multi-resource exercise takes students from the death of Patroclus in the *Iliad* to Odysseus' arrival in Ithaca.

- Classical Epic (Eugene Cotter, Seton Hall University)

  http://pirate.shu.edu/-cottereu/aeneid.htm

  Resources for a college course in classical epic (outlines of topics and questions on *Iliad, Odyssey*, and *Aeneid*).

- The Epic Cycle (Vergil's *Aeneid*: Commentary, The Vergil Project, Univ. Pennsylvania)

  http://vergil.classics.upenn.edu/comm2/sources/cycle/

  Description and discussion of post-Homeric Greek epic poems that complete the story of Homer's epics.

- The Epic Hero: Common Elements in Most Cultures (Bruce M. Johnson, Park View High School)

  http://www.hoocher.com/theepichero.htm

- Homer in the Roman Tradition (William Harris, Middlebury College)

  http://community.middlebury.edu/~harris/Humanities/homer.html

  Part of the article "Homer in a Changing Tradition."

- The Legend of the Trojan War (Ian Johnston, Malaspina University-College, BC)

  http://www.mala.bc.ca/~johnstoi/clas101/troy.htm

  Prose outline of the events of the Trojan War up to the escape of Aeneas; includes "The Cultural Influence of the Legend of the Trojan War."

- Outline of the Trojan War (Artzia.com)

  http://artzia.com/History/Ideas/Mythology/Troy/

  Summary of the events of the Trojan War up to the escape of Aeneas, with lists of participants on each side.

- Pages on the Trojan War and on Troy (Greek Mythology Link, Carlos Parada)

  http://homepage.mac.com/cparada/GML/Troy.html; see also,

  http://homepage.mac.com/cparada/GML/TrojanWar.html

- ThinkQuest website on Homer's *Iliad* and *Odyssey* (Tony Arkwright, et al.)

  http://library.thinkquest.org/19300/data/homer.htm

  Includes interactive "Virtual *Iliad*" and "Virtual *Odyssey*"; useful background information on Homer.

- The Trojan War: Mythological Background (Bruce M. Johnson, Park View High School)

  http://www.hoocher.com/trojanwar.htm

  Outline of major episodes of the Homeric poems involving gods and goddesses.

- The Underworld (Joan Jahnige, Kentucky Educational Television)

  http://www.dl.ket.org/latin1/mythology/1deities/underworld/intro.htm

  Includes links to characters and places, with some illustrations.

- "The Underworld Adventure of Aeneas in the *Aeneid*" and "*Aeneid* VI: Hades' Realm" (about.com)

  http://ancienthistory.about.com/library/weekly/aa082200a.htm

  With glossary entries, links to related subjects, and information on the corresponding passages in the *Odyssey*

- Wikipedia hypertext article on Homer

  http://en.wikipedia.org/wiki/Homer; for the Trojan War, see
  http://en.wikipedia.org/wiki/Trojan_War

- Yahoo/Geocities site on Homer and Troy

  http://www.geocities.com/Pentagon/Quarters/2471/Troy.html#Troy

  Hypertext archaeological and literary history of Troy, glossaries of gods
  and goddesses and Greeks and Trojans, images.

## The Augustan Age

- Augustan Sites on the Web (Resources for Augustan Studies, Eric Kondratieff, Forum Antiquum)

  http://www.sas.upenn.edu/-ekondrat/Augustus.html#Augsites

  Links to resources for the Augustan period, incl. link with The Latin
  Library text of the *Aeneid*.

- Augustus- Images of Power (Mark Morford, Univ. Virginia)

  http://etext.virginia.edu/users/morford/augimage.html

  Pictures and brief discussions of the visual symbols of Augustan
  propaganda.

- "Caesar Augustus, An Annotated Guide to Online Resources" (David Wilson-Okamura, virgil.org)

  http://virgil.org/augustus

- The Emergence of the Augustan Age (Bruce M. Johnson, Park View High
  School)

  http://www.hoocher.com/theemergenceoftheaugustanage.htm

  Convenient chronological outline of events in Roman history from the
  death of Caesar to 29 BCE.

- A Literary History of the Augustan Age (Bruce M. Johnson, Park View
  High School)

  http://www.hoocher.com/literaryhistory.htm

- Patron Augustus-Client Rome (Sondra Steinbrenner, ancienthistory.about.
  com)

  http://ancienthistory.about.com/gi/dynamic/offsite.htm?site=http://roman
  %2Dempire.net/articles/article%2D010.html

  Excellent exploration of the symbols of Augustan *auctoritas*.

- Princeps: The Life of Augustus Caesar (Suzanne Cross)

  http://augustus.fws1.com/

  Recent online appreciation of Octavian/Augustus.

- Rome: Republic to Empire ("Augustus and Tiberius," Barbara F. McManus, VRoma)

  http://www.vroma.org/~bmcmanus/romanpages.html

  Illustrated synopsis of the historical background of Augustan rule.

# Online Resources for Spot Questions

## Catullus

### Clodia/Lesbia

- Feminae Romanae: The Women of Ancient Rome (Suzanne Cross)

  http://dominae.fws1.com/Influence/Clodia/Index.html

- Resources for a college course "Women in the Roman World" (David Noy, Univ. Wales)

  http://www.lamp.ac.uk/~noy/roman4.htm

  Clodia and Cicero's *Pro Caelio*.

- VRoma (Henry Walker, Bates College)

  http://www.vroma.org/~hwalker/VRomaCatullus/Clodia.html

- One classicist's outline of the "Lesbia Cycle," cross-linked to his texts and translations. Wikipedia hypertext article on Clodia

  http://en.wikipedia.org/wiki/Clodia

## Cicero

### Roman Oratory

- Cicero on the Genres of Rhetoric (translated by John F. Tinkler, Towson State Univ.)

  http://www.towson.edu/~tinkler/reader/cicero.html

  Relevant excerpts on the nature of Roman oratory, translated from Cicero's oratorical works.

- Cicero's *Pro Archia Poeta*: Literature and the Foundations of a Legal Education (Kevin Patrick, Univ. Georgia)

  http://www.uga.edu/juro/2004/patrick2.htm

  Political and literary context of the speech, with notes and bibliography.

- Corax: The Crow's Nest (Thomas J. Kinney, Univ. Arizona)

  http://www.u.arizona.edu/~tkinney/resources/rhetoric.html#history

  A Web site devoted to ancient rhetoric, including elements, theory, and history.

- Roman Orator (Smith's *A Dictionary of Greek and Roman Antiquities* in Bill Thayer's Lacus Curtius Web site)

  http://penelope.uchicago.edu/Thayer/E/Roman/Texts/secondary/SMIG-RA*/Orator.html

  The making and function of a good orator; the status of oratory as a profession.

- Roman Oratory (Joseph T. Richardson, The Society for Ancient Languages)

  http://www.uah.edu/student_life/organizations/SAL/texts/misc/romanora.html

  Roman oratory to the time of Cicero; discussion of the five canons for the preparation and delivery of a good speech in Latin.

- Roman Oratory (Kelly A. MacFarlane, Univ. Alberta)

  http://www.ualberta.ca/~kmacfarl/CLASS_104/10.Oratory.html

  Includes methods of oratory: *controversiae* and *suasoriae*.

- Wikipedia: Rhetoric-Roman Rhetoricians

  http://en.wikipedia.org/wiki/Rhetoric

### Cicero's Philosophical Writings

- Cicero (The Internet Encyclopedia of Philosophy, Edward Clayton, Central Michigan Univ.)

  http://www.utm.edu/research/iep/c/cicero.htm

  On Cicero's philosophical works and his relationship to various schools of ancient philosophy, plus a brief synopsis of *De Amicitia*.

## Horace

See "The Augustan Age," above.

## Ovid

### Myth in the Metamorphoses

- Encyclopedia Mythica

  http://www.pantheon.org/mythica.html

  Compendium of articles on various subjects pertaining to ancient myth.

- Gods, Heroes, and Myth (Nikki Burke)

  http://www.gods-heros-myth.com/godpages/atlas.html

  Well-organized quick-studies of Greek, Roman, and Norse deities.

- Greek Mythology Link (Carlos Parada)

  http://homepage.mac.com/cparada/GML/

  Resources for a variety of topics on Greek myth. See especially

  http://homepage.mac.com/cparada/GML/METAMORPHOSES.html

  This page tracks the changes of gods, people, and things that are described in ancient literature. Literary sources are provided.

- Mythology in Western Art (Project Mythmedia, Ora Zehavi and Sonia Klinger, Univ. Haifa)

  http://lib.haifa.ac.il/www/art/mythology_westart.html

  Collection of art images relating to classical myth.

- The Olympian Gods (Classical Myth: The Ancient Sources, Laurel Bowman)

  http://web.uvic.ca/grs/bowman/myth/gods.html

  Images and text sources for the Olympian gods.

## Chapter 9

# Outlines and Summaries

This chapter provides you with quick-study outlines and summaries of the content of the Latin and English readings required for the AP Latin Exam. These outlines and summaries are designed to help you recall the content of your previous reading of the Latin. Be aware that the designation below of episodes in the *Aeneid*, Catullus 64, *Satire* 1.9, *Pro Archia Poeta*, and *De Amicitia* is subjective. For the *Aeneid*, familiar quotations from the Latin text are provided when they illustrate a topic or theme. When the Latin and English passages interlock on the syllabi for Vergil and Cicero, i.e., Latin then English then Latin, etc., summaries of the intervening English passages are provided for your convenience. For references to review materials found online, which are especially useful for those portions of the *Aeneid* and the *De Amicitia* to be read only in English, see Chapters 2, 3, and 12.

## Vergil

### Outline of the Twelve Books of the Aeneid by Episodes[1]
#### *Book 1 (Latin and English)*

**Lines to be read in Latin (1. 1–519)**

EPISODES

1–11      The theme of the poem and invocation to the Muse
                *Arma virumque cano, Troiae qui primus ab oris . . . .* (line 1)

12–13     Juno's jealousy and anger
                *Tantae molis erat Romanam condere gentem!* (line 33)

34–49     The Trojans leave for Sicily.

50–75     Juno appeals to Aeolus, god of the winds.

76–101    Aeolus complies with Juno's request.
                *O terque quaterque beati!* (line 94)

102–23    The storm shatters Aeneas' fleet

124–56    An angry Neptune ends the storm.
                Simile of the orator (lines 148–53)

---

[1] For a good reference map of the wanderings of Aeneas, see http://homepage.mac.com/cparada/GML/Aeneas.html.

157–79   The landing of the shipwrecked Trojans in Africa

180–97   Aeneas and Achates go hunting.

198–222  Aeneas encourages his comrades.

> *O socii. . .* (lines 198–207); *Forsan et haec olim meminisse iuvabit* (line 203)

223–53   Venus appears to Jupiter on behalf of her son Aeneas.

254–96   Jupiter reveals the destiny of Aeneas and of Rome

> *His ego nec metas rerum nec tempora pono; imperium sine fine dedi* (lines 278–79)

> *Romanos, rerum dominos, gentem togatam . . . .* (line 282)

297–304  Jupiter sends Mercury to Carthage to insure welcome for the Trojans.

305–34   Aeneas and Achates meet Venus, disguised as a huntress.

335–71   Venus describes Dido's flight from Tyre.

> *. . . dux femina facti* (line 364)

372–86   Aeneas tells the sad story of the Trojans.

387–417  Venus reveals herself and covers Aeneas and Achates with a cloud.

418–40   Aeneas and Achates make their way to Carthage.

> Simile of the bees (lines 430–36)

> *O fortunati, quorum iam moenia surgunt!* (line 437)

441–65   Aeneas and Achates view the Temple of Juno at Carthage

> *Sunt lacrimae rerum et mentem mortalia tangunt* (line 462)

466–93   The temple mural tells the story of the Trojan War.

494–519  Dido arrives at the temple.

> Simile of the goddess Diana's band (lines 498–504)

## Lines to be read in English (1. 520–756)

Queen Dido is formally addressed by Ilioneus, one of the Trojan survivors. Aeneas and Achates remain hidden in the mist. Ilioneus describes their search for Hesperia and the circumstances that had brought them to the north coast of Africa. Dido takes pity on the shipwrecked Trojans and sends scouts to search for Aeneas and Achates. The mist parts and Aeneas stands before Dido in all his glory. He addresses the queen with thanks and embraces his comrades. Dido replies that she is familiar with the story of Troy and invites the Trojans to a banquet so that she can hear more. Aeneas sends Achates back to the ships to inform Ascanius and to bid him return with gifts for the Carthaginians. Venus sends her son Cupid to substitute for Ascanius. Dido begins to have feelings for Aeneas and invites him to tell his story as they feast.

### Book 2 (Latin and English)

#### Lines to be read in Latin (2. 1–56)

| | |
|---|---|
| 1–13 | Aeneas begins his tale of the Trojan War. |
| | *Quorum magna pars fui* (line 6) |
| 14–39 | The Wooden Horse |
| 40–56 | Laocoon's warning |
| | *Equo ne credite. Quicquid id est, timeo Danaos et dona ferentes* (lines 48–49) |

#### Lines to be read in English (2. 57–198)

| | |
|---|---|
| 57–76 | The Greek Sinon is brought before Priam. |
| 77–104 | Sinon's story |
| 105–44 | Sinon's deceit |
| 145–98 | The Trojans take pity on Sinon. |

#### Lines to be read in Latin (2. 199–297)

| | |
|---|---|
| 199–233 | The death of Laocoon and his sons |
| | *Ecce autem gemini a Tenedo tranquilla per alta (horresco referens) immensis orbibus angues* (lines 203–4) |
| 234–49 | The Horse is taken into Troy. |
| | *Scandit fatalis machina muros feta armis* (lines 237–38) |
| 250–67 | The return of the Greeks |
| 268–86 | Aeneas' vision of Hector in a dream. |
| | *O lux Dardaniae, spes O fidissima Teucrum . . . .* (lines 281–86) |
| 289–95 | Hector's warning to Aeneas. |

#### Lines to be read in English (2. 298–468)

| | |
|---|---|
| 298–335 | Troy in flames |
| 336–54 | A rally by Aeneas and his comrades |
| 355–85 | The fury of the Trojans |
| 386–401 | The Trojans, in Greek armor, are initially victorious |
| 402–9 | The Trojans try to save Cassandra |
| 410–37 | The Trojans are mistaken for Greeks |
| 438–68 | The defense of Priam's palace |

**Lines to be read in Latin (2. 469–566)**

469–85    Achilles' son Pyrrhus enters the palace.

                Simile of the snake (lines 471–75)

486–505   Greeks swarm the palace.

506–25    The fate of Priam, king of Troy

526–43    The murder of Priam's son Polites

544–66    The death of King Priam

**Lines to be read in English (2. 567–734)**

567–87    Aeneas encounters Helen.

588–633   Venus intervenes.

                Simile of the ash tree (lines 626–31)

634–78    Anchises refuses to leave Troy.

679–704   An omen overcomes Anchises' objections.

705–34    Aeneas gives directions for flight.

**Lines to be read in Latin (2.735–804)**

735–67    The disappearance of Creusa and Aeneas' search

768–74    Aeneas sees a vision of Creusa.

                *Obstipui, steteruntque comae et vox faucibus haesit* (line 774)

775–94    Creusa advises Aeneas to leave Troy without her.

                *Longa tibi exsilia et vastum maris aequor arandum, et terram Hesperiam venies* (lines 780–81)

795–804   The Trojans take refuge in the mountains.

## Book 3 (English)

The fugitive Trojans make their way to Thrace, where they meet the ghost of Trojan Polydorus. Offerings of expiation for his murder are made, followed by the departure of the fleet to the south. They reach Delos where, after an omen, a priest of Apollo advises the Trojans to "seek out their ancient mother" (Italy). On to Crete, where a plague strikes. The Penates address Aeneas and bid him go to a land called Hesperia, source of the Trojan race. A storm drives them to the islands of the Strophades where dwell Phineus and Celaeno and the Harpies. After moving on, the Trojans meet Helenus, Priam's son, and now priest of Apollo and husband of Andromache, and another band of refugee Trojans. Helenus encourages the Trojans to continue their search for "the land of Ausonia."Aeneas learns of Scylla and Charybdis and then passes on to Sicily and Mt. Aetna, where the travelers meet Achaemenides, left behind by Odysseus, and the Cyclopes. Anchises later dies.

## Book 4 (Latin and English)

### Lines to be read in Latin (4. 1–449)

| | |
|---|---|
| 1–30 | Dido confesses to her sister Anna that she has fallen in love. |
| | *Degeneres animos timor arguit* (line 13) |
| 31–53 | Anna encourages Dido. |
| 54–64 | Dido sacrifices to the gods. |
| 65–89 | Dido's emotion |
| 90–104 | Juno approaches Venus. |
| 105–28 | Venus agrees to Juno's scheme to bring Dido and Aeneas together. |
| 129–59 | The hunting party |
| 160–72 | Aeneas and Dido take shelter in a cave. |
| 173–97 | Rumor spreads the story abroad. |
| | *Fama, malum qua non aliud velocius ullum* (lines 173–88) |
| 198–221 | The anger of Iarbas; Aeneas is compared to Paris for stealing another's bride. |
| 222–78 | Mercury is sent to warn Aeneas. |
| 279–95 | Aeneas makes plans to leave. |
| 296–304 | Dido's suspicions |
| | *Quis fallere possit amantem?* (line 296) |
| 305–30 | Dido reproaches Aeneas the first time. |
| 331–61 | Aeneas' reply |
| 362–92 | Dido's anger increases. |
| 393–407 | The Trojans prepare to depart. |
| | Simile of the ants (lines 402–7) |
| 408–36 | Dido's final appeal. |
| | *Improbe Amor, quid non mortalia pectora cogis!* (line 412) |
| 437–49 | Aeneas remains steadfast in his decision. |
| | Simile of the oak tree in a high wind (lines 441–49) |

### Lines to be read in English (4. 449–641)

| | |
|---|---|
| 450–73 | Dido's despair |
| 474–503 | Plans for the funeral pyre |
| 504–21 | Dido sacrifices to the gods below. |
| 522–53 | Dido's grief |

| 554–70 | Mercury again warns Aeneas. |
|---|---|
| | *Varium et mutabile semper femina* (lines 569–70) |
| 571–606 | Departure of the Trojans |
| 607–29 | Dido's curse |
| 630–41 | Dido asks nurse Barce to fetch Anna to "assist" in the ritual purification. |

**Lines to be read in Latin (4. 642–705)**

| 642–71 | Dido's death |
|---|---|
| | *Dulces exuviae . . . .* (lines 651–62) |
| 672–92 | Anna's grief |
| 693–705 | Dido's spirit is set free by the goddess Iris. |

## Book 5 (English)

The Trojan fleet heads for Sicily, where games are held to celebrate the anniversary of Anchises' death. Fellow Trojan Acestes hosts the games, which consist of a ship race (Cloanthus), foot race (Nisus and Euryalus), boxing match (Entellus and Dares), and an archery contest in which Acestes' arrow catches fire. Ascanius leads the young men in the "Trojan Games." Juno sends Iris to the Trojan women, who then, weary of war and traveling, set the ships afire. Nautes then advises that the weak be left in Sicily with Acestes and that the Trojans move on, with the aid of Neptune, whose help has been sought by Venus. Anchises appears to Aeneas in a dream. The helmsman Palinurus falls overboard and dies.

## Book 6

**Lines to be read in Latin (6. 1–211)**

| 1–13 | The Trojans reach Italy and arrive at Cumae. |
|---|---|
| 14–33 | The Temple of Apollo, whose doors depict the story of Daedalus and the Minotaur. |
| 34–55 | The Cumaean Sibyl |
| 56–76 | Aeneas prays to Apollo. |
| 77–101 | The Sibyl's prophecy |
| | *Tu ne cede malis* (line 95) |
| 102–23 | Aeneas asks to visit his father in the Underworld. |
| 124–55 | The Golden Bough |
| | *Facilis descensus Averno* (line 126) |
| 156–84 | The body of Misenus |
| 185–211 | The search for the Golden Bough |

**Lines to be read in English (6. 212–449)**

| | |
|---|---|
| 212–61 | Aeneas makes an offering to the deities of the Underworld. |
| 262–72 | The descent to the Underworld |
| 273–94 | Description of the entrance |
| 295–336 | Arrival at the River Styx; Charon, the ferryman |
| 337–83 | The ghost of the lost helmsman, Palinurus |
| 384–416 | Crossing the Styx |
| 417–25 | Cerberus |
| 426–39 | Ghosts of those who died prematurely |
| 440–49 | The Fields of Mourning (**Campi Lugentes**) |
| 450–76 | Aeneas meets Dido's ghost in the Underworld |

**Lines to be read in English (6. 477–846)**

| | |
|---|---|
| 477–93 | The ghosts of dead warriors |
| 494–534 | The fate of Deiphobus |
| 535–79 | Arrival in Tartarus |
| 580–607 | Some famous villains |
| 608–27 | Punishments of the wicked |
| 628–36 | The palace of Pluto |
| 637–65 | The Elysian Fields |
| 666–702 | Aeneas meets his father. |
| 703–23 | The River Lethe |
| 724–51 | Anchises philosophizes. |
| 752–87 | The Alban kings and Romulus |
| 788–807 | Anchises shows Aeneas the Julian descendants. |
| 808–25 | The "Parade of Heroes": Roman kings and heroes of the early Republic |
| 826–46 | Caesar, Pompey, and other heroes |

**Lines to be read in Latin (6. 847–901)**

| | |
|---|---|
| 847–853 | The mission of Rome<br>*Excudent alii spirantia mollius aera . . . .* (lines 847–53) |
| 854–92 | The young Marcellus |
| 893–901 | Return to the Upper World |

### Book 7 (English)

At last the Trojans arrive in Latium, where they meet Latinus, king of the Latins, and his daughter Lavinia. Latinus tells the story of Faunus. The Trojans "eat their tables," as prophesied. Aeneas sends a delegation, led by Ilioneus, to King Latinus and then begins to mark out the boundaries of a city. Stories are swapped, and Latinus learns that this was the original homeland of Trojan Dardanus. Latinus invites the Trojans to settle in Latium. A fearful Juno summons Allecto, changeling and dread goddess of the Underworld. Allecto stirs up trouble with Queen Amata and with the Rutulian hero Turnus, to whom Lavinia is betrothed. Ascanius, while hunting, wounds Silvia's stag, which leads to a confrontation, arranged by Allecto, between the Latins and the Trojans. Juno opens the gates of war. A great army is mustered from the Italic towns.

### Book 8 (English)

The river god Tiberinus appears to Aeneas and advises him to form an alliance with the Arcadians, enemies of the Latins. Aeneas sacrifices a white sow. At Pallanteum, the Arcadian king Evander, is receptive to Aeneas' proposal. The story of Hercules and Cacus is told at the ensuing feast, as well as the history of Arcadian Rome. Venus, fearful for her son, urges Vulcan to forge mighty arms for Aeneas. The formal alliance between Trojan and Arcadian is struck. The Shield of Aeneas, which depicts Rome's future history, including Romulus and Remus, the Rape of the Sabine Women, Porsenna's siege of Rome, the sack of the city by Gauls, Catiline and Cato, and the Battle of Actium.

### Book 9 (English)

Juno sends Iris to Turnus to inform him of the latest developments. He determines to attack the Trojans while Aeneas is away, and the Trojans retreat behind their newly-constructed battlements. Turnus then moves to burn the remaining Trojan ships, which, in answer to an old blessing, are changed into sea nymphs. There follows the tragic tale of the Trojan friends Nisus and Euryalus, who attempt to take word to Aeneas. The Latins attack the Trojan fortress, but Ascanius leads a counter-attack. Turnus turns the momentum but is trapped inside the Trojan stockade. He escapes by jumping into the Tiber River.

### Book 10 (Latin and English)

**Lines to be read in English (10. 1–419)**

| | |
|---|---|
| 1–15 | In a council of the gods on Olympus, Jupiter asks why the Italians and Trojans are fighting. |
| 16–61 | Venus holds Turnus and the Rutulians responsible and pleads, once again, for her son. |
| 62–95 | Juno's fierce rebuttal, in which she claims that it isn't her fault if Aeneas endeavors to marry someone else's bride (Lavinia). |
| 96–117 | The gods take sides and the situation escalates. Jupiter decrees that fate will determine the outcome. |

| | |
|---|---|
| 118–62 | As the battle rages, Aeneas arrives with a small Arcadian force led by Evander and with the huge army of Evander's Etruscan allies. |
| 163–214 | The "Catalogue of Ships" and their Trojan captains |
| 215–57 | The throng of recently-born sea nymphs meets the returning fleet, led by the Etruscan Tarchon, and speeds it along. |
| 258–361 | As the fleet approaches Italy, Turnus decides to abandon his attack and defend the coast. A Homeric battle scene ensues on the beach. |
| 362–420 | Evander's young son Pallas gives a stirring speech and charges into the enemy. More blood 'n' guts. |

## Lines to be read in Latin (10. 420–509)

| | |
|---|---|
| 420–38 | Pallas invokes the river god Tiber, slays the Rutulian Halaesus, and then is confronted by Lausus, the son of Mezentius. |
| | *Da hunc, Thybri pater, ferro, quod missile libro* (lines 421–23) |
| 439–56 | Turnus' sister Juturna warns him to go to the aid of Lausus. He does so. |
| | Simile of the lion and the bull. (Lines 454–56) |
| 457–78 | Pallas invokes Hercules, who is then advised by Jupiter that both heroes will soon meet their fate. Pallas casts his spear, with little effect. |
| | *Stat sua cuique dies, breve et irreparabile tempus omnibus est vitae; sed famam extendere factis, hoc virtutis opus* (lines 467–72) |
| 479–500 | Turnus spears Pallas and despoils the body while boasting of victory. |
| 501–20 | Vergil apostrophizes the death of Pallas and the fate of Turnus. |
| | *Nescia mens hominum fati sortisque futurae et servare modum, rebus sublata secundis!* (lines 501–2) |

## Lines to be read in English (10. 510–908)

| | |
|---|---|
| 520–605 | Bloody battle scenes, with Aeneas crazed with grief. |
| 606–32 | Jupiter and Juno discuss her request to save Turnus. |
| 633–88 | Juno spirits Turnus away from the field by creating a ghost, with the appearance of Aeneas, that lures him away from the fighting. |
| 689–768 | The deposed king of the Etruscans, cruel Mezentius, now becomes the star enemy warrior for the Latins and Rutulians. |
| | Simile of the boar (lines 707–15) |
| 769–76 | Aeneas seeks out Mezentius, who defies him with a boastful speech to his son Lausus. |

| 776–832 | Aeneas gravely wounds Mezentius with a spear. While delivering a hard-hearted speech, he then slays Lausus. |
|---|---|

Simile of the hailstorm (lines 803–10)

| 833–82 | Mezentius, while attempting to recover from his wounds, eulogizes his dead son and calls out for revenge upon Aeneas. |
|---|---|
| 883–908 | Aeneas strikes Mezentius' horse, which rears up and unseats the Etruscan. Aeneas finishes him off. |

### Book 11 (English)

Aeneas, grieving for the death of young Pallas, arranges for the body to be sent back to Evander at Pallanteum. A 12–day truce is called to allow time for burial of the dead. The prevailing feeling seems to be that Turnus and Aeneas should settle their differences in a duel. After an angry exchange in a council of the Latins and the Rutulians, Turnus agrees to fight Aeneas. Meanwhile, the Trojans attack, divided into two forces. Turnus moves out to meet one, led by Aeneas, and Camilla, female leader of the Volscians, remains behind to secure the defenses of Laurentum. Camilla is wounded by the Tuscan Arruns, but she is spirited away by the goddess Diana. Turnus is forced to return to the leaderless city.

### Book 12 (Latin and English)

#### Lines to be read in English (12. 1–790)

| 1–17 | Turnus realizes that the salvation of Laurentum lies with him alone. He determines to meet Aeneas in a duel and asks King Latinus to arrange this. |
|---|---|

Simile of the wounded African lion (lines 4–9)

| 18–70 | Latinus' attempts to appease the warrior fall on deaf ears. So do the entreaties of Amata. |
|---|---|
| 71–106 | Turnus, angry over the delay, arms himself for the fight and apostrophizes his spear. |

Simile of the bull charging a tree (lines 101–6)

| 107–33 | Aeneas also prepares, happy that the issue will finally be decided. The Rutulian and Trojan armies come together with great pomp to confirm the agreement. Aeneas prays to the gods regarding the outcome, either way. |
|---|---|
| 134–246 | Juno, afraid for Turnus, seeks help from his sister Juturna, a fountain nymph. Disguised as Camers, a noble Rutulian, Juturna spreads dissent among Turnus' followers. This happens while Latin and the chieftains are sacrificing to seal the agreement. |
| 247–65 | At this moment, a flock of wild swans is seen in the sky attacking an eagle that is trying to carry off one of them. The Rutulians, who outnumber the Trojans, immediately sieze upon this as a sign that they should attack the Trojans. |

266–310     A wild free-for-all ensues.

311–23     Aeneas, standing tall while trying to restore order, is wounded in the knee.

324–410     Turnus, with a sudden surge of new confidence, plunges into the fighting. Aeneas is carried away and his wounds tended.

Simile of Mars, the war-bringer (lines 331–39)

411–67     Venus heals the wound with a magic plant from Crete, and Aeneas plunges back into the fray.

Simile of the hailstorm (lines 451–58)

468–553     Both warriors rage on; Juturna, in the guise of his charioteer, guides Turnus' chariot away from Aeneas.

554–613     Aeneas suddenly turns his attention back to Laurentum and the Trojan army storms the walls. Queen Amata hangs herself in despair.

614–49     Turnus turns his attention to the beleaguered city, but is encouraged to remain in battle by Juturna.

650–71     Saces, a wounded Rutulian, rides up and confirms that the city is on the verge of collapse and that the queen is dead.

672–96     In anger, Turnus determines to meet Aeneas, once and for all.

Simile of the mountain rockfall (lines 684–90)

697–765     Aeneas and Turnus finally meet. Turnus' sword snaps when it strikes Aeneas' god-made shield (Turnus had grabbed his charioteer's sword by mistake). Aeneas pursues Turnus.

Simile of the hound and the stag (lines 749–57)

766–90     Aeneas' spear becomes stuck in an olive tree; Turnus prays to Faunus that the tree hold it fast. Meanwhile, Juturna has arrived with Turnus' own sword. Angry Venus comes down to free the spear for Aeneas.

### Lines to be read in Latin (12.790–842)

791–842     Jupiter intervenes and forbids Juno from interfering any further. He convinces her that the Trojans have suffered enough. Juno asks that the two sides become united under the Latin name.

*Quae iam finis erit, coniunx?* (lines 793–806)

*Occidit, occideritque sinas cum nomine Troia* (line 828)

*Es germana Iovis Saturnique altera proles: irarum tantos volvis sub pectore fluctus* (lines 830–40)

## Lines to be read in English (12. 843–86)

843–86    Jove sends one of the Furies to drive Juturna back to her fountain.

        Simile of the speeding arrow (lines 856–60)

## Lines to be read in Latin (12. 887–952)

887–918    The two warriors press on and taunt each other with angry words. But Turnus says that it is not Aeneas, but the gods, who terrify him, for Jupiter is his enemy. He heaves a huge boulder at Aeneas, but misses wildly.

        *Non me tua fervida terrent dicta, ferox: di me terrent et Iuppiter hostis* (lines 894–95)

        Simile of the dream-state (lines 908–14)

919–30    Aeneas hurls his spear with all his might and wounds Turnus in the thigh.

        Simile of the shot from a catapult (lines 921–23)

931–37    Turnus' last words are not a prayer for mercy, but rather an admission of guilt. "I have deserved this; you have conquered; Lavinia is your wife."

938–52    Aeneas, ready to spare Turnus, catches sight of Pallas' war-belt, which Turnus has worn ever since he slew the youth. Revenge and grief rise up in Aeneas' heart, and he plunges his sword into Turnus.

        *Tune hinc spoliis indute meorum eripiare mihi? Pallas te hoc vulnere, Pallas immolat et poenam scelerato ex sanguine sumit* (lines 947–49)

# Speeches in the *Aeneid*

**Who spoke the following and to whom? Try to recall the circumstances in which each speech was given. The answers are provided at the end of this chapter.**

## Book 1

1.    "Aeole, namque tibi divum pater atque hominum rex" (lines 65–75)

2.    "Tuus, O regina, quid optes, explorare labor" (lines 76–80)

3.    "O terque quaterque beati" (lines 94–101)

4.    "Tantane vos generis tenuit fiducia vestri?" (lines 132–41)

5.    "O socii (neque enim ignari sumus ante malorum)" (lines 198–207)

6.    "O qui res hominumque deorumque" (lines 229–53)

7.    "Parce metu, Cytherea; manent immota tuorum fata tibi" (lines 257–96)

8.  "Nulla tuarum audita mihi neque visa sororum, – quam te memorem, virgo?" (lines 323–34)

9.  "Quisquis es, haud, credo, invisus caelestibus auras vitalis carpis" (lines 387–401)

10. "Quid natum toties, crudelis tu quoque, falsis ludis imaginibus?" (lines 407–9)

11. "O fortunati, quorum iam moenia surgunt!" (line 437)

12. "Sunt lacrimae rerum et mentem mortalia tangunt" (line 462)

## Book 2

1.  "Infandum, regina, iubes renovare dolorem" (lines 3–13)

2.  "O miseri, quae tanta insania, cives?" (lines 42–49)

3.  "O lux Dardniae, spes O fidissima Teucrum" (lines 281–86)

4.  "Heu! fuge, nate dea, teque his," ait, "eripe flammis" (lines 289–95)

5.  "Quae mens tam dira, miserrime coniunx, impulit his cingi telis?" (lines 519–24)

6.  "At tibi pro scelere," exclamat, "pro talibus ausis di, si qua est caelo pietas, quae talia curet" (lines 535–43)

7.  "Referes ergo haec et nuntius ibis Pelidae genitori" (lines 247–50)

8.  "Quid tantum insano iuvat indulgere dolori, O dulcis coniunx?" (lines 776–89)

## Book 4

1.  "Soror, quae me suspensam insomnia terrent!" (lines 9–29)

2.  "O luce magis dilecta sorori, solane perpetua maerens carpere inventa" (lines 31–53)

3.  "Egregiam vero laudem et spolia ampla refertis tuque puerque tuus" (lines 93–104)

4.  "Quis talia demens abnuat aut tecum malit contendere bello?" (lines 107–14)

5.  "Iuppiter omnipotens, cui nunc Maurusia pictis gens epulata toris Lenaeum libat honorem" (lines 206–18)

6.  "Vade age, nate, voca Zephyros et labere pinnis Dardaniumque ducem" (lines 223–37)

7.  "Dissimulare etiam sperasti, perfide, tantum posse nefas tacitusque mea decedere terra?" (lines 305–30)

8.  "Ego te, quae plurima fando enumerare vales, numquam, regina, negabo promeritam" (lines 333–61)

9.  "Nec tibi diva parens, generis nec Dardanus auctor, perfide, sed duris genuit te cautibus horrens Caucausus" (lines 365–87)

10. "Inveni, germana, viam (gratare sorori), qui mihi reddat eum aut eo me solvat amantem" (lines 478–98)

11. "Praecipites vigilate, viri, et considite transtris" (lines 573–79)

12. "Pro Iuppiter! ibit hic," ait, "et nostris inluserit advena regnis?" (lines 590–629)

13. "Dulces exuviae, dum fata deusque sinebat, accipite hanc animam" (lines 651–2)

14. "Hoc illud, germana, fuit? Me fraude petebas?" (lines 675–85)

## Book 6

1. "Poscere fata tempus," ait. "Deus, ecce, deus!" (lines 45–46)

2. "O tandem magnis pelagi defuncte periclis (sed terra graviora manent)" (lines 83–97)

3. "Non ulla laborum, O virgo, nova mi facies inopinave surgit" (lines 101–23)

4. "Sate sanguine divum, Tros Anchisiade, facilis descensus Averno" (lines 125–55)

5. "Si nunc se nobis ille aureus arbore ramis ostendat nemore in tanto!" (lines 187–97)

6. "Infelix Dido, verus mihi nuntius ergo venerat exstinctam" (lines 456–66)

7. "Excudent alii spirantia mollius aera" (lines 847–53)

8. "Quis, pater, ille, virum qui sic comtatur euntem?" (lines 863–66)

## Book 10

1. "Da hunc, Thybri pater, ferro, quod missile libro" (lines 421–23)

2. "Tempus desistere pugnae; solus ego in Pallanta feror, soli mihi Pallas debetur; cuperem ipse parens spectator adesset" (lines 441–43)

3. "Per patris hospitium et mensas, quas advena adisti; te precor, Alcide, coeptis ingentibus adsis" (lines 459–63)

4. "Stat sua cuique dies, breve et inreparabile tempus omnibus est vitae; sed famam extendere factis, hoc virtutis opus" (lines 467–72)

5. "Arcades, haec," inquit, "memores mea dicta referte Evandro; qualem meruit, Pallanta remitto" (line 491–95)

## Book 12

1. "Quae iam finis erit, coniunx?" (lines 793–806)

2. "Es germana Iovis Saturnique altera proles: irarum tantos volvis sub pectore fluctus" (lines 830–40)

3. "Quae nunc, deinde mora est? Aut quid iam, Turne, retractas?" (lines 889–93)

4. "Non me tua fervida terrent dicta, ferox: di me terrent et Iuppiter hostis" (lines 894–95)

5. "Tune hinc spoliis indute meorum eripiare mihi? Pallas te hoc vulnere, Pallas immolat et poenam scelerato ex sanguine sumit" (lines 947–49)

# Catullus

**A quick-study of the forty-one poems of Catullus**

| Corpus | Meter | Length | Addressee | Topic |
|--------|-------|--------|-----------|-------|
| 1 | Hendec. | 10 | Nepos/Muse | Dedication |
| 2 | Hendec. | 10 | Sparrow | Lesbia |
| 3 | Hendec. | 18 | Sparrow | Lesbia |
| 4 | | 27 | Boat | Catullus abroad |
| 5 | Hendec. | 13 | Lesbia | Lesbia |
| 7 | Hendec. | 12 | Lesbia | Lesbia |
| 8 | | 19 | Catullus/Lesbia | Lesbia |
| 10 | Hendec. | 34 | Alfenus Varus | Caught in a lie |
| 11 | Sapphic | 24 | Furius and Aurelius | Lesbia |
| 12 | Hendec. | 17 | Marrucinus Asinius | Napkin stealer |
| 13 | Hendec. | 14 | Fabullus | Lesbia |
| 14a | Hendec. | 23 | Licinius Calvus | An unwanted gift |
| 22 | | 21 | Alfenus Varus | Suffenus |
| 30 | Hendec. | 12 | Alfenus Varus | Betrayal |
| 31 | | 14 | Sirmio | Catullus abroad |
| 35 | Hendec. | 18 | Papyrus page | "Lady of Dindymus" |
| 36 | Hendec. | 20 | Poems of Volusius | Lesbia |
| 40 | Hendec. | 8 | Raudus | Jealousy |
| 43 | Hendec. | 8 | (Ameana) | Lesbia |
| 44 | Hendec. | 21 | Catullus' farm | Self-rebuke |
| 45 | Hendec. | 6 | Acme and Septimius | Love |
| 46 | Hendec. | 11 | Catullus | Catullus abroad |
| 49 | Hendec. | 7 | Cicero | Thank you |
| 50 | Hendec. | 21 | Licinius Calvus | Poetry as love |

| Corpus | Meter | Length | Addressee | Topic |
|--------|-------|--------|-----------|-------|
| 51 | Sapphic | 16 | Lesbia | Lesbia |
| 60 | Hendec. | 5 | Lesbia | Lesbia |
| 64 | Hexameter | 203 | Peleus | Ariadne/Theseus |
| 65 | Elegaic | 24 | Hortalus | Brother's death |
| 68 | Elegaic | 40 | Manlius | Brother's death |
| 69 | Elegaic | 10 | Caelius Rufus | Smelly armpits |
| 70 | Elegaic | 4 | Lesbia | Lesbia |
| 72 | Elegaic | 8 | Lesbia | Lesbia |
| 76 | Elegaic | 26 | Catullus, The Gods | Lesbia |
| 77 | Elegaic | 6 | Caelius Rufus | Betrayal |
| 84 | Elegaic | 12 | Arrius | Speech problem |
| 85 | Elegaic | 2 | Lesbia | |
| 86 | Elegaic | 6 | About Quintia | Lesbia |
| 87 | Elegaic | 4 | | Lesbia |
| 96 | Elegaic | 6 | Licinius Calvus | Wife's death |
| 101 | Elegaic | 10 | Catullus' brother | Brother's death |
| 109 | Elegaic | 8 | Lesbia | Lesbia |
| 116 | Elegaic | 8 | Gellius | Feuding poets |

### Eighteen poems to be considered for inclusion in the "Lesbia Cycle"[2]

**Erotic Love:** 51, 5 and 7, 86 and 43, 2 and 3, 13

**Quarrel and Reconciliation:** 8, 36, 87 and 109

**Infidelity and Disillusionment:** 70, 72, 85, 60

**Farewell:** 76, 11

---

[2] Assignment of particular poems to the "Lesbia Cycle" is highly subjective. For one scholar's opinion, see http://www.vroma.org/~hwalker/VRomaCatullus/Clodia.html and for another, see Kenneth Quinn, *Catullus: An Interpretation*, London, B.T. Batsford, Ltd., 1972.

## An outline of Catullus 64, lines 50-253

The setting of this epyllion is the love and subsequent wedding of Peleus and Thetis. The scene moves to the wedding chamber in the house of Peleus, where the bed is draped with a wonderful coverlet. This is embroidered with stories of the deeds of ancient heroes, including the story of Theseus and Ariadne.

Lines 52–57   Ariadne awakens to find herself alone on an island beach, deserted by Theseus, whom she sees sailing away.

Lines 58–75   Ariadne's appearance in described. with both passion and despair. *Magnis curarum fluctuat undis.* (Line 62)

Lines 76–85   A brief account of the story of the Minotaur and Theseus' purpose in coming to Crete.

Lines 86–104   Ariadne swoons over Theseus.

Lines 105–11   The simile of the oak tree (the Minotaur) in a storm (Theseus)

Lines 112–15   Theseus escapes the labyrinth.

Lines 116–31   How Ariadne sacrificed the love of her family for Theseus.

Lines 132–201   Ariadne's lengthy soliloquy, which includes an apostrophe to Theseus.

*Nunc iam nulla viro iuranti femina credat.* (Line 143)

Men are never to be trusted after they get what they want. (Lines 144–48)

She reminds him that she saved him when he was facing death by the Minotaur (Lines 149–51).

Ariadne asks if she is to be left as prey for vultures and lie unburied. (Lines 152–53)

*Quod mare conceptum spumantibus exspuit undis?* (Line 155)

She then yields to her passion and admits that she would even have served him as a slave in his household. (Lines 158–63)

She wishes that Theseus had never arrived in Crete. (Lines 171–76)

Not only has Ariadne been rejected, but she has been deserted on a remote island. (Lines 177–91)

She then curses Theseus and calls down the Eumenides to avenge her. (Lines 192–201)

Lines 207–11   Theseus forgets to change the ship's sail as he approaches Athens.

Lines 212–37   The background of King Aegeus' instructions to his son Theseus to change to a white sail when safely within sight of home.

Lines 238–53   Aegeus, mistakenly believing his son to be dead, hurls himself from a cliff into the sea. Ariadne is avenged.

# Cicero

## *The Structure of the* Pro Archia

A forensic speech in the time of Cicero would contain the following elements, in some form or other. The sequence of these elements may sometimes change, and some may not appear in a particular speech.

**Exordium:**      opening statement

**Narratio:**      statement of facts of the case

**Refutatio:**      attempt to disprove opposition's case

**Confirmatio:**      defendant's version of events

**Peroratio:**      closing statement

## *Exordium (1-4)*

Cicero attempts to win the good will of the jury (**iudices**), who will decide the case, by mentioning his oratorical skills: **ingenium** (ability), **exercitatio** (experience), and **ratio** (selection of pertinent strategy). (By the way Cicero's brother Quintus, a praetor, presided over the tribunal!) He assigns credit for his success as an orator to his former teacher, A. Licinius Archias, the defendant. Furthermore, he begs the indulgence of the court to give him latitude in applying to this case a **novus genus dicendi** (new style of speaking). Cicero goes on to present a dissertation on the value of the liberal arts, a topic which he now introduces: "Indeed, all the arts that relate to humankind share a certain common bond (**commune vinculum**) and are inter-connected by a certain blood relationship (**cognatione**), as it were." (2)

## *Narratio (4-7)*

Cicero now presents Archias' personal background in order to begin laying the foundation for refuting the prosecution's charge that Archias was not a Roman citizen. He begins with Archias' birth in Antioch and proceeds to tell of Archias' journeys in Asia Minor and Greece, while developing a reputation as a poet. He had become a citizen of the allied town of Heraclea in Magna Graecia (southern Italy), a normal preliminary step towards attaining full Roman citizenship. While in Rome, he obtained the attention and patronage of a number of influential Romans, including Lucullus, whose political rivalry with Pompey may have led to the charges against him.

## *Refutatio (8-11)*

In this portion of Cicero's speech, he attempts to counter the prosecution's four main arguments:

1] that there was no written proof of Archias' citizenship at Heraclea

2] that Archias had not maintained a legal residence in Rome

3] that he had not appeared before the appropriate praetorian magistrate within the prescribed sixty-day period

4] that Archias' name was not to be found in official census records.

Cicero's counter-arguments are as follows:

1] the records in Heraclea had been lost in a fire during the Social War (but witnesses can attest to his citizenship)

2] Archias did indeed have a residence in Rome

3] although praetorian records are sometimes unreliable, Archias' name does appear in those of the praetor Metellus, whose records are trustworthy

4] Archias was away from Rome on a campaign with Lucullus when the census was taken and, therefore, was not in a position to have been enrolled.

### Confirmatio (12-30)

In this portion of his speech, Cicero delivers a lengthy discourse on the place of the **artes liberales** and **artes optimae** (liberal arts and fine arts) in a society. The value of the artist, such as Archias, is implicit in Roman civilization. He says, "How many pictures portraying the deeds of the most stalwart men have Greek and Roman writers left behind for us not only for our contemplation but also for our emulation?" (14) Cicero makes the following points about literature, which

1] furnishes rest and relaxation from the stress of daily life

2] provides incentives to noble action and moral courage

3] serves as a stimulus to youth and a diversion to old age

4] chronicles the deeds of great men in song

5] allows the writer to leave something of himself behind.

Cicero also makes several personal comments: that reading has helped to improve his oratorical powers and that Archias has even celebrated Cicero's consulship in a poem. He also quotes the Roman poet Ennius as calling poets **sancti** (holy) and makes the further point that other cities vie to be the birthplace of great poets, such as Homer, rather than calling into question their provenance.

### Peroratio (31-32)

At the closing of his case, Cicero presents an emotional appeal to the gentlemen of the jury to protect the citizenship and reputation of a man who has done much for Rome and who has much more to offer.

## The *De Amicitia*

Cicero's discourse on friendship, in the manner of a Greek philosophical treatise, takes the form of a dialogue between interlocutors: Laelius, a renowned orator of the 2nd century B.C., and his sons-in law, Q. Mucius Scaevola and Gaius Fannius Strabo. There are eleven chapters of the *De Amicitia*, 17–23 and 100–104, required for the choice author exam.

### Chapters 1-16 (English)

Cicero opens his treatise addressed to Atticus with the explanation that, as a boy, he had been left in the charge of the augur Q. Mucius Scaevola, the son-in-law of

Gaius Laelius, who was known as "the Wise." He explains that he will re-create as a dialogue a conversation on friendship that Laelius had had with Scaevola and another son-in-law, Gaius Fannius, following the death of Scipio Africanus. Cicero alludes to his work *De Senectute*, which he puts in the words of Cato the Elder, who was then an elderly man. Both Fannius and Scaevola comment on the composure shown by Laelius upon learning of his friend Scipio's death. Laelius ruminates on the subject of friendship, claiming that it is not he, Scipio, who has lost something but he, Laelius, who has lost a friend. There follows an exposition of Scipio's life as well-lived, which leads to acknowledgment of the Pythagorean belief that the soul exists separately from the body and that it survives death. Laelius speaks of the enjoyment he derives from recalling his friendship with Scipio. Fannius and Scaevola then ask Laelius to comment on the "theory and practice" of friendship.

### Chapters 17-23 (Latin)

- Laelius begins (Chapters 17–18) with the statement that friendship can only exist between those who are good, i.e., are in possession of these qualities: **fides** (loyalty), **integritas** (uprightness), **aequitas** (fairness), and **liberalitas** (generosity), plus freedom from passion, fickleness, and impudence, as well as displaying **constantia** (strength of character). He says, **Ego vos hortari tantum possum ut amicitiam omnibus rebus humanis anteponatis.**

- In Chapters 18–21, we learn that there exists between us a certain tie that grows stronger with our proximity to each other. Friendship is nothing other than accord (**consensio**) in all things, both human and divine, mixed with goodwill (**benevolentia**) and affection (**caritas**). It is second only to wisdom among the gifts of the gods.

- In Chapter 22, Cicero/Laelius discusses the fact that friendship allows us to share our joys and sorrows and that friendship that is real (**vera et perfecta**) is steadfast and ever present.

- Chapter 23 presents the idea that a friend is another self (**exemplar aliquod sui**). A true friend is "with you" even when you are alone. When the bond of goodwill (**coniunctio benevolentia**) is gone, what hope is there for either individuals or commonwealths?

### Chapters 100-104 end (Latin)

- In the four chapters that end the dialogue (100–104), the interlocutors discuss the fact that **virtus** (virtue) both creates and preserves the bond of friendship. Virtue consists of **convenientia rerum** (harmony), **stabilitas** (dependability), and **constantia** (steadfastness). Because the words friendship (**amicitia**) and love (**amor**) both come from the verb **amare**, love, with the idea of one who is cherished or esteemed, is an important part of the meaning of friendship. Laelius ends by speaking warmly of his great friendship for Scipio.

# Horace

## A Quick-Study of the Twenty Odes of Horace

| Corpus | Meter | Length | Addressee | Topic |
|--------|-------|--------|-----------|-------|
| **Book 1** | | | | |
| 1 | | 36 | Maecenas | Dedication |
| 5 | | 15 | Pyrrha | Love shipwrecked |
| 9 | Alcaic | 24 | Thaliarchus | Soracte (Carpe diem) |
| 11 | | 8 | Leuconoe | Carpe diem |
| 13 | | 20 | Lydia | Jealousy |
| 22 | Sapphic | 24 | Fuscus | Love for Lalage |
| 23 | | 12 | Chloe | Young love |
| 24 | | 24 | Melpomene, Vergil | Death of Quintilius |
| 25 | Sapphic | 20 | Lydia | Lydia's lost charms |
| 37 | Alcaic | 32 | Comrades | Cleopatra |
| 38 | Sapphic | 8 | Servant boy | Carpe diem |
| **Book 2** | | | | |
| 3 | Alcaic | 28 | Dellius | Carpe diem |
| 7 | Alcaic | 28 | Pompey | Amnesty for the soldier |
| 10 | Sapphic | 24 | Licinius | The Golden Mean |
| 14 | Alcaic | 28 | Postumus | Inevitability of death |
| **Book 3** | | | | |
| 1 | Alcaic | 48 | | Roman Ode - simplicity |
| 9 | | 24 | Lydia | Lovers' dialogue |
| 13 | Alcaic | 16 | Fons Bandusia | Horace's farm |
| 30 | | 16 | Melpomene | Horace's poetry |
| **Book 4** | | | | |
| 7 | | 28 | Torquatus | Carpe diem |

## An Index of First Lines of Horace's *Odes*

### Book 1

| | |
|---|---|
| 1 | Maecenas atavis edite regibus |
| 5 | Quis multa gracilis te puer in rosa |
| 9 | Vide ut alta stet nive candidum |
| 11 | Tu ne quaesieris – scire nefas – quem mihi, quem tibi |
| 13 | Cum tu, Lydia, Telephi |
| 22 | Integer vitae scelerisque purus |
| 23 | Vitas hinnuleo me simils, Chloe |
| 24 | Quis desiderio sit pudor aut modus |
| 25 | Parcius iunctas quatiunt fenestras |
| 37 | Nunc est bibendum, nunc pede libro |
| 38 | Persicos odi, puer, apparatus |

### Book 2

| | |
|---|---|
| 3 | Aequam memento rebus in arduis |
| 7 | O saepe mecum tempus in ultimum |
| 10 | Rectius vives, Licini, neque altum |
| 14 | Eheu fugaces, Postume, Postume |

### Book 3

| | |
|---|---|
| 1 | Odi profanum vulgus et arceo |
| 9 | "Donec gratus eram tibi" |
| 13 | O fons Bandusiae, splendidior vitro |
| 30 | Exegi monumentum aere perennius |

### Book 4

| | |
|---|---|
| 7 | Diffugere nives, redeunt iam gramina campis |

## Horace's *Satires* 1.9

Because of its similarity to Roman comedy, Horace's hexameter poem, popularly known as "The Pest" or "The Boor," will be outlined below as Acts in a drama.

### Act 1 (lines 1-12)

While strolling downtown, Horace is approached by someone slightly familiar to him. He makes it known, at first through hints and suggestions, and then by direct statement, that he would prefer to be by himself. The Pest presses on, insistent upon trying to impress Horace that he is a "poetry person." Finally, Horace invents the pretext of needing to visit a sick friend—across town. Alas, he is unsuccessful in freeing himself of the Pest.

### *Act 2 (lines 23-43)*

The Pest blathers on, celebrating his skill at speed writing, dancing, and singing, all of which are too bourgeois for Horace. After suggesting that the Pest attend to relatives—any relatives—("I've buried them all!" he retorts), Horace relates that he is fated by prophecy to die, not by poison or the sword, not by wheezing and coughing, or gout, but by prolonged exposure to a busy-body. They have now reached the Temple of Vesta at the time when courts are in session, and the Pest has an appointment as a defendant. Unfortunately, he chooses to stick with Horace.

### *Act 3 (lines 43-74)*

The Pest's inquiries from Horace about his patron Maecenas make it clear that the Pest has had ulterior motives in pursuing Horace. The poet, now piqued, does his best to set the busy-body straight and indicates that audiences are not sought in literary circles. At this moment, Horace's buddy Aristius Fuscus (see *Ode* 1.2) happens by and immediately spots an opportunity to have some fun at Horace's expense. He resists all of Horace's nods, winks, and outright begging, and quickly moves off to "another engagement," leaving Horace **sub cultro** (under the knife).

### *Act 4 (lines 74-78)*

Whereupon, the Pest's legal adversary arrives and issues a loud public challenge, defaming the Pest. Horace is recruited as a witness and now must face further time spent with the busy-body. With boisterous pushing and shoving, all make their way to the courts. Horace's final words, **Sic me servavit Apollo**, have been taken by some as ironic: "So <u>this</u> is how you've saved me, Apollo!"

# Ovid

## Daphne and Apollo (*Metamorphoses*, 1.452-567)

### *Episode*

Lines 452–65     Apollo was caused to fall in love with Daphne because of the jealousy of Cupid, who was peeved at Apollo for openly boasting about killing the Python and for belittling him. Apollo has never been in love before.

Lines 466–80     Cupid counters Apollo's boasts and claims power even over other gods. From Mt. Parnassus, he shoots Apollo with a golden arrow, forcing him to fall in love, and shoots Daphne with a leaden arrow, causing her to flee from love. Daphne heads for the woods to escape her many suitors.

Lines 481–502     Daphne's father, the river god Peneus, counsels her to marry and produce grandsons. Daphne replies by invoking the celibacy of the goddess Diana. Peneus yields. The stubble-field simile expresses the fiery passion of Apollo, who praises her physical beauty.

Lines 503–24    Apollo continues to pursue Daphne, asking her not to fear him and praising his own attributes as the son of the Jupiter. These include prophecy, music, and medicine, which alas cannot cure him of love.

Lines 525–39    Apollo continues to chase Daphne, which is described in the hare and hound simile.

Lines 540–52    About to be caught, Daphne calls upon her father to rescue her. She begins to transform into a tree.

Lines 553–67    Apollo, still in love with her, embraces her as a tree and vows to keep her with him always as his sacred symbol, to adorn his hair, lyre, and quiver. Reference is made to the laurel wreath as a symbol of victory and to the citizen's crown won by Augustus. As Apollo is ever-young, so shall the laurel be ever-green.

## Pyramus and Thisbe (*Metamorphoses*, 4.55-166)

Lines 55–64     Pyramus and Thisbe fall in love, but their parents forbid it. The lovers communicate with nods and signs.

Lines 65–80     The lovers discover a crack in the wall common to their houses and communicate through it. They address the wall in a lament over their separation.

Lines 81–104    The next day they meet at the usual spot and plot to sneak out that night to meet at Ninus' tomb and hide under a designated tree.

Lines 105–18    Thisbe, her face veiled, steals out and makes her way to the tree. A lioness suddenly appears at the spring nearby and frightens Thisbe, who flees to a nearby cave. The lioness tears at the veil, which Thisbe has left behind, and then moves on. Pyramus arrives and, drawing the conclusion that Thisbe has been killed, first invites the lion to kill him as well, and then stabs himself.

Lines 119–36    The leaky pipe simile leads to the fruit of the mulberry tree, sprinkled with the blood of Pyramus, which changes its color from white to red. Thisbe leaves the cave and, seeking out her lover, discovers him in the throes of death. Her countenance "shivers like the sea when a slight breeze ruffles its surface."

Lines 137–50    Thisbe embraces the dying Pyramus and calls his name. After he dies, Thisbe determines to stab herself also.

Lines 151–66    In Thisbe's lengthy death-speech, she prays that her parents will bury them in the same tomb and that the mulberry tree "keep the marks of our death and always bear the fruit of a dark color." She stabs herself and dies.

### Daedalus and Icarus (*Metamorphoses*, 8.183-235)

Lines 183–200   Daedalus plans his escape from Crete, where he is held prisoner by King Minos. With the help of his son Icarus, the famous craftsman fashions wings.

Lines 202–16   Icarus receives flying instructions.

Lines 217–35   While flying over the Aegean Sea, Icarus disobeys his father and falls to his death. Some fishermen witness the tragedy.

### Baucis and Philemon (*Metamorphoses*, 8.616-724)

Lines 616–36   Jupiter and Mercury visit the mortal world, where they are refused hospitality by everyone except a poor old couple, Baucis and her husband Philemon.

Lines 637–60   The gods (unrecognized by the couple) are invited into their humble home and preparations for a meal begin, including making ready the dining couch.

Lines 660–78   The meal begins.

Lines 679–702   A wonderful omen occurs, leading Baucis and Philemon to attempt a sacrifice of their only goose. Jove and Mercury reveal themselves as gods and make a startling promise.

Lines 703–24   The gods grant the couple a request, and Philemon expresses their wish to die together. Their house is transformed into a temple and husband and wife are changed into trees that will protect the sanctuary.

### Pygmalion (*Metamorphoses*, 10.238-97)

Lines 238–53   The Propoetides, daughters of the Cypriot Propoetus, refuse to acknowledge the divinity of Venus and are hardened into prostitutes. They are the reason why Pygmalion has become disenchanted with women and has determined to be celibate. He sculpts the statue of a woman and falls in love with it.

Lines 254–69   Pygmalion begins to believe that the statue is alive and begins to treat it as if it were a real woman, dressing and decorating it.

Lines 270–79   The festal day of Venus arrives and Pygmalion sacrifices and prays to the goddess for a wife. Venus agrees.

Lines 280–97   The statue comes alive. Venus then marries them and a child, Paphos, is born.

### *Amores* 1.1

Lines 1–20   Ovid claims that he was ready to write epic poetry (in dactylic hexameter) when Cupid stole a foot (making the line pentameter). An affronted Ovid challenges Cupid with the argument, "What if the gods changed roles?" and gives some examples. Ovid then tells Cupid to stick to what he knows best, love poetry, about which Ovid knows little and cares less.

Lines 21–30    In response, Cupid strings his bow and sends a shaft into Ovid, who now is constrained by his own feelings of love to write love poetry in elegaic meter (five feet, instead of six).

## *Amores* 1.3

Lines 1–6    Ovid asks Venus to hear his prayer that his girl love him.

Lines 7–16    The poet speaks of his qualifications: he does not have ancient ancestry nor abundant resources to offer, but Apollo and the Muses favor him. He enjoys steadfastness (**fides**), good character (**mores**), thrift (**simplicitas**), and modesty (**pudor**).

Lines 17–26    Mythological allusions celebrate the lasting power of song: Io, Leda, and Europa. Ovid and his girl will together achieve everlasting fame.

## *Amores* 1.9

Lines 1–16    This poem presents a detailed comparison between a lover and a soldier. The following points of comparison are noted in these lines: Both require youth; courage and vigor; remaining awake on guard through the night; following a "long road" to duty and withstanding rough terrain and the elements.

Lines 17–30    The comparison continues. Both are spies, one scouting the foe, the other keeping an eye out for a rival; both are sackers, the one besieging towns, the other the doorway of an unwilling mistress; both profit from sneak attacks, the one by surprising the enemy while asleep, the other taking advantage of a sleeping husband; both are sneaky and need to be able to pass through guards.

Lines 31–46    The poem ends with some comparisons from the Trojan War. Lovers are men of action. References are made to Achilles, Hector and Andromache, Agamemnon and Cassandra, and to the tale of Mars, Venus, and Vulcan. Ovid remarks about his own habits of idleness and vows to be "full of action and waging the wars of night."

## *Amores* 1.11

Lines 1–14    Ovid's handmaid Nape is of great help to him in arranging nighttime trysts with Corinna. Nape is charged here with the task of taking a message to her.

Lines 15–28    Nape is instructed to have Corinna read the tablets right away and to observe her reaction to what she reads. Ovid also wants a lengthy reply. He then changes his mind and asks only for the word

"Veni!" Ovid would then consider these tablets love trophies and hang them in the Temple of Venus, with a suitable inscription.

## *Amores* 1.12

| | |
|---|---|
| Lines 1–12 | This poem, which contains Corinna's answer to the invitation in 1.11, serves as its companion piece. It is an apostrophe to Ovid's tablets, which have been returned to him with the Roman equivalent of "Not tonight, I have a headache." In the opening lines, Ovid attempts to justify his rejection by alluding to the ill omen of Nape tripping over the threshold as she was departing. Ovid curses the wax of the tablets. |
| Lines 13–28 | Ovid continues to curse the tablets, this time the wood, which must have come from a hanging tree that was home to owls and vultures and other birds of ill-omen. These tablets would have been better used carrying the dry-as-dust accounts of some lawyer or banker. Ovid then prays that "rotten old age eat you away and that your wax grow colorless from neglect." |

## *Amores* 3.15

| | |
|---|---|
| Lines 1–20 | In this final poem of the *Amores*, Ovid celebrates his birthplace Sulmona, which he has made famous through his success as a writer. He makes reference to the birthplaces of Vergil and Catullus. Ovid bids goodbye to Cupid and to the writing of love elegies. |

# Answers to Speech Identifications in the *Aeneid*

## Book 1

1. Juno to Aeolus
2. Aeneas to Juno
3. Aeneas
4. Neptune to the winds
5. Aeneas to his comrades
6. Venus to Jupiter
7. Jupiter to Venus
8. Aeneas to Venus (as huntress)
9. Venus to Aeneas
10. Aeneas to Venus
11. Aeneas
12. Aeneas to Achates

## Book 2

1. Aeneas to Dido
2. Laocoon to the Trojans
3. Aeneas to Hector
4. Hector to Aeneas
5. Hecuba to Priam
6. Priam to Pyrrhus
7. Pyrrhus to Priam
8. Creusa to Aeneas

## Book 4

1. Dido to Anna
2. Anna to Dido
3. Juno to Venus
4. Venus to Juno
5. Iarbas to Jupiter
6. Jupiter to Mercury
7. Dido to Aeneas
8. Aeneas to Dido
9. Dido to Aeneas
10. Dido to Anna
11. Aeneas to crew
12. Dido
13. Dido to the pyre
14. Anna to dead Dido

## Book 6

1. Sibyl
2. Sibyl/Apollo
3. Aeneas to Sibyl
4. Sibyl to Aeneas
5. Aeneas
6. Aeneas to Dido
7. Anchises to Aeneas

## Book 10

1. Pallas to Tiberinus
2. Turnus to the Rutuli
3. Pallas to Hercules
4. Jupiter to Hercules
5. Turnus to the Arcadians

## Book 12

1. Jupiter to Juno
2. Jupiter to Juno
3. Aeneas to Turnus
4. Turnus to Aeneas
5. Aeneas to Turnus

# Chapter 10

# Figures of Speech

Figures of speech (also referred to as poetic techniques or rhetorical devices) present a way of saying something in a manner that is not obvious or ordinary. They allow poets to express their inner voices creatively. The *AP Latin Course Description* lists 34 figures of speech to be mastered for the AP Latin Exam. These are tested explicitly in context on the multiple-choice section and in the "spot" identification questions on the Latin Literature exam, as well as implicitly in the essay questions on the free-response section that ask for analysis of a writer's style. A frequency study of figures of speech appearing on AP Latin Exams from 2006–2001 indicates a preference for the following figures, in order of preference: chiasmus and synchysis, asyndeton, anaphora, metaphor, litotes, hendiadys, and tricolon crescens. Each of these appeared more than once, whereas assonance (no longer on the list), ellipsis, irony, metonymy, and simile each appeared one time. This information is provided not to suggest that these are the only figures of speech worth knowing, but to suggest that these particular figures may be considered among the most important for mastery.

In your review of figures of speech, pay particular attention to those figures that have similar functions or are easily confused, such as apostrophe and personification, chiasmus and synchysis, hendiadys and zeugma, metonymy and synecdoche, and metaphor and simile. It is unlikely, however, that you will be asked to distinguish between two easily-confused figures of speech, such as metonymy and synecdoche, in the same question. Of those figures not required for the exam but helpful to know in order to create a successful critical analysis of (poetic) style, review the following: anastrophe, assonance, condensation, irony, parallelism, and sound and word play (for which, see below).

As over 200 figures of speech have been recognized, it is best not to take any classification of function as absolute. Many figures can perform several functions simultaneously, e.g., hyperbaton and chiasmus: **speluncam Dido dux et Troianus eandem** (Dido and Aeneas are together in the same cave, *Aeneid* 4.124), or can achieve heightened effectiveness in conjunction with another figure, e.g., alliteration and onomatopoeia: **fit sonitus spumante salo** (describing the sound of the sea as the snakes slither along, *Aeneid* 2.209), or can accelerate words or actions, e.g., asyndeton and ellipsis: **Rapit in ius: clamor utrimque: undique concursus** (describing the hubbub as the plaintiff hauls the Pest off to court, Horace, *Satires* 1.9.77–78). These four words in Catullus, (Poem 51.11–12) – **gemina teguntur/lumina nocte** – contain a number of different figures of speech: antithesis (**lumina nocte**), assonance and rhyme (**gemina-lumina**), metaphor or metonymy (**lumina** for **oculi**), and transferred epithet (**gemina** to **lumina** from **nocte** or to **nocte** from **lumina**). There are two important things to remember about figures of speech:

1] a figure of speech is important only because of the <u>effect</u> that the figure has on the meaning of what is being expressed;

2] the listing and defining of figures of speech is never, by itself, an efficient or effective way to produce a style analysis of a passage of Latin. Consider only those which are obvious.

Some students believe that searching through a Latin passage for figures of speech is like collecting Easter eggs. The more you have, the better off you'll be. Such an approach never addresses the explicit analysis called for in a free-response essay question. Recognition and citation of a few <u>relevant</u> figures, with <u>explanation of their effect on the context</u> in which they are found, is certainly useful support for your analysis, but this will never substitute for a thoughtful and well-focused essay.

All the figures of speech required for the exam, as well as all others mentioned in this introduction, are reviewed below and are accompanied by practice activities for each of the five Latin authors. For further discussion on how these devices may be used in an analysis of style on the free-response section of the exam, see the example just below, the appropriate section of Chapter 7, and the detailed answers to the essay questions on the Practice Exams at the end of this book.

## Sample AP Latin Questions on Figures of Speech

### *Sample question of the type that might appear on the multiple-choice section:*

1.  The words <u>Figat tuus omnia, Phoebe, te meus arcus</u> (line 2) give an example of

    (A) personification

    (B) anaphora

    (C) litotes

    (D) chiasmus

**Answer:**

  **(D)** chiasmus

## Figures of Speech on the Free-Response Section

### Sample question from the spot or short identification question on Cicero, Horace, or Ovid:

> Dixit et eliso percussis aere pennis
> impiger umbrosa Parnasi constitit arce
> eque sagittifera prompsit duo tela pharetra
> diversorum operum.

### *Metamorphoses* 1.466–69

### Question:

Name the figure of speech that occurs in lines 1–2 (<u>dixit</u> . . . <u>arce</u>), and write out the Latin that illustrates it.

### Answer:

Line 1 provides an illustration of interlocked word order, or synchysis. The words <u>eliso percussis aere pennis</u> appear in an ABAB order, resulting in participle-noun combinations of <u>eliso aere</u> and <u>percussis pennis</u>. (Recognition of the alliteration of sibilants as suggestive of the whirring of Cupid's wings is also an acceptable answer.)

The following is a sample free-response essay question to illustrate the use of figures of speech in a poetic analysis. This question is an abbreviated version of a short essay.

> Fit sonitus spumante salo; iamque arva tenebant
> ardentesque oculos suffecti sanguine et igni
> sibila lambebant linguis vibrantibus ora.

### *Aeneid* 2.209–11

### Question:

In the passage above, Vergil presents a vivid description of two sea serpents, whose arrival in the story is critical to the story of the fall of Troy. In a short essay, discuss how the poet depicts the monsters in a manner that foreshadows the fall of Troy.

### Answer:

Through alliteration and onomatopoeia, the poet skillfully interweaves the sounds of the sea and the serpent, both of which bring destruction to Troy. The sea brings death in the form of both the Greek fleet and the two sea-dragons, the latter determined to kill Laocoon. In another part of this same passage, the serpents slither across the sea side-by-side, perhaps suggesting the flotilla of Greek ships. The sibilation (<u>sibila</u>, 3) of <u>sonitus spumante salo</u> (line 1) mimics both the sound of the surf and that of the hissing of the snakes. The hissing of snakes has a threatening effect on the reader. (Note the use of seven sibilants in lines 2–3.) The sounds in the next two lines reinforce the description of the twin serpents as something sinister and evil. Their flashing eyes (<u>ardentes oculos,</u> a metaphor) "suffused with blood and fire" (<u>suffecti sanguine et igni</u>) foreshadow the destruction of Troy. The flicking tongues (<u>linguis vibrantibus</u>) licking their hissing jaws come alive through the sounds and the rhythm of the multi-syllabic words, which also suggest the undulant movement of the serpents across the surface of the sea. Perhaps Vergil is continuing his portrayal of the deadly snakes by depicting their tongues (<u>linguis vibrantibus</u>) flicking from inside their hissing jaws (<u>sibila . . . ora,</u> line 3). The sea, the serpents, and the ships are all of a piece.

## Glossary of Figures Required for the AP Latin Exam

The first example or examples of each figure of speech are underlined, to assist you in your identification. Practice identifying the figure on your own in the remaining examples. Additional information is included to assist your understanding of the figure. As often as possible, at least one example is provided from each author.

- **allegory**: an extended metaphor. A narrative in which abstract ideas figure as circumstances or persons, such as the personification of **Fama** (Rumor) in *Aeneid* 4.173–97 or the use of Cupid's victory over Apollo to represent the triumph of passion over reason in Ovid's *Metamorphoses* 1.452–73.

  Effects: adds interest, teaches a moral lesson.

- **alliteration**: repetition of the same consonantal sound, usually at the beginning or within two or more successive words, e.g., **<u>m</u>agno <u>c</u>um <u>m</u>ur<u>m</u>ure <u>m</u>ontis**. Alliteration is often combined with **onomatopoeia** for which, see below.

  Effects:   emphasizes, enlivens.

  English:   Peter Piper picked a peck of pickled peppers.

  Let us go forth to lead the land we love. (John F. Kennedy)

  Latin:   **<u>V</u>eni, <u>v</u>idi, <u>v</u>ici.** (Emphatic; Julius Caesar)

  **Hic aliud <u>m</u>aius <u>m</u>iseris <u>m</u>ultoque tre<u>m</u>endu<u>m</u>.** (Awesome, ominous; *Aeneid* 2.19)

  **Taurus et in<u>c</u>ertam ex<u>c</u>ussit <u>c</u>ervi<u>c</u>e se<u>c</u>urim.** (The sound of cutting or chopping during the sacrifice of a bull. *Aeneid* 2.224)

  **Aut <u>v</u>ocem mutare <u>v</u>iros aut <u>v</u>ertere <u>v</u>estem.** (*Aeneid* 12.925)

  **Ut te postremo donarem munere mortis/et mutam nequiquam adloquerer cinerem.** (Note how the alliteration of the **m**'s gives a solemn, mournful sound in the context of Catullus' grief for his brother. Catullus, Poem 101.3–4; cf. Catullus, Poem 3.11–16)

**Non dubitavit Martis manubias Musis consecrare.** (Solemn, dignified. Cicero, *Pro Archia*, 27)

**Saxis, unde loquaces/lymphae desiliunt tuae.** (The water of Bandusia is lively, as well as life-giving. Note also the personification in the use of **loquaces**. Horace, *Odes* 3.13.15–16)

**O multum miseri meus illiusque parentes.** (Solemn, mournful; Thisbe speaks after Pyramus dies. Ovid, *Metamorphoses* 4.155)

Compare **assonance**: **paucis, si tibi di favent, diebus.** (Catullus, Poem 13.2)

Compare **onomatopoeia**: **namque mei nuper Lethaeo in gurgite fratris.** (Suggests the gurgling sound of water. Catullus, Poem 65.5)

- **anaphora**: repetition of a word, usually at the beginning of successive phrases, clauses, or lines. Anaphora, which appears frequently in all AP authors (particularly Vergil and Cicero) is often accompanied by **asyndeton**.

Effect: emphasizes.

English: Blessed are the poor in spirit . . ./Blessed are the meek . . ./Blessed are they who mourn. . . . (Beatitudes, *Gospel of Saint Matthew*)

We shall not flag or fail. We shall go on to the end. We shall fight in France, we shall fight on the seas and oceans . . . we shall never surrender. (Winston Churchill)

Latin: **Tu mihi quodcumque hoc regni, tu sceptra Iovemque/ concilias, tu das epulis accumbere divum.** (*Aeneid* 1.78–79)

**Dein mille altera, dein secunda centum,/deinde usque altera mille, deinde centum.** (Catullus, Poem 5. 8–9)

**Quantum** (six times! Cicero, *Pro Archia Poeta* 13)

**Nunc est bibendum, nunc pede libero/pulsanda tellus, nunc Saliaribus/ornare . . . tempus erat dapibus.** (Horace, *Odes* 1.37.1–4)

**Semper habebunt te coma, te citharae, te nostrae, laure, pharetrae.** (Ovid, *Metamorphoses* 1.558–59)

With **asyndeton**: **nostra sunt tropaea, nostra monumenta, nostri triumphi.** (Cicero, *Pro Archia Poeta* 21)

- **aposiopesis**: an abrupt break in a sentence, wherein the speaker is seemingly overwhelmed with anger, fear, excitement, or some other excessive emotion. An unfinished thought, the implied meaning of which is usually clear. The only example appearing in the Exam literature is provided here below.

See also **ellipsis**.

Effect: creates dramatic energy

English: He said he realized he was wro . . . I stopped mid-word, awestruck. His behavior was . . . but I blush to mention that. Oh, go to . . . !

Latin: **Quos ego ---! sed motos praestat componere fluctus.** (Neptune, *Aeneid* 1.135)

*Which I – but it is better to calm the troubled waters.*

Compare **ellipsis**: **Sic notus (est) Ulixes?** (*Aeneid* 2.44)

- **apostrophe:** a "turning away" from one to address another; often used to address an absent personified object or person. Apostrophe differs from **personification** in that it addresses an object directly, rather than merely describing it in human terms. Apostrophe appears frequently in Vergil and Catullus. See also **personification.**

Effects: expresses deep emotion and pathos; draws the reader into the situation

English: For Brutus, as you know, was Caesar's angel.

Judge, O you gods, how dearly Caesar loved him. (Shakespeare, *Julius Caesar*)

Alas, poor Yorick, I knew him, Horatio! (Shakespeare, *Hamlet*)

Latin: **O patria, O divum domus Ilium!** (*Aeneid* 2.241; cf. 2.56)

**Improbe Amor, quid non mortalia pectora cogis!** (*Aeneid* 4.412)

**O funde noster, seu Sabine seu Tiburs.** (Catullus, Poem 44.1)

**Invide, dicebant, paries, quid amantibus obstas?** (Ovid, *Metamorphoses* 4.73)

Compare **personification**: **et Claros et Tenedos Patareaque regia servit.** (Apollo's cult sites "serve" him as slaves do a master. Ovid, *Metamorphoses*, 1.516)

- **asyndeton:** the omission of connectors (**et, nec, vel,** etc.) in a closely related series in order to impress the reader by a rapid statement of ideas.

Effects: accelerates the words or actions; expresses non-stop action or violence.

English: But in a larger sense, we cannot dedicate, we cannot consecrate, we cannot hallow this ground. (Abraham Lincoln)

We shall pay any price, bear any burden, meet any hardships, support any friend, oppose any foe, to assure the survival and the success of liberty. (John F. Kennedy)

Latin:  **Saevus ubi Aeacidae telo iacet Hector, ubi ingens/Sarpe-don, ubi tot Simois correpta sub undis/scuta virum.** (*Ae-neid* 1.99–100)

**Chartae regiae, novi libri, novi umbilici, lora rubra, membranae.** (Catullus, Poem 22.5–7)

**Versatur urna serius ocius.** (Horace, *Odes* 2.3.26)

**Nec, quid Hymen, quid Amor, quid sint conubia, curat.** (Ovid, *Metamorphoses* 1.480)

Compare **polysyndeton: haec a te dictaque factaque sunt.** (Catullus, Poem 76.8)

- **chiasmus:** a criss-cross patterning of words, often nouns and adjectives, in the arrangement ABBA, e.g., noun-adjective-adjective-noun. Two corresponding pairs arranged in inverted or reverse, rather than parallel (ABAB) word order. The term comes from the shape of the Greek letter chi (X) and often emphasizes a contrast between the two pairs of words. Thus, **fracti** (A) **fatis** (B) **belloque** (B) **repulsi** (A) means *broken* (A) *by the fates* (B) *and by war* (B) *driven back* (A). In a broader sense, any ABBA word order may be considered chiastic, e.g., **vasto rex Aeolus antro**, but in sense the reversal isn't the same, i.e., *a vast king/Aeolus in a cave*. For more on such framing or embedding, see **hyperbaton**, below. Chiastic word order is commonly found in all AP Latin authors. See also **golden line**, **hyperbaton**, and **synchysis**.

Effects:  contrast.

          A     B          B       A

English:  The *cat* jumped in, out jumped the *mouse*.

Fair is foul, and foul is fair. (Shakespeare, *Macbeth*)

Renown'd for conquest, and in council skill'd. (Joseph Addison)

I am Sam, Sam I am. (Dr. Seuss, Theodor Geisel)

          A      B     B         A

Latin:  **Steteruntque comae et vox faucibus haesit.** (*Aeneid* 2.774)

**Oraclum Iovis inter sepulcrum/et Batti veteris sacrum sepulcrum**. (Catullus Poem 7.5–6)

**Gravedo frigida et frequens tussis.** (Catullus Poem 44.13)

**Spatium praeteriti temporis et pueritiae memoriam.** (Cicero, *Pro Archia Poeta* 1)

**Integer vitae scelerisque purus.** (Horace, *Odes,* 1.22.1)

**Hinc Thisbe, Pyramus illinc.** (Ovid, *Metamorphoses* 10.71)

          A        B       C     A      B

Compare **golden line: obviaque adversas vibrabant flamina vestes.** (Ovid, *Metamorphoses* 1.528–9)

|  | A | B | B | A |
|---|---|---|---|---|

Compare **hyperbaton**: **vox, huius hortatu praeceptisque, conformata.** (**Vox** and **conformata** frame the ablatives **hortatu praeceptisque**, creating chiasmus. Cicero, *Pro Archia Poeta* 1)

|  | A | B | A | B |
|---|---|---|---|---|

Compare **synchysis**: **paries domui communis utrique.** (Note how the walls of the houses of Pyramus and Thisbe interlock. Ovid, *Metamorphoses* 1.66)

- **ecphrasis:** a digression vividly describing a place, object, or event. In epic poetry, this device creates transition to a new scene.

  Effect: adds vividness, interest.

  Latin: See *Aeneid* 1.159–70 for the elaborate description of the harbor into which Aeneas' fleet limps after the storm, the murals in the Temple of Juno at Carthage (Book 4.456ff.), the description of the doors of the Temple of Apollo at Cumae (Book 6.20–33), or the description of Aeneas' shield in Book 8.626–728. In Catullus' epyllion, see the description of the bedspread in Poem 64, lines 50ff.

- **ellipsis:** omission of an easily understood or assumed word in order to avoid repetition, to secure rapidity of narration, or to accommodate the requirements of meter. The understood word is often a form of **esse**, but can also be a form of the verb **ago, dico, facio, inquit,** or **loquor**. See also **aposiopesis.**

  Effects: creates variety of style, accelerates the narrative.

  English: Ellipsis points are used in questions throughout the AP Latin Exam, e.g., "In lines 3–4 (<u>Melpomene</u> . . . <u>dedit</u>)."

  Latin: **(Suntne) tantae animis caelestibus irae?** (*Aeneid* 1.11)

  **Aeolus haec contra (dixit).** (*Aeneid* 1.76)

  **Vovit ... electissima pessimi poetae/scripta tardipedi deo daturam (esse).** (Catullus, Poem 36.6–7)

  **Tu ne quaesieris – scire nefas (est) – quem mihi, quem tibi.** (Horace, *Odes* 1.11.1)

  **Primus amor Phoebi Daphne Peneia (fuit).** (Ovid, *Metamorphoses* 1.452)

- **enjambment** (also spelled **enjambement**): in verse, the building of suspense by postponing to the next line a significant word or words related to the previous line. A run-on line. A favorite of Horace.

  Effect: develops suspense and creates surprise.

  English: That honourable grief lodged here which burns

  Worse than tears drown. (Shakespeare, *The Winter's Tale*)

> All in the valley of death
>
> rode the six hundred. (Tennyson)

Latin: **Litora – multum ille et terris iactatus et alto vi superum.** (*Aeneid* 1.3–4)

**Ac veluti magno in populo cum saepe coorta est seditio.** (*Aeneid* 1.149–50)

**Sed identidem omnium ilia rumpens.** (Catullus, Poem 11.19–29)

**Venator in campis nivalis Haemoniae, daret ut catenis fatale monstrum.** (Horace, *Odes* 1.37.20–21)

**Da mihi perpetua, genitor carissime, dixit, virginitate frui.** (Ovid, *Metamorphoses* 1.486–87)

- **hendiadys:** the use of two nouns connected by a conjunction and having the meaning of a single modified noun, e.g., **vulgus et multitudo**, *the rabble and mob* (= the common herd) and **vi et armis**, *by force and by arms* (= by force of arms). Often known as "two for one." Common in Vergil and Cicero.

Effect: amplifies, adds force.

English: He arrived despite the <u>rain and weather</u>. (= He arrived despite the <u>rainy weather</u>.)

It is nice and cool today! (= nicely cool)

Latin: **Hoc metuens, <u>molemque et montes</u> insuper altos** (= **molem montium**, a mass of mountains. *Aeneid* 1.61)

**Dirae ferro et compagibus artis/claudentur Belli portae.** (Here, the gates are closed by iron and close-fitting joints, instead of close-fitting iron joints. *Aeneid* 1.293–4)

**Non belle uteris in ioco atque vino** (= **in ebrioso ioco**, in drunken revelry. Catullus, Poem 12.2)

**Quod si, ut suspicor, hoc novum ac repertum** (= **novissime repertum**, newly discovered. Catullus, Poem 14a.8)

**In iudiciis periculisque** (= **in iudiciorum periculis**, Cicero, *Pro Archia Poeta* 3)

**Aurarum et silvae metu** (= **aurarum silvae**; not "breezes and the forest," but "breezes of the forest." Horace, *Odes* 1.23.4)

**Tecum Philippos et celerem fugam/sensi.** (Horace experienced with Pompey the swift rout at Philippi. Horace, *Odes* 2.7.9–10)

> **Mille domos adiere locum requiemque petentes** (= **locum requietis**, place of rest. Ovid, *Metamorphoses* 8.628)
>
> **Mollierant animos lectus et umbra meos** (= **umbrosus lectus**, shaded couch. Ovid, *Amores* 1.9.42)

Compare **zeugma: crudeles <u>aras</u> traiectaque <u>pectora</u> ferro <u>nudavit</u>.** (He <u>laid bare</u> the cruel <u>altars</u> <u>and</u> his <u>breast</u> pierced with steel, describing Sychaeus' death. *Aeneid* 1.355–56)

- **hyperbaton:** a significant distortion of normal word order. The separation of words, such as an adjective from its noun, that logically belong together. This figure enables the writer to place words in a <u>framing</u> or <u>bracketing</u> position for emphasis or sound, rather than grammar. Words can actually surround objects, which may be said to be "embedded," e.g., **vasto rex Aeolus <u>antro</u>** (Aeolus, king of the winds, is inside his cave, *Aeneid* 1.52). Cicero favors this figure, which is often accompanied by **asyndeton. Anastrophe** is also a distortion of normal word order, but one that expresses some kind of reversal, e.g., **te propter** for the more usual **propter te. Chiasmus, synchysis,** or **golden line** may be associated with the use of hyperbaton.

Effects:   emphasizes the first of the separated words; creates images and word play.

English:   Glistens the dew upon the morning grass.

Why should their liberty than ours be more? (Shakespeare, *Comedy of Errors*)

Size matters not! Judge me by my size, do you? (Yoda, *The Empire Strikes Back*)

Latin:   **<u>Tantae</u> animis caelestibus <u>irae</u>?** (*Aeneid* 1.11)

**<u>Speluncam</u> Dido dux et Troianus <u>eandem</u>.** (Dido and Aeneas are together in the same cave. *Aeneid* 4.124)

**<u>Totum</u> ut te faciant, Fabulle, <u>nasum</u>.** (The size of Fabullus' would-be nose is exaggerated by the distance between **totum** and **nasum**. Note the anastrophe of **totum** and **ut**. Catullus, Poem 13.14)

**Non immerenti quam mihi meus venter,/dum sumptuosas appeto, dedit, cenas.** (The verb of the relative clause, **dedit,** is postponed, and interrupts the **dum** clause. Catullus, Poem 44.8–9)

**Ratio aliqua ab optimarum artium studiis ac disciplina profecta.** (Cicero emphasizes the extent of his intellectual pursuits and formal training. Cicero, *Pro Archia Poeta* 1)

**Ad populi Romani gloriam laudemque celebrandam.** (Cicero, *Pro Archia Poeta* 19)

**Aequam memento rebus in arduis/servare mentem.** (The arduous circumstances are exaggerated by the long separation of **Aequam** from **mentem**. Horace, *Odes* 2.3.1–2)

**letique miserrima dicar/causa comes tui.** (Ovid, *Metamorphoses* 4.151–2)

- **hyperbole:** exaggeration for emphasis or rhetorical effect; overstatement. See the description of the bad odor of Rufus' armpit in Catullus 69. Its opposite is **litotes**, understatement.

Effect:   stresses the importance or seriousness of a situation; helps the reader to experience it with those involved.

English:   I must have walked a million miles this summer.

How do I love thee? Let me count the ways. I love thee to the depth and breadth and height my soul can reach. (Elizabeth Barrett Browning)

Publishing a volume of verse is like dropping a rose-petal down the Grand Canyon and waiting for the echo. (Don Marquis)

Latin:   **Fluctusque <u>ad sidera</u> tollit.** (The wind raises the waves to the stars. *Aeneid* 1.103)

**Cumulo praeruptus <u>aquae mons</u>.** (Referring to a wave of the sea as mountainous. *Aeneid* 1.105)

**Puto esse ego illi milia aut decem aut plura/perscripta.** (Catullus, Poem 22.4)

**Disertissime Romuli nepotum,/<u>quot sunt quotque fuere</u>, Marce Tulli,/<u>quotque post aliis erunt in annis</u>** (Catullus, Poem 49.1–3)

**Stravimus innumeris tumidum Pythona sagittis.** (Ovid, *Metamorphoses* 1.460)

Compare **litotes**: **Salve, <u>nec minimo</u>** (= **magno**) **puella naso.** (Catullus, Poem 43.1)

- **hysteron proteron:** reversal of the normal or expected sequence of events in order to put the more important idea, which logically would come later in time, first. "Later-earlier." Hysteron proteron has also been defined as "a chiasmus of ideas," e.g., "You ask who I am and how old I am? I am thirty-nine and my name is Bob."[1] An uncommon figure.

Effect:   emphasizes a particular word or idea, or stresses the result of an action.

English:   Put on your shoes and socks! (Socks go on before shoes.)

I fled when I saw the monster. (Although the sense requires that the monster <u>before</u> the fear arises, in the word order, the fleeing precedes the seeing.)

---

[1] Thanks to Professor Tom Benediktson, University of Tulsa.

Latin: **Fatisque deum defensus iniquis/inclusos utero <u>Danaos</u> et pinea furtim/<u>laxat claustra</u> Sinon.** (Sinon releases the Greeks inside the horse before releasing the bolt securing the trapdoor. *Aeneid* 2.257–59)

**Moriamus et in media arma ruamus**. (Let us die and rush into battle. *Aeneid* 2.353)

**Ut tecum loquerer simulque ut essem.** (Speaking is placed before being together. Catullus, Poem 50.13)

**Praedicari de se ac nominari volunt.** (One's name must be known, **nominari,** before it can be made public**, praedicari**. Cicero, *Pro Archia Poeta* 26)

**Quidlibet impotens/sperare fortunaque dulci/ebria.** (The hope for anything is placed before the drunkenness that should produce it. Horace, *Odes*, 1.37.10–12)

Compare **prolepsis: <u>misero</u> quod omnes/eripit sensus <u>mihi</u>.** (The poet is unhappy <u>before</u> he has lost his senses. Catullus, Poem 51.5–6)

- **interlocked word order** (see **synchysis**)

- **irony:** the expression of something contrary to what is intended, i.e., the words say one thing but actually mean another. This usage is a sort of humor, ridicule, or light sarcasm that states an apparent fact with the manifest intention of expressing its opposite. Common in Catullus, Cicero, and Ovid.

Effect: adds humor or sarcasm.

English: We brave men do quite enough if we merely stand there looking. (The supposition is that we are cowards and for that reason we do nothing.)

Yet Brutus says he (Caesar) was ambitious; and Brutus is an honorable man. (Shakespeare, *Julius Caesar*)

Latin: **Iunone secunda,** *with Juno's favor.* (The opposite is meant. *Aeneid* 4.45)

**scilicet in superis labor est,** *of course this is work for the gods.* (This implies that the gods would not be concerned with such trifles. *Aeneid* 4.379)

**tanto pessimus omnium poeta/quanto tu (Cicero) optimus omni um patronus,** as much as (I *am) the worst poet of all, so are you the best benefactor of all.* (This implies that Cicero is as good a benefactor as Catullus is a bad poet, which of course he would not admit! Catullus, Poem 49.6–7)

- **litotes:** an understatement or double negative. Litotes consists of a negative word, such as **non** or **nec/neque**, and a following adjective with a negative prefix, e.g., **<u>non indecoro</u> pulvere sordidi**, *soiled with <u>not unbecoming</u>*, *i.e., glorious, dust* (Horace, *Odes* 2.1.22). This figure usually asserts something by denying its opposite. Its opposite is **hyperbole**, overstatement.

Effect: emphasizes.

English: He is <u>not</u> a <u>bad</u> ballplayer. = He is a good ball player.

I <u>kid</u> you <u>not</u>. = I am serious.

It is <u>not</u> <u>unusual.</u> = It is normal.

Latin: **Neque enim ignari sumus.** (*Aeneid* 1.198)

**Non sane illepidum neque invenustum.** (Catullus 10.4)

**Et hic Romae propter tranquillitatem rei publicae non neglegebantur.** (Cicero, *Pro Archia Poeta* 5)

**Non sine (= cum) vano/. . . metu.** (Horace, *Odes* 1.23.3–4)

**Nec sumus ingrati: tibi nos debere fatemur.** (Ovid, *Metamorphoses* 4.76)

Compare **hyperbole: Servata centum clavibus et mero.** (Horace *Odes*, 2.14.26)

- **metaphor:** an implied comparison, made through the figurative use of words that <u>suggest</u> a likeness between what is actually being described and something else, e.g., **remigio alarum,** *the oarage of his wings* (speaking of Mercury's wings as ship's oars, *Aeneid* 1.301). Metaphors apply the qualities of something familiar to give form and substance to something less familiar. The comparison is made in the mind of the reader and is more often than not expressed in a single word. As figurative language, metaphor and **simile** are more common in poetry than prose.

Effect: creates interest, or further understanding of something unfamiliar; stimulates the imagination.

English: to bite the bullet; unbridled anger; don't count your chickens before they're hatched; that's a horse of a different color; to be on an even keel; to take the bull by the horns; a wildcat strike.

All the world's a stage,/and all the men and women merely players/they have their exits and their entrances. (Shakespeare, *As You Like It*)

A bad-tempered elbow. (V.S. Pritchett)

Latin: **Invadunt urbem somno vinoque sepultam** (Note also the foreshadowing in the word "buried" here. *Aeneid* 2.265)

**At regina gravi iamdudum saucia cura/vulnus alit venis et caeco carpitur igni.** (Dido is seriously wounded by her love for Aeneas. Note the interlocking of **regina gravi . . . saucia cura,** and the mixed images of nursing a wound [**vulnus alit**] and being consumed by blind fire [**caeco carpitur igni**]. *Aeneid* 4.1–2)

**Ignes interiorem edunt medullam.** (She's feeling the passion of love-fire. Catullus, Poem 35.15)

**Quae iacerent in tenebris omnia, nisi litterarum lumen accederet.** (All would lie in darkness, but for the "light" of literature. Cicero, *Pro Archia Poeta* 14)

**Aspera/nigris aequora ventis/(emirabitur insolens).** (The youth wonders at Pyrrha, who is compared to a storm at sea. Horace, *Odes* 1.5.6–7)

**uritur, et sterilem sperando nutrit amorem.** (Fire again is used as a metaphor for [Apollo's] passion. Ovid, *Metamorphoses*, 1.496)

Compare **simile**: **ac venti, <u>velut agmine facto</u>** (the winds are explicitly compared to a line of soldiers. *Aeneid* 1.82)

- **metonymy:** use of one noun for another which it suggests, such as the substitution of the name of a deity for an attribute, e.g., Ceres, goddess of agriculture, for grain. Metonymy is a benchmark of epic style. The distinction between metonymy and the closely-related figure **synecdoche** is subtle and confusing; many use metonymy as a term for both.

Effects: avoids commonplace words; conveys what is abstract in concrete terms.

English: jock for athlete, brass for military officers, salt for sailor, Band-Aid for bandage, Coke for soft drink, Kleenex for tissue, Xerox for photocopy.

He is a man of the cloth. (He wears a collar or vestment and is therefore a clergyman.)

The pen is mightier than the sword. (Discourse and diplomacy get better results than war.)

The White House (President of the United States) is too uncommunicative with the press. (News media)

Think outside the bun. (Television commercial referring to food that is not hamburger.)

Latin: **<u>Arma</u> (= bellum) virumque cano.** (*Aeneid* 1.1)

**Implentur veteris Bacchi pinguisque ferinae** (= **vini**. *Aeneid* 1.215)

**Tum omnibus una omnes surripuit Veneres** (= **pulchritudinem**. Catullus 86.6)

**Funus et imperio parabat.** (= **mortem**. Horace, *Odes* 1.37.8)

**In aeternum/exsilium impositura cumbae** (= Charon's skiff = the Underworld = death. Horace, *Odes* 2.3.27–28)

**Frustra cruento Marte carebimus.** (= **bellum**. Horace, *Odes* 2.14.13)

**Velut crimen taedas exosa iugales.** (Marriage torch substitutes for marriage. Ovid, *Metamorphoses* 1.483)

Compare **synecdoche: ibis in auratis aureus ipse <u>rotis</u>.** (Wheels for chariot. Ovid, *Amores* 1.3.42)

- **onomatopoeia:** "sound-sense," the poetic use of a single word whose sound suggests its meaning; often associated with alliteration. Ovid is wonderful at "creating verbal texture by weaving sounds through lines."[2] In **illa dedit turpes raucis bubonibus umbras,** note the noisy cry of the owl in **raucis** and the repetition of the "Hoo, Hoo" mimicked in **bubonibus** (Ovid, *Amores* 1.12.19)

  Effect:   creates interest and illustrates or reinforces lexical meaning.

  English:  Babble, bang, bobwhite, buzz, chickadee, click, crack, cuckoo, hiss, hum, meow, moo, murmur, quack, swish, thud

  Latin:    **Magnum cum <u>murmure</u> montis.** (The wind-cave echoes. *Aeneid* 1.55).

  **Qualis <u>mugitus</u>, fugit cum saucius aram**. (Mooing by a bull being sacrificed. *Aeneid* 1.223)

  **Lamentes gemituque et femineo ululatu**. (Women wailing or howling. *Aeneid* 4.667)

  **Ad solam dominam usque pipiabat.** (Suggests the chirping of a bird. Catullus, Poem 3.10)

  **Tintinant aures.** (Suggests the ringing of a bell. Catullus, Poem 51.11)

  **Quod mare conceptum spumantibus exspuit undis.** (With alliteration and consonance, the word **exspuit**, with **spumantibus . . . undis**, suggests the sound of the salt sea spray. Catullus, Poem 64.155)

  **Lenesque sub noctem susurri.** (The sibilation suggests gentle whispers at night. Horace, *Odes* 1.9.19)

- **oxymoron:** paradox, or the juxtaposition of opposite or contradictory words in the same phrase, e.g., **Festina lente**, *Make haste slowly* (Augustus, attributed by Suetonius). Oxymoron often appears as a noun and an adjective and is associated with **antithesis** and **juxtaposition**. This figure appears commonly in Horace.

  Effect:   creates surprise, curiosity.

  English:  Authentic reproduction, definite maybe, detailed summary, elevated subway, forward lateral, pretty ugly, jumbo shrimp, open secret, resident alien, silent alarm, uninvited guest, virtual reality, wireless cable

---

[2] Edward Hirsch, *How to Read a Poem and Fall in Love with Poetry*, San Diego, CA, A Harvest Book, Harcourt, Inc., 1999, p. 295.

The silence was deafening.

Hurts so good. (John Cougar Mellencamp)

Latin:  **Plenus sacculus est <u>aranearum</u>,** *a purse full of cobwebs.* (Here, cobwebs serve as a metaphor for emptiness, therefore the oxymoron is "full of emptiness." Catullus, Poem 13.8)

**Simplex munditiis.** (Simple in elegance. Horace *Odes,* 1.5.5)

**Virenti canities.** (Note the metaphors, green = youth, grey-white = old age. Horace, *Odes* 1.9.17)

**Arida nutrix.** (Dry wetnurse. Horace, *Odes,* 1.22.16)

**Insaniens . . . sapientiae.** (Horace, *Odes,* 1.34.2)

**Cum tacent, clamant.** (Cicero, *In Catilinam* 1.8)

Compare **antithesis** and **juxtaposition**: <u>omnes</u> <u>unius</u> **aestimemus assis.** (Catullus, Poem 5.3)

- **personification:** the attribution of human qualities to inanimate objects, animals, or concepts, in order to stimulate the reader's imagination and thus gain vividness. Abstractions are often capitalized when personified, e.g., **ante, Pudor, quam te violo aut tua iura resolvo**, *before, O Shame, I violate you or your laws* (Dido, *Aeneid* 4.27). See also, **prosopopeia**.

Effects:  stimulates the imagination and creates vividness; makes the abstract concrete.

English:  Mother nature.

Justice is blind.

The bowels of the earth.

Flowers danced about the lawn.

England expects every man to do his duty. (Lord Nelson)

Latin:  **Suadentque cadentia <u>sidera</u> somnos.** (Note how the spirants suggest the gentle, rhythmic breathing of sleep. *Aeneid* 2.9)

**<u>Phaselus</u> ille . . . <u>ait</u> fuisse navium celerrimus.** (Catullus' bean-boat is personified throughout this poem. Catullus, Poem 4.1–2)

**Aut quam sidera multa, cum tacet nox,/furtivos hominum vident amores.** (The stars see the lovers. Catullus, Poem 7.7–8)

**Luctantem Icariis fluctibus Africum.** (Winds and waves are wrestling. Horace *Odes* 1.1.15)

**Cui Pudor et Iustitiae soror, incorrupta Fides, nudaque Veritas.** (Personifications of the values of the Romans. Horace, *Odes* 1.24.6–7)

**Saxis, unde loquaces/(lymphae)** (Bandusia's waters are talkative. Horace, *Odes* 3.13.15)

> **Postero nocturnos Aurora removerat ignes.** (Note also the antithetical juxtaposition of **nocturnos Aurora** and the metaphor of **nocturnos ignes** for stars. Ovid, *Metamorphoses* 4.81)
>
> **Ferrea cum vestris bella, valete, modis.** (Ovid bids farewell to epic meter, i.e., epic poetry. Ovid, *Amores* 1.1.28)

Compare **apostrophe**: <u>passer</u>, **deliciae meae puellae.** (Catullus, Poem 3.1)

- **pleonasm:** the use of redundant, superfluous, or unnecessary words. The opposite is **ellipsis**. Common in Vergil.

Effects: clarifies, reinforces, or lends reassurance or an air of dignity.

English: I saw him do it with my very own eyes.

I'll meet you at 12 noon.

It's *deja vu* all over again. (Yogi Berra)

Latin: **Sic <u>ore</u> <u>effata</u>**, *and thus having spoken with her mouth.* (Hecuba, *Aeneid* 2.524)

**Et . . . in tenuem ex oculis evanuit auram.** (Creusa, *Aeneid* 4.278)

**Finem dedit ore loquendi**. (Aeneas, *Aeneid* 6.76)

Compare **ellipsis**: **facilis (est) descensus Averno.** (*Aeneid* 6.126)

- **polyptoton:** repetition of a word, but in a different form, such as **amant amantur** (Catullus Poem, 45.20). A favorite of Catullus.

Effect: adds interest, clarifies.

English: Winners never quit, and quitters never win.

With eager feeding food doth choke the feeder. (Shakespeare, *Richard II* )

The only thing we have to fear is fear itself. (Franklin D. Roosevelt)

Latin: **Quicum ludere, <u>quem</u> in sinu tenere/<u>cui</u> primum digitum dare appetenti.** (Catullus, Poem 2.2–3)

**Gemelle Castor et gemelle Castoris.** (Catullus, Poem 4.27)

**Tam te basia multa basiare.** (Catullus, Poem 7.9)

**Quae te ut paeniteat postmodo facti faciet tui.** (Catullus, Poem 30.12)

**tum Thetidis Peleus incensus fertur amore/tum Thetis humanos non despexit hymenaeos, tum Thetidi pater ipse iugandum Pelea sensit.** (Catullus, Poem 64.19–21)

**Regum timendorum in proprios greges/reges in ipsos imperium est Iovis.** (Note the parallelism and condensation. Horace, *Odes* 3.1.5–6)

**Ars adeo latet arte sua.** (Also oxymoron. Ovid, *Metamorphoses* 10.252)

- **polysyndeton:** the use of more conjunctions (**et, -que, atque, nec**) than is needed in a series of coordinate words, phrases, or clauses, such as **Quem non incusavi amens hominumque deorumque** (*Aeneid* 2.745). The opposite is **asyndeton**.

Effect:    produces a cumulative effect, a "heaping up."

English:  He ran <u>and</u> laughed <u>and</u> jumped for joy.

           (I love Rome) for its greatness, and its antiquity, and its beauty, and its populousness, and for its power, and its wealth, and its successes in war. (John Chryostom)

Latin:     **Eurusque Notusque ruunt creberque . . ./Africus.** (*Aeneid* 1.85–86)

           **Involvens umbra magna terramque polumque.** (*Aeneid* 2.251)

           **Et me recuravi otioque et urtica.** (Catullus, Poem 44.15)

           **Quin tu animo offirmas atque istinc teque reducis/et dis invitis desinis esse miser?** (Catullus, Poem 76.11–12)

           **Laudat digitosque manusque bracchiaque.** (Ovid, *Metamorphoses* 1.500–1)

Compare **asyndeton: sed pleni omnes sunt libri, plenae sapientium voces, plena exemplorum vetustas.** (Cicero, *Pro Archia Poeta* 14)

- **praeteritio:** this Ciceronian figure of persuasion draws attention to an idea by pretending to pass over it. This figure is also known as preterition or paraleipsis/paralipsis. It is uncommon.

Effect:    a kind of irony; draws more attention to something by pretending to ignore it.

English:  Not to mention . . ., or We need say nothing of . . ., or Far be it from me to say . . . .

           Pay no attention to the man behind the curtain. ("The Wizard of Oz")

           Let's not mention my opponent's habit of lying.

Latin:     **Illa nimis antiqua <u>praetereo</u>**, *I pass over those (next examples) as too distant in time*.

           **Obliviscor iam iniurias tuas, Clodia, depono memoriam doloris mei.**

           *I am forgetful of your injuries (to me), Clodia, and I am putting aside the memory of my pain.* (The injuries and pain are still mentioned! Cicero, *Pro Caelio*, 50)

- **prolepsis:** speaking of something future as already completed or existing; anticipation or preconception, a "looking forward." Often a noun that receives the action of an anticipatory verb follows it. See also **hysteron proteron**.

  Effect:    "flashforward," prioritizes or puts in prime position what is considered most important.

  English:  If my wife finds out, I'm a dead man!

              Precolonial United States (speaking of the U.S. before it was so designated)

              Consider the lilies of the field, how they grow.

  Latin:     **<u>Summersas</u> obrue puppes.** (The ships are sunk before they are overwhelmed. *Aeneid* 1.69)

              **<u>Vixi</u> et quem dederat <u>cursum</u> fortuna <u>peregi</u>.**

              *I have lived and I have followed the path that fortune had given (me).* (*Aeneid* 4.653)

  Compare **hysteron proteron**

- **prosopopoeia:** a Ciceronian prose figure, prosopoeia is the impersonation of an absent or imaginary speaker as speaking, for dramatic effect. In Cicero's speeches and philosophical works, he sometimes speaks in the person of another, as Laelius in *De Amicitia*. Prosopopoeia is a special type of **personification**.

  Effect:    adds drama.

  English:  If Miller Huggins were alive today, he'd be turning over in his grave. (Yogi Berra)

- **simile:** an <u>expressed</u> comparison introduced by words such as "like" or "as" (**qualis, similis, ut, velut**, **veluti**, and others). Similes in epic poetry are often lengthy. For extended similes, see Vergil (orator, *Aeneid* 1.148–53, bees, 1.430–36, the wounded deer, 4.68–72, the bacchant, 4.300–3, ants, 4.402–7, the oak tree, 4.441–6); Ovid, *Metamorphoses,* the burning field (1.492–96), the hare and the hound (1.533–39), the leaky pipe (4.122–24), and marble like beeswax (10.284–86).

  Effect:    describes or illustrates the unfamiliar by way of the familiar.

  English:  As heavy as lead, as light as a feather.

              My love is as a fever, longing still/For that which longer nurseth the disease. (Shakespeare, Sonnet 147)

              Reason is to faith as the eye to a telescope. (David Hume)

              Like ancient trees, we die from the top. (Gore Vidal)

  Latin:     **Ac <u>veluti</u> magno in populo cum saepe coorta est/<u>seditio</u>,** etc. (Neptune, in calming the seas, is compared to an orator calming riots in the Forum. *Aeneid* 1.148)

**Amorem,/qui illius culpa cecidit <u>velut</u> prati/ultimi <u>flos</u>.** (The poet compares his lost love to a flower. Catullus, Poem 11.22–23)

**Ut missum sponsi furtivo munere malum**, etc. (Catullus compares his forgetfulness about writing to a friend to a maiden who has forgotten about a love-gift apple. Catullus, Poem 65.19–24)

**Vitas inuleo me similis, Chloe.** (Chloe is like a fawn. Horace, *Odes* 1.23.1)

**Atqui non ego te tigris ut aspera/. . . frangere persequor** (Horace is like a tiger. Horace, *Odes* 1.23.9–10)

**Accipiter velut/molles columbas.** (Octavian is a hawk to Cleopatra's doves. Note the anastrophe of **accipiter velut**. Horace, *Odes* 1.37.17–18)

**Videt igne micantes/sideribus similes oculos.** (Daphne's eyes are compared to stars. Ovid, *Metamorphoses* 1.498–99)

**Exhorruit aequoris instar/quod tremit . . .** ([Thisbe's face] shivers like the sea, which ripples . . . . Ovid, *Metamorphoses* 4.135–36)

Compare **metaphor**: <u>raditur</u> hic <u>elegis</u> ultima <u>meta</u> meis, *The final turning-post is grazed by my elegies.* (Ovid, *Amores* 3.15.2)

- **synchysis** (also spelled **synchesis** and often referred to as **interlocked word order**): synchysis emphasizes specific words by varying the usual word order found in prose. Words are arranged so that one word of a pair is placed between the words of the other pair, in an ABAB pattern, e.g., adj. A, adj. B, noun A, noun B, such as **amissos longo socios sermone** (*Aeneid* 1.217). An adjective will usually precede the noun it modifies. This figure is favored by Ovid.

Effect: variety, emphasizes the close association of the word pairs and gives a closely-knit expression.

|   | A | B | A | B |
|---|---|---|---|---|

Latin: **Saevae memorem Iunonis ob iram.** (*Aeneid* 1.4)

**Aeternum hoc sanctae foedus amicitiae.** (Note how these words all share themselves with each other. Catullus, Poem 109.6)

**Aspera/nigris aequora ventis.** (Winds and waves are brought together, with the help of juxtaposition and transference. Horace, *Odes* 1.5.6–7)

**Damna tamen celeres reparant caelestia lunae.** (Note the juxtaposition of **caelestia** and **lunae**. Horace, *Odes* 4.7.13)

**Ista decent umeros gestamina nostros.** (The interlocking here allows Apollo's quiver, **gestamina**, to "hang" from his shoulders, **umeros nostros**. Ovid, *Metamorphoses* 1.457)

**In rigidum parvo silicem discrimine versae.** (The interlocking merges the image of the Propoetides becoming hardhearted and their transformation into stone. Ovid, *Metamorphoses* 10.242)

A      B      B      A

Compare **chiasmus**: **ut quos certus amor, quos hora novissima iunxit.** (Ovid, *Metamorphoses* 4.156)

A      A      B      C      C

Compare **golden line**: **Et scelerata fero consumite viscera morsu.** (Ovid, *Metamorphoses* 4.113)

- **synecdoche:** synecdoche is the use of the part for the whole (**pars pro toto**) for variety of expression. This figure often stresses an important feature, such as the material of which the object is made or an individual in place of a group. Vergil frequently uses **puppis** (properly the stern of a ship) in place of **navis** (the entire ship), or **tectum** (properly the roof of a house) for **domus** (the house itself). Synecdoche is often described as a type of metonymy and the two are often confused. When the distinction between metonymy and synecdoche is made, it is the following: when A is used to refer to B -- it is a synecdoche if A is a <u>part of</u> B, and a metonym if A is <u>commonly associated with</u> B, but is not a part of it. Here is a convenient summary of the distinction between **metonymy**, **synecdoche**, and **metaphor**.

  > Therefore, "The White House reported" would be a metonymy for the President and his staff, because the White House (A) is not a part of the President or his staff (B), it is merely closely associated with them because of physical proximity. On the other hand, asking for "All hands on deck" is a synecdoche because hands (A) are actually a part of the men (B) to whom they refer. There is an example which displays synecdoche, metaphor and metonymy in one sentence. "Fifty keels ploughed the deep", where "keels" is the synecdoche as it takes a part (of the ship) as the whole (of the ship); "ploughed" is the metaphor as it substitutes the concept of ploughing a field for moving through the ocean; and "the deep" is the metonym, as "deepness" is an attribute associated with the ocean.[3]

  Effect:    variety of expression.

  English:    "hands" referring to workers, "head" for cattle, "the law" for policemen, "mortal" for man, "sail" for ship, "shades" for sunglasses, "threads" for clothing, "wheels" for a car.

---

[3] Wikipedia "Metonymy" = http://en.wikipedia.org/wiki/Metonymy.

Friends, Romans, Countrymen, lend me your ears! (Antony in Shakespeare's *Julius Caesar*)

Wherever wood can swim, there I am sure to find this flag of England. (Napoleon)

Latin: **Incute vim ventis summersasque obrue puppes.** (Literally, the sterns of the ships. *Aeneid* 1.69)

**Labore fessi venimus larem ad nostrum. (Lares**, household gods, for home; this might also be considered metonymy. Catullus, Poem 31.9)

**Animus ex hoc forensi strepitu reficiatur et aures convicio defessae conquiescant.** (Cicero's mind and ears, as suggestive of his whole person, are given a rest from the noise of public life. Cicero, *Pro Archia Poeta*, 12)

**Caesar ab Italia volantem/remis adurgens.** (Oars for ships. Horace, *Odes* 1.37.16–17)

**Tutus caret obsoleti/sordibus tecti.** (Roof for house. Horace, *Odes* 2.10.6–7)

**Quoque erat accinctus, demisit in ilia ferrum.** (Iron for sword or weapon. Ovid, *Metamorphoses* 4.119)

Compare **metonymy: taedae quoque iure coissent/sed vetuere patres.** (Marriage torch for marriage. Ovid, *Metamorphoses* 4.60)

- **tmesis:** the separation of parts of a compound word by one or more intervening words, e.g., **circum dea fundit** (for **circumfundit**) (*Aeneid* 1.412). More common in poetry, especially Vergil, than prose.

Effect: stresses enclosed word/s, accommodates meter.

English: How heinous e'er it be (for However heinous it be.) (Shakespeare, *Richard II*)

whatsoever (for whatever)

any-old-how (for anyhow)

a-whole-nother (for another)

Latin: **Bis collo squamea circum/terga dati.** (For **circumdati**. *Aeneid* 2.218–19)

**Ante, pudor, quam te violo aut tua iura resolvo.** (For **antequam**. *Aeneid* 4.27)

**Non prius ex illo flagrantia declinavit/lumina, quam cuncto concrepit corpore flammam.** (For **priusquam**. Catullus, Poem 64.91–92)

**Lesbia mi praesente viro mala plurima dicit.** (For **maledicit**. Catullus, Poem 83.1)

> **Quem Fors dierum cumque dabit lucro**. (For **quem-cumque**. Horace, *Odes* 1.9.14)

- **transferred epithet:** an **epithet** is the consistent use of an adjective to characterize some person or thing, such as <u>swift-footed</u> Achilles, <u>rosy-fingered</u> Dawn, and <u>wine-dark</u> sea.

Latin:     **sum <u>pius</u> Aeneas** (*Aeneid* 1.378)

> A **transferred epithet** is an adjective that agrees grammatically with one noun but is placed close to, and shares its meaning with, another noun, e.g., **mare velivolum**, *sail-flying sea* (the ships, and not the sea, are "sail-flying," *Aeneid* 1.24). This use of an epithet reinforces or emphasizes by sharing the meaning of one word with two others, heightening the meaning of all.

Effect:    reinforces or emphasizes.

English:  The ploughman homeward plods his <u>weary</u> way (weary modifies way, grammatically, but more appropriately describes the ploughman.) (Thomas Gray)

> Here comes Jim in his <u>smartarse</u> leather coat (transferred from Jim to coat).

Latin:     **Templumque vetustum <u>desertae</u>/Cereris.** (It is the temple, and not Ceres, that is deserted, although she too, by association, is also abandoned. Therefore, **desertae** is taken grammatically with **Cereris** but has a meaning more appropriate to **templum** here. *Aeneid* 2.713–14)

> **Oraclum Iovis inter aestuosi.** (Both the oracle and Jove are "steamy." Catullus, Poem 7.5)

> **Tintinant aures, gemina teguntur/lumina nocte.** (Scansion of this line reveals that the **-a** at the end of **gemina** is long, and that therefore **gemina** modifies **nocte** grammatically (*twin night*). In sense it can also describe **lumina** (*twin eyes*). Catullus, Poem 51.11–12)

> **Ad aquae lene caput sacrae.** (Note the double transfer here of **lene** to both **aquas** and **caput** and **sacrae** to both **aquae** and **caput**. Horace, *Odes* 1.1.22)

> **Regina dementes ruinas.** (Cleopatra is insane, and not the ruins. Horace, *Odes* 1.37.7)

> **Plura locuturum timido Peneia cursu.** (Strictly speaking, it is Daphne, and not her flight, that is frightened; note the juxtaposition of **timido** and **Peneia**. Ovid, *Metamorphoses* 1.525)

- **tricolon crescens:** the use of three closely-connected or parallel descriptive elements, increasing in size and emphasis, to modify a person or thing. Also known as tricolon crescendo or ascending tricolon, this figure is often accompanied by **anaphora** and **asyndeton**. A tricolon is simply a sentence or line of verse with three separate but equal parts. Commonly used by Cicero.

Effect:   gives the impression of a series.

**tricolon:**

English:   A happy life is one spent in learning, earning, and yearning. (Lillian Gish)

... of the people, by the people, and for the people .... (Abraham Lincoln, *Gettysburg Address*)

Latin:   **Veni, vidi, vici.** (Julius Caesar)

**tricolon crescens:**

|  |  |
|---|---|
| 1 | 2 |

Latin:   **Nec te noster amor, nec te data dextera quondam/nec**

3

**moritura tenet crudeli funere Dido?** *Does neither our love, nor your right hand once given in pledge, nor Dido, about to die a cruel death, hold you?* (Note the anaphora. *Aeneid* 4.307–8)

**Quicum ludere, quem in sinu tenere,/cui primum digitum dare appetenti.** (The sparrow plays with Lesbia. Note the asyndeton and polyptoton of **qui**. Catullus, Poem 2.2–3)

**Hoc concursu hominum litteratissimorum, hac vestra humanitate, hoc denique praetore exercente iudicium,** etc. (Cicero lavishes praise on those hearing his case. Cicero, *Pro Archia Poeta*, 3)

**Sive per Syrtes iter aestuosas/sive facturus per inhospitalem/Caucasum vel quae loca fabulosus/lambit Hydaspes.** (Wherever the poet goes, Lalage will be with him. Horace *Odes* 1.22.5–8)

**Non incola montis,/non ego sum pastor, non hic armenta gregesque/(horridus observo).** (Apollo is not an ordinary man. Note the asyndeton. Ovid, *Metamorphoses* 1.512–14)

- **zeugma:** the use of one part of speech (usually a verb, but sometimes a noun) with two objects, when strictly speaking the word can be applied to only one of them. A condensed expression in which one word has two different senses simultaneously, one sense often being wrong. **Hendiadys** is "two for one," i.e., two words/nouns with a single meaning, such as, **umbram et silvam** petebat, *he sought shade and the woods,* instead of **umbrosam silvam**, *the shady woods.* **Zeugma** is "one for two," i.e., one word/verb with two meanings, for instance, **Aeneas tulit dolorem et patrem Troia**, *Aeneas carried grief and his father from Troy.*

Effect:   condenses.

English:   The farmers in the valley grew potatoes, peanuts, and bored.

We serve Devonshire cream, Beaujolais Nouveau, and 71 cities in Europe. (a magazine ad)

If we don't hang together, we shall hang separately. (Benjamin Franklin)

As Vergil guided Dante through the Inferno, the Sibyl Aeneas Avernus. (Roger D. Scott)

Latin: **Fatisque deum defensus iniquis/inclusos utero Danaos et pinea furtim/laxat claustra Sinon.** (The word **laxat** properly describes the release of the bolts, **claustra**, of the trapdoor securing the Greeks inside the wooden horse, rather than the Greeks themselves. See also **hysteron proteron**, above. *Aeneid* 2.257–59)

**Studium atque auris adhibere posset**. (He was able to lend his support and his ears. Cicero, *Pro Archia Poeta*, 5)

**Avium citharaeque cantus.** (Here, the singing comes from both the birds and the lyre. Horace, *Odes* 3.1.20)

**Illa redit, iuvenemque oculis animoque requirit.** (Here, **requirit** means "search for" with **oculis** and "long for" with **animo**. Ovid, *Metamorphoses* 4.129)

## Glossary of Additional Useful Figures of Speech

- **anastrophe:** the deliberate reversal of normal word order, often with the effect of emphasizing the word/s placed earlier. In Latin, anastrophe is commonly found as a conjunction that is delayed or a preposition following its object, such as **Karthago, Italiam contra**, *Carthage, opposite Italy* (*Aeneid* 1.13). Here, the preposition and its object are reversed to create the juxtaposition of Carthage and Italy. The term postposition is also used in the context of anastrophe. Postposition refers to the placement of any word later than expected, e.g., a clause may precede its antecedent in poetry. For example, **fidus quae tela gerebat Achates,** *weapons which the faithful Achates was carrying* (= **tela quae.** *Aeneid* 1.188). See also **hyperbaton**.

Effects: emphasizes the word appearing first; provides variety of style.

English: Up the hill went Jack and Jill.

When he himself might his quietus make. (Shakespeare, *Hamlet*)

What care I for my reputation? (George Jacques Danton)

Latin:

With prepositions:

**Errabant acti fatis maria omnia circum** (= **circum maria omnia.** *Aeneid* 1.32)

**Quos inter medius venit furor.** (*Aeneid* 1.348)

**Te propter Libycae gentes Nomadumque tyranni.** (*Aeneid* 4.320)

**Oraclum Iovis inter aestuosi.** (Catullus, Poem 7.5)

With conjunctions and adverbs:

**Accipiter velut (adurget)/molles columbas** (= velut accipiter .... Horace, *Odes* 1.37.17–19)

**Daret ut catenis/fatale monstrum.** (Horace, *Odes* 1.37.20–21)

**Saepe soporatos invadere profuit hostes/caedere et armata vulgus inerme manu.** (Ovid, *Amores* 1.9.22)

With relative clauses:

**Sum pius Aeneas, raptos qui ex hoste penates/. . . veho** (= qui penates raptos ex hoste . . . veho. *Aeneid* 1.378)

**Fractum qui veteris pedem grabati** (= qui fractum .... Catullus, Poem 10.22)

**Sancte puer, curis hominum qui gaudia misces** (= qui curis hominum gaudia misces. Catullus, Poem 64.95)

**Quae iacerent in tenebris omnia, nisi litterarum lumen accederet.** (= omnia quae .... Cicero, *Pro Archia Poeta* 14)

**Haberes/magnum adiutorem, posset qui ferre secundas** (= qui posset .... Horace *Satires* 1.9.45–46)

**In vacuo quae vulnera pectore fecit** (= quae in vacuo . . . pectore fecit. Ovid, *Metamorphoses* 1.520)

**Iusta precor: quae me nuper praedata puella est** (= puella quae .... Ovid, *Amores* 1.3.1)

Compare **hyperbaton: misero quod omnes eripit sensus mihi** (Catullus, Poem 51.5–6). This example also includes the postpositioned relative pronoun **quod**, which normally introduces the clause, i.e., precedes **misero = quod misero mihi omnes sensus eripit,** and chiasmus.

- **antithesis:** striking contrast of juxtaposed words or ideas, such as **Odi et amo**, *I hate and I love* (Catullus, 85.1). The figure **oxymoron** is necessarily a contrast between opposites and therefore includes antithesis. This figure is a favorite of Cicero.

Effect: contrast.

English: A time to be born, and a time to die. (*Ecclesiastes*, 3)

Not that I loved Caesar less, but that I loved Rome more. (Brutus, Shakespeare, *Julius Caesar*)

Love is an ideal thing, marriage a real thing. (Johann Wolfgang von Goethe)

Extremism in defense of liberty is no vice, moderation in the pursuit of justice is not virtue. (Barry Goldwater)

Latin:   <u>**Digna indigna**</u> **pati.** (Note also the asyndeton. *Aeneid* 12.811)

**At vobis male sit, malae tenebrae/Orci, quae omnia bella devoratis:/tam bellum mihi passerem abstulistis./O factum male!** (Catullus, Poem 3.13–16)

**Amant amantur.** (Note also the polyptoton and asyndeton. Catullus 45.20)

**Lumina nocte.** (Catullus, Poem 51.11–12)

**Cogit amare magis, sed bene velle minus.** (Catullus, Poem 72.8)

**Esset ... in Siciliam profectus et cum ex ea provincia ... decederet.** (Cicero, *Pro Archia Poeta*, 6)

Compare **oxymoron**: **virenti canities** (green = youth, grey-white = old age. Horace, *Odes* 1.9.17)

Compare **juxtaposition**: <u>**Ego te**</u>**, miseranda, peremi.** (Ovid, *Metamorphoses* 4.110)

- **assonance:** repetition of <u>internal</u> sounds, <u>usually vowels</u>, in successive words. The effect of assonance can be "musical" or onomatopoetic. What vowel sound seems to be emphasized in the line **multa tibi ante aras nostra cadet hostia dextra** (*Aeneid* 1.334)? Right, it is the vowel -**a**-. Distinguish this sound-effect from **alliteration**, which consists of the repetition of primarily <u>initial consonants</u>. Repetitions of sounds are common, particularly in poetry, and are often found in conjunction with **asyndeton**.

Effects:   emphasizes or draws attention; reinforces meaning; brings pleasure.

English:  Mankind can handle most problems. (assonance of a)

Fleet feet sweep by sleeping geeks. (assonance of e)

Try to light the fire. (assonance of i)

Thy kingdom come thy will be done. (assonance of o)

Latin:   **Acc<u>i</u>p<u>i</u>unt <u>i</u>n<u>i</u>m<u>i</u>cum <u>i</u>mbrem, r<u>i</u>m<u>i</u>sque fat<u>i</u>scunt.** (The sound of rain? *Aeneid* 1.123)

**Amicos longo socios sermone.** (*Aeneid* 1.217)

**Fit via vi.** (*Aeneid* 2.494)

**Vivamus, mea Lesbia, atque amemus.** (Light-hearted. Catullus, Poem 5.1)

**O fortunatam natam me consule Romam!** (Cicero, *De Consulatu*)

**Sperne puer neque.** (Horace, *Odes* 1.9.16)

**Lalagen amabo.** (Note the sing-song of **Lala**- and **ama**-. Horace, *Odes* 1.22.23)

**Sideribus similes oculos; videt oscula.** (Note the accompanying alliteration and the powerful assonance of the sound-a-likes **oculos** and **oscula**. Ovid, *Metamorphoses* 1.499)

- **condensation:** brevity or economy of expression. A word common to two or more parallel expressions is often expressed in the last one only, which is the opposite of the usual English practice. The appearance of such words as being "understood" or assumed is a characteristic feature of Latin. Condensation as a form of **ellipsis** is common in Latin poetry, especially in Ovid, and is commonly found with parallel phrasing, for which, see below.

Effect:  accelerates.

Latin:  **Hic amor, haec patria est.** (= **Hic amor [est], haec patria est**. *Aeneid* 4.347)

**Qui dare certa ferae, dare vulnera possumus hosti.** (= **Qui dare certa [vulnera] ferae [possumus], dare [certa] vulnera possumus hosti**. Note the asyndeton, and the use of poetic plural. Ovid, *Metamorphoses* 1.458)

**Fugat hoc, facit illud amorem** (= **fugat hoc [amorem], facit illud amorem**. Ovid, *Metamorphoses* 1.469)

**Sic deus et virgo; est hic spe celer, illa timore.** (Ovid, *Metamorphoses* 1.539)

**In frondem crines, in ramos bracchia crescunt.** (Note the anaphora and, again, the parallel phrasing. Ovid, *Metamorphoses* 1.550)

**Vota tamen tetigere deos, tetigere parentes.** (Ovid, *Metamorphoses* 4.164)

**Figat tuus omnia, Phoebe, te meus arcus.** (Ovid, *Metamorphoses* 1.463)

- **diminutive**: the suffixes **–ulus** (**-olus** after a vowel), **-(i)culus,** and **–ellus** (sometimes **–illus**) alter the meaning of a noun or adjective by diminishing its size. This often increases the level of affection, e.g., **caligula,** soldier's boot, a diminutive of **caliga,** producing Caligula, "L'il Boots." A favorite figure of Catullus.

Effect:  elicits feelings of affection and endearment.

English:  cigarette (-ette), duckling (-ling), kitty (-ey, -ie, -y), piglet (-let); German **–chen** or **–lein**, Italian, **-etta**, Russian **–chka** or **–ka,** Spanish **–ito.**

Latin:  **Ante fugam suboles, si quis mihi <u>parvulus</u> aula/luderet Aeneas.** (*Aeneid* 4.328)

**Vae miselle passer! . . ./Flendo turgiduli rubent ocelli.** (Catullus, Poem 3.16, 18)

**Ut Veraniolum meum et Fabullum.** (Catullus, Poem 12.17)

**Multum lusimus in meis tabellis/. . . scribens versiculos uterque nostrum.** (Catullus, Poem 50.2–4)

**Sideribus similes oculos; videt oscula.** (Ovid, *Metamorphoses* 1.499)

**Munera fert illi: conchas teretesque lapillos.** (Ovid, *Metamorphoses* 10.260)

- **golden line:** a form of interlocked or chiastic word in which a centrally-placed verb is surrounded by two adjectives on one side and two nouns on the other: ABCBA (= adjective A – adjective B – verb C – noun B – noun A). Only the hexameter line accommodates this figure. John Dryden described the golden line as a hexameter line "of two substantives and two adjectives with a verb betwixt to keep the peace" (preface to *Sylvae*). Commonly found in Ovid.

Effect:  draws attention.

A         B    C    B     A

Latin:  **Disiectam Aeneae toto videt aequore classem.** (*Aeneid* 1.128)

adj.      adj.     verb    noun    noun

**Aspera tum positis mitescent saecula bellis.** (*Aeneid* 1.291)

**Irrita ventosae linquens promissa procellae.** (Catullus, Poem 64.59)

**Omne capax movet urna nomen.** (Horace, *Odes* 3.1.16)

**Pulchra verecundo suffunditur ora rubore.** (Ovid, *Metamorphoses* 1.484)

- **Grecism (Hellenism):** a patronym (adj., patronymic), which is a component of a personal name based upon the name of one's father, often contains forms of the Greek suffix **–ides** or **–idos**, e.g., **Anchisiades** = Aeneas, son of Anchises. Ovid, in particular, likes to use periphrasis (circumlocution) in referring to the name of a hero or heroine.

Effect:  lends dignity and respect.

Latin:  **Saevus ubi Aeacidae telo iacet Hector.** (Descendant of Aeacus = Achilles. *Aeneid* 1.99)

**Defessi Aeneadae quae proxima litora cursu.** (Descendants/followers of Aeneas. *Aeneid* 1.157)

**Carmina uti possem mittere Battiadae** (= Callimachus, an inhabitant of Cyrene, whose father was Battus. Catullus, Poem 116.2; cf. Poems 7.6 and 65.16)

**Sisyphus Aeolides laboris.** (Sisyphus, son of Aeolus. Horace, *Odes* 2.14.20)

**Hoc deus in nympha Peneide fixit.** (Daphne, daughter of Peneus. Ovid, *Metamorphoses* 1.472)

**Venit Atlantides positis caducifer alis.** (Mercury, son of Atlas. Ovid, *Metamorphoses* 8.627)

Note:

Other Greek usages occur in poetry, wherein Greek endings are found on Greek names or words, e.g., **Ancona** (Catullus 36.13), **Acmen** (Catullus Poem 45.1), **Paphon** (Ovid, *Metamorphoses* 10.297), **barbiton** (Horace, *Odes* 1.1.34), **Lalagen** (Horace, *Odes* 1.22.10), **Geryonen Tityonenque** (Horace, *Odes* 2.14.8), **Chloen** (Horace, *Odes* 3.9.6) The Greek **−n** is the Latin **−m**.

- **parallelism:** the symmetrical arrangement of equal or balanced words, phrases, or clauses. Parallel structures are commonly joined by coordinating conjunctions, such as **et** or **vel**, but they are also found frequently with **asyndeton** and **condensation**. Parallelism oftens appears as a **tricolon**. Parallel phrases are found frequently in Cicero.

Effect:    creates equality and balance.

English:   In a larger sense, we cannot dedicate, we cannot consecrate, we cannot hallow this ground. (Abraham Lincoln)

. . . government of the people, by the people, and for the people shall not perish from this earth. (Abraham Lincoln)

Latin:     **Proximis censoribus . . . superioribus (censoribus) . . . primis (censoribus).** (Cicero, *Pro Archia Poeta* 11)

**Illum . . . maiores nostri in civitatem receperunt; nos hunc . . . de nostra civitate eiciamus?** (Note the asyndeton. Cicero, *Pro Archia Poeta* 22)

**Quod facit, auratum est et cuspide fulget acuta,/quod fugat, obtusum est et habet sub harundine plumbum**. (The two arrows of Cupid. Ovid, *Metamorphoses* 1.470–71)

**Saepe pater dixit, "Generum mihi, filia, debes"; saepe pater dixit, "Debes mihi, nata, nepotes."** (Peneus' speech to Daphne. Ovid, *Metamorphoses* 1.481–82)

**Nec prosunt domino, quae prosunt omnibus, artes!** (Apollo acknowledges to Daphne the ineffectiveness of his divine power. Note the anastrophe/postposition of **artes**. Ovid, *Metamorphoses* 1.524)

**Lux . . ./praecipitatur aquis, et aquis nox exit ab isdem.** (The sun sets and night falls. Ovid, *Metamorphoses* 4.92)

**Quique a me morte revelli/heu sola poteras, poteris nec morte revelli.** (Thisbe's speech to the dead Pyramus. Ovid, *Metamorphoses* 4.152–53)

- **poetic plural:** the use of the plural form of a pronoun or adjective in place of the singular, for metrical purposes or to create a more poetic expression, such as alliteration. Poetic schizophrenia!

Effect:   accommodates meter.

Latin:   **Tantaene animis caelestibus irae?** (*Aeneid* 1.11)

      **Crudeles aras traiectaque pectora ferro.** (Pygmalion's murder, *Aeneid* 1.355)

      **Illinc fas regna resurgere Troiae.** (*Aeneid* 2.210)

      **Soles occidere et redire possunt.** (The plurality of nature; Catullus, Poem 5.4; cf. 8.3)

      **Haec si, inquam attuleris, venuste noster.** (To Cat's good friend Fabullus. Catullus, Poem 13.6)

      **Me doctarum hederae praemia frontium/dis miscent superis.** (Horace, *Odes* 1.1.29)

      **Ista decent umeros gestamina nostros.** (Ovid, *Metamorphoses* 1.457)

- **sound play:** writers often simply like to play with the sounds of words. Sound play often accompanies or heightens the effect of another figure of speech, such as alliteration. "The sound must seem an echo to the sense," writes Alexander Pope. Ovid is especially good with sound effects. See also the examples accompanying **alliteration, onomatopoeia,** and **assonance.**

Effects:   illustrates, reinforces, heightens the sense.

Latin:   **Ac primum scilici scintillam excudit Achates.** (The striking of sparks from flint. *Aeneid* 1.174)

      **Stetit illa tremens, uteroque recusso/insonuere cavae gemitumque dedere cavernae.** (Note the trisyllables at the beginning of the line, reinforced by the repetition of **utero** and **recusso** and the **insonuere cavae ... dedere cavernae,** all suggesting the twanging back and forth of the spear shaft after it hits the wooden horse. *Aeneid* 2.52–3)

      **Ardentesque oculos suffecti sanguine et igne/sibila lambebant linguis vibrantibus ora.** (The twin serpents hissing. *Aeneid* 2.210–11)

      **Demissum lapsi per funem, Acamasque Thoasque.** (The sliding of the Greeks down the rope? *Aeneid* 2.262)

      **Nequiquam ingeminans iterumque iterumque vocavi.** (Note the redundancy of the mournful **m/n** sounds as Aeneas searches for the lost Creusa, and the contribution of the polysyndeton and rhetorical repetition of **iterum**. *Aeneid* 2.770)

**Sic ait et dextra crinem secat.** (Note the cutting sounds, as Iris severs a lock of Dido's hair. *Aeneid* 4.704)

**Cui dono lepidum novum libellum.** (Rhyme. Catullus, Poem 1.1)

**Qui nunc it per iter tenebricosum.** (The bird hopping into Hell? Catullus, Poem 3.11)

**Loquente saepe sibilum edidit coma.** (The rustling of leaves. Note the personification of **loquente . . . coma**. Catullus, Poem 4.12)

**Rumoresque senum severiorum.** (The whispering of gossipy old men. Catullus, Poem 5.2)

**Litus ut longe resonante Eoa/tunditur unda.** (Suggests the beating of the waves on the shore. Catullus, Poem 11. 3–4)

**Thyniam atque Bithynos**. (Suggests the boredom of Bithynia. Note the elision. Catullus, Poem 31.5)

**Nicaeaeque ager uber aestuosae.** (Catullus, Poem 46.5)

**Si quicquam mutis gratum acceptumve sepulcris** (on the death of Calvus' wife; the alliteration and consonance of –m- sounds are often used to express solemnity and sorrow. Catullus, Poem 96.1; cf. Poems 3 and 101)

**Te rursus in bellum resorbens/unda fretis tulit aestuosis.** (The salt sea seems to suck Pompeius back into the fray with its seething foam. Horace, *Odes* 2.7.15–16)

**Fractisque rauci fluctibus Hadriae.** (The harsh **c/t** sounds evoke the dangerous waters of the Adriatic. Horace, *Odes* 2.14.14; cf. *Odes* 1.1.15)

**Quod fugat, auratum est et cuspide fulget acuta.** (The hard **c/g** suggests the sharp cutting edge of the golden arrowhead. Ovid, *Metamorphoses* 1.417)

**Obviaque adversas vibrabant flamina vestes.** (The alliteration of **v** and **s** and the trisyllabic words suggest the rhythmic flapping of Daphne's clothes as she runs. Ovid, *Metamorphoses* 1.528)

**Murmure blanditiae minimo transire solebant.** (Note how the **m/n** alliteration suggests the gentle murmuring of the lovers. Ovid, *Metamorphoses* 4.70)

**Collocat . . . colla . . . mollibus.** (Rhyme. Ovid, *Metamorphoses* 10.267–69; cf. 280, 285)

**Corpus erat: saliunt temptatae pollice venae!** (the jumpy sounds perhaps mimic the lively beat of the pulse. Ovid, *Metamorphoses*, 10.289)

- **word play (word picture)**: word choice or position is used by poets to suggest something beyond the literal meaning. Often a "mind picture" is created. Word play often contains more than one figure of speech. Ovid is perhaps the most successful at doing this. See also the examples accompanying **chiasmus, hyperbaton,** and **synchysis**.

Effects: stimulates the imagination; reinforces sense.

Latin: **Sectaque intexunt abiete costas.** (The words are interwoven, **intexunt,** much as the ribs of the wooden horse; note the harsh **c**-sounds, perhaps the cutting of the wood? *Aeneid* 2.16)

**Uterumque armato milite complent.** (The belly is filled with armed men. *Aeneid* 2.20)

**Hic Dolopum manus, hic saevus tendebat Achilles,/classibus hic locus, hic acie certare solebant.** (Note the cinematic effect of a camera panning the shore, **hic . . . hic . . . hic . . . hic.** *Aeneid* 2.29–30)

**Scinditur incertum studia in contraria vulgus.** (The back-and-forth adjective-noun combinations suggest the uncertainty of the crowd. *Aeneid* 2.39)

**Sopor fessos complectitur artus.** (Sleep embracing the weary limbs [of the Trojans] suggests the previous strangling of and feeding on Laocoon by the serpent **in miseros morsu depascitur artus,** 2.215ff., *Aeneid* 2.253) Cf. the wooden horse as snake in **minans inlabitur urbi,** 240.

**Illum absens absentem auditque videtque.** (Dido is hallucinating. Note the polyptoton of **absens,** the polysyndeton, and the rhyming verbs, which all contribute to her "double vision."*Aeneid* 4.83)

**Passer mortuus est meae puellae.** (Death comes between the sparrow and Lesbia. Catullus, Poem 3.3)

**Orci, quae omnia bella devoratis.** (Hell devours all that is beautiful. Catullus, Poem 3.14)

**Paene insularum, Sirmio, insularumque.** (Sirmio is a promontory sticking out in the middle of the verse. Catullus, Poem 31.1)

**Manusque collo/ambas iniciens.** (The neck is embraced. Catullus, Poem 35.9–10)

**Sicine subrepsti mi atque intestina perurens/. . . nostrae crudele venenum/vitae.** (For his betrayal, Rufus is described in terms suggestive of a venomous snake. Note the hissing sibilation. Catullus, Poem 77, lines 3 and 5)

**Viridi membra sub arbuto.** (Limbs recline beneath an evergreen. Horace, *Odes* 1.1.21)

**Catulis cerva fidelis.** (The doe is surrounded by the trusty hounds. Horace, *Odes* 1.1.27)

**Teretes Marsus aper plagas.** (The boar is caught in the net. Horace, *Odes* 1.1.28)

**Quae nunc oppositis debilitat pumicibus mare.** (The cliffs and sea oppose each other. Horace, *Odes* 1.11.5)

**Saeviet circa iecur ulcerosum.** (Note the harsh sounds that surround Lydia's liver, the seat of passion, as the poet taunts her. Horace, *Odes* 1.25.15)

**Fortis et asperas/tractare serpentes.** (Cleopatra's asp. Horace, *Odes* 1.37.26–27)

**Post equitem sedet atra Cura.** (Gloomy Anxiety sits behind the horseman. Horace, *Odes* 3.1.40)

**Gelidos . . ./rubro sanguine rivos.** (The dark/hot blood mingling with the clear/cold water foreshadows the death of the kid-goat. Was the goat immersed in the spring? Horace, *Odes* 3.13.6–7)

**Lascivi suboles gregis.** (The herd protects its offspring. Horace, *Odes* 3.13.8)

**Cavis impositam ilicem/saxis.** (The oak grows out of the hollow rock. Horace, *Odes* 3.13.14–15)

**Eque sagittifera prompsit duo tela pharetra.** (The two arrows are inside the quiver. Ovid, *Metamorphoses* 1.468)

**Ut canis in vacuo leporem cum Gallicus arvo.** (The hound has trapped the hare in the field. Ovid, *Metamorphoses* 1.533)

**Vidit et obscurum timido pede fugit in antrum.** (Thisbe is actually enclosed in the dark cave. Ovid, *Metamorphoses* 4.100)

**Interea niveum mira feliciter arte sculpsit ebur.** (Note how the chiastic arrangement centers on **feliciter**, *successfully*; so that the "art is revealed by its art," as in **ars adeo latet arte sua.** Ovid, *Metamorphoses*, 10.247–48 and 252)

**Armata vulgus inerme manu.** (The unarmed mob is surrounded by those with weapons. Ovid, *Amores* 1.9.22)

## Practice Questions

The format and content of the following practice questions on figures of speech approximate those appearing on the AP Latin Exam. Occasionally you will find a question on a poetic technique or usage that is not required by the College Board. For additional practice on figures of speech, consult the resources listed in the Webliography section at the end of this chapter. Answers to all questions are also provided at the end of this chapter.

### VERGIL

1. ***Match the figure with its corresponding identification.***

_____ 1. Quos ego - - - !

_____ 2. In foribus letum Androgeo; tum pendere poenas/Cecropidae iussi (miserum!) septena quotannis/corpora natorum, etc.

_____ 3. Molemque et montes

_____ 4. Finem dedit ore loquendi

_____ 5. Summersas obrue puppes

_____ 6. Amissos longo socios sermone

_____ 7. Velut agmine facto

_____ 8. Invadunt urbem somno vinoque sepultam

_____ 9. Bis collo squamea circum/terga dati

_____ 10. Fluctusque ad sidera tollit

_____ 11. Fracti fatis belloque repulsi

_____ 12. Fit sonitus spumante salo

_____ 13. Facilis descensus Averno.

_____ 14. Crudeles aras traiectaque pectora . . . nudavit

_____ 15. Implentur veteris Bacchi

A. ellipsis

B. prolepsis

C. pleonasm

D. aposiopesis

E. metonymy

F. tmesis

G. interlocked (synchysis)

H. ecphrasis

I. zeugma

J. alliteration

K. metaphor

L. chiasmus

M. hyperbole

N. simile

O. hendiadys

2. **Select the correct answer. Each figure of speech is underlined for your convenience.**

1. What figure of speech occurs in <u>hic illius arma, hic currus fuit</u>?

   (A) simile                     (C) hyperbole

   (B) anaphora                   (D) tmesis

2. The word <u>desertae</u> in the phrase <u>templumque vetustum desertae Cereris</u> is

   (A) zeugma                     (C) personification

   (B) apostrophe                 (D) transferred epithet

3. The line <u>iamque faces et saxa volant, furor arma ministrat</u> contains an example of

   (A) ellipsis                   (C) asyndeton

   (B) tricolon crescens          (D) chiasmus

4. What figure of speech occurs in <u>involvens umbra magna terramque polumque</u>

   (A) tmesis                     (C) aposiopesis

   (B) polysyndeton               (D) alliteration

5. <u>Dulces exuviae, dum fata deusque sinebat</u> is an example of

   (A) enjambment

   (B) interlocked word order (synchysis)

   (C) apostrophe

   (D) polyptoton

6. <u>Ac velut magno in populo cum saepe coorta est/seditio</u> is

   (A) simile                     (C) zeugma

   (B) asyndeton                  (D) chiasmus

7. What figure of speech occurs in <u>multum ille et terris iactatus et alto/vi superum</u>?

   (A) interlocked word order (synchysis)

   (B) prolepsis

   (C) onomatopoeia

   (D) enjambment

8. The figure of speech in <u>saevus ubi</u> . . . <u>iacet Hector, ubi ingens Sarpedon, ubi tot</u> . . ./<u>scuta virum galeasque et fortia corpora solvit</u> is an example of

    (A) hendiadys
    (C) pleonasm
    (B) tricolon crescens
    (D) tmesis

9. <u>Longum per valles armenta sequuntur agmen</u> is an example of

    (A) hyperbaton
    (C) simile
    (B) aposiopesis
    (D) apostrophe

10. The figure of speech that appears in <u>sic ore effata</u> is

    (A) hyperbole
    (C) enjambment
    (B) personification
    (D) pleonasm

**3. Select the correct answer for each figure of speech. These examples come from Books 10 and 12. When there is no underlining, consider the entire sentence.**

1. <u>Sternitur</u> Arcadiae proles, <u>sternuntur</u> Etrusci/et vos. (Book 10.429–30)

    (A) polyptoton
    (C) metonymy
    (B) anaphora
    (D) tricolon crescens

2. O dolor atque decus magnum rediture parenti. (Book 10.507)

    (A) aposiopesis
    (C) enjambment
    (B) tmesis
    (D) apostrophe

3. <u>Sit</u> Latium, <u>sint</u> Albani per saecula reges,/<u>sit</u> Romana . . . propago. (Book 12.826–27)

    (A) assonance
    (C) hyperbole
    (B) anaphora
    (D) polysyndeton

4. Per patris <u>hospitium et mensas</u>, quas advena adisti. (Book 10.460)

    (A) transferred epithet
    (C) hendiadys
    (B) hyperbaton
    (D) litotes

5. <u>Infelix</u> umero cum apparuit alto/<u>balteus</u>. (Book 12.941–42)

    (A) zeugma
    (C) hyperbaton
    (B) pleonasm
    (D) anaphora

6. Hic Turnus ferro praefixum <u>robur</u> acuto. (Book 10.479)

    (A) apostrophe               (C) ellipsis

    (B) asyndeton              (D) synecdoche

7. Consurgunt gemitu Rutuli totusque <u>remugit</u>. (Book 12.928)

    (A) polyptoton             (C) personification

    (B) onomatopoeia        (D) transferred epithet

8. <u>Oculos dextramque</u> precantem/<u>protendens</u>. (Book 12.930–1)

    (A) transferred epithet      (C) zeugma

    (B) interlocked (synchysis)   (D) litotes

9. Volat <u>atri turbinis instar</u>. (Book 12.923)

    (A) asyndeton               (C) oxymoron

    (B) simile                 (D) prolepsis

10. Tempus desistere pugnae. (Book 10.441)

    (A) ellipsis                 (C) hyperbole

    (B) zeugma               (D) aposiopesis

## CATULLUS

***1. From the pool of figures provided below, match the poetic term with its English and Latin examples. Not all figures are used.***

| | | | | | |
|---|---|---|---|---|---|
| A. | anaphora | E. | diminutive | I. | alliteration |
| B. | personification | F. | litotes | J. | apostrophe |
| C. | transferred epithet | G. | onomatopoeia | K. | antithesis |
| D. | hyperbole | H. | metaphor | L. | metonymy |

**English Examples**

____ 1. Hunger sat shivering in the road.

____ 2. Plop, plop, fizz, fizz, O what a relief it is! (Alka Seltzer commercial)

____ 3. Nothing like a good glass of Bacchus to go with the pasta.

____ 4. My recollection of Latin grammar is minuscule.

____ 5. The moon is a ghostly galleon.

____ 6. We shall not flag or fail. We shall go on to the end. (Churchill)

___ 7. Sighted ship sank same. (WWII sub report)

___ 8. I must have taken a million Latin tests by now.

___ 9. The ice was so cold that it felt warm to the touch.

___ 10. Robin Williams is not an unfunny guy.

___ 11. Alas, poor Yorick, I knew him, Horatio! (Shakespeare)

**Latin Examples**

___ a. aut quam sidera multa, cum tacet nox/furtivos hominum vident amores

___ b. funditus atque imis exarsit tota medullis

___ c. tuae, Lesbia, sint satis superque

___ d. puto esse ego illi milia aut decem aut plura/perscripta

___ e. precesque nostras/oramus cave despuas

___ f. nec quae fugit sectare, nec miser vive

___ g. Salve, nec minimo puella naso

___ h. Annales Volusi . . . votum solvite pro mea puella

___ i. tum . . . omnes surripuit Veneres

___ j. nec somnus tegeret quiete ocellos

___ k. bellus ille et urbanus/Suffenus unus caprimulgus aut fossor

2.  *Identify the figure of speech underlined in each of the following lines from Catullus. When there is no underlining, consider the entire sentence.*

1.  Unam Septimius <u>misellus</u> Acmen/mavult.
    (A) enjambment          (C) apostrophe
    (B) diminutive          (D) hyperbole

2.  Eripite hanc <u>pestem perniciemque</u>.
    (A) hendiadys           (C) oxymoron
    (B) anaphora            (D) apostrophe

3. Iam <u>mens</u> praetrepidans <u>avet</u> vagari,/iam laeti studio <u>pedes vigescunt</u>.

   (A) hyperbaton            (C) personification

   (B) allegory             (D) hysteron proteron

4. Advenio has miseras, <u>frater</u>, ad inferias.

   (A) personification       (C) transferred epithet

   (B) aposiopesis          (D) apostrophe

5. <u>Phaselus</u> . . . <u>ait</u> fuisse navium celerrimus.

   (A) ellipsis             (C) asyndeton

   (B) interlocking (synchysis)     (D) personification

6. Quamvis candida <u>milies</u> puella . . . revocat.

   (A) transferred epithet    (C) hendiadys

   (B) hyperbole           (D) metaphor

7. Salve, <u>nec minimo</u> puella naso.

   (A) asyndeton          (C) litotes

   (B) prolepsis           (D) tmesis

8. Nescio, sed fieri sentio et <u>excrucior</u>.

   (A) transferred epithet    (C) hendiadys

   (B) metaphor           (D) asyndeton

9. Gravedo frigida et frequens tussis.

   (A) zeugma            (C) chiasmus

   (B) polysyndeton        (D) irony

10. Haec vestis priscis hominum variata figuris/heroum mira virtutes indicat arte.

    (A) ecphrasis           (C) polysyndeton

    (B) hyperbole          (D) tricolon crescens

11. Irrita ventosae linquens promissa procellae.

    (A) hysteron proteron     (C) enjambment

    (B) anaphora           (D) golden line

12. Electissima pessimi poetae scripta.

    (A) metaphor           (C) hyperbaton

    (B) asyndeton          (D) zeugma

13. Aeternum hoc sanctae foedus amicitiae.

    (A) prolepsis                 (C) interlocking

    (B) tricolon crescens (synchysis)    (D) alliteration

**3.** ***Each of the following lines contains at least two figures of speech. For each one, identify by name and write out the Latin that illustrates it.***

1. Gemina teguntur/lumina nocte.

2. O factum male! O miselle passer!

3. Mutuis animis amant amantur.

4. Nam Cytorio in iugo/loquente saepe sibilum edidit coma.

5. O quid solutis est beatius curis,/cum mens onus reponit, ac peregrino/labore fessi venimus larem ad nostrum,/desideratoque acquiescimus lecto?

6. Nam quo tempore legit incohatam/Dindymi dominam, ex eo misellae/ignes interiorem edunt medullam.

7. Salve, nec minimo puella naso/nec bello pede nec nigris ocellis.

8. Quaenam te genuit sola sub rupe leaena,/quod mare conceptum spumantibus exspuit undis, quae Syrtes, quae Scylla rapax, quae vasta Charybdis.

9. Tum omnibus una omnes surripuit Veneres.

10. Si quicquam mutis gratum acceptumve sepulcris.

**4.** ***Each of the following lines contains at least three figures of speech. For each one, identify by name and write out the Latin that illustrates it.***

1. Salve, o venusta Sirmio, atque ero gaude/gaudente, vosque, o Lydiae lacus undae, /ridete quidquid est domi cachinnorum.

2. Quaenam te mala mens, miselle Raude,/agit praecipitem in meos iambos?

3. Nunc audax cave sis, precesque nostras,/oramus, cave despuas, ocelle,/ne poenas Nemesis reposcat a te. Est vemens dea; laedere hanc caveto.

4. Ut effigies bacchantis, prospicit, eheu, prospicit et magnis curarum fluctuat undis.

5. Namque mei nuper Lethaeo in gurgite fratris/pallidulum manans alluit unda pedem.

6. Sicine subrepsti mi atque intestina perurens/ei misero eripuisti nostra bona?/ Eripuisti, eheu nostrae crudele venenum/vitae, eheu nostrae pestis amicitiae.

7. Naufragum ut eiectum spumantibus aequoris undis.

## 5. Match the figure with its corresponding identification.

| | | |
|---|---|---|
| ___ 1. | Totum ut te faciant, Fabulle, nasum | A. anaphora |
| ___ 2. | Vocaret aura, sive utrumque Iuppiter . . . | B. litotes |
| ___ 3. | Idem infaceto et infacetior rure | C. metonymy |
| ___ 4. | Facit delicias libidinesque | D. asyndeton |
| ___ 5. | Di magni, horribilem et sacrum libellum! | E. metaphor |
| ___ 6. | Nobis, cum semel occidit brevis lux | F. hyperbaton |
| ___ 7. | Aeternum hoc sanctae foedus amicitiae | G. chiasmus |
| ___ 8. | Iam me prodere, iam non dubitas fallere, perfide? | H. polyptoton |
| ___ 9. | Gravedo frigida et frequens tussis | I. interlocking (synchysis) |
| ___ 10. | Cena, non sine candida puella | J. diminutive |
| ___ 11. | Iocose lepide vovere divis | K. hendiadys |

## Cicero

### 1. Hyperbaton (framing or bracketing) is a common feature of Ciceronian prose. Locate and bracket the hyperbaton in each sentence or passage below. The first one is done for you.

a. Quod si [haec vox huius hortatu praeceptisque conformata] non nullis aliquando saluti fuit. . . .

b. Ut me pro summo poeta atque eruditissimo homine dicentem hoc concursu hominum litteratissimorum . . . .

c. Itaque hunc et Tarantini et Locrenses et Regini et Neopolitani civitate ceterisque praemiis donarunt, et omnes qui aliquid de ingeniis poterant iudicare cognitione atque hospitio dignum existimarunt.

d.  Adest vir summa auctoritate et religione et fide, M. Lucullus, qui se non opinari sed scire, non audisse sed vidisse, non interfuisse sed egisse dicit.

e.  Quam multas nobis imagines non solum ad intuendum verum etiam ad imitandum fortissimorum virorum expressas scriptores et Graeci et Latini reliquerunt!

2.  ***Select the correct answer to identify the following figures of speech, which are among Cicero's favorites. To assist you, the first few are underlined.***

1.  Est ridiculum ad ea quae habemus nihil dicere, quaerere quae habere non possumus . . . .

    (A)  personification
    (B)  litotes
    (C)  syncope
    (D)  asyndeton

2.  Cum esset cum M. Lucullo in Siciliam profectus et cum ex ea provincia cum eodem Lucullo decederet . . . .

    (A)  polyptoton
    (B)  antithesis
    (C)  alliteration
    (D)  oxymoron

3.  Dicentem hoc concursu hominum litteratissimorum, hac vestra humanitate, hoc denique praetore exercente iudicium . . . .

    (A)  polysyndeton
    (B)  simile
    (C)  anaphora
    (D)  synchysis

4.  Lectissimum virum . . . tanto conventu hominum ac frequentia, hoc uti genere dicendi.

    (A) hendiadys
    (B) transferred epithet
    (C) praeteritio
    (D) chiasmus

5.  Quaeso a vovis ut . . . detis hanc veniam accommodatam huic reo, vobis, quemadmodum spero, non molestam . . . .

    (A)  ecphrasis
    (B)  zeugma
    (C)  anastrophe
    (D)  chiasmus

6.  Ego multos homines excellenti animo ac virtute fuisse et sine doctrina, naturae ipsius habitu prope divino per se ipsos et moderatos et graves exstitisse fateor.

    (A)  hendiadys
    (B)  enjambment
    (C)  hyperbaton
    (D)  ecphrasis

7. Cum clarissimo imperatore L. Lucullo apud exercitum fuisse, superioribus cum eodem quaestore fuisse in Asia . . . .

   (A) ellipsis            (C) parallelism

   (B) allegory           (D) metonymy

8. Qui sedulitatem mali poetae duxerit aliquo tamen praemio dignam . . . .

   (A) hyperbaton        (C) juxtaposition

   (B) antithesis          (D) praeteritio

9. Fulvius non dubitavit Martis manubias Musis consecrare.

   (A) litotes             (C) chiasmus

   (B) hendiadys        (D) alliteration

10. Populus . . . Romanus aperuit . . . Pontum . . . ipsa natura et regione vallatum

    (A) metaphor         (C) polysyndeton

    (B) hendiadys        (D) personification

11. Qui ita se gerunt, ita vivunt, ut eorum probetur fides integritas aequitas liberalitas.

    (A) polsyndeton       (C) asyndeton

    (B) oxymoron        (D) simile

12. Ratio aliqua ab optimarum artium studiis ac disciplina profecta . . . .

    (A) litotes            (C) onomatopoeia

    (B) chiasmus         (D) prosopopeia

13. Quantum ceteris ad suas res obeundas, quantum ad festos dies ludorum celebrandos, quantum ad alias voluptates . . . .

    (A) hysteron proteron    (C) polysyndeton

    (B) alliteration       (D) anaphora

## Horace

**1. Match the figure of speech, as underlined, with its correct identification. These are among Horace's favorites.**

\_\_\_\_ 1. Manet sub <u>Iove</u> frigido/venator      A. asyndeton

\_\_\_\_ 2. <u>Aequam</u> memento rebus in arduis/ servare <u>mentem</u>      B. simile

\_\_\_\_ 3. Quis scit an adiciant <u>hodiernae crastina</u>/ <u>summae tempora</u> di superi?      C. onomatopoeia

___ 4. <u>Integer vitae scelerisque purus</u>          D. metaphor

___ 5. Saxis, unde <u>l</u>oquaces <u>l</u>ymphae desi<u>l</u>iunt tuae          E. hendiadys

___ 6. <u>Non</u>, Torquate, genus, <u>non</u> te facundia,          F. transferred epithet
<u>non</u> te/restituet pietas

___ 7. Omnes eodem cogimu<u>r, o</u>mnium/versatur urna          G. hyperbaton

___ 8. Daret ut catenis/<u>fatale</u> <u>monstrum</u>          H. personification

___ 9. <u>Aurarum et siluae</u> metu          I. interlocked (synchysis)

___ 10. Sublimi <u>feriam sidera</u> vertice          J. anaphora

___ 11. <u>Non sine</u> vano aurarum et siluae metu          K. alliteration

___ 12. Dum/. . . regina . . . <u>funus</u> et imperio parabat          L. litotes

___ 13. <u>Simplex</u> <u>munditiis</u>          M. chiasmus

___ 14. <u>Luctantem</u> Icariis fluctibus Africum          N. enjambment

___ 15. Vitas <u>inuleo</u> me <u>similis</u>, Chloe          O. hyperbole

___ 16. Regina <u>dementes</u> ruinas. . . parabat          P. metonymy

___ 17. Lenesque sub noctem <u>susurri</u> . . . repetantur          Q. oxymoron

## Ovid

### 1. *Underline the Latin that illustrates the figure of speech, as identified.*

1.  Ista decent umeros gestamina nostros          synchysis

2.  Gloria gentis ego,/quam sua libertas ad honesta coegerat arma          metonymy

3.  Raditur haec elegis ultima meta meis!          metaphor

4.  Comprimat ordinibus versus, oculosque moretur          chiasmus

5.  Mollierant animos lectus et umbra meos          hendiadys

6.  Sunt tibi magna, puer, nimiumque potentia regna          hyperbaton

7.   Iuvenemque oculis animoque requirit                    zeugma

8.   Vosque rotae frangat praetereuntis onus                 synecdoche

9.   Mille domos adiere locum requiemque petentes            hendiadys

10.  Effecere levem nec iniqua mente ferendo                 litotes

## 2.   Select the correct answer to identify each figure of speech. The first few are underlined to help you begin.

1.   Oscula dat reddique putat, loquiturque tenetque.
     (A)   anaphora                    (C)   tmesis
     (B)   litotes                     (D)   polysyndeton

2.   Quoque erat accinctus, demisit ilia <u>ferrum</u>.
     (A)   enjambment                  (C)   synecdoche
     (B)   oxymoron                    (D)   transferred epithet

3.   <u>Saepe</u> venire ad me dubitantem hortata Corinnam,/<u>saepe</u> laboranti fida reperta mihi.
     (A)   personification             (C)   polysyndeton
     (B)   anaphora                    (D)   polyptoton

4.   Ubi dicitur <u>altam</u>/coctilibus muris cinxisse Semiramis <u>urbem</u>.
     (A)   simile                      (C)   asyndeton
     (B)   personification             (D)   hyperbaton

5.   <u>Mars dubius, certa Venus</u>: victique resurgunt.
     (A)   hendiadys                   (C)   apostrophe
     (B)   asyndeton                   (D)   chiasmus

6.   Quidque tibi, lascive puer, cum fortibus armis?
     (A)   prolepsis                   (C)   ellipsis
     (B)   hyperbole                   (D)   polysyndeton

7.   Musa per undenos emodulanda pedes!
     (A)   tmesis                      (C)   pleonasm
     (B)   interlocked (synchysis)     (D)   hyperbole

8.  Ferrea cum vestris bella, valete, modis.
    - (A) litotes
    - (B) apostrophe
    - (C) simile
    - (D) ellipsis

9.  Ventilet accensas flava Minerva faces?
    - (A) asyndeton
    - (B) prolepsis
    - (C) hyperbole
    - (D) hyperbaton

10. Arma gravi numero violentiaque bella parabam.
    - (A) anaphora
    - (B) polysyndeton
    - (C) metonymy
    - (D) hyperbole

11. Ut Hymettia sole/cera remollescit.
    - (A) simile
    - (B) hyperbaton
    - (C) synecdoche
    - (D) chiasmus

12. Hoc habeat scriptum tota tabella "Veni!"
    - (A) litotes
    - (B) aposiopesis
    - (C) chiasmus
    - (D) alliteration

13. Militat omnis amans, et habet sua castra Cupido.
    - (A) metaphor
    - (B) transferred epithet
    - (C) polyptoton
    - (D) tricolon crescens

14. Ars adeo latet arte suo.
    - (A) apostrophe
    - (B) polyptoton
    - (C) onomatopoeia
    - (D) ellipsis

15. Tremebunda videt pulsare cruentum/membra solum.
    - (A) anaphora
    - (B) praeteritio
    - (C) interlocked (synchysis)
    - (D) tricolon crescens

16. Postera nocturnos Aurora removerat ignes.
    - (A) metaphor
    - (B) litotes
    - (C) polysyndeton
    - (D) zeugma

17. Nec sumus ingrati: tibi nos debere fatemur.
    - (A) metonymy
    - (B) pleonasm
    - (C) litotes
    - (D) ecphrasis

18. Invide, dicebant, paries, quid amantibus obstas?

    (A) transferred epithet          (C) chiasmus

    (B) oxymoron                     (D) apostrophe

19. Omnia possideat, non possidet aera Minos.

    (A) hendiadys                    (C) personification

    (B) chiasmus                     (D) aposiopesis

20. Mille domos clausere serae; tamen una recepit.

    (A) enjambment                   (C) anaphora

    (B) hyperbole                    (D) simile

21. Deus in flammas abiit, pectore toto/uritur.

    (A) metaphor                     (C) tmesis

    (B) polyptoton                   (D) polysyndeton

22. Rursus amans rursusque manu sua vota retractat.

    (A) alliteration                 (C) anaphora

    (B) synecdoche                   (D) asyndeton

23. Iuvenum pulcherrimus alter,/altera . . . praelata puellis.

    (A) hyperbaton                   (C) polysyndeton

    (B) chiasmus                     (D) tricolon crescens

24. Mille domos adiere locum requiemque petentes

    (A) chiasmus                     (C) hendiadys

    (B) ecphrasis                    (D) anaphora

25. Da mihi perpetua, genitor carissime, dixit/virginitate frui.

    (A) enjambment                   (C) oxymoron

    (B) personification              (D) ellipsis

**3. Select the correct answer for these poetic techniques and usages that are common, but are not required for the AP Latin Exam. The first few are underlined, to help you along.**

1. Videt . . . sideribus similes <u>oculos</u>, videt <u>oscula</u>.

    (A) antithesis                   (C) anaphora

    (B) dyspepsia                    (D) sound play

2. Tota domus duo sunt, idem <u>parent</u>que <u>iubent</u>que.
   - (A) diminutive
   - (B) colloquialism
   - (C) anastrophe
   - (D) antithesis

3. Puer Icarus . . . <u>quas</u> vaga moverat aura,/captabat <u>plumas</u>.
   - (A) anastrophe
   - (B) poetic plural
   - (C) parallelism
   - (D) allusion

4. <u>Ego</u> <u>te</u>, miseranda, peremi.
   - (A) juxtaposition
   - (B) anastrophe
   - (C) transferred epithet
   - (D) embolism

5. Et parvas v<u>o</u>lucres et fl<u>o</u>res mille c<u>o</u>l<u>o</u>rum.
   - (A) golden line
   - (B) assonance
   - (C) parenthetical expression
   - (D) Grecism

6. Ille graves urbes, hic durae limen amicae/obsidet.
   - (A) juxtaposition
   - (B) condensation
   - (C) euphemism
   - (D) poetic plural

7. Et scelerata fero consumite viscera morsu.
   - (A) anastrophe
   - (B) archaism
   - (C) golden line
   - (D) parallelism

8. His (tabellis) ego commisi nostros insanus amores.
   - (A) poetic plural
   - (B) euphemism
   - (C) chiasmus
   - (D) alliteration

9. Summissoque humiles intrarunt vertice postes.
   - (A) poetic plural
   - (B) juxtaposition
   - (C) euphemism
   - (D) golden line

10. Hortaturque sequi damnosasque erudit artes.
    - (A) juxtaposition
    - (B) anastrophe
    - (C) foreshadowing
    - (D) antithesis

11. Corniger increpuit thyrso graviore Lyaeus.
    - (A) allusion
    - (B) antithesis
    - (C) parallelism
    - (D) juxtaposition

12. Genae maduere seniles,/et patriae tremuere manus.
    (A) golden line            (C) diminutive
    (B) archaism            (D) foreshadowing

13. Et lux . . ./praecipitatur aquis, et aquis nox exit ab isdem.
    (A) parenthetical expression     (C) hypoxia
    (B) antithesis            (D) archaism

14. Venit Atlantiades positis caducifer alis.
    (A) juxtaposition          (C) euthanasia
    (B) antithesis            (D) Grecism

15. Sic deus et virgo; est hic spe celer, illa timore.
    (A) golden line            (C) condensation
    (B) colloquialism         (D) diminutive

**4. Find the word picture in each example and indicate how the word order contributes to the meaning. The first few are underlined to help you get started.**

a.    Ut canis in vacuo leporem cum Gallicus arvo

b.    Vidit et obscurum timido pede fugit in antrum

c.    Conditaque in liquida corna autumnalia faece

d.    Cingere litorea flaventia tempora myrto

e.    Velut ales, ab alto/quae teneram prolem produxit in aera nido

f.    Geminas opifex libravit in alas

g.    Sunt tibi magna, puer, nimiumque potentia regna

h.    Sagittifera prompsit duo tela pharetra

i.    Saepe, ubi constiterant hinc Thisbe, Pyramus illinc

j.    Fissus erat tenui rima . . . paries

k.    Caedere et armata vulgus inerme manu

l.    Oraque caerulea patrium clamantia nomen/excipiuntur aqua

5. **Indicate how each word play, as identified, contributes to the sense of the context in which it is found.**

a.  Interea niveum mira feliciter arte sculpsit ebur (chiasmus)

b.  Turpe senex miles, turpe senilis amor (anaphora, parallelism)

c.  Vota tamen tetigere deos, tetigere parentes (alliteration)

d.  Cura deum di sint, et, qui coluere, colantur (polyptoton)

e.  Frondere Philemona Baucis,/Baucida conspexit senior frondere Philemon. (synchysis, chiasmus, condensation)

f.  Ars adeo latet arte sua (oxymoron)

g.  Mollia cinguntur tenui praecordia libro (synchysis)

h.  Quod facit, auratum est et cuspide fulget acuta,/quod fugit, obtusum est et habet sub harundine plumbum (parallelism)

i.  Pes modo tam velox pigris radicibus haeret (chiasmus, antithesis/juxtaposition)

j.  Et denso mixtas perferet imbre nives (synchysis)

6. **Given the context, identify the sound effect and then explain how it contributes to the meaning of each example. There may be more than one sound effect.**

a.  Obviaque adversas vibrabant flamina. (The sound of Daphne's clothing as she runs)

b.  Quod datus est verbis ad amicas transitus aures. (The lovers whisper at the wall)

c.  Conciderant ictae nivea cervice iuvencae. (A heifer is sacrificed at the festival of Venus)

d.  Corpus erat: saliunt temptatae pollice venae! (The statue has come to life)

e.  Hos petit in socio bella puella viro. (A lover is like a soldier)

f.  Cum vitiato fistula plumbo/scinditur et tenui stridente foramine longas/ eiaculatur aquas et ictibus aera rumpit. (Pyramus' wound is like a leaky pipe)

g.  Eliso percussis aere pennis. (Cupid takes to the air)

h.  Iuppiter est genitor. (Apollo boasts of his lineage)

## Vergil – Passage Analysis

### Passage A

       Haec ubi dicta, cavum conversa cuspide montem
       impulit in latus: ac venti velut agmine facto,
       qua data porta, ruunt et terras turbine perflant.
*Line*  Incubuere mari totumque a sedibus imis
   5   una Eurusque Notusque ruunt creberque procellis
       Africus et vastos volvunt ad litora fluctus:
       insequitur clamorque virum stridorque rudentum.
       Eripiunt subito nubes caelumque diemque
       Teucrorum ex oculis; ponto nox incubat atra.
   10  Intonuere poli et crebris micat ignibus aether
       praesentemque viris intentant omnia mortem.

                                    ***Aeneid* 1.81–91**

Identify the following poetic techniques in the passage above, underline them, and label with the appropriate letter in the nearest margin. Some figures may have more than one example. The techniques are <u>not</u> listed in the order in which they appear in the text.

| | | | |
|---|---|---|---|
| a. | ellipsis | f. | sound play |
| b. | alliteration | g. | polysyndeton |
| c. | metonymy | h. | interlocked word order (synchysis) |
| d. | hyperbole | i. | personification |
| e. | simile | j. | alternate perfect tense |

### Passage B

       Talia iactanti stridens Aquilone procella
       velum adversa ferit, fluctusque ad sidera tollit.
       Franguntur remi, tum prora avertit et undis
*Line*  dat latus, insequitur cumulo praeruptus aquae mons.
   5   Hi summo in fluctu pendent; his unda dehiscens
       terram inter fluctus aperit, furit aestus harenis.

                                      ***Aeneid* 1.102–107**

Identify the three examples of <u>hyperbole</u> that appear in this passage and discuss the poetic effect of this figure on Vergil's description of the storm.

### Passage C

Iunonem interea rex omnipotentis Olympi
adloquitur fulva pugnas de nube tuentem:
"Quae iam finis erit, coniunx? Quid denique restat?
*Line* Indigetem Aenean scis ipsa et scire fateris
5 deberi caelo fatisque ad sidera tolli.
Quid struis? Aut qua spe gelidis in nubibus haeres?
Mortalin decuit violari vulnere divum?
Aut ensem (quid enim sine te Iuturna valeret?)
ereptum reddi Turno et vim crescere victis?

**Aeneid 12.791–99**

Identify by name the following poetic techniques and usages that appear in this
passage:

Iunonem . . . tuentem (1–2)

omnipotentis (1)

Quid . . . Quid (3,6)

Aenean (4)

deberi caelo fatisque . . . tolli (5)

ad sidera (5)

Mortalin . . . divum (7)

violari vulnere divum (7)

ereptum reddi (9)

## Catullus – Passage Analysis

### Passage D

O misero frater adempte mihi,
tu mea tu moriens fregisti commoda, frater,
tecum una tota est nostra sepulta domus;
omnia tecum una perierunt gaudia nostra
quae tuus in vita dulcis alebat amor.

**Catullus 68.20–24**

Write out the Latin illustrating each of the following figures that appear in the
passage above. The techniques are not listed in the order in which they appear in
the text.

a.  anaphora            e.  chiasmus

b.  anastrophe          f.  hyperbaton

c.  apostrophe          g.  metaphor

d.  assonance           h.  poetic plural

## Horace – Passage Analysis

### Passage E

Te flagrantis atrox hora Caniculae
nescit tangere, tu frigus amabile
  fessis vomere tauris

*Line*   praebes et pecori vago.
 5 Fies nobilium tu quoque fontium,
  me dicente cavis impositum ilicem
   saxis, unde loquaces
    lymphae desiliunt tuae.

**Horace, *Odes* 3. 13.9–16**

Explore these two stanzas in order to locate the following figures. Write out the Latin that illustrates each one and then briefly comment on how each contributes to the meaning. Line numbers are provided to help you zero in.

| | |
|---|---|
| alliteration | (lines 2 and 7–8) |
| antithesis | (lines 1–2) |
| apostrophe | (line 5) |
| asyndeton | (line 2) |
| chiasmus | (lines 3–4) |
| diminutive | (line 1) |
| framing | (lines 1 and 6–7) |
| personification | (line 7) |
| polyptoton | (lines 1–2) |
| word play | (lines 3 and 6–7) |

## Ovid – Passage Analysis

### Passage F

Ite hinc, difficiles, funebria ligna, tabellae,
  tuque, negaturis cera referta notis . . . .
At, tamquam minio penitus medicata, rubebas—

*Line*  ille color vere sanguinulentus erat!
 5 Proiectae triviis iaceatis, inutile lignum,
  vosque rotae frangat praetereuntis onus. . . .
Illa (arbor) dedit turpes raucis bubonibus umbras,
  vulturis in ramis et strigis ova tulit. . . .
Ergo ego vos rebus duplices pro nomine sensi—
 10 auspicii numerus non erat ipse boni!

**Ovid, *Amores* 1.12.7–8, 11–14, and 19–28**

In this passage, Ovid curses his note-tablets for failing to bring back good news from Corinna. Locate and underline the following figures of speech that contribute to his depiction of the tablets.

     a. personification

     b. hyperbaton/framing

     c. apostrophe

     d. diminutive

     e. metaphor

     f. synecdoche

     g. onomatopoeia

     h. juxtaposition

     i. golden line

     j. word play

### Passage G

     Et <u>modo</u> blanditias adhibet, <u>modo</u> grata puellis
     munera fert illi: <u>conchas teretesque</u> lapillos
     <u>et parvas volucres</u> et flores <u>mille colorum</u>
*Line*  iliaque pictasque pilas et ab arbore lapsas
  5   Heliadum <u>lacrimas</u>. Ornat quoque vestibus artus,
     dat digitis gemmas<u>, d</u>at longa monilia collo;
     <u>aure leves bacae, redimicula pectore pendent</u>—
     cuncta decent.

**Ovid, *Metamorphoses* 10.259–66**

With reference to the passage above, identify by name in the sequence that they appear, the underlined figures of speech used by Ovid to describe and emphasize the gifts that Pygmalion bestows on his love-statue. Note that the figure in line 2 extends into line 3 and in line 7 there are as many as three.

## Answers Vergil

### Question 1

| | | |
|---|---|---|
| 1. D | 6. G | 11. L |
| 2. H | 7. N | 12. J |
| 3. O | 8. K | 13. A |
| 4. C | 9. F | 14. I |
| 5. B | 10. M | 15. E |

## Question 2

1. (B) anaphora
2. (D) transferred epithet
3. (C) asyndeton
4. (D) polysyndeton
5. (C) apostrophe

6. (A) simile
7. (D) enjambment
8. (B) tricolon crescens
9. (A) hyperbaton
10. (D) pleonasm

## Question 3

1. (A) polyptoton
2. (D) apostrophe
3. (B) anaphora
4. (C) hendiadys
5. (C) hyperbaton

6. (D) synecdoche
7. (B) onomatopoeia
8. (C) zeugma
9. (B) simile
10. (A) ellipsis

# Catullus

## Question 1

### English Examples

1. (B) personification
2. (G) onomatopoeia
3. (L) metonymy
4. (E) diminutive
5. (H) metaphor
6. (A) anaphora

7. (I) alliteration
8. (D) hyperbole
9. (K) antithesis
10. (F) litotes
11. (J) apostrophe

### Latin Examples

a. (B) personification
b. (H) metaphor
c. (I) alliteration
d. (D) hyperbole
e. (G) onomatopoeia
f. (A) anaphora

g. (F) litotes
h. (J) apostrophe
i. (L) metonymy
j. (E) diminutive
k. (K) antithesis

## Question 2

1. (B) diminutive
2. (A) hendiadys
3. (D) hysteron proteron
4. (D) apostrophe
5. (D) personification
6. (B) hyperbole
7. (C) litotes
8. (B) metaphor
9. (C) chiasmus
10. (A) ecphrasis
11. (D) golden line
12. (C) hyperbaton
13. (C) interlocking/synchysis

## Question 3

Note that the identifications of figures are given in alphabetical order.

1. Antithesis (**lumina nocte**); assonance/rhyme/sound play/ (**gemina . . . lumina**); metaphor (**lumina = oculi**); transferred epithet (**gemina**: from **nocte** to **lumina**)

2. Anaphora (**O**); apostrophe (**O factum male! O miselle passer!**); diminutive (**miselle**)

3. Assonance (**animis amant amantur**); asyndeton (**amant amantur**); polyptoton (**amant amantur**)

4. Alliteration (**saepe sibilum**); onomatopoeia (**sibilum**); personification (**loquente . . . coma**)

5. Anastrophe (**larem ad**); metonymy (**larem**); tricolon (**cum . . . reponit, ac . . . nostrum, desideratoque . . . lecto**)

6. Alliteration (**Dindymi dominam**); diminutive (**misellae, medulla**); metaphor (**ignes edunt**)

7. Anaphora (**nec . . . nec . . . nec**); assonance (**nec bello pede nec . . . ocellis**); diminutive (**ocellis**); litotes (**nec minimo, nec bello, nec nigris**)

8. Alliteration (**sola sub, spumantibus exspuit undis**); anaphora (**Quae . . . quae . . . quae**); onomatopoeia (**exspuit**)

9. Antithesis (**una omnes**); metonymy (**Veneres**); word play (**omnibus una omnes**)

10. Hyperbaton (**mutis [gratum acceptumve] sepulcris**); transferred epithet (from **sepulcris** to the deceased); consonance of **m**'s

## Question 4

1. Alliteration (**Lydiae lacus**); apostrophe (**O venusta Sirmio**); onomatopoeia (**cachinnorum**): personification (**gaude, ridete**): polyptoton (**gaude, gaudente**); transferred epithet (**Lydiae** from **undae** to **lacus**); tricolon crescens (**Salve; ero gaude gaudente; ridete . . . cachinnorum**)

2. Alliteration (**mala mens**), diminutive (**miselle**), hyperbaton (**te ... praecipitem**), synecdoche (**iambos**)

3. Anaphora (**cave** ), assonance of a and e, diminutive (**ocelle**), onomatopoeia (**despuas**), poetic plural (**nostras, oramus**) 4. Anaphora (**prospicit**); hyperbaton (**magnis [curarum fluctuat] undis**); metaphor (**magnis curarum fluctuat undis**); parenthesis (**eheu**); simile (**Ut effigies bacchantis**)

5. Allusion (**Lethaeo**); diminutive (**pallidulum**); euphemism (**pallidulum ... pedem**); hyperbaton/ framing (**mei ... fratris**; **pallidulum ... pedem**); onomatopoeia (**gurgite**)

6. Anaphora (**eheu nostrae**); metaphor (**venenum vitae, pestis amicitiae**); parallelism (**eheu nostrae crudele ... amicitiae**); poetic plural (**nostra, nostrae**); interlocking/synchysis (**nostrae ... venenum vitae... nostrae pestis amicitiae**); syncope (**subrepsti**); enjambment (**sicine subrepsti mi, vitae**).

7. Alliteration (**spumantibus aequoris undis**); anastrophe (**Naufragum ut**) onomatopoeia (**spumantibus**); simile (**Naufragum ut**)

## Question 5

| | | | | | |
|---|---|---|---|---|---|
| 1. | F | 5. | J | 9. | G |
| 2. | C | 6. | E | 10. | B |
| 3. | H | 7. | I | 11. | D |
| 4. | K | 8. | A | | |

# CICERO

## Question 1

Note that Question (a) has been answered.

b. Ut [me pro summo poeta atque eruditissimo homine dicentem] hoc concursu hominum litteratissimorum . . . .

c. Itaque [hunc et Tarantini et Locrenses et Regini et Neopolitani civitate ceterisque praemiis donarunt, et omnes qui aliquid de ingeniis poterant iudicare cognitione atque hospitio dignum] existimarunt.

d. Adest [vir summa auctoritate et religione et fide, M. Lucullus], qui se non opinari sed scire, non audisse sed vidisse, non interfuisse sed egisse dicit.

e. Quam multas nobis [imagines non solum ad intuendum verum etiam ad imitandum fortissimorum virorum expressas] scriptores et Graeci et Latini reliquerunt!

## Question 2

1. (D) asyndeton
2. (B) antithesis (contrast)
3. (C) anaphora
4. (A) hendiadys
5. (D) chiasmus
6. (C) hyperbaton
7. (C) parallelism

8. (A) hyperbaton
9. (D) alliteration
10. (B) hendiadys
11. (C) asyndeton
12. (B) chiasmus
13. (D) anaphora

# HORACE

## Question 1

1. P
2. G
3. I
4. M
5. K
6. J

7. A
8. N
9. E
10. O
11. L
12. D

13. Q
14. H
15. B
16. F
17. C

# OVID

## Question 1

1. <u>Ista</u> decent <u>umeros</u> <u>gestamina</u> <u>nostros</u> — synchysis
2. Gloria gentis ego,/quam sua libertas ad honesta coegerat <u>arma</u> — metonymy
3. <u>Raditur</u> haec elegis <u>ultima</u> <u>meta</u> meis! — metaphor
4. <u>Comprimat</u> ordinibus <u>versus,</u> <u>oculosque</u> <u>moretur</u> — chiasmus
5. Mollierant animos <u>lectus</u> <u>et</u> <u>umbra</u> meos — hendiadys
6. Sunt tibi <u>magna</u>, puer, nimiumque potentia <u>regna</u> — hyperbaton
7. Iuvenemque <u>oculis</u> <u>animoque</u> <u>requirit</u> — zeugma
8. Quoque erat accinctus, demisit in ilia <u>ferrum</u> — synecdoche
9. Mille domos adiere <u>locum</u> <u>requiemque</u> <u>petentes</u> — zeugma
10. Effecere levem <u>nec</u> <u>iniqua</u> mente ferendo — litotes

## Question 2

1. (D) polysyndeton
2. (C) synecdoche
3. (B) anaphora
4. (D) hyperbaton
5. (D) chiasmus
6. (C) ellipsis
7. (B) interlocking (synchysis)
8. (B) apostrophe
9. (D) hyperbaton
10. (C) metonymy
11. (A) simile
12. (D) alliteration
13. (A) metaphor
14. (B) polyptoton
15. (C) interlocking (synchysis)
16. (A) metaphor
17. (C) litotes
18. (D) apostrophe
19. (B) chiasmus
20. (B) hyperbole
21. (A) metaphor
22. (C) anaphora
23. (B) chiasmus
24. (C) hendiadys
25. (A) enjambment

## Question 3

1. (D) sound play
2. (D) antithesis
3. (A) anastrophe
4. (A) juxtaposition
5. (B) assonance
6. (B) condensation
7. (C) golden line
8. (C) poetic plural
9. (D) golden line
10. (C) foreshadowing
11. (D) allusion
12. (D) foreshadowing
13. (B) antithesis
14. (D) Grecism
15. (C) condensation

## Question 4

a. The hare is "trapped" by the Gallic hound.

b. Thisbe is "inside" the dark cave.

c. The autumnal cherries are "suspended" in the liquid wine-dregs.

d. The golden locks are "wreathed" in sea-grown myrtle.

e. The young bird (**teneram prolem**) is "nestled" in the middle of the nest (**alto . . . nido**).

f. Daedalus "hangs suspended" between the two wings.

g. **Magna . . . nimiumque potentia regna** extends and magnifies Cupid's realms.

h. Two arrows are "hanging" in the arrow-bearing quiver.

i. Thisbe and Pyramus "face each other" through the wall.

j. The tiny crack "separates" or "divides" the wall.

k. The unarmed mob is "surrounded" by the armed band.

l. Icarus, shouting his father's name, is "drowning" in the sky-blue water (**caerulea . . . aqua**).

## Question 5

a. In this line, Ovid displays the skill that he describes by placing the key word **feliciter** in the center of the chiastic arrangement of **niveum . . . ebur** surrounding **mira . . . arte**, suggesting the beauty sculpted in the marble.

b. The anaphora and parallelism here bring out the comparison between the old soldier and the old lover.

c. Note the alliteration of -t- in **Vota tamen tetigere deos, tetigere parentes.**

d. The play on the verb **colo, colere (coluere, colantur)** emphasizes Ovid's point about respecting the gods.

e. Both the chiastic arrangement (**Philemona Baucis ... Baucida ... Philemon**) and synchysis of **Frondere ... Baucis ... frondere Philemon** of this line, plus condensation, help to express the fact that Baucis and Philemon are transforming into trees simultaneously.

f. In an oxymoron, Ovid literally "conceals" his art so that it can't be seen as art (this is true of his poetry, as well as Pygmalion's statue). The word **latet** lies "hidden" or embedded inside the sentence.

g. The tender bark (**tenui . . . libro**), through synchysis, literally blends or merges with Thisbe's soft breasts (**Mollia . . . praecordia**).

h. The parallel phrasing of the two **quod** clauses compares Cupid's two arrows: **Quod facit** matches with **quod fugit**; **auratum est** with **habet . . . plumbum**; and **cuspide fulget acuta** with **obtusum est.**

i. The juxtaposition and contrast of **velox** with **pigris** amplifies the transformation of swift-footed Thisbe into slow-rooted Thisbe.

j. The hard rain (**denso . . . imbre**) literally mixes with the snow (**mixtas . . . nives**).

## Question 6

a. The alliteration or redundancy of the **v** and **s** sounds suggests the sound of Daphne's clothing flapping as she runs.

b. The appearance of seven **s**'s in the line (sibilation) expresses the lovers whispering at the crack in the wall.

c. The hard **c**-sounds bring to mind the cutting or chopping sound of the heifer's sacrifice.

d. The jumpy sounds of the words in this line (**saliunt temptatae pollice**) suggest the up-and-down beating of a pulse (**saliunt . . . venae**).

e. The rhyming play of the sounds of **bella** and **puella** suggests a double meaning: the girl is pretty (**bella**) and the girl is contrasted with war (**bella**). A lover, by implication, is like a soldier.

f. The words **eiaculatur** and **ictibus** perhaps suggest the stop-and-go sound of water spurting through a crack in a leaky pipe. Also the trisyllabic and rhythmic words **fistula, scinditur, stridente,** along with **ictibus**, contribute.

g. The sibilant words **eliso, percussis, and pennis** evoke the whooshing sound of Cupid rising into the air with flapping wings.

h. The rhyme of **Iuppiter** with **genitor** draws attention to the fact that Jove is Apollo's father.

# Vergil – Passage Analysis

## *Passage A*

a. ellipsis: **dicta (sunt)**, line 1

b. alliteration: **cavum conversa cuspide** (line 1); **venti velut** (line 2); **terras turbine** (line 3); **vastos volvunt** (line 6).

c. metonymy: **poli**, line 10

d. hyperbole: **volvunt ad sidera fluctus**, line 6

e. simile: **velut venti agmine facto**, line 2

f. sound play: **cavum conversa cuspide**, line 1; **stridorque rudentum**, line 7

g. polysyndeton: **Eurusque Notusque**, line 5; **clamorque virum stridorque rudentum**, line 7; **caelumque diemque**, line 8

h. interlocked word order (synchysis): **clamorque virum stridorque rudentum**, line 7

i. personification: **Eripiunt . . . nubes**, lines 8–9

j. alternate perfect tense: **incubuere**, line 4; **intonuere**, line 10

## *Passage B*

1. **fluctusque ad sidera tollit**, line 2

2. **cumulo praeruptus aquae mons**, line 4

3. **unde dehiscens terras inter fluctus aperit**, lines 5–6

Conclusion: these examples of hyperbole exaggerate the force of the storm and thus the danger to Aeneas.

## *Passage C*

**Iunonem . . . tuentem**: hyperbaton/framing

**omnipotentis**: transferred epithet (from **Olympi** to **rex**)

**Quid . . . Quid**: anaphora
**Aenean**: Greek form
**deberi caelo fatisque . . . tolli**: chiasmus
**ad sidera**: hyperbole
**Mortaline . . . divum**: antithesis/contrast
**violari vulnere divum**: alliteration
**ereptum reddi**: antithesis/contrast

## Catullus – Passage Analysis
### Passage D

a. anaphora     **tu** line 2, **frater** 1–2, **tecum una** 3–4
b. anastrophe     **est sepulta**, 3
c. apostrophe     **O . . . frater**, 1
d. assonance     o's in 1, 3
e. chiasmus     dative-vocative-vocative-dative, 1
f. hyperbaton     **omnia . . . gaudia nostra**, 4
g. metaphor     **alebat**, 5
h. poetic plural     **nostra**, 3, 4

## Horace – Passage Analysis
### Passage E

alliteration: **loquaces lymphae desiliunt, nescit tangere tu**
antithesis: **flagrantis** with **frigus** (although not the same part of speech)
apostrophe: **Fies nobilium tu quoque fontium**
asyndeton: **tangere, tu**
chiasmus: **fessis . . . tauris . . . pecori vago**
diminutive: **Caniculae**
framing: **flagrantis . . . Caniculae; cavis . . . saxis**
personification: **loquaces**
polyptoton: **te** and **tu**
word play: the bulls "pull" the plough, **vomere tauris**; the oak is "planted" in the rocks, **cavis impositum ilicem/saxis.**

## Ovid – Passage Analysis
### Passage F

a. personification: **Ite . . . tabellae** (1); **rubebas** (3); **iaceatis** (5)
b. hyperbaton/framing: **difficiles . . . tabellae** (1); **negaturis . . . notis** (2); **turpes . . . umbras** (7); **auspicii . . . boni** (10)

c. apostrophe: **funebria ligna, tabellae** (1); **tuque ... cera** (2); **inutile lignum** (5)

d. diminutive: **tabellae** (1)

e. metaphor: **sanguinulentus** (4), the color red (cf. **rubebas**) suggests that Ovid is "bleeding" from the wound of his rejection.

f. synecdoche: **rotae** (6)

g. onomatopoeia: **raucis** (7), **bubonibus** (7)

h. juxtaposition: **ego vos** (9)

i. golden line: **auspicii numerus non erat ipse boni** (10)

j. word play: the word **duplices** describes both the two-fold tablet and its two-faced or duplicitous character!

### *Passage G*

**modo ... modo**: anaphora

**conchas teretes ... et parvas volucres**: chiasmus

**lapillos**: diminutive

**mille colorum**: hyperbole

**iliaque pictasque**: polysyndeton

**(ab arbore lapsas Heliadum) lacrimas**: metaphor

**gemmas, dat**: asyndeton

**aure leves bacae (pendent), redimicula pectore pendent**: condensed line, parallel clauses, diminutive

# Webliography on Figures of Speech

## General Web Sites

- Figures of Speech (T. Abney, teacher's web site)
  http://abney.homestead.com/files/aeneid/tropedefinitioncards.htm
  Clickable exercise asking for definitions of 22 figures.

- Figures of Speech (Bruce M. Johnson, teacher's web site)
  http://www.hoocher.com/figuresofspeech.htm
  Definitions of required figures, with examples from Catullus and the *Aeneid*.

- A Glossary of Rhetorical Terms with Examples (Ross Scaife, Univ. Kentucky
  http://www.uky.edu/AS/Classics/rhetoric.html
  Twenty-six of the 34 figures required by the College Board are found here, with English and Latin examples.

- Interpreting Poetry (Joan Johnige, Kentucky Educational Television)

  http://www.dl.ket.org/latinlit/carmina/index.htm

  Definitions with examples of figures from Catullus and Horace.

- Literary Devices (Jerard White, teacher's web site)

  http://www.fralibrary.com/teachers/white/literary_devices.htm

  Figures are designated as AP or non-AP; includes the 34 for AP, plus anastrophe, caesura, elision, framing, the golden line, hiatus, and rhetorical question.

- Mr. Prueter's Literary Devices (teacher's web site)

  http://www.prueter.org/bill/literarydevices.html

  English and Latin examples.

- *Quia* java games (Ruth Sameth)

  http://www.quia.com/jg/11339.html

  Concentration, flashcards, matching, word search on figures of speech. See also http://www.quia.com/hm/80390.html

- Silvae Rhetoricae (Gideon O. Burton, Brigham Young University)

  http://humanities.byu.edu/rhetoric/Figures/Figures-Overview.htm

  Contains a useful search engine (Search the Forest); English and Latin examples.

**The following sites are by and for English students, but are also useful to the Latin student.**

- Literary Terms (maintained by students in Ted Nellen's high school Cyber English class)

  http://www.tnellen.com/cybereng/lit_terms/

- Mrs. Dowling's Literature Terms

  http://www.kidskonnect.com/FigurativeLanguage/FigurativeLanguage-Home.html

- Virtual Salt: A Handbook of Rhetorical Devices (Robert A. Harris)

  http://www.virtualsalt.com/rhetoric.htm

  Thoroughgoing list, with numerous examples in English and a self-test. Produced by a writer.

## Web Sites for Figures of Speech in AP Latin

### Vergil

- AP Vergil's *Aeneid* (Tim Abney, teacher's web site)

  http://abney.homestead.com/aeneid.html

Click-and-drag matching exercises for many figures found in the required Books of the *Aeneid*; a valuable resource! See also,

http://abney.homestead.com/files/aeneid/aeneid2tropes6b1flashcards.htm

Flashcards for figures in the *Aeneid*; 50 items drawn from entire *Aeneid*.

### Catullus

- Figures of Speech (T. Abney, teacher's web site)

  http://abney.homestead.com/files/catullus/catullustropeflashcards1.htm

  Flashcards for figures in Poems 64, 65, 68, 69, 76, 77, 85, 109, 116.

### Cicero

- Test: Figures of Speech in Cicero (Robert Patrick)

  http://www.quia.com/quiz/259156.html

  Twenty-five clickable multiple-choice questions on Cicero's favorites (you will receive a score, but not the correct answers).

### Horace

- The World of Horace's *Odes* (Ortwin Knorr)

  http://www.willamette.edu/cla/classics/faculty/knorr/horace/Horace_c.1.1.html

  This promises to be a useful site, but it is still under construction. Good for *Odes* 1.1.

### Ovid

- Ovid (Tim Abney, teacher's web site)

  http://abney.homestead.com/ovid1.html

  Click-and-drag matching activities on figures from the *Amores* and from each of the five required myths of the *Metamorphoses*.

# Chapter 11

# Meter and Scansion

## Meter and Scansion on the AP Latin Exam

Meter (the metrical structure of verse) and scansion (the analysis of the metrics of verse) are essential for mastery of Latin poetry and are therefore evaluated on the AP Latin Exam. This chapter presents for you a quick-study of both meter and scansion.

Each syllable in a line of Latin verse is characterized by a vowel, diphthong, or elision consisting of a long or short sound. The combination of these long and/or short sounds is called a foot, which originally equalled the time it took, while dancing, to raise one foot and then lower it to the ground. (Conceptually, a poetic foot is equal to a bar in music.) Several Latin poets rest their claim for immortality on their success in adapting Roman themes to Greek meter (or vice versa).

Two of the meters required for the AP Latin Exam have repeating lines. One is dactylic hexameter, used by all four AP Latin poets, and the other is the hendecasyllable, an eleven-syllable line that was a favorite of Catullus. Catullus and Ovid both use the elegiac couplet, which consists of a hexameter line (six feet) paired with a pentameter line (five feet). The final two required meters consist of four-line strophes, Alcaic and Sapphic, named after Greek poets from the island of Lesbos. <u>On the exam, for each of these meters, as appropriate to your author/s, you are expected to be able to identify elisions and to mark the sound of a vowel as long or short.</u> You need not concern yourself with separating the line into feet (although this is helpful!) or with the more technical aspects of scansion. Because of the ambiguity of the anceps syllable in the final foot of a line of Latin verse, <u>you are allowed to mark the final syllable long in all meters.</u> For additional information about how Latin poets use sound and rhythm, see the previous chapter.

## The Required Meters

The following meters are required for the AP Latin Exam. Cicero, of course, wrote in prose.

| AP Latin Status | Author | Required Meter | Poems |
|---|---|---|---|
| Required author | **Vergil** | dactylic hexameter | *Aeneid* |
| Required author | **Catullus** | hendecasyllabic | Most Poems 1–60 |
| | | elegiac couplet | Poems 65–116 |
| | | dactylic hexameter | Poem 64, lines 50–253 |
| Choice author | **Ovid** | dactylic hexameter | *Metamorphoses* |
| | | elegiac couplet | *Amores* |
| Choice author | **Horace** | Alcaic strophe | *Odes* |
| | | Sapphic strophe | *Odes* |
| | | dactylic hexameter | *Satires* 1.9 |

## How Metrics and Scansion Are Evaluated on the AP Latin Exam

The meters listed for Vergil and Catullus are tested on the multiple-choice sections of the respective Vergil and Latin Literature exams. Most passages of verse on the multiple-choice section have at least one question, and up to three, on scansion (2–5 percent of your grade on this section). Because in the hexameter line the pattern of sounds in the final two feet is always the same, i.e., dactyl and spondee, only the first four feet of a hexameter line are tested, using this format on the multiple-choice section:

The metrical pattern of the first four feet of line 3 (nec quisquam . . . videt) is

(A) spondee-dactyl-dactyl-spondee

(B) dactyl-spondee-dactyl-spondee

(C) spondee-spondee-dactyl-spondee

(D) dactyl-spondee-spondee-dactyl

In the multiple-choice sections of the two most-recently released AP Latin Exams (1999 and 2005), five questions on the hexameter line appeared, plus two on the first line of the elegiac couplet (i.e., a hexameter line), and one on the hendecasyllable.

Scansion of the meters used by the choice authors are tested in the spot question of the free-response section of the Latin Literature exam (for these questions, see Chapter 8). You are asked to write out and scan one line from the relevant poem or passage. The effect of the rhythm on the sense is not evaluated. Only two questions on metrics appeared in the spot question of the free-response sections on exams from 2006–2001: hexameter (*Satires* 1.9, line 35, 2003) and Alcaic (*Odes* 2.7, line 4, 2004).

# The Language of Meter

For the actual metrical patterns of the various meters, see the next section.

- **Alcaic:** the Alcaic strophe, named after the Greek poet Alcaeus, contains four lines, the <u>first two</u> of which are alike, followed by two shorter lines that differ. This was Horace's favorite meter, which he used for poems on patriotic or stately themes, including the six Roman Odes. Also *Odes* 1.9, 1.37; 2.3, 2.7, 2.14; 3.1 and 3.13.

- **anceps**: meaning "two-headed," a syllable that can be either long or short. This is usually indicated by ū or by x.

- **dactyl**: one long syllable followed by two short syllables, ‑ u u.

- **diphthong**: a double vowel with a single sound, e.g., **ae (a͟estas), au (Pla͟utus), eu (ehe͟u),** or **oe (co͟epit)**. All diphthongs are long. Double vowels that have two sounds are not diphthongs, e.g., **filia**. The vowel combination **ei** also consists of two syllables, e.g., **deinde = de + inde**.

- **elegiac couplet**: the elegiac couplet consists of a hexameter line (six feet) paired with a pentameter line (five feet). Of the AP Latin authors, elegiac was used by Catullus and Ovid.

- **elision** (verb, elide): to slur an end vowel with an initial vowel (**quaeque ipse**), an end vowel with an initial **h (meminisse͟ horret)**, or a final –**m** with an initial vowel (**quamqua͟m animus**). In some texts, elisions are indicated by contraction, e.g., **meast** for **mea est**. Sometimes an elision does not occur where expected (**hiatus**), in order to achieve a particular poetic effect. Such lines are not tested on the AP Latin Exam.

- **foot**: a metrical unit consisting of a poetic unit such as a dactyl or spondee.

- **hendecasyllable** (adj., hendecasyllabic; also known as Phalaecian): an eleven-syllable repeating line preferred by Catullus. Many of the poems in the first half of the Catullan corpus (1–60) are written in this meter, which is lively and used for poems of fun or romance.

- **hexameter**: a line of verse containing six (hexa-) metrical units. Dactylic hexameter, also known as the "heroic hexameter," appears in Vergil's *Aeneid*, Catullus, Poem 64, Horace's *Satires*, and Ovid's *Metamorphoses*.

- **Sapphic**: the Sapphic strophe or stanza, named after Sappho, the Greek poetess from Lesbos, contains four lines, the <u>first three</u> of which are alike, followed by a short line. A substitution is allowed in the second foot. This meter is used by Horace in *Odes* 1.22, 1.25, 1.38, and 2.10 and also by Catullus in Poems 11 and 51. Sapphic is used for lighter-hearted po- ems (*Odes* 1.22, 1.25, and 1.38) or sometimes for more serious philosophy (2.10).

- **scansion** (verb, scan): the determination of the length of each syllable in a line of verse as long or short.

- **spondee**: two long syllables, -- --.

- **stanza** (or **strophe**): a division of a poem that contains a repeated pattern of meter.

- **strophe**: see **stanza**.

- **syllable**: a vowel, diphthong, or elision.

- **syncope**: the omission of an alphabetic component within a word, e.g., **norat** for **noverat**. Latin words, usually verbs, are often abbreviated or shortened to accommodate the meter in poetry. Note the difference be- tween syncope and **elision**.

# Scansion

In scansion, every syllable of a Latin word, that is, every vowel, diphthong, or elision, is assigned a long or short sound. Whether the sound is long or short re- flects the length of time the sound was held when spoken. The determination of elision, or slurring between a final and an initial vowel or between a final –**m** and an initial vowel, is also a part of the process of scanning. Macrons (long marks) are not provided on the AP Latin Exam (except in prose passages, in order to make grammatical distinctions between **puellā** and **puella,** for example). For poetry, it is assumed that you will be able to use scansion in order to determine the length of an ambiguous syllable, and therefore its grammatical function.

## Dactylic Hexameter

Each line of hexameter verse contains six feet. The basic metrical unit of a line of dactylic hexameter, the "fingers and feet" meter, is the dactyl (the Greek word for finger, i.e., one long knuckle and two short ones). In sound-sense, the rhythm – u u is equivalent to "dum-diddy-diddy." The following English hexameter may help you to remember the rhythm:

/    /  /  /    /  /   /     /  /
*Down in a deep dark dell sat an old cow munching a beanstalk.*

A spondee may be substituted for a dactyl in any of the first four feet in order to provide the poet with more opportunities for variety of rhythm. As mentioned above, for the purpose of the AP Latin Exam, the final two feet are always to be considered a dactyl and a spondee in succession, that is, - u u / - -.

The detailed rules for the assignment of long and short values to syllables lie outside the scope of this book. To review these, ask your teacher, consult your textbook or reader, or go online (see the Web sites suggested below). In general, sounds are long if they are long by nature, i.e., have a naturally long sound when pronounced, such as the final vowels in the ablative singular form **servo**, the ablative plural form **servis**, and the accusative plural form **servos**. You may know these simply by having learned the correct pronunciation of Latin. Also long are diphthongs and vowels followed by two or more consonants in the same or different words, e.g., the ¯o- in **po̲ssumus** is long <u>by position</u>, i.e., it is followed by two ¯s's, as is the second ¯u- in **po̲ssumu̲s legere,** i.e., it is followed by the consonants ¯s and l̄-. (Yes, sounds cross over between words in Latin scansion.) In general, if there is no reason for a syllable to be long, it is to be considered short. Logic and deduction are also useful strategies to apply when determining the length of a syllable in Latin, e.g., a single short syllable cannot appear between two long syllables in a hexameter line, which consists of units of ¯ u u and ¯ ¯. <u>You are not required to designate foot-breaks in your scansion of a line on the exam</u>, but it helps to do so in order to determine whether or not you have accurately scanned each of the first four feet. Don't be reluctant to work out scansion directly on the question sheet of the exam.

Here below you will find an example of the scansion of a hexameter line. Note that the first and last syllables are always long and remember that no substitutions are allowed in the fifth and sixth feet.

$$\overline{\phantom{x}} \quad \overline{\phantom{x}} \quad \overline{\phantom{x}} \quad \overline{\phantom{x}}$$

| Syllables | ¯ u u / ¯ u u / ¯ u u / ¯ u u / ¯ u u / ¯ ¯ |
|-----------|---------------------------------------------|
| Feet | 1   2   3   4   5   6 |

## Steps in Scanning a Line of Dactylic Hexameter

1. Check to see if there are any elisions in the line and mark them.

   **Arma virumque cano Troiae qui primus ab oris**

   There are no elisions in this line.

2. Mark the initial syllable long and the final two syllables long, so that the last foot is a spondee.

   **Arma virumque cano Troiae qui primus ab oris**

3. Mark the fifth, fourth, and third syllables from the end a dactyl, which is formulaic. The last two feet of any dactylic line on the AP Latin Exam should look like this: ¯ u u / ¯ ¯. So far, we have

   **Arma virumque cano Troiae qui primus ab oris**

4. You need not mark the feet on the exam, but it is helpful to do so in order to determine where the feet begin and end, so that you can determine if you have scanned the line successfully. Remember that only the first four feet are required. Remember, too, that a single short cannot appear between two longs. Mark all syllables that are long by nature or are a diphthong:

<pre>
 -              -    - -    -    - u u  - -
</pre>
**Arma virumque cano Troiae qui / primus ab / oris**

Note 1:

> The final **-o** of verbs is always long by nature. The **-o** in **cano** is also long by position (see below).

Note 2:

> The **-o-** in **Troiae** is long because one short cannot appear between two longs in a hexameter line. The **i** is consonantal (= **j**).

Note 3:

> The double-vowels **-ae** and **-ui** are diphthongs.

6. Mark all syllables that are long by position, i.e., are followed by two or more consonants or by **x** or **z** (which have the sounds of double consonants).

<pre>
  -         -            -    - -   -    - u u   - -
</pre>
**Arma virumque cano Troiae qui / primus ab / oris**

7. Mark the remaining syllables short and divide the line into feet to make sure that you have the first four feet accounted for as containing either a dactyl or a spondee.

<pre>
  -   u u -   u  u  -   - -    -   - u u   - -
</pre>
**Arma vir/umque ca/no Troi/ae qui / primus ab / oris**
<pre>
       1       2       3      4       5          6
</pre>

Note:

> The enclitic **-que** is not a diphthong. Its quantity is determined by its position in the line, e.g.,

<pre>
                          u
</pre>
**fracti bello fatisque repulsi** (short)

<pre>
                              -
</pre>
**aedificant sectaque intexunt abiete costas** (long by position).

When a hexameter line consists primarily of dactyls, i.e., a predominance of short syllables, the effect is one of rapidfire or staccato action or an expression of high emotion. Observe these examples from the *Aeneid*:

- The urgency of Hector's warning to Aeneas is evident in the jumpy interplay of dactyls and spondees:

<pre>
 - -  u u  - u u -   -    -    u u  - u u  -    -
</pre>
**heu fuge, nate dea, teque his, ait, eripe flammis** (*Aeneid* 2.289)

- The uproar in Priam's palace when the Greeks break through with a rush:

<pre>
 -   u u - uu-  u u-  uu- u u  - -
</pre>
**At domus interior gemitu miseroque tumultu / miscetur** (*Aeneid* 2.486)

- Dido's agitation on discovering Aeneas' plans to leave Carthage:

<pre>
 -  u u-  uu-  u  u-  - -u u  -  -
</pre>
**posse nefas tacitusque mea decedere terra** (*Aeneid* 4.306)

A predominance of spondees produces a slow or somber effect and/or creates a more thoughtful or deliberate pace.

- Nightfall settles on the land, concealing the treachery of the Greeks:

$$- - \quad - \quad - \quad - \quad - \quad - - \quad - \quad u \quad u \quad - \quad -$$
**involvens umbra magna terramque polumque** (*Aeneid* 2.251)

- Priam has been slain by Pyrrhus, his life ebbing away as he witnesses the death throes of his city. The scansion gives the appearance of an electro-cardiograph's readout on a failing heart, doesn't it?

$$- \quad u \quad u \quad - \quad - \quad - \quad - \quad - \quad - \quad - \quad u \quad u \quad - \quad -$$
**sorte tulit, Troiam incensam et prolapsa videntem / Pergama**
(*Aeneid* 2.554–56)

- Cocytus, a river of the Underworld, is slow and sluggish in its flow:

$$- - - \quad - - \quad - \quad - \quad - - \quad - \quad u \quad u \quad - \quad -$$
**Cocytus sinu labens circumvenit atro** (*Aeneid* 6.132)

## Hendecasyllable

The metrical pattern for the hendecasyllabic, or eleven-syllable line, is:

$$- - / - u u / - u / - u / - -$$

Catullus prefers that the first foot be a spondee (- -), but it can also be either – u or u –. For the remaining feet the pattern is regular and predictable:

$$- \quad - \quad - \quad u \, u \, - \quad u \, - \quad u \, - \, -$$
**sed contra accipies meros amores** (Catullus, Poem 13.9)

$$- \quad - \quad - \quad u \, u \, - \quad u \, - \quad u \quad - \, -$$
**quod tu / cum olfaci/es, de/os ro/gabis** (Catullus, Poem 13.13)

- The interplay of long and short sounds gives a feeling of vitality. Lesbia's pet sparrow hops around on her lap:

$$- \quad - \, - \quad u \, u \, - \quad u \quad - \quad u \quad - \, -$$
**sed circumsiliens modo huc modo illuc** (Catullus, Poem 3.9)

## Elegiac Couplet

The elegiac couplet consists of a hexameter line (six feet) paired with a pentameter line (five feet). The pentameter line has as its centerpiece, or middle foot, a "mega-dactyl" of four-syllables (- - u u). The pentameter line can also be thought of as having two equal halves, each of which contains two and one-half dactylic feet, that is - $\overline{u\,u}$ / - $\overline{u\,u}$ / -. The pattern is:

$$- u\,u / - u\,u / - u\,u / - u\,u / - u\,u / - - \qquad \text{(hexameter line)}$$

$$- u\,u / - u\,u / - - u\,u / - u\,u / - \qquad \text{(pentameter line)}$$

‐ ‐ ‐ u u ‐ u u ‐ u u ‐ u u ‐ ‐
**Quae bello est habilis, Veneri quoque convenit aetas.**

‐ u u ‐ ‐ ‐ ‐ u u ‐ u u ‐
**Turpe senex miles, turpe senilis amor.** (Ovid, *Amores* 1.9.2–3)

- Of Ovid's favorite meter, Samuel Taylor Coleridge, in his poem "Ovidian Elegaic Metre," writes:

  In the hexameter rises the fountain's silvery column,

  In the pentameter aye falling in melody back.

- Poems written in this meter are sometimes called epigrams. The two lines in a couplet often interact with one another, either by reinforcing or reversing the thought expressed. The two lines of a couplet also often consist of a single, self-contained idea. Here is an example of an elegaic couplet that could easily be a complete epigram:

  ‐ u u ‐ ‐ ‐ ‐ ‐ ‐ ‐ u u ‐ ‐ ‐
  **Lesbia formosa est, quae cum pulcherrima tota est,**

  ‐ ‐ u u ‐ ‐ ‐ ‐ u u ‐ u u ‐
  **tum omnibus una omnes surripuit Veneres.** (Catullus, Poem 86.5–6)

## Alcaic Strophe (or Stanza)

The Alcaic strophe contains four lines, the first two of which are alike, followed by two shorter lines that differ. The first and last syllables of each line may be marked long. The foot count for each line is 6 + 6 + 5 + 4. There are no substitutions in this meter. Here is the pattern:

Line 1     - / - u / - - / - u u / - u / -

Line 2     - / - u / - - / - u u / - u / -

Line 3     - / - u / - - / - u / - -

Line 4        - u u / - u u / - u / - -

‐ ‐ u ‐ ‐ ‐ u u ‐ u ‐
**Vives ut alta stet nive candidum**

‐ ‐ u ‐ ‐ ‐ u u ‐ u ‐
**Soracte, nec iam sustineant onus**

‐ ‐ u ‐ ‐ ‐ u ‐ ‐
**silvae laborantes, geluque**

‐ u u ‐ u u ‐ u ‐ ‐
**flumina constiterint acuto?** (Horace, *Odes* 1.9.1–4)

## Sapphic Strophe (or Stanza)

The Sapphic strophe, named after the Greek lyric poetess Sappho, also contains four lines, the <u>first three</u> of which are alike, followed by a short line. The first and last syllable of each line may be marked long. <u>Note the anceps in the fourth syllable of the first three lines.</u> Remember the format of Catullus 11 and 51 to help you distinguish the Sapphic from the Alcaic stanza. The foot count is 5 + 5 + 5 + 2. The pattern is:

Line 1     - u / - u / - u u / - u / - -    (dactyl in the center foot)

Line 2     - u / - u / - u u / - u / - -

Line 3     - u / - u / - u u / - u / - -

Line 4        - u u / - -

**Integer vitae scelerisque purus**

**non eget Maurus iaculis neque_arcu**

**nec venenatis gravida sagittis,**

**Fusce, pharetra.** (Horace, *Odes* 1.22.1–4)

# A Summary of Meter and Scansion on the AP Latin Exam

## You are:

- expected to be able to identify elisions and to mark the sound of a vowel as long or short
- allowed to mark the final syllable long in all meters

## You are not:

- provided with macrons
- required to mark feet or other pertinent items, such as caesura
- tested on unusual lines

## Practice Questions on Elision

Mark the elisions in the following lines and then explain how the elision contributes to the meaning. For elision, see above under "The Language of Meter." The answers are provided below.

## Vergil

1. Turbine corripuit scopuloque infixit acuto. (*Aeneid* 1.45)

2. Incute vim ventis summersasque obrue puppes. (*Aeneid* 1.69)

3. Velum adversa ferit, fluctusque ad sidera tollit. (*Aeneid* 1.103)

4. Peragro / Europa atque Asia pulsus. (*Aeneid* 1.385)

5. Taurus et incertam incussit cervice securim. (*Aeneid* 2.224)

6. Vitam exhalantem; subiit deserta Creusa. (*Aeneid* 2.563)

7. Indulge hospitio causasque innecte morandi. (*Aeneid* 4.51)

8. Fama . . . pariter facta atque infecta canebat. (*Aeneid* 4.190)

9. Corde premit gemitum lacrimasque effundit inanes. (*Aeneid* 10.465)

10. Saxum antiquum ingens, campo quod forte iacebat. (*Aeneid* 12.897)

## Catullus

11. Vivamus, mea Lesbia, atque amemus. (Catullus, Poem 5.1)

12. Nox est perpetua una dormienda. (Catullus, Poem 5.6)

13. Non belle uteris in ioco atque vino. (Catullus, Poem 12.2)

14. Di magni, horribilem et sacrum libellum. (Catullus, Poem 14a.12)

15. Atque in perpetuum, frater, ave atque vale. (Catullus, Poem 101.10)

## Ovid

16. Exuviis gaudens, innuptaeque aemula Phoebes. (Ovid, *Metamorphoses* 1.476)

17. Fugit, cumque ipso verba imperfecta reliquit. (Ovid, *Metamorphoses* 1.526)

18. Eiaculatur aquas, atque ictibus aera rumpit. (Ovid, *Metamorphoses* 4.124)

19. Dicitur atque unum surripuisse pedem. (Ovid, *Amores* 1.1.4)

20. Quantaculaque estis, vos ego magna voco. (Ovid, *Amores* 3.15.14)

## Practice Questions on Syncope

For syncope, see above under "The Language of Meter." In addition to syncope, two other variations in spelling occur commonly in poetry.

1.  Do not confuse the verb ending --**ere**, which can be a substitute for the third person plural perfect tense ending –**erunt**, with that of an infinitive. Look for the perfect stem!

    **Conticuere omnes intentique ora tenebant** (= **conticuerunt**; note the perfect stem **conticu-**) (*Aeneid* 2.1)

    **sed haec prius <u>fuere</u>: nunc recondita / senet** (= **fuerunt**) (Catullus, Poem 4.25)

    **<u>Diffugere</u> nives, redeunt iam gramina campis** (= **diffugerunt**) (Horace, *Odes* 4.7.1)

    **Flete meos casus: tristes <u>rediere</u> tabellae** (=**redierunt**) (Ovid, *Amores* 1.12.1)

2.  Another variation also appears to be an infinitive but it is, in fact, the second person singular of the present or future passive:

    **Haec ara tuebitur omnes, aut <u>moriere</u> simul** (= **morieris**) (*Aeneid* 2.524)

    **qui te lenirem nobis, neu <u>conarere</u>** (= **conareris**) (Catullus, Poem 116.3)

    **ante fores stabis, mediamque <u>tuebere</u> quercum** (= **tueberis**) (Ovid, *Metamorphoses* 1.563)

In the items below, identify the contracted or shortened forms and then indicate their normal prose equivalents.

### Vergil

1.  Vi superum, saevae memorem Iunonis ob iram. (*Aeneid* 1.4)

2.  Audierat Tyrias olim quae verteret arces. (*Aeneid* 1.20)

3.  Imperio premit ac vinclis et carcere frenat. (*Aeneid* 1.54)

4.  Incubuere mari totumque a sedibus imis. (*Aeneid* 1.85)

5.  O Danaum fortissime gentis / Tydide! (*Aeneid* 1.96)

6.  Scuta virum galeasque et fortia corpora volvit! (*Aeneid* 1.101)

7.  Nec latuere doli fratrem Iunonis et irae. (*Aeneid* 1.130)

8.  Monstrarat, caput acris equi; sic nam fore bello. (*Aeneid* 1.445)

9. Pabula gustassent Troiae Xanthumque bibissent. (*Aeneid* 1.473)

10. Exstinxti te meque, soror, populumque patresque. (*Aeneid* 4.682–83)

## Catullus

11. Nam mellitus erat suamque norat. (Catullus, Poem 3.6)

12. Fulsere quondam candidi tibi soles. (Catullus, Poem 8.3)

13. Natum dicitur esse, comparasti / ad lecticam homines. (Catullus, Poem 10.15–16)

14. Utor tam bene quam mihi pararim. (Catullus, Poem 10.32)

15. Donarunt Veneres Cupidinesque. (Catullus, Poem 13.12)

16. Quem tu scilicet ad tuum Catullum / misti continuo. (Catullus, Poem 14a.14)

17. Nec sanctam violasse fidem, nec foedere ullo. (Catullus, Poem 76.3)

18. Sicine subrepsti mi atque intestina perurens. (Catullus, Poem 77.3)

## Horace

19. Virides rubum / dimovere lacertae. (Horace, *Odes* 1.23.6–7)

20. Dispeream, ni / summosses omnes. (Horace, *Satires* 1.9.47–48)

## Ovid

21. Adnuit, utque caput visa est agitasse cacumen. (Ovid, *Metamorphoses* 1.567)

22. Sed vetuere patres; quod non potuere vetare. (Ovid, *Metamorphoses* 4.61)

23. Corpora cum forma primae vulgasse feruntur. (Ovid, *Metamorphoses* 10.241)

24. In me militiae signa tuere tuae. (Ovid, *Amores* 1.11.12)

# Practice Questions on Scansion

## General Scansion and Dactylic Hexameter

1. Which letter is <u>not</u> considered a vowel, if any?

   a    e    i    o    u    h    y

2. Why is dactylic hexameter called the "heroic hexameter"?

3. Name five ancient poets who composed in hexameter verse.

4. Which one of the Catullan poems required for the AP Latin Exam was written in hexameters?

5. Which poem/s of Ovid were written in hexameter? Which poem/s of Horace?

6. What is the minimum number of syllables found in a hexameter line?

   8    10    13    15    20

   How many feet are found in a hexameter line?

   4    5    6    7    8    9    10

7. The hexameter also serves as the first line of which of the following meters?

   Alcaic strophe    elegiac couplet    Sapphic strophe    hendecasyllable

8. The metrical unit − u u is known as

   (A) a spondee    (C) a trochee

   (B) an iamb    (D) a dactyl

9. The metrical unit - - is known as

   (A) an iamb    (C) a dactyl

   (B) a spondee    (D) a trochee

10. For the purposes of the AP Latin Exam, the last two feet of a dactylic line consist of, in order:

    (A) two dactyls    (C) dactyl and spondee

    (B) two spondees    (D) spondee and dactyl

11. Which of the meters required for the AP Latin Exam, if any, does/do not contain a dactyl?

    dactylic hexameter    hendecasyllable    elegiac    Alcaic    Sapphic

12. True or False? Elided syllables are always long.

13. A vowel followed by two consonants is long or short by position?

14. True or False? The noun **proelia** contains two diphthongs.

15. How many elisions, if any, are found in each of the following lines? Mark them.

    Flores amoenae ferre iube rosae.            0 1 2 3 4 5

    Umbram hospitalem consociare amant.     0 1 2 3 4 5

    Atque id sincere dicat et animo.             0 1 2 3 4 5

    Quam modo qui me unum atque unicum amicum habuit.   0 1 2 3 4 5

    Exsilium impositura cumbae.             0 1 2 3 4 5

16. How many spondees do you find in the first four feet of each of these hexameter lines?

    Quod mare conceptum spumantibus exspuit undis.    0 1 2 3 4

    Fit sonitus spumante salo; iamque arva tenebant.     0 1 2 3 4

    Gnate, ego quem in dubios cogor dimittere casus.     0 1 2 3 4

17. Scan the following to determine whether **sola** is nominative with **leaena,** or ablative, modifying **rupe**.

    Quaenam te genuit sola sub / rupe leaena

**Note: the verse lines in Exercises 18–23 are in dactylic hexameter.**

18. The metrical pattern of the first four feet of <u>huc se provecti deserto in litore condunt</u> is

    (A) spondee – dactyl – spondee – spondee

    (B) spondee – spondee – spondee – spondee

    (C) spondee – spondee – spondee – dactyl

    (D) spondee – dactyl – spondee – dactyl

19. The metrical pattern of the first four feet of <u>panduntur portae iuvat ire et Dorica castra</u> is

    (A) spondee – spondee – dactyl – spondee

    (B) spondee – spondee – spondee – dactyl

    (C) spondee – dactyl – spondee – spondee

    (D) dactyl – spondee – dactyl – spondee

20. The metrical pattern of the first four feet of <u>idque audire sat est, iamdudum sumite poenas</u> is

    (A) spondee – dactyl – dactyl – spondee

    (B) dactyl – dactyl – spondee – spondee

    (C) spondee – spondee – dactyl – dactyl

    (D) spondee – dactyl – spondee – spondee

21. The metrical pattern of the first four feet of <u>dividimus muros et moenia pandimus urbis</u> is

    (A) dactyl – spondee – spondee – dactyl

    (B) dactyl – dactyl – spondee – spondee

    (C) spondee – dactyl – spondee – dactyl

    (D) spondee – dactyl – dactyl – spondee

22. The metrical pattern of the first four feet of <u>involvens umbra magna terramque polumque</u> is

    (A) spondee – dactyl – spondee – spondee

    (B) dactyl – spondee – spondee – dactyl

    (C) spondee – dactyl – spondee – dactyl

    (D) spondee – spondee – spondee – spondee

23. The metrical pattern of the first four feet of <u>corripiunt spirisque ligant ingentibus; et iam</u> is

    (A) dactyl – spondee – spondee – dactyl

    (B) dactyl – spondee – dactyl – spondee

    (C) spondee – dactyl – spondee – dactyl

    (D) dactyl – dactyl – spondee – spondee

24. How does the meter or rhythm contribute to the meaning of the following excerpts?

    (A) Involvens umbra magna terramque polumque. (Night falls. *Aeneid* 2.251)

    (B) Nequiquam ingeminans iterumque iterumque vocavi. (Aeneas seeks Creusa. *Aeneid* 2.770)

    (C) Si bene quid de te merui, fuit aut tibi quicquam / dulce meum, miserere domus labentis et istam. (Dido confronts Aeneas. *Aeneid* 4.317–18)

    (D) Et Thybrim multo spumantem sanguine cerno. (The Sibyl speaks of Rome's destiny. *Aeneid* 6.87)

## Hendecasyllable

25. There are 3, 7, 10, or 11 syllables in every line of this meter.

26. The metrical pattern of <u>ignes interiorem edunt medullam</u> is

    (A)  - - / - u u / - - / - u / - -

    (B)  - u / u u u / - u / - u / - -

    (C)  - - / - u u / - u / - u / - -

    (D)  u - / - u u / - u / - - / - -

27. Scan the following line:

    agit praecipitem in meos iambos

28. Which of the following is likely, based upon its theme as you know it, to have been written in the hendecasyllabic meter?

    ___ Multas per gentes et multa per aequora vectus / advenio has miseras, frater, ad inferias.

    ___ Siqua recordanti benefacta priora voluptas / est homini, cum se cogitat esse pium.

    ___ Quod mihi fortuna casuque oppressus acerbo / conscriptum hoc lacrimis mittis epistolium.

    ___ Cenabis bene, mi Fabulle, apud me / paucis, si tibi di favent, diebus.

## Elegiac Couplet

29. What two AP Latin authors write in this meter?

    Vergil     Catullus     Horace     Ovid

30. The elegiac couplet consists of a hexameter line of ___ feet and a pentameter line of ___ feet.

31. If you were trying to determine the meter of the following poem, what criteria would you use?

    Odi et amo. Quare id faciam, fortasse requiris.
    Nescio, sed fieri sentio et excrucior.

    **Catullus, Poem 85**

32. The metrical pattern of the first four feet of line 3 is

> Nulla potest mulier tantum se dicere amatam
> vere, quantum a me Lesbia amata mea es.
> Nulla fides ullo fuit umquam foedere tanta,
> quanta in amore tuo ex parte reperta mea est.

**Catullus, Poem 87**

(A) dactyl – spondee – dactyl – spondee

(B) spondee – spondee – dactyl – spondee

(C) dactyl – spondee – dactyl – dactyl

(D) dactyl – spondee – spondee – spondee

33. The metrical pattern of the fourth line of the poem above is

(A) - - / - - / - - u u / - u u / -

(B) - u u / - - / - - u u / - u u / -

(C) - - / - u u / - u - u / - u u / -

(D) - u u / - u u / - - u u / - u u / -

## Alcaic and Sapphic Strophes

34. Identify the following strophes as either Alcaic or Sapphic.

1. Pone me pigris ubi nulla campis
arbor aestiva recreatur aura,
quod latus mundi nebulae malusque
Iuppiter urget

2. Ausa et iacentem visere regiam
vultu sereno, fortis et asperas
tractare serpentes, ut atrum
corpore combiberet venenum

35. The first ____ lines of the Sapphic strophe are the same, as are the first ____ lines of the Alcaic.

36. Which strophe, Alcaic or Sapphic, permits a substitution in a line?

37. True or False? The final line of both Alcaic and Sapphic contains a dactyl.

38. The following excerpt, because of its theme or content, is likely to have come from a poem written in which of the following meters? Alcaic or Sapphic

> Hic generosior / descendat in Campum petitor, / moribus hic meliorque fama / contendat, illi turba clientium / sit maior.

39. Scan this stanza from the Soracte Ode and name the meter.

> Donec virenti canities abest
> morosa. Nunc et campus et areae
>   lenesque sub noctem susurri
>     composita repetantur hora.

**Horace, *Odes* 1. 9.17–20**

40. Scansion of the first three lines of this Sapphic strophe indicates that Horace prefers which choice for the substitution in the second foot, spondee (- -) or trochee (- u)?

> Rectius vives, Licini, neque altum
> semper urgendo neque, dum procellas
> cautus horrescis, nimium premendo
>     litus iniquum.

**Horace, *Odes* 2. 10.1–4**

# Practice Questions on Rhythm and Meaning

## Question 1

> Mittitur infestos alter speculator in hostes,
>   in rivale oculos alter, ut hoste, tenet.
> Ille graves urbes, hic durae limen amicae
>   obsidet; hic portas frangit, at ille fores.

**Ovid, *Amores* 9.17–20**

Discuss how Ovid uses elegiac couplets to compare the lover with the soldier in the poem above. In your answer, refer directly to how the Latin is organized.

## Question 2

> Si quicquam mutis gratum acceptumve sepulcris
>   accidere a nostro, Calve, dolore potest,
> quod desiderio veteres renovamus amores
>   atque olim amissas flemus amicitias,
> certe non tanto mors immatura dolori est
>   Quintiliae, quantum gaudet amore tuo.

**Catullus, Poem 96**

(a)  How does the rhythm of this poem reflect its meaning? Write out and scan line 1 to prove your point.

(b)  What consonantal sound predominates in this poem? What is its effect?

## Question 3

"Fer, pater," inquit, "opem, si flumina numen habetis! . . .
Qua nimium placui, mutando perde figuram!"

**Ovid,** *Metamorphoses* **1.545, 547**

Scan these lines, name the meter, and then discuss how the rhythm contributes to the way in which the poet expresses Daphne's emotion.

## Question 4

Omne capax movet urna nomen.

**Horace,** *Odes* **3.1.16**

How does the rhythm of this line suggest its meaning? (This is the final line of an Alcaic stanza.) How does the syllabification of the words contribute to this effect? What is the ultimate effect of the sound and rhythm on the meaning of this line?

# Answers to Practice Questions on Elision

## Vergil

1.  Turbine corripuit scopulo_que inf_ixit acuto.
    The elision actually "fixes" or attaches Ajax to the cliff.

2.  Incute vim ventis summersas_que obr_ue puppes.
    The slurring of the words suggests the sound of the ship as it rolls over.

3.  Vel_um adv_ersa ferit, fluctus_que ad_ sidera tollit.
    The waves are "connected to" the stars.

4.  Peragro / Europ_a atque A_sia pulsus. The journey is "lengthened" by the multiple elisions.

5.  Taurus et incert_am inc_ussit cervice securim. This elision suggests the errant blow of the axe on the neck of the sacrificial bull.

6.  Vit_am exh_alantem; subiit deserta Creusa.
    Perhaps Anchises' dying gasp?

7. Indulge hospitio causasque innecte morandi.

Anna suggests that Dido "connect" herself more closely to Aeneas and "weave together" reasons for him to stay in Carthage.

8. Fama . . . pariter facta atque infecta canebat.

The joining of "(events) done and undone" emphasizes both.

9. Corde premit gemitum lacrimasque effundit inanes.

"Tears" and "pour out," when elided, have an obvious effect.

10. Saxum antiquum ingens, campo quod forte iacebat.

The age and size of the boulder are magnified by their joining with the boulder itself.

## Catullus

11. Vivamus, mea Lesbia, atque amemus.

Lesbia is linked directly with love.

12. Nox est perpetua una dormienda.

The perpetual night of death is joined to its singularity, or oneness.

13. Non belle uteris in ioco atque vino.

When joined to "wine," "good times" are exaggerated.

14. Di magni, horribilem et sacrum libellum.

When linked with **sacrum**, **horribilem** ("a dreadful and accursed book"), the meaning of both words is intensified.

15. Atque in perpetuum, frater, ave atque vale.

Catullus magnifies both his farewell and the fact that it is forever.

## Ovid

16. Exuviis gaudens, innuptaeque aemula Phoebes.

Daphne's likeness to Diana is heightened by her connection to "unmarried."

17. Fugit, cumque ipso verba imperfecta reliquit.

Apollo's words are literally "left incomplete" by the slurring of "words unfinished."

18. Eiaculatur aquas, atque ictibus aera rumpit.

    This elision contributes to the image of the water spurting from the leaky pipe.

19. Dicitur atque unum surripuisse pedem.

    The syllable/foot is actually "stolen" here!

20. Quantaculaque estis, vos ego magna voco.

    Ovid uses a huge word (but a diminutive, **quantaculaque**) to describe his tiny hometown (which has become "big and famous" because of the poet himself) and actually lengthens it with the elision in a small but significant tribute.

## Answers to Practice Questions on Syncope

### Vergil

| | | | |
|---|---|---|---|
| 1. | superum = superorum | 6. | virum = virorum |
| 2. | audierat = audiverat | 7. | latuere = latuerunt |
| 3. | vinclis = vinculis | 8. | monstrarat = monstraverat |
| 4. | incubuere = incubuerunt | 9. | gustassent = gustavissent |
| 5. | Danaum = Danaorum | 10. | exstinxti = exstinxisti |

### Catullus

11. norat = noverat
12. fulsere = fulserunt
13. comparasti = comparavisti
14. pararim = paraverim
15. donarunt = donaverunt
16. misti = misisti
17. violasse = violavisse
18. subrepsti = subrepsisti

### Horace

19. dimovere = dimoverunt
20. summosses = summovisses

### Ovid

21. agitasse = agitavisse
22. vetuere = vetuerunt patres; potuere = potuerunt

23.  vulgasse = vulgavisse

24.  tuere = tueris

# Answers to Practice Questions on Scansion

## General Scansion and Dactylic Hexameter

1.  All are considered vowels in Latin poetry.

2.  Dactylic hexameter was used in "heroic" or epic verse, e.g., the Homeric poems and the *Aeneid*.

3.  Vergil, Catullus, Horace, Ovid, and Homer (gotcha!)

4.  Poem 64

5.  The *Metamorphoses*, the *Satires*

6.  Thirteen; six

7.  Elegiac couplet

8.  (D) a dactyl

9.  (B) a spondee

10.  (C) dactyl and spondee

11.  All contain at least one dactyl.

12.  False, elided syllables are not always long.

13.  A vowel followed by two consonants is (usually) long by position.

14.  False, the noun **proelia** contains one diphthong, **-oe-**.

15.  How many elisions, if any, are found in each of the following lines? Mark them.

| | |
|---|---|
| Flores amoenae ferre iube rosae. | 0 |
| Umbr<u>am ho</u>spitalem consociar<u>e a</u>mant. | 2 |
| Atqu<u>e id</u> sincere dicat et animo. | 1 |
| Quam modo qui m<u>e unum atqu</u>e unic<u>um amic</u>um h<u>a</u>buit. | 5 |
| Exsili<u>um im</u>positura cumbae. | 1 |

16.

    ‾ u u ‾ ‾ ‾    ‾ ‾ u u ‾ uu ‾ ‾
Quod mare conceptum spumantibus exspuit undis.    3

    ‾ u u‾ ‾ ‾ u u‾ ‾    ‾ u u ‾ ‾
Fit sonitus spumante salo; iamqu<u>e a</u>rva tenebant.    3

    ‾ ‾ ‾ ‾ ‾‾ ‾   u u‾ ‾ ‾ ‾ ‾ u u ‾ ‾
Gnate, ego quem in dubios cogor dimittere casus.    3

17.           ‾ ‾  ‾ u u ‾ ‾ ‾ ‾  ‾ u u ‾ ‾
      Quaenam te genuit sola sub / rupe leaena.    ablative with rupe

18.  (B) spondee – spondee – spondee – spondee

19.  (A) spondee – spondee – dactyl – spondee

20.  (D) spondee – dactyl – spondee – spondee

21.  (A) dactyl – spondee – spondee – dactyl

22.  (D) spondee – spondee – spondee – spondee

23.  (B) dactyl – spondee – dactyl – spondee

24.  How does the meter contribute to the meaning of the following excerpts?

         ‾ ‾ ‾  ‾  ‾  ‾ ‾ ‾  ‾ u u ‾  ‾

   (A) involvens umbra magna terramque polumque (slow approach of night-fall; all spondees. *Aeneid* 2.251)

         ‾ ‾   ‾ ‾ u u ‾  u u ‾   u u  ‾  u  u ‾ ‾

   (B) nequiquam ingeminans iterumque iterumque vocavi (redundancy of dactyls suggests the echoes of Aeneas calling for Creusa. *Aeneid* 2.770)

         ‾ u  u ‾  ‾ ‾  u u ‾ u u ‾  u u  ‾   ‾

   (C) Si bene quid de te merui, fuit aut tibi quicquam

         ‾ u  u ‾   u u ‾ u u  ‾ ‾ ‾ u u ‾  ‾

   dulce meum, miserere domus labentis et istam (the words are rapid-fire and mono- and disyllablic, as Dido confronts Aeneas. *Aeneid* 4.317–18)

         ‾  ‾ ‾ ‾  ‾ ‾ ‾  ‾  ‾ u u ‾  ‾

   (D) et Thybrim multo spumantem sanguine cerno (the Sibyl speaks of Rome's destiny in a solemn, somber, slow rhythm. *Aeneid* 6.87)

## Hendecasyllable

25.  There are 11 syllables in every line.

26.  (C) ‾ ‾ / ‾ u u / ‾ u / ‾ u / ‾ ‾

27.  ‾ ‾   ‾ u u   ‾   u ‾ u ‾  ‾
agit praecipitem in meos iambos

28.  Cenabis bene, mi Fabulle, apud me / paucis, si tibi di favent, diebus (light-hearted theme)

## Elegiac Couplet

29.  Catullus and Ovid

30.  Six feet and five feet

31.  Couplet format, serious (love) theme, corpus number above 60, i.e., 85

32.  (A) dactyl – spondee – dactyl – spondee

33.  (D) ‾ u u / ‾ u u / ‾ ‾ u u / ‾ u u / ‾

## Alcaic and Sapphic Strophes

34. The first strophe is Sapphic and the second, Alcaic.

35. The first three lines of the Sapphic strophe are the same, as are the first two lines of the Alcaic.

36. Sapphic

37. True, the final lines of Alcaic and Sapphic each contain a dactyl.

38. Alcaic, because of the nature of its topic here, which is Roman politics.

39. Alcaic

> ‾ ‾  u ‾  ‾ ‾ u u ‾ u ‾
> donec virenti canities abest
>
> ‾ ‾ u  ‾ ‾ ‾  u u ‾ u ‾
> morosa. Nunc et campus et areae
>
> ‾ ‾ u ‾  ‾ ‾  u ‾ ‾
> lenesque sub noctem susurri
>
> ‾  u u ‾ u u ‾ u  ‾ ‾
> composita repetantur hora.

40. Horace prefers a spondee in the second foot.

> ‾ u ‾ ‾  u u ‾ u  ‾ ‾
> Rectius vives, Licini, neque altum
>
> ‾  ‾ ‾ ‾  ‾ u u ‾  u ‾ ‾
> semper urgendo neque, dum procellas
>
> ‾ ‾  ‾ ‾ ‾  u u ‾  u ‾ ‾
> cautus horrescis, nimium premendo

# Answers to Practice Questions on Rhythm and Meaning

## Question 1

Both the soldier and the lover are mentioned in each of the two couplets. The soldier alternates with the lover through the anaphora of **alter** in the first couplet, and the alternation of **ille** (soldier) with **hic** (lover) and **hic** (soldier) with **ille** (lover) in the second couplet. The appearance of synchysis (**hic portas ... ille fores**), end-line placement (**Mittitur ... tenet**), and condensation in the second couplet, e.g., **Ille graves urbes (obsidet)** and **at ille fores (frangit)** all contribute to the "doubling effect" resulting from the use of couplets.

## Question 2

```
   -  -  --      -  -  -    -  -  -  u u - -
```
(a)   Si quicquam mutis grat<u>um ac</u>ceptumve sepulcris

   Since this a poem of consolation for the death of a friend's wife, Catullus slows down the rhythm by using spondees instead of dactyls.

(b)   The sound of **m** is used numerous times in this poem; this sound is slow to articulate, and it is therefore heavy and solemn, which is fitting for a poem about death.

## Question 3

```
   -  u u  -  u    u -    - -  u u - u  u - -
```
"Fer, pater," inquit, "opem, si flumina numen habetis! . . .

```
   -  u u -    u u -  - -   -  -   u u - -
```
Qua nimium placui, mutando perde figuram!"

The meter is (dactylic) hexameter. The alternation of long and short sounds suggests the urgency of Daphne's plea to her father.

## Question 4

When scanned, the sounds of this line suggest the shaking of the lots in the urn, which is reinforced by the redundant rhythm of the five disyllabic words:

```
   -  u u -  u u - u - u
```
omne capax movet urna nomen.

# Webliography for Meter and Scansion

- Examples of Greek and Latin Meters in English Verse (Rosemary Wright)

  http://www.cornellcollege.edu/classical_studies/meters.shtml

  An example of dactylic hexameter from English verse.

- *Hexametrica*: An Introduction to Latin Hexameter Verse (Dan Curley, Skidmore College)

  http://www.skidmore.edu/academics/classics/courses/metrica/scansion.html

  Thorough presentation of all aspects of the hexameter line, geared toward students of Vergil.

- Latin Poetic Meter (Ben Johnson, Hampden Academy, Hampden, ME)

  http://www.ha.sad22.us/BenJohnson/scansion.html

  A one-page quick-study of hexameter and elegiac.

- Meter and Scansion (Iona College)

  http://www.iona.edu/latin/meter.html

  Hexameter, elegiac, and Sapphic as background for the Catullus poems on the Web site.

- Scansion (Kentucky Educational Television)

  http://www.dl.ket.org/latinlit/carmina/scansion/index.htm

  Good for rules about elision and for poetic terms.

- Scansion of Latin Poetry (Marc Moskowitz, via N.S.Gill)

  http://ancienthistory.about.com/od/scansion1

  The basic rules for scansion.

- Tutor.BestLatin.net (Laura Gibbs, under construction)

  http://tutor.bestlatin.net/about/meter_dachex.htm

  Includes audio examples of hexameter from Aesop's fables and from Theobaldus, Avianus, and others, in Latin. Also, elegiac couplet and Sapphic stanza. A fun site, including *Bestiaria Latina* with a Legend of the Day, *Mythologiae* (Ritchie's *Fabulae Faciles*), *Biblia Vulgata*, and *Legenda Aurea* (the Lives of the Saints).

- *Viva Voce* – Roman Poetry Recited (V. Nedeljkovic, University of Belgrade)

  http://dekart.f.bg.ac.yu/-vnedeljk/VV

  Several passages of hexameters from Vergil and Juvenal read aloud.

# PART II

## Taking and Scoring the AP Latin Exam

# Chapter 12

# Taking and Scoring the AP Latin Exam

## Final Preparations for Taking the Exam

If you are reading this chapter, you have done all the hard work of preparing for success on the AP Latin Exam, usually administered during the third week in May. Be aware that recently the AP Latin Exam has been scheduled in the very last testing slot, so those of you who are taking multiple AP exams should plan ahead. You have spent three, four, or five years of study, at school or at home, to prepare for this exam, in order to show yourself, your friends, your parents, your teachers, and your selected college or university, that you have mastered a difficult language and a difficult exam syllabus. You are to be commended!

You have "talked the talk," and now it's time to "walk the walk." It is most important that you do your best, within the pace of your formal coursework, to have completed the syllabus required for your particular author or authors. If you have not, you will be faced with the question of quality versus quantity: Should I review what I have already done, or use the final hours to make up for lost time? In the author's opinion, you are better served to do what you <u>can</u> do well. Cramming at the end of your AP Latin course will only serve to make you anxious about what you do not know. In recent years, there has been much discussion, among those who teach AP Latin, about the demanding expectations of the College Board Latin syllabi, as compared to semester courses on Vergil or Catullus now taught in colleges and universities. Regardless, the best way to find success on the AP Latin Exam is to 1) prepare the required readings as thoroughly as possible, and 2) do as much sight reading as you can. The former is a product of your classwork in school. The latter often takes a more personal commitment, whether by taking the extra step of approaching your daily assignments as sight passages, by practicing reading Latin without preparation, or by utilizing the resources provided online by The College Board.

There are a number of ways to review for the AP Latin Exam. One or two weeks is a standard amount of review time, which of course depends first upon your early completion of the syllabus, and then upon your regular class and final exam schedule, your additional AP courses, and the other year-end academic and non-academic activities that draw on your time. If you have not been practicing with AP-style questions you are encouraged to do so now, using those provided in this book or online at The College Board AP Latin Web site. Here are some tips for effective review:

## Long Term:

- Make your review for the Exam easier by committing yourself to finishing the required reading.

- Do the "grunt work" of thoroughly preparing each daily assignment throughout your AP Latin course.

- Peer tutoring is a good way to review your basic skills in preparation for the Exam. Share the wisdom of your experience with younger students throughout the year.

- Take full advantage of this book!

## Short Term:

- Make the most of any formal review provided by your teacher. Most likely, you will be stretched for time at this point in the school year, especially if you are preparing for more than one AP exam. Make a personal review plan and stick to it!

- Review with classmates, either at school or at home. Misery loves company and confidence springs from shared experience. (Be sure to obtain the appropriate permissions if you plan a study session in someone's home!)

- Play at **Sortes Vergilianae**. Open your Latin text at random to see if you can identify the content and context of the Latin on the page that turns up. Doing this for passages not required for the exam is also a good way to practice your sight reading skills!

- As you review for the Exam, think about passages that might make good compare-and-contrast questions.

- Visit with an AP Latin Exam veteran for advice on how best to use your time at this stage.

- Go back over the tests that you took during your AP Latin course and try to learn from your previous mistakes.

- Some students like to read English translations of the required authors/passages during their review, in order to get "the big picture," which is sometimes sacrificed in the haste to get to the finish line. This is especially true of Vergil. Don't feel guilty about using for review the various online resources suggested in this book, especially those quick-study sites suggested in this chapter.

- After taking the Practice Tests provided at the end of this book, spend time examining the reasons for whatever difficulties you may have had. Since you are now taking an AP Exam, you have probably reached the point in your education where you are "AP-savvy." This means that you know that you should get a good night's rest before the exam, eat a good breakfast (or lunch), and, above all, relax! For the exam, bring several #2 pencils (for the machine-graded bubble sheet used in the multiple-choice section), a black or blue pen (required for the free-response section), and a highlighter (useful during the 15–minute reading period). Also, bring an energy-boosting snack for the 10–minute break between the multiple-choice and free-response sections.

## Taking The AP Latin Exam

First of all, the tips presented below presume that you have taken practice AP Latin Exams (especially the ones provided in this book or on The College Board AP Latin Web site) and that you are familiar with the format, directions, and level of difficulty of the questions. This is important because you will want to direct all your mental energy during the Exam on the Latin. You have already met some of the following tips in previous chapters, but it doesn't hurt to give you a reminder, does it?

### Multiple-Choice Section

- Before you answer the questions, skim each Latin passage quickly. Use the reading title and the vocabulary assistance to help you understand the general theme or message. As you look over each passage, focus on noun-adjective combinations, pronoun references, verb forms (particularly participles, infinitives, and subjunctives), and the special words that define and bind together phrases, clauses, and sentences.

- Do not attempt to translate the entire multiple-choice reading passage. Translate only when the question requires you to do so.

- Read each question carefully.

- Know that the questions are asked in the sequence in which the answers are found in the Latin passage and that all questions contain both line references (lines 1–2) and citation of the Latin needed to answer the question. There are usually one or two questions per Latin sentence.

- Do not blind guess (remember that you are penalized for wrong answers). If you can narrow your choices to two, then answer the question by making an educated guess. You are not expected to know the answer to every question or to answer every question in order to achieve a "good" score on this part of the Exam.

- Do not rush, but work at a steady pace. You should average about one minute per question (50 questions in 60 minutes).

### Free-Response Section

- Use the 15–minute reading period productively. Look over every question in your green booklet and try to recognize the Latin passages being tested and the essential element/s of each essay question. Use a highlighter or other means to underscore or otherwise emphasize relevant Latin in the text and the "prompt" within the question. You may write directly on your green test booklet (this is returned to your teacher and will not be considered by the Readers in evaluating your performance). During this time, be sure to "flag" in some way the three questions on the correct choice author, so that you do not become disoriented while writing under the stress of time.

- When you are underway, re-read each question thoroughly and <u>answer the question asked</u>! Avoid blathering or telling everything you know about the author or the passage. Quality, not quantity, will earn you top marks.

- Be familiar with the following terms and their relevance to the Exam: <u>literal, well-developed, short, and long</u>.

- In essay questions, <u>refer to the Latin throughout the passage or passages</u>.

- <u>Document your discussions on essays by citing and translating or closely paraphrasing the relevant Latin</u>.

- <u>Write your essays with attention to providing a beginning, a middle, and an end</u>.

- <u>Remember that you must begin the answer to each question on a fresh page</u> of your pink free-response booklet. (This does not apply to different sections of the same question.) Be sure to label each question, or section of a question, accurately. Skip lines as you write, to allow for editing later in the testing session.

- <u>Answer the questions in whatever sequence makes you feel the most confident</u>. You may wish to begin by addressing those questions which you find the easiest. If you are confronted with an unfamiliar passage, you are perhaps best served to leave this until last and then apply the principles of successful sight reading that you have learned during your time in Latin. In such situations, you will presumably have the advantage of being familiar with the literary context of the passage, even though you do not recognize it immediately.

- It is customary to <u>underline the Latin cited</u>. Underlining the relevant Latin "highlights" your ability to make use of the Latin text accurately and thoughtfully in your discussion. Remember that ellipsis points may be used in citing longer clauses or sentences, however, it is a good idea to <u>limit the length of your citations to a few relevant words</u>. (Refer back to Chapter 7 for reminders about how to cite Latin correctly and effectively on essays.)

## Point Systems Used for Scoring the AP Latin Exams

**Multiple-Choice Score** = number correct out of 50 (see below for information about weighting)

**Free-Response Score:**

| Required Authors | Translation 1 | Translation 2 | Long Essay | Short Essay | Back- ground |
|---|---|---|---|---|---|
| **Vergil** | 9 points | 9 points | 6 points | 6 points | 6 points |
| **Catullus** | 9 points | 6 points | 6 points | | |

| Choice Authors | Short Essay | Translation | Spot | |
|---|---|---|---|---|
| **Cicero, Horace, Ovid** | 6 points | 9 points | 8 points | |

### Scores on Multiple-Choice Questions

To provide you with a general reference point, statistics taken from scores on the multiple-choice section both of the 2005 AP Latin Exams suggest that if you had answered 23 out of 49 questions correctly, you would have had a good chance to earn an overall test score of 5.[1] One College Board publication points out, "Generally, to obtain a total grade of 3 or higher on an AP Exam, students need to answer about 50 percent[2] of the multiple-choice questions correctly and to do acceptable work on the free-response section."

### Average Scores on Free-Response Questions

Here are the mean scores for the free-response questions on the 2005 AP Latin Exam.[3] The mean score is the average score earned by all students who answered that question. Again, this is to be taken as a point of reference and not as a summary of student performances on any other AP Latin Exam.

| Vergil | Translation 1 | Translation 2 | Long Essay | Short Essay | Back- ground |
|---|---|---|---|---|---|
| | 4.43 out of 9 | 3.03 out of 9 | 3.34 out of 6 | 3.28 out of 6 | 3.33 out of 6 |
| | 49 percent | 34 percent | 56 percent | 55 percent | 56 percent |

[1] *2005 AP Latin Literature and AP Latin Vergil Released Exams*, pp. 178 and 181.

[2] The College Board, *A Guide to the Advanced Placement Program*, May 1999, p. 46.

[3] *2005 AP Latin Literature and AP Latin Vergil Released Exams*, indicated by question.

| Latin Lit | Translation | Long Essay | Short Essay | Short Essay | Translation | Spot |
|---|---|---|---|---|---|---|
| **Catullus** | 3.44 out of 9 | 2.75 out of 6 | 2.45 out of 6 | 38 percent | 46 percent | 41 percent |
| **Cicero** | 2.32 out of 6 | 3.57 out of 9 | 3.97 out of 8 | 39 percent | 40 percent | 50 percent |
| **Horace** | | | | 2.70 out of 6 | 4.17 out of 9 | 5.41. out of 8 |
| | | | | 45 percent | 46 percent | 68 percent |
| **Ovid** | | | | 3.16 out of 6 | 3.01 out of 9 | 3.58 out of 8 |
| | | | | 53 percent | 33 percent | 45 percent |

## Sample Scoring Worksheet: Vergil[4]

### Section I: Multiple-Choice (Vergil)

[_____ − 1/3 × _____] × .9796 = _____

Number correct    Number wrong    Weighted Section I
Score
(Do not round scores.)

### Section II: Free-Response Section (Vergil)

Question 1 (Translation 1) _____ × 1.2 = _____

Question 2 (Translation 2) _____ × 1.2 = _____

Question 3 (Long Essay) _____ × 4.2 = _____

Question 4 (Short Essay) _____ × 2.4 = _____

Question 5 (Background) _____ × 1.8 = _____

Sum = _____

Weighted Section II
Score

---

[4] 2005 *AP Latin Literature and AP Latin Vergil Released Exams*, p. 180.

## Composite Score

_____ + _____ = _____

    Weighted Section I     Weighted Section II     Composite Score
        Score               Score         (Round to nearest
                                           whole number)

## AP Grade Conversion Chart: Vergil[5]

| Composite Score Range | AP Grade |
|:---:|:---:|
| 79–120 | 5 |
| 68–78 | 4 |
| 50–67 | 3 |
| 36–49 | 2 |
| 0–35 | 1 |

# Sample Scoring Worksheet: Latin Literature[6]

## Section I: Multiple-Choice (Latin Literature)

[_____ − 1/3 × _____] × .9796 = _____

    Number correct           Number wrong         Weighted Section I
                                                 Score
                                            (Do not round scores)

## Section II: Free-Response Section (Latin Literature)

### Catullus

Question 1 (Translation)   _____ × 1.2 = _____

Question 2 (Long Essay)   _____ × 2.4 = _____

Question 3 (Short Essay)   _____ × 1.8 = _____

### Choice Author (Cicero, Horace, or Ovid)

Question 4, 7, 10 (Short Essay)  _____ × 2.4  = _____

Question 5, 8, 11 (Translation)  _____ × 1.2  = _____

Question 6, 9, 12 (Short Id.)    _____ × 1.35 = _____

                                                     Sum = _____

                                                     Weighted Section II
                                                     Score

---

[5] Composite score ranges are determined formulaically each year by the Chief Reader. The composite score ranges provided here are accurate for the 2005 AP Vergil Exam.

[6] *2005 AP Latin Literature and AP Latin Vergil Released Exams*, p. 177.

## Composite Score

_____ + _____ = _____

Weighted Section I    Weighted Section II       Composite Score
Score      Score    (Round to nearest
whole number)

## AP Grade Conversion Chart: Latin Literature[7]

| Composite Score Range | AP Grade |
|:---------------------:|:--------:|
| 79–120 | 5 |
| 60–75 | 4 |
| 43–59 | 3 |
| 32–42 | 2 |
| 0–31 | 1 |

# What Does My AP Latin Exam Score Mean?

As you have seen, your AP Latin Exam score of 5, 4, 3, 2, or 1 is calculated using a formulaic numerical assessment of your performance on the multiple-choice and free-response sections, the sum of which is converted from a composite score to the 5–point AP scale given below:[8]

| AP Grade | Qualification |
|:--------:|:--------------|
| 5 | Extremely well qualified |
| 4 | Well qualified |
| 3 | Qualified (considered by many to be "passing") |
| 2 | Possibly qualified |
| 1 | No recommendation |

---

[7] The composite score ranges provided here are accurate for the 2005 AP Latin Lit Exam.

[8] For many (but not all!) institutions, the AP Exam scoring scale approximates the grading scale of a college course, e.g., 5 = A, 4 = B, 3 = C, etc.

For your information, on the 2005 AP Latin Exams the breakdown of (rounded) scores was:

| Vergil | Latin Literature |
|---|---|
| 5 = 19 percent | 5 = 18 percent |
| 4 = 17 percent | 4 = 19 percent |
| 3 = 29 percent | 3 = 24 percent |
| 2 = 16 percent | 2 = 15 percent |
| 1 = 19 percent | 1 = 23 percent |

Contact the Admissions or Classics departments of your chosen college or university for information about the graduation requirement in foreign language and about what placement or credit you may earn from your performance on the AP Latin Exam. You may also gather information from your teacher, college or guidance counsellor, school or college alumni, catalogues and bulletins, or college/university or Classics Department Web sites.[9] Remember that the location of classics courses varies from institution to institution. In major universities and many small liberal arts colleges, you will find a Department of Classics. Latin may have its own department or be taught within a classical civilization or other humanities department, such as English, comparative literature, history, or languages. Also, be aware that there is some difference among higher institutions with regard to how they view a given score on the AP Latin Exam. Although more students are taking the AP Latin Exam, paradoxically, fewer colleges and universities seem to be accepting even high scores for credit or placement (the reasons for this vary from institution to institution).[10] Even having had the experience of taking an AP Latin course and/or Exam, you may be asked to take an "in house" test designed by the college/university or the department that determines placement or credit. If you are asked to do this, your chances for a successful experience will certainly be increased by your background in the Advanced Placement Program. Comparability studies conducted by the AP Program every five to seven years indicate that secondary students who have studied an AP subject score higher on the AP Exam than those who have had an equivalent course in college and who take the Exam. Remember, that there is much to be said for your participation in a seminar-sized class of able and motivated Latin students, led by an enthusiastic and capable in-

---

[9] The College Board provides online a current list of 200 top colleges ranked by those "receiving the greatest number of AP grades." Go to apcentral.collegeboard.com, click on "Programs," then "AP Research and Data," then "Exam Data 2005," then "Other Information and Data."

[10] To the knowledge of the author there are no hard data for this claim, but the comments made by Latin teachers at professional conferences and at AP workshops, in journals and newsletters, and on The College Board's AP Latin Electronic Discussion Group, suggests that, indeed, this can and does happen.

structor, all of whom are willing to accept and grow from academic challenge. This is, perhaps, more to the point of preparing for success in college. You <u>have</u> taken part in what many students have considered one of their best academic experiences in high school.

In the moments before you take the AP Latin Exam, relax, breathe deeply, remember that you have worked hard, and know that you will do your best. **Bona fortuna!**

# Online Review Resources for the AP Vergil Exam

## Quick Studies

- Bookrags

  http://www.bookrags.com/notes/and/SUM.htm

  Contains glossaries of characters, names/places, quotes, articles on the role of gods and goddesses, historical subtexts, omens and prophecies, women, discussion/thought topics, detailed hypertext summaries by book.

- Wikipedia hypertext article on the *Aeneid*

  http://en.wikipedia.org/wiki/Aeneid

  An excellent quick study.

## Outlines, Summaries, and Study Guides

- Outline of Vergil's *Aeneid* (Ross Scaife, University of Kentucky)

  http://www.uky.edu/AS/Classics/aeneidout.html

  Book-by-book outline of the high points, with line numbers; support for a college course on Vergil.

- Study Guide for the *Aeneid* (University of Central Oklahoma)

  http://www.libarts.ucok.edu/english/faculty/spencer/worldlit/aeneid1.html

  Synopses of Books 1, 2, 4, and 6.

- Vergil Study Guide (Diane Thompson, Northern Virginia Community College)

  http://novaonline.nvcc.edu/eli/eng251/virgilstudy.html

  Includes "Aeneas-A New Kind of Hero," "The Dido Problem-Passion and Politics," "Gods, the Will Of Jupiter, Destiny/Fate." Also, a glossary of characters and deities in the *Aeneid*.

## Study Questions on the *Aeneid*

- AP Vergil site (Tim Abney, Marquette High School)

  http://abney.homestead.com/aeneid.html

  Valuable for clickable interactive exercises on content, vocabulary, sight reading, scansion, and figures of speech, by book of the *Aeneid*, including Books 10–12.

- *Aeneid*: Exercises in Reading Comprehension and Interpretation (Ablemedia, Classics Technology Center)

  http://ablemedia.com/ctcweb/netshots/vergil.htm

  Exercise in reading comprehension and interpretation: Books 1, 2, 4, 6, 8, and 12.

- Quick Summary Outline of the *Aeneid* (Eugene Cotter, Seton Hall University)

  http://pirate.shu.edu/~cottereu/aeneid.htm

  Twelve individual topics and themes, with discussion questions.

- Review Questions over the Myths of Early Rome and the *Aeneid* (Jean Alvares, Montclair State University)

  http://chss2.montclair.edu/classics/aeneidetc.htm

  Clickable multiple-choice questions, with answers.

- Self-Quiz on Vergil's *Aeneid* (Brooklyn College, CUNY)

  http://academic.brooklyn.cuny.edu/classics/hansen/assign3.htm (Books 1, 2, 4, and 12)

  http://academic.brooklyn.cuny.edu/classic/wilson/core/aeneid6q.htm (Book 6)

- Study Guide for Vergil's *Aeneid* (Robin Mitchell-Boyask, Temple University)

  http://www.temple.edu/classics/aeneidho.html

  Analytical review of Books 1, 2, 4, 6, 7, and 12, with questions.

- Vergil, *Aeneid*: Study Questions for Books 1–6 (RJS, Columbia University)

  http://humanities.psydeshow.org/reference/aeneid-study-qq-1.htm#

- Virgil's *Aeneid* (David Silverman, Reed College)

  http://academic.reed.edu/humanities/110Tech/Aeneid.html

  FAQs and basic facts; modern critics on the *Aeneid*.

# Online Review Resources for the AP Latin Lit Exam

For additional resources, see Chapters 3 and 8.

## Review aids for Catullus

- AP Catullus Page (Tim Abney, Marquette High School)

  http://abney.homestead.com/catullus.html

  See activities for scansion and figures of speech under "Working with Individual Poems."

- Love and Romance in Greece and Rome (John Gruber-Miller, Cornell College, IA)

  http://www.cornellcollege.edu/classical_studies/lit/catullusguide.shtml

  Brief study guide for Catullus.

- Rudy Negenborn (Utrecht, Netherlands) [**Latin texts with translations**]

  http://www.negenborn.net/catullus/

  Translations in many languages, Latin texts, sample scansions.

- Shocked Catullus (Robert Larson, Kent State University) [**Latin hypertexts**]

  http://www.personal.kent.edu/~rlarson/catullus/

  Needs Shockwave plug-in. Does not include syllabus poems added in 2005, but excellent hypertexts for reading practice.

- Henry Walker (Bates College, V Roma) [**Latin texts with translations**]

  http://www.vroma.org/~hwalker/VRomaCatullus/

- Latin text with facing line-by-line translation. Linked to Merrill's Perseus text. Wikipedia hypertext article on Catullus

  http://en.wikipedia.org/wiki/Catullus

## Review aids for Cicero

### *Pro Archia Poeta*

- Claude Pavur (Saint Louis Univ.) [**Latin text**]

  http://www.slu.edu/colleges/AS/languages/classical/latin/tchmat/readers/accreaders/cicero/archia.htm

  The Latin text of *Pro Archia Poeta* is laid out in what the College Board would consider sense units, or "segments."

- Joseph T. Richardson (The Society for Ancient Languages) [**Latin text with translation**]

  http://www.uah.edu/student_life/organizations/SAL/texts/latin/classical/cicero/proarchia.html

  Translation of *Pro Archia Poeta*, with introduction and notes

- Wikipedia hypertext article on Cicero

  http://en.wikipedia.org/wiki/Cicero

### De Amicitia

- California State University-Northridge

  http://www.csun.edu/~hcfll004/amicitia.html

  An outline of *De Amicitia*.

- *De Amicitia* (Joseph T. Richardson, The Society for Ancient Languages) [**Latin text with translation**]

  http://www.uah.edu/student_life/organizations/SAL/texts/latin/classical/cicero/deamicitia.html

  Text with facing English translation.

## Review aids for Horace

### Odes

- *Odes* (Joseph T. Richardson, The Society for Ancient Languages) [**Latin texts**]

  http://www.uah.edu/student_life/organizations/SAL/texts/latin/classical/horace/carmina.html

  Includes an introduction to the *Odes*.

- Shocked Horace (Robert Larson, Kent State University) [**Latin hypertexts**]

  http://www.personal.kent.edu/~rlarson/horace/

  Hypertexts of all AP Horace poems, save *Satires* 1.9. Excellent for reading practice!

- Wikipedia hypertext article on Horace

  http://en.wikipedia.org/wiki/Horace

### Satires 1.9

- Kentucky Educational Television (Joan Jahnige) [**Latin text**]

  http://www.dl.ket.org/latinlit/carmina/index.htm

  Wonderful color-coded Latin hypertext of *Satires* 1.9, with pop-up windows.

- *Satires* 1.9 (Joseph T. Richardson, The Society for Ancient Languages) **[Latin hypertext]**

  http://www.uah.edu/student_life/organizations/SAL/texts/latin/classical/horace/sermones.html

  Includes introduction and translation notes available as a frame below the Latin text.

## Review aids for Ovid

### *Metamorphoses*

- AP Ovid (Tim Abney, Marquette High School)

  http://abney.homestead.com/ovid1.html

  Valuable site for interactive exercises on scansion and figures of speech for both *Metamorphoses* and *Amores*.

- Bookrags: *Metamorphoses*

  http://www.bookrags.com/notes/met/

  Bio, one-page plot summary, character descriptions, object/place descriptions, theme tracker (revenge, violence, women), book-by-book summaries of the mythological stories.

- Ovid's *Metamorphoses* (Larry A. Brown)

  http://larryavisbrown.homestead.com/files/xeno.ovid1.htm

  An intro and commentary, with discussion of myths and links to sources and influences in art and literature. Some analysis and thematic cross-linked summaries.

- The Structure of the *Metamorphoses* (Joseph Farrell, Univ. Pennsylvania)

  http://ccat.sas.upenn.edu/~jfarrell/courses/spring96/myth/metstruc.html

- Wikipedia hypertext article on Ovid

  http://en.wikipedia.org/wiki/Ovid

### *Amores*

- Diotima article on the *Amores* (John Svarlien and Diane Arnson Svarlien, stoa.org)

  http://www.stoa.org/diotima/anthology/amores_index.shtml

  Good background information by William W. Batstone.

# PART III
## Review of Grammar and Syntax

# Nouns, Pronouns, Adjectives, and Adverbs

## Chapter 13A: Nouns

### Quick Study of Noun Forms*

|          | 1st      | 2nd      | 2nd N.      | 3rd     | 3rd N.    | 4th     | 5th      |
|----------|----------|----------|-------------|---------|-----------|---------|----------|
| **Singular** |      |          |             |         |           |         |          |
| Nom.     | tibia    | nasus    | bracchium   | pes     | caput     | manus   | facies   |
| Gen.     | tibiae   | nasi     | bracchi     | pedis   | capitis   | manus   | faciei   |
| Dat.     | tibiae   | naso     | bracchio    | pedi    | capiti    | manui   | faciei   |
| Acc.     | tibiam   | nasum    | bracchium   | pedem   | caput     | manum   | faciem   |
| Abl.     | tibia    | naso     | bracchio    | pede    | capite    | manu    | facie    |
| **Plural** |        |          |             |         |           |         |          |
| Nom.     | tibiae   | nasi     | bracchia    | pedes   | capita    | manus   | facies   |
| Gen.     | tibiarum | nasorum  | bracchiorum | pedum   | capitum   | manuum  | facierum |
| Dat.     | tibiis   | nasis    | bracchiis   | pedibus | capitibus | manibus | faciebus |
| Acc.     | tibias   | nasos    | bracchia    | pedes   | capita    | manus   | facies   |
| Abl.     | tibiis   | nasis    | bracchiis   | pedibus | capitibus | manibus | faciebus |

* For a more thorough review of the basics of Latin grammar and syntax, see the author's book, *The Best Test Preparation for the SAT Subject Test: Latin*, Research & Education Association, 2006.

## Quick Study of Noun Syntax

| Case | Function | Description of Function | Example |
|------|----------|-------------------------|---------|
| **Nominative** | | | |
| | subject | expresses who or what is performing the action | **Servus laborat.** *The slave is working.* |
| | predicate nominative | restates the subject | **Senex servus est.** *The old man is a slave.* |
| **Genitive** ("of," -'s or -s') | | | |
| | possessive | expresses whose, of whom, or of what; links two nouns | **amica pueri** *the girlfriend of the boy or the boy's girlfriend.* |
| | descriptive | with accompanying adjective, describes another noun | **femina magnae pulchritudinis** *a woman of great beauty.* |
| | partitive | indicates a part of the whole | **satis temporis; plus vini** *enough (of) time; more wine* |
| | objective | expresses object of emotion | **cupiditas pecuniae** *the desire for money,* lit., *of money* |
| | with special words | requires translation "of" | **plenus irae; amoris gratia** *full of anger; for the sake of love* |
| **Dative** ("to" or "for") | | | |
| | indirect object | indicates "to" or "for" whom something is done, shown, told, or given | **Puer puellae osculum dedit.** *The boy gave a kiss to the girl, The boy gave the girl a kiss.* |
| | possession | shows ownership | **Est canis puero.** *The boy has a dog,* lit., *there is a dog to/for the boy* |

| Case | Function | Description of Function | Example |
|---|---|---|---|
| **Dative** ("to" or "for") *(cont.)* | | | |
| | reference | indicates "with reference" to whom an action is done | **Militi periculum belli verum est.** *With reference to or For the soldier, the danger of war is real.* |
| | double dative | dative of reference + dative of purpose | **suis saluti fuit** *he was the salvation of his men,* lit., *for the salvation for his men.* |
| | with verbs | intransitive verbs | **crede mihi.** *trust me,* lit., *be trusting to me.* |
| | | impersonal verbs | **licet mihi,** *I am permitted,* lit., *it is permitted to me* |
| | | compound verbs | **occurrere amico** *to meet a friend* |
| | with adjectives | adjectives that require the meaning "to" or for" | **similis patri** *similar to the father* |
| | agent | the person who must perform a necessary action | **tibi agendum est** *you must do it,* lit., *it must be done by you* |
| **Accusative** | | | |
| | direct object | receives action of verb | **Brutus Caesarem necavit.** *Brutus killed Caesar.* |
| | object of preposition | accompanies **per, prope**, etc. | **per viam; prope arborem** *along the road; near the tree* |
| | place to which | expresses motion towards with **ad** | **ad urbem** *toward the city* |

| Case | Function | Description of Function | Example |
|------|----------|------------------------|---------|
| **Accusative** *(cont.)* | | | |
| | duration of time | expresses passage of time | **tres dies; abhinc duos menses** <br> *for three days; two months ago* |
| | subject of infinitive | subject of infinitive in indirect statement | **Audio <u>theatrum clausum</u> esse**. <br> *I hear that the <u>theater</u> was closed.* |
| | gerundive of purpose | **ad** + gerundive expresses purpose or intent | **<u>ad forum videndum</u>** <br> *<u>to see the forum</u>* |
| | exclamatory | expresses an exclamation | **Me miserum!** <br> *How unhappy I am!* |
| **Ablative** ("by," "from," "with," etc.) | | | |
| *With a preposition* | | | |
| | place where | used with prepositions, e.g., **in** (*in, on*), **sub**, etc., to indicate location | **in mensa; sub plaustro** <br> *on the table; beneath the wagon* |
| | accompaniment | expresses partnership (*with*) | **Puer <u>cum cane</u> ambulat**. <br> *The boy walks <u>with his dog</u>.* |
| | personal agent | indicates the person who completes the action of a passive verb (*by*) | **Luna <u>ab amantibus</u> conspicitur**. <br> *The moon is seen <u>by the lovers</u>.* |
| | place from | used with prepositions, e.g., **a/ab, de,** or **e/ex**, to express motion away | **ab urbe, de caelo, e villis** <br> *away from the city, down from the sky, from the villas* |

| Case | Function | Description of Function | Example |
|------|----------|------------------------|---------|
| **Ablative** ("by," "from," "with," etc.) *(cont.)* | | | |
| ***With or without a preposition*** | | | |
| | manner | indicates how (*with*) | **magno (cum) murmure** *with a great rumbling* |
| | separation | indicates the distancing of one person/thing from another, following certain verbs (with or without **a/ab** or **e/ex**) | **(e) timore se liberavit** *he freed himself from fear* |
| | cause | "because of," with or without **a/ab, de, e/ex** | **(ex) vulnere dolebat** *he was in pain from (because of) his wound* |
| ***Without a preposition*** | | | |
| | time when | expresses a point in time (*in, on, at*) | **sexto anno; aestate** *in the sixth year; in the summer* |
| | time within | expresses time during which (*in, within*) | **quinque mensibus** *(with)in five months* |
| | means | indicates the instrument or tool with which an action is performed (*with, by*) | **Miles gladio hostem vulneravit.** *The soldier wounded his enemy with a sword* |
| | comparison | expresses comparison between two persons or things | **Hic mons altior illo est.** *This mountain is higher than that.* |
| | degree of difference | indicates the extent to which one person/thing differs from another (*much, less*) | **Hic mons multo altior est.** *This mountain is much higher,* lit., *higher by much.* |

| Case | Function | Description of Function | Example |
|------|----------|------------------------|---------|
| **Ablative** ("by," "from," "with," etc.) *(cont.)* | | | |
| *With or without a preposition* *(cont.)* | | | |
| | description | with accompanying adjective, describes some characteristic (a person *of...*) | **Erat vir magna fortitudine.** *He was a man of great courage.* |
| | respect or specification | expresses in what regard or respect something is true | **mea sententia** *in my opinion* |
| | with certain verbs | accompanies specific deponent verbs | **Fruamini vitā.** *You should enjoy life.* |
| | ablative absolute | phrase consisting of pro/noun+ participle in ablative | **hoc facto** *after this is/was/had been done (after, when, since, while, etc.)* |
| | | | **multis clamantibus** *while many are/were/will be shouting* |
| | | | **Caesare consule** *while Caesar is/was/will be consul* |
| **Vocative** | | | |
| | direct address | naming or speaking directly to a person | **"Tite, claude ianuam."** *"Titus, close the door."* |
| | | | **"Fer auxilium matri, fili."** *"Help your mother, son."* |
| **Locative** (*in* or *at*) | | | |
| | place where | indicates location without a preposition (names of cities, small islands, **domus, rus**) | **Romae maneo.** *I am staying in Rome.* |

## Practice Questions: Nominative Case*

1.  <u>Ignavo servo mandata dedit</u>. The subject of this sentence is
    - (A) Ignavo
    - (B) servo
    - (C) mandata
    - (D) he (in the verb <u>dedit</u>)

2.  Quis erat . . . ?
    - (A) vilicum
    - (B) vilici
    - (C) vilico
    - (D) vilicus

3.  Bacillus Bombacem** . . . punire vult.
    - (A) servum
    - (B) servus
    - (C) servo
    - (D) servorum

4.  Bacillus . . . non erat.
    - (A) dominum
    - (B) domino
    - (C) dominus
    - (D) domine

## Practice Questions: Genitive Case

1.  Bombax plus . . . semper vult.
    - (A) cibus
    - (B) cibum
    - (C) cibo
    - (D) cibi

2.  Bombax servus . . . erat.
    - (A) magnae ignaviae
    - (B) magnam ignaviam
    - (C) magnas ignavias
    - (D) magna ignavia

3.  The life of a slave was often <u>full of misery</u>.
    - (A) plena miseriā
    - (B) plena miseriae
    - (C) plena miseria
    - (D) plena cum miseria

4.  Canes vestigia <u>fugitivae ancillae</u> secuti sunt.
    - (A) of the runaway maid
    - (B) with the runaway maid
    - (C) for the runaway maid
    - (D) toward the runaway maid

---

\* The answers to all review questions are found at the end of each chapter.

\*\* The sentences in these practice questions include the fictional characters Bombax, a ne'er-do-well slave, Bombax, his overseer, and Palaestra, Bombax's heartthrob.

5. For a slave, the price <u>of freedom</u> was hard work.

   (A) libertatum        (C) libertatis

   (B) libertati          (D) libertate

6. Bombax <u>aliquid mali</u> semper agebat.

   (A) of something bad      (C) something bad

   (B) for something bad     (D) with someone bad

7. . . . nomen non habebat.

   (A) Unus e servis        (C) Uno servo

   (B) Unum servum      (D) Unius servi

8. Servus <u>gratiam benefici</u> agit.

   (A) gratitude and kindness (C)     gratitude for kindness

   (B) gratitude or kindness    (D) kind gratitude

9. Bombax quinque milia . . . ambulare non poterat.

   (A) passus            (C) passus

   (B) passum         (D) passuum

## Practice Questions: Dative Case

1. Will the master give <u>the slave</u> her freedom?

   (A) servam         (C) servae

   (B) serva          (D) serva

2. Bombacis tunica <u>idonea cenae</u> non erat.

   (A) suitable with dinner    (C) a suitable dinner

   (B) suitable for dinner      (D) for a suitable dinner

3. Necesse est . . . parcere.

   (A) miseros servos      (C) miserorum servorum

   (B) miseri servi        (D) miseris servis

4. <u>Dominus filio servi pecuniam libertati dedit.</u>

   (A) The master gave the slave's son freedom for his money.

   (B) The slave's son gave the master money for his freedom.

   (C) The master gave the slave's son money for his freedom.

   (D) The slaves gave the master's son money for their freedom.

5. <u>Licebatne Bacillo servis praeesse?</u>

   (A) Is he permitted to place Bacillus in charge of the slaves?

   (B) Did he place the slaves in charge of Bacillus?

   (C) Was Bacillus permitted to be in charge of the slaves?

   (D) Was Bacillus permitting the slaves to be in charge?

6. <u>Nihil pecuniae Bombaci erat.</u>

   (A) Bombax never has money.

   (B) Bombax had no money.

   (C) Bombax has no money.

   (D) There is no money for Bombax.

7. Bombax . . . epistulam amoris misit.

   (A) Palaestram      (C) Palaestra

   (B) Palaestrae      (D) ad Palaestram

8. The overseer Bacillus was <u>a great help to his master</u>.

   (A) magnum auxilium domini

   (B) magno auxilio ad dominum

   (C) magnum auxilium domino

   (D) magno auxilio domino

9. Cena . . . ponenda erat.

   (A) ab Palaestra      (C) Palaestrā

   (B) Palaestrae      (D) Palaestra

## Practice Questions: Accusative Case

1. Bombax napped <u>for eight hours</u>.

   (A) octo horis      (C) octo horas

   (B) octava hora      (D) octavam horam

2. Bacillus iratus erat propter . . . servi.

   (A) fuga      (C) fuga

   (B) fugae      (D) fugam

3. Bombax cum Palaestra <u>tres horas</u> in horto sedebat.

   (A) three hours ago      (C) within three hours

   (B) for three hours      (D) at the third hour

4. In horto, statua . . . piscinam posita erat.

(A) prope                     (C) de

(B) pro                        (D) sine

5. Bombax ad villam <u>abhinc quattuor menses</u> pervenit.

(A) four months later       (C) within four months

(B) after four months       (D) four months ago

6. "Noli <u>in me</u> baculum vertere!" implorabat Bombax.

(A) in me                  (C) into me

(B) against me          (D) on me

7. <u>Triginta milia passuum abhinc septem dies iter fecit.</u>

(A) In seven days, he traveled three miles.

(B) Seven days ago, he traveled three thousand miles.

(C) Seven days ago, he traveled for thirty miles.

(D) Within seven days, he traveled thirty miles.

8. Bombax <u>Delphos</u> iter facere volebat.

(A) from Delphi           (C) to Delphi

(B) near Delphi           (D) in Delphi

9. Bombax in agros cucurrit <u>ad fugiendum.</u>

(A) as he was fleeing       (C) at the point of flight

(B) in order to flee         (D) towards the fugitive

10. Nemo cogitat . . . diligentem servum esse.

(A) Bombax            (C) Bombace

(B) Bombacem        (D) Bombacis

## Practice Questions: Ablative Case

1. Radix <u>magnitudine</u> boletorum felix erat.

(A) by means of the size       (C) because of the size

(B) according to the size       (D) except for the size

2. <u>Within three hours</u>, the dessert will have been served.

(A) Tertia hora           (C) Tres horas

(B) Tribus horis         (D) Tertias horas

3. Gustatio huius cenae dignissima . . . erat.

   (A) laudis           (C) laudi

   (B) laude           (D) laus

4. Secunda mensa <u>magna cura</u> parata erat.

   (A) with great care

   (B) because of great care

   (C) by means of great care

   (D) with respect to great care

5. Radix optimus coquus . . . dubio erat.

   (A) pro           (C) sub

   (B) de           (D) sine

6. <u>Bombax paulo altior Bacillo erat.</u>

   (A) Bacillus was much taller than Bombax.

   (B) Bombax was a little taller than Bacillus.

   (C) Bombax was much taller than Bacillus.

   (D) Bacillus was a little taller than Bombax.

7. For the dinner, Radix created dishes <u>of great beauty.</u>

   (A) magna pulchritudo

   (B) magnae pulchritudini

   (C) magna pulchritudine

   (D) magnam pulchritudinem

8. Radix convivas <u>culina</u> prohibebat.

   (A) from the kitchen           (C) in the kitchen

   (B) by means of the kitchen           (D) with respect to the kitchen

9. Bombax had loved Palaestra <u>for two years.</u>

   (A) secundo anno           (C) duobus annis

   (B) duos annos           (D) secundum annum

10. Bacillus Bombacem . . . verberabat.

    (A) cum baculo           (C) baculo

    (B) baculum           (D) a baculo

11. Coquus . . . salis semper utebatur.

    (A)  nimium               (C)  nimio

    (B)  nimius                (D)  nimiam

12. <u>Altero servo a Bacillo verberato</u>, Bombax diligentius laborabat.

    (A)  While Bacillus was beating another slave

    (B)  After Bacillus had been beaten by another slave

    (C)  As Bacillus is beating another slave

    (D)  Because another slave had been beaten by Bacillus

## Practice Questions: Vocative Case

1. . . . Catulle, desinas ineptire. (Catullus)

    (A)  Misere               (C)  Miser

    (B)  Miseri               (D)  Misero

2. "Extende manum, . . .!" admonuit iratus Tuxtax.

    (A)  Erronius            (C)  Erroni

    (B)  Erronii             (D)  Erronio

3. Ignosce mihi, . . . .

    (A)  grammaticus       (C)  grammaticum

    (B)  grammatici        (D)  grammatice

4. The vocative singular of <u>my friend</u> is

    (A)  mi amice           (C)  mi amico

    (B)  meus amicus      (D)  mei amici

## Practice Questions: Locative

1. Aeneas classem . . . ducebat.

    (A)  Italiam             (C)  ad Italiam

    (B)  Italiae              (D)  Italia

2. Aeneas cum Sibylla <u>Cumis</u> profectus est.

    (A)  from Cumae        (C)  up to Cumae

    (B)  to Cumae          (D)  near Cumae

3.   After leaving Troy, Odysseus sailed <u>for home</u>.

    (A)   domus                    (C)   ad domum

    (B)   domum                  (D)   in domum

4.   Navigavitne Aeneas <u>Syracusas</u>?

    (A)   away from Syracuse      (C)   to Syracuse

    (B)   in Syracuse           (D)   within Syracuse

5.   Dum Aeneas . . . manebat, Dido eum amabat.

    (A)   Carthagine          (C)   Carthaginem

    (B)   Carthagini           (D)   Carthaginibus

6.   Vergilius <u>Brundisio</u> <u>Neapolim</u> iter fecit.

    (A)   from Brundisium to Naples

    (B)   to Brundisium from Naples

    (C)   up to Brundisium from Naples

    (D)   from Brundisium and Naples

7.   Vergilius <u>ruri</u> morari semper volebat.

    (A)   from the country       (C)   in the country

    (B)   to the country         (D)   into the country

## Practice Questions on All Nouns

1.   Filius senatoris . . . est.

    (A)   miles                   (C)   militis

    (B)   militem               (D)   milite

2.   Cleopatra <u>veneno</u> mortem sibi intulit.

    (A)   without poison        (C)   for poison

    (B)   poison                 (D)   with poison

3.   Aeger morbo . . . mortuus est.

    (A)   quinto die            (C)   quinti diei

    (B)   quinque dies        (D)   quintum diem

4.   Eratne Caesar parvus <u>magnitudine</u>?

    (A)   by means of his size    (C)   despite his size

    (B)   with respect to his size   (D)   instead of his size

5.  Silvae sunt plenae <u>arborum</u>.
    - (A) with trees
    - (B) of trees
    - (C) trees
    - (D) from trees

6.  Liberi aliquid . . . semper volunt.
    - (A) novum
    - (B) novi
    - (C) novus
    - (D) novo

7.  <u>Erat auxilio amico</u>.
    - (A) He helped a friend.
    - (B) A friend helped him.
    - (C) The help was friendly.
    - (D) His friend was helpful.

8.  <u>Viginti annos</u> vir pauper erat.
    - (A) After twenty years
    - (B) Within twenty years
    - (C) For twenty years
    - (D) On the twentieth year

9.  Puer rumpens per ianuam clamavit, "Ignosce . . . !"
    - (A) me
    - (B) meum
    - (C) mihi
    - (D) mei

10. Manus utiles <u>multis rebus</u> sunt.
    - (A) for many tasks
    - (B) with many tasks
    - (C) many tasks
    - (D) because of many tasks

11. Adulescens . . . cum parentibus habitabat.
    - (A) domo
    - (B) domum
    - (C) domus
    - (D) domi

12. Cicero . . . erat.
    - (A) consulem
    - (B) consule
    - (C) consuli
    - (D) consul

13. Hospites . . . manebant.
    - (A) in ianuam
    - (B) propter ianuam
    - (C) per ianuam
    - (D) ad ianuam

14. <u>Duobus mensibus</u> <u>Athenas</u> navigabit.

    (A) Within two months/from Athens

    (B) After two months/from Athens

    (C) For two months/to Athens

    (D) In two months/to Athens

15. Multi Romam . . . visitare volunt.

    (A) urbs aeterna

    (B) urbis aeternae

    (C) urbem aeternam

    (D) urbe aeterna

16. Hannibal in Italia <u>sedecim annos</u> manebat.

    (A) within sixteen years

    (B) for sixteen years

    (C) after sixteen years

    (D) sixteen years

17. Catilina erat vir <u>parvae dignitatis</u>. The expression equivalent in meaning to the underlined phrase is

    (A) parvae dignitati

    (B) parva dignitate

    (C) parvam dignitatem

    (D) parva dignitas

18. Roma maior urbs . . . erat.

    (A) Brundisium

    (B) Brundisio

    (C) Brundisi

    (D) Brundisiis

19. <u>Illa nocte</u> multi senatores <u>Roma</u> fugerunt.

    (A) For that night/to Rome

    (B) After that night/from Rome

    (C) On that night/from Rome

    (D) Because of that night/to Rome

20. Milites <u>in hostes</u> impetum faciebant.

    (A) toward the enemy

    (B) against the enemy

    (C) from the enemy

    (D) through the enemy

21. Scelesti servi digni . . . sunt.

    (A) supplicio

    (B) supplicium

    (C) supplicii

    (D) supplicia

22. <u>Multa servis facienda sunt.</u>

    (A) Many things must be done to the slaves.

    (B) Slaves have to do many things.

    (C) Many slaves must do things.

    (D) The slaves are doing many things.

23. Quot amicos habes, . . . ?

    (A) Publius          (C) Publi

    (B) Publium          (D) Publio

24. <u>Mihi nomen est Perdix.</u>

    (A) My name is Perdix.          (C) Perdix gave me a name.

    (B) Perdix has my name.          (D) Perdix was my name.

25. <u>Senex prudentia carebat.</u>

    (A) Age and wisdom were lacking.

    (B) The old man lacked wisdom.

    (C) The wise man was old.

    (D) He lacked the wisdom of age.

26. Cena . . . placebat.

    (A) imperatori          (C) imperatore

    (B) imperatorem          (D) imperatoris

# Answers: Nominative Case

1. **(D)**

   The sentence reads "<u>He</u> gave orders to the lazy slave." The subject is in the verb, as none of the other forms can serve as the subject. Answers (A) **Ignavo** and (B) **servo** are in the dative case and **mandata** is (neuter) plural, whereas the verb **dedit** is singular.

2. **(D)**

   **Vilicus** is a predicate nominative because it follows the verb and restates the subject. (A), the most likely wrong choice because the verb **erat** cannot take a direct object. Answer (B) is genitive singular or nominative or vocative plural and (C) dative or ablative singular.

3.  **(A)**

This question is designed to test the fact that a noun in apposition must agree with the noun that it defines or limits and is generally found next to the noun it defines. Therefore, the answer is **servum**, modifying **Bombacem**. Answer (B) is nominative singular and could modify **Bacillus**, but the position of the missing word makes it more likely to be taken with **Bombacem** than with **Bacillus**, and the case is wrong. Answer (C) is dative or ablative singular and (D) genitive plural, neither of which are correct choices for apposition with **Bacillum**.

4.  **(C)**

**Dominus** is the correct answer because a predicate nominative, restating the subject, is required by the context. The obvious answer is perhaps (A) **dominum**, but an accusative direct object cannot be found with **erat**. Answer (B) is dative/ablative and (D) vocative, neither of which fits the context.

## Answers: Genitive Case

1.  **(D)**

The irregular noun **plus** is found with the partitive genitive, therefore, **plus cibi** "more of food (= more food)" is the best choice to complete the sentence. Answer (A) **cibus** is a distractor because it has the same ending as **plus** (which is neuter). Answers (B) accusative and (C) dative/ablative are not justifiable in the context of this sentence.

2.  **(A)**

The missing expression is a genitive of description, giving the meaning "Bombax was a slave <u>of great idleness</u>." Answer (B) is accusative, which can't follow a form of **esse**. Answer (C) is plural and the context is singular and (D) is nominative and not appropriate here.

3.  **(B)**

This question tests knowledge of the genitive case used with certain adjectives, here, **plenus, -a, -um**. So, "full of misery" is correctly translated as **plena miseriae**. Answers (A) and (C) do not make sense, as the nouns accompanying **plena** are not in the genitive, but in the ablative and nominative cases, respectively. Neither does Answer (D) "full with misery" make sense.

4.  **(A)**

This question asks for recognition of **fugitivae ancillae** as genitive, rather than dative. The context of the sentence requires the sense "of the runaway maid" rather than "to/for the runaway maid," so the resulting phrase must be (A) genitive, not (C) dative. Answers (B) and (D) are ablative and accusative phrases, respectively, and therefore are not appropriate choices here.

5.  **(C)**

This question simply asks for knowledge of the genitive singular ending of the 3rd declension noun **libertas**, which is **libertatis**. The other answers are (A) **libertatum**, genitive plural, (B) **libertati**, dative singular, and (D) **libertate**, ablative singular, none of which correctly translates "of freedom."

6.  **(C)**

**Aliquid mali** is a partitive genitive, meaning "something (of) bad." The sentence reads, "Bombax was always doing <u>something bad</u>." Answer (A) is a distractor that incorrectly translates the genitive phrase and Answers (B) and (D) are dative "for" and ablative "with," respectively, neither of which translates the genitive form **mali** correctly.

7.  **(A)**

Given the choices, this sentence requires an alternative to the partitive genitive, which is Answer (A) **Unus e servis** "one of the slaves." Answers (B), (C), and (D) do not make sense in the context of this sentence, which reads, "<u>One of the slaves</u> did not have a name."

8.  **(C)**

This is an example of the objective genitive, requiring the sense of "for" for **gratiam benefici**, e.g., "The slave is giving gratitude <u>for (a) kindness</u>." The translations offered in Answers (A) and (B) require conjunctions such as **et** and **aut/vel** in the Latin, which are not found in the sentence, and (D), "kind" is an indefensible translation of the noun **benefici**.

9.  **(D)**

Numbers are used in expressions of the partitive genitive, as here, **milia passuum**, "thousands of paces," or "miles." Answer (A) is genitive, but singular, and **quinque** and **milia** both require a plural to complete their meaning. Answer (B) **passum** could serve as the accusative direct object of **ambulare**, but does not link grammatically with **milia**. Answer (C) is the nominative singular of the 4th declension noun **passus** and does not have a function in this sentence, as **Bombax** is the subject.

## Answers: Dative Case

1.  **(C)**

This is an example of the dative as indirect object. The gender is not an issue, as all forms are in the 1st declension and feminine. Answer (A) is accusative, (B) ablative, and (D) nominative, none of which suit the context. The phrasing of the English suggests that "the slave" should be accusative, but the direct object is clearly "freedom."

2.   **(B)**

This question examines familiarity with the dative case accompanying adjectives whose essential meaning includes the word "to/for," as here, **idonea cenae**, "suitable for dinner." The sentence reads, "Bombax did not have a tunic <u>suitable for dinner</u>." Answer (A) is an ablative phrase and (C) "a suitable dinner" incorrectly translates **idonea** as modifying **cenae**. Answer (D) is a distractor that requires the Latin to read **idoneae cenae**, "for a suitable dinner" rather than **idonea cenae**, "suitable for dinner."

3.   **(D)**

**Parcere** is a verb that takes a dative object, hence, **miseris servis parcere**, "to be sparing to the unfortunate slaves." Answer (A) is the obvious (but incorrect!) answer as the accusative direct object of the verb, (B) is nominative plural, intended to simulate 3$^{rd}$ declension dative singular forms, and (C) genitive plural, does not fit the meaning of the sentence.

4.   **(C)**

This intricate sentence contains two uses of the dative: indirect object (**filio**) and purpose (**libertati**). The noun **servi** in the genitive singular serves as a distractor. Translation (A) incorrectly swaps the phrase **pecuniam libertati**, "money for freedom" with "freedom for money." Translation (B) misinterprets the functions of the nouns **dominus filio**, as **dominus** is nominative and **filio** dative rather than dative and nominative, respectively. In Answer (D), if slaves (**servi**) were the subject, a plural verb would be necessary, but the verb **dedit** is singular.

5.   **(C)**

This sentence contains two uses of the dative, one with an impersonal verb, Licebatne Bacillo, "Was Bacillus permitted," lit., "Was it permitted to Bacillus," and the other with a compound verb, servis praeesse, "to be in charge of the slaves". Answer (A) makes the common error of confusing the verb praeesse, "be in charge of," with praeficere, "place in charge of." Answer (B) is defensible, grammatically, but makes less sense than Answer (C) and gives the impersonal verb Licebat a personal subject ("he"). Answer (D) makes Bacillus the personal subject of Licebat and mistranslates praeesse as praeficere.

6.   **(B)**

**Nihil . . . Bombaci erat** is an example of the possessive dative, equivalent to **Bombax pecuniam non habet**. This sentence also contains an example of the partitive genitive, **nihil pecuniae**, "nothing of money = no money." Answers (C) and (D) do justice to the Latin, but the verb tense in each should be past, not present. In Answer (A), "never" does not render **nihil** correctly.

7.  **(D)**

Because motion is implied in the verb **misit**, Bombax is sending the love letter "toward" Palaestra and the preposition **ad** + accusative is used. Therefore, the dative case in Answer (B) is inappropriate here. Answer (A) "to send someone something" misrepresents an indirect object ("someone") as a direct object.

8.  **(D)**

**Magno auxilio domino** is a double dative, expressing both reference ("to his master") and purpose ("a great help"). Answer (C) seems the most likely answer because it replicates the English, but Latin requires a dative of purpose (**magno auxilio**) rather than a predicate nominative or accusative (**magnum auxilium**) in this context. The Latin of Answer (A) incorrectly reads "a great help of the master." In the phrase **ad dominum** in (B), **ad** means "toward" and implies motion, which is not evident in the English here.

9.  **(B)**

The passive periphrastic requires a dative of agent when a person is performing the obligatory action of the verb, hence, **Palaestrae**, "by Palaestra." This sentence reads, "The dinner had to be served <u>by Palaestra</u>." Answer (A), and perhaps (C), as ablatives of agent, are tempting answers, but the dative, and not the ablative, is found with a passive periphrastic such as **ponenda erat**. Answer (D) **cena** is preferable to **Palaestra** as the nominative subject, given the sense.

# Answers: Accusative Case

1.  **(C)**

"For eight hours" expresses extent of time, therefore the accusative case is needed. The ablative case, expressing other elements of time, appears in two of the other options: Answer (A) "(with)in eight hours" and Answer (B) "in/on the eighth hour." Note in this mistaken translation the use of the ordinal "eighth" (**octavam**) rather than the cardinal number "eight" (**octo**). Answer (D) **octavam horam**, "for the eighth hour" expresses an extent of time.

2.  **(D)**

The preposition **propter** takes the accusative case, hence **fugam**. If **propter** is properly identified as a preposition, the two choices are Answers (A) ablative and (D) accusative. Answer (B) is a red herring, as the meaning of **propter**, "because of," might suggest an object in the genitive case, however, this is incorrect. Answer (C) **fuga**, a subject form, does not fit the grammatical requirements.

3.  **(B)**

This is another accusative extent of time, this time in Latin. Answer (A) is provided as a distractor because the word "ago" in the answer would be expressed in the accusative case (i.e., **abhinc tres horas** "three hours ago"), however the adverb **abhinc** is missing. "Within three hours" and "at the third hour," indicating a point in time, require the ablative.

4.  **(A)**

This question requires a specific knowledge of which prepositions are found with the accusative case and which with the ablative. **Prope** is the only choice found with the accusative, hence, **prope piscinam**, "near the fishpool."

5.  **(D)**

This sentence reads, "Bombax arrived at the villa <u>four months ago</u>." Answers (A) and (B) require that the Latin be **post quattuor menses** or **quattuor post mensibus**, and Answer (C) the ablative phrase **quattuor mensibus**.

6.  **(B)**

This question asks you to discriminate among various meanings of the preposition "in." The sentence reads, "'Don't turn the switch against me,' implored Bombax." Answers (A) and (D) are incorrect because in meaning "in" or "on" is found with the ablative case. Answer (C) "into me" makes less sense than "against me."

7.  **(C)**

This sentence contains two constructions with the accusative: extent of distance, **triginta milia passuum**, "for thirty thousand paces = 30 miles," and a time expression, **abhinc septem dies**, "seven days ago." In Answer (A) the time frame and mileage are incorrect; in (B) the time frame is correct, but the mileage is not; and in (D) the distance is correct, but the time frame is incorrect.

8.  **(C)**

The preposition **ad** is understood with the name of a city in the accusative of place to which. The context of the sentence implies that Bombax wished to travel to or from Delphi because the idiom **iter facere** expresses motion. This eliminates Answers (B) and (D) as choices, due to sense. As **Delphos** has an accusative ending (plural because the name **Delphi** is plural) with the understood preposition **ad,** Answer (C) is correct. For (A) to have been correct, the form **Delphis** (= **e Delphis**) would have been necessary.

9.  **(B)**

In this sentence, **ad fugiendum** is a gerund of purpose, meaning "for the purpose of fleeing" or "(in order) to flee." Answer (D) is omitted because **fugiendum** does not mean "fugitive." The translations in neither (A) "as" nor (C) "at the point of" correctly translate the preposition **ad**.

10. **(B)**

The noun **Bombacem** is accusative singular and serves as the subject of the infinitive **esse** in this indirect statement. Answer (A) **Bombax**, which might be taken as the obvious answer, is incorrect because the form is nominative. Answers (C) and (D) are eliminated because **Bombace** and **Bombacis** are in the wrong cases, i.e., ablative and genitive, respectively.

## Answers: Ablative Case

1.   Ablative of description (C) The sentence reads, "Radix was happy <u>because of the size</u> of the mushrooms." Answers (B) and (D) do not make sense in this context and are not justifiable grammatically from the Latin provided. Answer (A) is justifiable, as **magnitudine** could conceivably be an ablative of means, but **magnitudo** is not an implement.

2.   Ablative of time (within which) (B) This sentence reads "<u>Within three hours</u>, the dessert will have been served." Answer (A) **tertia hora** is singular and therefore incorrect, as is Answer (D) **tertias horas**, because the ordinal number **tertius** appears, instead of the cardinal **tres**. Answer (C) is an example of extent of time with the accusative "for three hours" and is therefore an incorrect translation of **tribus horis**.

3.   Ablative with special adjective (B) Because the adjective **dignus, -a, -um** "worthy of" nearly always takes the ablative case, Answer (B) **(dignissima) laude** "most worthy of praise," is the correct response. Answer (A) accusative is not plausible, nor is Answer (C), which is dative. Answer (D) is tempting because **dignissima** is feminine nominative singular, as is **laus**. However, the sentence does not make sense with **dignissima laus** as the subject (which is **gustatio**).

4.   Ablative of manner (A) "With great care" makes the best sense of the choices given. The sentence reads, "The dessert course had been prepared <u>with great care</u>." This answers the question "How or in what manner had the dessert been prepared?" The word **magna** in the ablative preceding a noun in the ablative strongly suggests that **magna cura** is ablative of manner. Answers (B) and (C) do not make sense in this context and the wording of (C) requires that **magna cura** be taken as an ablative of means, but **cura** is not an implement.

5.   Ablative with preposition (D) All options contain prepositions that take the ablative case, but only **sine** supplies a word whose meaning is consistent with the context: "Radix was the best cook, <u>without a doubt</u>."

6.   Ablatives of degree of difference and comparison (B) This sentence contains an ablative of degree of difference (**paulo altior**, "a little taller"), together with an ablative of comparison (**Bacillo**, "than Bacillus"). The sentence is comparing Bom-

bax with Bacillus, so Answers (A) and (D) are out. Answer (C) is not appropriate because **paulo** is translated as "much."

7. Ablative of description (C) The appearance of the word "of" in the phrase "of great beauty" tempts an identification as genitive of description, but there is no genitive option among the answers. Since the ablative case may also be used to describe someone or something, Answer (C) is correct. Answer (B) looks temptingly like a genitive, but is in fact a dative, which is unsuited to the context here. The nominative and accusative in Answers (A) and (D), respectively, have no grammatical justification for expressing the phrase "of great beauty."

8. Ablative of separation (A) The meaning of the verb **prohibebat** suggests the answer "from the kitchen" by default. This is a verb of separation, because it means to keep someone or something away. The translations in Answers (B) "by means of," (C) "in," and (D) "with respect to," are not consistent with the meaning of this verb. Therefore, **culina prohibebat** is an example of the ablative of separation, "(Radix) kept the guests (away) <u>from the kitchen</u>."

9. Accusative, duration of time (B) This is a sneaky one, as it tests your knowledge of the accusative of duration of time, reviewed in the previous chapter. Answer (A) "in the second year," is an ablative of time when. Answer (C) means "(with)in two years," an ablative of time within which, and Answer (D), "for the second year," an extent of time, but is singular with an ordinal number and not plural with a cardinal number.

10. Ablative of means (C) The clause "Bacillus was beating Bombax . . ." sets up use of the ablative of means or instrument, since it suggests the use of an implement or tool, i.e., Bombax was being beaten <u>with</u> something. Since the ablative of means is found without a preposition, Answers (A) and (D) are out. Answer (B) makes no sense in this context, as **Bacillus** is the subject and **Bombacem** the direct object.

11. Ablative with a special verb (C) As an alert Latin student, you no doubt immediately spotted the deponent verb **utebatur**, one of the special deponents that takes an object in the ablative case, which is **nimio** in this sentence. The other forms are (A) nominative/accusative neuter, (B) nominative, and (D) accusative, respectively. Complicating matters is the appearance of the partitive genitive in this sentence, **nimio salis**, "too much (of) salt." If you answered this one correctly, way to go!

12. Ablative absolute (D) The underlined portion of this sentence is an ablative absolute, which you haven't yet reviewed. This ablative absolute contains a past participle, **verberato**, which means that the action of the beating has already taken place, relative to the working (**laborabat**). The action in (A) and (C) is happening at the same time as that of the main verb (-ing), so these must be omitted

from consideration. Answers (B) and (D) are both translated in the past, but it is the <u>slave</u> who has been beaten, not Bacillus, therefore (B) is incorrect.

## Answers: Vocative Case

1. **(C)**

This line from Poem 8 reads, **Miser Catulle, desinas ineptire**, "<u>Poor</u> Catullus, stop playing the fool."As an adjective modifying **Catulle**, which is vocative, **Miser** must therefore also be vocative. Answer (A) **Misere** is an adverb that might mislead you into thinking that the adjective **miser** must have the same ending as its noun, **Catulle**. Neither (B) **Miseri,** genitive singular or nominative or vocative plural, nor (D) **Misero**, dative or ablative singular, agrees with **Catulle**.

2. **(C)**

The context requires the vocative form of the name **Effluvius**, based upon the answers provided. Since this name ends in **–ius**, the **–us** is dropped, leaving **Effluvi** as the vocative. Answer (A) is nominative singular, (B) nominative plural, and (D) dative or ablative singular and irrelevant to the context.

3. **(D)**

Given the forms of the answers, the word **grammaticus** "teacher" clearly belongs to the 2nd declension, leading to the choice of (D) **grammatice**, as the correct answer. The imperative **Ignosce** in the sentence requires that the missing form be vocative singular. Answer (A) is nominative, (B) genitive singular or nominative plural, and (C) accusative singular.

4. **(A)**

The correct translation of "my friend" as a vocative requires familiarity with the fact that the vocative form of the possessive adjective **meus** is irregular. Thus, **mi amice** is correct. Answer (B) is nominative, not vocative. Answer (C) **mi amico** is the contracted form of **mihi** + the dative form of **amicus**. Answer (D) **mei amici** is nominative or vocative plural.

## Answers: Locative Case

1. **(C)**

Italy is a "country," not a city or small island, and therefore requires the preposition **ad**. The other cases are irrelevant, although Answer (A) **Italiam**, is a sneaky attempt to get you to nibble a red herring!

2. **(A)**

   **Cumis** is either the ablative or dative form of **Cumae** (a name which is plural), meaning either "from Cumae" or the locative "in Cumae." Because the verb **profectus est**, "he set out," predisposes the former meaning, **Cumis** must mean "from Cumae," giving the sentence the meaning "Aeneas set out <u>from Cumae</u> with the Sibyl."

3. **(B)**

   "Sailed for home" is motion towards a place, therefore **ad** + accusative is expected. However, the word **domus** gets special treatment among place expressions and drops the preposition, thereby omitting Answers (C) and (D). The nominative **domus** in Answer (A) has no meaning here.

4. **(C)**

   Among the choices, Answers (B) and (D) can be omitted because one can't sail in a city. Since **Syracusas** is accusative (the name **Syracusae** is plural), the place preposition **ad** is understood, giving "to Syracuse." Answer (A) requires **Syracusis**, "from Syracuse."

5. **(B)**

   The sentence in this question begins, "While Aeneas remained . . . ," implying "at" or "in" Carthage. These prepositions require the locative case, which for the singular 3ʳᵈ declension noun **Carthago** is equivalent to the dative, **Carthagini**. None of the other answers makes sense with **manebat**: Answer (A) means "from Carthage," (C) "to Carthage," and (D) does not translate.

6. **(A)**

   The ablative **Brundisio** (= **e Brundisio**) and accusative **Neapolim** (= **ad Neapolim**) mean "from Brundisium" and "to Naples." Answers (B) and (C) require **Brundisium Neapoli**, (D) **Brundisio et Neapoli**.

7. **(C)**

   The verb **morari,** "to stay," creates a context that requires the locative case, meaning "in or at place." The locative form **ruri** thus means "in the countryside." Remember that **rus** is a word that does not take a preposition in place expressions. Answer (A) "from the country" requires the ablative form **rure** and (B) "to the country" and (D) "into the country" require the accusative form **rus,** which is neuter.

## Answers: Practice Questions on All Nouns

1. (A) pred. nom.
2. (D) abl. means
3. (A) abl. time
4. (B) abl. respect
5. (B) gen. w/ adj.
6. (B) partitive gen.
7. (A) double dative
8. (C) acc. extent time
9. (C) dat. with verb
10. (A) dat. with adj.
11. (D) locative
12. (D) pred. nom.
13. (D) acc. prep. phrase
14. (D) abl. time within, acc. place to which
15. (C) apposition
16. (B) acc. extent time
17. (B) abl. descr.
18. (B) abl. compar.
19. (C) abl. time; abl. place from
20. (B) acc. prep. phrase
21. (A) abl. with adj.
22. (B) dative of agent
23. (C) vocative
24. (A) dat. possession
25. (B) abl. separation
26. (A) impersonal, w/**cena** as subject

# Chapter 13B: Pronouns

## Quick Study of Demonstrative Pronouns

### Hic, Haec, Hoc

|  | Singular | | | Plural | | |
|---|---|---|---|---|---|---|
|  | **M** | **F** | **N** | **M** | **F** | **N** |
| Nom. | hic | haec | hoc | hi | hae | haec |
| Gen. | huius | huius | huius | horum | harum | horum |
| Dat. | huic | huic | huic | his | his | his |
| Acc. | hunc | hanc | hoc | hos | has | haec |
| Abl. | hōc | hāc | hōc | his | his | his |

### Ille, Illa, Illud

|  | Singular | | | Plural | | |
|---|---|---|---|---|---|---|
|  | **M** | **F** | **N** | **M** | **F** | **N** |
| Nom. | ille | illa | illud | illi | illae | illa |
| Gen. | illius | illius | illius | illorum | illarum | illorum |
| Dat. | illi | illi | illi | illis | illis | illis |
| Acc. | illum | illam | illud | illos | illas | illa |
| Abl. | illo | illā | illo | illis | illis | illis |

### Is, Ea, Id

|  | Singular | | | Plural | | |
|---|---|---|---|---|---|---|
|  | **M** | **F** | **N** | **M** | **F** | **N** |
| Nom. | is | ea | id | ei | eae | ea |
| Gen. | eius | eius | eius | eorum | earum | eorum |
| Dat. | ei | ei | ei | eis | eis | eis |
| Acc. | eum | eam | id | eos | eas | ea |
| Abl. | eo | eā | eo | eis | eis | eis |

# The Forms of Demonstrative Pronouns

The demonstrative pronoun (**demonstrare**, *point out*), which can serve as both a pronoun and an adjective, designates a particular person or thing. The demonstrative pronouns are:

| Singular | Plural |
|---|---|
| **hic**, **haec**, **hoc**, *this one here* | *these ones here* |
| **ille**, **illa**, **illud**, *that one over there* or *this one, that one* | *those ones over there* *they, these ones, those ones* |
| **is**, **ea**, **id** | *he, she, it,* |
| **īdem**, **eadem**, **idem**, *the same one* | *the same ones* |
| **iste**, **ista**, **istud**, *that one over there (often shows contempt)* | |

Notes:

- The pronoun **īdem**, **eadem**, **idem** consists of **is**, **ea**, **id** + the suffix -**dem**. The following forms vary from **is**, **ea**, **id** (the letter –**m** changes to –**n** in these forms for reasons of pronunciation):

    acc. sing., masc. and fem.: **eundem** and **eandem**

    gen. pl.: **eorundem**, **earundem**, **eorundem**

- The neuter plural form **eadem**, *the same (things)* is often used as a substantive.

- The demonstrative **iste**, **ista**, **istud** has the same forms as **ille**, **illa**, **illud**.

# The Uses of Demonstrative Pronouns

**Hic** and **ille** have the same distinctions in meaning as in English, i.e., **hic** refers to this one right here, and **ille** to that one over there. When used as adjectives, these words have the same forms and meanings as the pronouns, but simply modify a noun in the sentence, e.g,

| Demonstrative pronoun: | **hic in foro ambulabat**. |
|---|---|
| | *this man (or he) was strolling in the forum.* |
| Demonstrative adjective: | **Hic vir in foro ambulabat.** |
| | *This man was strolling in the forum.* |

In the first sentence, with no other information as to the identity of the person or thing to which the pronoun refers, **Hic** is translated as "This man" or "He" because the pronoun is masculine.

Notes:

- Use the context to distinguish the feminine form **haec** from the neuter form **haec**, which appears often as a pronoun, *these things*, and the feminine form **illa** from the neuter form **illa**.

- Don't confuse the demonstrative **hic**, *this*, with the adverb **hīc**, *here*.

It is important to note that the demonstrative pronoun **is**, **ea**, **id**, *this one, that one,* substitutes for the pronoun of the third person, *he, she, it,* which Latin does not have. (This demonstrative will be discussed more thoroughly in the section on personal pronouns.)

## Practice Questions on Demonstrative Pronouns

1.  The accusative singular of īdem is
    (A) idem
    (B) eandem
    (C) eundem
    (D) eorundem

2.  Noli <u>ei</u> credere!
    (A) them
    (B) him
    (C) that
    (D) yourself

3.  Tribunus <u>haec</u> dixit quod iratus erat.
    (A) this thing
    (B) those things
    (C) these things
    (D) that thing

4.  Senatores in Curia congregant. Vidistine . . . ?
    (A) eum
    (B) ei
    (C) ea
    (D) eos

5.  In Curia <u>hic</u> senator prope <u>illos</u> sedebat.
    (A) that. . .this man
    (B) these. . .those men
    (C) this. . .them
    (D) this. . .these men

6.  <u>That acquaintance of yours</u> always disrupts public assemblies.
    (A) Īdem
    (B) Is
    (C) Hic
    (D) Iste

7.  Censor nomina <u>illorum</u> in tabula scribit.
    (A) his
    (B) their
    (C) them
    (D) that

8.  Does a praetor do <u>the same things</u> as a consul?
    (A) illa
    (B) istos
    (C) eos
    (D) eadem

9.   Frater huius senator est.

(A)   This senator has a brother.

(B)   The brother of that man is a senator.

(C)   This man's brother is a senator.

(D)   He is the brother of this senator

10.   Dabatne aedilis his illa?

(A)   these things to her

(B)   those things to them

(C)   that thing to them

(D)   her to these

11.   Is eis de hoc dicet.

(A)   He will tell this about them.

(B) He is telling him about this.

(C)   He is telling them about that.

(D)   He will tell them about this.

## Quick Study of the Relative Pronoun

|        | Singular | | | Plural | | |
|--------|------|------|------|--------|--------|--------|
|        | **M** | **F** | **N** | **M** | **F** | **N** |
| Nom.   | qui   | quae  | quod  | qui    | quae   | quae   |
| Gen.   | cuius | cuius | cuius | quorum | quarum | quorum |
| Dat.   | cui   | cui   | cui   | quibus | quibus | quibus |
| Acc.   | quem  | quam  | quod  | quos   | quas   | quae   |
| Abl.   | quo   | qua   | quo   | quibus | quibus | quibus |

# The Uses of the Relative Pronoun

The relative pronoun **qui, quae, quod**, *who, which, that*, is so called because it introduces an explanatory or descriptive clause that "relates" to another word or other words in its sentence or in a previous sentence. The verb of this clause is in the indicative and therefore its meaning is expressed as a fact. The noun or pronoun that the relative clause modifies is known as the antecedent, which is usually found immediately prior to the relative pronoun. The pronoun that introduces the relative clause agrees with its antecedent in gender and number, but not necessarily in case. In its clause, the relative pronoun performs a function independent of that of its antecedent, e.g.,

acc.                                                                          nom.

**Spurius [quem audivi orationem habentem] erat senator.**

relative clause

*Spurius was the senator [whom I heard giving a speech].*

The relative pronoun **quem** agrees with its antecedent **senator** in gender (masculine) and number (singular), but not in case. **Senator** serves as the predicate nominative in the main clause and **quem** is the direct object of the verb **audivi** in the relative clause. When reading, be sure to relate the relative pronoun to its antecedent.

## Tips on Translating the Relative Pronoun

- When the antecedent is a <u>person</u>, use *who, whom,* or *whose* when translating. When the antecedent is a <u>thing</u>, use *which* or *that*.

- The relative pronoun can also introduce other types of clauses that have their verbs in the subjunctive mood. These clauses, such as the relative clause of purpose and the relative clause of characteristic, will be presented in a later chapter.

- The relative clause is a self-contained unit of thought, often framed by commas. When translating a relative clause, it is helpful to bracket the clause as a separate sense unit within the sentence, e.g., **Oratio [quam audivi] erat longa**, *The speech [that I heard] was long.* When translating, <u>avoid pulling words out of the relative clause and inserting them into the main clause, and vice versa.</u>

- The antecedent of a relative pronoun is sometimes given in the context of the preceding sentence, leading to a situation where the relative pronoun is found at the beginning of the succeeding sentence. When translating this "linking **qui**," substitute a demonstrative, such as *this* or *these*, or a personal pronoun, such as *him*, e.g.,

> **Spurius de rebus urbanis dicebat. <u>Quibus</u> verbis dictis, omnes eum laudabant.**
>
> *Spurius was speaking about urban affairs. <u>These</u>, lit., Which, words having been spoken, everyone praised him.*

> **<u>Quem</u> octo servi e foro lectica ferebant.**
>
> *Eight slaves carried <u>him</u>, lit., whom, from the Forum in a limo.*

In the first set of sentences, the form **quibus** refers to Spurius' speech about urban affairs, **de rebus urbanis**, mentioned in the previous sentence. In the second example, the relative pronoun **quem** refers back to **eum** (Spurius) in the previous sentence. In such situations, English requires that you avoid translating a word such as **quem** as a relative pronoun (*whom, which,* etc.)

## The Interrogative Pronoun

| | Singular | | |
|---|---|---|---|
| | **M** | **F** | **N** |
| Nom. | quis | quis | quid |
| Gen. | cuius | cuius | cuius |
| Dat. | cui | cui | cui |
| Acc. | quem | quem | quid |
| Abl. | quo | quo | quo |

Note:

- The plural of the interrogative pronoun is the same as that of the relative pronoun **qui, quae, quod**.

# Practice Questions on Relative and Interrogative Pronouns

1. Senes . . . in foro vidi senatores erant.
   - (A) quis
   - (B) qui
   - (C) quem
   - (D) quos

2. The accusative singular feminine of <u>quis</u> is
   - (A) quam
   - (B) quem
   - (C) quae
   - (D) qua

3. Aedificium <u>quod</u> faciebant basilica erat.
   - (A) when
   - (B) that
   - (C) because
   - (D) since

4. <u>At what hour</u> will the citizens leave the assembly?
   - (A) Quam horam
   - (B) Quae hora
   - (C) Qua hora
   - (D) Quid horae

5. Consul <u>cui</u> fasces dati sunt imperium tenebat.
   - (A) whose
   - (B) whom
   - (C) who
   - (D) to whom

6. The senators <u>with whom</u> the consul was walking were his enemies.

   (A) quocum

   (B) post quos

   (C) quibus

   (D) quibuscum

7. Consul <u>cui</u> nomen Cicero erat senatum consultum ultimum tenebat.

   (A) whom

   (B) who

   (C) whose

   (D) with whom

8. . . . legi cives semper parent?

   (A) Quo

   (B) Quem

   (C) Cui

   (D) Quis

9. <u>Which laws</u> did Roman citizens disregard?

   (A) Quas leges

   (B) Quae leges

   (C) Quarum legum

   (D) Quibus legibus

10. <u>A quibus</u> omnes leges parebuntur?

    (A) For whom

    (B) From whom

    (C) From which

    (D) By whom

11. Qui <u>quae</u> vult dicit, <u>quae</u> non vult audiet. If stated, the antecedent of each <u>quae</u> would be the form

    (A) eas

    (B) eam

    (C) ea

    (D) id

12. Plebes <u>qui ambulabant</u> per Viam Sacram ad comitiam ibant. The most accurate substitute is

    (A) ambulaturi

    (B) postquam ambulaverant

    (C) ambulantes

    (D) quod ambulabant

13. Saxa <u>quibus</u> basilica aedificata erat gravissima fuerunt.

    (A) for whom

    (B) with which

    (C) to which

    (D) by whom

14. Pericula timidus <u>quae</u> non sunt videt. The antecedent of <u>quae</u> is

    (A) dangers

    (B) the fearful person

    (C) those things (understood)

    (D) she (understood)

15. <u>Sunt quibus diversae opiniones essent</u>.

   (A) There are those who had different opinions.

   (B) They are the ones whose opinions are different.

   (C) Those who had opinions were different.

   (D) They are the different ones who had opinions.

### Quick Study of Indefinite Pronouns and Adjectives

| Indefinite Pronoun | | | Indefinite Adjective | | |
|---|---|---|---|---|---|
| M | F | N | M | F | N |
| **qui**dam, **quae**dam, **quod**dam, *a certain one* | | | **qui**dam, **quae**dam, **quod**dam, *a certain* | | |
| ali**quis**, *some/anyone*, ali**quid**, *some/anything* | | | ali**qui**, ali**qua**, ali**quod**, *some, any* | | |
| **quis**que, **quid**que, *each one, everyone* | | | **quis**que, **quae**que, **quod**que, *each, every* | | |
| **quis**quam, *anyone*, **quid**quam/ quicquam, *anything* | | | (**ullus, -a, -um**, *any*) | | |

# Practice Questions on Indefinite Pronouns and Adjectives

1. Suntne <u>aliquae leges</u> malae?

   (A) all laws            (C) some laws

   (B) many laws        (D) certain laws

2. The Senate wishes to remove <u>certain praetors</u> from their provinces.

   (A) quidam praetores     (C) aliquos praetores

   (B) quosdam praetores    (D) quosque praetores

3. Si <u>quis</u> in forum ierit, splendida aedificia videbit.

   (A) who              (C) someone

   (B) anyone         (D) whoever

4. <u>Quisquis</u> amat, valeat; pereat qui nescit amare! (Pompeiian wall inscription)

   (A) Anyone         (C) a certain one

   (B) Someone       (D) Whoever

5. <u>Aliquis aliquid de quoquam dicere potest</u>.

    (A) He can say anything whatever about this.

    (B) Some people can speak about anything to anyone.

    (C) Every person has something to say about this certain person.

    (D) Anyone can say anything about anyone.

6. <u>Alicui quidem roganti quam iubenti libentius paremus</u>. This sentence means

    (A) You can catch more flies with honey than with vinegar.

    (B) Oil and water don't mix.

    (C) Birds of a feather flock together.

    (D) The end justifies the means.

7. <u>Īdem</u> is to <u>eundem</u> as <u>quidam</u> is to

    (A) quorundam        (C) quendam

    (B) quemquam       (D) quemque

8. Can there be a reason <u>for anyone</u> to speak out against his own country?

    (A) quicquid         (C) quibusque

    (B) quodam         (D) cuiquam

9. . . . . remedia graviora periculis sunt.

    (A) Quadam        (C) Quidam

    (B) Quaedam       (D) Quoddam

## Quick Study of Personal Pronouns

|  | First person, "I," "we/us" | | Third person, "you" | |
|  | Singular | Plural | Singular | Plural |
|---|---|---|---|---|
| Nom. | ego | nos | tu | vos |
| Gen. | mei | nostrum, nostri | tui | vestrum, vestri |
| Dat. | mihi | nobis | tibi | vobis |
| Acc. | me | nos | te | vos |
| Abl. | me | nobis | te | vobis |

# The Pronoun of the Third Person (*He, She, It, and They*)

The demonstrative pronoun **is, ea, id** designates the person or thing about which the speaker or writer is talking or writing and therefore serves as the pronoun of the third person, *he, she, it*. The subject plurals are **ei, eae, ea,** *they*. Here are examples of the use of this demonstrative as the pronoun of the third person:

**Noli dicere ea ei.**
*Don't say those things to him/her.*

**Mitte epistulam ad eum.**
*Send the letter to him.*

**Nos eos non amamus.**
*We do not like them.*

**Ite cum eis!**
*Go with them!*

**Eis id facient.**
*They will do it for them.*

**Is eam amat.**
*He likes her.*

Note:

- Remember that third person pronouns may cross gender boundaries when expressing meaning, e.g., **Accepistine epistulam?** *Did you receive the letter?* **Eam accepi.** *I did receive it (not her).*

## Personal Pronouns and Possessive Adjectives

| | Singular | | Plural | |
|---|---|---|---|---|
| | **Personal Pron.** | **Possessive Adj.** | **Personal Pron.** | **Possessive Adj.** |
| 1st person | **ego** *I* | **meus, -a, -um** *my, mine* | **nos** *we* | **noster, nostra, nostrum** *our/s* |
| 2nd person | **tu** *you* (alone) | **tuus, -a, -um** *your/s* (sing.) | **vos** *you* (all) | **vester, vestra, vestrum** *your/s* (pl.) |
| 3rd person | **is, ea, id** *he, she, it* | | **ei, eae, ea** *they* | |

Notes:

- To express possession in the third person, Latin uses either a pronoun or an adjective. As there is no possessive adjective corresponding to the third person pronoun **is, ea, id,** the genitive form of the pronoun **eius (ejus)**, *of him, of her, of it* (= *his, hers, its*) is used. (Note how much the Latin word **eius** sounds like the English word *his!*) The plurals are **eorum, earum, eorum,** *of them* (= *their, theirs*):

  **Fortuna eius bona est.**
  *His/Her luck, i.e., the luck of him/her, is good.*

- Possession in the third person can also be expressed by using the adjective **suus, -a, -um**. This adjective corresponds to the reflexive pronoun **se** (for which, see below). The reflexive adjective **suus, -a, -um** can be singular or plural and has the meaning *his own*, *her own,* or *their own.* Here are some examples to illustrate the distinction in meaning between the use of **eius** as a possessive pronoun and that of **suus, -a, -um** as a reflexive adjective:

Possessive pronoun:     **Pater se culpavit quod filium non agnovit.**
                        *Father blamed himself because he did not recognize*
                        *recognize his (someone else's) son.*
                        **Nonne matres filios earum agnoscere possunt?**
                        *Surely mothers can recognize their sons (the sons of others)?*

Reflexive adjective:    **Pater se culpavit quod filium suum non agnovit.**
                        *Father blamed himself because he did not recognize his own son.*
                        **Nonne matres filios suos agnoscere possunt?**
                        *Surely mothers can recognize their own sons?*

## Practice Questions on Possessive Pronouns and Adjectives

1.    . . . omnes liberi esse volumus.

    (A)  Nobis            (C)  Ei

    (B)  Vos              (D)  Nos

2.    The plural of tibi is

    (A)  vobis            (C)  vestrum

    (B)  vos              (D)  tui

3.    Amici, Romani, cives, . . . venite!

    (A)  nobiscum         (C)  cum vobis

    (B)  ad vestros       (D)  cum nobis

4.    Illum librum emi sed eum non legi.

    (A)  him              (C)  it

    (B)  his              (D)  them

5. <u>Te tua, me mea delectant</u>.

    (A)   My things please you, your things please me.

    (B)   Your things please me, my things please you.

    (C)   Your and my things please both you and me.

    (D)   Your things please you, my things please me.

6. <u>Dic mihi haec</u>.

    (A)   She is speaking to me.      (C)   Tell her this for me.

    (B)   Tell me these things.      (D)   This woman is talking to me.

7. <u>Nec tecum possum vivere nec sine te</u>. (Martial)

    (A)   I can live neither with you nor without you.

    (B)   I can live with you and I cannot live without you.

    (C)   You can neither live with me nor without me.

    (D)   I not am able to live with you or near you.

8. He lost <u>his (someone else's) money</u>.

    (A)   eorum pecuniam      (C)   suam pecuniam

    (B)   eius pecuniam      (D)   eam pecuniam

9. Not <u>for ourselves</u> alone.

    (A)   nos      (C)   nobis

    (B)   nostris      (D)   ad nos

10. Videsne . . . in speculo?

    (A)   te      (C)   vestrum

    (B)   vos      (D)   tibi

11. <u>I am helping you</u>.

    (A)   Tuli auxilium ad te.      (C)   Tu auxilium mihi das.

    (B)   Vobis auxilio sum.      (D)   Auxilium tibi venit.

# Reflexive and Intensive Pronouns

| Singular and Plural | |
| --- | --- |
| | **M, F,** and **N** |
| Nom. | _____ |
| Gen. | **sui** |
| Dat. | **sibi** |
| Acc. | **se** |
| Abl. | **se** |

# Tips on Translating Reflexive and Intensive Pronouns

- Distinguish between the reflexive and the intensive pronoun by looking at both the placement of the word and its function. With the reflexive pronoun, the action of the verb is directed at the subject. Unlike the intensive pronoun, the case function of a reflexive pronoun is <u>independent</u> of that of the noun to which it refers, e.g.,

  nom.  acc.
  **Pater <u>se</u> culpavit.**
  *Father blamed <u>himself</u>.*

Intensive pronouns generally follow the nouns with which they combine and (unless they are substantives) behave like adjectives, i.e., agree with the noun in case, gender, and number:

  nom.  nom.
  **Pater <u>ipse</u> me non agnovit.**
  *Father <u>himself</u> did not recognize me.*

# Practice Questions on Reflexive and Intensive Pronouns

*Enjoy the following "sentence story"!*

1. Ille consul <u>sibi</u> potestatem habere volebat.

    (A) himself
    (B) for himself
    (C) for him (someone else)
    (D) for them

2. The senators blamed <u>him</u> for his rival's death.

    (A) eum
    (B) ipse
    (C) ipsum
    (D) se

3.  <u>Consul dicit suum competitorem se occidisse.</u>

    (A)  The consul says that his rival killed him (someone else).

    (B)  The consul says that he (someone else) killed his rival.

    (C)  The consul says that his (someone else's) rival killed himself.

    (D)  The consul says that his rival killed himself.

4.  Some senators called for <u>his</u> removal.

    (A)  sui                    (C)  eius

    (B)  suum                   (D)  ipsius

5.  Iste sciebat <u>quosdam</u> senatores sibi inimicos esse.

    (A)  some                   (C)  any

    (B)  all                    (D)  several

6.  <u>Certe irati senatores consuli ipso se opposuerunt.</u>

    (A)  Surely the consul himself confronted the angry senators.

    (B)  Surely the angry senators themselves confronted the consul.

    (C)  Surely the consul confronted the angry senators themselves.

    (D)  Surely the angry senators confronted the consul himself.

7.  <u>Senatores suos secum ducebant.</u>

    (A)  The senators brought his men with them.

    (B)  They were bringing with them the senators' men.

    (C)  The senators brought their men with them.

    (D)  The senators brought their men with him.

8.  "You must give <u>yourself</u> up to justice!" shouted someone from the crowd.

    (A)  se                     (C)  tu

    (B)  vobis                  (D)  te

9.  "<u>I myself</u> am not a crook!" exclaimed the consul.

    (A)  Meus ipse              (C)  Ille ipse

    (B)  Ego ipse               (D)  Me ipse

10. Iste <u>se ipsum</u> puniendum esse non credidit.

    (A)  they themselves        (C)  he (someone else)

    (B)  he himself             (D)  that one

## Quick Study of All Pronouns

| Latin Form | Translation | Type | Function |
|---|---|---|---|
| **hic, ille, is** | *this one, that one* | demonstrative | points out specifically |
| **qui, quae, quod** | *who, which, that* | relative | describes, explains |
| **quis, quis, quid** | *who? what?* | interrogative | introduces a question |
| **quidam, aliquis** | *a certain one, someone, anyone* | indefinite | identifies vaguely |
| **ego, tu, is, ea, id** | *I, you, he, she, it* | personal | designates with reference to writer |
| **me, te, se** | *myself, yourself, him/herself/itself* | reflexive | restates the subject |
| **ipse, ipsa, ipsum** | *he himself, she herself, it (itself)* | intensive | emphasizes |

# Answers: Demonstrative Pronouns

1.  **(C)**
     The form **eundem** is the equivalent of the pronoun **eum** + the suffix **–dem**, which is accusative singular. Answer (A) is neuter, (B) has the correct case but the incorrect gender (feminine), and (D) the correct gender but the incorrect case and number (genitive plural).

2.  **(B)**
     The verb **credere** takes an object in the dative, accounting for the appearance of **ei**, which is dative singular. Answer (A) misdirects you into considering **ei** as the nominative plural masculine form, which would produce the translation "them," actually a translation of an accusative form (vs. the nominative **ei**, "they"). This does not fit the context here. Answer (C) "that" cannot be a translation of the demonstrative **ei** without a meaning such as "that person" as a pronoun. Answer (D) requires that the **ei** be the personal/reflexive pronoun **tibi**, "yourself" (singular because the imperative is singular).

3.  **(C)**
     This question examines your ability to discriminate between singular and plural forms of the demonstrative pronoun **hic, haec, hoc**, and between the meanings of "this" and "that." Since this demonstrative pronoun means "this/these," Answers (B) and (D) are not options because they contain translations of **ille**, i.e., "that" and "those." The context requires that **haec** be the accusative direct object of **dixit**. Familiarity with the forms of this pronoun leads to the conclusion that

**haec** is accusative plural neuter, "these things." The sentence reads, "The tribune said <u>these things</u> because he was angry."

4. **(D)**
This sentence completion calls for the simple direct object form **eos**, "Did you see <u>them</u>?" referring to the senators (masculine and plural). Answer (A) is singular, the incorrect number, (B) is dative singular or nominative plural, the incorrect cases, given the context of this sentence, and (C) is **ea,** feminine singular or nominative or accusative plural neuter. Answer (C) as a neuter plural form **ea,** "those things," is justifiable grammatically, but **ea** has no possible antecedent (**senatores** is not neuter and **Curia** is not plural). Furthermore, **ea,** as the 3rd person form "she," could not be the subject of **vidistine**.

5. **(C)**
This questions asks for discrimination between the meanings of **hic** and **ille** and between their functions as adjective and pronoun. **Hic**, as a demonstrative adjective, modifies **senator** "this (senator)" and **illos** "them" serves as the pronoun object of the preposition **prope**. For Answer (A), the Latin would be **ille. . .hunc**. In (B), the answer "these" is plural and in the sentence **hic** is singular. For (D), the correct Latin would be **hic** and **hos**. The sentence reads, "In the Senate House, <u>this</u> senator was sitting near <u>those</u> (senators)."

6. **(D)**
The English translation of the underlined phrase contains an overtone or suggestion of contempt or distaste, requiring that the answer be (D) **iste**. The pronouns supplied in the other answers do not carry such meaning.

7. **(B)**
**Illorum** is a genitive (plural) form of the demonstrative pronoun, which can be deduced from the context. Answer (B) "their" is the only plural answer that expresses the idea of possession. Answer (A) "his" (Latin **eius**) is singular, (C) "them," is not genitive ("of them" would be correct), and (D) "that," is both singular and an adjective, despite having the proper basic meaning of **ille, illa, illud**.

8. **(D)**
The phrase "the same things" in the question requires a neuter plural pronoun in Latin. Answer (A) fills the bill, but does not include the meaning of "the same." Answers (B) and (C), although plural, are both masculine and therefore do not accurately translate "things." Furthermore, as with **illa** in (A), these pronouns do not carry the meaning of "the same" found in **eadem**.

9. **(C)**
This sentence is tricky, because your mind's eye wants to read it as Answer (D) "He is the brother of this senator," or something equivalent. The sentence reads, "The brother of this (man) is a senator." The genitive form **huius** does not agree with **senator** or **frater**, which are nominative. Answer (A) is incorrect because **est** does not mean "has" and (B) **huius** has a meaning of "this," rather than

"that." Note that the apostrophe is used instead of the more familiar word "of" to indicate possession in the translation given in the correct answer, (C).

10.  **(B)**
"Was the aedile giving <u>those things to them</u>?" The verb of giving implies the appearance of both a direct object (here, **illa**, "those things") and an indirect object (here, **his**, "to them"). Answer (A) "these things to her" requires that the Latin be **haec ei**, (C) "that thing to them," **illud eis,** and (D) "her to those," **his eam**.

11.  **(D)**
The fact that **dicet** is in the future tense eliminates Answers (B) and (C), which have verbs in the present tense. In Answer (A), the meanings of **hoc** and **eis** are transposed, leaving Answer (D), "He (Is) will tell (dicet) (to) them (eis) about this (de hoc).

## Answers: Relative Pronoun and Interrogative Pronoun and Adjective

1.  **(D)**
The context of the missing relative pronoun suggests the word "whom" to complete the meaning of the verb, i.e., "I saw whom." As "whom" is an object form in English, an object form in Latin is required, leaving the choices of Answers (C) and (D), which are both accusative. Since the antecedent **senes** is plural, (C) **quem**, which is singular, must be eliminated. Answer (A) **quis** is an interrogative pronoun and does not relate back to an antecedent and (B) **qui** is a relative pronoun in the nominative case, which seems to be the correct answer, at first glance. Remember that the function of a relative pronoun in its clause is separate from that of its antecedent. The sentence reads, "The old men <u>whom</u> I saw in the forum were senators."

2.  **(B)**
Option (A) **quam** seems the obvious correct answer, but this form is the accusative singular feminine form of the relative pronoun **quae** and not that of the interrogative pronoun **quis**. Answer (C) **quae,** is feminine nominative (singular or plural) and (D) **qua** is the feminine ablative singular form of the relative **quae**.

3.  **(B)**
The relative pronoun **quod** in this sentence modifies **aedificium** and is the direct object of the verb **faciebant**, i.e., "The building <u>that</u> they were making." Answer (A) "when" is not an option for translating **quod**. **Quod** can have a causal meaning, i.e., "because" or "since," as in Answers (C) and (D), but these meanings do not make sense in the context of this sentence.

4.  **(C)**
The underlined phrase "At what hour" requires an ablative of time. Since the sentence is a direct question, an interrogative adjective is needed. The underlined

phrase "At what hour" requires an ablative of time. Since the sentence is a direct question, an interrogative adjective is needed. The ablative singular form of **qui, quae, quod**, which serves as the interrogative adjective, is therefore, **qua**. **Qua hora**, "At what hour?" accurately completes the meaning of the sentence. The accusative, nominative, and partitive genitive phrases in Answers (A), (B), and (D), respectively, have no grammatical meaning in this context.

5. **(D)**
   In this sentence, **dati sunt** takes a dative indirect object **cui** "to whom," the antecedent of which is **consul**. The sentence reads, "The consul <u>to whom</u> the fasces were given held the imperium." Answer (A) "whose" is possessive genitive, the form of which would be **cuius**. Answer (B) "whom" is object accusative, the form of which is **quem**, and (C) "who" is subject nominative, the form of which is **qui**.

6. **(D)**
   "With whom" is a phrase requiring the preposition **cum**. Since the antecedent **senatores** is plural, the relative pronoun must also be plural. Hence, Answer (A), which is singular, must be eliminated. Answer (B) **post quos** "after whom," changes the meaning of the original prepositional phrase and (C) breaks the general rule that the ablative of accompaniment must be found with the preposition **cum**. 7. (C) **Cui** is the dative singular form of the relative pronoun in a dative of possession with **erat**, "The consul to whom the name was Cicero . . . ," i.e., who had the name Cicero." In the Latin sentence, Answer (A) requires the accusative form **quem**, (B) the nominative form **qui**, and (D) the ablative form **quocum**.

8. **(C)**
   This is a bit tricky. Success on this question requires that you know that the verb **parere** takes a dative object. Only **cui** is dative and is therefore the correct answer. This form is an interrogative adjective modifying **legi**. Answer (A) **quo,** is ablative, (B) **quem**, perhaps the most obvious answer, accusative, and (D) **quis**, nominative. The sentence reads, "<u>Which</u> law do (the) citizens always obey?"

9. **(A)**
   Basically, this question asks you to decide whether the English phrase "Which laws?" serves as the subject or direct object of the verb. By turning the sentence around, "Roman citizens disregarded which laws?" you can determine that the answer must be the object accusative, e.g., **quas leges**. Answer (B) **quae leges** is nominative, (C) **quarum legum** is genitive, and (D) **quibus legibus** dative or ablative.

10. **(D)**
    This sentence contains the simple prepositional phrase **A quibus**, "By whom?" as the interrogative phrase to be translated. Answer (A) "For whom" is dative. Answers (B) "From whom" and (C) "From which" are ablative, but require the prepositional phrase **E quo** or **E quibus**. The sentence reads, "<u>By whom</u> will all laws be obeyed?"

11. **(C)**

This sentence says, "He who says (the things) <u>that</u> he wants will hear (the things) <u>that</u> he does not want (to hear)." Since the sense requires that the form **quae** be the neuter plural of the relative pronoun, the antecedent is understood as the neuter plural "things." Since "that" is the direct object in both instances, the only pronoun among the answers that is accusative plural neuter is **ea (quae)**. If Answer (A) **eas** were the antecedent, the relative would be **quas**; if (B) **eam**, the relative would be **quam**; if (D) **id**, then **quod.**

12. **(C)**

This question asks you to substitute a similar construction for the relative clause **qui ambulabant**. The present active participles **ambulantes** can be translated as the relative clause "who were walking." Answer (A) **ambulaturi** "about to walk" is a future active participle, (B) **postquam ambulaverant** "after they had walked" is a time clause, and (D) **quod ambulabant** "because they were walking," a causal clause.

13. **(B)**

**Quibus** is tricky here because it is an ablative without a preposition, leading to some contextual guesstimation. The form could also be dative, of course, but the sense does not permit this use, unless it would be incorrectly taken as a possessive dative with the verb **erat**. Therefore Answers (A) and (C), which are dative, are eliminated. So, "The stones . . . the basilica had been built were extremely heavy." Answer (D) "by whom" does not relate to **saxa**, the antecedent of **quibus**, nor is a preposition found before **quibus**, which would be required for an ablative of agent, also meaning "by whom," with the passive verb. Such a sentence would not make sense, i.e, "The stones by whom. . . ." **Saxa quibus** must mean, "The stones with which or by means of which. . . ."

14. **(A)**

This sentence by Publilius Syrus says, "The fearful (person) sees dangers <u>that</u> are not even (there)." Among the answers, the antecedent of **quae** that gives the most meaningful translation is "dangers," **Pericula**, which is the direct object of **videt**. **Quae** agrees with **Pericula** as a neuter plural, leading to the meaning "Dangers that. . . ." **Quae** does not agree with Answer (B) **timidus** in gender or number. Answer (C) is grammatically conceivable, but the ensuing translation does not make sense, and (D) requires that the relative clause have a singular verb.

15. **(A)**

This sentence reads, literally, "There are those to whom there were different opinions,"i.e., who had different opinions. Thus, **quibus diversae opiniones essent** is an example of dative of possession. Also, the antecedent of the relative pronoun **quibus** is missing. In the sentence, the adjective **diversae** clearly modifies **opiniones**, which removes Answers (C) and (D). The translations of the relative pronoun and verb tense are wrong in Answer (B). The relative clause of characteristic with the subjunctive, **quibus . . . essent**, that appears in this sentence will be covered below.

# Answers: Indefinite Pronouns and Adjectives

1.  **(C)**
    Selecting the correct answer here requires knowledge of the meaning of the indefinite adjective **aliqui, aliqua, aliquod**, "some" or "any." The Latin of Answer (A) would be **omnes leges**, (B) **multae leges**, and (D) **quaedam leges**. The sentence reads, "Are <u>some</u> laws bad?"

2.  **(B)**
    Proper translation of the underlined phrase requires knowledge of the meaning of the adjective **quidam, quaedam, quoddam** "a certain," which the context requires in its accusative plural form, **quosdam.** Answer (A) has the correct adjective, but in the wrong form, i.e., nominative instead of accusative. Answers (C) and (D) have the correct case endings, but neither is the correct Latin word: **aliquos** means "some" or "any" and **quosque** means "each" or "every."

3.  **(B)**
    When introduced by conjunctions such as **si**, the pronoun **quis** means "anyone." Translation (A) "who" for **quis,** requires that the pronoun be an interrogative and that the sentence be a direct question, which it is not. Answers (C) "someone" and (D) "whoever" are not acceptable meanings of the pronoun **quis**. The Latin for the former would be **aliquis** and for the latter **quicumque** or **quisquis**. The sentence reads, "If <u>anyone</u> comes into the forum, he will see magnificent buildings."

4.  **(D)**
    This quote is part of a Pompeiian wall inscription about love. The indefinite pronoun **quisquis** is the nominative subject of the sentence and means "whoever." The Latin for Answers (A) and (B) is **aliquis**. For Answer (C), **quidam**. The sentence reads, "<u>Whoever</u> loves, let him prosper; he who does not know (how) to love, let him be undone." Note the appearance of the jussive subjunctives **valeat** and **pereat**, "Let him. . . ."

5.  **(D)**
    This sentence contains a mouthful of three indefinite pronouns: **aliquis** "anybody," **aliquid** "anything," and a form of **quisquam** (or **quicquam**) "anyone" (or "anything"). The first is the nominative subject, the second the accusative direct object, and the third the object of an ablative preposition. Answers (A), (B), (C), all containing various elements of correctness, are designed to test your knowledge of the meanings of various indefinite pronouns. In (A), the object **aliquid** cannot mean "whatever." In (B), **quisque** does not mean "some people" nor does **de quoquam** mean "to anyone." The "about this certain person" of Answer (C) requires the ablative of the indefinite pronoun **quidam**, which is **quodam**, not **quoquam**.

6.  **(A)**
    This sentence says, literally, "We more readily obey someone (who is) asking (rather) than ordering." The verb **parere** takes a dative object, hence the parti-

cipial phrase **alicui . . . roganti quam iubenti.** Don't be fooled into thinking that **quidem** in this sentence is another indefinite pronoun!

7.   **(C)**
      This analogy compares the singular subject and object forms of the demonstrative pronoun **idem** with the indefinite pronoun **quidam**. These forms illustrate the effect of assimilation in producing the spelling changes of **eundem** and **quendam**. 8. (D) "For anyone" requires the dative of **quisquam**, which is **cuiquam**. Answer (A) **quicquid** is nominative or accusative singular neuter, meaning, "whatever." Answer (B) **quodam** is ablative singular of **quidam** "a certain person" and (C) **quibusque** is a plural of **quisque**, which does not fit the singular sense here.

9.   **(B)**
      The various possible answers tell you that what is missing is a form of **quidam**, **quaedam**, **quoddam**, the indefinite adjective. The missing adjective modifies **remedia**, which is the neuter plural subject of the verb **sunt**. Of the choices, the neuter plural form of the adjective that agrees with **remedia** is **quaedam**. Answer (A) **quadam** is ablative singular feminine, (C) **quidam** is nominative singular masculine, and (D) **quoddam** is nominative/accusative singular neuter. This sentence reads, "Some solutions are worse than the problems."

## Answers: Personal Pronouns

1.   **(D)**
      The missing pronoun must be **Nos**, in order to agree with the verb **volumus** "we wish." The appearance of the pronoun in addition to the personal ending of the verb, emphasizes that it is <u>we</u> who wish to be free. Answer (A) is the wrong form of the pronoun and neither (B) **Vos** "you" nor (C) **Ei** "they" agrees with the verb. The sentence reads, "<u>We</u> all (or All of us) wish to be free.

2.   **(A)**
      **Tibi** is dative singular. Therefore, its plural is **vobis**. Answer (B) **vos** is nominative or accusative plural, (C) **vestrum** is genitive plural, and (D) **tui** genitive singular.

3.   **(A)**
      **Nobiscum** to accompany **venite**, "You (pl.) come <u>with us</u>," makes the best sense. Answers (B) **ad vestros** "toward yours" and (C) **cum vobis** "with you" make no sense in the context of this sentence. Remember that the preposition **cum** is attached to the pronoun, eliminating Answer (D).

4.   **(C)**
      This question asks you to remember that a masculine pronoun can be translated "it" when referring to a thing (e.g., **librum**). Answer (A) "him" is a possible translation of the pronoun **eum**, but this meaning does not make sense in the

specific context given. Answer (B) "his" is not a possible translation of **eum** and (D) "them" is plural, whereas **eum** is singular. This sentence reads, "I bought that book, but I didn't read <u>it</u>."

5.   **(D)**
   This sentence reads, "<u>Your (things)</u> please you (and) <u>my (things)</u> please me." The pronouns **te** and **me** are in the accusative singular and serve as direct objects in this sentence. **Tua** and **mea**, "yours" and "mine," serve as corresponding possessive adjectives used as neuter substantives, "your things" and "my things," since no nouns are provided. Answers (A) and (B) are the same, but the wording is reversed. (This is a confusing sentence!) The translation in (C) does not give the meaning of the Latin, wherein each person is pleased by his own things, not both persons by both things.

6.   **(B)**
   **Dic** "Tell" is an imperative, immediately eliminating Answers (A) and (D), which do not contain imperatives. In Answer (C), the translation "her" is incorrect for the demonstrative **haec**, which can be feminine, but is not in the dative case, as required by the translation "Tell (to) her. . . ." This form would be **huic**. In the correct answer, **haec** serves as a pronoun in the accusative plural neuter form, meaning "these things."

7.   **(A)**
   The meaning of this sentence depends upon correct translation of **nec . . . nec**, "neither . . . nor," and upon seeing that **cum** and **sine** are opposites, and that therefore their prepositional phrases **tecum** "with you" and **sine te** "without you" contrast. Answer (B) says the same thing in both clauses, (C) turns the thought around, and (D) **sine**, is mistranslated as "near."

8.   **(B)**
   In Answer (A), the pronoun **eorum** "their" is plural, whereas "his" is required in the sentence. Answer (C) contains the reflexive adjective "his own," but the sentence reads "his ("someone else's"). In Answer (D), **eam** serves as a demonstrative adjective "this or that (money)," which does not indicate possession. Answer (B) may be rendered "his money", i.e., the money of someone other than the subject.

9.   **(C)**
   The word "for" in the English sentence suggests the use of the dative case. Therefore, Answer (A) **nos**, which is nominative or accusative and not dative, (B) **nostros**, which is accusative and adjective, and (D) **ad nos**, which is a prepositional phrase requiring a verb of motion, are all inappropriate.

10.   **(A)**
   The appearance of the word **speculo** "mirror" suggests that someone is looking at himself or herself, requiring the reflexive/personal pronoun "you." This is because the subject of **vides** is in the second person, i.e., "you are looking at

yourself." Answers (A) and (B) are both possible, but the verb is singular, therefore (B) is incorrect because the object pronoun **vos** is plural. Answer (C) **vestrum** "of you" or "your" does not fit the sense, and (D) is in the dative case, which is not justifiable here. The sentence reads, "Do you see <u>yourself</u> in the mirror?"

11.   **(B)**
     "I am helping you" may be rendered in Latin as a double dative, "I am for a help to/for you," i.e., **Vobis auxilio sum**. Answer (A) has the verb in the wrong tense, (C) transposes "you" and "me," and (D) "Help is coming to/for you" does not indicate from whom the help is coming.

## Answers: Reflexive and Intensive Pronouns

1.   **(B)**
     "For himself" requires the dative form of the reflexive pronoun **se**, which is **sibi**. The Latin of Answer (A) is the intensive pronoun **(ille consul) ipse**, "that consul himself." Answer (C) requires the pronoun of the third person **ei** "for him" (a second party) and (D) "for them" is not reflexive, as the subject is **ille consul** "that consul."

2.   **(A)**
     The pronoun **eum** fits the need for an accusative form of the third person pronoun, referring to the consul. Answers (B) and (C) are intensive (nominative singular masculine and nominative/ accusative singular neuter), neither of which is appropriate to the sense here. The pronoun **se** is a reflexive pronoun of the third person in the accusative, but must refer back to **senatores** as its antecedent, which doesn't fit the sense.

3.   **(D)**
     This sentence contains both a reflexive adjective (**suum**) and a reflexive pronoun (**se**), both referring to the consul's rival (**competitorem**), which is found within an indirect statement. Therefore, the sentence reads, "The consul says that his (own) rival killed himself." Answers (A) and (B) require **eum**, rather than **se** (note the ambiguity of the Latin here), and Answer (C) requires the substitution of **eius** for **suum.**

4.   **(C)**
     "His" is not a reflexive adjective because the subject to which it refers is **senatores**, which is plural. Therefore, Answers (A) and (B) are to be discounted. Answer (D) **ipsius** is, indeed, genitive and suggests the idea of possession found in the word "his," but the meaning of the sentence does not provide an opportunity for the use of an intensive pronoun.

5.   **(A)**
     This question reviews the material in a previous chapter. The indefinite pronoun **quidam** can mean "some" in the plural. The sentence reads, "That one (i.e.,

the consul) knew that some senators were unfriendly to him." Answer (B) requires **omnes,** (C) **aliquos,** and (D) the adjective **complures.**

6.  **(D)**
    This sentence contains both an intensive pronoun, **(consuli) ipso** "(the consul) himself," which is dative after the compound verb **opposuerunt**, and a reflexive pronoun, **se (opposuerunt)** "(opposed) themselves (to)." In Answer (A) the translation wrongly has the consul confronting the senators. In (B), the Latin requires that the intensive pronoun be **ipsi** to modify **senatores** instead of the consul. Answer (C) is a combination of the variations found in (A) and (B), and is therefore incorrect.

7.  **(C)**
    The reflexive adjective **suus, -a, -um** sometimes serves as a substantive, as here, where **suos** without a modified noun means "their (own) men." Note the masculine gender. **Secum** "with themselves" behaves as other reflexive pronouns when found with **cum**, which is enclitic. In Answer (A), the translation "his men" is not reflexive with regard to the subject **senatores**, which is plural. Answer (B) omits **suos** in its translation and (D) "with him," does not correctly translate **se-cum**, which is reflexive.

8.  **(D)**
    The sentence illustrates the use of the personal pronoun as reflexive. "Yourself" or **te** is the direct object of the verb "give up" and refers back to the subject of that verb, "you." Answer (A) is in the wrong person (third) and (B) and (C) are in the wrong case, dative and nominative, respectively.

9.  **(B)**
    This sentence illustrates the use of the intensive pronoun emphasizing a personal pronoun, which is a common type of expression. Therefore, **Ego ipse** is the correct rendering of "I myself." Answer (A) offers an impossible combination of a possessive adjective (**meus,** "my") and an intensive pronoun (**ipse,** "himself"). Answer (D) is not an intensive, but a reflexive, pronoun in the third person and is found in the incorrect case (accusative). Answer (C) **Ille ipse** gives the incorrect meaning, "He himself." 10. (B) This sentence, which combines an intensive with a reflexive, reads, "That one (i.e., the consul) believed that he himself must not be punished." **Se ipsum** serves as the subject accusative of the infinitive **puniendum esse** in an indirect statement and refers back to the subject of the main clause, **iste**. Answer (A) "they themselves" is impossible as a translation because **se ipsum** is singular. Answer (C) "he (someone else)" is not reflexive, as required by **se ipsum** in the sentence. Answer (D) is rendered by the pronoun **illum** or **istum** in Latin.

# Chapter 13C: Adjectives and Adverbs

The forms of adjectives are the same as or similar to those of nouns. Adjectives modify nouns and can even stand as nouns themselves. They are organized into two classes, based on their forms. One class has endings of the first and second declensions of nouns and is identified by the masculine, feminine, and neuter forms of the nominative singular, e.g., **laetus, laeta, laetum** (in dictionary format, **laetus, -a, -um**). The other class has endings of the third declension, e.g., **tristis, tristis, triste (tristis, -is, -e)**.

| | |
|---|---|
| First/second declension adjective: | **Romani qui ruri habitabant <u>laeti</u> saepe erant.** |
| | *Romans who lived in the country were often <u>happy</u>.* |
| Third declension adjective: | **Romani qui in urbe habitabant <u>tristes</u> saepe erant.** |
| | *Romans who lived in the city were often <u>unhappy</u>.* |

An adjective must agree with its noun in case, number, and gender. In the first example above, **laeti** modifies **Romani**. Both are nominative, plural, and masculine. In the second example, **tristes** also modifies **Romani**, and both are also nominative, plural, and masculine. <u>However, an adjective is not required to have the very same ending as the noun in order for it to agree with the noun.</u> If the adjective belongs to a different declension from the noun, the endings will be spelled differently, e.g.,

**Same Declensions:**

First/second declension adjective and first/second declension noun **laeti Romani**, *happy Romans*

Third declension adjective and third declension noun **agrestis amnis**, *country stream*

**Different Declensions:**

Third declension adjective and second declension noun **tristes Romani**, *unhappy Romans*

First/second declension adjective and third declension noun **periculosum flumen**, *dangerous river*

# Adjectives in the Positive, Comparative, and Superlative Degrees

| | | Singular | | | Plural | | |
|---|---|---|---|---|---|---|---|
| | | **Masc.** | **Fem.** | **Neut.** | **Masc.** | **Fem.** | **Neut.** |
| **Nom.** 1st/2nd | | **laetus** | **laeta** | **laetum** | **laeti** | **laetae** | **laeta** |
| | | laetior | laetior | laetius | laetiores | laetiores | laetiora |
| | | laetissimus | laetissima | laetissimum | laetissimi | laetissimae | laetissima |
| | 3rd | **tristis** | **tristis** | **triste** | **tristes** | **tristes** | **tristia** |
| | | tristior | tristior | tristius | tristiores | tristiores | tristiora |
| | | tristissimus | tristissima | tristissimum | tristissimi | tristissimae | tristissima |
| **Gen.** 1st/2nd | | **laeti** | **laetae** | **laeti** | **laetorum** | **laetarum** | **laetorum** |
| | | laetioris | laetioris | laetioris | laetiorum | laetiorum | laetiorum |
| | | laetissimi | laetissimae | laetissimi | laetissimorum | laetissimarum | laetissimorum |
| | 3rd | **tristis** | **tristis** | **tristis** | **tristium** | **tristium** | **tristium** |
| | | tristioris | tristioris | tristioris | tristiorum | tristiorum | tristiorum |
| | | tristissimi | tristissimae | tristissimi | tristissimorum | tristissimarum | tristissimorum |
| **Dat.** 1st/2nd | | **laeto** | **laetae** | **laeto** | **laetis** | **laetis** | **laetis** |
| | | laetiori | laetiori | laetiori | laetioribus | laetioribus | laetioribus |
| | | laetissimo | laetissimae | laetissimo | laetissimis | laetissimis | laetissimis |
| | 3rd | **tristi** | **tristi** | **tristi** | **tristibus** | **tristibus** | **tristibus** |
| | | tristiori | tristiori | tristiori | tristioribus | tristioribus | tristioribus |
| | | tristissimo | tristissimae | tristissimo | tristissimis | tristissimis | tristissimis |
| **Acc.** 1st/2nd | | **laetum** | **laetam** | **laetum** | **laetos** | **laetas** | **laeta** |
| | | laetiorem | laetiorem | laetius | laetiores | laetiores | laetiora |
| | | laetissimum | laetissimam | laetissimum | laetissimos | laetissimas | laetissima |
| | 3rd | **tristem** | **tristem** | **triste** | **tristes** | **tristes** | **tristia** |
| | | tristiorem | tristiorem | tristius | tristiores | tristiores | tristiora |
| | | tristissimum | tristissimam | tristissimum | tristissimos | tristissimas | tristissima |
| **Abl.** 1st/2nd | | **laeto** | **laeta** | **laeto** | **laetis** | **laetis** | **laetis** |
| | | laetiore | laetiore | laetiore | laetioribus | laetioribus | laetioribus |
| | | laetissimo | laetissima | laetissimo | laetissimis | laetissimis | laetissimis |
| | 3rd | **tristi** | **tristi** | **tristi** | **tristibus** | **tristibus** | **tristibus** |
| | | tristiore | tristiore | tristiore | tristioribus | tristioribus | tristioribus |
| | | tristissimo | tristissima | tristissimo | tristissimis | tristissimis | tristissimis |

## Adjectives as Nouns

Plural forms of both first/second and third declension adjectives are sometimes used as nouns. When an adjective substitutes for, or "takes the substance of," a noun in this way, it is called a substantive, which means that it can "stand by itself." Substantive adjectives appear in English, as in the title of the classic film *The Good, the Bad, and the Ugly*. **Labor omnia vincit**, *Labor conquers all (things)*, serves as the motto of the State of Oklahoma.

> **Multi in Campaniam se moverunt.**
> *Many (people) have moved into Campania.*

> **Tuleruntne omnes bona secum?**
> *Did they all bring their possessions with them?*

The following adjectives are commonly found as substantives:

| **First/Second Declension** | **Third Declension** |
| --- | --- |
| **bona,** *the goods (property)* | **maiores,** *ancestors* |
| **boni/mali,** *good/bad people* | **minores,** *descendants* |
| **multa,** *many things* | **omnes,** *all men, everyone* |
| **multi/pauci,** *many/few people* | **omnia,** *all things, everything* |
| **Romani,** *Romans* | |

## Adjectives as Adverbs

Where English uses an adverb, Latin often uses an adjective. When you translate, let the best sense dictate the phrasing, e.g.,

> **Aestate laeti ad oram maritimam proficiscuntur.**
> *In the summertime, they gladly go to the seacoast*, rather than *the glad (people) go to the seacoast*.

## Variable Adjectives (*Alius, Nullus,* etc.)*

Nine common adjectives of the first and second declensions are irregular in that they have −**ius** in the genitive singular and −**i** in the dative singular in all genders, e.g.,

> **Estne pomerium terminus totius urbis Romae?**
> *Is the pomerium the boundary of the entire city of Rome?*

Except for the variation in the nominative and accusative singular neuter, these two cases have the same endings as the demonstrative pronoun **ille, illa, illud** (for which, see the previous chapter). These irregular adjectives are:

| | |
| --- | --- |
| **alius, alius, aliud,** *another* | **alter, altera, alterum,** *the other* |
| **nullus, -a, -um,** *none* | **neuter, neutra, neutrum,** *neither* |
| **solus, -a, -um,** *alone* | **uter, utra, utrum,** *which (of two)* |
| **totus, -a, -um,** *whole, entire* | |
| **ullus, -a, -um,** *any* | |
| **unus, -a, -um,** *one* | |

---

* These adjectives are often designated by the term "irregular." The term "variable" is used here to distinguish these adjectives from other irregular adjectives, for which, see below.

Use UNUS NAUTA to remember these adjectives, i.e., Unus, Nullus, Ullus, Solus, then Neuter, Alter, Uter, Totus, Alius.*

### Quick Study of the Comparison of Irregular Adjectives

| Positive | Comparative | Superlative |
|---|---|---|
| **bonus, -a, -um**, *good* | **melior, melius**, *better* | **optimus, -a, -um**, *best* |
| **malus, -a, -um**, *bad* | **peior, peius**, *worse* | **pessimus, -a, -um**, *worst* |
| **magnus, -a, -um**, *big* | **maior, maius**, *bigger* | **maximus, -a, -um**, *biggest* |
| **parvus, -a, -um**, *small* | **minor, minus**, *smaller* | **minimus, -a, -um**, *smallest* |
| **multus, -a, -um**, *many, much* | **plus, pluris** (gen.), *more* | **plurimus, -a, -um**, *most* |

## Practice Questions

1. Roma . . . quam Pompeii erat.

   (A) paulo minor       (C) multo minor

   (B) paulo maior       (D) multo maior

2. Hard work overcomes <u>all things</u>.

   (A) omnes       (C) omnia

   (B) omni       (D) omnibus

3. Caesar was more powerful <u>than Cicero</u>.

   (A) Cicerone       (C) quam Cicerone

   (B) Cicero       (D) Ciceronis

---

* See David Pellegrino, http://latinteach.com/adjmnemonics.html.

4. Eratne Caesar . . . Romanus omnium?

   (A) nobilissimus
   (C) nobilissimum

   (B) nobilius
   (D) nobilior

5. <u>Bonum</u> is to <u>melius</u> as <u>multum</u> is to

   (A) plurimus
   (C) plurimum

   (B) plurium
   (D) plus

6. The genitive singular of <u>alter</u> is

   (A) alteri
   (C) alteris

   (B) alterius
   (D) altero

7. <u>Pauci sed boni.</u>

   (A) The few are the good.
   (C) The good are few.

   (B) Few men, but good ones.
   (D) Few possessions, but good ones.

8. <u>Facile consilium damus alii.</u>

   (A) We give easy advice to others.

   (B) We are giving someone else advice about that which is easy.

   (C) We give advice to another easily.

   (D) The easiest advice is that which we give to others.

# Adverbs

## Quick Study – Comparison of Regular Adjectives and Adverbs

|  | Adjectives | Adverbs |
|---|---|---|
| Positive | **laetus, -a, -um,** *happy* | **laete,** *happily* |
| Comparative | **laetior, laetior, laetius,** *happier* | **laetius,** *more happily* |
| Superlative | **laetissimus, -a, -um,** *happiest* | **laetissime,** *most happily* |

## Quick Study – Comparison of Irregular Adjectives and Adverbs

| | Positive | | | Comparative | | Superlative | | |
|---|---|---|---|---|---|---|---|---|
| | **M** | **F** | **N** | **M & F** | **N** | **M** | **F** | **N** |
| Adjective | **bonus, -a, -um**, *good* | | | **melior, melius,** *better* | | **optimus, -a, -um,** *best* | | |
| Adverb | **bene,** *well* | | | **melius,** *better* | | **optime,** *best* | | |
| Adjective | **malus, -a, -um,** *bad* | | | **peior, peius,** *worse* | | **pessimus, -a, -um,** *worst* | | |
| Adverb | **male,** *badly* | | | **peius,** *worse* | | **pessime,** *worst* | | |
| Adjective | **magnus, -a, -um,** *great* | | | **maior, maius,** *greater* | | **maximus, -a, -um,** *greatest* | | |
| Adverb | **magnopere,** *greatly* | | | **magis,** *more* | | **maxime,** *most* | | |
| Adjective | **parvus, -a, -um,** *small* | | | **minor, minus,** *smaller* | | **minimus, -a, -um,** *smallest* | | |
| Adverb | **paulum,** *little* | | | **minus,** *less* | | **minime,** *least* | | |
| Adjective | **multus, -a, -um,** *many, much* | | | **plus** (**pluris,** gen.), *more* | | **plurimus, -a, -um,** *most* | | |
| Adverb | **multum,** *much* | | | **plus,** *more* | | **plurimum,** *most* | | |

**N.B.** Be aware that a few adjectives are compared by using the adverbs **magis**, *more*, and **maxime**, *most*, e.g., **magis idoneus**, *more suitable*, and **maxime idoneus**, *most suitable*.

## Practice Questions

1.  Flores in horto prope arbores <u>dulces</u> redolent odores. Based on the sense, the noun modified by <u>dulces</u> is

    (A)  Flores

    (B)  horto

    (C)  arbores

    (D)  odores

2.  Crescuntne flores <u>celerius</u> arboribus?

    (A)  quickly

    (B)  more quickly

    (C)  as quickly as

    (D)  most quickly

3.  The form of the adverb that means <u>too easily</u> is
    (A)  facilius
    (B)  facilis
    (C)  facillime
    (D)  magis facilis

4.  Which of the following adverbs has a meaning pertaining to place?
    (A)  postridie
    (B)  paulisper
    (C)  undique
    (D)  vix

5.  <u>Italia est pulcherrima</u> means
    (A)  Italy is rather beautiful.
    (B)  Italy is very beautiful.
    (C)  Italy is too beautiful.
    (D)  Italy is beautiful.

6.  Nonne sol maior <u>quam luna</u> est? The best substitute for the underlined phrase is
    (A)  lunā
    (B)  luna
    (C)  lunam
    (D)  lunae

7.  Illud opus in horto non . . . est.
    (A)  facilis
    (B)  facilium
    (C)  facile
    (D)  facilibus

8.  The positive adverb of the adjective <u>gravis</u> is
    (A)  grave
    (B)  gravius
    (C)  graviter
    (D)  gravidus

9.  <u>Libere, liberius, liberrime.</u>
    (A)  freely, very freely, too freely
    (B)  freely, too freely, relatively freely
    (C)  free, rather free, very free
    (D)  freely, rather freely, most freely

10. Hoc flumen . . . quam illud fluit.
    (A)  lentior
    (B)  lentissime
    (C)  lente
    (D)  lentius

11. Heri vesperi per ripam <u>quam diutissime</u> ambulabamus.
    (A)  for a long time
    (B)  for as long as possible
    (C)  for a very long time
    (D)  for a rather long time

12. Canis nomine Fido . . . est.

   (A) fidelissimus omnium        (C) fidelissime omnium

   (B) fidelissimus omnibus       (D) maxime fidelis omnium

13. <u>Parvus</u> is to <u>paulum</u> as <u>magnus</u> is to

   (A) magis                   (C) magnopere

   (B) maxime                 (D) magnum

14. <u>Multa ignoscendo fit potens potentior.</u> (Publilius Syrus)

   (A) Many things become more powerful through forgiveness.

   (B) By being forgetful of power, many become more powerful.

   (C) By forgiving many things, a powerful man becomes more powerful.

   (D) Being so powerful over many things, he becomes forgiving.

15. Hi horti . . . quam illi sunt. Qui horti . . . omnium sunt?

   (A) minores / minimi         (C) minores / minime

   (B) minori / minimorum      (D) minoribus / minimi

## Answers: Adjectives

1. **(D)**

This sentence expresses a comparison between Rome and Pompeii. Since you should know that Rome was much larger than Pompeii, Answer (D) is preferable to (B). Answers (A) **paulo minor** "a little smaller" and (C) **multo minor** "much smaller" are not correct because they are not true. This comparative construction is an example of the ablative of degree of difference. This sentence reads, "Rome was <u>much bigger</u> than Pompeii."

2. **(C)**

**Omnia** "all things" appears as a substantive in this sentence. Answer (A) **omnes** can be accusative plural, as required, but would have the meaning "all people" as the masculine/feminine form. Answer (B) is dative or ablative singular and (D) dative or ablative plural, neither of which fits the meaning of "all things" as the direct object in this sentence.

3. **(A)**

**Cicerone** is an ablative of comparison. Answer (B) is only possible if it is accompanied by **quam**, which it is not. In (C), both options that express comparison appear together, i.e., **quam** and the ablative, which is incorrect. Answer (D) is genitive and irrelevant to the required English meaning.

4.   **(A)**
"Was Caesar the <u>most noble</u> Roman of all?" The appearance of **omnium** in this sentence keys the need for the superlative adjective "<u>most</u> .... of all." Based on the answers provided, a form of the adjective **nobilis** is missing. This adjective must modify **Romanus**, which is a nominative in apposition to the subject **Caesar**. This requirement eliminates (C), which is a superlative adjective, but in the accusative case. Answers (B) and (D) are comparative forms, respectively, neither of which correctly completes the idiomatic use with **omnium**. Because of its similarity to **Romanus**, the neuter comparative form **nobilius** surely distracted you!

5.   **(D)**
This analogy compares positive and comparative forms of irregular adjectives in the neuter gender. As **melius** is the comparative form of **bonum**, you are asked to provide the comparative form of **multum** "much," which is **plus** "more." Answers (A) and (C) are both superlative, not comparative, and in (B) the genitive plural form **plurium** is reminiscent of the nominative or accusative singular neuter ending –**um**, but the declension is wrong.

6.   **(B)**
**Alter** is an irregular adjective, which takes the unexpected genitive and dative singular endings of –**ius** and –**i**, respectively. The remaining forms of **alter, altera, alterum** have endings of the regular first/second declension adjective. Answer (A) is nominative or dative, (C) dative or ablative plural, and (D) ablative singular, which are all inconsistent with the requested genitive singular form.

7.   **(B)**
This sentence contains examples of adjectives used as substantives. **Pauci** = "the few" or "few people," just as **boni** means "the good" or "good people." The sentence reads, "Few men, but good ones." (A form of the verb **esse** is often understood in mottoes.) Answers (A) and (C) omit the conjunction **sed** from their translations and (D) would require that the substantives be neuter, as implied by the word "possessions," i.e., goods. 8. (C) This sentence provides an example of the neuter form of the adjective **facilis** used as an adverb, **facile,** "easily." In Answer (A) **alii** cannot be translated as "to others," which would require the dative plural form **aliis**. The translation in Answer (B) does not render **facile** correctly. Answer (D) "easiest" translates the superlative and not the positive degree as required by the form **facile** in the sentence. Also, as mentioned, "to others" is not the correct translation of **alii**.

## Answers: Adverbs

1.   Adjective   **(D)**
This sentence reads, "The flowers in the garden near the trees give off a <u>sweet</u> scent." Based purely on the ending, the adjective **dulces** could modify **Flores, arbores**, or **odores**, but based upon the sense, **odores** is the most likely noun modified. The position of the noun **odores**, perhaps a poetic counterpart to **Flores** at

the front of the sentence, is meant to distract you, as **odores** would logically be found beside **dulces**.

2.    Adverb    **(B)**
    The form **celerius** can be a comparative adjective in the nominative or accusative singular neuter form, or a comparative adverb. If **celerius** were an adjective, it would modify either the noun **flores** or the noun **arboribus**, which are neither singular nor neuter. Therefore, **celerius** must be an adverb modifying the verb **crescunt**. As an adverb, the form **celerius** is comparative, hence Answer (B), "more quickly." The Latin of Answer (A) is **celeriter**, the positive adverb, (C) the correlative expression **tam celeriter quam...**, and (D) the superlative adverb **celerrime**. The sentence reads, "Do flowers grow <u>more quickly</u> than trees?"

3.    Adverb    **(A)**
    "Too easily" is a comparative ("too") adverb ("easily"). "Too . . ." is one of the options for translating the comparative degree of adjectives and adverbs. Of the forms provided, Answer (A) **facilius** is correct. Answer (B) **facilis** is a positive adjective "easy," (C) **facillime** a superlative adverb "very easily," and (D) **magis facilis** "more easily," which is an improper use of the comparative adverb **magis**.

4.    Adverb    **(C)**
    Answers (A) **postridie** "on the next day" and (B) **paulisper** "for a short while" pertain to time and (D) **vix** "scarcely" expresses manner, leaving **undique** "on all sides" as an adverb answering the question "Where?" and expressing place.

5.    Adjective    **(B)**
    This question tests knowledge of the potential variations used to express the meaning of the superlative adjective. Here, the form is **pulcherrima**. Answers (A), (C), and (D) are all unacceptable. Answers (A) "rather beautiful" and (C) "too beautiful" are variations of ways to express the comparative degree, and Answer (D) "beautiful" expresses the positive degree.

6.    Adjective    **(A)**
    This sentence, which reads "Isn't the sun larger <u>than the moon?</u>" contains an expression of comparison between the sun and the moon. Of the choices offered, only the ablative of comparison, Answer (A) **luna** can substitute for the **quam** comparative construction that appears in the sentence. Answer (B) **luna** is nominative, (C) **lunam** is accusative, and (D) **lunae** genitive or dative.

7.    Adjective    **(C)**
    The demonstrative adjective **illud** reveals the gender of **opus** to be neuter. Therefore, by the rules of agreement, the missing adjective must have a neuter ending. Furthermore, the adjective must have a nominative case ending, because it is modifying the subject, **opus**. The question of degree doesn't arise, because all answers appear in the positive degree. These limitations rule out Answer (A) **facilis**, which does not have a neuter ending, and (D) **facilibus**, which is not singular,

but plural. Answer (B) provides distraction because it has an ending that is identifiable as a potential nominative or accusative neuter form of the 2nd declension. However, it is not. **Facilium** is genitive and plural. The sentence reads, "The work in the garden is not <u>easy</u>."

8.  Adverb  **(C)**

Only two of the four answers can be adverbs: Answers (B) **gravius** the comparative and (C) **graviter** the positive. Since the positive is requested, the correct answer is **graviter**. Answers (A) **grave** and (D) **gravidus** are positive adjectives.

9.  Adverb  **(D)**

This series represents the sequence of the various degrees of the adverb **libere**. The meaning of the word is irrelevant, as all answers have to do with being free. You should be concerned with 1) the correct part of speech, adjective or adverb, and 2) the appropriate sequence of the translations relative to the forms. Since the forms are adverbs and are given in the standard order of positive, comparative, and superlative, the correct answer is (D). Answer (C) translates adjectives, rather than adverbs. Answer (A) reverses the comparative and superlative and (B) gives redundant translations of the comparative form.

10.  Adverb  **(D)**

The need for a comparative adverb to accompany **quam illud** in order to complete the meaning of the sentence, "This river flows <u>more slowly</u> than that one," leads to Answer (D) **lentius**. Answer (A) **lentior** is comparative, but is an adjective. Answers (B) **lentissime** and (C) **lente** are incorrect forms of the degree of the adverb required by the context here.

11.  Adverb  **(B)**

The idiomatic expression **quam** + superlative is translated "as . . . as possible," which makes Answer (B) **quam diutissime** correct. Answer (A) requires the positive adverb **diu**, (B) the superlative adverb **diutissime** by itself, and (D) the comparative adverb **diutius**. The sentence reads, "Yesterday evening we walked along the riverbank <u>for as long as possible</u>."

12.  Adjective  **(A)**

Given the answers, the missing part of the sentence is the common phrase containing the superlative adjective plus the genitive plural form **omnium**, ". . .-est of all." The best immediate choices are (A) and (C), both of which contain a superlative. Answer (A) is correct because Answer (C) **fidelissime** is an adverb, and an adjective is needed to modify **Fido**, as the sense suggests. Answer (B) **fidelissimus omnibus** contains the wrong form of **omnis** and (D) provides a tempting, but incorrect, phrase using the superlative adverb **maxime**.

13.  Adjective  **(C)**

As **paulum** "little" is the positive adverb corresponding to the positive irregular adjective **parvus** "small" you are looking for the adverbial equivalent of the positive irregular adjective **magnus** "big." This is Answer (C) **magnopere**, "greatly." Answer (A) **magis** is the <u>comparative</u> adverb formed from **magnus**, (B) is the <u>superlative</u> adverb formed from **magnus**, and (D) **magnum** is the positive adjective of **magnus** in the neuter form, which matches, incorrectly, with the positive adverb **paulum**.

14. Adjective  **(C)**
    Don't let the gerund in this sentence fool you into translating the adjectives incorrectly. **Multa** is used as a substantive, "many things," here, as is **potens**, "a/the powerful man." In Answer (A), the translation makes **multa** the subject, which it is not posssible because the verb **fit** is singular. This version also omits the word **potens**. In Answer (B), the object of **ignoscendo** is "many things," not "power," nor does **potentior** agree with **multa**. Answer (D) omits the word **potentior** and ignores the substantive adjective **potens** as the subject of the verb **fit**. The sentence reads, "By overlooking many things (or much), a powerful (man) becomes more powerful."

15. Adjective  **(A)**
    Read these sentences as, "These gardens are <u>smaller</u> than those. Which gardens are the <u>smallest</u> of all?" These translations require comparative and superlative forms of the irregular adjective **parvus** to complete their meanings. In both sentences, the adjectives modify the nominative subject **horti**. Answer (B) **minori** is not a nominative form, but dative, and **minimorum** is genitive. The missing adjective in the second sentence must modify **horti** and not the genitive plural form **omnium**. Answer (C) contains an adverb **minime** and Answer (D) **minoribus** is in the ablative case, which is a diversion to fool you into considering the possible need for the ablative of comparison here.

# The Indicative Mood of Verbs

## Chapter 14 A: Indicative Verbs, Active and Passive

### Indicative and Subjunctive

This chapter is devoted to helping you recall the forms of regular finite verbs in the indicative mood, the most common category of verbs in Latin. The indicative mood expresses a fact or an assertion, as well as a direct question, whereas the subjunctive mood expresses hypothetical situations:

Indicative: **Catella passerem <u>habet</u> qui ad solam dominam pipiat.**
(Fact) *Catella <u>has</u> a songbird that sings only to its mistress.*

Subjunctive: **Utinam hic passer mihi <u>pipiet</u>.**
(Non-fact) *If only this sparrow <u>would sing</u> for me.*

There are six tenses of the indicative, active and passive. Because indicative verbs are the most frequently found in Latin, you probably learned these first and extended from them your knowledge of additional verb forms. In this chapter, the forms of the indicative mood will be presented together in the active and passive voices, according to tense. Note: the forms and meanings of the imperative, participle, and infinitive will be covered in subsequent chapters.

### Active and Passive

Voice is the aspect of the verb that expresses who is doing the action. The active voice expresses the doer of the action and the passive voice expresses the action of the verb as done to the subject:

Active: **Cum passer mortuus est, Catella <u>lugebat</u>.**
*When her songbird died, Catella <u>mourned</u>.*

Passive: **Cum passer mortuus est, a Catella <u>lugebatur</u>.**
*When the songbird died, <u>it was mourned</u> by Catella.*

In the form charts provided below, the third conjugation verb **mitto, mittere, misi, missus** appears. Verbs from the third conjugation are the most commonly used verbs in Latin literature.

## The Present System of Verbs

### Present Indicative: Active and Passive

**mitto, mittor,**
*I send, am sent*

**mittimus, mittimur,**
*we send, are sent*

**mittis, mitteris,**
*you (alone) send, are sent*

**mittitis, mittimini,**
*you (all) send, are sent*

**mittit, mittitur,**
*he sends, is sent*

**mittunt, mittuntur,**
*they send, are sent*

### Imperfect Indicative: Active and Passive

**mittebam, mittebar,**
*I was sending, was sent*

**mittebamus, mittebamur,**
*we were sending, were sent*

**mittebas, mittebaris,**
*you were sending, were sent*

**mittebatis, mittebamini,**
*you were sending, were sent*

**mittebat, mittebatur,**
*he was sending, was sent*

**mittebant, mittebantur,**
*they were sending, were sent*

### Future Indicative: Active and Passive

**mittam, mittar,**
*I will send, will be sent*

**mittemus, mittemur,**
*we will send, will be sent*

**mittes, mittēris,**
*you will send, will be sent*

**mittetis, mittemini,**
*you will send, will be sent*

**mittet, mittetur,**
*he will send, will be sent*

**mittent, mittentur,**
*they will send, will be sent*

### "Telling the Future"

- Know the principal parts of the verbs in question. In a third conjugation verb, e.g., **docet**, the vowel **-e-** is the stem vowel of the present tense, as indicated in the first principal part **doceo**. In a third conjugation verb, e.g., **discet**, the vowel **-e-** represents the future tense.

- Look for other indications of the future tense in the context of the sentence, e.g., the adverb **cras**, *tomorrow,* or a verb having a more obvious form of the future tense, e.g., **docebit**.

- Guess future! There are many more verbs in the third conjugation than in the second, making it much more likely that a verb with an **-e-** vowel is in the future tense than in the present.

- Avoid confusing the present passive form **mitteris**, *you are being sent,* or the future passive form **mittēris**, *you will be sent,* with the future perfect active **miseris**, *you will have sent.*

- Future time may also be expressed by the use of the active periphrastic, consisting of the future active participle + forms of **esse**, e.g., **missurus est**, *he is about to send, going to send.* The active periphrastic is a more emphatic or definitive expression of the future tense and will be discussed further in Chapter 16A.

# The Perfect System of Verbs

## Perfect Indicative: Active and Passive

**misi, missus sum,**
*I sent, have been sent*

**misisti, missus es,**
*you sent, have been sent*

**misit, missus est,**
*he sent, has been sent*

**misimus, missi sumus,**
*we sent, have been sent*

**misistis, missi estis,**
*you sent, have been sent*

**miserunt, missi sunt,**
*they sent, have been sent*

## Pluperfect Indicative: Active and Passive

**miseram, missus eram,**
*I had sent, had been sent*

**miseras, missus eras,**
*you had sent, had been sent*

**miserat, missus erat,**
*he had sent, had been sent*

**miseramus, missi eramus,**
*we had sent, had been sent*

**miseratis, missi eratis,**
*you had sent, had been sent*

**miserant, missi erant,**
*they had sent, had been sent*

## Future Perfect Indicative: Active and Passive

**misero, missus ero,**
*I will have sent, will have been sent*

**miseris, missus eris,**
*you will have sent, will have been sent*

**miserit, missus erit,**
*he will have sent, will have been sent*

**miserimus, missi erimus,**
*we will have sent,*
*will have been sent*

**miseritis, missi eritis,**
*you will have sent,*
*will have been sent*

**miserint, missi erunt,**
*they will have sent,*
*will have been sent*

### Quick Study Synopsis of an Indicative Verb in the Active and Passive Voice

| | Active | Passive |
|---|---|---|
| | **mitto, mittere, misi, missus** | |
| **Present System** | | |
| Present | **mittit**, *he is sending, sends* | **mittitur**, *he is being sent, is sent* |
| Imperfect | **mittebat**, *he was sending, kept on sending* | **mittebatur**, *he was being sent, was sent* |
| Future | **mittet**, *he will send* | **mittetur**, *he will be sent* |
| **Perfect System** | | |
| Perfect | **misit**, *he sent, has sent, did send* | **missus est**, *he has been sent, was sent* |
| Pluperfect | **miserat**, *he had sent* | **missus erat**, *he had been sent* |
| Fut. Perf. | **miserit**, *he will have sent* | **missus erit**, *he will have been sent* |

## Practice Questions

1. The future passive equivalent of <u>scribit</u> is
   - (A) scribitur
   - (B) scribebatur
   - (C) scriptus est
   - (D) scribetur

2. The perfect tense equivalent of <u>audis</u> is
   - (A) auditus est
   - (B) audivisti
   - (C) audiebas
   - (D) auditis

3. Heri <u>legisti</u> librum quem priore die emeras.
   - (A) you are reading
   - (B) you did read
   - (C) you will read
   - (D) you want to read

4. The active equivalent of <u>tenebamini</u> is
   - (A) tenebas
   - (B) tenebatis
   - (C) tenetis
   - (D) tenebaris

5. The active of <u>missus erat</u> is
   - (A) mittebat
   - (B) mittebatur
   - (C) miserat
   - (D) missus est

6. Pater suum filium <u>cognoverat</u>.
   - (A) recognized
   - (B) had recognized
   - (C) has recognized
   - (D) was recognizing

7. <u>Vocabamur</u> a parentibus nostris.
   - (A) We will be called
   - (B) We are called
   - (C) We were called
   - (D) We were calling

8. The plural of <u>tenuit</u> is
   - (A) tenuerant
   - (B) tenuerunt
   - (C) tenuerint
   - (D) tenent

9. Prima luce sol <u>surget</u>.
   - (A) arose
   - (B) will rise
   - (C) has risen
   - (D) rises

10. The future tense of <u>duco</u> is
    - (A) ducam
    - (B) ducebam
    - (C) ducemus
    - (D) ducor

11. <u>Dormiebat</u>ne ignavus discipulus?
    - (A) Will...sleep?
    - (B) Can...sleep?
    - (C) Was...sleeping?
    - (D) Were...sleeping?

12. The personal subject of <u>trahimini</u> is
    - (A) tu
    - (B) ego
    - (C) nos
    - (D) vos

13. Proximo mense ad Hispaniam <u>mittēris</u>.
    - (A) you will be sent
    - (B) you are being sent
    - (C) you will have sent
    - (D) you will send

14. The singular of <u>parabamus</u> is
    - (A) paramus
    - (B) parabo
    - (C) paro
    - (D) parabam

15. Which of the following belongs to the second conjugation?

    (A) custodio            (C) iungo

    (B) navigo             (D) iubeo

16. The passive of <u>portaverunt</u> is

    (A) portati erant        (C) portati erunt

    (B) portati sunt         (D) portantur

17. <u>Duxi</u> equum ad aquam.

    (A) I lead             (C) I led

    (B) Lead              (D) To have led

18. Di homines semper <u>amaverint</u>.

    (A) they had loved      (C) they will have loved

    (B) they did love        (D) they will love

19. Baculum a cane <u>receptum est</u>.

    (A) has been fetched     (C) is being fetched

    (B) had been fetched     (D) has fetched

20. Si ad Cretam navigaveris, a piratis <u>capieris</u>.

    (A) you are being captured     (C) you are capturing

    (B) you will have captured     (D) you will be captured

21. Consul <u>facturus es</u>.

    (A) you are becoming       (C) you have become

    (B) you are about to become   (D) you will have become

## Answers

| | | | | | | | | | |
|---|---|---|---|---|---|---|---|---|---|
| 1. | (D) | 5. | (C) | 9. | (B) | 13. | (A) | 17. | (C) |
| 2. | (B) | 6. | (B) | 10. | (A) | 14. | (D) | 18. | (C) |
| 3. | (B) | 7. | (C) | 11. | (C) | 15. | (D) | 19. | (A) |
| 4. | (B) | 8. | (B) | 12. | (D) | 16. | (B) | 20. | (D) |
| | | | | | | | | 21. | (B) |

# Chapter 14 B: Deponent Verbs

## Passive Verbs and Deponent Verbs

Deponent verbs have "put aside" (**deponere**) their active forms and passive meanings. Therefore, they are verbs that have only <u>passive forms</u> and <u>active meanings</u>, e.g., **loquitur**, *he is speaking* (not *he is being spoken*). Such verbs have also been called "fake passives." Deponent verbs occur in all four conjugations and have the same forms as regular passive verbs. Even forms such as the perfect passive participle have active meanings, e.g., **locutus**, *having spoken* (not *having been spoken*).

## Deponent Verbs

Note that deponent verbs have only <u>three</u> principal parts:

| | |
|---|---|
| **loquor** | (I speak, first person singular, present tense passive) |
| **loqui** | (to speak, present passive infinitive) |
| **locutus sum** | (I have spoken, first person singular, perfect tense passive) |

As with non-deponent verbs, the conjugation of a deponent verb is determined from its second principal part: first **hortari**, second **vereri**, third **loqui**, and fourth **oriri**. The deponent verb given above belongs to the third conjugation because its present infinitive form is **loqui**. (The forms of passive and deponent infinitives will be discussed further in Chapter 16C.) The present active stem is then **loque-** (from the hypothetical present active infinitive form **loquere**). The deponent verb has a present active stem that is used in some forms, such as the gerundive, e.g., **loquendum**, or the imperfect subjunctive, e.g., **loqueretur**. There are no deponent verbs in English, but there are a large number in Latin, many of which are found in compound forms. Here are some examples of how deponent verbs are translated in context:

> **Glukos medicus se ipsum curare <u>conatus est</u>. <u>Mortuus est</u>.**
>
> *Dr. Glukos <u>tried</u> to cure himself. <u>He died</u>.*

### Synopsis of a Deponent Verb

| loquor, loqui, locutus sum | |
|---|---|
| Present | **loquuntur**, *they are speaking* |
| Imperfect | **loquebantur**, *they were speaking* |
| Future | **loquentur**, *they will speak* |
| Perfect | **locuti sunt**, *they have spoken* |
| Pluperfect | **locuti erant**, *they had spoken* |
| Future Perfect | **locuti erunt**, *they will have spoken* |

Note:

> Other forms of deponent verbs, such as imperatives, participles, and infinitives, will be covered in subsequent chapters.

## COMMON DEPONENT VERBS

### First Conjugation

**arbitror, arbitrari, arbitratus sum**, *think, judge*

**conor, conari, conatus sum**, *try, attempt*

**hortor, hortari, hortatus sum**, *encourage, urge on*

**miror, mirari, miratus sum**, *wonder*

**moror, morari, moratus sum**, *stay, remain*

### Second Conjugation

**polliceor, polliceri, pollicitus sum**, *promise*

**reor, reri, ratus sum**, *think*

**tueor, tueri, tutus sum**, *protect, aid*

**vereor, vereri, veritus sum**, *fear, be afraid*

### Third Conjugation

**loquor, loqui, locutus sum**, *speak, talk*

**nanciscor, nancisci, nactus sum**, *obtain*

**nascor, nasci, natus sum**, *be born*

**proficiscor, proficisci, profectus sum**, *set out, depart*

**queror, queri, questus sum**, *complain, lament*

**sequor, sequi, secutus sum**, *follow*

**utor, uti, usus sum** (+ abl.), *use*

### Third-*io* Conjugation

**egredior, egredi, egressus sum**, *go out, leave*

**ingredior, ingredi, ingressus sum**, *go in, enter*

**morior, mori, mortuus sum**, *to die*

**patior, pati, passus sum**, *to endure, suffer, allow*

**progredior, progredi, progressus sum**, *go forward, proceed*

**regredior, regredi, regressus sum**, *go back, return*

## Fourth Conjugation

**experior, experiri, expertus sum**, *test, try*

**orior, oriri, ortus sum**, *rise, get up*

**potior, potiri, potitus sum** (+ abl. or gen.), *possess, obtain*

# Some Additional Information About Deponent Verbs

## Semi-Deponent Verbs

The subcategory of deponent verbs called <u>semi-deponents</u> consists of verbs that are active in the present system and passive in the perfect system, e.g., **audeo, audere, ausus sum**, *I dare, to dare, I (have) dared*. In addition to **audeo**, the most common semi-deponents are **gaudeo, gaudere, gavisus sum**, *rejoice, be glad*, and **soleo, solere, solitus sum**, *be accustomed*. Note that all three verbs belong to the second conjugation. Be careful to distinguish between **audeo** and **audio**!

> **Nuper vespillo Diaulus nunc medicus fieri <u>ausus est</u>.**
> *Diaulus, recently an undertaker, now <u>has dared</u> to become a doctor.*

## Deponent Verbs with the Ablative Case

In Chaper 13A, you met a small number of deponent verbs that take their direct objects in the <u>ablative</u> case, rather than the accusative.

> **Symmachus <u>discipulis</u> qui manus gelatas habebant utebatur.**
> *Symmachus kept using <u>apprentices</u> who had cold hands.*

These verbs are:

**fruor, frui, fructus sum** (+ abl.), *enjoy, have benefit of*

**fungor, fungi, functus sum** (+ abl.), *perform, discharge*

**potior, potiri, potitus sum** (+ abl. gen.), *obtain, get possession of*

**utor, uti, usus sum** (+ abl.) *to use, make use of*

**vescor, vesci** (+ abl.), *to eat, feed on*

Note:

- Use the memory device PUFFV ("puffy") to remember these deponent verbs with the ablative case.*

## Several Additional Points

1) Note that the common deponent **morior** in the perfect system means *is dead* as well as *died*, i.e., **mortuus est** means *he is dead*, as well as *he died*.

2) The verb **videre** has a special sense when it appears in the passive, i.e., *to be seen* means *to seem*. In its passive forms, this verb can behave like a deponent verb, i.e., can have an active meaning: **videor, videri, visus sum**, *I seem, to seem, I have seemed*. (For this verb as an impersonal with the dative case, see Chapter 14D.)

---

* David Pellegrino, http://latinteach.com/casemnemonics.html.

## Tips on Translating Deponent Verbs

Deponent verbs may be recognized through familiarity or from context. First, know the principal parts of the most common deponents, i.e., know which verbs are deponent. Secondly, use common sense to help you to determine whether a verb is passive or deponent, e.g.,

> **Aegri multum dolorem <u>patiebantur</u>.**
> *The sick <u>were enduring</u> much pain.*

> You can deduce the fact that **patiebantur** is deponent because its meaning as a passive verb, *were being endured*, does not make sense in this context.

- Be alert to the peculiarities of some deponent verbs, e.g., semi-deponents and deponents with ablative objects.

- When working with deponent verbs, take care to distinguish among those that look alike, e.g., **miror,** *wonder at*, **morior,** *die*, and **moror,** *delay*, or **nanciscor,** *obtain*, and **nascor,** *be born*.


## Practice Questions

1. Iuvenalis <u>loquebatur</u>, "Mens sana in corpore sano."

    (A) was said            (C) was saying

    (B) will say             (D) kept on being said

2. Glukos in cubiculum <u>ingressus est</u> ut cum aegra Anemia loqueretur.

    (A) entered           (C) has been entered

    (B) is entering        (D) having entered

3. "Anemia, it is important for you <u>to get out of</u> the house every day," advised Glukos.

    (A) egredere          (C) egressus esse

    (B) egrediendi       (D) egredi

4. Anemia mortua a Mercurio ad inferos <u>ducetur</u>.

    (A) will lead          (C) is leading

    (B) is led             (D) will be led

5. Quamobrem Mercurius . . . <u>potitus est</u>?

    (A) caduceum        (C) caduceos

    (B) caduceo          (D) caduceorum

6. <u>Vererisne</u> mori? The closest meaning to that of the underlined word is

    (A)  Timetisne             (C)  Timebisne

    (B)  Timesne               (D)  Timeresne

7. Aesculapius omnes Romanos <u>tuetur</u>.

    (A)  will protect          (C)  is being protected

    (B)  should protect       (D)  protects

8. Medici Romani se ipsos curare <u>ausi sunt</u>.

    (A)  were dared           (C)  have been dared

    (B)  dared               (D)  are daring

## *Sententiae Antiquae*

1. Cura pecuniam crescentem. . . . (Horace)

    (A)  sequitur            (C)  secuturus esse

    (B)  sequi               (D)  secutus es

2. Non nobis solum <u>nati sumus</u>. (Cicero)

    (A)  we have been born     (C)  we were being born

    (B)  we are being born      (D)  we had been born

3. In bibliothecis . . . defunctorum immortales animae. (Pliny the Elder)

    (A)  loquebatur         (C)  loquor

    (B)  locuti erant        (D)  loquuntur

4. <u>Non progredi est regredi</u>. (Motto)

    (A)  We're advancing backwards rapidly.

    (B)  The good old days were best.

    (C)  Man never accomplished anything without hard work.

    (D)  Forward not backward.

5. "Stick to the subject, the words <u>will follow</u>." (Cato)

    (A)  sequuntur         (C)  sequantur

    (B)  secuta erunt       (D)  sequentur

**Stumper**:   "O <u>passi</u> graviora, dabit deus his quoque finem!" (Vergil)

    (A) to suffer (B) having been suffered (C) having suffered (D) they suffered

# Answers

1. **(C)**
   **Loquebatur** is in the imperfect tense and therefore is translated "he was saying." The sentence reads, "Juvenal <u>was saying</u>, 'A sound mind in a sound body.'" Answers (A) and (D) also express the meaning of the imperfect tense, but in the passive voice, whereas **loquor** is a deponent verb. Answer (B) requires the future tense form **loquetur**.

2. **(A)**
   As with verbs in the regular passive voice, verb forms such as **ingressus est** provide the various past tenses of deponent verbs. **Ingressus est** is a form of the perfect tense, therefore Answer (A) "entered" is correct. The sentence reads, "Glukos <u>entered</u> the room to speak with the ill Anemia." Answer (C) is also given in the perfect tense, but is passive. Answer (B) "is entering" is a common incorrect translation of a passive form of the perfect system because of the appearance of the verb **est**. Answer (D) would require the past participle **ingressus**, which is only a component of the perfect passive verb form.

3. **(D)**
   The phrase "to get out of" is expressed by the infinitive **egredi**. Although Answer (A) **egredere** appears to be an infinitive, it is not, because **egredior** is a deponent verb and has forms only in the passive. This form is an alternative to the second person singular present tense form **egrederis**. Answer (B) **egrediendi** is a gerund or gerundive and (C) **egressus esse** is an infinitive, but appears in the wrong tense (perfect).

4. **(D)**
   The appearance of a regular passive verb form is designed to "keep you honest." **Ducetur** "she will be led" is the future tense of the passive of the regular verb **ducere**. The sentence reads, "The deceased Anemia <u>will be led</u> by Mercury to the underworld." The other answers give translations in the active voice, in anticipation of the incorrect identification of **ducetur** as a deponent verb.

5. **(B)**
   This question tests your alertness to the fact that certain deponent verbs take a direct object in the ablative case. **Potior** is one of these verbs, therefore **caduceo** is the correct answer, leading to the meaning "For what reason did Mercury come into possession of the <u>caduceus</u>?" Answer (A) is the anticipated incorrect answer, as **caduceum** is accusative. Answers (C) and (D) are in the plural and therefore incorrect here, since "caduceus" is singular.

6. **(B)**
   **Vererisne** is in the present tense, second person singular, "Are you afraid?" The equivalent in the active voice is **times**. Answer (A) is plural and (B) is future tense. **Vereri** is a second conjugation verb and therefore **vereris** is present tense,

not future, which is **Vereberis**. Answer (D) is a form of the imperfect subjunctive. Note the deponent infinitive **mori**, "to die."

7. **(D)**

In this question, you are to decide between the present and future tenses, either of which could conceivably be expressed by the form **tuetur**. Since this verb belongs to the second conjugation, the form is in the present tense, making (D), and not (A), the correct answer. The Latin of (B) "should protect" is the subjunctive form **tueatur**. Answer (C) is not possible, since the translation "is being protected" is passive, and **tueor** is a deponent verb. The sentence reads, "Aesculapius protects all Romans." (For the ambiguity between forms of the present and future tenses, see above.)

8. **(B)**

**Audeo** is a semi-deponent verb, which has active meanings in the perfect system. **Ausi sunt** is in the perfect tense and has **medici Romani** as its subject. The sentence therefore reads, "Roman doctors ventured to take care of themselves." Answers (A) and (C) offer translations that are passive, which are not appropriate for a deponent form. Answer (D) is a red herring, because it contains the translation "are," a meaning of **sunt**, but not of **ausi sunt**.

## *Sententiae Antiquae* Answers

1. **(A)**

Horace's sentence reads, "Worry follows increasing money." Therefore, a main verb is necessary to complete the meaning of the sentence. Answers (B) and (C), which are infinitives, do not serve this function. Answer (D) **secutus es** "you have followed" does not have a personal ending that agrees with the nominative subject **cura**.

2. **(A)**

Cicero's sentence reads, "We have not been born for ourselves alone." Because of the meaning "be born" in English, the verb **nascor** appears to be passive, but is deponent. Therefore, the underlined form **nati sumus** is a form of the perfect tense, which is translated "we have been born," or better, "we are born" = "we are alive." The translations in Answers (B), (C), and (D) are in the wrong tenses, i.e., present, imperfect, and pluperfect.

3. **(D)**

Pliny says, "The undying souls of the dead speak in libraries." The nominative subject **immortales animae** requires a plural verb, a fact that drops Answers (A) and (C) from consideration. Answer (B) appears to be a likely option, but the verb **locuti erant** does not agree in gender with the subject **animae**.

4.  **(D)**
    The Latin reads literally, "Not to go forward is to go backward." The deponent infinitives **progredi** and **regredi** are examples of the subjective infinitive, i.e., the infinitive used as a noun subject ("going forward" and "going backward"). (For the subjective infinitive, see Chapter 16C.)

5.  **(D)**
    "Will follow" requires a future tense in the Latin, so **sequentur** is the correct answer, as **sequor** belongs to the third conjugation. Answer (A) **sequuntur** means "they are following," (B) **secuta erunt** "they will have followed," and (C) **sequantur** "let them follow," a form of the jussive subjunctive. Only the 1st person singular form of the future tense contains an –a- vowel, i.e., **sequar**.

## Stumper:

**(C)**
**Passi** is the past participle of **patior** which, by the way, gives the English derivative "passive." Perfect passive participial forms may only be translated (literally) in the active voice if the verb is deponent, i.e., "having suffered" rather than "having been suffered," i.e., Answer (B). Answer (A) "to suffer" translates the infinitive form **pati**, which is similar in appearance to the participial form **passi**. Answer (D) "they suffered" expresses a main verb, **passi sunt**, which includes the past participle in its form.

# Chapter 14C:  Review of Irregular Verbs

## Regular and Irregular Verbs

Look at the list of principal parts provided below. You will remember that irregular verbs do not conform to the patterns found in regular verbs. Irregular verbs are among the most commonly used verbs in Latin, as they are in many languages. They can stand alone, like **est**, become parts of other verb forms, such as **missus est** or **missus esse**, or be combined with prepositional prefixes to form a host of verbs that are related to them in meaning, e.g., **abesse**. Some tenses of irregular verbs conform to the patterns of regular verbs and contain familiar personal endings, but many of the forms of irregular verbs are unpredictable and must be memorized.

### Principal Parts of Irregular Verbs

> **sum, esse, fui**, *be*
>
> **possum, posse, potui**, *be able, can*
>
> **eo, ire, ii** (or **ivi**), *go*
>
> **fero, ferre, tuli, latus**, *carry, bring*
>
> **volo, velle, volui**, *wish, want*
>
> **nolo, nolle, nolui**, *be unwilling*
>
> **malo, malle, malui**, *prefer*
>
> **fio, fieri, factus sum**, *become, happen*

Examples of irregular verbs in context:

> **Habentne magistri in memoria se discipulos fuisse?**
> *Do teachers ever remember that they themselves were students?*

> **Romani Athenas ierunt ut linguam Graecam discerent.**
> *Romans went to Athens in order to learn the Greek language.*

> **Velitne quisquam magister fieri?**
> *Would anyone wish to become a teacher?*

## The Present Indicative Active of Irregular Verbs

The forms of the present tense of irregular verbs are the most unpredictable of the six tenses. Here are the forms of the present indicative of the common irregular verbs listed above, except for **nolo** and **malo**, which approximate those of **volo**. Look for patterns within the irregularities and try to remember what you have previously learned about these verbs. Notice from the principal parts given above that only two irregular verbs, **fero** and **fio**, have passive forms.

## Conjugations of the Present Tense of Irregular Verbs

| | esse, *be* | | posse, *be able* | | ire, *go* | |
|---|---|---|---|---|---|---|
| | **Sing.** | **Pl.** | **Sing.** | **Pl.** | **Sing.** | **Pl.** |
| 1st | **sum** | **sumus** | **possum** | **possumus** | **eo** | **imus** |
| 2nd | **es** | **estis** | **potes** | **potestis** | **is** | **itis** |
| 3rd | **est** | **sunt** | **potest** | **possunt** | **it** | **eunt** |
| | fero, *bring* | | velle, *wish* | | fieri, *become* | |
| | **Sing.** | **Pl.** | **Sing.** | **Pl.** | **Sing.** | **Pl.** |
| 1st | **fero** | **ferimus** | **volo** | **volumus** | **fio** | **fimus** |
| 2nd | **fers** | **fertis** | **vis** | **vultis** | **fis** | **fitis** |
| 3rd | **fert** | **ferunt** | **vult** | **volunt** | **fit** | **fiunt** |

# Indicative Active of Irregular Verbs

All tenses of irregular verbs, except for the forms of the present, behave as their regular verb counter-parts (stem + ending). For complete conjugations of these forms, consult your textbook.

### Quick Study Synopses of Irregular Verbs

| | esse | posse | ire |
|---|---|---|---|
| Pres. | **est**, *he is* | **potest**, *he is able* | **it**, *he is going* |
| Impf. | **erat**, *he was being* | **poterat**, *he was able* | **ibat**, *he was going, went* |
| Fut. | **erit**, *he will be* | **poterit**, *he will be able* | **ibit**, *he will go* |
| Perf. | **fuit,** *he has been, was* | **potuit,** *he has been able, could* | **iit** (or **ivit**), *he has gone, went* |
| Plupf. | **fuerat**, *he had been* | **potuerat**, *he had been able* | **ierat** (or **iverat**), *he had gone* |
| Fut. Pf. | **fuerit**, *he will have been* | **potuerit**, *he will have been able* | **ierit** (or **iverit**), *he will have gone* |

|        | ferre | velle | fieri |
|--------|-------|-------|-------|
| Pres.  | **fert**, *he is bringing* | **vult**, *he is wishing* | **fit**, *he is becoming* |
| Impf.  | **ferebat**, *he was bringing* | **volebat**, *he was wishing* | **fiebat**, *he was beoming* |
| Fut.   | **feret**, *he will bring* | **volet**, *he will wish* | **fiet**, *he will become* |
| Perf.  | **tulit**, *he has brought* | **voluit**, *he has wished* | **factus est**, *he has become* |
| Plupf. | **tulerat**, *he had brought* | **voluerat**, *he had wished* | **factus erat**, *he had become* |
| Fut. Pf. | **tulerit**, *he will have brought* | **voluerit**, *he will have wished* | **factus erit**, *he will have become* |

Note:

For the forms, functions, and translations of imperatives, participles, and infinitives of these verbs, see the following chapters.

## Sum, esse, fui, *be, exist*

1. The forms of **esse** vary the most of any irregular verb. Remember that the third person plural of the future tense is **erunt**. Be careful to distinguish this form from that of the third person plural of the perfect tense, **fuerunt**.

2. Although both **eram** and **fui** may be translated *I was*, the former is in the imperfect tense and thus the action is understood as <u>ongoing</u>, i.e., *I was, over a period of time*. **Fui** is in the perfect tense and shows <u>completed</u> action, i.e., *I was, and am no longer*.

3. Forms of the irregular verb **esse** may accompany participles in order to create other verb forms, e.g., **missus <u>erat</u>, missus <u>esset</u>, missus <u>esse</u>, missurus <u>esse</u>, mittendus <u>est</u>**. Note that when this type of combination occurs, there is a change in the meaning of the form of **esse**, e.g., **missus <u>est</u>** means *he <u>has been</u> sent*, not *he <u>is</u> sent*.

4. In a line of verse, forms of **esse** may be omitted from a two-part verb, such as **missurus (esse)**, due to considerations of meter or dramatic effect.

   Note:

   Do not confuse the irregular verb **sumus**, *we are*, with the adjective **summus, -a, -um**, *the top of*.

## Possum, posse, potui, *be able, can*

1. The forms of **posse** derive from the adjective **potis**, meaning *able, capable*, which is attached as a prefix to various forms of **esse**. Before forms of **esse** beginning with **s-**, the **-t-** of **potis** is altered or assimilated to **-s-**, hence **potis + sum = possum** (as opposed to **potsum**). The **-t-** is retained before a vowel, e.g., **poteram** or **potuisti**.

2. In English, the past tense of *can* is *could*.

3. When translating, be careful to distinguish the imperfect indicative **poteram** from the pluperfect indicative **potueram**, and the forms of the verb **posse** from those of the regular verb **pono, ponere, posui, positus**, *put, place*.

## Eo, ire, ii (ivi), *go*

1. This verb behaves as the regular fourth conjugation verb **audio** except for the future tense, where it changes to first and second conjugation forms, e.g., **ibo, ibis, ibit**, etc.

2. The alternative perfect tense form **ivi** is found much less often than **ii**, i.e., the form **iveram** appears less commonly than **ieram**. The forms of the perfect tense of **ire** made from the **i**-stem are **ii, isti, iit** and **iimus, istis, ierunt**. Those made from the stem **iv-** are **ivi, ivisti, ivit** and **ivimus, ivistis, iverunt**.

   Note:
   - Distinguish **eo**, *I go*, from the adverb **eo**, *to this place*, by using context.

## Fero, ferre, tuli, latus, *bring, carry*

1. This irregular verb has the endings of a regular third conjugation verb, such as **mittere**, in the present system, although the stem vowel −**e**- is missing occasionally, e.g., **ferre**, *to bring*.

2. This verb has a passive voice, the forms of which are constructed and translated in a regular manner, e.g., the synopsis **feritur, ferebatur, feretur, latus est, latus erat, latus erit**. Note:

   Note:
   - Avoid confusing the forms of **fero, ferre** with those of **ferio, ferire**, *strike, hit*.

## Volo, velle, volui, *wish, want*; nolo, nolle, nolui, *be unwilling, not wish*; malo, malle, malui, *prefer, want more*

1. These verbs often have the endings of regular third conjugation verbs, except for forms in the present tense (see the chart above, and also note the irregular forms of the present infinitives **velle, nolle**, and **malle**). The tenses of the perfect system are regularly formed.

2. Remember that the verb **nolo** (**non** + **volo**) can become a compound form in the present tense, i.e., singular, **nolo, non vis, non vult,** and plural, **nolumus, non vultis, nolunt.**

> Notes:
> - **Volo, velle**, should be carefully distinguished from **volo, volare**, *fly*, and from forms of the noun **vis**, *force, strength*, by using the context.
>
> - Be careful not to confuse forms of the irregular verb **malo** (**magis** + **volo**, *wish more*) with those of the adjective **malus, -a, -um**, *bad*.

## Fio, fieri, factus sum, *become, happen*; *be made*

**Fio** has forms much like the regular fourth conjugation verb **audio**. This irregular verb serves as the passive of the present system of the verb **facere**, e.g., **faciuntur**, *they are being made* = **fiunt**, *they become*. In the perfect system, passive forms appear as deponent verbs, e.g., **facti sunt**, *they have become*. **Fieri** can have either the meanings *become, occur*, or *happen*, or the passive meanings *be done* or *be made*. Consider both options when translating.

## Tips for translating irregular verbs

Practice with the forms of irregular verbs and know the principal parts so that you are familiar with the patterns within the irregularity of each verb. Be able to make distinctions in tense and meaning among forms that are similar, e.g., **erunt, fuerunt, ierunt** or **erant, fuerant, ierant**.

- It is important to remember that forms of the imperfect tense **eram, eras, erat**, etc., refer to <u>ongoing action</u> in the past and the forms of the perfect tense, **fui, fuisti, fuit**, etc., refer to <u>completed</u> action in the past. Remember that, although the word "been" is used in translating forms of verbs in the perfect system of **esse**, i.e., **fuit**, *he has been*, the verb has a meaning in the active voice.

- Remember that the forms of the irregular verb **fio, fieri, factus sum** may be translated with meanings that are either active (*become, happen*) or passive (*be done* or *be made*), depending upon the context.

- The irregular verbs **ferre, ire**, and **sum** have many compound forms. These often exhibit assimilation, e.g., **afferre** (**ad** + **ferre**), *carry toward*, and **auferre** (**ab** + **ferre**), *carry away*.

# Practice Questions

1. The perfect active indicative of <u>sunt</u> is

    (A) fuerunt

    (B) fuerint

    (C) fuerant

    (D) fuissent

2. The perfect active indicative of <u>potes</u> is
   (A) potuistis
   (B) potueras
   (C) potueris
   (D) potuisti

3. Ego magister <u>factus eram</u>.
   (A) I was being made
   (B) I was becoming
   (C) I had become
   (D) I have been made

4. When <u>will we be able</u> to live in peace and harmony?
   (A) potuerimus
   (B) poteramus
   (C) poterimus
   (D) possumus

5. <u>We went</u> to school.
   (A) imus
   (B) eamus
   (C) iimus
   (D) ieramus

6. Which verb is <u>not</u> in the present tense?
   (A) fuit
   (B) fert
   (C) vult
   (D) it

7. Coals <u>had been brought</u> to Newcastle.
   (A) ferebant
   (B) lati erant
   (C) ferebantur
   (D) lati sunt

8. Ubi leges non valent, <u>poterit</u>ne populus liber esse?
   (A) will be able
   (B) was able
   (C) is able
   (D) will have been able

9. <u>Does</u> any student <u>prefer</u> to stay at home?
   (A) Maluitne?
   (B) Malebatne?
   (C) Mavultne?
   (D) Maletne?

10. <u>Non feremus</u>.
    (A) We are not enduring.
    (B) We shall not be endured.
    (C) We shall not endure.
    (D) We have not endured.

**Stumper:** The prince <u>had become</u> a pauper.
   (A) factus est
   (B) factus erat
   (C) fecit
   (D) fecerat

## Sententiae Antiquae

1.  <u>Anni eunt modo fluentis aquae</u>. (Ovid) The basic meaning of this thought is

    (A)  Time flies.                         (C)  Seize the day.

    (B)  O the times, O the values!          (D)  Make haste slowly.

2.  If <u>you prefer</u> peace and quiet, take a wife of equal station. (Quintilian)

    (A)  malebas                             (C)  mavis

    (B)  malueras                            (D)  maluisti

3.  In this Republic, <u>there were</u> once men of great character and reliability. (Cicero)

    (A)  fuerant                             (C)  essent

    (B)  erant                               (D)  sunt

4.  <u>Possunt quia posse videntur</u>. (Vergil)

    (A)  They could since they seemed to be able.

    (B)  They can since they seemed to be able.

    (C)  They could since they seem to be able.

    (D)  They are able since they seem to be able.

5.  <u>Magnae res non fiunt sine periculo</u>. (Terence)

    The basic meaning of this thought is

    (A)  Always carry an umbrella.

    (B)  No pain, no gain.

    (C)  Only the simple things matter.

    (D)  We have nothing to fear but fear itself.

## Answers

1.  **(A)**
    The perfect tense forms of **esse** have regular endings. Answer (B) is in the future perfect tense, (C) the pluperfect indicative, and (D) the pluperfect subjunctive.

2.  **(D)**
    The verb **posse** has the endings of regular verbs in the perfect tense, plus the stem **potu-**, hence **potuisti** "you were or have been able" is equivalent in the perfect tense to the present tense form **potes** "you are able." Answer (A) is in the perfect tense and is in the 2nd person, but is plural. Answer (B) **potueras** is pluper-

fect, "you had been able" and (C) **potueris** is future perfect, "you will have been able."

3.   **(C)**
  The perfect system of the passive voice of **facere** is translated as a deponent verb, i.e., with the active meaning of "happen" or "become." The form **factus eram** is in the pluperfect tense, therefore the verb means "I had become." Answers (A) and (B) require **fiebam** and (C), **factus sum**.

4.   **(C)**
  Answer (A) is to be distinguished from the correct answer (C) because the perfect stem is found in (A) **potuerimus**, making this form future perfect. The underlined translation "will we be able" in the sentence calls for **poterimus,** a form in the future tense. Answer (B) **poteramus** is pluperfect, "we had been able," and (D) **possumus** present, "we are able."

5.   **(C)**
  "We went" requires a form of the imperfect or perfect tense of the verb **ire**. Since no form of the imperfect tense is available among the choices, Answer (C) **iimus**, is correct. Answer (A) **imus** is in the present indicative and (B) **eamus** is in the present tense of the subjunctive mood. Answer (D) is pluperfect, "we had gone."

6.   **(A)**
  Answer (A) **fuit,** contains the perfect stem **fu-** and therefore is a form of the perfect tense of **esse**, "he has been" or "he was." Answers (B), (C), and (D) are all in the present tense.

7.   **(B)**
  The translation "had been brought" requires a passive form of the pluperfect tense of **ferre**, thus, **lati erant**. Answer (A) is in the active voice and Answers (C) and (D) are in the wrong tenses, i.e., imperfect and perfect. Remember that among irregular verbs, only **fero** and **fio** have passive forms.

8.   **(A)**
  **Poterit** is in the future tense and is thus translated "will be able." The sentence reads, "When the laws are not strong, <u>will</u> the people <u>be able</u> to be free?" Answer (B) translates a verb in the imperfect or perfect tense, (C) in the present tense, and (D) in the future perfect.

9.   **(C)**
  "Does prefer" requires the present tense in Latin, leading to the answer **mavult**, which is a compound form of the verb **volo**. Answer (A) **maluit** is perfect tense (note the tense indicator –**u**-), (B) **malebat** is imperfect tense, and (D) **malet** is future tense.

10. **(C)**

The –**e**- vowel present in **feremus** makes this a form of the future tense. It cannot be translated in the present tense because **ferre** is an irregular verb, rather than a verb of the 3rd conjugation. Answer (A) requires the present tense **(ferimus)**, (B) the future passive **(feremur)**, and (D) the perfect tense **(tulimus)**.

**Stumper: (B)**

The tense of the underlined verb is pluperfect, eliminating Answers (A) and (C), which are in the perfect tense. Since "had become" = "had been made," the passive form **factus erat** is required, rather than the active form **fecerat**.

## *Sententiae Antiquae* Answers

1. **(A)**

Ovid's sentence reads, "The years go (by) in the manner of flowing water." The verb **eunt** is the present tense of **ire**. The subject of this sentence is **anni** "years" which leads to the immediate conclusion that the sentence has something to do with time.

2. **(C)**

"You prefer" requires the present tense of the irregular verb **malle** in the 2nd person, which is **mavis**. Answer (A) **malebas** means "you were preferring," (B) **malueras** "you had preferred," and (D) **maluisti,** "you (have) preferred."

3. **(B)**

The underlined verb "there were" is translated by a form of the imperfect tense of the verb **esse**, which is **erant**. (**Fuerunt** is not an option given here.) Answer (A) **fuerant** "they had been" is pluperfect tense, (C) **essent** is imperfect tense, but subjunctive, and (D) **sunt** "they are" is present tense.

4. **(D)**

This question tests command of forms of the verb **posse** and also the use of the passive of **videre** as a deponent verb. The correct answer is "They are able since they seem to be able." Since **possunt** is in the present tense, Answers (A) and (C), containing the translation "could," which expresses the past tense in English, are incorrect. Answer (B) translates the present tense form **videntur** as "seemed," which is in the past tense, and therefore also incorrect.

5. **(B)**

Terence's sentence reads, "Great events don't come about without risk." Of the answers available, the closest in meaning to this is Answer (B) "No pain, no gain."

# Chapter 14D: Review of Impersonal Verbs

Impersonal verbs are found in the third person singular and have the ending **-t** and the non-personal subject "it," e.g., **Claudio placet**, *it is pleasing (to) Claudius* or *Claudius is pleased*. Some impersonal verbs, such as **placet**, can be used personally, that is, the subject is expressed: **Boleti placent Claudio**, *Mushrooms please Claudius*. Impersonal verbs may also appear as gerunds or infinitives. There are about fifteen or so of these verbs that appear commonly in Latin, many of which belong to the second conjugation. Most are followed by an infinitive phrase, but some may also be followed by a subjunctive clause. When there is need for variation in tense, the tense change appears in the impersonal, e.g., **placet, placebat, placebit**. Forms of the impersonal verb are found in both the indicative and subjunctive moods. Since impersonal verbs are common in Latin but rarely appear in English, the literal translation of an impersonal construction in Latin should be rephrased in English, as in this example:

> **Pudebatne Claudium claudum esse?**

> *Was Claudius ashamed to be lame?* lit., *Was it shaming Claudius to be lame?*

The subject of the sentences in this chapter is the life and times of the emperor Claudius, as he is portrayed in the film series *I, Claudius*.

## Impersonal Verbs (accusative or dative) + (infinitive or subjunctive)

### Impersonal Verb with the Accusative Case and an Infinitive

Observe the function of the impersonal verbs **necesse erat** in the sentence below. Note that the impersonal is accompanied by a noun in the accusative case, plus an infinitive:

acc.             infin.

**Caligula occiso, necesse erat <u>milites</u> novum imperatorem <u>eligere</u>.**

> *When Caligula was killed, it was necessary for the soldiers to select a new emperor.*

Impersonal verbs with the accusative:

> **accidit, accidere, accidit**, *it happens*

> **decet, decere, decuit**, *it is proper, fitting; one should*

> **iuvat, iuvare**, *it pleases*

> **necesse est**, *it is necessary*

> **oportet, oportere, oportuit**, *it is fitting; one ought* or *must*

## Impersonal Verb with the Dative Case and an Infinitive

Observe the function of the impersonal verbs **libebat** in the sentence below. Note that the impersonal is accompanied by a noun in the dative, plus an infinitive:

dat.              infin.

**Libebatne <u>Claudio</u> imperator <u>fieri</u>?**

*Was it agreeable <u>to Claudius</u> to become (that he become) emperor?*

Impersonal verbs with the dative:

> **libet, libere, libuit**, *it is pleasing, agreeable*
>
> **licet, licere, licuit**, *it is allowed, permitted; one may*
>
> **opus est**, *there is need, it is necessary*
>
> **placet, placere, placuit**, *it pleases; one likes*
>
> **videtur, videri**, *it seems*

## Impersonal Verb with the Subjunctive

The sentence below illustrates the use of an impersonal verb followed by an subjunctive clause, with or without **ut**. This serves as an alternative to the impersonal verb accompanied by an infinitive, described above. The same rules apply regarding the used of the accusative or dative case;

subjunctive

**Licebatne Claudio (ut) filiam fratris uxorem duceret?**

*Was Claudius permitted to marry (that he marry) his niece?*

# Impersonal Verbs (accusative + genitive or infinitive)

This type of impersonal verb expresses <u>feelings or emotion</u> and is followed by the accusative (of the person or persons feeling the emotion) and the genitive (of the cause or reason for the emotion), e.g.,

acc.       gen.

**Non taedebat <u>Tiberium</u> <u>vitae</u> Capreis.**

*It was not boring <u>Tiberius</u> <u>of life</u> on Capri.* (literal)

When such impersonal verbs are used, some rephrasing of the English is necessary in order to clarify the meaning of the Latin. For example, the sentence above, when rendered in better English, reads, *Tiberius was not bored with life on Capri.* Such verbs may be accompanied alternatively by an infinitive phrase, in place of the genitive case, e.g,

acc.       infin.

**Non paenituit Tiberium Roma <u>egredi</u>.**

*Tiberius did not regret <u>leaving</u> Rome*, lit., *it did not make Tiberius feel regret to leave from Rome.*

Impersonal verbs that are found with the accusative + genitive (or infinitive). Note that all belong to the second conjugation:

> **miseret, miserere, miseruit**, *it makes one* (acc.) *feel pity or feel sorry for something* (gen.)
>
> **paenitet, paenitere, paenituit**, *it makes one* (acc.) *regret or repent of something* (gen.)
>
> **piget, pigere, piguit**, *it annoys, disgusts, causes one* (acc.) *to be ashamed of something* (gen.)
>
> **pudet, pudere, puduit**, *it shames, makes one* (acc.) *ashamed of something* (gen.)
>
> **taedet, taedere, taesum est**, *it bores, makes one* (acc.) *tired of something* (gen.)

## Passive Verbs Used Impersonally

Intransitive verbs, i.e., verbs that do not take a direct object, may be used in the third person singular of the passive, with the implied subject "it," e.g.,

> **Ab imperatore ad munera <u>perventum est</u>**.
>
> *The emperor <u>arrived</u> at the public show,* lit., *It was arrived by the emperor....*

Such verbs are used impersonally when the writer or speaker wishes to emphasize the <u>action</u>, rather than the person/s performing the action. Good English requires rephrasing of passive verbs used impersonally, e.g., **fortiter pugnabatur**, *the fighting was fierce,* lit., *it was fought fiercely.* Verbs such as **parco**, *spare*, **persuadere**, *convince*, **pugnare**, *fight*, and compound forms of **venire**, e.g., **pervenire**, *arrive*, among others, appear impersonally in the passive.

## Tips on Translating Impersonal Verbs

An impersonal verb differs from a personal verb by requiring the non-personal subject "it," in most cases. After working out the meaning of the impersonal verb and its accompanying forms, recast the wording in comprehensible English.

- The impersonal verb is often found at the front of a Latin sentence, but may be located anywhere.

- Be alert to the fact that the case of the noun or pronoun that accompanies the impersonal verb can be accusative, dative, and/or genitive.

- Note the tense of the impersonal verb and also whether it is accompanied by an infinitive phrase or a subjunctive clause.

- The semi-deponent verb **soleo, solere, solitus sum**, *be accustomed, usual*, and the verb **debeo, debere, debui, debitus**, *owe, ought, be obligated, should*, can appear to be impersonal verbs because their forms are often found in the third person and are accompanied by an infinitive. However, they always have personal subjects, e.g.,

    > **Caligula <u>solebat</u> crudelis esse.**
    >
    > *Caligula <u>was in the habit of</u> being cruel.*

    > **Caligula <u>debet</u> propter crudelitatem puniri.**
    >
    > *Caligula <u>ought</u> to be punished for his cruelty.*

## Practice Questions

1.  In pictura moventi "Sum Claudius," multos veneno necare . . . placebat.

    (A)  Liviae          (C)  Livia
    (B)  Liviam          (D)  Liviā

2.  Non decebat Caligulam dicere "Oderint, dum metuant."

    (A)  Caligula was not allowed
    (B)  It was not necessary for Caligula
    (C)  Caligula was not ashamed
    (D)  It was not appropriate for Caligula

3.  Julia was weary of exile.

    (A)  Iulia exsili taedebat.       (C)  Iuliam exsili taedebat.
    (B)  Iuliae exsilium taedebat.    (D)  Iuliam exsilium taedebat.

4.  Videbatur . . . Claudium stultum esse.

    (A)  Livia          (C)  Liviae
    (B)  Liviam         (D)  Liviā

5.  Piget Liviam linguae haesitationis Claudi. The basic meaning of this sentence is that

    (A)  Claudius feels pity for Livia's stuttering.
    (B)  Claudius' stuttering is agreeable to Livia.
    (C)  Livia permits Claudius to stutter.
    (D)  Claudius' stuttering disgusts Livia.

6.  "Oportuit Germanos signa legionum reddere!" exclamabat Augustus.

    (A)  Ought          (C)  Can
    (B)  Did            (D)  Might

7.  Debebatne Claudius Britanniam vincere?

    (A)  was forbidden      (C)  was obligated
    (B)  was permitted      (D)  was encouraged

8.  Women were not allowed to be emperors.

    (A)  Feminis non licet       (C)  Feminae non licebant
    (B)  Feminae non licebat     (D)  Feminis non licebat

9. Tacitus scripsit Neronem Romam incendere <u>non paenitere</u>.

    (A)  did not regret         (C)  is not punished

    (B)  is not permitted        (D)  ought not

10. Caligula imperatore, <u>accidit</u> ut equus senator fieret.

    (A)  it happened           (C)  it pleased

    (B)  it was appropriate     (D)  it was necessary

## *Sententiae Antiquae*

1. Infamiae suae neque <u>pudet et taedet</u>. (Cicero, on Verres) These words refer to

    (A)  shame and weariness     (C)  misery and repentence

    (B)  regret and pity          (D)  pleasure and pain

2. A liar <u>ought</u> to have a good memory. (Quintilian)

    (A)  licet               (C)  oportet

    (B)  placet             (D)  decet

3. <u>Decet verecundum esse adulescentem</u>. (Plautus)

    (A)  It is shameful for a young person to be modest.

    (B)  A young person can regret being modest.

    (C)  It is proper for a young person to be modest.

    (D)  There is need for young people to be modest.

4. Quodque libet facere . . . licet. (Seneca)

    (A)  victor             (C)  victori

    (B)  victorem         (D)  victoris

5. Placeat. . . quidquid deo placuit. (Seneca)

    (A)  hominem         (C)  homini

    (B)  homo            (D)  homine

**Stumper:**  <u>Aedificare in tuo proprio solo non licet quod alteri noceat</u>. (Legal)

    (A)  You are allowed to build whatever you like on your own property.

    (B)  If someone hurts himself while building on your property, you are at fault.

    (C)  You are allowed to build on your own property only what does not harm another.

    (D)  No one should harm another while in a building on your property.

## Answers

1.   **(A)**
When used impersonally, **placere** takes a dative object, therefore the missing form of the word **Livia** should appear in the dative case, which is Answer (A). The sentence reads, "In the movie 'I, Claudius,' it was pleasing <u>to Livia</u> to kill many (people) with poison." Answer (B) **Liviam**, an accusative, is an obvious, but incorrect, answer. Answers (C) **Liviā** and (D) **Livia** have no function in this sentence.

2.   **(D)**
As all the verbs are given in the imperfect tense, you are asked to select the correct meaning of **(non) decebat (Caligulam)**, which is "it was (not) appropriate (for Caligula)." The sentence reads, "It was not appropriate for Caligula to say, 'Let them hate (me), so long as they fear (me).'" Answer (A) "was allowed" requires **licebat**, (B) "was necessary" requires **necesse erat**, and (C) "was ashamed" **pudebat**.

3.   **(C)**
**Taedebat**, as a verb expressing emotion, takes an accusative of the person and a genitive of the cause or reason for the emotion. In Answer (C), **Iuliam** is accusative and **exsili** genitive, giving the literal meaning "It was not wearying <u>Julia of exile</u>." Answers (A), (B), and D) do not have the correct combination of accusative and genitive forms: (A) has nominative and genitive, (B) dative/genitive and accusative, and (D) accusative and accusative.

4.   **(C)**
This sentence reads, "It seemed to Livia that Claudius <u>was</u> foolish." The missing noun must be the dative form **Liviae** after the impersonal verb **videbatur** (ses Chapter 14B). Answers (A), (B), and (D) are all in the incorrect case, i.e., nominative, accusative, and ablative, respectively.

5.   **(D)**
**Piget**, another verb expressing emotion, is found with the accusative, **Liviam**, and genitive, **linguae haesitationis**. (**Claudi** is simply a possessive genitive, unrelated to the use of the impersonal verb here.) Answer (A) would require an exchange of Livia and Claudius in the sentence and the appearance of the look-alike verb **pudet**. Answers (B) and (C) mistranslate **piget** as "is agreeable" and "permits," respectively.

6.   **(A)**
Of the choices of meanings for **oportuit** in this sentence, "ought" is the most appropriate. Answer (B) "did" simply translates the tense of **oportuit**. Answers (C) "can" requires the verb **posse** and (D) "might" the subjunctive mood. The sentence reads, "'The Germans <u>ought</u> to return the legionary standards,' exclaimed Augustus." The accusative form **Germanos** is consistent with the appearance of the irregular verb **oportuit**.

7. **(C)**

   This question tests your knowledge of the meaning of the verb **debere**, which has the sense of obligation, that is, something one ought to do or should do. Hence, the sentence reads, "<u>Was</u> Claudius <u>obliged</u> to conquer Britain?" The answers "forbid," "permit," and "encourage," require other verbs.

8. **(D)**

   The impersonal verb **licebat** is found with the dative case, therefore Answer (D) **feminis licebat** is correct. Answer (A) **feminis licet** has the incorrect tense. Answer (B) **feminae** is singular when a plural is required ("women") and Answer (C) **feminae** incorrectly serves as the subject of the impersonal verb.

9. **(A)**

   The impersonal verb **paenitet** means "regret" (as in penance and penitant), therefore Answer (A) is correct. The sentence reads, "Tacitus writes that Nero <u>did not</u> <u>regret</u> burning Rome." The infinitive **paenitere** is used in an indirect statement. Answer (B) requires the verb **licere**, (C) the verb **punire** (etymologically akin to **paenitere**), and (D) **oportere**.

10. **(A)**

    This sentence reads, "While Caligula was Emperor, <u>it happened that</u> a horse became a senator." The meaning of the verb **accidit** is "it happens" or "it happened." The imperfect tense of the subjunctive **fieret** in the substantive result clause requires that **accidit** be translated as a past tense in this sentence. Answer (B) requires **decebat** in the Latin, (C) **placebat**, and (D) **necesse erat**.

## *Sententiae Antiquae* Answers

1. **(A)**

   Since the meanings of the impersonals **pudet** and **taedet** are "it is shameful" and "it is wearisome," respectively, Answer (A) is correct. Answer (B) requires the verbs **paenitet** and **miseret**, and (C) and (D) require words that do not relate to impersonal verbs. The sentence reads, "(Verres) <u>is</u> neither <u>ashamed</u> of nor <u>bored</u> with his own ill fame."

2. **(C)**

   The word "ought" requires the impersonal verb **oportet**. Answer (A) **licet** means "permitted" or "allowed," (B) **placet** "pleased," and (D) **decet** "fitting" or "appropriate."

3. **(C)**

   Since **decet** means "it is fitting or appropriate," Answer (C) is the best response. Answers (A) "shameful" and (B) "regret" do not give acceptable meanings of the impersonal verb **decet**. Answer (D) gives the wrong sense of **decet** and translates **adulescentem** as plural.

4.   **(C)**
Seneca's statement, "A victor <u>is allowed</u> to do whatever he likes," requires that the word **victor** be in the dative case after the impersonal verb **licet**, i.e., "it is permitted <u>to the victor</u>." The nominative, accusative, and genitive cases found in Answers (A), (B), and (D) are not relevant in this sentence.

5.   **(C)**
This sentence reads, "Let whatever has been acceptable to god be acceptable to <u>mankind</u>." The dative form **deo** with the impersonal verb **placuit** prompts recognition of the fact that the case of the missing noun will also be dative, i.e., **homini**. Answer (A) is accusative, (B) nominative, and (D) ablative. Note the appearance of the independent jussive subjunctive form **placeat**, "let it be acceptable."

**Stumper:**

**(C)**
Neither Answer (B) nor Answer (D) contains in its translation the proper meaning of the impersonal verb **licet**. Answer (A) seems likely, until you notice that "whatever you like" does not correctly render **quod alteri noceat,** which means "(the type of thing) which may be harmful to another" in the original sentence. This is a relative clause of characteristic with the subjunctive. (For the dative case with certain verbs, see Chapter 13A.)

# Chapter 15

# The Imperative Mood of Verbs

## The Imperative Mood

You will remember that the term mood indicates the way in which a verb functions in a sentence. Now that you have reviewed the indicative, you will review the second mood of the three, the imperative, which expresses a command or prohibition. The imperative mood appears less often than the indicative and subjunctive moods. This chapter will present the positive and negative imperatives of regular, deponent, and irregular verbs, as well as the vocative case of nouns, which is often found in association with imperatives. Although the imperative has forms in both the present and future tenses, only the present tense will be reviewed in this book. The review questions will include the commonly used question words **Nonne?**, **Num?**, and the enclitic **–ne?**

### Quick Study of the Imperatives of Regular Verbs

|  | Singular | Plural |
|---|---|---|
| First conjugation (**stare**) | **sta,** *(you alone) stand* | **state,** *(you all) stand* |
| Second conjugation (**sedere**) | **sede,** *(you alone) sit* | **sedete,** *(you all) sit* |
| Third conjugation (**legere**) | **lege,** *(you alone) read* | **legite,** *(you all) read* |
| Fourth conjugation (**audire**) | **audi,** *(you alone) listen* | **audite,** *(you all) listen* |

Notes:

- The verbs **dicere, ducere, facere**, and **ferre** have irregular forms of the present imperative: **dic, duc, fac,** and **fer**. The plurals are regular: **dicite, ducite, facite**, and **ferte** (but note the dropped **–i-** in **ferte**). This rhyme may help your memory: "**Duc, dic, fac**, and **fer**, should have an **–e**, but it isn't there."*

- Avoid translating the word **Noli** in a negative command or prohibition as *I don't want*, e.g., *Noli cadere!* means not *I don't want to fall!* but *Do not fall!*

---

* Keith Berman; see David Pellegrino, http://latinteach.com/verbmnemonics.html.

## Practice Questions

1. . . . bene, discipule!
   - (A) Notate
   - (B) Nota
   - (C) Notare
   - (D) Nolite notare

2. Semper . . . veritatem, Doofe.
   - (A) dicite
   - (B) nolite dicere
   - (C) dic
   - (D) dici

3. <u>Doofus is here, isn't he</u>?
   - (A) Num Doofus adest?
   - (B) Nonne Doofus adest?
   - (C) Estne hic, annon?
   - (D) Adestne Doofus?

4. . . . diem, discipuli!
   - (A) Carpe
   - (B) Carpite
   - (C) Noli carpere
   - (D) Carpi

5. <u>Noli obdormire!</u>
   - (A) Don't fall asleep!
   - (B) I don't want to fall asleep!
   - (C) Don't want to fall asleep!
   - (D) I wish you wouldn't fall asleep!

6. <u>Num studes?</u> The expected answer is
   - (A) Ita vero
   - (B) Non scio
   - (C) Studeo
   - (D) Minime

## *Sententiae Antiquae*

1. <u>Disce aut discede.</u> (School motto)
   - (A) Teach or leave.
   - (B) Learn or leave.
   - (C) Behave or depart.
   - (D) Dance or die.

2. <u>Saepe stilum verte bonum libellum scripturus.</u> (Horace) (<u>stilum vertere</u> = *to turn over the stilus, to erase*)
   - (A) Good reading leads to good writing.
   - (B) Write much to write well.
   - (C) Use a good pencil when writing.
   - (D) Much editing makes for good writing.

3. . . . , O Veneres Cupidinesque! (Catullus)

   (A) Luge                 (C) Lugete

   (B) Lugeri             (D) Lugere

4. . . . in arma properare, Romani! (Anon.)

   (A) Non                (C) Nolle

   (B) Noli               (D) Nolite

5. <u>Nonne iubebis</u> Catilinam in vincula duci? (Cicero)

   (A) You won't order, will you?     (C) Surely you won't order?

   (B) Will you order?              (D) You will order, won't you?

6. Ludi magister, . . . simplici turbae. (Martial)

   (A) parce              (C) parcere

   (B) parcite            (D) parsus

## Answers

1. **(B)**
   The punctuation reveals this sentence to be a direct command. Since **discipule**, a single student, is being addressed, the answer must be a singular form of the imperative, which is Answer (B) **Nota**. Answer (A) is plural, (C) an infinitive, and (D) a negative command.

2. **(C)**
   The implied meaning of this sentence requires the singular command, since **Doofe** is in the vocative case. The verb **dico** has an irregular form of the singular imperative, which is **dic**. The remaining answers are incorrect because (A) and (B) are in the plural and (D) is a present passive infinitive.

3. **(B)**
   The phrasing of the original sentence calls for a question word in the Latin that produces a positive answer. Thus, **Nonne Doofus adest** is correct. Answer (A) reads "Doofus isn't here, is he? (C) "Is he here, or not?" and (D) "Is Doofus here?"

4. **(B)**
   This sentence tempts you to choose Answer (A) **Carpe**, to complete Horace's famous saying, but the vocative form **discipuli** is plural, requiring (B) **Carpite**. Answer (C) doesn't make sense, given the implied meaning of the command, and (D) is a present passive infinitive, which could easily be mistaken as a form of the imperative, if the verb **carpere** belonged to the 4th conjugation.

5. **(A)**

This sentence provides an example of a singular negative command or prohibition, "Don't fall asleep!" Answers (B) and (C) are typical mistaken translations of the negative imperative and (D) requires a subjunctive verb expressing a wish.

6. **(D)**

The interrogative particle **Num** in the sentence reading "You don't study, do you?" prompts the answer **Minime** "No, I don't." Answer (A) **Ita vero** means "Yes," (B) **Non scio** "I don't know," and (C) **Studeo**, "I do study."

## *Sententiae Antiquae* Answers

1. **(B)**

This motto plays on the imperative singular forms of the verbs **discere** "learn" and **discedere** "leave." Answer (A) requires familiarity with the meaning of the verb **discere**, which is not "teach" (this is **docere**). Answer (C) suggests, wrongly, that **disce** might mean "behave," given the derivative "discipline." Answer (D) is for fun.

2. **(D)**

Horace's saying reads, "Turn (your) stilus often (if you're) going to write a book (that's) good." He means by "turn your stilus often," that erasing or frequent editing is necessary for good writing. **Verte** is a singular command addressed to the reader and **scripturus** is a future active participle modifying you, the reader (the subject of **Verte**).

3. **(C)**

You might be familiar with this famous opening line from Poem 3. The punctuation requires an imperative, which must be plural, since the vocatives **Veneres** and **Cupidines** are plural. Answer (C) **Lugete** fits the requirements. Answer (A) **Luge** is a singular imperative, (B) **Lugeri** a present passive infinitive, and (D) **Lugere** a present active infinitive, none of which fits the context of the sentence.

4. **(D)**

This sentence is a negative command in the plural, as required by the punctuation and by the vocative plural form **Romani**. **Nolite** is the form needed to supplement the infinitive **properare**, therefore completing the negative imperative. The sentence reads, "<u>Don't rush</u> to arms, Romans!" Answer (A) **Non** has no sense here, (B) **Noli** is the singular imperative, and (C) **Nolle** the present active infinitive.

5. **(D)**

The interrogative particle **Nonne** requires phrasing in translation that produces a positive response. This is Answer (D) "You will, won't you?" The sentence reads, "<u>You will order</u> that Catiline be put into chains, won't you?" Answers (A) and (C) require the negative particle **Num** and (B) the enclitic –**ne**.

6.   **(A)**

This quote from Martial asks the teacher to "spare the simple crowd," i.e., the students. The context requires a singular imperative, **parce**, because the person addressed (**magister**) is singular. Answer (B) **parcite,** is a plural imperative, (C) **parcere,** a present active infinitive, and (D) **parsus,** a perfect passive participle, none of which fits the context here.

# Advanced Grammar

## Chapter 16 A: Participles and the Ablative Absolute

### Quick Study of Participles

| mitto, mittere, misi, missus | | |
|---|---|---|
| | **Active** | **Passive** |
| Present | **mittens** (stem **mittent-**), *sending* | |
| Perfect | | **missus, -a, -um**, *having been sent* |
| Future | **missurus, -a, -um**, *about to send* | **mittendus, -a, -um**, *about to be sent* (also known as the gerundive)* |

### The Present Active Participle

- Use the letters **–ns** (**mittens**) to recognize the form of the <u>n</u>ominative <u>s</u>ingular of the present participle. The nominative singular lacks the **-nt-** of the remaining forms. Use the **-nt-** of the Latin form, e.g., **mittent-**, to identify the participle as prese<u>nt</u>.

- For greater clarity in English, translate the participle as a clause:

  **Exercens in palaestra, Erroneus sudat.**

  As a verbal adjective: *Exercising in the palaestra, Erroneus is sweating.*

  As a clause: *While (he is) exercising in the palaestra, Erroneus is sweating.*

---

* Gerunds and gerunds will be covered in Chapter 16B.

- The action of the present participle takes place <u>continuously</u> and <u>at the same time as</u> the action of the main verb in a sentence. Therefore, if the main verb is found in the past tense, the present participle, in order to express contemporary action, must be translated *was ___ -ing,* and not *is ___ -ing.* Use the words *while* or *as* to translate the present participle:

  Present                 Present

  **Exercens in palaestra, Erroneus sudat.**
  > *While (he is) exercising in the palaestra, Erroneus is sweating.*
       Present                             Present

  Present                 Past

  **Exercens in palaestra, Erroneus sudabat.**
  > *While (he was) exercising in the palaestra, Erroneus was sweating.*
       Past                             Past

## The Perfect Passive Participle

- The perfect passive participle is the fourth principal part of the regular verb. You met this form when reviewing the perfect passive system of indicative verbs, e.g., **missus est**, *he has been sent.* As the perfect passive participle of the verb, **missus, -a, -um** is translated *having* (perfect) *been* (passive) *sent.* Latin does not have a perfect active participle, although past participles of deponent verbs have active meanings.

  **Erroneus <u>unctus</u> e palaestra egressus est.**
  > *Erroneus, <u>having been oiled</u>, left the exercise area.*

- Unlike the action of the present participle, the action of the past participle is <u>completed</u> and takes place <u>prior</u> in time to the action of the main verb in the sentence. In the sentence just above, Erroneus was oiled down <u>before</u> he left the exercise area. Past participles of deponent verbs are translated as active, e.g.,

  **Senex, in caldario nimis <u>passus</u>, in frigidarium iniit.**
  > *The old man, <u>having suffered</u> too much in the hot room, entered the cold room.*

  The sense of the context and knowledge of the principal parts of deponent verbs will assist you in the correct translation of the participles of deponent verbs.

- Here are some common ways to translate a perfect passive participle, using the sentence **Erroneus <u>unctus</u> egressus est:**

  > *Erroneus, having been oiled, left.*
  >
  > *Erroneus left when he was/had been oiled.*
  >
  > *Erroneus left after he was/had been oiled.*
  >
  > *Erroneus left because he was/had been oiled.*
  >
  > *Erroneus, who was oiled, left.*
  >
  > *Erroneus was oiled and then left.*

# The Future Active Participle

- Remember that a form such as **missurus** is a participle in the future tense by noting that the **-ur-** in the form reflects the –ur– in the English word "fut<u>ur</u>e."

   > **Erroneus <u>dimissurus</u> servum plus unguenti poposcit.**
   > *Erroneus, <u>about to send away</u> the slave, asked for more oil.*

- Here are some ways of expressing the future active participle in English:

   | | | |
   |---|---|---|
   | *About to...* | *Intending to...* | *Planning to...* |
   | *Going to...* | *On the point of...* | *Ready to...* |

- These sentences illustrate the translation of the future active participle as a clause:

   > **Erroneus senatori in thermas <u>ingressuro</u> occurrit.**
   > *Erroneus happened upon the senator <u>who was going to enter</u> the baths.*

   > **Erroneus senatorem subsequens, "Nos <u>lavaturi</u> te salutamus!" clamavit.**
   > *Erroneus, tagging along after the senator, proclaimed, "We <u>who are about to bathe</u> salute you!"*

# The Ablative Absolute

- The ablative absolute is a participial phrase that is <u>grammatically independent of the rest of the sentence</u> ("absolute," fr. **absolvere**, *set free, separate*). It generally consists of a noun or pronoun that is accompanied by a present or past participle, with both forms found in the ablative case, e.g,

   > **<u>Thermis aedificatis</u>, Erroneus salubritate fruebatur.**
   > *<u>After the public baths were built</u>, Erroneus enjoyed good health.*

   Compare the following sentence:

   > **<u>Vinum bibentes</u>, viri inter se colloquebantur.**
   > *<u>While drinking wine</u>, the men gossiped among themselves.*

   How do these two sentences differ in structure? In the second example, the participial phrase is <u>not</u> an ablative absolute because there is a <u>direct connection</u> between the participial phrase **vinum bibentes** and **viri... colloquebantur**, the main part of the sentence. That is, the participle **bibentes** modifies the subject of the main clause, **viri**. This participial phrase is not "absolute" or separate from the main sentence. In the first sentence, the meaning of the ablative absolute **Thermis aedificatis** is separate from that of the main clause, **Erroneus salubritate fruebatur**, i.e., Erroneus did not build the baths (but he did enjoy them!).

- In Latin, the subject of the perfect passive participle in an ablative absolute is not the same as that of the main verb; however, in English it may be expressed as such if the identity of the two subjects is clearly the same, e.g.,

   > **<u>Vestimentis exutis</u>, Erroneus aliquid unguenti poscebat.**
   > *<u>After he had taken off his clothes</u>, Erroneus asked for some oil, lit.,*
   > *After the clothes had been taken off, Erroneus....*

In this sentence, the person who is disrobing and Erroneus are clearly the same, therefore the ablative absolute may be changed from the passive to the active voice in translation. When translating in such situations, be sure to express the action of the past participle as preceding that of the main verb.

- Because there is no present active participle of the verb **esse**, this participle is understood and expressed in the English translation of a Latin sentence in which the ablative absolute seems to lack a participial form, e.g.,

With an adjective: **Erroneo aegro, in caldario manere non iam poterat.**
> *Since Erroneus was ill, he was not able to stay in the hot room any longer.*

With a noun: **Servo custode, vestimenta non surripientur.**
> *While a slave is on guard, the clothes will not be stolen.*

The tense of the understood participle correlates with that of the main verb.

## Quick Study of the Ablative Absolute

---

**Type 1 (with the perfect passive participle, action precedes that of the main verb)**

> **Linteo a balneatore accepto, Erroneus se ipsum strenue defricabat.**
> *After the towel had been received from the attendant,* lit., *the towel having been received from the attendant, Erroneus vigorously rubbed himself dry.*

**Type 2 (with the present active participle, action contemporary with that of the main verb)**

> **Erroneo in popina bibente, amicus suus in caldario madefacit.**
> *While Erroneus is drinking in the snack-bar, his friend is soaking in the hot room.*

> **Erroneo in popina bibente, amicus suus in caldario madefaciebat.**
> *While Erroneus was drinking in the snack-bar, his friend was soaking in the hot room.*

**Type 3 (with no participle)**

> **Erroneo balneatore, accipietne aliquis linteum?**
> *If Erroneus is the bath attendant, will anyone receive a towel?*

> **Aqua frigidiore, Erroneus in frigidarium intrare non voluit.**
> *The water being too cold, Erroneus did not wish to enter the cold room.*
> Better English, *Since the water was too cold....*

---

## Recognizing an Ablative Absolute

- Every ablative absolute must contain at least <u>two</u> elements, the noun or pronoun and the participle or its substitute (a second noun, an adjective, or a pronoun).

- Often the noun or pronoun and participle are found in close proximity, but there may be additional, intervening words. The noun or pronoun regularly appears before the participle.

- The ablative absolute usually appears early in the sentence.

- As an independent thought unit in a sentence, the ablative absolute is usually (but not always) set off by commas from the rest of the sentence.

## Translating an Ablative Absolute

The "Type 1" ablative absolute, that is, the ablative absolute containing a past participle, is by far the most common. When translating, begin by rendering the participle literally, i.e., **Thermis aedificatis**, *The baths having been built*. Use *having been* _____ as your memorized or default translation of the past participle. Then move on to other possibilities that might better express the meaning in English. As with other participial constructions, the ablative absolute can be translated as a clause that expresses time (*after, when*) and cause (*since*), as well as condition (*if*), concession (*although*), or relation (*who*). The decision is up to you, the reader, to determine the best contextual sense of an ablative absolute, e.g.,

**<u>Thermis aedificatis, cotidie multi se lavare poterant.</u>**

Temporal:     *After/When the baths had been built...*

Causal:     *Since/Because the baths had been built...*

The ablative absolute may also coordinate with the main clause and serve as a second main verb, e.g., *The baths had been built <u>and</u>.....*

Here are some additional examples of ablatives absolute translated as clauses:

**<u>Erroneo morante</u>, amici in apodyterium intraverunt.**
     *<u>While Erroneus was loitering</u>, his friends entered the dressing room.*

**<u>Vestimentis exutis</u>, Erroneus amicos deridentes eum audiebat.**
     *<u>After he had taken off his clothes</u>, Erroneus heard his friends laughing at him.*

**<u>Hoc audito</u>, Erroneus linteo se celavit.**
     *<u>When he (had) heard this</u>, Erroneus hid himself with a towel.*

**Amicus molestus, <u>Erroneo verecundo</u>, linteum surripuit.**
     *<u>Since Erroneus was (being) bashful</u>, his pesky friend stole away the towel.*

## Tips on Translating Participles

Please refer to the following sentence with respect to the tips below:

> **Erroneus unguentum et strigilem <u>ferens</u>, in pavimento lapsus est.**
>
> *While Erroneus <u>was carrying</u> the oil and strigil, he slipped on the tiled floor.*

- Participles are verbal adjectives and must modify a noun or pronoun in the sentence. The participle follows the rules of noun-adjective agreement in Latin. When translating a participle, locate the participle (**ferens**) and then link it with the pronoun or noun modified (**Erroneus**).

- The participle **ferens** represents one of two actions in the sentence in which it appears. The expression in English of the time of the action of the participle depends upon the tense of the main verb of the sentence. **Ferens** is expressed as *was carrying* because the main verb **lapsus est** is in the past tense.

- The participle as a verbal adjective is found in a participial phrase, which is a group of words without a subject or verb and containing a participle, e.g., **unguentum et strigilem ferens**. In Latin, the participle is found at the end of the phrase, as **unguentum et strigilem <u>ferens</u>**, whereas in English, the participle is found at the beginning, *carrying oil and a strigil*.

- Participial phrases are usually translated as subordinate clauses that express particular circumstances of time (*while, when*), cause (*since, because*), condition (*if*), concession (*although*), or relation (*who*). The phrase underlined above is expressed as a temporal clause, *while Erroneus was carrying*.

- Participial phrases can be found at the beginning, middle, or end of a Latin sentence.

- The word modified by the participle usually precedes it: **Erroneus...ferens**.

- The phrase in which a participle is found is often framed by commas.

## Practice Questions on Participles and the Ablative Absolute

1. Cives, <u>furibus vestes surripientibus</u>, custodes conducebant.

   (A) because the clothes had been stolen by the thieves

   (B) since the thieves had stolen the clothes

   (C) because the thieves were stealing the clothes

   (D) while the thieves are stealing the clothes

2. Cicero scripsit, "Signa rerum <u>futurarum</u> a dis ostenduntur."

   (A) having been        (C) about to be

   (B) being             (D) had been

3.  The voices of the men <u>singing</u> annoyed me <u>while I was soaking</u> in the hot bath.

    (A)  cantantium/madefaciens

    (C)  cantantium/madefacientem

    (B)  cantantis/madefacientes

    (D)  cantantes/madefaciente

4.  The girls <u>were going to hurry</u> into the changing room.

    (A)  festinaturae erant

    (C)  festinaturae sunt

    (B)  festinaturae fuerant

    (D)  festinaturi erant

5.  Select the translation of the sentence that is <u>not</u> correct.

    > Servi strigilibus homines unctos defricabant.

    (A)  While the men were being oiled down, the slaves were scraping them with strigils.

    (B)  The slaves were scraping with strigils the men who had been oiled down.

    (C)  The slaves were oiling down the men and then scraping them with strigils.

    (D)  After the men had been oiled down, the slaves scraped them with strigils.

6.  <u>His rebus factis</u>, athletae in palaestram ierunt.

    (A)  While these things were being done

    (B)  After these things were done

    (C)  About to do these things

    (D)  While doing these things

7.  <u>Exercens</u> athleta plus unguenti rogat.

    (A)  While exercising

    (C)  Having exercised

    (B)  About to exercise

    (D)  Who was exercising

8.  "We <u>who are about to bathe</u> salute you!" the men proclaimed to the attendants.

    (A)  lavantes

    (C)  lavandi

    (B)  lauturi

    (D)  lauturos

9.  Select the translation of the underlined participial phrase that is <u>not</u> correct.

    > Illa, <u>vix patiens vaporem</u>, e caldario egrediebatur.

    (A)  since she was barely enduring the steam

    (B)  barely enduring the steam

    (C)  because she is barely enduring the steam

    (D)  who was scarcely enduring the steam

## Sententiae Antiquae

1. Quidquid id est, timeo Danaos et dona . . .! (Vergil)

   (A) ferentia            (C) ferens

   (B) ferentem          (D) ferentes

2. Why are you laughing? <u>When the name has been changed</u>, the story is told about you. (Horace)

   (A) Mutans nomen      (C) Mutatis nominibus

   (B) Mutato nomine      (D) Mutatum nomen

3. A word <u>to the wise</u> is sufficient. (Terence)

   (A) sapienti           (C) sapientes

   (B) sapiens          (D) sapientem

4. O vos . . . graviora, dabit deus his quoque finem. (Vergil)

   (A) passa            (C) passi

   (B) passus          (D) passos

5. The skill of an orator <u>about to recite</u> pleases those <u>who are going to listen</u>. (Quintilian)

   (A) dicturi/auditura      (C) dicti/auditos

   (B) dicentis/audientes    (D) dicturi/audituros

## Answers

1. Ablative absolute   **(C)**

   This question tests your ability to translate an ablative absolute containing a present participle when the main verb is in a past tense. The present participle must be translated in the past because its action must be contemporary with that of the main verb, which is past. The translations in Answers (A) and (B) provide past actions that are completed, "had been stolen" and "had stolen," which would require perfect passive participles. The translation in Answer (D) "are stealing" is not contemporary with the time of the main verb **conducebant**, which is in the imperfect tense.

2. Future participle   **(C)**

   Answer (C) translates the underlined form **futurarum** correctly as the future participle of the verb **esse**. The sentence reads, "Indications <u>of future events</u>, lit., things about to be are revealed to the world by the gods." Answer (A) translates a perfect active participle, which doesn't exist as a form except in the case of deponent verbs. Answers (B) and (D) are in the wrong tenses.

3. Present participle **(C)**

"Of the men singing" requires a form that is genitive plural and "annoyed me (while I was) soaking" a form that is accusative singular to modify **me**, leading to **cantantium/madefacientem**. Although the verbs may be unfamiliar, their forms should not. **Madefaciens** in Answer (A) is nom. sing. and does not agree with **me**, the direct object of the verb "annoyed" in the sentence. Answer (B) contains forms that are gen. sing. and nom./acc. pl., which are incorrect. Answer (D) contains forms that are also in the incorrect case and number (nom./acc. pl. and abl. sing.)

4. Active periphrastic **(A)**

This question tests your familiarity with the active periphrastic. "(They) were going to hurry" requires a future active participle "going to hurry" and the auxiliary verb "(they) were," which is **erant**. Answer (B) translates as "had been about to hurry," and (C) "are about to hurry." Answer (D) "were about to hurry" provides the correct translation, but the participle **festinaturi** has a masculine ending where a feminine ending, modifying "the girls," is required.

5. Perfect passive participle **(A)**

This sentence reads literally, "The slaves were scraping with strigils the men having been oiled down." The participle is **unctos**, the perfect passive participle of **unguere** modifying **homines**, which is the direct object of the verb **defricabant**. Answer (A) requires a present participle to render the meaning "while," which is an action contemporary with that of the main verb, rather than prior to it, as required by the perfect passive participle **unctos**.

6. Ablative absolute **(B)**

"After these things were done" is a condensation of "these things having been done," a more literal translation of the ablative absolute **His rebus factis**. Answer (D) requires the present participle "while doing" (**facientes**) and (C) the future participle "about to do" (**facturi**), both directly modifying **athletae** and thus not ablatives absolute. Answer (A) renders a present passive participial form ("were being done"), which is inexpressible in Latin.

7. Present participle **(A)**

**Exercens** is the nominative singular form of the present participle modifying **athleta**, the subject of the sentence. Answer (B) "about to exercise" translates the future participle **exerciturus**, (C) "having exercised" gives an impossible meaning of **exercens**, and (D) "was exercising" requires that the main verb be **rogabant**, a past tense. The sentence reads, "While exercising, the athlete is requesting more oil." Note the appearance of the partitive genitive.

8. Future participle **(B)**

This sentence requires a future participle, "about to bathe," modifying the subject "we,"which is the form **lauturi** (remember that the masculine ending is preferred when the gender is not specified). Answer (A) **lavantes** is a present participle, "bathing," and (C) **lavandi** a gerund or gerundive form that is not appropriate in this context. Answer (D) **lauturos** is a future participle, but has an accusative ending, rather than the necessary nominative.

9. Present participle   **(C)**

**Vix patiens vaporem** is a present participial phrase that must be rendered as continuous action in the past tense in order to be contemporary with the time of the main verb **egrediebatur**, which is in the imperfect tense. Answer (C) is incorrect because the translation "is enduring" cannot properly render **patiens**, since the main verb is in the past tense.

10. **(A)**

This question tests your awareness that participles may be translated as clauses. The meaning of the present participle **morantibus** "lingering" can also be rendered as **qui morabantur** "while they were lingering." The sentence reads, "We gave money to the beggars (who were) <u>lingering</u> in the entryway." Answer (B) **moraturis** is translated "about to linger," (C) **cum morati erant** "when/since they had lingered," and (D) **quamquam morantur** "although they are lingering." (See Segment A6.)

11. **(A)**

**Postquam cives detersi erant**, "After the citizens had been dried off," can also be rendered in Latin by the ablative absolute as a temporal clause, i.e., **civibus detersis**. The sentence reads, "<u>After the citizens had been dried off</u>, the bathman gathered the towels into one place." Answers (B), (C), and (D) all express continuous action in past time (**detergebantur, detergerentur**, and **detergebant** are all in the imperfect tense), whereas the verb **detersi erant** expresses completed action in past time.

## *Sententiae Antiquae* Answers

1. Present participle   **(D)**

The missing participle, which must be in the present tense, given the possible answers, agrees with the direct object **Danaos**, according to the sense required by the context. Answer (A) is misleading, as you are tempted to use **ferentia** to modify **dona**. But the "gifts" are not doing the "bringing"! Answer (B) **ferentem** is a singular form where a plural is required and (C) **ferens** is a nominative singular form where an accusative plural is required. The sentence reads, "Whatever it is (i.e., the wooden horse), I fear Greeks even <u>bearing (or when they bear)</u> gifts."

2. Ablative absolute **(B)**

The ablative absolute **mutato nomine** correctly translates the time clause "When the name has been changed." Answer (A) **mutans nomen** contains a present participle, which does not correctly render the meaning. Answer (C) **mutatis nominibus** is an ablative absolute, but has forms in the plural, whereas the singular is required. Answer (D) **mutatum nomen** is a phrase with the past participle, but does not make sense in the context.

3.  Present participle, substantive   **(A)**
    This question presents the participle **sapiens** as a substantive, i.e., "the one being wise, " "the wise." Since the English requires a dative form, "to the wise," **sapienti** is the correct answer. Answer (B) is nominative, (C) nom/acc. plural, and (D) accusative singular, none of which fits the context.

4.  Past participle, deponent   **(C)**
    All answers are in the perfect passive participial form of the deponent verb **patior, pati, passus sum**. This participle, when translated in the active voice, means "having suffered." All that's left to do is to determine the function, or case, of the missing participle. The form modifies the vocative form **vos**, given the sense, so it must be vocative plural, ergo, **passi**. Answer (A) tempts you to use the participle to modify **graviora**, but this word serves as the (neuter plural substantive) direct object. Answer (B) **passus** is singular, not plural, and (D) **passos** is accusative, not vocative, as required by the context. The sentence reads, "O you having suffered (who have suffered) rather serious trials, god will make an end to these, too."

5.  Future participle   (D)
    "About to recite" and "going to listen" both require future active participles. The first participle modifies "of an orator," which requires a form in the genitive case. The clause "who are going to listen" modifies "those," which serves as the accusative direct object. (There are no dative forms offered as answers, so a verb other than **placere** for "please" must be assumed.) The forms in Answer (D) **dicturi/audituros** fulfil all the requirements and provide the correct answer. Answer (A) **dicturi/auditura** contains future participles, but **auditura** does not modify "those (people)," which is personal and not neuter. Answers (B) and (C) contain participles other than those in the future tense, i.e., **dicentis** (present) and **dicti/auditos** (past).

# Chapter 16 B: The Gerund, Gerundive, and Supine

## The Gerund

The gerund is a verbal noun that has characteristics of both a verb and a noun, e.g.,

**Possumus discere multa de deis Romanis legendo.**
We can learn much about the Roman gods by reading.

The gerund is formed by adding **–nd-** to the present stem of the verb, together with the endings of the second declension singular noun in all cases but the nominative. The gerund serves the functions of a noun in these cases and is translated with *–ing*, e.g., *reading.*

| | **Forms** | **Common Uses** |
|---|---|---|
| Nom. | _____ | |
| Gen. | **legendi**, *of reading* | purpose with **causa** or **gratia** |
| Dat. | **legendo**, *to, for reading* | indirect object or with special adjectives |
| Acc. | **legendum**, *reading* | purpose with **ad** |
| Abl. | **legendo**, *by, with reading* | means/instrument or with **de, e/ex,** or **in** |

Note:

- There is no nominative form of the gerund. The subjective infinitive **legere**, *reading*, is substituted. (For this type of infinitive, see Chapter 16C.)

## The Gerundive (Future Passive Participle)

The gerundive is a verbal adjective formed by adding **–ndus, -a, -um** to the present stem of the verb, e.g., **legendus, -a, -um.** As a verbal adjective, the gerundive agrees with a noun:

**Possumus discere de deis Romanis fabulis legendis.**
*We can learn about the Roman gods by reading stories*, lit., *by stories about to be read.*

In the sentence given above, note that the gerundive **legendis** is attracted into the ablative case in agreement with the noun **fabulis**, *by (means of) stories.* You would normally expect the accusative form **fabulas** to serve as the direct object of **legendis**, but the Romans preferred to use a gerundive, i.e., **fabulis legendis,** instead of a gerund, i.e., **fabulas legendo**, when a direct object was involved.

Notes:

- The form of both the gerund and gerundive may be recognized by the **–nd-**, deriving from **gerendus, -a, -um**, *about to be done*, which is the gerundive form of the Latin verb **gerere**.

- You may remember that the gerundive serves as a verbal adjective by learning the phrase "The gerundive is an adjective."

## Simple Gerundive

The gerundive is found in all noun cases, e.g.,

Dative: **Orpheus apud inferos lyram modulatus est acquirendae uxori.**

*Orpheus played his lyre in the underworld to gain possession of his wife.*

Ablative: **Lyrā modulandā, Orpheus bestias flexit.**

*Orpheus charmed the beasts by playing his lyre.*

## Gerundive of Purpose (with *Ad, Causa,* or *Gratia*)

The gerundive accompanying **ad** (+ acc.), *to, in order to,* **causa** (+ gen.) or **gratia** (+ gen.), *for the purpose of, for the sake of,* indicates purpose or intent, e.g.,

**Icarus alte volabat caeli tangendi causa.**
*Icarus flew high for the sake of touching the sky.*

**Daedalus mare investigabat ad filium mortuum inveniendum.**
*Daedalus searched the sea in order to find his dead son.*

## Passive Periphrastic (or Gerundive of Obligation)

The gerundive is commonly used with a form of the verb **esse** to express necessity or obligation. When the gerundive has this function, it has meanings such as *must be, ought to be, should be.* This use is known either as the passive periphrastic (a time honored Greek term which roughly means "roundabout") or the gerundive of obligation. Any tense of the verb **esse** may be used, e.g.,

**Medusa necanda est.**    *Medusa has to be (must be) killed.*

**Medusa necanda erat.**    *Medusa had to be killed.*

**Medusa necanda erit.**    *Medusa will have to be killed,* etc.

Note:

- The gerundive of obligation is frequently used in indirect statements and indirect questions. For more on these constructions, see Chapters 16C and 16D, Section 5, respectively.

Indirect statement:    **Perseus scit Medusam necandam esse.**
*Perseus knows that Medusa must be killed.*

Indirect question:    **Perseus non rogavit cur Medusa necanda esset.**
*Perseus did not ask why Medusa had to be killed*

When an intransitive verb, that is, a verb which does not take a direct object, appears in the passive periphrastic, the gerundive is translated <u>impersonally</u>, i.e., has "it" as its subject. For better English, transform the passive voice to the active, e.g.,

> **Ad Graias Perseo eundum est.**
>> *Perseus must go to the Graiae,* lit., *It must be gone by Perseus to the Graiae.*

You will note in the previous example that **Perseo** is expressed in the <u>dative</u> case. In the passive periphrastic, the person who must perform the obligation expressed in the verb is found in the dative case, a use known as the dative of agent. (The ablative of personal agent with **a/ab** is <u>not</u> used with this construction. For this usage, see Chapter 13A.)

## Quick Study of the Gerund and the Gerundive

| The Gerund | The Gerundive |
|---|---|
| is a verbal noun; | is a verbal adjective; |
| corresponds to the English verbal noun in *–ing*, e.g., **mittendum**, *sending*; | agrees with a noun or pronoun, e.g., **ad epistulam mittendam**, *for the purpose of sending the letter*; |
| is present and active in meaning; | is future and passive in meaning; |
| is found only in the gen., dat., acc., and abl., sing. forms of the second declension | is found in all case forms of the first/second declension adjective |

## The Supine

Just as the gerund is a verbal noun, so is the supine. It is formed from the fourth principal part of the verb, but has a different meaning from that of the perfect passive participle. Only two cases invite review: the accusative, e.g., **narratum**, and the ablative, **narratu.** Note that the endings of the supine are those of the fourth declension noun. The supine is used with the accusative to express purpose, e.g., **narratum**, *to tell*, and with the ablative to express respect or specification, e.g., **narratu**, *with respect to telling.* Use the context to distinguish between **narratum** as a supine, *to tell*, and **narratum** as a perfect passive participle, *having been told.*

Supine showing purpose:  **Hercules ad inferos Cerberum <u>captum</u> iit.**
> *Hercules went to the underworld <u>to capture</u> Cerberus.*
> (Note that the meaning of **captum** as "having been captured" does not make sense here.)

Supine showing respect:  **Cerberus tria capita habebat (horribile <u>visu</u>!)**
> *Cerberus had three heads (horrible <u>to see</u>!)*

Notes:

- Verbs that govern the accusative supine usually express motion, as in the example just above.
- The supine as ablative of respect is found with certain neuter adjectives, e.g., **facile/difficile**, *easy/difficult*, **horribile**, *dreadful*, **mirabile**, *remarkable*, **miserabile**, *wretched*, and **optimum**, *best*. (For the ablative of respect, see Chapter 13A.)

## Practice Questions

1.  <u>Quod erat demonstrandum.</u>
    - (A)  What was being shown
    - (B)  What has to be shown
    - (C)  What had to be shown
    - (D)  What is being shown

2.  Prometheus ignem surripuit hominis . . . causa.
    - (A)  adiuvandus
    - (B)  adiuvandi
    - (C)  adiuvandis
    - (D)  adiuvandum

3.  Minotauro necato, . . . domum redeundum est.
    - (A)  Theseus
    - (B)  Theseum
    - (C)  Theseo
    - (D)  Thesea

4.  Theseus navigavit ad Cretam <u>ut Minotaurum necaret</u>. The best substitute for this clause is
    - (A)  necare Minotaurum
    - (B)  ad Minotaurum necandum
    - (C)  quod Minotaurus necabitur
    - (D)  Minotauro necato

5.  <u>Sisyphus scivit saxum sibi semper volvendum esse.</u>
    - (A)  Sisyphus knows that he will always roll the stone.
    - (B)  Sisyphus knew that he must roll the stone forever.
    - (C)  Sisyphus knew that the stone had always been rolled by him.
    - (D)  Sisyphus knew that he was going to roll the stone forever.

6.  Arachne melius Minerva . . . texere poterat.
    - (A)  mirabilis dictu
    - (B)  mirabile dictum
    - (C)  mirabile dictu
    - (D)  mirabilis dictum

7. Multi venerunt <u>ad videndum Pegasum</u>. The construction that has the same basic meaning is

   (A) Pegasum visum

   (C) Pegaso viso

   (B) quod Pegasum videbant

   (D) videntes Pegasum

8. <u>Daphne fugiente, Apollini celerrime currendum erat</u>. The basic meaning of this sentence is that

   (A) Daphne had to run after Apollo

   (B) Apollo had to run after Daphne

   (C) Apollo has to run after Daphne

   (D) Apollo was running from Daphne

9. Hercules duodecim labores complevit <u>laborando</u> diligenter.

   (A) for working

   (C) about to work

   (B) by working

   (D) having worked

10. <u>Pyramus Thisben visam amavit</u>. Which of the following is <u>not</u> correct?

    (A) Pyramus loved to look at Thisbe.

    (B) Pyramus saw Thisbe and fell in love with her.

    (C) Pyramus loved Thisbe after seeing her.

    (D) When he had seen her, Pyramus loved Thisbe.

## Sententiae Antiquae

1. Wise thinking is the source <u>of writing</u> well. (Horace)

   (A) scribendum

   (C) scribendi

   (B) scribendae

   (D) scribendorum

2. Gossip gains strength <u>by going</u> (as it goes). (Vergil)

   (A) iens

   (C) eundo

   (B) eundum

   (D) euntem

3. <u>Caesari omnia uno tempore erant agenda</u>. (Caesar)

   (A) Everything was being done by Caesar at the same time.

   (B) Caesar had to do everything at the same time.

   (C) Caesar was about to do everything at the same time.

   (D) Everything was done to Caesar at the same time.

4. <u>Mea Musa a componendo carmine teneri non potest</u>. In this sentence, Ovid says that

   (A) creating his verse cannot be kept from the Muse.

   (B) his Muse keeps him from creating verse.

   (C) his Muse cannot keep him from creating verse.

   (D) his Muse cannot be kept from creating verse.

5. <u>Regulus laudandus est in conservando iure iurando</u>. (Cicero)

   (A) Regulus ought to be praised for keeping his oath.

   (B) Regulus is praising those who keep their oath.

   (C) Regulus had to be praised for keeping his oath.

   (D) Regulus is being praised for keeping his oath.

## Answers

1. Passive periphrastic   **(C)**
   **Demonstrandum** is a gerundive modifying the relative pronoun **quod,** whose antecedent is the unstated pronoun **id**. The appearance of the verb **erat** defines the construction **erat demonstrandum** as a gerundive in a passive periphrastic, meaning "(that) which had to be demonstrated (was, in fact, demonstrated)." This Latin phrase, abbreviated Q.E.D., is often found at the end of mathematical proofs.

2. Gerundive of purpose   **(B)**
   This question evaluates your knowledge of the gerundive of purpose with **causa**. The sentence reads, "Prometheus stole fire <u>for the sake of helping</u> mankind." Since **causa** takes the genitive case, its object is **hominis,** to be modified by the gerundive **adiuvandi**. Answer (A) is nominative singular, (B) dative/ablative plural, and (D) masculine accusative singular or neuter nominative/accusative singular, all designed to prompt consideration because of the similarity of their endings to those already found in the sentence.

3. Dative of agent   **(C)**
   The periphrastic **redeundum est** in this sentence requires that Theseus be dative of agent, i.e., **Theseo**. The sentence reads, "After the Minotaur was killed, <u>Theseus</u> was obliged to return home." **Theseo...redeundum est**, which is an example of the passive periphrastic used with an intransitive verb, reads, literally, "It must be returned home by Theseus...." Answer (B) might seem to be a good choice, since **Theseum** appears to agree with **redeundum est**, but the accusative case is not justifiable. Answers (A) and (D) have no sense here.

4. Gerundive of purpose   **(B)**
   The gerundive of purpose, **ad Minotaurum necandum,** "for the purpose of killing the Minotaur," may be substituted for **ut Minotaurum necaret**, which

is an **ut** clause of purpose with the subjunctive. The infinitive in Answer (A) is not generally used to express purpose. Answer (C) is a causal clause, "because the Minotaur will be killed," which changes the meaning, and the ablative absolute in Answer (D) expresses that the Minotaur had already been killed.

5.   Passive periphrastic   **(B)**
    The periphrastic **volvendum esse** is found in the context of an indirect statement following the verb **scivit**. This construction requires the use of an infinitive. The sentence reads, literally, "Sisyphus knew that he must roll the stone forever, lit., that the stone must always be rolled by him." Note that **sibi**, the dative of agent, replaces the accusative form **se**, which would ordinarily be the subject accusative of the infinitive.

6.   Supine   **(C)**
    The supine phrase **mirabile dictu**, a favorite of Vergil, here completes the sentence "Arachne was able to weave better than Minerva (remarkable to say!)" The supine as ablative of respect ("remarkable with respect to saying so") is found with the neuter form of **mirabilis**, hence, Answers (A) and (D) must be omitted, as **mirabilis** is masculine/feminine. Because the meaning of this sentence does not require a supine of purpose, Answer (B) **mirabile dictum** may be eliminated.

7.   Gerundive of purpose; supine   **(A)**
    The acceptable substitute for the gerundive of purpose, **ad videndum Pegasum**, is the supine phrase **Pegasum visum**. The sentence reads, "Many came to see Pegasus." Answer (B) is a causal clause that does not express purpose, nor do the participial phrases given in Answers (C) and (D).

8.   Passive periphrastic   **(B)**
    The sentence reads, "Since Daphne was fleeing, Apollo had to run very quickly." The passive periphrastic construction with an intransitive verb, **currendum erat**, expresses necessity in past time. **Apollini** is dative of agent. Answers (A) and (D) reverse the meaning, and Answer (C), which is not in past time, requires the form **currendum est**.

9.   Gerund   **(B)**
    Since **laborando** serves the function of a noun in this sentence, Answer (B) "by working," which serves as an ablative of means, is correct. If **laborando** were a gerundive, it would modify another word. The sentence reads, "Hercules completed the twelve Labors by working tirelessly." Answer (C) "about to work" translates a future active participle and (D) "having worked" translates a perfect active participle, which has no form in Latin. Answer (A) is a potential translation of **laborando**, but has no contextual meaning in this sentence.

10.   Perfect passive participle   **(A)**
    "To look at" incorrectly translates the perfect passive participle **visam** as a supine. The accusative form of the supine ends in –**um**, i.e., **visum**. Answers (B), (C), and (D), are acceptable ways of translating **visam** as a past participle.

## *Sententiae Antiquae*

1.  Gerund **(C)**
    "Of writing" is a noun, therefore requiring that the gerund **scribendi** have its ending in the genitive case. Answer (A) **scribendum** could be a gerund, but is not in the genitive case. Answers (B) **scribendae** and (D) **scribendorum** must be gerundives, because of their adjectival endings.

2.  Gerund **(C)**
    "By going" is a gerund, here serving the function of the ablative of means. This quote from Vergil's *Aeneid* is the source of the motto of the State of New Mexico, **Crescit eundo**. All answers are forms of the irregular verb **ire**: Answer (A) **iens** is a present participle in its nominative (masculine, feminine, neuter) or accusative singular (neuter) form and (D) **euntem** is an accusative singular form of the present active participle, neither of which may be translated as "by going." Answer (B) **eundum** may be seen as a gerund, but the accusative case is not justified by the context.

3.  Passive periphrastic **(B)**
    This sentence contains the passive periphrastic **erant agenda**, with **Caesari** serving as dative of agent. Answers (A), (C), and (D) do not express the idea of necessity or obligation, but of past continuous action ("was being done"), future action ("was about to do"), or past completed action ("was done"), respectively. Note the word order of **erant agenda**.

4.  Gerundive **(D)**
    The core of the meaning of this sentence is the prepositional phrase that includes a gerundive, **a componendo carmine**, "from composing verse." The use of the ablative here contains the idea of separation. Answer (A) is incorrect because the prepositional phrase given above does not serve as the subject of the sentence. In Answers (B) and (C), the Muse is not "keeping him from creating verse," as there is no Latin pronoun "him" in the original sentence. This sentence translates, "However, my Muse cannot be kept from creating verse."

5.  Passive periphrastic **(A)**
    The correct answer to this question centers on the expression of the meaning of the periphrastic, **laudandus est**. Answers (B) "is praising" and (D) "is being praised" can be eliminated because they do not express obligation. Answer (C) "had to be praised" can be eliminated because it expresses past time.

# Chapter 16C: Infinitives and Indirect Statement

## Quick Study of Infinitives

| mitto, mittere, misi, missus | | |
|---|---|---|
| | **Active** | **Passive** |
| Present | **mittere**, *to send* | **mitti,** *to be sent* |
| Perfect | **misisse**, *to have sent* | **missus esse**, *to have been sent* |
| Future | **missurus esse**, *to be about to send* | **missus iri**, *to be about to be sent* (rare) |

## Quick Study of the Infinitives of Irregular Verbs

| Present | Perfect | Future |
|---|---|---|
| **esse**, *to be* | **fuisse**, *to have been* | **futurus esse**, *to be about to be* |
| **posse**, *to be able* | **potuisse**, *to have been able* | |
| **ire**, *to go* | **iisse**, *to have gone* | **iturus esse**, *to be about to go* |
| **ferre**, *to bring* | **tulisse**, *to have brought* | **laturus esse**, *to be about to bring* |
| **velle**, *to wish* | **voluisse**, *to have wished* | |
| **nolle**, *to be unwilling* | **noluisse**, *to have been unwilling* | |
| **malle**, *to prefer* | **maluisse**, *to have preferred* | |
| **fieri**, *to become* | **factus esse**, *to have become* | |

Notes:
- **Fero** is the only irregular verb with passive infinitive forms: **ferri**, *to be brought*, and **latus esse**, *to have been brought*.
- The word **fore** is often used as a substitute for **futurum esse**.

# Uses of the Infinitive

## Subjective infinitive and objective infinitive

The infinitive, usually the present active infinitive, may be used as a subject or object of the main verb. Subjective infinitives are considered neuter singular nouns:

subjective

**Dulce et decorum est pro factione <u>mori</u>.**

> *It is sweet and glorious <u>to die</u> for one's racing team*, i.e., <u>*Dying*</u> *is sweet....*\*

The infinitive may also serve as the direct object of a verb:

objective

**<u>Vincere</u> quam <u>vinci</u> auriga mavult.**

> *A charioteer prefers <u>victory</u> to <u>defeat</u>*, lit., *to win, rather than to be defeated.*

## Complementary infinitive

The complementary (not complimentary!) infinitive completes the meaning of another verb. The other verb is often irregular, e.g.,

> **Potestne Limax hoc certamen <u>vincere</u>?**
> *<u>Is</u> Limax <u>able to win</u> this race?*

> **Nonne Limax metam <u>vitare</u> <u>vult</u>? Eheu!**
> *Surely Limax <u>wants to avoid</u> the turning post? Oops!*

> **Quadrigas <u>fregisse</u> <u>videtur</u>.**
> *He <u>seems to have broken</u> his chariot.*

# Tips on Translating Infinitives

- When translating, consider the context of the sentence in which the infinitive is found. Look for a <u>controlling verb</u> in the case of a complementary infinitive.

- The literal translation of an infinitive, *to ___*, will not always be appropriate to the context in which the infinitive is found, e.g., as a subject or object or in indirect statement. Be alert for the use of an adjective + **esse** that may appear to be a perfect passive infinitive, e.g.,

  | | |
  |---|---|
  | Adjective + **esse**: | **Auriga putat se <u>peritum</u> esse.** |
  | | *The charioteer thinks that he (himself) <u>is</u> <u>experienced</u>.* |
  | Perfect Passive Infinitive: | **Auriga putat se victorem <u>pronuntiatum esse</u>.** |
  | | *The charioteer thinks that he (himself) <u>was</u> <u>declared</u> the winner.* |

---

\* After the famous saying by Horace, **Dulce et decorum est pro patria mori**, *It is sweet and glorious to die for one's country.*

- The literal translation of an infinitive rarely shows or expresses purpose, i.e., *in order to___*. For the latter, a gerund or gerundive of purpose (**ad** or **causa/gratia** + the gerund or gerundive) or a clause of purpose (**ut** + subjunctive) is used. (For the gerund/gerundive of purpose, see the previous chapter. For the purpose clause with **ut**, see Chapter 16D, Section 4.

- Also, especially in poetry, an alternative form of the perfect tense, such as **sumpsere**, may fool you into thinking that it is the present infinitive **sumere**. Closer inspection reveals that it is the perfect stem, e.g., **sumps** –, that precedes what appears to be an infinitive ending. The form **sumpsere** is, in fact, an alternative to the third person plural of the perfect tense, **sumpserunt**, *they have obtained*, and not the present active infinitive **sumere**, *to obtain*.

- Subjunctive verbs formed from the present and perfect active infinitives are not to be confused with the infinitives themselves, e.g., **esse** is a present infinitive, whereas **essem** is an imperfect subjunctive, and **egisse** is a perfect infinitive, while **egisset** is a pluperfect subjunctive. (The subjunctive will be reviewed in Chapter 16D.)

## Indirect Statement

The infinitive may be used to report what someone hears, says, thinks, etc. This grammatical construction is known as indirect statement or accusative and infinitive. The following sentences illustrate the grammatical differences between direct and indirect statement:

| | |
|---|---|
| Direct statement: | **Auriga quadrigas magna arte agit.** |
| | *The charioteer drives the chariot with great skill.* |
| Indirect statement: | **Dicit aurigam quadrigas magna arte agere.** |
| | *He says that the charioteer drives the chariot with great skill.* |

Verbs of mental or verbal action, e.g., **dicit**, are followed by a subject accusative, e.g., **aurigam**, and an infinitive, e.g., **agere**, unless they introduce a direct quotation. Such verbs should be remembered, because of the frequency with which the indirect statement occurs in Latin. (This might lead you to think that the ancient Romans were gossipy!) A memory device such as "M and M (mind and mouth) verbs" may help you to remember the following verbs that commonly introduce indirect statements in Latin:

| | |
|---|---|
| **arbitrari,** *think* | **negare,** *deny* |
| **audire,** *hear* | **putare,** *think* |
| **cognoscere,** *recognize* | **scire,** *know* |
| **credere,** *believe* | **sentire,** *feel, perceive* |
| **dicere,** *say* | **sperare,** *hope* |
| **intellego,** *know, understand* | **videre,** *see* |

An infinitive has a definite relationship in time with that of the main verb of the sentence. Look at the following examples:

> **Conspiciebamus Limacem equos <u>pascere</u>.**
> *We saw that Limax <u>was feeding</u> his horses.*

> **Limax putabat Velocem optimum equum <u>fuisse</u>.**
> *Limax thought that Velox <u>had been</u> the best horse.*

Because the infinitive **pascere** in the first example is given in the present tense, its action is contemporary with or happening at the same time as that of the main verb **conspiciebamus**, which is past tense. Therefore, the "feeding" and the "seeing" must be expressed as happening <u>at the same time</u>. In the second example, the infinitive **fuisse** is in the past tense, indicating that its action has already happened relative to that of the main verb **putabat**. But the action of the main verb **putabat** is also past tense, leading to the conclusion that Velox had been the best horse <u>before</u> Limax thought about it. This relationship may be thought of as "past (main verb) – past (infinitive) – *had*." In the table below, note that infinitives in the <u>present</u> tense are translated <u>at the same time as</u> the main verb, those in the <u>perfect</u> tense are translated at a time <u>before</u> the main verb, and those in the <u>future</u> tense at a time <u>after</u> the main verb.

## Quick Study of Indirect Statement

| | The Active Infinitive in Indirect Statement | |
|---|---|---|
| Present Main | **Limax <u>dicit</u> se quadrigas <u>agere</u>.** <br> *Limax <u>says</u> that he <u>drives</u> (is driving) the chariot.* | Present Infinitive |
| Present Main | **Limax <u>dicit</u> se quadrigas <u>egisse</u>.** <br> *Limax <u>says</u> that he <u>drove</u> (has driven) the chariot.* | Past Infinitive |
| Present Main | **Limax <u>dicit</u> se quadrigas <u>acturum esse</u>.** <br> *Limax <u>says</u> that he <u>will drive</u> the chariot.* | Future Infinitive |
| Past Main | **Limax <u>dicebat</u> se quadrigas <u>agere</u>.** <br> *Limax <u>said</u> that he <u>was driving</u> the chariot,* i.e., he said this at the same time as he was driving | Present Infinitive |
| Past Main | **Limax <u>dicebat</u> se quadrigas <u>egisse</u>.** <br> *Limax <u>said</u> that he <u>had driven</u> the chariot,* i.e., he drove before he spoke about it. | Past Infinitive |
| Past Main | **Limax <u>dicebat</u> se quadrigas <u>acturum esse</u>.** <br> *Limax <u>said</u> that he <u>would drive</u> the chariot.* | Future Infinitive |

| The Passive Infinitive in Indirect Statement | | |
|---|---|---|
| Present Main | **Limax <u>dicit</u> a se quadrigas <u>agi</u>.** <br> *Limax <u>says</u> that the chariot <u>is (being) driven</u> by him.* | Present Infinitive |
| Present Main | **Limax <u>dicit</u> a se quadrigas <u>actas esse</u>.** <br> *Limax <u>says</u> that the chariot <u>has been driven</u> by him.* | Past Infinitive |
| Past Main | **Limax dicebat a se quadrigas <u>agi</u>.** <br> *Limax <u>said</u> that the chariot <u>was (being) driven</u> by him*, i.e., he said this at the same time that he was driving. | Present Infinitive |
| Past Main | **Limax <u>dicebat</u> a se quadrigas <u>actas esse</u>.** <br> *Limax <u>said</u> that the chariot <u>had been driven</u> by him*, i.e., he drove before he spoke about it. | Past Infinitive |

## Tips on Translating Indirect Statement

- Look for a verb of mental or verbal action that introduces an infinitive with a subject accusative.

- Distinguish between reflexive and non-reflexive subjects of the infinitive, e.g., **se**, *himself*, and **eum**, *him*, i.e., someone other than the subject of the main verb. (For reflexive pronouns, see Chapter 13B.)

- In indirect statement, when the infinitive has a compound or two-part form, i.e., perfect passive or future active, the participial portion of the infinitive agrees in gender and number with its subject, which will be accusative, e.g.,

   Perfect passive: **Auriga vidit mappam demissam esse**.
   *The charioteer saw that the white starting cloth had been dropped.*

   Future active: **Sperabat <u>se</u> metam primo circumiturum esse.**
   *He was hoping that he (himself) would go around the turn post first.*

- The indirect statement will <u>never</u> have quotes around it.

- For the best sense, insert the word "that" after the main verb in the English translation, even though this word does not appear in the Latin. Do not use the word "to" when translating an infinitive in an indirect statement, e.g.,

   **Limax dicit se victorem <u>esse</u>.**
   Incorrect:    *Limax says he (himself) <u>to be</u> the winner.*
   Correct:      *Limax says <u>that</u> he (himself) <u>is</u> the winner.*

- Remember that it is the <u>time relationship</u> between the main verb and the infinitive that you are translating, i.e., it is the <u>tense of the infinitive rela-</u>

tive to that of the main verb that determines the meaning of the indirect statement. Take special care with sentences containing a main verb in the past tense, e.g., **dicebat**, *he was saying*, when found with an infinitive either in the present tense, e.g., **esse**, *was*, or the past tense, e.g., **fuisse**, *had been*. When faced with an example of the latter, where the tenses of both the main verb and the infinitive are past, remember the acronym PPH, "past-past-*had*." If you are uncertain about how to express the time relationship, turn the indirect statement into a direct statement:

Indirect:   **Limax dicebat se quadrigas egisse**. (Note that the infinitive is in
            *Limax said that he _____ the chariot.*   the past tense.)

Direct:     Limax said, "*I drove the chariot.*"
            i.e., he had already driven the chariot at the time he spoke.

Therefore:  *Limax said that he had driven the chariot.*

- The form **esse** is often omitted from the perfect or future active infinitive, e.g., **missum (esse)** or **missurum (esse),** and their meanings assumed or understood from context.

## Practice Questions

1.  "Don't fall out of your chariot, Limax!" laughed the spectators.

    (A)  Non cadere              (C)  Noli cadere

    (B)  Nolite cadere           (D)  Non licet cadere

2.  Finire : finiri :: vincere : _____

    (A)  vinci                   (C)  vince

    (B)  vici                    (D)  victi

3.  Spectator animadvertit that charioteer e curru cecidisse.

    (A)  ille auriga             (C)  illi aurigae

    (B)  illum aurigam           (D)  illos aurigas

4.  Limax putavit se a multis non fautum esse.

    (A)  has not been favored    (C)  was not favored

    (B)  is not favored          (D)  had not been favored

5.  Infelix auriga semper sperat crastinum diem melius _____ .

    (A)  fuisse                  (C)  fuerat

    (B)  fore                    (D)  erit

6. Limax dixit se scire <u>velle</u> quot factiones contenderent.

   (A) has wanted

   (B) was wanting

   (C) wants

   (D) will want

7. <u>Making an effort is noble</u>.

   (A) Conans est nobilis.

   (B) Conari est nobile.

   (C) Conatus est nobiliter.

   (D) Nobiliter conatur.

8. "Miror tot milia virorum cupere equos et in curribus homines videre," inquit Plinius.

   (A) Pliny doesn't understand why so many people like chariot racing.

   (B) Pliny wonders what it would be like to be a charioteer.

   (C) Pliny thinks that everyone should experience chariot racing.

   (D) Pliny says that both horses and charioteers often act like children.

9. Limax scivit <u>sibi carceres purgandos esse</u>.

   (A) that he is going to clean out the stalls

   (B) that he must have the stalls cleaned out

   (C) that he must clean out the stalls

   (D) that he will be invited to clean out the stalls

10. <u>Sperat auriga diu se victurum</u>.

    (A) The charioteer, going to live for a long time, is hopeful.

    (B) The charioteer hoped that he would live for a long time.

    (C) He hopes that the charioteer will live for a long time.

    (D) The charioteer hopes that he will live for a long time.

## *Sententiae Antiquae*

1. Identify the item that is <u>not</u> one of the three components necessary for an indirect statement.

   <u>Ait omnia pecunia effici posse</u>. (Cicero)

   (A) Ait

   (B) posse

   (C) omnia

   (D) effici

2. We often see that the victor <u>has been overcome</u> by the vanquished. (Dionysius Cato)

   (A) superavisse

   (B) superatum esse

   (C) superare

   (D) superaturum esse

3.  <u>If you wish to be loved, love</u>! (Seneca)

    (A)  Si vis amari, ama!    (C)  Si vis amari, amate!

    (B)  Si vis amare, ama!    (D)  Si vis amatus esse, ama!

4.  He preferred <u>to be</u> good rather than <u>to seem</u> good. (Sallust)

    (A)  esse...videre     (C)  fuisse...visus esse

    (B)  esse...videri     (D)  esse...vidisse

5.  . . . quid antequam natus sis acciderit id est semper esse puerum. (Cicero)

    (A)  Noli nescire     (C)  Nesciendus

    (B)  Nescire      (D)  Nesciri

6.  Pudor doceri non potest, nasci potest. (Publilius Syrus)

    (A)  Modesty cannot be learned, it can be obtained.

    (B)  One cannot be taught modesty, one is born with it.

    (C)  Teaching is not shameful, it can be a product of birth.

    (D)  He cannot teach modesty, but he can obtain it.

7.  He is ungrateful who denies that <u>he has received</u> a kindness that he has received. (Cicero)

    (A)  accipi      (C)  accipere

    (B)  acceptum esse    (D)  accepisse

8.  Ego verum amo; verum volo mihi <u>dici</u>. (Plautus)

    (A)  to be spoken    (C)  to speak

    (B)  to have spoken    (D)  to have been spoken

9.  <u>Making a mistake is human</u>. (Seneca)

    (A)  Errans est humanus.   (C)  Errare humanum est.

    (B)  Esse humanus est error.  (D)  Errans est humanus.

## Answers

1.  Prohibition **(C)**

    The negative command "Don't fall," **Noli cadere,** represents one of the varied uses of the infinitive. Answer (A) is not a negative command, (B) is plural (Limax is being addressed in the original sentence), and (D) is not a command, but an infinitive phrase with an impersonal verb.

2. Present passive infinitive   **(A)**

The present active infinitive of **finio** is to the present passive as the present active infinitive of **vinco** is to the present passive, which is **vinci**. Answer (B) **vici** is the third principal part or perfect tense, first person singular. Answer (C) **vince** is the present imperative and (D) **victi** a form of the perfect passive participle.

3. Subject accusative   **(B)**

The subject of an infinitive in an indirect statement is in the accusative case. Of the choices provided, **illum aurigam** is in the accusative case and in the singular, as required by "that charioteer." Answer (A) **ille auriga** presents what would have been the subject of the direct statement. Answer (C) **illi aurigae** is dative and (D) **illos aurigas** is plural.

4. Indirect statement   **(D)**

This sentence contains an example of "past-past-*had*," that is, both the main verb **putavit** and the infinitive **fautum esse** are in the past tense, resulting in the translation "had been favored." Answer (A) "has (not) been favored" and (C) "was (not) favored" are only possible if the main verb is in the present tense. Answer (B) "is not favored" is **(non) faveri**, which is a present passive infinitive. The sentence reads, "Limax knew that he <u>had not been favored</u> by many."

5. Indirect statement with **fore**   **(B)**

In this sentence, the verb **sperat** is a verb of mental action, which prompts an indirect statement, of which **crastinum diem** is the subject and **fore** (= **futurum esse**) the infinitive. The sentence reads, "The unsuccessful charioteer always hopes that tomorrow <u>will be</u> better." Answer (A) **fuisse** translates as "has been" and (C) and (D) are not infinitives, but pluperfect and future tense forms of the verb **esse**.

6. Indirect statement   **(B)**

The main verb **dixit** in this sentence keys an indirect statement, the subject of which is **se** and the infinitive **velle**. The combination of the main verb in the past tense and the infinitive in the present tense leads to the translation "was wanting." Answer (A) "has wanted," is **voluisse**. Answer (C) "wants" is a literal translation of the infinitive **velle**, but, given the context, the infinitive cannot have this meaning. Answer (D) "will want" cannot translate the present active infinitive **velle**. The sentence reads, "Limax said that he <u>was wanting</u> to know how many racing teams were in contention."

7. Subjective infinitive   **(B)**

This sentence contains the subjective infinitive of the deponent verb **conari** "to try" = "trying." Therefore **Conari est nobile** is the correct answer. Since a subjective infinitive is considered equivalent to a neuter noun, the adjective **nobile**, which is neuter, is correct. The obvious but incorrect answer is (A), while (C) **Conatus est nobiliter** expresses the action in past time. Answer (D) **Nobiliter conatur**, meaning "He is trying nobly," is also incorrect.

8.    Indirect statement   **(A)**
      Pliny said, "I wonder that so many thousands of men want to watch horses and people standing in chariots." Answers (B), (C), and (D) contain various inaccuracies in their translations. Note that there are two indirect statements following the main verb **miror** and connected by **et.**

9.    Indirect statement with passive periphrastic   **(C)**
      This sentence contains an indirect statement in which the infinitive consists of **purgandos esse**, a gerundive in the passive periphrastic construction, which expresses necessity. The subject of the infinitive has reverted from accusative to dative as the agent of the necessary action. Therefore, **se** becomes **sibi.** Answer (A) "is going to clean out" is **(se)... purgaturum esse.** Answer (B) "must have the stalls cleaned out" is in colloquial English and cannot express the Latin in the original sentence because it makes it sound as though someone else will do it. In Answer (D) the Latin for "he will be invited" is not found in the original. Poor Limax, who even has to clean out the stalls!

10.   Indirect statement   **(D)**
      The sentence reads, "The/A charioteer hopes that he will live for a time." The subject of the sentence, **auriga,** is put in a secondary position to tempt you into thinking that it is the subject of the infinitive, which is **se**. Note the ellipsis of the future infinitive **victurum (esse)**. Answer (A) requires a future participle in the nominative case, **(auriga) victurus**. Answer (B) requires a main verb that is in the past tense and not the present. Answer (C) requires that **auriga** be **aurigam** in order to serve as the accusative subject of the infinitive **victurum (esse)**. Remember that **auriga** is masculine.

## *Sententiae Antiquae* Answers

1.    **(D)**
      **Effici** is a complementary infinitive dependent upon **posse** in this sentence. **Posse**, the subject of which is **omnia**, is the infinitive in the indirect statement following **ait**. The sentence reads, "He says that all things can be accomplished with money."

2.    Indirect statement   **(B)**
      The underlined phrase "has been overcome" requires an infinitive that is perfect and passive, e.g., **superatum esse.** Answer (A) **superavisse** is active, and (C) **superare** and (D) **superaturum esse** are in the wrong tenses and voices (present and future active).

3.    Complementary infinitive   **(A)**
      Answer (B) is incorrect because the infinitive **amare** is active and does not correctly express "to be loved." In Answer (C) the imperative is plural, whereas the singular is required, as indicated by the 2nd person singular form **vis**. Answer (D) offers the incorrect translation in the past tense, "If you wish to have been loved, love!"

4.    Complementary infinitive  **(B)**
Answer (C) is immediately rejected because **fuisse**, "to have been" does not correctly translate the infinitive "to be," as required in the original sentence. Answers (A) and (D) have the incorrect form of the infinitive, as **videre** means "to see" and **vidisse** "to have seen." "To seem" requires the present passive infinitive, which is **videri**, "to be seen" = "to seem."

5.    Subjective infinitive  **(B)**
Cicero's famous thought contains a subjective infinitive, **nescire**, "not knowing." The sentence reads, "<u>Being unaware</u> of what happened before you were born is always to be a child." The infinitive acts as the antecedent of the pronoun **id**. Note the two subjunctive clauses within this sentence: **quid...acciderit** and **antequam natus sis**.

6.    Complementary infinitive  **(B)**
In Answer (A) **doceri** is incorrectly translated as "learned" (this is **disci**). Answer (C) "Teaching is not shameful" reverses the thought of the original sentence, "Shame cannot be taught." Answer (D) incorrectly translates the passive infinitive **doceri** as active and misreads **nasci** as the infinitive of **nanciscor**, "obtain," rather than **nascor**, "be born."

7.    Indirect statement  **(D)**
The verb "denies," which introduces the indirect statement "that he has received," is in the present tense and active voice. The corresponding form of the infinitive "he has received" is the perfect active form **accepisse**. Answer (A) **accipi** is present passive, which has a contextual meaning "he is received." Answer (B) **acceptum esse** is perfect passive, "he has been received," and (C) **accipere** is present active, "he is receiving."

8.    Complementary infinitive  **(A)**
**Dici** is the present passive infinitive of the verb **dicere**. The sentence reads, "I love (what is) true, i.e., the truth; I wish the truth <u>to be spoken</u> to me." Answer (B) "to have spoken" is the perfect active infinitive **dixisse**, (B) "to speak," the present active form **dicere**, and (D) "to have been spoken" the perfect passive form **dictum esse**. Note the substantive adjective **verum.**

9.    Subjective infinitive  **(C)**
This famous saying contains the subjective infinitive **errare** modified by the neuter adjective **humanum**, a gender required by the use of the infinitive as a noun.

## Section 1: Forms of the Subjunctive

### The Subjunctive Mood*

The subjunctive is the third of the three moods of finite verbs. Remember from your review of the indicative and imperative moods that mood indicates the function of a verb in a sentence. You have met the <u>indicative</u> mood, which indicates a statement of fact or an assertion, as well as a direct question, and the <u>imperative</u> mood, which expresses a command. The third mood, the <u>subjunctive</u>, is used to express a non-factual or hypothetical action, such as a possibility or wish, often requiring in English an auxiliary or helping verb such as *might, should,* or *would*:

Indicative: **Libertus gladiator esse <u>volebat</u>.**
*The freedman <u>wanted</u> to be a gladiator.*

Imperative: **"Noli esse gladiator!" dicebat amicus.**
*"Don't be a gladiator!" his friend said.*

Subjunctive: **Amicus mirabatur cur libertus gladiator esse <u>vellet</u>.**
*The friend wondered why the freedman <u>wished</u> to be a gladiator.*

The use of the subjunctive, such as "I wish I <u>were</u> in Rome now" (not "was"!) or "<u>Be</u> it ever so humble...," has virtually disappeared from English. In Latin, verbs found in the subjunctive mood have a variety of uses, including serving as the verb with independent meaning found in a main clause or as the verb in a variety of subordinate or dependent clauses. The subjunctive appears most commonly as the verb of a dependent clause, as in the example provided above. This is evident from the meaning of its Latin root **subiungere**, *to subjoin, subordinate.* It has been observed that the subordinating nature of the Latin language, that is, the fact that a single main idea can establish control or priority over secondary or dependent thoughts in a sentence, reflects the martial character of the Romans and the direct authority that they established over other peoples.

There are four tenses of the subjunctive, with no forms in the future or future perfect tenses. The expression of the tense of a subjunctive verb is the same as

---

*For an excellent online presentation of the subjunctive mood, see Greta Ham, "The Subjunctive in Latin: Some Basic Functions," http://www.facstaff.bucknell.edu/gretaham/Teaching/latin102/latin/subjunctive_main.html.

its indicative equivalent, e.g., the imperfect subjunctive **mitteret**, *he was sending*, translates just as the imperfect indicative **mittebat**, *he was sending*. The meaning of a subjunctive verb is dependent upon and derived from its context.

## Present Subjunctive: Active and Passive

|  | 1st Conj. | 2nd Conj. | 3rd Conj. | 4th Conj. |
|---|---|---|---|---|
| Present Active | **pugnet** | **deleat** | **mittat** | **custodiat** |
| Present Passive | **pugnetur** | **deleatur** | **mittatur** | **custodiatur** |

Notes:
- Formation: The vowel that marks the present subjunctive for the second, third, and fourth conjugations is -**a**-, e.g., **deleat, mittat**, and **custodiat**. Since the stem vowel of the first conjugation in the indicative is already -**a**-, the present subjunctive of that conjugation is formed using the vowel -**e**-, e.g., **pugnet**. "Let's <u>e</u>at c<u>a</u>v<u>ia</u>r" or "W<u>e</u> h<u>ea</u>r <u>a</u> l<u>ia</u>r" are memory devices that might help you remember the stem vowels of the four conjugations that are found in the present subjunctive.*

- The first person singular, or "I" form, of each tense in the active voice ends in **–m**, e.g., **mitta<u>m</u>, mittere<u>m</u>, miseri<u>m</u>, misisse<u>m</u>**. The remaining personal endings for all tenses of the subjunctive are the same as those of indicative verbs. The present subjunctive is most often found by itself in a main clause and also in "should . . . would" conditional clauses. For these uses, see sections of this chapter.

## Imperfect Subjunctive: Active and Passive

|  | 1st Conj. | 2nd Conj. | 3rd Conj. | 4th Conj. |
|---|---|---|---|---|
| Imperfect Active | **pugnaret** | **deleret** | **mitteret** | **custodiret** |
| Imperfect Passive | **pugnaretur** | **deleretur** | **mitteretur** | **custodiretur** |

Note:
- The imperfect subjunctive is regularly used in purpose, result, and **cum** clauses, present contrary to fact conditions, and optative subjunctive expressions with **utinam**. It is perhaps the most commonly used of subjunctive forms. For these uses, see sections of this chapter.

---

* David Pellegrino, http://latinteach.com/verbmnemonics.html.

## Perfect Subjunctive: Active and Passive

|  | 1st Conj. | 2nd Conj. | 3rd Conj. | 4th Conj. |
|---|---|---|---|---|
| Perfect Active | **pugnaverit** | **deleverit** | **miserit** | **custodiverit** |
| Perfect Passive | **pugnatus sit** | **deletus sit** | **missus sit** | **custoditus sit** |

Notes:

- The perfect tense active gives the appearance of the future perfect tense active (for which, see Chapter 14A). Note, however, that the first person singular of the perfect active subjunctive is **miserim**, whereas that of the future perfect indicative is **misero**. All other forms are the same.

- The perfect tense appears the least often of the four tenses of the subjunctive. It occurs independently as a potential subjunctive, and in conditional, result, and indirect question clauses. For these uses, see sections of this chapter.

## Pluperfect Subjunctive: Active and Passive

|  | 1st Conj. | 2nd Conj. | 3rd Conj. | 4th Conj. |
|---|---|---|---|---|
| Pluperfect Active | **pugnavisset** | **delevisset** | **misisset** | **custodivisset** |
| Pluperfect Passive | **pugnatus esset** | **deletus esset** | **missus esset** | **custoditus esset** |

Note:

- The pluperfect tense of the subjunctive appears frequently in past contrary to fact conditions, in **cum** clauses, and as an optative subjunctive expressing an unfulfilled wish in past time. For these uses, see the following chapters.

### Quick Study Synopsis of Subjunctive Verbs

|  | Active | Passive |
|---|---|---|
| Present | **mittat** | **mittatur** |
| Imperfect | **mitteret** | **mitteretur** |
| Perfect | **miserit** | **missus sit** |
| Pluperfect | **misisset** | **missus esset** |

## Synopses of Deponent Verbs in the Subjunctive

|  | 1st conj: | **hortor, hortari, hortatus sum** |
|--|--|--|
|  | 2nd conj: | **vereor, vereri, veritus sum** |
|  | 3rd conj: | **loquor, loqui, locutus sum** |
|  | 4th conj: | **orior, oriri, ortus sum** |

|  | 1st Conj. | 2nd Conj. | 3rd Conj. | 4th Conj. |
|--|--|--|--|--|
| Pres. | **hortetur** | **vereatur** | **loquatur** | **oriatur** |
| Imperf. | **hortaretur** | **vereretur** | **loqueretur** | **oriretur** |
| Perf. | **hortatus sit** | **veritus sit** | **locutus sit** | **ortus sit** |
| Pluperf. | **hortatus esset** | **veritus esset** | **locutus esset** | **ortus esset** |

## Synopses of Irregular Verbs in the Subjunctive

| **sum, esse, fui** | | **eo, ire, ii/ivi** | | **volo, velle, volui** | |
|--|--|--|--|--|--|
| **possum, posse, potui** | | **fero, ferre, tuli, latus** | | **fio, fieri, factus sum** | |
| Pres. | **sit** | **possit** | **eat** | **ferat** | **velit** | **fiat** |
| Imperf. | **esset** | **posset** | **iret** | **ferret** | **vellet** | **fieret** |
| Perf. | **fuerit** | **potuerit** | **ierit** **iverit** | **tulerit** | **voluerit** | **factus sit** |
| Pluperf. | **fuisset** | **potuisset** | **isset** **ivisset** | **tulisset** | **voluisset** | **factus esset** |

Notes:

- Be reminded that the perfect stem of the verb **ire** is found variously as **i-** and **iv-**. Thus, **isset** and **ivisset** are both correct.

- In addition to the passive forms of **fieri**, given above, the verb **ferre** contains passive forms of the subjunctive, e.g., present tense, **feratur**, imperfect tense, **ferretur**, perfect tense, **latus sit,** and pluperfect tense, **latus esset**.

# Tips on Mastering Forms of the Subjunctive

The present and perfect subjunctive forms are sometimes mistaken for their present, future, and future perfect indicative counterparts, e.g., the present subjunctive **mittat** can be mistaken for the present or future indicative, **mittit** or **mittet.** You should assume that a verb form containing the ending vowel **–a–** is in the present subjunctive, since this vowel characterizes the present subjunctive of three conjugations (second, third, and fourth), whereas it characterizes the indicative of only one, the first. Therefore, such a verb form has a much greater chance of being subjunctive than indicative.

Use the context to distinguish the perfect subjunctive **miserit** from the future perfect indicative form **miserit**. (Remember, however, that the first person singular of the perfect subjunctive is **-erim**, e.g, **miserim**, whereas the future perfect indicative form is **−ero**, e.g., **misero**.) To differentiate between ambiguous forms, know principal parts and use contextual clues. As was mentioned in the previous chapter on infinitives, the imperfect and pluperfect tenses of the subjunctive, both active and passive, are formed from the present and perfect infinitives. Avoid confusing forms of the subjunctive with those of the infinitive.

Remember that a verb in the subjunctive mood can be found both independently as a main verb and in a clause that is dependent upon the main verb.

The tenses of the subjunctive are rendered in the same manner as those of the indicative. In a clause, the subjunctive verb depends upon the tense of the main verb for its meaning.

Subjunctive verbs, whether independent or dependent, express non-factual or hypothetical situations. Use words such as *can, could, may, might, should,* or *would* when translating.

# Section 2: The Subjunctive Used Independently

A subjunctive verb may be found independently in a sentence, i.e., by itself in a main clause, as opposed to serving as the verb in a dependent clause:

Independent (main clause):   **Omnes gladiatores fortiter <u>pugnent</u>!**
*<u>Let</u> all gladiators <u>fight</u> bravely!*

Dependent (subordinate clause): **Gladiatores pugnant <u>ut vivant</u>.**
*Gladiators fight <u>in order to live</u>.*

The presentation in this chapter is limited to independent uses of the subjunctive, which include <u>polite command</u> and encouragement (jussive and hortatory), <u>questions</u> in which the speaker or writer expresses doubt or disbelief by "thinking aloud" (deliberative), <u>wishes</u> that cannot or may not be fulfilled (optative), and the <u>possibility</u> that something may happen or might have happened (potential). The actions of such verbs in the subjunctive, as opposed to those in the indicative, may not actually take place or have taken place and are therefore to be considered hypothetical. English words such as *can, could, may, might, should,* and *would* best express the meaning of the various uses of the independent subjunctive. You should concentrate on determining the suitable English meaning from context. For example, **Ne pugnent** has meanings such as, *Let them not fight, If only they wouldn't fight,* or *They should not fight,* depending upon the circumstances. For the forms of the independent subjunctive, which are found most often in the present tense, see section 1 of this chapter.

## Uses of the Independent Subjunctive

### Jussive and hortatory subjunctives

Perhaps the most common uses of the independent subjunctive are the jussive and the hortatory.

> Jussive: **"Cedant togae armis!" exclamabant gladiatores.**
> *"Let the togas yield to arms!" yelled the gladiators.*

> Hortatory: **Ne pugnemus, mi Maxime, atque vivamus.**
> *Let us not fight, my Maximus, and let us live.*

| Descriptive Label | Function | Tense Used | Negative |
|---|---|---|---|
| **Jussive (iubere/ jubere**, *order*) | polite command | present (*Let him/them...*) | **ne** |
| **Hortatory (hortari,** *urge*) | encouragement | present (*Let us...*) | **ne** |

Notes:

- Because the uses and meanings of the jussive and hortatory are substantially identical (distinguished by whether the first or third person is being addressed), the forms are often combined into a single category and translated "*Let....*" You may enjoy remembering this usage as the "Caesar salad" subjunctive, i.e., *Lettuce do this, lettuce do that.**

- For an example of the jussive subjunctive, keep in mind the well-known saying **Caveat emptor**, *Let the buyer beware,* i.e., be an informed consumer.

- When the second person (*you*) is required in the expression of a command, Latin prefers the imperative mood of the verb, e.g., **Cape consilium in arena!** *(You) make your plan in the arena!***

- The perfect tense of the subjunctive is sometimes used to express a negative command or prohibition, e.g., **Ne ceperis consilium in arena**, *Don't make your plan in the arena*. This is an alternative to the more common **noli/ nolite** + infinitive (for which, see Chapter 15).

---

* From a roundtable sharing discussion, Oklahoma Classics Association workshop, 1996.

** The example sentences in this section derive from Roman *sententiae*: **Cedant arma togae**, *Let arms yield to the toga* (Cicero), i.e., the military should be subordinate to the government; **Vivamus, mea Lesbia, atque amemus**, *Let us live, my Lesbia, and let us love* (Catullus); **Gladiator in arena consilium capit**, *The gladiator makes his plan in the arena* (Seneca), i.e., the gladiator must be able to think on his feet and adjust to circumstances.

## Deliberative subjunctive

Unlike the direct question, which is found with the indicative mood (see Chapter 14), the deliberative question with the subjunctive is expressed as a question to oneself, with no answer expected. This type of question can imply doubt, indignation, surprise, or confusion, e.g.,

**Androcles leoni se oppositurus erat. "Quid faciam?" gemuit.**
*Androcles was about to face the lion. "What should I do?" he groaned.*

| Descriptive Label | Function | Tenses Used | Negative |
|---|---|---|---|
| **Deliberative** (**deliberare**, *consider*) | self-question | present (*Am I to? Should I?*) imperfect (*Was I to?*) | **non** |

Note:

- The difference between a direct question with the indicative and a deliberative question is that the former expresses a fact and the latter a non-fact:

    Direct question:      **Quod consilium in arena capis?**
    *What plan are you making in the arena?*

    Deliberative question:      **Quod consilium in arena capias?**
    *What plan should you make in the arena?*

## Optative subjunctive

The optative subjunctive expresses a wish felt or spoken by the speaker or writer. It is found either independently or as a clause, and most often with the particle **utinam** (negative **utinam ne**), which has the meanings *if only, would that, I wish (that), may*. A clause introduced by **utinam** usually expresses a wish incapable of fulfilment, or a regret. It is most often found with the imperfect or pluperfect tense:

Imperfect tense:      **Lanista cogitabat, "Utinam meliores gladiatores haberem."**
*The trainer was thinking, "I wish that I had better gladiators (but I do not)" or "I regret that I do not have...".*

Pluperfect tense:      **Utinam naumachiam in amphitheatro vidissemus.**
*If only we had seen a sea battle in the amphitheater (but we did not) or "I regret that we did not see...".*

| Descriptive Label | Function | Tenses used | Negative |
|---|---|---|---|
| **Optative** (**optare**, *choose*) | wish | present (*if only, may, hope, possible future*) imperfect (*if only...were, unaccomplished present*) pluperfect (*if only...had, unaccomplished past*) | **ne** |

Notes:

- The present tense is used when the wish is conceived of as possibly coming true in the future:

  **Utinam <u>sis</u> victor, Anxi.**
  > *If only <u>you would be</u> the victor, Anxius* or
  >
  > *<u>May you be</u> the victor, Anxius (and you very well may be).*

- For testing purposes, the optative subjunctive is usually found with **utinam**. However, the optative may also appear independently of this particle when its meaning has the effect of a jussive/hortatory or a conditional, as in a prayer, e.g.,

  **Di me <u>adiuvent</u>.**
  > *<u>May</u> the gods <u>help</u> me* or *If only the gods would help me.*

- The imperfect tense is used when the wish is not capable of fulfillment now:

  **Utinam victor <u>esses</u>, Anxi.**
  > *If only <u>you were</u> (or <u>might be</u>) the victor, Anxius (but you aren't).*

- The pluperfect tense is used when the wish was not capable of fulfillment in the past:

  **Utinam victor <u>fuisses</u>, Anxi.**
  > *If only <u>you had been</u> the victor, Anxius (but you weren't).*

## Potential subjunctive

The potential subjunctive is an independent subjunctive that expresses an action as possible or conceivable in past, present, or future time. It is translated as *can, could, may, might, should,* or *would* in the present (occasionally the perfect) tense when referring to present or future time and *could have, might have,* or *would have* in the imperfect tense when referring to past time.

Present or Future time:   **Spartacus Romanos <u>superet</u>.**
> *Spartacus <u>may defeat</u> the Romans (and there is the possibility that he might).*

Past time:   **Nemo hoc <u>crederet</u>.**
> *No one <u>would have believed</u> this (but there is the possibility that they might have).*

| Descriptive Label | Function | Tenses used | Negative |
|---|---|---|---|
| **Potential (posse,** *be able***)** | possibility | present (*may, could, would, should,* present or future) <br> imperfect (*might have, could have, would have,* past) | **non** |

## Quick Study of Independent Subjunctives

| Present Time | | | |
|---|---|---|---|
| **Romae vivam.** | *Let me live in Rome.* | hortatory | exhortation |
| **(Utinam) Romae vivam.** | *May I live in Rome.* | optative | wish |
| | *I wish I could live in Rome.* | optative | wish |
| | *If only I might live in Rome.* | optative | wish |
| **Romam vivam.** | *I could live in Rome.* | potential | possibility |
| | *I may* or *might live in Rome.* | potential | possibility |
| **Romae vivat.** | *Let him live in Rome.* | jussive | polite command |
| **Vivamne Romae?** | *Should I live in Rome?* | deliberative | self question |
| Past Time | | | |
| **Viveremne Romae?** | *Was I to live in Rome?* | deliberative | self question |
| **Utinam Romae viverem.** | *If only I were to live in Rome.* | optative | wish |
| **Utinam Romae vixissem.** | *If only I had lived in Rome.* | optative | wish |
| **Romae viverem.** | *I might have/could have/ would have lived in Rome.* | potential | possibility |

# Tips on Translating Independent Subjunctives

- The present tense is the tense most often found in the various uses of the independent subjunctive.
- When in the process of identifying and translating a subjunctive verb as independent, look carefully at the environment of the verb. When translating, observe the context to help you to make an "educated guess" about whether or not the verb is subjunctive. For instance, observe this sentence from Horace:

  **Non omnis <u>moriar</u>, multaque pars mei vitabit Libitinam.**
  *I will not perish altogether, and indeed a great part of me will elude Libitina (goddess of the dead.)*

- The verb **moriar** could mean either *I will die* (future indicative) or *Let me die* (present subjunctive). The context of this verb, which includes the more obvious future form **vitabit**, will help you to determine that the best meaning is *I will die*. (Of course, you've probably already decided this since you know that **non** negates **moriar** here, whereas **moriar** as a hortatory subjunctive would be negated by **ne**!)

- Translation of the present subjunctive can be confusing, because of the variety of its functions (exhortation, wish, possibility, etc.) Similar blurring of intent or tone has taken place in English, e.g., "I would be careful" could be conceived of as advice (hortatory), a wish (optative), the main clause of a condition ("if I were you"), etc. It is important to let the context of the sentence dictate how you express the meaning of the present subjunctive. Use words such as *can, could, may, might, should,* and *would,* as well as *let*.

## Practice Questions

1. May she rest in peace.
   - (A) Requiescit
   - (B) Requiescens
   - (C) Requiesce
   - (D) Requiescat

2. Sit tibi terra levis. (= S.T.T.L., often inscribed on Roman tombstones.)
   - (A) The earth is gentle upon you.
   - (B) Be gentle upon the earth.
   - (C) You are resting gently in the earth.
   - (D) May the earth be gentle upon you.

3. Palmam qui meruit, ferat. (Lord Nelson)
   - (A) Whoever deserves the palm will display it.
   - (B) He who has earned the palm, let him display it.
   - (C) He is displaying the palm which he earned.
   - (D) Whoever wants the palm should display it.

4. Would that we had been less desirous of life. (Cicero)
   - (A) fuissemus
   - (B) essemus
   - (C) fueramus
   - (D) fuerimus

5. Sit. (The Beatles)
   - (A) It is.
   - (B) He can.
   - (C) Let it be.
   - (D) Would that it were.

6. Quid agam? (Cicero)
   - (A) What should I do?
   - (B) What was I to do?
   - (C) What have I done?
   - (D) What had I done?

7. <u>Dum inter homines sumus, colamus humanitatem</u>. (Seneca)

    (A) While we are among men, let us cherish humanity.

    (B) We must cherish humanity while we are among men.

    (C) We do cherish humanity as long as we are among men.

    (D) While we were among men, we should have cherished humanity.

8. <u>Let us hope</u> for what we want, but <u>let us endure</u> whatever happens. (Cicero)

    (A) Speramus...ferimus          (C) Speramus...feramus

    (B) Speremus...feremus          (D) Speremus...feramus

9. Utinam populus Romanus unam cervicem . . . ! (Suetonius, quoting Caligula)

    (A) habet                       (C) haberet

    (B) habuerat                    (D) habebat

10. Quod sentimus loquamur; quod loquimur sentiamus. (Seneca)

    If we were to negate the subjunctive verbs in this sentence, we
    would use the word . . . .

    (A) non                         (C) nihil

    (B) ne                          (D) nonne

11. Utinam ratio <u>duxisset</u>, non fortuna. (*pace* Livy)

    (A) might guide                 (C) had guided

    (B) would guide                 (D) was guiding

12. <u>Utinam liberorum nostrorum mores non ipsi perderemus</u>. (Quintilian)

    (A) Would that we might not ruin our children's character.

    (B) I wish that we will not ruin our children's character.

    (C) If only we had not ruined our children's character.

    (D) We were not ruining our children's character.

13. <u>Let us rejoice</u>, therefore, while we are young! (Medieval song)

    (A) Gaudemus                    (C) Gaudete

    (B) Gaudebimus                  (D) Gaudeamus

14. Which word is <u>not</u> appropriate for translating the independent subjunctive?

    (A) should                      (C) may

    (B) might                       (D) will

**Stumper:** Fortunam citius <u>invenias</u> quam retineas. (Publilius Syrus)

    (A)  you will find             (C)  you may find

    (B)  you find                 (D)  you might have found

## Answers

1.    Jussive  **(D)**
     The famous epitaph R.I.P., **Requiescat in pace**, is an example of the jussive subjunctive in the present tense. Answer (A) **Requiescit** is in the present indicative form, (B) **Requiescens** is the present participle, and (C) **Requiesce** the singular form of the present imperative.

2.    Jussive  **(D)**
     The verb **sit** in this epitaph is also a jussive subjunctive. Answer (A) requires a verb that is present indicative and (B) a present imperative. Answer (C) also requires a present indicative and mistranslates the other words in the epitaph.

3.    Jussive  **(B)**
     Since **ferat** is a form of the present subjunctive, Answer (B) "...let him display it" is the best translation. Answer (A) requires the future tense **feret** and (C) the present tense **fert**. Answer (D) translates **meruit** incorrectly.

4.    Optative  **(A)**
     "Would that" introduces the subjunctive of a wish, therefore, "we had been" must be a subjunctive form in the pluperfect tense. This is **fuissemus**. Answer (B) **essemus** is in the wrong tense (imperfect), (C) **fueramus** is in the correct tense (pluperfect) but wrong mood (indicative), and (D) **fuerimus** is in the wrong tense and mood (future perfect indicative, "we will have been") or simply the incorrect tense (perfect subjunctive, "we have been").

5.    Jussive  **(C)**
     "Let it be" is an obvious answer if you're a Beatles' fan! Answers (A) and (B) call for the indicative mood and (D) is optative in past time.

6.    Deliberative  **(A)**
     **Quid agam**? is a classic example of the use of the subjunctive mood in a deliberative question. The real question here is, "What is the tense of the verb **agam**?" Well, the answer is the present tense, leading to Answer (A) "What <u>am I to do</u>?" Answers (B) "What was I to do," (C) "What have I done," and (D) "What had I done," all have incorrect verb tenses.

7.    Hortatory  **(A)**
     In this sentence, you should focus your thinking on the mood and tense of the main verb **colamus**. Since the verb **colo, colere** belongs to the third conjugation, this form is a hortatory subjunctive in the present tense, i.e., "Let us cherish."

Answer (B) "We must cherish (humanity)" requires a construction that expresses necessity or obligation, e.g., **(humanitas) nobis colenda est**, (C) "We do cherish," is **colimus** and (D) "We should have cherished" is **coluerimus**.

8. Hortatory **(D)**

Determining the correct answer to this question requires familiarity with the principal parts or forms of the regular verb **spero, sperare** and the irregular verb **fero, ferre**. (These may be deduced from the answers provided.) **Sperare** belongs to the first conjugation, so Answers (A) and (C) are incorrect, since **speramus** is in the present indicative and the hortatory or present subjunctive is required by the English meaning. Answer (B) **feremus** is in the future tense, leaving **feramus** as the correct answer.

9. Optative **(C)**

The appearance of the particle **utinam** defines this sentence as a wish, which requires a subjunctive verb. Since **haberet** is the only subjunctive appearing among the choices, it is the correct answer. Answer (A) is present indicative, (B) pluperfect indicative, and (D) imperfect indicative. In this wish, Caligula wanted the people to have one head so he could decapitate them all at once.

10. Hortatory **(B)**

The hortatory subjunctive forms **loquamur** and **sentiamus** require the negative **ne**. Answers (C) and (D) do not require the subjunctive and Answer (B), when found with the subjunctive, is most commonly used in the context of the result clause, i.e., **ut non**.

11. Optative **(C)**

The subjunctive verb **duxisset** in this wish is in the pluperfect tense, hence, "had guided" is the correct response. (Note that all forms in the answers appear in the active voice.) Answers (A) "might guide" and (B) "would guide" are in the present tense (**ducat**) while (D) "was guiding" is in the imperfect tense (**duceret**).

12. Optative **(A)**

The tense of the verb **perderemus** in this wish introduced by **utinam** is imperfect, which nullifies the translations in Answers (B) and (C). These contain verbs in the future and pluperfect tenses, respectively. Answer (D) is not possible because the translation is phrased as a (factual) assertion, not a wish, therefore requiring the indicative mood.

13. Hortatory **(D)**

This famous song, often sung or played at graduations, is an encouragement to celebrate. Therefore, the hortatory subjunctive **Gaudeamus** "Let us rejoice" is correct. Answer (A) **Gaudemus** "We are rejoicing" is in the present indicative, (B) **Gaudebimus** "We shall rejoice" is in the future indicative, and (C) **Gaudete** "Rejoice!" is a plural imperative.

14. **(D)**
The word "will" is only used in the indicative mood, because it implies a statement that is going to come true. The words "should," "might," and "may" are all used to express meanings that are only potentially true, and are thus subjunctive.

**Stumper:** Potential **(C)**
This sentence, which reads, "You <u>may come upon</u> fortune sooner than (you may) hold onto it, "contains two potential subjunctives, **invenias** and **retineas**, expressing possibilities capable of realization. Answers (A) and (B) are in the future and present tenses of the indicative, respectively, and as such make assertions of fact, rather than possibility. Answer (D) "you might have found" translates a potential subjunctive in the imperfect tense (**invenires**), rather than the present (**invenias**), and expresses past time.

# Section 3: Conditional Sentences

Conditional, or "if-then," sentences in Latin are complex in that they really express two ideas, one in a main or independent clause, the other in a subordinate or dependent clause, e.g., "If you understand this, then you understand conditional sentences." A conditional sentence contains a conditional clause, or condition, which consists of the *if*-clause introduced by **si** (or its negative equivalent **nisi**, *if....not, unless*) and ending with a verb. In the conditional sentence given above, the conditional clause is "If you understand this." The *then*-clause serves as the main or independent clause, also known as the conclusion. In the sentence above, the main clause is "then you understand conditional sentences." The *if*-clause is traditionally known as the <u>protasis</u> (Greek for "premise"), and the *then*-clause as the <u>apodosis</u> (Greek for "outcome"). Note that the word "then" is not necessarily expressed in the English translation.

condition/subordinate or dependent clause/protasis
**[Si Lesbia Catullum amabit], ipse laetus erit.**
conclusion/main or independent clause/apodosis

*[If Lesbia will love / loves Catullus], (then) he will be happy.*

The clauses in conditional sentences may be found with verbs in either the indicative or the subjunctive mood, and in any tense. There are three main types of conditional sentences, which are classified as simple, future less vivid or "should... would," and contrary to fact. Simple conditionals have the indicative in both clauses, the future less vivid conditional has the present subjunctive in both clauses, and contrary to fact conditionals have a past tense of the subjunctive in both clauses. In this chapter you will read about the Roman poet Catullus, who had a love affair with a woman to whom he gave the name "Lesbia."

# Conditionals with the Indicative Mood

## Simple Conditional Sentences

This type of conditional sentence, also known as a "factual" or "open" condition, makes a simple statement. Simple conditionals have verbs in the <u>indicative mood in both clauses</u>. Use of the indicative implies that the condition is happening or is likely to happen. Any tense may be used. If the tense used is future or future perfect in the *if*-clause and future in the *then*-clause, then the sentence is classified as a <u>future more vivid conditional</u>. Here are some examples:

Simple Conditions:

> **Si Lesbia Catullum <u>amat</u>, ipse laetus <u>est</u>.**
> *If Lesbia <u>loves</u> Catullus (and very possibly she does), (then) <u>he is</u> happy.*

> **Si Lesbia <u>amabat</u> Catullum, ipse laetus <u>erat</u>.**
> *If Lesbia <u>loved</u> Catullus (and very possibly she did), <u>he was</u> happy.*

Future More Vivid Conditions:

> **Si Lesbia Catullum <u>amabit</u>, ipse laetus <u>erit</u>.**
> *If Lesbia <u>will love</u> Catullus, (and very possibly she will), <u>he will be</u> happy.*

> **Si Lesbia Catullum <u>amaverit</u>, ipse laetus <u>erit</u>.**
> *If Lesbia <u>will have loved</u> Catullus (and very possibly she will have), <u>he will be</u> happy.*

Note:

- In simple and future more vivid conditional clauses, it is better to translate verbs in the future and future perfect tenses as present tenses in English, e.g.,

> **Si Lesbia Catullum <u>amaverit</u>, ipse laetus erit.**
> *If Lesbia <u>loves</u>, lit., will have loved, Catullus, he will be happy.*

# Conditionals with the Subjunctive Mood

## Future Less Vivid ("should . . . would") Conditional Sentences

This type of conditional, sometimes called "ideal," expresses a remote future possibility, i.e., a condition that may possibly (but improbably) be true or realized in the future. These appear with the <u>present subjunctive in both clauses</u> and may be translated traditionally, if somewhat archaically, by "should" in the *if*-clause and "would" in the *then*-clause, e.g.,

**Si Lesbia Catullum <u>amet</u>, ipse laetus <u>sit</u>**.
*If Lesbia <u>should love</u> Catullus (and it is possible, but unlikely, that she does), <u>he would be</u> happy.*

Note:

- This type of conditional sentence is less frequent than the other two types.

## Contrary to Fact (or Contrafactual) Conditional Sentences

Such conditionals express conditions and conclusions that could not possibly happen or be true. The verbs of these conditionals, which are also known as "imaginary" or "unreal," are both subjunctive. In present time, or <u>present contrary to fact</u>, the <u>imperfect subjunctive</u> appears in both clauses; in past time, or <u>past contrary to fact</u>, Latin uses the <u>pluperfect subjunctive</u> in both clauses:

**Si Lesbia Catullum <u>amaret</u>, ipse laetus <u>esset</u>.**
*If Lesbia <u>were to love</u> Catullus (but she does not), <u>he would be</u> happy (but he is not).*

**Si Lesbia Catullum <u>amavisset</u>, ipse laetus <u>fuisset</u>.**
*If Lesbia <u>had loved</u> Catullus (but she did not), he <u>would have been</u> happy (but he was not).*

## Mixed Conditions

The tenses or moods of both clauses in a conditional sentence need not be the same. Mixed conditionals may be found containing clauses 1) with different tenses of the subjunctive, 2) with an indicative paired with an independent subjunctive, 3) with a subjunctive *if*-clause paired with an imperative, or with various other combinations. The meaning of such sentences is usually apparent from the sense implied by the context, e.g.,

Mixed tenses: **<u>Essetne Catullus laetus, si Lesbia eum amavisset</u>?**
*<u>Would Catullus be</u> happy (now), if Lesbia <u>had loved</u> him (previously)?*

Mixed moods: **Si Lesbia Catullum <u>amat</u>, <u>gaudeamus</u>.**
*If Lesbia <u>does love</u> Catullus, <u>let us be delighted</u>.*

Mixed moods: **Si <u>putatis</u> Lesbiam Catullum amare, <u>gaudete</u>!**
*If <u>you think</u> that Lesbia does love Catullus, <u>be glad</u>!*

## Quick Study of Conditional Sentences

| Type | Verbs in Clauses | Meanings of Verbs Dependent clause | Main clause |
|---|---|---|---|
| Simple (likely to happen) | indicative | *If he does..., then he is....* *If he did,..., then he was....* | |
| Future more vivid (likely to happen) | future, future perfect indicative | *If he will (have)..., then he will....* (Best translated in the present) | |
| Future less vivid (possible, but unlikely) | present subjunctive | *If he should..., then he would...* | |
| Present contrary to fact (impossible or unreal) | imperfect subjunctive | *If he were to..., then he would....* | |
| Past contrary to fact (impossible or unreal) | pluperfect subjunctive | *If he had..., then he would have....* | |

# Tips on Translating Conditional Sentences

- Conditional sentences present few problems in translation because they are very similar to English.

- The conclusion or *then*-clause may precede the condition or *if*-clause in the word order of a Latin sentence for emphasis or other considerations. Always read through in Latin the entirety of a Latin sentence before determining its meaning.

- In the *if*-clause or condition, translate future and future perfect tenses in the present tense.

- Note that all three types of conditional sentences in Latin reveal something about the truth of what is being said or written, i.e., simple conditions reveal that it is likely that the condition is true, future less vivid conditions reveal the possibility that the condition may be true, and contrary to fact conditions express that it is impossible that the condition is true.

# Practice Questions on Conditional Sentences

*Catullus is to be imagined as speaking in many of these sentences.**

1. <u>Si vales, Lesbia, gaudeo</u>.
   - (A) If you are well, Lesbia, I am happy.
   - (B) If you should be well, Lesbia, then I would be happy.
   - (C) If you were well, Lesbia, then I would be happy.
   - (D) If you will be well, Lesbia, then I am happy.

2. Si pulchram Lesbiam vidisses, certe eam <u>amavisses</u>.
   - (A) you would love
   - (B) you had loved
   - (C) you would have loved
   - (D) you were loving

3. O di, <u>si vitam puriter agam</u>, <u>eripiatis</u> hanc pestem perniciemque mihi.
   - (A) If I will lead an upright life, you will take away . . . .
   - (B) If I should lead an upright life, you would take away . . . .
   - (C) If I were to lead an upright life, you would take away . . . .
   - (D) If I am leading an upright life, you should take away . . . .

4. <u>Si cum passere ludere possem</u>, tristes curas animi levarem.
   - (A) If I can play with the sparrow
   - (B) If I am able to play with the sparrow
   - (C) If I were able to play with the sparrow
   - (D) If I should be able to play with the sparrow

5. Si Lesbiam in matrimonium ducere <u>velim</u>, dicatne "Ita vero"?
   - (A) should wish
   - (B) will wish
   - (C) am wishing
   - (D) was wishing

6. <u>Mortuus essem, nisi mea puella mihi mille basia daret</u>.
   - (A) I would die if I gave my girl a thousand kisses.
   - (B) Unless I were to give my girl a thousand kisses, I would die.
   - (C) If I would not have given my girl a thousand kisses, I would die.
   - (D) I would die unless my girl were to give me a thousand kisses.

---

*Several answers in this practice exercise are derived directly from the poems of Catullus: question 3, Poem 76.19-20; question 4, Poem 2.9-10; question 6, Poems 5 and 7; question 7, Poem 77.3-4; and question 10, Poem 13.4-7.

7. <u>Si meam Lesbiam ames, Rufe, misero mihi intestina eripias</u>. This sentence tells us that

   (A) There is no information as to whether or not Rufus loves Lesbia.

   (B) It is possible, but unlikely, that Rufus loves Lesbia.

   (C) Rufus could not, in any way, love Lesbia.

   (D) It is a fact that Rufus loves Lesbia.

8. Sepulcrum mei fratris visam, <u>si ego ipse ad Bithyniam iero</u>.

   (A) if I go to Bithynia            (C) if I would have gone to Bithynia

   (B) if I had gone to Bithynia      (D) if I were going to Bithynia

9. Si navis mihi non fuisset, ad Sirmionem navigare non. . . . .

   (A) potero              (C) potuissem

   (B) possem              (D) poteram

10. Si candidam puellam et vinum <u>attuleris</u>, mi Fabulle, bene cenabis.

    Which of the following is <u>not</u> an acceptable translation of <u>attuleris</u>?

    (A) you will have brought      (C) you will bring

    (B) you bring                  (D) you brought

## Sententiae Antiquae

1. Discere <u>si quaeris</u>, doce. Sic ipse doceris. (Medieval)

   (A) if you will seek            (C) if you will be sought

   (B) if you are sought           (D) if you seek

2. If anyone <u>should violate</u> this, I wish that he would live for a long time in pain. (From a tombstone)

   (A) violaverit              (C) violavisset

   (B) violaverat              (D) violabat

3. <u>Si ea defendes quae ipse recta esse senties</u>. (Cicero)

   (A) If only you will stand by what you feel to be correct.

   (B) If only you should stand by what you would feel to be correct.

   (C) If only you had stood by what you would have felt to be correct.

   (D) If only you were standing by what you saw to be correct.

4. The whole world <u>would perish</u> if compassion <u>were</u> not <u>to end</u> bad feelings. (Seneca the Elder)

   (A) pereat . . . finiat        (C) periret . . . finiret

   (B) periet . . . finiet        (D) perebat . . . finiebat

5. Salus omnium una nocte amissa esset, nisi Catilina captus esset. (Cicero) The tense and voice of the subjunctive verbs in this sentence are

   (A) imperfect passive        (C) pluperfect passive

   (B) imperfect active        (D) present passive

6. Minus saepe erres, <u>si scias quid nescias</u>. (Publilius Syrus)

   (A) If you knew what you did not know

   (B) If you know what you did not know

   (C) If you should know what you do not know

   (D) If you knew what you do not know

**Stumper:** Which of the following conditional sentences contains a future more vivid condition?

   (A) Dices "heu" si te in speculo videris. (Horace)

   (B) Si tu eo die fuisses, te certo vidissem. (Cicero)

   (C) Laus nova nisi oritur, etiam vetus amittitur. (Publilius Syrus)

   (D) Si quietem mavis, duc uxorem parem. (Quintilian)

# Answers

1. Simple   **(A)**
   This is a simple conditional sentence with the indicative, stating as a fact that if Lesbia is well, then Catullus is happy. Answer (B) "If you should be well" contains a translation that requires a "should...would" condition, (C) "If you were well" a present contrary to fact condition, and (D) "If you will be well" a future more vivid condition with the future tense. This sentence greets Lesbia as if in a letter or note.

2. Past contrary to fact   **(C)**
   This condition is revealed by the appearance of the pluperfect subjunctive form **amavisses**. The sentence reads, "If you had seen the gorgeous Lesbia, <u>you would have loved</u> her." Answer (A) requires the imperfect subjunctive form **amares** in a present contrary to fact condition. Answer (B) "you had loved," although in the proper tense, is a statement requiring the indicative mood, i.e., **amaveras**, as is (D) "you were loving," i.e., **amabas**.

3. Future less vivid   **(B)**
   That this sentence is a "should...would" conditional is indicated by the present subjunctive form **eripiatis**. The verb **agam** could, of course, be a form of the future indicative, but this possibility is negated by the appearance of **eripiatis**. This sentence, taken from Catullus Poem 76, reads, "O gods, <u>if I should lead an upright life, you would snatch away</u> from me this plague and pestilence" (i.e., Lesbia). Answers (A) and (D) require the indicative mood. Answer (C) is phrased as a

present contrary to fact clause, "If I were to lead...," which would require a verb in the imperfect subjunctive, i.e., **agerem**.

4.   Present contrary to fact   **(C)**

The underlined clause is part of a present contrary to fact conditional sentence. The appearance of the verb **possem** in the imperfect tense of the subjunctive leads to the translation "If I were able." Answers (A) and (B) express the same thing in different ways, both requiring the indicative, since they are assertions. Answer (D) "If I should be able..." translates a future less vivid clause, which is **Si ... possim**. This sentence, from Catullus Poem 2, reads, "If I were able to (could) play with the songbird, I would relieve the sad cares of my heart."

5.   Future less vivid   **(A)**

This condition sentence contains a "should...would" condition, requiring the present subjunctive **(velim)** in the protasis, or *if*-clause, and in the apodosis, or *then*-clause **(dicat)**. Answer (B) "will" requires the future indicative **(volam)**, (C) the present indicative **(volo)**, and (D) the imperfect indicative or subjunctive **(volebat** or **vellet)**.

6.   Present contrary to fact   **(D)**

This sentence is a present contrary to fact condition, containing the verbs **essem** and **darem**, both in the imperfect tense. Unless Lesbia were to give Catullus a thousand kisses (which she will not), he would die (but he will not). Answer (A) does not translate **nisi** correctly, (B) turns the thought around and has Catullus giving Lesbia the kisses, and (C) translates the tense of the verb **darem** incorrectly as "would have given."

7.   Future less vivid   **(B)**

This is a "should...would" conditional sentence, expressing the fact that it is possible, but unlikely, that if Rufus should love Lesbia, he would tear out Catullus' guts. Answer (C) requires a contrary to fact condition, which is impossible, given the present tenses of the verbs, and (D) requires that the Latin express a simple factual condition, but the verbs are subjunctive.

8.   Future more vivid   **(A)**

This sentence reads, "If Catullus goes to Bithynia, he will visit his brother's grave." The use of the future and future perfect tenses **visam** and **iero** reveal this sentence to be a future more vivid conditional. Remember that in English the present tense may be used to express future time in such a context. Answers (B) and (D) are past contrary to fact conditions requiring the pluperfect subjunctive and (C) is a present contrary to fact condition, which requires the imperfect subjunctive. The verb **ierit** in the *if*-clause is a future perfect indicative form (or a perfect subjunctive, which doesn't fit the context).

9.   Past contrary to fact   **(C)**

This sentence reads, "If I had not had a ship, I would not have been able to sail to Sirmio." This is a past contrary to fact condition, which requires the pluperfect subjunctive in both the protasis and apodosis of the sentence. Answer (A) **potero** is future indicative, (B) **possem** is imperfect subjunctive, and (D) **poteram** imperfect indicative.

10.  Future more vivid   **(D)**
     The future indicative verb form **cenabis** reveals that **attuleris** is in the future perfect tense in a sentence that expresses a future more vivid condition. As a past tense, Answer (D) "you brought" is the only translation that does not have an acceptable meaning of the future perfect tense. (See Segment A.)

## *Sententiae Antiquae* Answers

1.  Simple   **(D)**
    This simple conditional sentence reads, "<u>If you seek</u> to learn, teach. And so you yourself are taught." The verb **quaeris** is present active indicative. Answer (A) requires the future tense (**quaeres**), (B) the present passive (**quaereris**), and (C) the future passive (**quaēreris**).

2.  Future less vivid   **(A)**
    The perfect subjunctive may appear in "should...would" conditions such as this. The non-factual nature of the statement removes Answers (B) and (D), which are indicative, from consideration. Answer (C) **violavisset**, which is in the pluperfect tense, cannot produce the translation "should violate," which expresses a meaning that derives from the present system of verbs.

3.  Future more vivid   **(A)**
    This sentence expresses the future more vivid condition **Si . . . defendes**, "If you (will) defend...," **senties**, "(then) you will feel." The translation in Answer (B) "If you should stand" requires a "should...would" condition with the present subjunctive, (C) "If you had stood" requires a past contrary to fact condition with the pluperfect subjunctive, and (D) "If you were standing," a present contrary to fact condition with the imperfect subjunctive.

4.  Present contrary to fact   **(C)**
    Seneca's thought expresses a contrary to fact condition in present time, as the imperfect subjunctive is suggested by the translation "were to end." Thus, the forms **periret** and **finiret** are correct. Answer (A) contains verbs in the present subjunctive, (B) in the future indicative, and (D) in the imperfect indicative, none of which fit the sense required.

5.  Past contrary to fact   **(C)**
    **Amissa esset** and **captus esset** are forms of the pluperfect passive subjunctive in a past contrary to fact conditional sentence. The sentence reads, "The safety of everyone <u>would have been lost</u> in a single night, if Catiline <u>had</u> not <u>been captured</u>."

6.    Future less vivid    **(C)**

This sentence reads, "You would be wrong less often, <u>if you (should) know (that) which you do not know</u>." The main clause of this future less vivid condition contains the indirect question **quid nescias**. The translations in Answers (A) and (D) contain verbs in the past tense, which the original sentence does not contain. The meaning of the sentence in Answer (B) is rendered by the indicative in a simple condition.

**Stumper:    (A)**

The correct answer reads, "You will say 'Ugh!' if you see yourself in the mirror." This sentence contains verbs in the future (**Dices**) and future perfect (**videris**) tenses. Answer (B) reads, "If you had been (there) on that day, I surely would have seen you," a past contrary to fact condition. Answer (B) reads, "Unless brand new praise is forthcoming, even the previous (praise) is lost," a simple condition. Answer (D) "If you prefer peace, marry a wife of equal (station)" is another simple condition with the indicative.

# Section 4: Subordinate Clauses With *Ut*

## Subordinate Clauses With the Subjunctive

As you have been reminded in the past two chapters, subjunctive verbs are found both independently in main clauses and as verbs in dependent clauses, which are also known as secondary or subordinate clauses. In Chapter 13B, you reviewed dependent clauses with the indicative, introduced by the relative pronoun **qui, quae, quod**. Dependent clauses with the subjunctive are usually introduced by words such as **si, quis, cum**, or, as presented in this section, the adverb **ut**, e.g.,

main/independent clause        subordinate/dependent clause

**Omnes milites ferociter pugnant [ut hostes superent].**

*All soldiers fight hard [in order to defeat the enemy].*

In the sentence above, the main thought is that all soldiers fight hard. Secondary to this thought and dependent upon it is the purpose clause "in order to defeat the enemy," which gives additional information about the main thought. Such clauses can be "triggered" or set off by a word in the main clause that provides a context for the dependent clause, such as **tam** with this result clause:

**Milites <u>tam</u> ferociter pugnabant [ut hostes superarentur].**

*The soldiers fought <u>so hard</u> [that the enemy was defeated].*

Subjunctive verbs, whether independent or in dependent clauses, express wishes, possibilities, doubts, opinions, and so forth, whereas indicative verbs express statements of fact. In this and the next two sections, you will review the ways to identify various subjunctive clauses, as well as the ways in which they differ in meaning. Only the most common subordinate clauses with the subjunctive are presented in these chapters, because these types appear most frequently in Latin literature. The presentations for review are organized according to the word that introduces the dependent clause, such as **ut**, **quid**, or **cum**. In this chapter, you will review four clauses introduced by the adverb **ut**: purpose, result, indirect command, and fear. Brackets [ ] are used to designate the subordinate clause.

## Types of *Ut* Clauses with the Subjunctive

The adverb **ut** introduces several different types of subjunctive clauses and is also found in a clause with the indicative. The negative of these clauses varies with the type of clause. The terms used to identify **ut** clauses, such as purpose or result, give insight into their meanings.

### Purpose Clause with *Ut*

Although there are several different ways to express in Latin the idea of the purpose or intent of an action, the **ut** clause is perhaps the most common. This clause is also known as a "final" clause. The negative is **ne.** When translating, use wording such as *to, in order to, so that,* or *for the purpose of,* and render the verb by using the helping verbs *may* or *might*. Most often, the present or imperfect tense is found in a purpose clause, e.g.,

> **Gloriosus miles esse vult [ut ipse praeclarissimus fiat].**
> *Gloriosus wants to be a soldier [in order to become famous].*

> **Gloriosus praeclarissimus esse volebat [ut puellae eum amarent].**
> *Gloriosus wanted to be famous [so that girls might like him].*

Notes:

- Whereas the infinitive is used in English to express purpose, this use appears rarely in Latin, and then only in poetry.

- For the relative purpose clause and a summary of purpose constructions in Latin, see the next section.

### Result Clause with *Ut*

The result clause, also called a "consecutive" clause, begins with **ut** (negative **ut non**) and ends with a subjunctive verb, usually in the present or imperfect tense. This clause, however, is set up by a "trigger word," such as **adeo, ita, sic,** or **tam,** which mean *so, to such an extent,* **talis, -is, -e,** *of such a kind,* **tantus, -a, -um,** *of such a size,* or **tot,** *so many.* Such words appear outside of and preceding the **ut** clause. When translating **ut** in a result clause, use the word *that* (= *with the result that*):

> **Gloriosus <u>tam</u> defessus est [ut Rubiconem transire non possit].**
> *Gloriosus is <u>so</u> weary [that he cannot cross the Rubicon River]*

**Rubico flumen <u>ita</u> vivum fluebat [ut Gloriosus lapsus in aquam caderet].**

*The Rubicon River was running <u>so fast</u> [that Gloriosus slipped and fell in].*

Notes:

- Sometimes the perfect subjunctive, instead of the imperfect, is found in the result clause if the past event whose action is being described <u>actually occurred</u>:

  **Gloriosus <u>talis</u> conspiciebatur [ut alii milites riserint].**

  *Gloriosus was such a sight [that the other soldiers (in fact) laughed].*

- A variation of the result clause, often referred to as a <u>substantive (noun) clause of result</u>, appears with verbs of causing or happening, such as **facere ut**, *to bring it about that*, or with several impersonal verbs, such as **accidit ut, evenit ut**, or **fit/fiebat ut**, *it happens/happened that*, or **fieri potest ut**, *it may be that, it is possible that*. For example,

  **Caesar <u>faciebat</u> [ut Romani urbem Romam oppugnarent].**

  *Caesar <u>was bringing it about</u> [that Romans were attacking Rome].*

## Indirect Command

You might expect a highly structured and militaristic society such as that of the Romans to have several different ways to express the idea of command. You have reviewed the direct command (imperative mood, Chapter 15) and the independent subjunctive with the force of a gentle command (jussive and hortatory, Chapter 16D, Section 2). The indirect command expresses or reports a command as second hand communication, i.e., states what the original command was. Also known as the jussive clause, jussive noun clause, or substantive noun clause of purpose, the indirect command is a substantive or noun clause that consists of **ut** (or **ne**) + the subjunctive and answers the implied question "What is commanded?" A substantive is anything that takes the place of a noun, including a verbal clause:

**Centurio Glorioso imperat.**

*The centurion gives an order to Gloriosus.*

What order does the centurion give? **"Desili de nave."**

The order "Jump down from the ship" becomes the direct object of the verb **imperat**, i.e., that which was ordered. The direct command **"Desili de nave"** now becomes the substantive clause, or indirect command, **ut de nave desiliret**. The translation of **ut** in this type of subjunctive clause is *to...* or *that...*, e.g.,

Direct command:    **"Desili de nave, Gloriose!" centurio imperat.**

*The centurion commands, "Jump down from the ship, Gloriosus!"*

Indirect command:   **Centurio Glorioso <u>imperat</u> [ut de nave desiliat].**

*The centurion <u>commands</u> Gloriosus [to jump down from the ship].*

Notes:

- The above sentence could be written alternatively as:

    **Centurio imperat [ut Gloriosus de nave desiliat].**
    *The centurion orders [that Gloriosus jump down from the ship].*

    In this sentence, Glorious is not the direct recipient of the centurion's command (the word **Gloriosus** is found inside the dependent clause), but receives the command through another.

- For the Romans, the use of verbs that mean *bid, order, request,* as well as *invite, persuade, beg,* or *pray,* carried weight and required a response. The following verbs introduce an indirect command:

| | |
|---|---|
| **hortari,** *encourage, urge* | **orare**, *plead, pray* |
| **imperare** (+ dat.), *order* | **persuadere** (+ dat.), *persuade, convince* |
| **invitare,** *invite* | **petere,** *ask* |
| **mandare**, *command* | **praecipere** (+ dat.), *instruct* |
| **monere,** *advise, warn* | **rogare,** *ask* |
| **obsecrare**, *beg, beseech* | |

- Remember the verbs listed above by using the convenient, if goofy, acronym "HIPPIPROMMO."

- Most of the verbs above take a direct object in the accusative case. The verbs **imperare, persuadere**, and **praecipere**, however, take the <u>dative</u> case (for which, see Chapter 13A).

- The verb **iubere**, which also has the meaning *order*, is not followed by the indirect command but takes the infinitive with subject accusative, e.g.,

    **Centurio Gloriosum <u>desilire</u> iubebat.**
    *The centurion was ordering Gloriosus <u>to jump down</u>.*

## Fear Clause

Fear clauses are structured like other **ut** clauses with the subjunctive, except that the meanings of **ut** and **ne** are unique. Their meanings are reversed, that is, **ut** and **ne** have meanings that are the opposite of those found in other **ut** clauses. They express in a different way what was originally an independent jussive clause in the context of the emotion of fear or apprehension, e.g., **Vereor. Ne cadas**! *I'm scared. May you not fall!* became **Vereor ne cadas**, *I'm scared that you may fall.* Thus, **ne** expresses the positive, *that...*, and **ut** the negative, *that...not*, following words that suggest or mean fear or apprehension. That which is feared is expressed in the fear clause. The fear clause, like the indirect command, is a noun or substantive clause, in that it serves as the direct object of the main verb and answers the implied question "What is feared?" Verbs that introduce a fear clause include **metuere, pavere, timere,** and the deponent **vereri**, e.g.,

**Gloriosus <u>veretur</u> [ut scuto defendatur].**
*Gloriosus <u>fears</u> [that he may not be protected by his shield].*

**Timebatne Gloriosus [ne in testudine nigresceret]?**
<u>*Was*</u> *Gloriosus <u>afraid</u> [that it would be dark inside the "tortoise"]?*

Notes:

- Alternatively, the verbs of fearing listed above may be accompanied by an infinitive, e.g.,

  **Gloriosus metuebat a castris <u>discedere</u>.**
  *Gloriosus was afraid <u>to leave</u> camp.*

## Quick Study of *Ut* Clauses with the Subjunctive

| Type Clause | Main Clause Cue | Introductory Word | Meaning of Clause | Subjunctive |
|---|---|---|---|---|
| Purpose | [none] | **ut** <br> **ne** | *to, in order that,* <br> *so that* <br> *so that...not, not* <br> *to...* | present, <br> imperfect |
| Example: | **Gloriosus se celabat ut diu dormiret.** <br> *Gloriosus was hiding in order to sleep for awhile.* | | | |
| Result | **adeo, ita, sic,** <br> **tam**, etc. | **ut** <br><br> **ut non** | *that, with the* <br> *result that* <br> *that...not* | present, <br> imperfect, <br> perfect |
| Example: | **Iste <u>tam</u> bene se celaverat ut centurio eum invenire non posset.** <br> *He had hidden <u>so</u> successfully that the centurion couldn't find him.* | | | |
| Indirect Command | verb of command or persuasion | **ut** <br> **ne** | *that* <br> *that...not* | present, <br> imperfect |
| Example: | **Scelesto invento, centurio ei <u>imperavit</u> ut matellas vacuefaceret.** <br> *When the rascal had been found, the centurion ordered him to empty the chamber pots.* | | | |
| Fear | word of fearing | **ne** <br> **ut** | *that* <br> *that...not* | present, <br> imperfect |
| Example: | **Gloriosus <u>timuerat</u> ne centurio ei noceret.** <br> *Gloriosus had feared that the centurion might harm him.* | | | |

## Tips on Translating *Ut* Clauses

- When translating **ut** clauses, look for a cue word in the main clause that may "trigger" or set up the specific meaning of the subordinate clause, e.g., **ita** or **tam** (result), **hortari** or **imperare** (indirect command), or **timere** or **vereri** (fear). Remember that "trigger words" are found outside of and preceding the subjunctive clause. It is helpful to bracket the subjunctive clause in order to indicate that it contains information which is separate from that of the main clause of the sentence.

- **Ut** clauses are generally found with the present or imperfect subjunctive and follow the rules of sequence of tenses.

- Most **ut** clauses are best translated using the words *that...*or *to....*

- The adverb **ut** may also be found with a verb in the indicative, in which case it has the meaning of *as* or *when*, e.g.,

> **Gloriosus, <u>ut</u> centurio <u>imperaverat</u>, de nave desiluit.**
> *Gloriosus, <u>as</u> the centurion <u>had ordered</u>, jumped down from the ship.*

## Practice Questions

1. Admonebitne Caesar suos <u>ut Britanni suas facies tingant</u>?
   - (A) that the Britons dye their faces
   - (B) to dye his own face like the Britons
   - (C) that his men will dye the faces of the Britons
   - (D) that the Britons dye the faces of centurions

2. Suntne tot barbari in Gallia. . .Caesar eos vincere . . . ?
   - (A) non . . . potest
   - (B) ut . . . non possit
   - (C) ne . . . potest
   - (D) ne . . . possit

3. Are soldiers afraid <u>to die</u>?
   - (A) ut . . . moriantur
   - (B) ne . . .moriuntur
   - (C) ut . . . morerentur
   - (D) ne . . . moriantur

4. Traiano imperatore, accidit ut Dacii . . . .
   - (A) victi sunt
   - (B) victuri sint
   - (C) vincerentur
   - (D) vincebantur

5. Miles bibebat <u>ad bellum obliviscendum</u>. Which answer provides the closest substitute?
   - (A) ut bellum oblivisceretur
   - (B) bello oblito
   - (C) quia bellum obliviscebatur
   - (D) obliviscens bellum

6.  . . . superbus Gloriosus erat ut multos amicos non haberet.

    (A) Tamen               (C) Tandem

    (B) Tam                 (D) Tunc

7.  Gloriosus, <u>ut hostes conspexit</u>, arborem ascendit.

    (A) in order to see the enemy

    (B) to see the enemy

    (C) with the result that he saw the enemy

    (D) when he saw the enemy

## *Sententiae Antiquae*

1.  <u>Non ut edam vivo sed ut vivam edo.</u> (Quintilian)

    (A) I do not eat to live, but I live to eat.

    (B) I should not live to eat, but I should eat to live.

    (C) I do not live to eat, but I eat to live.

    (D) I will not live so that I may eat, but I will eat so that I may live

2.  The fruit vendors ask <u>that you make</u> M. Holconius Priscus aedile. (from a Pompeiian election poster)

    (A) ut vos facitis         (C) ne vos faciatis

    (B) ut vos faceretis       (D) ut vos faciatis

3.  Feminae spectatum veniunt et veniunt ut ipsae . . . . (Ovid)

    (A) spectentur             (C) spectent

    (B) spectarentur           (D) spectantur

4.  Orandum est <u>ut sit</u> mens sana in corpore sano. (Juvenal)

    (A) that there will be     (C) that there be

    (B) that there was         (D) that there must be

5.  Nemo adeo ferus est ut mitescere non <u>possit</u>. (Horace)

    (A) was not able           (C) has not been able

    (B) will not be able       (D) is not able

6.  Cito scribendo non fit <u>ut bene scribatur</u>; bene scribendo fit ut cito. (Quintilian)

    (A) that it is written well      (C) in order to write well

    (B) as it should be well written (D) that it was written well

**Stumper:** Hortatur eos <u>ne animo deficiant</u>. Caesar's direct command would have been:

(A)  Noli deficere!  (C)  Deficite!

(B)  Nolite deficere!  (D)  Non deficere

# Answers

1.  Indirect command   **(A)**

The appearance of the verb **Admonebit** defines the clause **ut...tingant** as an indirect command with its subjunctive verb in primary sequence. The sentence reads, "Will Caesar advise his men <u>that the Britons dye their faces</u>?" For various reasons, the remaining answers do not translate the Latin correctly. Answers (C) and (D) translate as part of the subordinate clause elements that are really part of the main clause.

2. Result clause   **(B)**

The word **tot** preceding the clause cues this as a result clause. The sentence reads, "Are there so many barbarians in Gaul <u>that</u> Caesar <u>cannot</u> defeat them?" This **ut** result clause requires a subjunctive verb in primary sequence, as the main verb is in the present tense, which removes Answers (A) and (C) from consideration. The negative of a result clause is not **ne**, as in Answer (D), but **ut non**.

3. Fear clause   **(D)**

This fear clause is in primary sequence, which requires that the subjunctive be in the present tense, as in the clause **ne...moriatur**. Remember that the meanings of **ut** and **ne** are reversed in fear clauses! Answer (A) disregards this fact, (B) does not contain a subjunctive verb, and in (C), the tense of the verb **moreretur** is not justifiable, given the present tense of the main verb.

4.  Substantive result clause   **(C)**

This sentence reads, "While Trajan was emperor, it came to pass (happened) that the Dacians <u>were conquered</u>." The appearance of **accidit** sets up a result clause requiring a subjunctive verb, which eliminates Answers (A) **victi sunt** and (D) **vincebantur**. Answer (B) **victuri sint** is subjunctive, but has a meaning in the active voice, i.e., "about to conquer," which does not fit the context. Therefore, Answer (C) **vincerentur** is correct.

5.  Purpose clause   **(A)**

The purpose clause **ut...obliviceretur** "(in order) to forget the war" is the best substitution for the underlined gerundive of purpose **ad bellum obliviscen-dum**. The original sentence reads, "The soldier drank <u>for the purpose of forgetting the war</u>." Answer (B) is an ablative absolute, (C) a causal clause, and (D) a present participial phrase, none of which fit the context. (For the gerundive of purpose, see Chapter 16B.)

6.  Result clause  **(B)**
    The sense of the thought here, "Gloriosus was *so* arrogant that he did not have many friends," leads to the conclusion that this sentence contains a result clause. Of the choices, the word **tam**, "so...," introduces the result clause **ne... haberet** in secondary sequence. None of the adverbs in Answers (A), (B), and (C) are relevant to defining an **ut** clause with the subjunctive.

7.  **Ut** + indicative  **(D)**
    This sentence reads, "When he saw the enemy, Gloriosus climbed a tree." Because the verb **conspexit** is indicative, **ut** must be translated "as" or "when." Answers (A) and (B) call for purposes clauses, and (C) for a result clause, all requiring subjunctive verbs.

## *Sententiae Antiquae* Answers

1.  Purpose clause  **(C)**
    Quintilian's sentence contains two purpose clauses, **ut...edam** and **ut vivam**. Answer (A) reverses the two clauses, Answer (B) requires independent subjunctives in the present tense, and (D) mistranslates the tenses of the verbs **vivere** and **edere**.

2.  Indirect command  **(D)**
    **Ut vos faciatis** idiomatically translates "that you vote." This clause is an indirect command introduced by the verb "ask" in the main clause of the English sentence and requiring a subjunctive verb in primary sequence. Answer (A) is not a subjunctive clause, (B) has the verb in the wrong tense, and (C) **ne vos faciatis**, incorrectly negates the original positive statement.

3.  Purpose clause  **(A)**
    This sentence, which reads, "They come to see (and) to be seen themselves," referring to women at the races, contains a purpose clause with its verb in primary sequence (**spectentur**, after **veniunt**). Answer (B) **spectarentur** is in the imperfect tense in secondary sequence, (C) **spectent** is active and doesn't fit the context, and (D) **spectantur** is in the indicative mood. Note the supine of purpose, **spectatum**, for which, see Chapter 16B.

4.  Indirect command  **(C)**
    **Ut sit** is an indirect command after the verb **orare** in the periphrastic **orandum est**. Juvenal's famous statement says, "(We) must maintain that there be a sound mind in a sound body." Answer (A) requires the "future subjunctive" form (**futura sit**), (B) the imperfect tense (**esset**), and (D) an expression of necessity in the clause.

5.   Result clause   **(D)**

The appearance of **adeo** keys the result clause **ut non mitescere possit**. The present tense of the subjunctive verb **possit** is correctly translated "is not able" or "cannot." The sentence reads, "No one is so fierce that he cannot be tamed."

6.   Substantive result clause   **(A)**

The underlined clause is a substantive result clause following the verb **fit**. Quintilian's thought reads, "Not by writing quickly does it come about <u>that it is written well</u>; by writing well, it comes about that (it is written) quickly." Note the condensation of the Latin, with the omission of **scribatur** in the second half of the sentence. In Answer (B), the translation "as" for **ut** requires an indicative verb, whereas **scribatur** is subjunctive. Answer (C) "in order to" is phrased as a purpose clause and has the verb in the active voice, and (D) incorrectly translates the tense of **scribatur** as imperfect.

**Stumper:**   Indirect command   **(B)**

The particle **ne** negates the indirect command in the sentence "He is urging them <u>not to lose heart</u>" (lit., "that they not be lacking in spirit"). Since Caesar is urging **eos**, "them," the command must be plural, as well as negative, giving the answer **Nolite deficere** as the original direct command in Latin. Answer (A) **Noli deficere** is singular, (C) **Deficite** is a positive command, rather than negative, and (D) is an improperly constructed prohibition.

# Section 5: Subordinate Clauses with Q-Words

During your review, you have met the relative, or **qui**, clause with the indicative, e.g., **Cicero qui consul erat**, *Cicero who was a consul* (Chapter 13B) and the deliberative question with the independent subjunctive, e.g., **Quid agam**? *What should I do?* (Chapter 13D, Section 2). There are several different types of subjunctive clauses that are introduced in Latin by question words or by a word that begins with the letter **q**. Because of the similarity in the appearance of these clauses, it is appropriate to consider them together.

## Types of Subjunctive Clauses Introduced by Q-Words

The most common subjunctive clauses introduced by a **q**-word are the indirect question, relative clause of characteristic, and causal clause. In the context of these clauses, we will also review doubt clauses and the relative, or **qui**, purpose clause.

## Indirect Question

Indirect questions are to direct questions as indirect commands are to direct commands. They express the fact that someone is reporting a direct question, e.g.,

Direct question: **"Quid agis?" Cicero rogabat.**
*"How are you doing?" Cicero asked.*

Indirect question: **Cicero rogabat [quid agerem].**
*Cicero asked [how I was doing].*

An indirect question consists of a dependent subjunctive clause that is introduced by a "question word" such as **cur, quid, quis, quomodo, ubi,** or **unde**. Such clauses are set up or "triggered" by an indicative verb of asking, wondering, or knowing, such as **quaerere, mirari,** or **scire**, respectively. The indicative verb of the main clause is the same type of verb as that which introduces an indirect statement (for which, see Chapter 16D). When working out the meaning of a Latin sentence containing an indirect question, look for the following components: a verb of verbal or mental action, a question word, and a subjunctive verb, e.g.,

verb of verbal action       question word

Indirect question: **Atticus <u>rogat</u> Scribacem [<u>cur</u> epistulas nondum**

subjunctive verb
**<u>scripserit</u>].**

> *Atticus is asking (his scribe) Scribax [why he has not yet written the letters].*

verb of mental action    subj. acc.           infinitive

Indirect statement: **Atticus <u>nescivit</u> <u>Scribacem</u> stilum suum <u>amisisse</u>.**
*Atticus did not know that Scribax had lost his pen.*

The subjunctive verb in an indirect question is translated in the same tense as it would be if it were an indicative verb. Remember that indirect questions in Latin will never contain question or quotation marks. Use your "I.Q.!"

Notes:

- Take care to distinguish the indirect question clause from other types of **q**-clauses, such as the relative clause found with the indicative (for which, see Chapter 13B).

- In an indirect question, the Romans often preferred to emphasize the question by placing it first in the sentence, e.g.,

  **[Quid sit futurum cras] fuge quaerere.** (Horace)
  *Stop asking [what may happen tomorrow].*

- Since a direct question may be expressed by using a verb in the future tense, it should be remembered that, in an indirect question, the <u>active periphrastic</u> (future participle + form of **esse** in the subjunctive) may be used to express future time, e.g.,

  **Scribax scire voluit quot epistulas ipse <u>scripturus esset</u>.**
  *Scribax wanted to know how many letters <u>he was about to transcribe</u>.*

## Double Indirect Questions

Indirect questions can be alternative or double, i.e., more than a single question may be asked in a sentence, such as the following questions introduced by **utrum... an**, *whether...or*:

> **Atticus mirabatur [utrum Scribax ignavus an strenuus esset].**
>
> *Atticus was wondering [whether Scribax was lazy or energetic].*

## Indirect Clauses Expressing Doubt

An indirect question may express doubt in the following ways:

1) the subjunctive clause of doubt is introduced by the words **num** or **an**, *whether*, preceded by a verb of questioning or doubting, such as a form of the verb **dubitare,** *doubt*, or the phrase **dubium est**, *there is doubt that*, e.g,

> **Aliqui dubitant [num Cicero carmina scripserit].**
>
> *Some people doubt [whether Cicero wrote poetry].*

Note:

- Remember that the interrogative particle **num** can also introduce a direct question with the indicative, to which a negative answer is expected.

2) the negative subjunctive clause of doubt is introduced by the word **quin** (*that*), preceded by the stated or implied negative of the doubting word or expression, e.g., **non dubitare** or **non dubium est** (= **sine dubio**):

> **Est non dubium [quin Caesar ad Ciceronem epistulas scripserit].**
>
> *There is no doubt, or It is doubtless [that Caesar wrote letters to Cicero].*

## Relative Clause of Characteristic

This type of subjunctive clause, which is introduced by a relative pronoun, describes a type of person or thing, rather than one that is actual or specific. This type of relative clause describes a general quality or characteristic of the antecedent. Such clauses follow indefinite words phrases such as **nemo est qui** (*there is no one who...*), **is est qui** (*he is the type* or *kind of person who...*), and **sunt qui** (*there are those of the sort who...*). The relative clause of characteristic is generally found with the present subjunctive. Be especially careful to distinguish the relative characteristic clause with the subjunctive from the explanatory relative clause with the indicative. The explanatory clause provides (more) factual information about the antecedent:

Relative clause with the indicative:   **Tiro est scriba [qui diligens est].**
                                        *Tiro is the (particular) scribe [who is careful].*

Relative clause with the subjunctive:  **Tiro est scriba [qui diligens sit].**
                                        *Tiro is the (type of) scribe [who is careful].*

Additional examples of relative clauses of characteristic:

**Nemo est [qui omnes epistulas Ciceronis legerit].**

*There is no one (in the opinion of the writer) [who has read all of Cicero's letters].*

**Erant [qui dicerent] Tironem scribam optimum omnium esse.**

*There were those [who said] that Tiro was the best secretary of all.*

## Relative Purpose Clause

The relative, or **qui**, clause with the subjunctive can also be used to express purpose:

**Cicero Terentiae dedit <u>epistulam</u> [quam legeret].**

*Cicero gave Terentia <u>a letter</u> [to read, i.e. that she was to read].*

In such situations, the relative pronoun (**quam**), refers back to a particular antecedent (**epistulam**), while at the same time indicating purpose or intent (**legeret**).

Note:

- When translating a relative clause, identify the antecedent of the relative pronoun, determine if the verb of the clause is indicative or subjunctive, and then consider the contextual sense of the **qui** clause carefully before deciding upon its meaning. Does the relative clause give a factual description of something or someone? (Indicative) Does it describe a general type of person? (Subjunctive) Does it indicate the purpose of some other action? (Subjunctive)

## Causal Clauses

Causal clauses are dependent clauses introduced by explanatory words such as **quod, quia,** or **quoniam**, all meaning *because, since*. Such clauses are found with either the indicative or the subjunctive. When the <u>indicative</u> is used, the writer/speaker is taking responsibility for the reason, i.e., the reader must assume that the explanation is viewed by the writer as <u>a known fact</u>. When the <u>subjunctive</u> is found in the dependent clause, the reason is viewed as that of someone other than the writer/speaker, i.e., it is <u>alleged</u>, e.g.,

Indicative (fact):

**Cicero orationes Philippicas habebat [quod Antonius tyrannus <u>erat</u>].**

*Cicero delivered the Philippics [because Antony <u>was</u> a tyrant, as far as the speaker of the sentence is concerned].*

Subjunctive (allegation):

**[Quia Cicero rem publicam <u>servavisset</u>], "Pater Patriae" salutabatur.**

*[Since Cicero <u>had saved</u> the state, in the opinion of someone other than the writer], he was saluted as "Father of his Country."*

Note:

- When **quod** is found in a clause with its verb in the indicative mood, be careful to use context in order to determine whether **quod** has the meaning *because* (causal) or *which, that* (relative):

**Quod** causal (indicative-factual):

> **Cicero scripsit De Natura Deorum [quod credit] deos esse.**
> *Cicero wrote On the Nature of the Gods [because he believes] that the gods exist.*

**Quod** relative (indicative-factual):

> **Placebatne Ciceroni nomen [quod ei datum erat]?**
> *Was Cicero pleased with the name [that had been given to him]?*

## Quick Study of Q-Clauses

| Type of clause | Introductory word | Meaning | Function |
|---|---|---|---|
| **Indicative (factual)** | | | |
| Relative | **qui, quae, quod** | *who, which, that* | explains, describes |
| Causal | **quod, quia, quoniam** | *since, because* | gives a reason as a fact |
| **Subjunctive (non-factual)** | | | |
| Indirect question | **cur, quid, quis, quomodo, ubi**, etc. | *why, what, who, how, when,* etc. | restates a question |
| Double indirect question | **utrum . . . an** | *whether...or* | restates more than one question |
| Doubt clauses | **num** <br><br> **quin** | *whether* <br><br> *that* | expresses uncertainty **(dubitare, dubium est)** <br> expresses certainty **(non dubitare)** |
| Rel. characteristic | **qui, quae, quod** | *the type who...* | describes a type |
| Relative purpose | **qui, quae, quod** | *to, in order to* | indicates purpose (relates to antecedent) |
| Causal | **quod, quia, quoniam** | *since, because* | gives a reason as an allegation |

## Practice With Q-Clauses

Look carefully at the prior and succeeding context of a **q**-word in the clause in order to determine its meaning. Is there a word in the main clause that "sets up" the meaning expressed in the subordinate clause? Does an indicative or subjunctive verb appear in the dependent clause? Now review what you know about **q**-word clauses by bracketing the clause in each sentence below and then inspecting its context. Finally, translate the entire sentence:

1. **Antonius qui inimicus Ciceronis erat illum necare voluit**.
2. **Quot senes libellum De Senectute legerint, Cicero scire vult.**
3. **Estne Cicero qui virtutem optimam esse credat?**
4. **Cicero de philosophia scripsit quod cara Tullia mortua esset**.
5. **Cicero orationem habebat quae Milonem defenderet**.
6. **Legimus orationes Ciceronis quod de Romanis nos certiores faciunt.**

## Answers

1. **[Qui ... erat]**

   *Antony, who was a personal enemy of Cicero, wished to kill him.*

2. **[Quot ... legerint]**

   *Cicero wants to know how many elderly men have read his treatise "On Old Age."*

3. **[qui ... credat]**

   *Is Cicero the type of man who believes that virtue is the greatest (good)?*

4. **[quod ... mortua esset]**

   *Cicero wrote about philosophy because his dear Tullia had died.*

5. **[quae ... defenderet]**

   *Cicero gave a speech to defend Milo.*

6. **[quod ... faciunt]**

   *We read the speeches of Cicero because they inform us about the Romans.*

## Discussion of answers

Sentence 1 contains a relative clause of fact with the indicative (see Chapter 13B). Sentence 6 contains a **quod** causal clause with the indicative, also indicating a factual statement. The remaining sentences contain clauses with subjunctive verbs. Remember that subjunctive verbs are used in clauses that express hypothetical or non-completed actions. In Sentence 2, Cicero does not yet know for a fact how many men have read his essay (indirect question). Sentence 3 describes the type of man Cicero might be (relative clause of characteristic). In Sentence 4, the subjunctive is used because it is the opinion of someone other than the writer that Cicero wrote philosophy because his daughter had died (causal clause with the subjunctive). The use of the subjunctive in the clause in Sentence 5 tells us that Cicero gave the speech in order to defend Milo (relative purpose clause).

## Practice with Indirect Expressions

You have now met three different types of expressions that are "indirect": an infinitive clause and two subjunctive clauses. Each reports in second-hand fashion an original statement, command, or question. To test your command of indirect expressions, translate the following sentences and then create in English the original direct expression:

| | |
|---|---|
| Indirect statement: | **Multi sciunt Ciceronem Arpini natum esse.** |
| Indirect command: | **Aliquis Ciceroni persuasit ut Tusculi habitaret.** |
| Indirect question: | **Scitne quisquam in quo loco Cicero mortuus sit?** |

### Answers

| | |
|---|---|
| Indirect statement: | *Many know that Cicero was born at Arpinum.* |
| Direct statement: | "Cicero was born at Arpinum." |
| Indirect command: | *Someone persuaded Cicero to live in Tusculum.* |
| Direct command: | "Live in Tusculum, Cicero!" |
| Indirect question: | *Does anyone know where Cicero died?* |
| Direct question: | "Where did Cicero die?" |

### Quick Study of Expressions of Purpose

| | |
|---|---|
| **Gerundive of purpose** | |
| **Cicero iter facit <u>ad amicum visendum</u>.** <br> *Cicero is traveling <u>to visit</u> a friend.* | See Chapter 16B. |
| **Supine** | |
| **Cicero iter facit <u>visum amicum</u>.** <br> *Cicero is traveling <u>to visit</u> a friend.* | See Chapter 16B. |
| **Ut** purpose clause | |
| **Cicero iter facit <u>ut amicum visat</u>.** <br> *Cicero is traveling <u>to visit</u> a friend.* | See Chapter 16D.4. |
| **Relative purpose clause** | |
| **Cicero epistulam mittet <u>quae dicat</u> se venire.** <br> *Cicero will send a letter <u>to say</u> that he is coming.* | See above. |

## Practice Questions

1. Cicero scire vult <u>quis</u> sibi nomen "Tully" <u>dederit</u>.

   (A) who will have given       (C) who had given

   (B) who was giving       (D) who has given

2. Cicero Milonem . . . quia Clodium per Viam Appiam occidisset.

   (A) defendebat       (C) defenderet

   (B) defendet       (D) defenditur

3. Non dubium erat . . . Cicero clementiam Caesaris . . . .

   (A) qui . . . colat       (C) quin . . . coleret

   (B) ne . . . coleret       (D) quin . . . colebat

4. Quid agas, cura ut sciam.

   (A) Take care that I know where you are going.

   (B) Take care to know who you are.

   (C) Take care that I know how you are doing.

   (D) Take care to know what you are doing.

5. Cicero mirabatur quomodo cum senatoribus <u>gratiam habiturus esset</u>.

   (A) has gained favor       (C) is going to gain favor

   (B) was going to gain favor       (D) will be able to gain favor

6. <u>Erant qui non credidit Ciceronem militem fuisse.</u>

   (A) There are those who do not believe that Cicero was a soldier.

   (B) There were those who believe that Cicero was not a soldier.

   (C) There were those who did not believe that Cicero had been a soldier.

   (D) There were those who did not believe that Cicero was a soldier.

7. Nemo scivit utrum Hortensius an Cicero optimus orator <u>factus esset</u>.

   (A) has become       (C) had become

   (B) was becoming       (D) was about to become

8. <u>Nemo est qui dubitet quin Cicero bonus consul fuerit.</u>

   (A) There is no one who will doubt that Cicero would have been a good consul.

   (B) There is no one who does not doubt that Cicero was a good consul.

   (C) There is no one who doubts that Cicero was a good consul.

   (D) There is no one who doubts that Cicero was not a good consul.

## Sententiae Antiquae

1.  Videtis quantum scelus contra rem publicam vobis <u>nuntiatum sit</u>. (Cicero, on Catiline)

    (A)  has been reported     (C)  was being reported

    (B)  had been reported     (D)  is reported

2.  Scire ubi aliquid invenire . . . , ea maxima pars eruditionis est. (Anon.)

    (A)  posses     (C)  potueras

    (B)  potes     (D)  possis

3.  <u>Quod</u> cum animadvertisset Caesar naves militibus compleri iussit. (Caesar)

    (A)  Because     (C)  The fact that

    (B)  What     (D)  This

4.  Malum est consilium quod mutari non . . . . (Publilius Syrus)

    (A)  potuerit     (C)  potuisset

    (B)  posset     (D)  potest

5.  Odi et amo. <u>Quare id faciam</u>, fortasse requiris. (Catullus)

    (A)  Why I have done this     (C)  Why I do this

    (B)  Why I will do this     (D)  Why I will have done this

6.  Multi cives ea pericula <u>quae imminent</u> neglegunt. (Cicero)

    (A)  which might be imminent     (C)  which were imminent

    (B)  which are imminent     (D)  which will be imminent

7.  <u>Quis dubitet num in virtute felicitas sit</u>? (Cicero)

    (A)  Who would doubt whether there is happiness in virtue?

    (B)  Who would doubt whether or not there is happiness in virtue?

    (C)  Who doubts whether virtue is happiness?

    (D)  Who will doubt whether he is happy in his virtue?

8.  Caesar milites reprehendit <u>quod sibi ipsi iudicavissent quid agendum esset</u>. (Caesar)

    (A)  because they had (in fact) decided for themselves what had to be done.

    (B)  because they were deciding for themselves what he must do.

    (C)  because they did the thing which they had decided.

    (D)  because they had (according to others) decided for themselves what had to be done

**Stumper:**   Do both of the following have the same meaning?

(A)   Yes                                        (B)   No

*Exegi monumentum aere perennius. (Horace)*

*Nihil est manu factum quod tempus non consumat. (Cicero)*

# Answers

1. Indirect question   **(D)**
    This sentence contains an indirect question in primary sequence, with the main verb in the present tense and the subjunctive verb **dederit** in the perfect tense. The sentence reads, "Cicero wants to know who has given him the name "Tully." **Dederit** could be identified as a future perfect tense, as is suggested in Answer (A) "who will have given," but the question word **quis** requires that the verb be subjunctive in an indirect question. Answers (B) and (C) require verbs in secondary sequence, which do not correlate with the tense of the main verb.

2.   Causal clause   **(A)**
    A main verb in the past tense is required because the subjunctive verb of the causal clause, **quia...occidisset**, is in the pluperfect tense. Answers (B) and (D) are in the future and present tenses, respectively, and Answer (C) is in the imperfect tense, but is subjunctive, which does not fit the context of the main or independent clause. The sentence reads, "Cicero was defending Milo since he had killed Clodius along the Appian Way."

3.   Doubt clause   **(C)**
    The words **non dubium** introduce a doubt clause with its verb in secondary sequence after **erat**. This sentence reads, "There was no doubt that Cicero respected Caesar's clemency." The verb in Answer (A) is in the wrong tense of the subjunctive, Answer (B) contains **ne**, an incorrect particle for a doubt clause, and (D) **quin...gaudebat** is a clause with a verb in the indicative, rather than the required subjunctive.

4.   Indirect question and indirect command   **(C)**
    This sentence, which contains two subjunctive clauses, reads, "Take care that I know how you're doing." **Quid agas** is an indirect question following the verb **sciam**. **Ut sciam**, after **cura**, has the force of an indirect command. Answer (A) mistranslates the indirect question that contains the idiomatic expression **Quid agis?** "How are you?" Answers (B) and (D) imply that the subject of the verb **sciam** is in the second person, rather than the first. (For indirect command, see the previous chapter.)

5.   Indirect question   **(B)**
    This sentence contains an example of the "future subjunctive," that is, the use of the future active participle with a subjunctive form of the verb **esse** as an active periphrastic (see Chapter 16A). The **q**-word **quomodo** introduces the indi-

rect question clause. The sentence reads, "Cicero was wondering how <u>he was going to gain favor</u> with the senators." Answers (B) and (C) incorrectly translate **esset** in the perfect and present tenses, respectively, and the translation in (D) assumes the future tense of the verb **posse**, which does not appear in the sentence.

6.   Relative clause with the indicative   **(C)**
     The accuracy of the translation of this sentence depends upon the correct rendering of the tenses of the three verbs: **erant, credidit**, and **fuisse**. **Qui non credidit** is a relative clause with the indicative, indicating that it was considered a fact that some did not believe that Cicero had been a soldier. The verb **erant** is in the imperfect tense, eliminating Answer (A). In Answer (B), **non** incorrectly negates **esse** and in (D), the infinitive is translated incorrectly, that is, "was a soldier" requires the infinitive **esse** instead of **fuisse**. (See Chapter 13B.)

7.   Indirect question   **(C)**
     This sentence reads, "No one knew whether Hortensius or Cicero <u>had become</u> the best orator." **Factus esset** is the subjunctive of the verb **fieri** in the pluperfect tense, completing the double indirect question **utrum...an...factus esset**. Answer (A) "has become" requires the perfect tense, which would be in the incorrect time sequence. Answer (B) "was becoming" requires the form **fieret** rather than **factus esset**, and (D) "was about to become," the active periphrastic **facturus esset** (for which, see Chaper 16A).

8.   Relative clause of characteristic and doubt clause   **(C)**
     The correct translation is "There is no one who doubts that Cicero was a good consul." This sentence contains two subordinate clauses with the subjunctive. **Qui dubitet** is a relative clause of characteristic with a verb in the present subjunctive in primary sequence, describing a type of person who doubts. The appearance of **dubitet** in this clause introduces a clause of doubt, **quin . . . fuerit**. Answer (A) incorrectly translates **dubitet** as a future tense, therefore making the original characteristic clause an explanatory relative clause. The translation in Answer (B) "does not doubt" incorrectly negates the verb **dubitet**, creating a meaning that is the opposite of that of the original sentence. In the same way, Answer (D) incorrectly negates the subordinate verb **fuerit**.

## *Sententiae Antiquae* Answers

1.   Indirect question   **(A)**
     **Nuntiatum sit** is a form of the perfect passive subjunctive (for which, see Appendix 12), here found in an indirect question introduced by **quantum**. The sentence reads, "You see how much evil against the State (i.e., by the Catilinarian conspirators) <u>has been reported</u> to you all." The remaining answers translate the verb **nuntiatum sit** in the incorrect tense, i.e., (B) pluperfect (**nuntiatum esset**), (C) imperfect (**nuntiaretur**), and (D) present (**nuntiatur**).

2. Indirect question  **(D)**

As all the verbs in this sentence are found in the present tense, the primary sequence is used, eliminating Answer (A), which is in the imperfect tense. The subjunctive mood is required because the missing form completes an indirect question introduced by **ubi**, thereby eliminating Answers (B) **potes** and (C) **potueras**, which are both indicative. The sentence reads, "Knowing (To know) where <u>you can</u> find something, that is the most important part of being educated."

3. (Ambush question!)  **(D)**

The form **quod** is a relative pronoun refering to some previous antecedent that is neuter singular. Answers (A), (B), and (C) do not fit the context of the meaning, which is, "When Caesar had noticed <u>this</u>, he ordered the ships to be filled up with soldiers." It is tempting to connect **quod** with the following subjunctive verb **animadvertisset**, but this verb follows **cum** in a circumstantial clause. (This will be reviewed in the next chapter.)

4. Relative clause with the indicative  **(D)**

**Quod . . . potest** is a simple relative clause, describing **malum consilium**. An indicative verb is therefore required in the subordinate clause, hence **potest**. The sentence reads, "It is a bad plan that <u>cannot</u> be changed." Answer (A) as a form of the future perfect indicative does not make sense, and as a form of the perfect subjunctive, is out of place in an explanatory relative clause. Answers (B) and (C) are subjunctive, and not justifiable in the context of this sentence.

5. Indirect question  **(C)**

The indirect question **quare id faciam**, dependent upon **requiris**, is found in Catullus, Poem 85. This sentence reads, "I hate and I love. <u>Why I do this</u>, perhaps you ask." As the verbs are all in the present tense, the sequence is primary. Answer (A) mistranslates the tense of **faciam** as perfect, (B) as a future indicative, and (D) as a future perfect indicative.

6. Relative clause with the indicative  **(B)**

The relative clause **quae imminent** describes its antecedent **ea pericula**, and thus requires the indicative mood. The sentence reads, "Many citizens disregard those dangers <u>which are imminent</u>." Answer (A) "might be imminent," as a non-fact, requires the subjunctive. Answers (C) and (D) translate the tense of **imminent** incorrectly as imperfect and future.

7. Doubt clause  **(A)**

The doubt clause **num . . . sit** is introduced by the deliberative question **Quis dubitet**? "Who would doubt?" Answers (B) and (C) incorrectly negate the verb **sit** and (D) contains two errors: the verb **dubitet** is not in the future tense and **felicitas** is not an adjective, but a noun.

8. Causal clause and indirect question  **(D)**

This sentence contains two subjunctive clauses, a causal clause with the subjunctive, **quod . . . iudicavissent (iudicavissent)**, indicating that the speaker/writer is doubtful of the reason given by Caesar, and an indirect question, **quid agendum esset**, whose verb is a passive periphrastic. Answer (A) is incorrect because it suggests that the statement is factual, which would require the verb **iudicaverit**, in the indicative mood. The verb tense of **iudicavissent** in Answer (B) is translated incorrectly, and Answer (D) gives a wholesale mistranslation of the Latin.

**Stumper:   (B)**

Horace's line reads, "I have built a monument more lasting than bronze," i.e., something timeless. Cicero says, "There is nothing made by (man's) hand that time does not consume," i.e., all things are transitory. These statements obviously oppose one another in meaning.

# Section 6: Subordinate Clauses with *Cum*

The word **cum** has two basic functions in Latin: as a preposition governing an object in the ablative case, e.g., **cum laude**, *with praise*, and as a conjunction that joins a dependent clause to a main clause, e.g., **[Cum strenuissime laboravisset], summam laudem recepit,** *[Since he had worked the hardest], he received the greatest praise*. There are three major types of **cum** clauses found with the subjunctive: causal, circumstantial, and concessive (the "three C's"). In such clauses, the word **cum** means *since, when*, or *although*, depending upon the context. A variation of the circumstantial clause that expresses action at a specific time appears with its verb in the indicative mood. **Cum** clauses with verbs in the subjunctive are found in the imperfect and pluperfect tenses and follow the rules for sequence of tenses.

## Types of *Cum* Clauses

### *Cum* Causal Clause (*Since, Because*)

When the **cum** clause expresses the reason why the action of the main clause occurred, **cum** means *since* or *because* and is followed by a subjunctive verb, e.g.,

> **[Cum Troianos superare non possent], Graeci equum ligneum aedificaverunt.**
>
> *[Since they were unable to defeat the Trojans], the Greeks constructed a wooden horse.*

> **Laocoon [cum hasta equum percussisset] a serpentibus necatus est.**
>
> *Laocoon, [because he had struck the horse with a spear], was killed by serpents.*

Notes:

- **Cum** clauses are generally located close to the front of the sentence.
- The clause **quae cum ita sint**, *since these things are so*, appears often in prose.
- For causal clauses introduced by **q**-words, see the previous section.

## *Cum* Time Clauses (*When*)

### *Circumstantial and Temporal Clauses*

When a dependent **cum** clause expresses the general circumstances, situation, or conditions in which the action of the clause occurs, a subjunctive verb is used, and **cum** means *when*. The circumstantial clause is found with the imperfect or pluperfect subjunctive and refers to past time. **Cum** meaning *when* may also be found with a past tense of the indicative, but in this case, the **cum** clause indicates or dates a specific or precise point in time, and is sometimes accompanied by a clarifying phrase or word, such as **eo tempore**, *at that time,* or **tum**, *then*. When the clause has this meaning, it is generally referred to as a temporal clause.

Circumstantial (+ subjunctive):

> **[Cum manes ad Acherontem flumen pervenissent]**, **Charon eos scapha transportavit.**
>
> *[When souls had reached the river Acheron], Charon carried them across in a boat.*

Temporal (+ indicative):

> **[Cum ad Acherontem pervenerat], tenuitne Aeneas obolum?**
>
> *[(At the time) when he had reached the Acheron], did Aeneas have the fare?*

Notes:

- A famous example of the **cum** temporal clause is Cicero's saying, **Cum tacent, clamant**, *When they are silent, they cry aloud*, meaning that they (i.e., the senators) have made their feelings clear without having to express them. In **cum** clauses, the appearance of **cum** with the indicative is much less frequent than with the subjunctive.

### *Time Clauses with the Indicative* (When, As soon as)

Temporal or time clauses introduced by words such as **ubi,** *when,* and **simul atque** or **simul ac,** *as soon as,* are found with the indicative and express pure time.

### *Clause of Anticipation* (Before)

Time clauses introduced by anticipatory words such as **antequam** and **priusquam**, *before,* are found with both indicative and subjunctive verbs. In indicative clauses, which refer strictly to the time of something that has actually occurred, the present, perfect, and future perfect tenses are used. In subjunctive clauses, when expectancy or action that did not actually occur is expressed in past time, the imperfect tense is used:

Indicative (actually happens/happened):

> **[Priusquam Aeneas ad Italiam <u>pervenerat</u>], magna tempestas coorta est.**
> *[Before Aeneas <u>had reached</u> Italy], a great storm arose.*

Subjunctive (anticipated as happening):

> **[Antequam omnes naves <u>delerentur</u>], vis tempestatis cecidit.**
> *[Before all the ships <u>were destroyed</u>], the force of the storm weakened.*

## Dum *Clauses with the Indicative*

The adverbs **dum** or **donec** + the <u>indicative</u> express an actual fact in pure time and mean *while, as long as*, depending upon the context:

> **[Dum Troiani (Trojani) ad Italiam navigabant], Palinurus in mare cecidit.**
> *[While the Trojans were sailing to Italy], Palinurus fell overboard.*

## Dum *Clauses with the Subjunctive*

**Dum** or **donec** also can have the meaning *until* when expressing expectancy or anticipation. In this case the verb of the dependent clause is <u>subjunctive</u>:

> **Aeneas multa passus est [dum conderet] urbem.** (Vergil)
> *Aeneas endured many things [until he could found] the city.*

## Provisional Clauses

**Dum** (often strengthened by **modo** = **dummodo**) + the present or imperfect <u>subjunctive</u> can also be translated *provided that* or *if only*, in which case the clause is known as a clause of proviso:

> **Oderint [dum metuant].** (Attributed to Caligula by Suetonius)
> *Let them hate me [provided that they fear me].*

# Cum Concessive Clause *(Although)*

The word concessive implies that the statement within the **cum** clause is granted or assumed as true by the speaker or writer. In this context, **cum** means *although* and introduces a clause with its verb in the subjunctive mood. The concessive **cum** clause is often (but not always) accompanied by the word **tamen**, *nevertheless*, in the main clause:

> **[Cum Vergilius de armis viroque caneret], (tamen) de femina optime scripsit.**
> *[Although (or Granted that) Vergil sang about arms and a man], (nevertheless) he did his best writing about a woman.*

Note:

- The words **quamquam** and **etsi**, meaning *although*, also introduce concessive clauses, either with the indicative or the subjunctive, depending upon whether or not the clause contains a statement of fact.

## Tips on Translating *Cum* Clauses

When translating **cum** clauses, which are almost all grammatically identical, try one meaning of **cum**, then another, etc., to see which meaning makes the best sense in the context of the sentence. **Cum** clauses are regularly found with subjunctive verbs in either the imperfect or pluperfect tense. Be especially alert for the appearance of **cum** as a preposition. Questions on standardized tests are not designed to be misleading and will rarely present you with a grammatical decision that is not clearly defined.

### Quick Study of *Cum* Clauses

| Type of clause | Cue in main clause | Meaning of clause | Function |
|---|---|---|---|
| **Indicative** | | | |
| Temporal | **eo tempore, tum** | *when, whenever* | specific time |
| **Subjunctive** | | | |
| Causal | | *since, because* | gives a reason |
| Circumstantial | | *when* | general circumstance |
| Concessive | **tamen** | *although* | truth granted by writer |

## Quick Study of Time Clauses

| Type of clause | Introd. word | Meaning of clause | Function |
|---|---|---|---|
| **Indicative** | | | |
| Temporal | **ubi** <br> **simul atque/ac** | *when* <br> *as soon as* | pure time |
| | **dum*** <br> **donec*** | *while, until* <br> *as long as* | fact in real time |
| | **cum** | *when* | specific time |
| **Subjunctive** | | | |
| Circumstantial | **cum** | *when* | general circumstance |
| Anticipatory | **antequam**** | *before* | anticipation |
| | **priusquam**** | | |
| | **dum** | *until* | intention, expectancy |
| Provisonal | **dum(modo)** | *provided that* | conditional wish |

# Practice Questions

1.  <u>Cum</u> Augustus novam Romam aedificare vellet, tamen dicebat "O fortunati, quorum iam moenia surgunt!"

    (A) When

    (B) Because

    (C) Provided that

    (D) Although

2.  <u>Cum Aeneas Carthagine excessisset</u>, Dido se necare constituit.

    (A) Since Aeneas left Carthage

    (B) When Aeneas leaves Carthage

    (C) When Aeneas had left Carthage

    (D) Since Aeneas was leaving Carthage

3.  <u>When Troy had been captured, it was burned</u>.

    (A) Troia (Troja) cum capta esset, incensa est.

    (B) Troia (Troja) dum capiebatur, incensa est.

    (C) Troia (Troja) capta, incensa erat.

    (D) Troia (Troja) cum caperetur, incendebatur.

---

\* These clauses are also found with their verbs in the subjunctive.

\*\* These clauses are also found with their verbs in the indicative.

4.  Vergilius <u>cum</u> apibus avibusque ruri libenter habitabat.
    (A) when                          (C) since
    (B) with                          (D) although

5.  <u>Cum Vergilius mortuus sit</u>, Aeneis non completa est.
    (A) While Vergil was dying        (C) When Vergil dies
    (B) After Vergil died             (D) Because Vergil died

6.  When Aeneas <u>heard</u> Cerberus barking, the Sibyl said, "Cave canem, Cave canem, Cave canem!"
    (A) audiret                       (C) audivisset
    (B) auditus erat                  (D) audit

7.  Eodem tempore cum Vergilius de Marcello . . . , Augustus lacrimavit.
    (A) legit                         (C) legat
    (B) l egeret                      (D) legisset

8.  Romani, <u>cum crederent</u> Aeneam gentem togatam condidisse, Aeneidem legebant.
    (A) since they believed           (C) after they believed
    (B) whenever they believe         (D) although they believe

9.  Troianis fugientibus, cum Creusa e conspectu . . . tum Aeneas ad urbem rediit.
    (A) abiisset                      (C) abit
    (B) abeat                         (D) abierat

10. <u>Cum Augustus de Livia certior factus esset</u>, cogitavit, "Dux femina facti."
    (A) Because Augustus is informed about Livia
    (B) When Augustus was informed about Livia
    (C) When Augustus had been informed about Livia
    (D) Since Augustus was being informed about Livia

## *Sententiae Antiquae*

1.  A man is outside of his body at that very moment <u>when he is angry.</u> (Publilius Syrus)
    (A) cum iratus est                (C) cum iratus sit
    (B) cum iratus esset              (D) cum iratus esse potest

2. <u>Satis est beatus qui potest cum vult mori</u>. (Publilius Syrus)

   (A)  He is happy enough who wants to die when he can.

   (B)  Happy enough is the one who can die when he wants.

   (C)  He who dies can be happy enough whenever he wants.

   (D)  Because he wants to die, he who is happy enough can.

3. <u>Quae cum ita sint</u>, Catilina, . . . . (Cicero)

   (A)  Since these things are this way    (C)  Although this was the case

   (B)  Whenever this is true    (D)  Whatever things are so

4. Quod bellum oderunt, cum fide de pace . . . . (Livy)

   (A)  agerent    (C)  egissent

   (B)  agebant    (D)  aguntur

5. You hope (to see) a fox's tail at the very moment <u>when you see</u> his ears. (Medieval)

   (A)  cum vidisti    (C)  cum videas

   (B)  cum vides    (D)  cum visurus es

**Stumper:**  <u>Cum essent</u> civium domini, libertorum erant servi. (Pliny the Younger)

   (A)  Seeing that they were    (C)  Since they had been

   (B)  Although they were    (D)  Provided they are

## Answers

1.  Concessive  **(D)**
    The appearance of the word **tamen** in the main clause cues the **cum** clause in this sentence as concessive. The sentence reads, "<u>Although</u> Augustus wished to build a new Rome, nevertheless he said, 'O fortunate are they whose walls are already rising!'" which is a quote from Book 2 of the *Aeneid*. The translations in Answer (A) "When" and (B) "Because" are possible grammatically, but less likely than "Although," because of **tamen**. Answer (B) "Provided that," which is a provisional clause, does not fit the context.

2.  Circumstantial  **(C)**
    This sentence requires decisions about the type of clause and the tense of the verb. Since the verb **excessisset** is in the pluperfect tense, Answers (A), (B), and (D) are incorrect because they offer translations in the simple past, present, and imperfect tenses, respectively. The clause is translated as circumstantial because the only answer with the subordinate verb in the correct tense is introduced by the word "when." The sentence reads, "<u>When Aeneas had left Carthage</u>, Dido decided

to kill herself." (For the forms of the various tenses of the subjunctive, see Chapter 16D.1.)

3.  Circumstantial **(A)**
    The subordinate clause in this sentence can be found either with an indicative or a subjunctive verb. Answer (B) provides Latin that does not give the translation "When Troy had been captured." Answer (C) is incorrect because the verb of the main clause, the pluperfect form **incensa erat**, does not translate "it was burned" correctly. Answers (A) and (D) contain subjunctive verbs, so the decision becomes one of tense. The original sentence reads "had been captured," which requires a pluperfect passive verb form in the subordinate clause. This is **capta esset**. Answer (D) gives the verb **caperetur** in the imperfect tense.

4.  Prepositional phrase **(B)**
    This question is included to "keep you honest" about the possibility that **cum** can be a preposition followed by a noun in the ablative case, as here: **cum apibus avibusque**. The sentence reads, "Vergil gladly lived in the country <u>with the birds and bees</u>."

5.  Causal **(D)**
    The **cum** clause in this sentence makes the best sense as a causal clause, "Because Vergil died, the *Aeneid* was not completed." Answers (A) "While Vergil was dying" and (C) "When Vergil dies" do not translate the perfect subjunctive form **mortuus sit** correctly. Answer (B) "After Vergil died" does not give an appropriate rendering of the conjunction **cum**.

6.  Circumstantial **(A)**
    Since the choices of answers provide two verbs in the indicative and two in the subjunctive, the decision must be made on the basis of tense. Answers (B) and (C) are incorrect because they are pluperfect and the imperfect or perfect is required to translate "When Aeneas heard...." Answer (C) **audit** is in the present tense, leaving **audiret**, an imperfect subjunctive form in secondary sequence, as the correct answer. Hopefully, you enjoyed the humor of this sentence!

7.  Temporal **(A)**
    The time phrase "at the moment" specifies the time of the action of the verb in the **cum** clause, thus requiring an indicative verb in a temporal clause. As Answers (B) **legeret**, (C) **legat**, and (D)     **legisset** are all forms of the subjunctive, Answer (A) **legit** is correct.

8.  Causal **(A)**
    This sentence reads, "<u>Since</u> the Romans believed that Aeneas had founded the toga-ed race, they read the *Aeneid*." Answers (B) and (C) do not correctly translate the **cum** of the subordinate clause in this sentence. Answer (D) "although" is possible grammatically, but even if the clause **cum crederent** were concessive (note that the following "trigger word" **tamen** is missing), this clause does not make sense when translated as concessive.

9.  Temporal  **(D)**
    The correlative "time words," **tum...cum**, "at the time when...," specify the time of the action of the clause, thereby establishing it as a temporal clause with the indicative. The correct answer is therefore **abierat.** Answers (B) and (C) are in the present tense, which is incorrect in a sentence that contains **rediit**, a verb that requires the secondary sequence in the subordinate clause. Answer (A) **abiisset,** would make the clause circumstantial and the time element more generalized. The sentence reads, "While the Trojans were fleeing, Aeneas returned to the city at the time when Creusa <u>had vanished</u>."

10. Circumstantial  **(C)**
    The tense of the verb in the subordinate clause determines which answer is correct. As **factus esset** is a form of the pluperfect passive, Answer (C) is correct. Answer (A) requires the present tense and Answers (B) and (D) "was informed" and "was being informed" require the imperfect tense.

## *Sentientiae Antiquae* Answers

1.  Temporal  **(A)**
    The appearance of "at that very moment" in the sentence creates a specific time frame for the action of the subordinate clause, which is a temporal clause with the indicative. Answers (B) and (C) contain subjunctive clauses with subjunctive verbs in the imperfect and present tenses, respectively, and Answer (D) is not a correct translation because the verb **potest** does not appear in the original sentence.

2.  Temporal  **(B)**
    The use of the indicative in the subordinate clause **cum vult** means that Publilius Syrus is saying that he who dies at the very moment that he wishes is happy. Answers (A), (C), and (D) all change the meaning of the original statement by altering the elements contained in the **cum** clause.

3.  Causal  **(A)**
    Answer (C) contains a mistranslation of the present subjunctive verb **sint** and (D) a mistranslation of the relative pronoun **quae**, which refers to some antecedent that is unidentified here. When **cum** means "whenever," the indicative mood is used, eliminating Answer (B).

4.  Prepositional phrase  **(B)**
    **Cum fide** is a prepositional phrase, which removes from consideration the use of **cum** in a subordinate clause and any need for the subjunctive, eliminating Answers (A) and (C) The present passive form in Answer (D) does not make sense in the context here. The sentence reads, "Because they hated war, they were acting <u>with reliability</u> concerning peace."

5.  Temporal **(B)**
Answer (A) **cum vides** is the only choice that contains a verb in the correct tense. Answers (A) and (D) all contain verbs in incorrect tenses, i.e., perfect indicative and the future tense in an active periphrastic construction. Answer (C) is incorrect because **cum** circumstantial clauses are found with verbs in the imperfect or pluperfect tenses, and **videas** is in the present tense. This sentence indicates that at the specific time when you see the ears of a fox, i.e., his head, then he probably sees you, and you may be in danger. At the time when you see the tail, i.e., his back, he has passed by and you are safe.

**Stumper:  (B)**
Answers (C) and (D) are incorrect because they contain incorrect translations of the underlined verb **essent**, which is in the imperfect tense. Answer (A) contains a verb that is correctly translated ("they were") but has a less acceptable meaning than that of Answer (B) in its context. The sentence reads, "<u>Although they were</u> the masters of the citizens, they were the slaves of freedmen." Note the omission of **tamen**.

## Quick Study of Subordinate Clauses

| **Indicative (Factual)** | |
| --- | --- |
| 1.  Relative<br>*who, which, that* | **Plinius homo erat [cui imperator credidit].**<br>*Pliny was a person [<u>whom</u> the emperor trusted].* (Chapter 13B; see also #s 11 and 12, below) |
| 2.  **Quod** Causal<br>*because, since* | **Plinius praefectus creatus est [quod officiosus erat].**<br>*Pliny was appointed an official [<u>because</u> (it was a fact that) he was dutiful].* (Chapter 16D.5; see also #13, below) |
| 3.  **Cum** Temporal<br>*when* | **[Eo tempore <u>cum</u> Plinius natus est], suus pater Comi habitabat.**<br>*[At the time <u>when</u> Plinus was born], his father was living at Comum.* (Chapter 16D.6; see also #s 14, 15, and 16, below) |
| **Dum** Temporal<br>*while, as long as, until* | **[Dum in Bithynia erat], Plinius multas epistulas ad imperatorem misit.**<br>*[<u>While</u> Pliny was in Bithynia], he sent many letters to the emperor.* (Chapter 16D.6; see also #19, below) |
| Anticipatory<br>*before* | **Plinius consul Romae erat [<u>priusquam</u> proconsul in Bithynia fuit].**<br>*Pliny was a consul in Rome [(in fact) <u>before</u> he was governor in Bithynia].* (Chapter 16D.6; see also #18, below) |

| Subjunctive (non-factual) | |
|---|---|
| 4. Conditional<br>*if* | **[Nisi Mons Vesuvius erupuisset], urbs Pompeii mansisset.**<br>*[If Mount Vesuvius had not erupted], the city of Pompeii would have remained.* (past contrary to fact, Chapter 16D.3) |
| 5. **Ut** Purpose<br>*to, in order that* | **Quintilianus Plinium docebat [ut melius scriberet].**<br>*Quintilian taught Pliny [to write better].* (Chapter 16D.4; see also # 12, below) |
| 6. **Ut** Result<br>*that* | **Tantum periculum erat [ut multi Pompeiis fugerent].**<br>*The danger was so great [that many fled from Pompeii].* (Chapter 16D.4; see also #7, below) |
| 7. Substantive Result<br>*that* | **Plinius effecit [ut complures proconsules damnarentur].**<br>*Pliny brought it about [that several governors were condemned].* (Chapter 16D.4; see also #6, above) |
| 8. Indirect Command<br>*that* | **Plinius Christianis imperabat [ne in unum locum congregarent].**<br>*Pliny ordered the Christians [not to gather together in one place].* (Chapter 16D.4) |
| 9. Fear<br>*(that)* | **Hodie multi timent [ne Vesuvius iterum erupturus sit].**<br>*Today many are afraid [that Vesuvius is going to erupt again].* (Chapter 16D.4) |
| 10. Indirect Question<br>*who, what, why* | **Secundus cognoscere voluit [cur amicus Tacitus annales scripsisset].**<br>*Secundus wanted to know [why his friend Tacitus had written the Annals].* (Chapter 16D.5; see also #17, below) |
| 11. Relative Characteristic<br>*the type who, that* | **Secundus homo erat [qui eruditionem magni aestimaret].**<br>*Secundus was the type of person [who thought highly of education].* (Chapter 16D.5; see also #s 1 and 12) |
| 12. Relative Purpose<br>*to, in order to* | **Plinius legatum misit [qui imperatorem de Christianis certiorem faceret].**<br>*Pliny sent an envoy [to inform the emperor about the Christians].* (Chapter 16D.5; see also #s 1 and 11, above) |

| **Subjunctive (non-factual)** *(continued)* | |
|---|---|
| 13. **Quod** Causal<br>*since, because* | **[Quod multi Christiani essent], multi delatores erant.**<br>*[Because there were many Christians], there were many informers.* (Chapter 16D.5; see also #2 and 14) |
| 14. **Cum** Causal<br>*since, because* | **[Cum Christiani in provincia essent], Plinius consilium Traiani petebat.**<br>*[Since there were Christians in the province], Pliny sought the advice of Trajan.* (Chapter 16D.6; see also #s 1 and 13, above) |
| 15. **Cum**<br>Circumstantial<br>*when* | **[Cum Plinius proconsul in Bithynia esset], cives florebant.**<br>*[When Pliny was proconsul in Bithynia], the citizens were prosperous.* (Chapter 16D.6; see also #s 3, 14, and 16) |
| 16. **Cum**<br>Concessive<br>*although* | **[Cum Bithynia provincia Romana esset], tamen cives Graece loquebantur.**<br>*[Although Bithynia was a Roman province], nevertheless the citizens spoke Greek.* (Chapter 16D.6; see also #s 3, 14, and 15, above) |
| 17. Doubt<br>*doubt that* | **Est non dubium [quin Plinius suum patruum dilexerit].**<br>*There is no doubt [that Pliny held his uncle in high regard].* (Chapter 16D.5; see also #10, above) |
| 18. Anticipatory<br>*before* | **[Priusquam de Vesuvio scribere posset], patruus Plini mortuus est.**<br>*[Before he could write about Vesuvius], Pliny's uncle died.* (Chapter 16D.6; see also #3, above) |
| 19. Anticipatory<br>*until* | **Plinius exspectabat [dum audiret] nuntium ex imperatore.**<br>*Pliny was waiting [to hear,* lit., *until he should hear] news from the emperor.* (Chapter 16D.6; see also #s 3 and 18, above.) |
| 20. Proviso<br>*provided that,*<br>*if only* | **Licebat servis custodes in Bithynia esse [dummodo fideles essent].**<br>*Slaves were allowed to be guards in Bithynia, [provided that they were trustworthy].* (Chapter 16D.6; see also #3, above) |

# Chapter 16E: Latin Sentence Structure

## Conjunctions

Although conjunctions are rarely considered an important feature of reading Latin, they are the "connective tissue" of a Latin sentence and therefore are important for translation and comprehension. Conjunctions are indeclinable words that join together words, phrases, clauses, and sentences. They are used to connect two ideas of equal importance (coordinating) or to attach a dependent or secondary idea to a main thought (subordinating). Since dependent clauses appear frequently in Latin, subordinating conjunctions are most important for understanding the relationship between the dependent clause and the main clause:

Coordinating conjunction: **Cicero in rostra ascendit <u>et</u> orationem habuit.**

*Cicero mounted the Rostra <u>and</u> gave a speech.*

Subordinating conjunction: **Orationem habuit <u>ut</u> Pompeium laudaret**.

*He gave the speech <u>to</u> praise Pompey.*

### Important Coordinating Conjunctions

| | | | |
|---|---|---|---|
| et<br>-que<br>atque<br>ac | *and* | neque<br>nec | *nor, and not* |
| aut<br>vel<br>-ve | *or, either* | sive<br>seu | *whether, or* |
| sed<br>at | *but* | autem | *however* |
| nam<br>enim | *for* | quare (qua re)<br>quamobrem<br>  (quam ob rem) | *wherefore, for<br>which reason* |
| ergo<br>itaque<br>igitur | *therefore* | | |

## Important Subordinating Conjunctions

| | | |
|---|---|---|
| Causal: | **cum**<br>**quod**<br>**quia**<br>**quando**<br>**quoniam** | *because, since* |
| Conditional: | **si**<br>**nisi** | *if*<br>*if not, unless* |
| Concessive: | **cum**<br>**etsi**<br>**quamquam** | *although* |
| Interrogative: | **num**<br>**utrum**<br>**utrum . . . an** | *whether*<br><br>*whether . . . or* |
| Purpose/<br>Result | **ut**<br>**ne**<br>**ut . . . non** | *to, in order to, that, so that*<br>*that . . . not, lest*<br>*so that...not* (result) |
| Temporal: | **cum** | *when* |

## The Conjunction -*que*

The conjunction –**que**, which means *and*, is usually joined to the second of a combination of two words that are closely connected in meaning, e.g., (**in**) **terra marique**, *on land and sea,* or **Senatus Populusque Romanus (SPQR)**, *the Senate and People of Rome*. Here is an example in context:

> **Servi Ciceronis <u>fortiter fideliterque</u> ei serviebant.**
> *Cicero's slaves served him <u>bravely and faithfully</u>.*

When connecting clauses, -**que** is usually attached to the first word of the connected clause. The conjunction does not always connect the word to which it is attached with the word or those words immediately preceding it, but may be separated by intervening words:

> **Atticus Ciceroni [<u>discedenti</u>] e Curia [<u>procedentique</u>] ad bibliopolam occurrit.**
> *Atticus happened upon Cicero [<u>who was leaving</u> the Senate House] <u>and</u> [<u>proceeding</u> to the bookseller].*

> **[Epistula a Tirone <u>scripta est</u>], [iussu<u>que</u> Ciceronis ad Atticum <u>missa est</u>].**
> *[The letter <u>was transcribed</u> by Tiro] <u>and</u> [<u>was sent</u> to Atticus at Cicero's bidding].*

## Words that Correlate and Coordinate

Latin sentences often contain words that correlate, that is, they have partners or are paired. Such words are known as correlatives. These words are usually separated within the sentence, so, as you begin to comprehend the meaning, it is best to be alert to the possibility that their partners may appear further along. Here are some common examples of correlatives:

| | |
|---|---|
| **ibi . . . ubi** | *there . . . where* |
| **non solum . . . sed etiam** | *not only . . . but also* |
| **talis . . . qualis** | *uch . . . as* |
| **tantus . . . quantus** | *so great . . . .as (great)* |
| **tot . . . quot** | *so many . . . as (many)* |
| **tum . . . cum** | *then . . . when* |

In addition, some adverbs, as well as conjunctions, coordinate with one another, that is, they are found in pairs, e.g.,

| | |
|---|---|
| **aut . . . aut** (or **vel . . . vel**) | *either . . . or* |
| **cum . . . tum** | *while . . . so also* or *at the same time* |
| **et . . . et** (or **–que . . . -que**) | *both . . . .and* |
| **modo . . . modo** | *now . . . .now* |
| **neque . . . neque** (**nec . . . nec**) | *neither . . . nor* |
| **nunc . . . nunc** (or **iam . . . iam**) | *now . . . now* |
| **sive** (**seu** or enclitic **-ve**) **. . . sive** (**seu** or enclitic **-ve**) | *whether . . . or, if . . . if* |
| **tam . . . quam** | *so (as) . . . as* |

The following pairs of indefinite pronouns are also used in this way:

| | |
|---|---|
| **alius . . . alius** (pl., **alii . . . alii** | *the one . . . another some . . . others)* |
| **alter . . . alter** | *the one . . . the other* |

## Examples of How Correlatives Work

In the following example of the use of correlatives, **quam** correlates with **tam**:

**Ea <u>tam</u> antiqua est <u>quam</u> Amphitheatrum Flavium!**
> *She is <u>so</u> (or <u>as</u>) old <u>as</u> the Colosseum!*

Such sentences are often condensed. The expanded original reads:

**Ea tam antiqua est quam Amphitheatrum Flavium (antiquum est).**
> *She is so (or as) old as the Colosseum (is old).*

In the following sentence, note the relationship between **tantam** and **quanta**:

> **Dives <u>tantam</u> pecuniam habebat <u>quanta</u> erat numquam satis.**
> *The rich man had <u>so</u> (or as) <u>much</u> money <u>as</u> was never enough, lit., so much money as much (as) was never enough.*

The relative adjective **quanta** must agree in gender and number (feminine singular) with that of its correlative antecedent **tantam**, but observe also that its case (nominative) is determined by how it functions within its clause, i.e., **quanta** (**pecunia**) serves as the subject of its clause, whereas **tantam pecuniam** serves as the direct object of the main clause.

## Idioms

An idiom (fr. Greek, "one's own," "personal") is an expression in one language that cannot be expressed precisely in another or has a meaning that requires familiarity with the cultural context of the language, e.g., English "to bum a ride." Idioms are found regularly in Latin and should be considered in any thorough review of the language. Here are some common Latin idioms:

| | |
|---|---|
| **bellum gerere**, *to wage war* | **in memoriam habere,** *to remember* |
| **certior facere**, *to inform* | **orationem habere,** *to deliver a speech* |
| **consilium capere**, *to make a plan* | **proelium committere,** *to begin battle* |
| **gratias agere**, *to thank* | **iter facere,** *to make a journey, travel* |
| **in animo habere**, *to intend* | **vitam agere,** *to live one's life* |

## Thoughts About the Structure of a Latin Sentence

Remember that Latin, when expressing a thought, makes use of participles and dependent clauses more often than English does. When in Rome, do as the Romans do. Think like a Roman!

> Latin: *After this was done, he did that.*
>
> English: *He did this and then he did that.*

- Latin regularly (but not always!) places the most emphatic words at the beginning and end of a clause or sentence. The intervening words contribute to the overall sense.

- The words within word groups or "sense units" in a Latin sentence are not mixed together except in poetry, when a particular effect is desired by the poet. Consider the following prose sentence:

> **Urbe Roma condita, multi mirabantur num Romulus deus facturus esset.**
> *After Rome had been founded, many wondered whether Romulus would become a god.*

Words from the main clause **multi mirabantur** may not intrude upon or interject themselves into the ablative absolute **urbe Roma condita**. No elements from either of these constructions may intrude upon the dependent clause **num . . . facturus esset**, and so forth. However, one word group may contain another.

• Patterns of word order do appear in Latin sentence structure (see more below). "Normal" word order in a Latin sentence consists of subject – indirect object – direct object – adverb and prepositions – verb, with the result that the subject and verb "bookend" the thought. Remember that such a pattern is common, but not obligatory.

• Remember, too, that the functional meaning of a Latin word derives from its ending, which forces your mind's eye to work from right to left, or backwards, through a word, e.g., in translating **mittebat**, you read -**t**, *he*, -**ba**-, *was*, **mitte**-, *sending*. This puts your mind, which is trained to read English from left to right, at odds with itself and creates a sort of mental tension that must be reduced through practice in translation.

• No doubt you have observed that Latin can express the same thought in fewer words than English. As the Romans, at least early in their history, were spare and economical by nature, their language is often condensed or elliptical, leaving out verbal elements whose meaning is "understood," i.e., must be deduced from context:

> **Qui non est hodie, cras minus aptus erit.**
> *(He) who is not (ready) today will be less ready tomorrow.*

If the Latin were expanded, it would read:

> **(Is) qui non (aptus) est hodie, cras (ille) minus aptus erit.**

# Some Observations About Word Order

## A Word or Two about Adjectives and Word Order

Roman writers, especially poets, often separated an adjective from its noun for visual or phonetic effect, e.g.,

> **"O <u>miseri</u>, quae tanta insania, <u>cives</u>?"** (Laocoon, in the *Aeneid*)
> *O <u>pitiable</u> <u>citizens</u>, what madness is this?"*

In the following line, Horace describes a maid embraced by a youth while both are surrounded by roses:

> Quis <u>multa</u> **gracilis** [ te ] **puer** in <u>rosa</u>?
> *What **slender boy** (embraces) [you] amid <u>many a rose</u>?*

Although an adjective or adverb generally precedes the word that it modifies (with a few exceptions, such as **res publica** or **populus Romanus**), an adjective can also be found after the noun it modifies. When two adjectives modify the same noun, they can be connected with **et**, e.g., **Tiberis erat flumen celere et turbidum**, *the Tiber was a swift, wild river*. Note that the conjunction is omitted in English. It is most important to be familiar with the forms of adjectives and nouns and to think clearly about your options regarding the words that may or may not go together in a noun-adjective combination.*

## Some Additional Observations Regarding Word Order

- The first position in a sentence is emphatic.
- The more unusual the position of a word, the more emphatic its meaning.
- A name or a personal pronoun often stands in an emphatic place.
- Demonstrative, interrogative, and possessive adjectives regularly proceed their nouns, e.g., **haec mater**, **Quae mater**? and **mea culpa**.
- The adjective precedes the noun modified, just as the adverb precedes the verb. Adjectives used as attributes are usually placed after the noun modified, e.g., **senator prudens, servus ignavissimus**.
- Certain common conjunctions, such as **itaque**, regularly come first in a sentence, whereas words such as **autem, enim, igitur, quidem, quoque**, and **vero** are never found first. **Quidem** and **quoque** immediately follow the words they emphasize.
- A preposition regularly precedes its noun, e.g., **in hoc signo vinces**; a prepositional phrase often immediately precedes the verb to which it is connected.
- When a form of **esse** is used as the main verb, it regularly stands first, or before its subject, e.g., **Est prudens**, *He is wise*.
- The negative, such as **haud, non, neque**, precedes the word it affects.

## Steps to Use When Translating a Latin Sentence

- Read through the entire sentence to see all of its words in context. Get a feel for the meaning from the particular vocabulary used and from the way in which the forms associate with one another. Warning: do not use derivatives as meanings when rendering a Latin word in English, as the meaning of the Latin root and its English derivative often vary, e.g., **tradere**, *hand over*, not *trade*.
- Take the words in the order in which they were written and develop the sense as you proceed. Focus on recognizing the way the sentence is structured, i.e., the main clause/s, dependent clause/s, and phrase/s in the sequence in which they are found. As you move through the sentence, divide it into "sense" units by placing real or imagined brackets around word groups, e.g.,

---

* See also "How Latin Poetry Differs From Prose," Chapter 7.

| ablative absolute | main clause | dependent clause (indirect question) |
|---|---|---|

**[Urbe Roma condita], [multi mirabantur] [num Romulus deus facturus esset].**

*[After Rome had been founded], [many wondered] [whether Romulus would become a god].*

<u>It is most important that you understand the meaning of the thought in the Latin sentence before expressing it in English.</u>

- Since much of how Latin expresses meaning depends on the relationship of dependent clauses to main clauses, as well as to other dependent clauses, be familiar with how these interact.

- The main subject or object of a sentence is found in the main clause, not the dependent clause. Avoid identifying the verb of the dependent clause as the main verb.

**Commovebaturne Remus quod paucas aves modo viderat?**

*Was Remus upset because he had seen only a few birds?*

Note that the verb **viderat,** while found in the slot normally occupied by the main verb, actually serves as the verb of the dependent **quod** clause.

- Think of the words in a clause as a self-contained unit of thought. Don't pull words out of a main clause or a dependent clause and place them somewhere else in the sentence (see above). Use brackets to help you visualize by containing or holding together the words in a clause or sense unit:

**[Cum Remus moenia urbis Romae derideret], Romulus iratus factus est.**

*[Because Remus was mocking the city walls of Rome], Romulus became angry.*

Once you have begun to articulate the meaning of a dependent clause, complete the meaning of that clause before moving further into the sentence.

- The meaning of a dependent clause usually relates to a specific word or phrase in the main clause, which regularly precedes the dependent clause. Continue to look backward as you move forward through the sentence and try your best to retain what has come before. Use graphic symbols such as arrows to link one part of a sentence to another.

- The emphatic words in both main and dependent clauses are usually found at the beginning and end of their sense units. Look for additional "directional signals" provided by the placement of important words or word groups as you proceed through the sentence. (Remember, the Romans did not use punctuation as we do!) In the following sentence, note how the word **hominem** is common to two different grammatical constructions:

**Nonne nemo credit [hominem (qui suum fratrem occiderit) deum fieri posse]?**

*Surely no one believes [that a man (who has killed his own brother) can become a god]?*

This sentence contains the dependent clause **qui . . . occiderit** within the indirect statement **(credit) hominem . . . posse.** The relative clause describes its antecedent **hominem,** which also serves as the subject of the infinitive in indirect statement and therefore binds together the two constructions.

- Your initial translation may result in a sort of "translationese," which will require further exploration of the possible meaning through the juggling of words, phrases, and clauses. Rephrasing and the application of English idiom are often required to make the sense clear.

# PRACTICE EXAMS

## AP Latin: Vergil

# PRACTICE EXAM 1

### This exam is also on CD-ROM in our special interactive AP Latin TEST*ware*®

## AP Latin: Vergil

## Multiple-Choice Section

**TIME:** 60 Minutes
50 Questions

---

**DIRECTIONS:** Each reading passage is followed by a series of questions and incomplete statements that are related to the passage. Select the best answer or completion and fill in the appropriate oval on your answer sheet.

---

### A sad time in the Underworld

"O nate, ingentem luctum ne quaere tuorum;
ostendent terris hunc tantum fata neque ultra
esse sinent. Nimium vobis Romana propago
*Line* visa potens, superi, propria haec si dona fuissent.
5   Quantos ille virum magnam Mavortis ad urbem
campus aget gemitus! Vel quae, Tiberine, videbis
funera, cum tumulum praeterlabere recentem! . . .
Heu! miserande puer, si qua fata aspera rumpas,
tu Marcellus eris! Manibus date lilia plenis,
10  purpureos spargam flores animamque nepotis
his saltem accumulem donis et fungar inani
munere."

1.  This speech is given by whom to whom?
    (A) the Cumaean Sibyl to Aeneas
    (B) Venus to Juno
    (C) Jupiter to Hercules
    (D) Anchises to Aeneas

2. The common prose equivalent of the grammatical construction ne quaere (line 1) is

   (A) non quaere
   
   (B) noli quaerere
   
   (C) nolite quaerere
   
   (D) ne quaeras

3. In lines 1–3 (O . . . sinent), the speaker is advising the listener not to grieve because

   (A) the fates will not allow it

   (B) the departed person is not related to the listener

   (C) the entire Roman Empire will be mourning

   (D) the deceased is not destined to live long

4. Line 4, the missing word that completes visa is

   (A) est
   
   (B) esse
   
   (C) sum
   
   (D) esset

5. Si dona fuissent (line 4) is translated as

   (A) If the gifts had been . . .

   (B) If the gifts are . . .

   (C) If the gifts were to be . . .

   (D) If the gifts should be . . .

6. The case of virum (line 5) is

   (A) accusative
   
   (B) genitive
   
   (C) vocative
   
   (D) nominative

7. Which of the following figures of speech is found in lines 5–6 (Quantos . . . gemitus)?

   (A) personification
   
   (B) ellipsis
   
   (C) hyperbaton
   
   (D) asyndeton

8. Line 5–6 (Quantos . . . gemitus) imply that

   (A) the god Mars will bring grief to the city

   (B) there will be a funeral in the Campus Martius

   (C) Mars will be acknowledged as patron god of Rome

   (D) in the Campus Martius many men will die

9. The verb <u>praeterlabere</u> (line 7) is translated

   (A) to glide past

   (B) glide past

   (C) you will glide past

   (D) about to glide past

10. Which of the following figures of speech is found in lines 8–9 (<u>Heu</u> ... <u>eris</u>)?

    (A) polysyndeton     (C) chiasmus

    (B) apostrophe     (D) aposiopesis

11. As an historical figure, Marcellus (line 9) was destined to be

    (A) Julius Caesar's son

    (B) conqueror of Hannibal

    (C) the son of Romulus

    (D) Augustus' heir

12. In lines 9–12 (<u>Manibus</u> . . . <u>munere</u>), we learn that Anchises wants to

    (A) honor his ancestors

    (B) remember past times

    (C) say prayers

    (D) perform a ritual burial

13. The metrical pattern of the first four feet of line 11 is

    (A) spondee-dactyl-spondee-spondee

    (B) spondee-dactyl-dactyl-spondee

    (C) dactyl-spondee-spondee-spondee

    (D) dactyl-spondee-spondee-dactyl

## The Sabine women prevent war

Iam stabant acies ferro mortique paratae
    iam lituus[1] pugnae signa daturus erat,
cum raptae veniunt inter patresque virosque
*Line*    inque sinu natos, pignora[2] cara, tenent.
 5  Ut medium campi scissis tetigere capillis,
    in terram posito procubuere genu,
et quasi sentirent, blando clamore nepotes
    tendebant ad avos[3] bracchia parva suos . . .
Tela viris animique cadunt, gladiisque remotis
10    dant soceri[4] generis accipiuntque manus,
laudatasque tenent natas, scutoque[5] nepotem
    fert avus: hic scuti dulcior usus erat.

1 lituus, -i, m.: bugle, war trumpet
2 pignus, pignoris, n.: pledge, token
3 avus, -i, m.: grandfather
4 socer, soceri, m.: father-in-law
5 scutum, -i, n.: shield

14. In lines 1–2 (Iam . . . erat), we learn that
    (A) the battle lines were ready
    (B) the signal for battle had been given
    (C) the fighting was just under way
    (D) the fighting was fierce and to the death

15. Which of the following figures of speech occurs in line 1 (Iam . . . paratae)?
    (A) transferred epithet    (C) prolepsis
    (B) synecdoche    (D) polysyndeton

16. In line 3, raptae is translated
    (A) having captured    (C) about to capture
    (B) while capturing    (D) having been captured

17. In line 4, the subject of tenent is
    (A) raptae (line 3)
    (B) patresque virosque (line 3)
    (C) natos (line 4)
    (D) pignora (line 4)

18. In line 5, <u>tetigere</u> is translated
    (A) touch
    (B) they touched
    (C) to have touched
    (D) to touch

19. In lines 5–8 (<u>Ut</u> . . . <u>suos</u>), we learn that
    (A) the women covered their heads
    (B) the women embraced their husbands around the knees
    (C) the young children held out their arms to their grandfathers
    (D) the older folk wept and grieved for their misfortune

20. In line 7, <u>quasi sentirent</u> is translated
    (A) as if they understood
    (B) which they understood
    (C) so that they might understand
    (D) since they understand

21. In line 8, <u>ad avos</u> . . . <u>suos</u> means
    (A) to his own grandfather
    (B) to someone else's grandfathers
    (C) to the grandfathers themselves
    (D) to their own grandfathers

22. Which of the following figures of speech occurs in lines 9–10 (<u>Tela</u> . . . <u>manus</u>)?
    (A) metaphor
    (B) chiasmus
    (C) zeugma
    (D) polyptoton

23. In line 9, <u>gladiis remotis</u> is translated
    (A) while putting away their swords
    (B) after they had put away their swords
    (C) when their swords were being put away
    (D) as they were about to put away their swords

24. In lines 11–12 (<u>laudatasque</u> . . . <u>usus erat</u>), we learn that
    (A) gifts were exchanged by the adversaries
    (B) grandfathers carried their grandsons on their shields
    (C) sons praised and embraced their fathers
    (D) children were returned to their parents

25. In line 12, <u>dulcior</u> means

(A) sweeter

(C) rather sweetly

(B) very sweet

(D) much sweeter

### Why Fabricius recommended an enemy for the consulship

Fabricius Luscinus magnā glorīa vir magnisque rebus gestis fuit. P. Cornelius Rufinus manu quidem strenuus et bellator bonus militarisque disciplinae peritus admodum fuit, sed furax homo[1]
*Line* et avaritiā acri erat. Hunc Fabricius non probabat neque amico
5 utebatur osusque eum morum causā fuit. Sed cum in temporibus rei publicae difficillimis consules creandi forent et is Rufinus peteret consulatum competitoresque eius essent inbelles quidam et futtiles,[2] summa ope adnixus est Fabricius uti Rufino consulatus deferretur. Eam rem plerisque admirantibus, quod hominem avarum cui esset
10 inimicissimus, creari consulem vellet, "Malo," inquit, "civis me compilet,[3] quam hostis vendat."

1 <u>osus</u>, -a, -um, adj: having hated
2 <u>futtilis</u>, -is, -e, adj.: good for nothing, worthless
3 <u>compilo</u>, -are, -avi, -atus: to rob

26. In lines 2–3 (<u>P. Cornelius</u> . . . <u>fuit</u>), we learn that Rufinus was

(A) antagonistic and vengeful

(B) skilled in matters of war

(C) inexperienced as a leader

(D) tough but undisciplined

27. The case of <u>disciplinae</u> (line 3) depends on

(A) <u>bellator</u> (line 2)

(C) <u>peritus</u> (line 2)

(B) <u>militarisque</u> (line 2)

(D) <u>fuit</u> (line 2)

28. Lines 3–4 (<u>sed</u> . . . <u>erat</u>) tell us that Rufinus was also

(A) cruel

(C) ambitious

(B) clever

(D) greedy

29. In lines 4–5 (<u>Hunc</u> . . . <u>fuit</u>), we are told that Fabricius
    (A) respected Rufinus, but did not like him
    (B) thoroughly disliked Rufinus because of his character
    (C) considered Rufinus a friend, despite his shortcomings
    (D) disapproved of Rufinus, but did not hate him

30. In lines 5–6 (<u>Sed</u> . . . <u>forent</u>), we learn that, during the Republic, consuls
    (A) had to be elected in troubled times
    (B) made the times more difficult
    (C) could be appointed rather than elected
    (D) sometimes failed to deal with a crisis

31. In line 6, <u>forent</u> is an alternative to the more traditional form
    (A) <u>fuerunt</u>          (C) <u>essent</u>
    (B) <u>futurum esse</u>     (D) <u>fuisse</u>

32. In lines 6–7 (<u>et</u> . . . <u>futtiles</u>), we learn that
    (A) the enemies of Rufinus were seeking the consulship
    (B) Rufinus intended to make war on the consuls, who were his enemies
    (C) His rivals for the consulship planned to kill Rufinus
    (D) Rufinus' political adversaries were weak

33. In line 6, <u>peteret</u> is subjunctive because it completes
    (A) a causal clause (since)
    (B) an indirect statement
    (C) a concessive clause (although)
    (D) a purpose clause

34. The –<u>que</u> (line 7) connects
    (A) <u>Rufinus</u> and <u>competitores</u> (lines 6–7)
    (B) <u>peteret</u> and <u>essent</u> (lines 6–7)
    (C) <u>consulatum</u> and <u>competitores</u> (line 7)
    (D) <u>competitores</u> and <u>inbelles</u> (line 7)

35. In line 8 (<u>summa</u> . . . <u>deferretur</u>), we learn that Fabricius
    (A) worked hard to defeat Rufinus
    (B) requested that Rufinus postpone his bid for office
    (C) used all his resources to support Rufinus' candidacy
    (D) purchased the consulship for himself

36. The case of <u>plerisque admirantibus</u> (line 9) depends upon

    (A)  <u>Eam rem</u> (line 9)

    (B)  <u>esset inimicissimus</u> (lines 8–9)

    (C)  <u>creari consulem vellet</u> (line 10)

    (D)  <u>inquit</u> (line 10)

37. Lines 9–10 (<u>Eam</u> . . . <u>vellet</u>) tell us that many people were wondering

    (A)  why Fabricius wanted a personal enemy to become consul

    (B)  if Fabricius himself wanted to become consul

    (C)  whether a greedy man could become consul

    (D)  why Rufinus wanted to become consul

38. Lines 10–11 (<u>Malo</u> . . . <u>vendat</u>) are translated

    (A)  The citizen who robs me and then sells me to the enemy is wicked.

    (B)  I prefer that a citizen rob me than an enemy sell me.

    (C)  The citizen who sells me to an enemy, robs me.

    (D)  I would rather have a citizen rob me than an enemy.

### Martial describes an acquaintance

Vicinus meus est manuque tangi
de nostris Novius potest fenestris.
Quis non invideat mihi putetque

*Line*   horis omnibus esse me beatum,

5   iuncto cui liceat frui sodale?[1]
Tam longe est mihi quam Terentianus,
qui nunc Niliacam regit Syenen.[2]
Non convivere, nec videre saltem,[3]
non audire licet, nec urbe tota

10   quisquam est tam prope tam proculque nobis.
Migrandum est mihi longius vel illi.
Vicinus Novio vel inquilinus[4]
sit, si quis Novium videre non vult.

1  <u>sodalis, -is</u>, m.: close friend
2  <u>Niliacam</u> . . . <u>Syenen</u>: Syene, located on the Nile River
3  <u>nec</u> . . . <u>saltem</u>: "not even"
4  <u>inquilinus, -i</u>, m.: fellow tenant

39. In lines 1–2 (<u>Vicinus</u> . . . <u>fenestris</u>), we learn that Martial and Novius

    (A) use the same window

    (B) like to leave windows open

    (C) are close neighbors

    (D) share a room

40. In line 3, <u>Quis non invideat mihi</u> is translated

    (A) Who does not envy me

    (B) Who would not envy me

    (C) Whom would I not envy

    (D) He who does not envy me

41. In line 5 (<u>iuncto</u> . . . <u>sodale</u>), why does Martial think that most people would consider him fortunate?

    (A) His friends envy him.

    (B) He has a friend close by.

    (C) His friends enjoy getting together with him.

    (D) He makes his friends happy.

42. The noun-adjective combination <u>iuncto</u> . . . <u>sodale</u> (line 5) takes its case from

    (A) the pronoun <u>cui</u>

    (B) the verb <u>liceat</u>

    (C) the verb <u>frui</u>

    (D) the general sense of the context

43. In line 6, the words <u>Tam</u> . . . <u>quam</u> mean

    (A) Now . . . then        (C) As . . . as

    (B) So . . . than         (D) So . . . that

44. Martial's point in lines 6–7 (<u>Tam</u> . . . <u>Syenen</u>) is that

    (A) Terentianus is as far from him as the Nile is from Syene.

    (B) Rome is a less friendly place than Africa.

    (C) Novius has a friend in Africa named Terentianus.

    (D) Novius might as well be in Africa.

45. The case of <u>Syenen</u> (line 7) is

    (A) nominative        (C) accusative

    (B) genitive          (D) vocative

46. In lines 8–10 (<u>Non</u> . . . <u>nobis</u>), Martial declares that

    (A)  no one is farther away from him than his neighbor

    (B)  he enjoys the company of his neighbors

    (C)  there is no one in the entire city, near or far, who is not his friend

    (D)  people in a large city should avoid each other

47. Which of the following figures of speech occurs in lines 8–10 (<u>Non</u> . . . <u>nobis</u>)?

    (A)  litotes                    (C)  zeugma

    (B)  anaphora                   (D)  chiasmus

48. Line 11 (<u>Migrandum</u> . . . <u>illi</u>) is translated

    (A)  He and I ought to move away together.

    (B)  I should move closer to him.

    (C)  He intends to move farther away from me.

    (D)  I must move farther away or he must.

49. In line 13, <u>sit</u> is translated

    (A)  he is                      (C)  I wish that he were

    (B)  let him be                 (D)  Be!

50. The figure of speech that appears in lines 12–13 (<u>Vicinus</u> . . . <u>vult</u>) is

    (A)  alliteration               (C)  chiasmus

    (B)  polyptoton                 (D)  ellipsis

## STOP

**This is the end of the Multiple-Choice Section of the AP Latin: Vergil Exam. If time remains, you may check your work only in this section. Do not begin the Free-Response Section until instructed to do so.**

# PRACTICE EXAM 1

## AP Latin: Vergil

### Free-Response Section

**TIME:** 2 hours (including a 15-minute reading period)

---

**DIRECTIONS:** Answer ALL FIVE of the questions in this Section, following directions carefully.

---

### Question 1 – Vergil (15 percent)
(Suggested time – 10 minutes)

> "Romulus excipiet gentem et Mavortia condet
> moenia Romanosque suo de nomine dicet.
> His ego nec metas rerum nec tempora pono;
> *Line*    imperium sine fine dedi. Quin aspera Iuno,
> 5      quae mare nunc terrasque metu caelumque fatigat,
> consilia in melius referet, mecumque fovebit
> Romanos, rerum dominos, gentemque togatam."
>
> ***Aeneid*** **1.276–82**

Give a literal translation of the passage above.

# Question 2 – Vergil (15 percent)

## (Suggested time – 10 minutes)

Begin your answer to this question on a fresh page.

Tum genitor natum dictis adfatur amicis:
"Stat sua cuique dies, breve et inreparabile tempus
omnibus est vitae; sed famam extendere factis,
*Line* hoc virtutis opus. Troiae sub moenibus altis
5 tot gnati cecidere deum, quin occidit una
Sarpedon, mea progenies; etiam sua Turnum
fata vocant metasque dati pervenit ad aevi."

*Aeneid* **10.466–72**

Give a literal translation of the passage above.

# Question 3 – Vergil (35 percent)

## (Suggested time – 45 minutes)

Begin your answer to this question on a fresh page.

(A)

"Quid tantum insano iuvat indulgere dolori,
O dulcis coniunx? Non haec sine numine divum
eveniunt; nec te hinc comitem asportare Creusam
*Line* fas, aut ille sinit superi regnator Olympi.
5 Longa tibi exsilia et vastum maris aequor arandum,
et terram Hesperiam venies, ubi Lydius arva
inter opima virum leni fluit agmine Thybris:
illic res laetae regnumque et regia coniunx
parta tibi; lacrimas dilectae pelle Creusae."

*Aeneid* **2.776–84**

(B)

"O tandem magnis pelagi defuncte periclis
(sed terrae graviora manent), in regna Lavini
Dardanidae venient (mitte hanc de pectore curam),
*Line* sed non et venisse volent. Bella, horrida bella,
5 et Thybrim multo spumantem sanguine cerno.
Non Simois tibi nec Xanthus nec Dorica castra
defuerint; alius Latio iam partus Achilles,
natus et ipse dea; nec Teucris addita Iuno
usquam aberit, cum tu supplex in rebus egenis
10 quas gentes Italum aut quas non oraveris urbes!

Causa mali tanti coniunx iterum hospita Teucris
externique iterum thalami."

*Aeneid* **6.83–94**

In these speeches, Aeneas receives two pictures of what his fate in Italy will be. In a well-developed essay, compare and contrast these two speeches, commenting on how the tone reflects the circumstances in which each is given.

(Remember to support what you say by making direct reference to the Latin **throughout** each passage. Cite and translate or closely paraphrase the relevant Latin. Do <u>not</u> simply summarize or paraphrase what the poem says.)

## Question 4 – Vergil (20 percent)

### (Suggested time – 20 minutes)

Begin your answer to this question on a fresh page.

(A)

> "Agnosco veteris vestigia flammae.
> Sed mihi vel tellus optem prius ima dehiscat
> vel pater omnipotens abigat me fulmine ad umbras,
> *Line*  pallentes umbras Erebo noctemque profundam,
> 5   ante, pudor, quam te violo aut tua iura resolvo.
> Ille meos, primus qui me sibi iunxit, amores
> abstulit; ille habeat secum servetque sepulcro."

*Aeneid* **4.23–29**

(B)

> Illa solo fixos oculos aversa tenebat
> nec magis incepto vultum sermone movetur
> quam si dura silex aut stet Marpesia cautes.
> *Line*  Tandem corripuit sese atque inimica refugit
> 5   in nemus umbriferum, coniunx ubi pristinus illi
> respondet curis aequatque Sychaeus amorem.

*Aeneid* **6.469–74**

In the passages above, Dido first contemplates breaking her vow to her dead husband and then suffers the consequences of her decision to do so. In a **short** essay, discuss how the actual consequences reflect those foreseen by the queen.

(Remember to support your observations from the **entire text** of each passage and be sure to cite and translate or closely paraphrase directly from the Latin text.)

# Question 5 – Vergil (15 percent)

## (Suggested time – 20 minutes)

Begin your answer to this question on a fresh page.

*Hybris* is a Greek term that means exaggerated pride, which is often accompanied by stubbornness. In ancient literature, this flaw often led to dishonor, punishment, or even death. **Choose one character from Group A and one character from Group B.** In a **short** essay, discuss how the behavior of these two characters illustrates the idea of *hybris*. Provide specific details in your discussion.

| Group A | Group B |
| --- | --- |
| Allecto, one of the Furies | Dares or Entellus, boxers at the funeral games |
| Amata, queen of the Latins | Mezentius, Etruscan ally of the Rutuli |
| Juturna, sister of Turnus | Turnus, king of the Rutuli |

**END OF AP LATIN: VERGIL
PRACTICE EXAM 1**

# PRACTICE EXAM 1

## AP Latin: Vergil

## Answer Key

## List of Authors and Passages Appearing on This Exam

### Multiple-Choice[1]

#### Required Author Passage

"A sad time in the Underworld" (*Aeneid* 6.868–74, 882–86)

#### Sight Passages

"The Sabine women prevent war" (Ovid, *Fasti* 3.215–22, 225–28)

"Why Fabricius recommended an enemy for the consulship" (Aulus Gellius, *Noctes Atticae* 4.8)

"Martial describes an acquaintance" (Martial, *Epigrams* 1.86)

### Free-Response

Translation 1: *Aeneid* 1.276–82

Translation 2: *Aeneid* 10.466–72

Long Essay: *Aeneid* 2.776–84, 6.83–94

Short Essay: *Aeneid* 4.23–29, 6.469–74

Identification: Allecto, Amata, and Juturna; Dares/Entellus, Mezentius, and Turnus

---

[1] Translations of all multiple-choice passages are provided below.

## Answers to the Multiple-Choice Questions:
## Vergil, Practice Exam 1

| "A Sad Time" | "Sabine Women" | "Fabricius" | "Martial" |
|---|---|---|---|
| 1. (D) | 14. (A) | 26. (B) | 39. (C) |
| 2. (B) | 15. (B) | 27. (C) | 40. (B) |
| 3. (D) | 16. (D) | 28. (D) | 41. (B) |
| 4. (D) | 17. (A) | 29. (B) | 42. (C) |
| 5. (A) | 18. (B) | 30. (A) | 43. (C) |
| 6. (B) | 19. (C) | 31. (C) | 44. (D) |
| 7. (C) | 20. (A) | 32. (D) | 45. (C) |
| 8. (B) | 21. (D) | 33. (A) | 46. (A) |
| 9. (C) | 22. (C) | 34. (B) | 47. (B) |
| 10. (B) | 23. (B) | 35. (C) | 48. (D) |
| 11. (D) | 24. (B) | 36. (D) | 49. (B) |
| 12. (D) | 25. (A) | 37. (A) | 50. (A) |
| 13. (A) |  | 38. (B) |  |

# PRACTICE EXAM 1

## AP Latin: Vergil

## Detailed Explanations of Answers to Multiple-Choice Questions

### "A sad time in the Underworld"

1. **(D)**
   The mention of the Underworld in the title cues the fact that this passage is from Book 6 of the *Aeneid*. **O nate**, my son (line 1), refers to Aeneas, as throughout the *Aeneid*. This passage comes from the "Parade of Heroes," where Anchises describes to Aeneas the future history of Rome. In this particular passage, Anchises mournfully describes the fact that Marcellus, waiting for passage to the Upperworld, is destined to die young (see lines 8–9). In line 1, he advises Aeneas not to mourn for "one of your own" (**tuorum**), referring to Marcellus as his future ancestor. Marcellus, son of Augustus' sister Octavia and Augustus' heir-designate, died in 23 BCE. He was buried in Augustus' own mausoleum (see lines 6–7) and his name was memorialized in the Theater of Marcellus. Vergil himself died a few years later.

2. **(B)**
   The particle **ne** + the present imperative is a common poetic substitute for the imperative of **nolo** + present infinitive found in prose. For review of the imperative, see Chapter 15.

3. **(D)**
   Lines 2–3 translate "The fates will only reveal him to the earth nor will they allow him to stay longer." Cf. line 8, "if only you could break the harsh (bonds of) fate." Thus, Answer (D) "the deceased is not destined to live long" is correct.

4. **(D)**
   Answer **(D) esset** is correct because visa esset is the pluperfect subjunctive form necessary to complete the then–clause of the condition si . . . fuissent, to mean "if the gifts had been . . . (then) the Roman race would have seemed . . . ." The omission of esset due to ellipsis. The subject of visa esset is Romana propago

(line 3). For subjunctive forms, see Chapter 16D, Section 1, and for conditional sentences, see Chapter 16D, Section 3.

5.  **(A)**
    **Si dona fuissent** (line 4), "If the gifts had been," is the conditional or *if*-clause in a past contrary to fact conditional sentence. The tense of **fuissent** is pluperfect. The tense of the translated subjunctive verb in Answer (C) "If the gifts were to be" requires the imperfect tense (**essent**) in a present contrary to fact condition. For conditional clauses, see Chapter 16D, Section 3.

6.  **(B)**
    **Virum** is syncope for **virorum**, genitive plural, as often in Vergil. **Virum** completes (**Quantos**) . . . **gemitus** (line 6), the direct object of **aget**. For syncope, see Chapter 11.

7.  **(C)**
    The adjective-noun combination **Quantos . . . gemitus** (lines 5–6) frames the entire sentence and emphasizes the extent of the grief being described, hence this figure is hyperbaton. **Quantos . . . gemitus** is the accusative direct object of **ille . . . campus . . . aget** (lines 5–6), referring to the grief that Marcellus' death will elicit. For figures of speech, see Chapter 10.

8.  **(B)**
    Answer (B) "there will be a funeral in the Campus Martius" is correct because lines 5–6 say, "How much grieving (**Quantos . . . gemitus**) of men (**virum**) will that Field (**ille . . . campus**) bring (**aget**) to the great city of Mars!"

9.  **(C)**
    **Praeterlabere** = **praeterlabēris**, which is the second person, future indicative passive form of the deponent verb **praeterlabor, praeterlabi, praeterlapsus sum**, *to pass by*. **Praeterlabere** means something like "you will glide past." The subject is **Tiberine**, the river god Tiber, which is in the vocative singular. For variations in the spelling of Latin verbs, see Chapter 11.

10. **(B)**
    Anchises digresses to address Marcellus directly, **miserande puer . . . tu Marcellus eris**, in lines 8–9. This is an example of apostrophe, for which, see Chapter 10.

11. **(D)**
    Marcellus was the first choice of Augustus to succeed him as Emperor. This is a background fact question.

12. **(D)**
    The Latin translates, "Give me lilies with full hands (i.e., handsful of lilies, still a flower commonly associated with funerals), let me scatter the purple flowers and at least heap up the dead soul of my ancestor with these gifts and perform this

meaningless ritual (i.e., the gesture will be meaningless because it won't prevent Marcellus from dying young).

13.  **(A)**
Don't forget to incorporate the elision of **saltem** with **accumulem** into your scansion. The line reads

        -    -      -    u  u -      -  -  -    -    u  u -  -
**his saltem accumulem donis et fungar inani**. For scansion, see Chapter 11.

## "The Sabine women prevent war"

14.  **(A)**
Answer (A) is correct, because the Latin of lines 1–2 does not give any indication that the battle (between the Romans and the Sabine men) was already under way. These lines are translated, "Now the battle lines (**acies**) were standing fast (**stabant**), prepared for the sword and for death (**ferro mortique paratae**), now the bugle (**lituus**) was ready to give the signal (**signa daturus erat**) for attack (**pugnae**)."

15.  **(B)**
The word **ferro**, iron or steel, the material of which the weapon is made, substitutes in line 1 for the weapon itself. This is an example of synecdoche. For figures of speech, see Chapter 10.

16.  **(D)**
**Raptae** is a perfect passive participle of **rapio, rapere, rapui, raptus**, serving here as a substantive, i.e., "those women (note the feminine ending) having been abducted," "the abducted women" (hence, the "rape" of the Sabine women). For more on participles, see Chapter 16A.

17.  **(A)**
The subject of **tenent**, as it is of **veniunt**, previously, is **raptae** (line 3). See the previous answer for the use of a participle as a noun. This part of the sentence translates, "when the abducted women (**raptae**) came between (**veniunt inter**) the fathers and husbands (not simply "men" for **virosque**) and held to their bosoms (**in sinu . . . tenent**) their sons, dear pledges (of love) (**pignora cara**)".

18.  **(B)**
**Tetigere** is a poetic alternative for **tetigerunt**, the third person plural of the perfect active indicative = "they touched." Thus, Answer (B) is correct. For alternative verb forms, see Chapter 11.

19.  **(C)**
This sentence says, "When they reached (**tetigere**) the middle of the field, their hair shorn (in grief) (**scissis . . . capillis**) they sank (**procubuere**) to the ground on bended knee (**posito . . . genu**) and, as if they understood, with a per-

suasive call (**blando clamore**), the grandsons reached out their tiny arms to their grandfathers." Thus, Answer (C) "the younger children held out their arms to their grandfathers" is correct.

20.  **(A)**
**Quasi sentirent** is a present contrary to fact conditional clause. The verb is imperfect subjunctive, because the idea that the children understood what was happening was imaginary or could not possibly happen, which emphasizes the importance of what was actually happening, i.e., that they were being encouraged to make contact with their grandfathers (**tendebant ad avos bracchia parva suos**). Thus, Answer (A) "as if they understood (but they did not)" is the correct answer. For conditionals, see Chapter 16D, Section 3.

21.  **(D)**
Answers (A) and (C) are incorrect because each child was calling his grandfather (**avum** is accusative). Answer (B) is incorrect because the child was seen by the grandfather, rather than vice versa (**visum** [**est**] is passive). Thus, Answer (D) "to their own grandfathers" is correct.

22.  **(C)**
In line 11 we find a "one for two," an example of zeugma. The subjects of the single verb **cadunt** are both **tela**, "weapons," and **animi**, "their hostility," i.e., how they felt. Thus, the men are dropping both an object and a feeling. For more on figures of speech, see Chapter 10.

23.  **(B)**
**Gladiisque remotis** is an ablative absolute, "after they had put away their swords." The key to the correct answer is the word "after," since **remotis** is a past participle. Answer (A) "while . . . " indicates an action contemporary with that of the main verb, i.e., a present participle. Answer (C) "were being" is an ongoing or continuous action, whereas in a past participle such as **remotis**, the action has been completed. In Answer (D) "were about to" the meaning is in the future tense. The translation in Answer (A) is acceptable in the active voice because the identity of those putting away their swords is made clear by the context. Technically, **gladiis remotis** means "(their) swords having been put away," with no understanding of who it was that had put them away. For the ablative absolute, see Chapter 16A.

24.  **(B)**
Answer (C) is tempting, but **natas** means daughters, not sons (gotcha!) Nothing was exchanged or returned, so Answers (A) and (D) are incorrect. The Latin that leads to the correct answer (B) translates, "(each) grandfather carried his grandson on his shield: this was a sweeter use of the shield."

25. **(A)**
**Dulcior** is a comparative adjective modifying **usus**. The correct answer is therefore (A) "sweeter." Answer (B) "very sweet" is in the superlative degree (**dulcissimus**), Answer (C) "rather sweetly" is a comparative adverb (**dulcius**), and Answer (D) "much sweeter" (**multo dulcior**) is an example of the ablative of degree of difference, for which, see Chapter 13A. For forms of adjectives and adverbs, see Chapter 13C.

# "Why Fabricius recommended an enemy for the consulship"

26. **(B)**
Lines 1–2 tell us that Rufinus was skilled in hand-to-hand combat (**manu . . . strenuus**) and a fine warrior (**bellator bonus**), who was thoroughly experienced in military training (**militarisque disciplinae peritus**). Thus, Rufinus may be said to have been "skilled in matters of war" (Answer A).

27. **(C)**
**Disciplinae** is genitive because this case is required by the meaning of the adjective **peritus, -a, -um**, "experienced in" (literally "experienced of"). The genitive case usually establishes a connection between two nouns or between a noun and certain adjectives. See Chapter 13A.

28. **(D)**
The answer is (D) greedy, because we are told in lines 2–3 that Rufinus was thievish (**furax**) and fiercely greedy (**avaritia acri**).

29. **(B)**
**Hunc Fabricius non probabat** tells us that "Fabricius did not approve of him (**Hunc** =Rufinus)," **neque amico utebatur**, that "he did not accept him as a friend," and **osusque eum morum causa fuit**, that "he (Fabricius) hated him because of his character (**morum causa**)." Thus, Answer (B) is correct. Answers (A), (C), and (D) all require some degree of acceptability of Rufinus by Fabricius, which is not indicated in the Latin.

30. **(A)**
The grammar of the clause **cum . . . creandi forent** (line 4) makes this sentence tricky. **Forent** is a substitute for the more common form of the imperfect subjunctive, which is **essent.** In its more familiar form, **creandi essent** is a passive periphrastic whose subject is **consules**, giving the meaning "the consuls must be or had to be elected." The subjunctive mood is required in the form **essent** because **creandi essent** completes a **cum** causal clause, according to the best sense of the context. Thus, this part of the sentence reads, "But since in the very troubled times (**in temporibus . . . difficillimis**) of the Republic (or state, **rei publicae**), consuls had to be elected . . . . " For the passive periphrastic construc-

tion, see Chapter 16B; for **cum** clauses with the subjunctive, see Chapter 16D, Section 6.

31. **(C)**

See the answer to the previous question.

32. **(D)**

In line 5, the subjunctive clause **is Rufinus peteret consulatum** and is the second clause introduced by **cum,** which is found at the beginning of the sentence. This clause tells us that Rufinus was seeking the consulship. A third subjunctive clause, also dependent upon **cum,** is **competitoresque . . . futtiles,** which tells us that Rufinus' (**eius**) adversaries for the consulship were **inbelles** (also spelled **imbelles**). . . **et futtiles** (also spelled **futiles**), meaning "unwarlike and ineffective." Thus, Answer (D) "Rufinus' political adversaries were weak" is correct.

33. **(A)**

As indicated previously, the sense of the sentence in lines 4–6 (**Sed . . . deferretur**) requires that **cum . . . forent . . . peteret . . . essent** be translated as causal clauses, "Since . . . . " Answer (B) is impossible because there is no infinitive in this sentence; the **cum** concessive clause in Answer (C) is usually found with **tamen**; and, although an **ut** purpose clause does appear in this sentence (**uti . . . . deferretur**), it is separate and grammatically distinct from the **cum** clauses found in the earlier part of the sentence. Thus, Answer (A) causal clause is correct. For **ut** clauses, see Chapter 16D, Section 4; for **cum** clauses, see Chapter 16D, Section 6.

34. **(B)**

The enclitic **‑que** connects the two clauses **is Rufinus peteret consulatum** and **competitoresque eius essent inbelles quidam et futtiles,** hence Answer (B) **peteret** and **essent** is correct. When connecting clauses, **‑que** is usually attached to the first word of the connected clause. The conjunction does not always connect the word to which it is attached with the word or those words immediately preceding it, but may be separated by intervening words. For the use of **‑que,** see Chaper 16E.

35. **(C)**

In lines 5–6, **summa ope ādnixus est Fabricius** tells us that Fabricius labored with great resources so that the consulship would be given to Rufinus (**uti Rufino consulatus deferretur**). Thus, Answer (C) "used all his resources to support Rufinus' candidacy" is correct. There is no indication in this passage that Fabricius himself had political ambitions (Answer D), or that he had interfered in any other way with Rufinus' candidacy (Answers A and B).

36. **(D)**

**Plerisque admirantibus** is in the dative case after **inquit** in the next line. This has the meaning, "To many wondering . . . , he said . . . . " The adjective **in-**

**imicus**, "unfriendly to" (Answer B) is found with the dative case, but it is not to be considered in the context of the participial phrase **plerisque admirantibus**. For the dative case, see Chapter 13A.

37.  **(A)**
Lines 6–7 (**Eam . . . vellet**) tell us that "To many (people) wondering at the state of affairs wherein he (Fabricius) wanted a greedy man, to whom he was most unfriendly, to be elected consul." Thus, Answer (A) "why Fabricius wanted a personal enemy to become consul" is correct. The Latin does not support the other interpretations.

38.  **(B)**
Fabricius' punchline says, "I prefer that a citizen rob me than (that) an enemy sell (me)." The other answers do not do justice to the Latin as it stands.

## "Martial describes an acquaintance"

39.  **(C)**
In lines 1–2, Martial indicates that he and Novius are close neighbors by saying, "Novius is my neighbor and can be reached (by hand) from my window." **Nostris**, incidentally, is an example of the use of poetic plural (= **meis**). Answers (A) and (B) use the word **fenestris** as a distractor. Answer (D) goes too far past the meaning of **vicinus**.

40.  **(B)**
This is a deliberative question with the subjunctive, "Who would not envy me?" Answer (B), as a statement of fact, requires the indicative mood, but **invideat** is subjunctive. Answer (C) swaps **Quis** with **mihi**, which is the dative object of invideat, making the sentence in Latin, **Cui ego non invideam?** Answer (D) is not a question. For this use of the independent subjunctive, see Chapter 16D, Section 2.

41.  **(B)**
Lines 3–4 set up the answer to this question. "Who would not envy me and (who would not) think that I am happy all the time, I who (**cui**) am allowed (**licet**) to enjoy (**frui**) close companionship (**iuncto sodale**)?" Martial is saying that a neighbor who lives as close as Novius does to him, and the companionship that this implies, is ordinarily cause for feelings of satisfaction.

42.  **(C)**
The deponent verb **fruor, frui, fructus sum**, "to enjoy," takes the ablative case, therefore Answer (C) the verb **frui** is correct. **Cui** itself is the dative object of **liceat** (Answers A and B). For special deponent verbs, see Chapter 14B.

43.  **(C)**
**Tam** and **quam** are correlatives, which requires that they take their meaning as a pair. The sentence in which these words are found (line 6) reads, "(He) is <u>as</u> far

away from me <u>as</u> Terentianus." Answer (C) is therefore correct. For correlatives, see Chapter 16E.

44. **(D)**

The sentence in lines 6–7 reads, "(He) is as far away from me as Terentianus, who now governs Syene, on the Nile." This implies that Novius might as well be in Africa with Terentianus, which is Answer (D).

45. **(C)**

**Syenen** (line 7) is accusative (the name of the city is Greek). The Greek ending **–n** becomes the Latin ending **–m**; both are accusative singular. See Chapter 10.

46. **(A)**

In lines 8–9, the series of instances in which Martial may not rely upon his neighbor Novius (neither enjoying his company nor seeing nor hearing him) leads to the conclusion in lines 9–10 that "there is no one in the entire city so near and yet so far from me." Answer (A) "no one is farther away from him than his neighbor" is therefore correct; the other answers give inaccurate meanings. Note the reappearance of the poetic plural, **nobis**.

47. **(B)**

The repetitions of **non, nec,** and **tam** in lines 8–10 are all examples of anaphora, which creates a cumulative effect. For figures of speech, see Chapter 10.

48. **(D)**

The passive periphrastic **migrandum est** is impersonal, requiring the subject "it" literally, "It must be moved." **Mihi**, a dative of agent, is the one who "must be moved." To create better sense, the passive is turned around to become active, i.e., "It must be moved by me" becomes "I must move." **Illi**, which refers to Novius, also serves as a dative of agent with **Migrandum est**. Thus, the correct answer is (D) "I must move farther away or he must (move farther away)." For the use of a gerundive in a passive periphrastic, see Chapter 16A.

49. **(B)**

In lines 12–13, Martial explains what he meant in the previous line. **Sit** is the jussive use of the present subjunctive, requiring the translation "let," e.g., "Let the one who does not want to see Novius be his neighbor or his roommate." Answer (A) requires the Latin word **est**, (C) **(velim) esset**, and (D) **esto.**

50. **(A)**

Note the emphatic use of the letter **v** in the final two lines: <u>V</u>icinus No<u>v</u>io <u>v</u>el . . . No<u>v</u>ium <u>v</u>idere . . . <u>v</u>ult. For alliteration and other figures of speech, see Chapter 10.

# Translations of the Multiple-Choice Passages

## "A sad time in the Underworld"

"O son, do not ask about the immense sorrow of your (people); the fates will only reveal him (Marcellus) to the earth and not allow him to remain any longer. The Roman race (would have) seemed too mighty to you, gods, if these gifts (i.e., Marcellus) had been lasting. How much grieving of men that Field (of Mars) will bring to the great city of Mars! Or what funeral service, O Tiber, will you see when you will glide past the freshly-built tomb! . . . Woe, pitiable youth, if in any way you could disrupt the fates, you will be Marcellus! Give me lilies with full hands, let me scatter the purple flowers and at least heap up the dead soul of my ancestor with these gifts and perform this hollow/empty gesture."

## "The Sabine women prevent war"

Now the battle lines were standing fast, prepared for the sword and for death, now the bugle was ready to give the signal for attack, when the abducted women came between the fathers and husbands and held to their bosoms their sons, dear pledges of love. When they reached the middle of the field, their hair shorn (in grief), they sank to the ground on bended knee and, with a persuasive call, the grandsons, as if they understood, reached out their tiny arms to their grandfathers. The weapons and hostility dropped away from the men and, their swords having been put away, the fathers-in-law gave and received the hands (i.e., shook the hands) of their family (members) [or, the fathers-in-law of the family gave and received hands, i.e., shook hands], and praised their daughters and held onto them, and (each) grandfather carried his grandson on his shield: this was a sweeter use of the shield.

## "Why Fabricius recommended an enemy for the consulship"

Fabricius Luscinus was a man of great reputation and great deeds. P. Cornelius Rufinus, indeed was skillful in hand-to-hand (combat) and a fine warrior and completely experienced in military matters, but a man thievish and fiercely greedy. Fabricius did not approve of him nor associated with him as a friend, and hated him because of his character. But since there was need of electing consuls during the trying times of the Republic, and Rufinus sought the consulship and his political opponents were unwarlike and feeble, Fabricius strove with great resources in order that the consulship should be given to Rufinus. To many wondering at this state of affairs, the fact that he wanted a greedy man to whom he was a sworn enemy to be elected consul, Fabricius said, "I would prefer that a citizen rob me, than an enemy sell me."

## "Martial describes an acquaintance"

Novius is my neighbor and can be touched by hand from my window. Who would not envy me and think me happy all the time, I who am permitted the joy of close companionship? He is as far away from me as Terentianus, who now governs Syene on the Nile. I may not enjoy his company, nor even see or hear him, who is so near and yet so far from me. Either I must move away or he must. If anyone does not want to see Novius, let him be his neighbor or roommate.

# Answers to Free-Response Section

## Question 1

### Translation

"Romulus will take up the line and found the walls of Mars and will call (the people) Romans after his own name. Upon these I place boundaries of neither territory nor time; I have granted empire without limit. Yes, even harsh Juno, who now in her fear harrasses the sea, the lands, and the sky, will change her counsel for the better, and with me will cherish the Romans, masters of the world, and the toga-ed race."

### Grading

**9 pts. total, one-half point for each segment. Round up your score.**

1. Romulus excipiet gentem
2. et Mavortia condet moenia
3. Romanosque . . . dicet
4. suo de nomine
5. his ego . . . pono
6. nec metas . . . nec tempora
7. rerum
8. imperium . . . dedi
9. sine fine

10. quin aspera Iuno

11. quae . . . metu . . . fatigat

12. mare nunc terrasque . . . caelumque

13. consilia . . . referet

14. in melius

15. mecumque

16. fovebit Romanos

17. rerum dominos

18. gentemque togatam

## Acceptable Translations for Translation Question 1, Vergil: Practice Exam 1

For instructional purposes, more grammatical and syntactical information is provided here than is usually found in the grading reports on the translation question.

1. **Romulus:** Romulus

   **excipiet:** (he) will accept/take up/receive

   **gentem:** line/people/race/nation/offspring/descendants/clan

2. **et:** [connects **excipiet** and **condet**]

   **Mavortia:** of Mars/deriving from or coming from the god Mars/Martian [modifies **moenia**]

   **condet:** (he) will found/establish/set up/build [future tense]

   **moenia:** walls/city walls/city fortifications

3. **Romanosque:** Romans/the Romans/Roman people/Roman race

   **dicet:** (he) will call/name/designate/denote [future tense]

4. **suo de nomine**: after/from/by/according to his own name ["his own" or "his" are both acceptable for **suos**]

5. **his:** on these/upon these/with respect to these [the reference is to **Romanos**, line 2]

   **ego pono:** I put/place/set/establish//lay out

6. **nec . . . nec:** neither . . . nor **metas:** boundary/limit [the literal meaning of **metas** as "turning posts" or "goals" may be used; singular or plural]

   **tempora**: time/period or extent of time [singular or plural]

7. **rerum:** of empire/of the world [= **orbis terrarum**; may be taken with both **metas** and **tempora**]

8. **imperium:** empire/command/rule/mastery/authority/sovereignty

   **dedi:** (I) gave/granted/bestowed/offered ["have given" or "did give' is acceptable]

9. **sine fine:** without end/limit/boundary/border [must be construed with **imperium**]

10. **quin:** yes even/rather/nay rather/but indeed **aspera:** harsh/bitter/cruel/wild/rough/difficult [modifies **Iuno**]

    **Iuno:** Juno

11. **quae:** who [the antecedent is **Iuno**, the subject of **fatigat**]

    **metu:** because of/in her fear/apprehension/dread/anxiety [take with **fatigat**; ablative of cause]

    **fatigat:** (she) harrasses/wears out/wearies/tires/fatigues/vexes

12. **mare nunc terrasque . . . caelumque:** now the sea, (and) the lands, and the sky [direct objects of **fatigat**]

13. **consilia:** counsel/plans/resolve/judgment/deliberation [must be the direct object of **referet**; may be singular]

    **referet:** change//bring back/return/restore [future tense]

14. **in:** for the better/in or with respect to **melius:** the better

15. **mecum:** and with me/and together with me/and along with me

    **-que:** [combines **referet** and **fovebit**]

16. **fovebit:** (she) will cherish/foster/support [favor is also acceptable; future tense]

    **Romanos:** the Romans/the Roman people/the Roman race [direct object of **fovebit**]

17. **rerum:** of empire/of the world [= **orbis terrarum**; cf. line 3]

    **dominos:** masters/lords/possessors/owners [in apposition to **Romanos**]

18. **gentemque togatam:** the toga-ed race/the nation or race wearing or clad in togas [also in apposition to **Romanos**]

# Question 2

## Translation

Then the father (Jupiter) addresses his son (Hercules) with kindly words: "To each person his own day is designated; brief and irretrievable is the time of life for all; but to extend (your) reputation by actions, this is the task of courage. Beneath Troy's high walls so many sons of gods fell (died), indeed together (with them) Sarpedon, my own son, died; and so his own destiny summons Turnus and he has arrived at the limit of his life that has been assigned."

## Grading

*9 pts. total, one-half point for each segment. Round up your score.*

1. tum genitor

2. natum . . . adfatur

3. dictis . . . amicis

4. stat sua . . . dies

5. cuique

6. breve et inreparabile

7. tempus omnibus est vitae

8. famam extendere factis

9. hoc . . . opus virtutis

10. sub moenibus altis Troiae

11. tot gnati . . . deum

12. cecidere

13. quin occidit una Sarpedon

14. mea progenies

15. etiam sua Turnum fata vocant

16. pervenit

17. metasque . . . ad

18. dati . . . aevi

## Acceptable Translations for Translation Question 2, Vergil: Practice Exam 1

For instructional purposes, more grammatical and syntactical information is provided here than is usually found in the grading reports on the translation question.

1. **tum:** then/next/thereupon/at that time

   **genitor:** father/forefather/Jupiter

2. **natum:** son/child/offspring [Hercules is acceptable here]

   **adfatur:** (he) addresses/approached/speaks to [deponent verb]

3. **dictis:** word/speech [ablative of means]

   **amicis:** kindly/friendly/favorable/pleasing

4. **stat:** (it) is designated/appointed/exists/stands/remains/is fixed **sua:** one's own/his or her own [modifies **dies**]

   **dies:** day/lifetime/span of life [subject of **stat**]

5. **cuique:** each person/every person/everybody/each one [dative of reference]

6. **breve:** brief/short/small/quick/short-lived/fleeting [modifies **tempus**]

   **et:** [joins **breve** and **inreparabile**]

   **inreparabile:** irretrievable/unrecoverable/irreplaceable/temporary [modifies **tempus**]

7. **tempus**: time

   **omnibus**: for all or everyone/with respect to all or everyone [may be rendered as "everyone's"; dative of reference]

   **est**: (it) is [the subject is **tempus**]

   **vitae**: of/for [dative of purpose in double dative with **omnibus**]

8. **famam:** reputation/fame/public opinion/repute

   **extendere:** extend/prolong/expand/stretch out/embellish/enlarge [subjective infinitive: to extend = extending, which is the subject of the verb **est**, understood in the next line.]

   **factis:** action/deed/act/exploit [ablative of means]

9. **hoc:** this [referring to the previous infinitive phrase, **sed famam extendere factis**]

   **opus:** task/work/labor/job [subject of the understood verb **est**, an ellipsis]

   **virtutis:** courage/valor/strength/manliness/bravery

10. **sub:** under/beneath **moenibus:** the walls/city walls/city fortifications

    **altis:** high/tall/lofty/towering/soaring/steep [take with **moenia**]

    **Troiae:** of Troy/Troy's

11. **tot:** so many

    **gnati**: son/offspring/progeny/ [= **nati**, subject of **cecidere**]

    **deum:** god/the divine/deity [syncope for **deorum**; must be genitive plural, "of the gods" or "the gods"]

12. **cecidere:** (they) fell/fell down/dropped/died/were destroyed or killed [alternative form of the third person plural perfect active indicative, **ceciderunt**]

13. **quin:** yes even/rather/nay rather/but indeed **occidit:** (he) died/fell dead/perished/was killed [perfect tense, *ala* **cecidere**]

    **una:** together/with [i.e., the other sons of gods mentioned previously]

    **Sarpedon:** Sarpedon [subject of **occidit**]

14. **mea progenies:** my son/progeny/offspring/child/ [in apposition to **Sarpedon**]

15. **etiam:** also/besides/even

    **sua ... fata:** his (Turnus') own fate/destiny/future [may be singular; subject of **vocant**]

    **Turnum:** Turnus [direct object of **vocant**]

    **vocant:** (they) summon/call/beckon/designate

16. **pervenit:** (he) has arrived/arrived at/reached/come to/approached [perfect tense, as scansion determines that the -**e**- in **venit** is long, but may

be translated as present, "(he) reaches or attains"; the subject is Turnus, understood]

17. **metasque:** the boundary/limit/turning post/goal [may be singular] **ad**: [note the anastrophe of the prepositional phrase **metasque . . . ad**, which accompanies **pervenit**]

18. **dati:** (having been) assigned/alloted/given/provided/apportioned/meted out [perfect passive participle modifying **aevi**]

    **aevi:** life/age/life-time/span of life/period of years [genitive singular with **metasque**]

# Question 3

## Long Essay

For the grading scale used for evaluating essays, see Chapter 7. Here are some high points of each speech to consider in your comparative analysis, followed by a sample essay. Such observations, which will set up your formal essay, may be made in writing during the 15–minute reading period. The sample essays may seem overly thorough, but the author is attempting to accommodate the wide range of answers that will be given by users of this book.

(A)  *Aeneid* 2.776–84:

   - Creusa takes her leave of Aeneas after Troy has fallen
   - Creusa reassures the worried Aeneas (insano . . . dolori, frantic grief) that what she is doing is sanctioned by the gods (Non . . . eveniunt).
   - Jupiter, ruler of the high gods, does not allow him (nec fas [est] . . . sinit) to take Creusa from here as his companion.
   - Aeneas will experience lengthy exile (longa exsilia) and wander the vast ocean (vastum arandum) before reaching Hesperia.
   - He will find there the Lydian/Etruscan Tiber flowing with gentle stream (leni fluit agmine) among the rich fields (arva opima).
   - There Aeneas will find happiness (res laetae), a kingdom (regnum), and a royal wife (regia coniunx).
   - Creusa continues to reassure Aeneas by advising him not to mourn (lacrimas pelle) and that she knows that he loves her (dilectae Creusae).

(B)  *Aeneid* 6.83–94:

   - The Cumaean Sibyl foretells Aeneas' destiny
   - The Sibyl begins by reassuring Aeneas that he has already survived the great perils of the sea (magnis pelagi periclis), but tempers this with a warning of dangers ahead on land (terrae graviora manent).
   - She also reassures the Trojans (mitte hanc de pectore curam) that they will reach their goal in the realm of Lavinium, but will regret coming (non et venisse volent).

- The Sibyl speaks of grim wars and the Tiber flowing with blood. There will be rivers like those at Troy, and a Greek camp (<u>Dorica castra</u>). There will be another Achilles (=Turnus), who will also be goddess-born.

- Juno will continue to harrass the Trojans (<u>nec usquam aberit</u>) and force them to seek aid (<u>cum tu supplex in rebus egenis</u>) from those already settled in Hesperia, i.e., Evander and the Arcadians.

- The cause of the hostilities will again be a foreign bride (<u>coniunx hospita</u>) and an immigrant marriage (<u>externique thalami</u>). <u>Iterum</u> alludes to Lavinia as a second Helen.

## Sample Long Essay

These two speeches, the first of which (A) was given by Creusa and the second (B) by the Cumaean Sibyl, have several things in common and many differences. They are both addressed to Aeneas by women and both outline his future as leader of the Trojans; however, they differ in factual detail and in tone. The first speech may be said to be "Odyssean" in that it focuses on the upcoming journey of Aeneas after the fall of Troy (<u>longa . . . venies</u>) and the rewards of finding "home" (lines 6–8). The second speech may be seen as "Iliadic," in that it focuses on the conflict upon the Trojan arrival in Italy (<u>sed terrae graviora manent</u> and <u>bella . . . cerno</u>, lines 2–5).

In Speech (A), Creusa attempts to reassure her husband, as they are soon to be parted, that Aeneas' destiny is the will of the gods (i.e., Jupiter), as opposed to Speech (B), which, although somewhat reassuring that the Trojans will gain a foothold in Italy (<u>in regna . . . curam</u>, lines 2–3), emphasizes the fact that Juno will continue to haunt them (<u>nec Teucris . . . aberit</u>, lines 8–9).

In Speech (A), the tone is upbeat – when Aeneas reaches Hesperia, he will find the gentle flow of the Lydian Tiber (Lydia was the reputed home of the Etruscans, who were countrymen of the Trojans in both Asia Minor and Italy) and fertile farmland (<u>arva inter opima</u>, lines 6–7). He will find happiness (<u>res laetae</u>), a kingdom (<u>regnum</u>) and a royal wife (<u>regia coniunx</u>). On the other hand, in Speech (B), the Sibyl, in graphic and foreboding terms (<u>sed terrae graviora manent</u> . . . <u>sed non et venisse volent</u>, lines 2–4), warns Aeneas of the trials to come. Note the contrast between the description of the Tiber with its gentle flow (<u>leni fluit agmine Thybris</u>) in Speech (A) and the Tiber foaming with blood (<u>Thybrim multo spumantem sanguine</u>) in Speech (B). These trials include war and bloodshed (<u>bella . . . cerno</u>, lines 4–5), and a second battle for survival against new "Greeks" and a new Achilles (Turnus, lines 7–8), the cause of which will be a foreign bride, Lavinia (<u>coniunx iterum hospita</u> and <u>externique thalami</u>, lines 11–12), just as Helen was the cause of the Trojan War. In Speech (A), emphasis is given to what Aeneas will find in Hesperia, i.e., "a land of milk and honey" (<u>ubi Lydius. . . Thybris</u>, lines 6–7). In Speech (B), the Sibyl mentions what Aeneas will not find, i.e., welcome assistance (<u>cum tu supplex . . . urbes</u>, lines 9–10).

On the other hand, each speaker briefly adopts the tone of the other in describing the realities of Aeneas' situation. Creusa warns Aeneas that "long exile" and "the vasty deep" lie ahead (A, line 5). The Sibyl congratulates Aeneas on surviving thus far (O tandem . . . periclis, B1–2, and mitte . . . curam, B3). The tone of Speech (A) then is one of cautious optimism because Creusa is trying to persuade her husband to look forward, and not back. The tone of Speech (B) is more foreboding and pessimistic, if not realistic: Dardanidae venient . . . sed non et venisse volent (B, lines 3–4).

Creusa's speech is more calming and reassuring (note the various noun-adjective combinations dulcis coniunx, comitem Creusam, arva opima, leni agmine, res laetae, and dilectae Creusae). She still loves her husband (O dulcis coniunx, line 2, and know that he loves her, dilectae . . . Creusae, line 9). Creusa is hopeful and encouraging, which reassures both Aeneas and the reader. On the other hand, the Sibyl's speech is threatening and ominous (note the pejorative accumulation of horrida, spumantem sanguine, in rebus egenis, mali tanti, coniunx hospita, externique thalami). Through these grim words, Vergil elicits in the reader feelings of sympathy and compassion for Aeneas and the Trojans. The edgy tone of the Sibyl in Speech (B) reminds both Aeneas and the reader that, although many hardships have been endured (magnis . . . periclis), the struggle is not yet over. Ultimately it is Aeneas' triumph over such misfortunes that makes him truly pius and that allows him to enjoy the fruits of his labors of which Creusa speaks.

# Question 4

## Short Essay

For the grading scale used for evaluating essays, see Chapter 7. Here are some high points of each passage to consider in your comparative analysis.

(A)  At the beginning of Book 4, Dido speaks of her temptation to fall in love with Aeneas in the context of the pledge of fidelity to her husband.

- Dido feels love again (Agnosco . . . flammae). The word flammae is a metaphor for love and contrasts with pudor (line 5), below.

- She has reservations about her feelings (sed) and begins to feel guilty, as she has made a pledge to her husband (ante, pudor, . . . resolvo) and claims that her love for him has survived his death (ille . . . sepulcro). The use of the jussive subjunctives habeat and servet (line 7) makes it appear that Dido still loves Sychaeus, or at least feels that she must. The anaphora of ille in 6–7 is emphatic of her concern for her husband and for her pledge.

- Her initial feelings of guilt raise terrible spectres of doom in her mind, in which she imagines suffering torments in Hades for breaking her vow (Sed mihi . . . noctemque profundam). The words violo and tua iura resolvo are charged and suggest that Dido acknowledges the seriousness of her pledge. The images of the earth opening up and swallowing her (tellus . . . ima dehiscat), being cast to Hades by Jove's thunderbolt (pater . . . ad umbras), and experiencing the bloodless shades and deep darkness of Erebus (pallentes . . . profundam) all speak to her fear of divine retribution.

(B)   Dido is met in the Underworld by Aeneas.

- Dido turns away (from Aeneas) and stares (fixos oculos) at the ground at her feet (Illa . . tenebat). Illa for Dido; the loss of her name suggests, symbolically, Dido's loss of herself.

- She does not change her facial expression (nec . . . vultum movetur), as Aeneas speaks.

- Dido is compared to hard flint (dura silex) or Marpesian rock (Marpesia cautes = Hellenic marble). She is passive, not active.

- She finally tears herself away (corripuit sese) and flees into a shady grove (in nemus umbriferum). She is characterized here as inimica, a personal enemy of Aeneas.

- Dido meets her husband (pristinus coniunx), who "comforts her troubles" (respondet curis) and "gives her love back in measure equal to her own" (aequatque . . . amorem). There is implicit comparison between Sychaeus and Aeneas, who is now a personal enemy.

## Sample Short Essay

In Dido's speech in Passage (A), she speaks of the pangs of love, indicated by the use of the metaphor flammae. She has loved no one since the death of her husband, to whom she had pledged her undying loyalty. However, these "traces of the old love" cause her pangs of shame or guilt, for she has made a pledge and she is a woman of her word. Note the contrast between flammae, passion, and pudor, shame, which is personified through the apostrophe in line 5. In Passage (A), she imagines the worst by conjuring up spectres of the divine punishment that awaits her if she breaks her vow: the earth swallowing her up (tellus . . . dehiscat, A2), Jove casting her into Hades with his thunderbolt (pater . . . ad umbras, A3), and the bloodless shades and deep darkness of Erebus haunting her (pallentes . . . profundam, A4). She ends her speech emphatically (note the anaphora of ille = Sychaeus) by seeming to renew her vows to her dead husband. She reminds herself that he was her first love (Ille . . . primus . . . me sibi iunxit, A6) and prays that he keep her love with him even in the tomb (ille . . . sepulcro, A7). Note here the use of the jussive subjunctive (habeat and servet), which often appears in the context of vows or prayers. Elsewhere in Book 4, she is described as having erected a shrine to her dead husband, where she receives portents of death.

In Passage (B), we learn that Dido is now, indeed, in the Underworld. She is not tormented by eternal punishment, as she predicted in Passage (A), but suffers in silence, her eyes staring at the ground (solo fixo oculos . . . tenebat, line 1) and her facial expression unmoving (nec . . . vultum movetur, line 2). She is now a woman as hard and inert as flint. Contrast the metaphors dura silex and Marpesia cautes here with that of flammae in Passage A. She is now in both a literal and metaphorical darkness, like the moon behind passing clouds (says Vergil elsewhere): the overtones here of the word shadowy, umbriferum (line 5), reflect the death-like darkness of umbras and noctemque profundam portrayed in Passage (A), lines 3 and 4. She is now lifeless and one of the pallentes (A4), a mere shadow of her former self. (Note the contrast between umbras and pallentes in A3–4.) But she remains a devoted spouse. Dido is with Sychaeus, who still loves her (coniunx . . . amorem), bringing us full-circle to the end of Passage (A), where she renews her promise to love him even unto death. She has kept her promise.

Essentially, Dido has been able to "have her cake and eat it, too." The consequences in Passage (B) of breaking her vow to Sychaeus do not seem to be as terrible as she had imagined in Passage (A). However, she, "the woman scorned," is suffering her own self-imposed hellfire in the Underworld. For Dido, Hell is not active but passive. Her torment is psychological, not physical. Her suicide has made her an inimica of Aeneas now, rather than the lover suggested by flammae in Speech (A) and she has returned to and found consolation in her husband, her first love.

# Question 5

Because it is difficult to do justice to this question in the space provided here (there are nine possible combinations of characters that can be discussed), you are given some information about each character which is relevant to the topic of *hybris*. Compare the content of your own answer with those given below. On the actual AP Vergil Exam, a short analytical essay is expected.

## Group A

**Allecto:** One of three Furies who drove their victims insane (furor). Allecto serves as Juno's henchwoman in Book 7, first stirring up trouble by alienating both Amata and Turnus to the idea of a Trojan presence in Italy, using the vision of a terrible snake, then by causing Ascanius to wound a pet stag of the Latins while hunting. Although it was the nature of the Furies to stand for the rightness of things and the natural order, they often persecuted mortals who broke "natural laws." It was in regard to the latter that Allecto was hybristic, because her duties as accomplice to Juno took her "out of bounds" with respect to what had been preordained by the Fates, i.e., Aeneas' success.

**Amata:** From her first appearance in Book 7, when Aeneas and the Trojans arrive in Latium, to her suicide in Book 12, Amata attempts to "get her way" by promoting the cause of Turnus as Lavinia's true future husband. Despite the oracle that Lavinia is to marry a foreigner, Amata remains steadfast in her self-destructive plans for her daughter (although she becomes more reasonable when she joins King Latinus in attempting to persuade Turnus to withdraw during a truce). In Book 7, she yields to the poisonous words of the Fury Allecto and hides Lavinia in the woods and continues thereafter to interfere with what others consider are the best interests of her daughter. At the end of the Aeneid, on the mistaken assumption that Turnus is dead, she hangs herself. That Amata's single-minded determination is the cause of her own downfall is an example of hybris.

**Juturna:** Juturna, Turnus' sister, is active in the story of Book 12. She is less a victim of her own choices than the other characters on this list, as she is manipulated by Juno to protect her brother and thus to interfere with the destiny of the Trojans in Italy. She assumes the guise of Turnus' charioteer and saves him more than once on the battlefield. Her resolute, almost obsessive, concern for her brother does not lead to her destruction, as she is a water nymph. Juturna jumps into a river and disappears from the story at the end of Book 12.

## Group B

**Dares or Entellus:** Dares and Entellus were contestants in the boxing event at the funeral games for Anchises described in Book 5. Dares' attitude toward himself and his opponent was something like that of a modern professional wrestler: disdain and arrogance. Entellus, after defeating Dares, showed poor sportsmanship by bragging about his feat and flaunting his victory over Dares. The moral is clear: humility is a virtue, arrogance (hybris) a vice.

**Mezentius:** Etruscan king and father of Lausus, Mezentius appears primarily in Book 10, where he is an ally of Turnus against Aeneas and the Trojans. He had been exiled from his home city for cruelty. Mezentius has the character of Plautus' Miles Gloriosus, a swaggering braggart. After Lausus, who had defended his father in battle, is killed by Aeneas, Mezentius' shame at the fact that his son died in his place drove him into a frenzy of rage and despair. Fearless and defiant until his death, Mezentius was subsequently killed by Aeneas. Excessive pride was Mezentius' downfall.

**Turnus:** Turnus is the anti-hero (some would say hero) of Books 7–12 because he serves as the chief antagonist of Aeneas. In fighting against the newcomer Trojans, he proves himself valiant but hot-headed. Turnus shows a moment of nobility when he takes exception to Juno saving him from battle by tricking him with a ghost-phantom of Aeneas. But it is in Book 10 where Turnus sows the seeds of his own destruction by slaying Pallas, the young son of King Evander, and then by mocking the dead youth and taking his swordbelt. His provocative, if not sacrilegious, behavior earned him an apostrophe from Vergil declaring that it was Turnus' time to die. At the end of Book 12, it is Aeneas' recognition of the swordbelt on Turnus' shoulder that causes him to kill Turnus on behalf of Pallas.

# PRACTICE EXAM 2

## AP Latin: Vergil

## Multiple-Choice Section

**TIME:** 60 Minutes
50 Questions

**DIRECTIONS:** Each reading passage is followed by a series of questions and incomplete statements that are related to the passage. Select the best answer or completion and fill in the appropriate oval on your answer sheet.

### Aeneas confronts Turnus

Stetit acer in armis

Aeneas volvens oculos dextramque repressit;
et iam iamque magis cunctantem flectere sermo
*Line* coeperat, infelix umero cum apparuit alto
5   balteus et notis fulserunt cingula bullis
Pallantis pueri, victum quem vulnere Turnus
straverat atque umeris inimicum insigne gerebat.
Ille, oculis postquam saevi monimenta doloris
exuviasque hausit, furiis accensus et ira
10  terribilis: "Tune hinc spoliis indute meorum
eripiare mihi? Pallas te hoc vulnere, Pallas
immolat et poenam scelerato ex sanguine sumit."

1.   In lines 1–2 (<u>Stetit . . . repressit</u>), we learn that Aeneas is

   (A)   taking the fight to Turnus

   (B)   convinced that the fight is over

   (C)   vigilant but non-combative

   (D)   lacking the weapons to continue the fight

2.  <u>Cunctantem</u> (line 3) is
    (A)  a noun                          (C)  a gerundive
    (B)  an active periphrastic           (D)  a participle

3.  The noun <u>sermo</u> in the context of line 3 refers to the previous speech of
    (A)  Turnus                          (C)  Jupiter
    (B)  Juturna                         (D)  the Rutulians

4.  In lines 3–4 (<u>et</u> . . . <u>coeperat</u>), we learn that Aeneas had begun to
    (A)  speak                           (C)  grow more confident
    (B)  change his mind                 (D)  interrupt Turnus

5.  Which figure of speech appears in lines 4–6 (<u>infelix</u> . . . <u>pueri</u>)?
    (A)  asyndeton                       (C)  simile
    (B)  hyperbaton                      (D)  transferred epithet

6.  <u>Quem</u> (line 6) refers to
    (A)  the swordbelt
    (B)  Pallas
    (C)  the wound inflicted by Turnus
    (D)  Turnus

7.  In line 7, <u>straverat</u> is translated
    (A)  he was throwing down
    (B)  he threw down
    (C)  he had thrown down
    (D)  he had been thrown down

8.  In lines 4–7 (<u>infelix</u> . . . <u>gerebat</u>), we learn that Aeneas
    (A)  saw Pallas' dead body on the ground
    (B)  wept upon seeing Pallas' wounds
    (C)  noticed Turnus wearing Pallas' swordbelt
    (D)  tore the swordbelt from Turnus' shoulder

9.  The metrical pattern of the first four feet of line 7 is
    (A)  dactyl-spondee-spondee-dactyl
    (B)  spondee-dactyl-dactyl-spondee
    (C)  spondee-spondee-dactyl-dactyl
    (D)  dactyl-dactyl-dactyl-spondee

10. The figure of speech that appears in lines 8–9 (<u>oculis</u> . . . <u>hausit</u>) is

    (A) hendiadys           (C) chiasmus

    (B) asyndeton         (D) transferred epithet

11. The case of <u>indute</u> (line 10) is

    (A) ablative            (C) nominative

    (B) accusative        (D) vocative

12. In line 11, (<u>Tune</u>) . . . <u>eripiare mihi</u>? is translated

    (A) Are you snatching me away?

    (B) Are you being snatched away from me?

    (C) Will I snatch you away?

    (D) Are you to be snatched away from me?

13. In lines 11–12 (<u>Pallas</u> . . . <u>sumit</u>), who is represented figuratively as striking Turnus' death blow?

    (A) Mars

    (B) the goddess of vengeance

    (C) Aeneas

    (D) Pallas

### Romulus reacts to news of his brother's death

Haec ubi rex didicit,[1] lacrimas introrsus obortas
    devorat et clausum pectore vulnus habet.
Flere palam non vult exemplaque fortia servat,
*Line*    "Sic"que "meos muros transeat hostis," ait.
5   Dat tamen exsequias[2] nec iam suspendere fletum
    sustinet, et pietas dissimulata patet,
osculaque applicuit posito suprema feretro[3]
    atque ait, "Invito frater adempte, vale!"
Arsurosque artus unxit. Fecere, quod ille,
10   Faustulus et maestas Acca soluta comas.
Tum iuvenem nondum facti flevere Quirites.
    Ultima plorato subdita flamma rogo[4] est.

1 <u>Haec ubi rex didicit</u>: in this version of the story, Remus had been killed by Celer, who had been put in charge of building Rome's walls.
2 <u>exsequiae</u>, -<u>arum</u>, f.pl.: funeral rites
3 <u>feretrum</u>, -<u>i</u>, n.: bier to carry the body to the grave
4 <u>rogus</u>, -<u>i</u>, n.: funeral pyre

14. In lines 1–2 (<u>Haec</u> . . . <u>habet</u>), we learn that Romulus

    (A) could not contain his grief

    (B) suppressed his grief

    (C) increased his grief

    (D) felt no grief

15. In line 1, the verbal form <u>obortas</u> is a

    (A) deponent          (C) gerund

    (B) present subjunctive    (D) main verb

16. As indicated in line 3 (<u>Flere</u> . . . <u>servat</u>), it appears that Romulus

    (A) wept openly

    (B) was pleased at the news

    (C) did what everyone expected

    (D) grieved privately

17. In line 4, <u>transeat hostis</u> is translated

    (A) let the enemy go across

    (B) the enemy is passing over

    (C) the enemy will go over

    (D) he may overtake the enemy

18. In line 5, the phrase <u>nec iam</u> means

    (A) not only now        (C) and yet not

    (B) no longer           (D) never again

19. In lines 5–8 (<u>Dat</u> . . . <u>vale</u>), we learn that Romulus was unable to conceal his grief

    (A) during the funeral rites

    (B) after he had buried his brother

    (C) when he kissed the funeral bier

    (D) after he had bid his brother farewell

20. Which of the following figures of speech appears in lines 7–8 (<u>osculaque</u> . . . <u>vale</u>)?

    (A) hendiadys

    (B) interlocked word order (synchysis)

    (C) hyperbole

    (D) polysyndeton

21. In line 8 (<u>Invito</u> . . . <u>vale</u>), Romulus' final words to his brother imply that

    (A) his brother had welcomed death

    (B) his brother's body had been stolen

    (C) his brother had died prematurely

    (D) he had wanted his brother to die

22. <u>Arsurosque artus unxit</u> (line 9) is translated

    (A) He cremated the body and then annointed it.

    (B) He annointed the body about to be cremated.

    (C) With great skill, he prepared the body to be cremated.

    (D) He embraced the body before cremation.

23. In line 9, the form <u>Fecere</u> is

    (A) future indicative     (C) present infinitive

    (B) perfect indicative     (D) present imperative

24. Which of the following figures of speech is found in line 10 (<u>Faustulus</u> . . . <u>comas</u>)?

    (A) transferred epithet     (C) litotes

    (B) metonymy     (D) aposiopesis

25. Line 12 (<u>Ultima</u> . . . <u>est</u>) is translated

    (A) The final lament is given over the burning pyre.

    (B) Romulus, as a final act of grief, ignited the pyre.

    (C) After the pyre was arranged, the wretched fire was finally lit.

    (D) At last the fire has been placed beneath the lamentable pyre.

### Pliny congratulates a friend

Recte fecisti, Valeri, quod gladiatorum munus Veronensibus nostris
promisisti, a quibus olim amaris suspiceris ornaris. Inde etiam uxorem carissimam tibi et probatissimam habuisti, cuius memoriae aut

*Line*
opus aliquod aut spectaculum atque hoc potissimum, quod maxime
5  funeri, debebatur. Praeterea tanto consensu rogabaris, ut negare
non constans, sed durum videretur. Illud quoque egregie, quod tam
facilis tam liberalis in edendo fuisti; nam per haec etiam magnus
animus ostenditur. Vellem Africanae[1], quae coemeras plurimas, ad
praefinitum diem occurrissent: sed licet cessaverint[2] illae tempestate
10  detentae, tu tamen meruisti ut acceptum tibi fieret, quod quo minus
exhiberes non per te stetit. Vale.

1 Africanae, -arum, f.pl.: = Africanae ferae, panthers
2 licet cessaverint: "granted that they were late"

26. In lines 1–2 (Recte . . . ornaris), we learn that Valerius

    (A)  is a well-known gladiator in Verona

    (B)  wants to win votes by sponsoring games

    (C)  is being honored by gladiatorial games

    (D)  has sponsored games in Verona

27. The figure of speech that occurs in lines 1–2 (Recte . . . ornaris) is

    (A)  alliteration        (C)  hyperbole

    (B)  asyndeton        (D)  ellipsis

28. In lines 2–5 (Inde . . . debebatur), we learn that Valerius' wife

    (A)  was deceased

    (B)  was a wealthy and powerful woman

    (C)  was not loved or respected by her husband

    (D)  cared little for the games

29. The case of the noun memoriae (line 3) depends upon

    (A)  uxorem (line 2)        (C)  funeri (line 5)

    (B)  cuius (line 3)         (D)  debebatur (line 5)

30. Complete the following translation of lines 5–6 (Praeterea . . . videretur): "Moreover, you were asked by so many people . . . "

    (A) that to deny that you were not strong-minded would seem shameless

    (B) that to refuse would seem not resolute, but rude

    (C) that those who did not seem to agree with you were considered harsh, rather than steadfast

    (D) that no one appeared to deny your determination and toughness

31. In line 6, Illud is the direct object of

    (A) fecisti (understood from line 1)

    (B) edendo (line 7)

    (C) fuisti (line 7)

    (D) the verb est (understood)

32. In the context of line 7, edendo is translated

    (A) must sponsor

    (B) having sponsored

    (C) sponsoring

    (D) about to be sponsored

33. In lines 6–8 (Illud . . . ostenditur), Pliny characterizes Valerius as generous because

    (A) Verona had never had gladiatorial games before

    (B) he had honored his wife with the show

    (C) he was efficient and lavish in giving the games

    (D) public games were usually financed by the state

34. The form Vellem (line 8) is

    (A) present infinitive       (C) imperfect subjunctive

    (B) present indicative       (D) present subjunctive

35. The words Vellem Africanae . . . ad praefinitum diem occurrissent (lines 8–9) are translated

    (A) I wished that the panthers had arrived on the appointed day.

    (B) I want you to know the panthers will arrive as scheduled.

    (C) I wished I knew on what day the panthers would arrive.

    (D) If only the panthers had arrived on the day I wished.

36. In lines 9–10 (<u>sed</u> . . . <u>detentae</u>), we learn that the panthers

    (A)   arrived on time despite a storm

    (B)   did not arrive at all

    (C)   were unwilling to travel because of the weather

    (D)   did not arrive on time because of a storm

37. The clause that ends with the subjunctive verb <u>exhiberes</u> (line 11) is introduced by

    (A)   <u>licet</u> (line 7)       (C)   <u>quod</u> (line 8)

    (B)   <u>ut</u> (line 8)       (D)   <u>quo minus</u> (line 8)

38. In lines 10–11 (<u>tu</u> . . . <u>stetit</u>), Pliny assures Valerius that

    (A)   Pliny will take responsibility for what happened

    (B)   Valerius deserves credit for his intentions

    (C)   Valerius can display the panthers at another time

    (D)   No one will blame him

### A festival celebrates the blessings of the farm

> Luce sacra requiescat humus, requiescat arator,
>    et grave suspenso vomere[1] cesset opus.
> Solvite vincla iugis; nunc ad praesepia[2] debent
> *Line*    plena coronato stare boves capite.
> 5  Omnia sint operata deo;[3] non audeat ulla
>    lanificam pensis[4] imposuisse manum.
> Vos quoque abesse procul iubeo, discedat ab aris,
>    cui tulit hesterna gaudia nocte Venus.
> Casta placent superis: pura cum veste venite
> 10    et manibus puris sumite fontis aquam.
> Cernite, fulgentes ut eat sacer agnus ad aras
>    vinctaque post olea[5] candida turba comas.

1 <u>vomer</u>, <u>vomeris</u>, m.: ploughshare
2 <u>praesepium</u>, -<u>i</u>, n.: manger; corn crib
3 <u>deo</u>: Bacchus or Ceres
4 <u>pensum</u>, -<u>i</u>, n.: a portion of wool weighed out to a spinner as a day's task; "a day's work"
5 <u>olea</u>, -<u>ae</u>, f.: the olive (tree, branch, leaf, fruit)

39. As we learn from lines 1–2 (<u>Luce</u> . . . <u>opus</u>), the poet asks that the festival include

    (A) a day of rest for all

    (B) more rigorous work than usual

    (C) postponement of all work but the ploughing

    (D) only light chores

40. In line 2 (<u>et</u> . . . <u>opus</u>), the noun <u>vomere</u> is ablative

    (A) of means or instrument

    (B) in an ablative absolute

    (C) of comparison

    (D) of manner

41. In lines 3–4 (<u>Solvite</u> . . . . <u>capite</u>), we learn that

    (A) the farm equipment should be cleaned

    (B) corn cribs should be decked with wreaths

    (C) oxen are to be prepared for sacrifice

    (D) the cattle should be fed well

42. In line 5, <u>Omnia sint operata deo</u> is translated

    (A) All things have been done for the god

    (B) Let the god do all things

    (C) Let all things be done for the god

    (D) All things are being done by the god

43. In line 6, the case of <u>pensis</u> depends upon

    (A) <u>Omnia</u> . . . <u>deo</u> (line 5)  (C) <u>lanificam</u> . . . <u>manum</u> (line 6)

    (B) <u>audeat</u> (line 5)  (D) <u>imposuisse</u> (line 6)

44. In lines 7–8 (<u>Vos</u> . . . <u>Venus</u>), we learn that those who have been recent lovers

    (A) are especially welcome at the festival

    (B) must stay away from the festival

    (C) may be present, but not at the altars

    (D) may be together only the night of the festival

45. In line 8, <u>Venus</u> is an example of which figure of speech?

    (A) transferred epithet  (C) metonymy

    (B) hendiadys  (D) onomatopoeia

46. In lines 9–10 (<u>Casta</u> . . . <u>aquam</u>), we learn that festival celebrants are to
    (A) wash their garments in the pure spring water
    (B) draw the spring's water with pure hands
    (C) make chaste offerings to the gods
    (D) purify themselves after they arrive

47. Line 11 (<u>Cernite</u> . . . <u>aras</u>) is translated
    (A) See how the shining lamb goes to the sacred altars
    (B) O shining ones, tell us when the sacred lamb will go to the altars
    (C) Determine whether the sacred lamb will go to the shining altars
    (D) Observe how the sacred lamb goes to the shining altars

48. In line 11 (<u>Cernite</u> . . . <u>aras</u>), which figure of speech occurs?
    (A) hyperbaton          (C) anaphora
    (B) hyperbole           (D) polysyndeton

49. The case and number of <u>olea</u> (line 12) are
    (A) nominative singular    (C) ablative singular
    (B) nominative plural      (D) accusative plural

50. Line 12 (<u>vinctaque</u> . . . <u>comas</u>) describes the
    (A) celebrants annointing their heads with oil
    (B) harvesting of olive branches
    (C) celebrants in festival attire
    (D) honoring of the farm's crops

## STOP

**This is the end of the Multiple-Choice Section of the AP Latin: Vergil Exam. If time remains, you may check your work only in this section. Do not begin the Free-Response Section until instructed to do so.**

# PRACTICE EXAM 2

## AP Latin: Vergil

### Free-Response Section

**TIME:** 2 hours (including a 15-minute reading period)

**DIRECTIONS:** Answer ALL FIVE of the questions in this Section, following directions carefully.

### Question 1 – Vergil (15 percent)
(Suggested time – 10 minutes)

"Dis equidem auspicibus reor et Iunone secunda
hunc cursum Iliacas vento tenuisse carinas.
Quam tu urbem, soror, hanc cernes, quae surgere regna
*Line* coniugio tali! Teucrum comitantibus armis
5 Punica se quantis attollet gloria rebus!
Tu modo posce deos veniam, sacris litatis
indulge hospitio causasque innecte morandi."

***Aeneid* 4.45–51**

Give a literal translation of the passage above.

# Question 2 – Vergil (15 percent)

## (Suggested time – 10 minutes)

Begin your answer to this question on a fresh page.

> Sic Turno, quacumque viam virtute petivit,
> successum dira dea negat. Tum pectore sensus
> vertuntur varii; Rutulos aspectat et urbem
> *Line* cunctaturque metu letumque instare tremescit,
> 5    nec quo se eripiat, nec qua vi tendat in hostem,
> nec currus usquam videt aurigamve sororem.
>
> *Aeneid* **12.913–18**

Give a literal translation of the passage above.

# Question 3 – Vergil (35 percent)

## (Suggested time – 45 minutes)

Begin your answer to this question on a fresh page.

(A)
> At domus interior gemitu miseroque tumultu
> miscetur, penitusque cavae plangoribus aedes
> femineis ululant; ferit aurea sidera clamor.
> *Line* Tum pavidae tectis matres ingentibus errant
> 5    amplexaeque tenent postes atque oscula figunt.
> Instat vi patria Pyrrhus: nec claustra nec ipsi
> custodes suffere valent.
>
> *Aeneid* **2.486–92**

(B)
>            It clamor ad alta
> atria; concussam bacchatur Fama per urbem.
> Lamentis gemituque et femineo ululatu
> *Line* tecta fremunt, resonat magnis plangoribus aether,
> 5    non aliter, quam si immissis ruat hostibus omnis
> Karthago aut antiqua Tyros, flammaeque furentes
> culmina perque hominum volvantur perque deorum.
>
> *Aeneid* **4.665–71**

In each of these two passages, a household is thrown into an uproar. In a well-developed essay, compare and contrast the manner in which each each is described.

(Remember to support what you say by making direct reference to the Latin **throughout** the passages. Cite and translate or closely paraphrase the relevant Latin. Do <u>not</u> simply summarize or paraphrase what the poem says.)

## Question 4 – Vergil (20 percent)
### (Suggested time – 20 minutes)

Begin your answer to this question on a fresh page.

> Constitit et lacrimans, "Quis iam locus," inquit "Achate,"
> quae regio in terris nostri non plena laboris?
> En Priamus. Sunt hic etiam sua praemia laudi;
> *Line*    sunt lacrimae rerum et mentem mortalia tangunt.
>    5    Solve metus; feret haec aliquam tibi fama salutem."
> Sic ait atque animum pictura pascit inani
> multa gemens, largoque umectat flumine vultum. . .
> Ter circum Iliacos raptaverat Hectora muros
> exanimumque auro corpus vendebat Achilles.
>    10    Tum vero ingentem gemitum dat pectore ab imo,
> ut spolia, ut currus, utque ipsum corpus amici
> tendentemque manus Priamum conspexit inermes.
>
> *Aeneid* 1.459–65, 483–87

In this passage, Aeneas expresses deep emotions with regard to what he and Achates are seeing. In a **short** essay, discuss now the poet uses his craft to develop sympathy for Aeneas and the Trojans.

(Remember to support your observations from the **entire text** of each passage and be sure to cite and translate or closely paraphrase directly from the Latin text.)

# Question 5 – Vergil (15 percent)

## (Suggested time – 25 minutes)

Begin your answer to this question on a fresh page.

In the *Aeneid*, lesser deities often appear in the story to further the interests of another character or an event. **Select one deity from each group below** and discuss the way in which that deity furthers the cause of an individual or an incident in the story. The deities in Group A might be considered to have a positive effect, whereas the deities in Group B a negative one.

| Group A | Group B |
|---|---|
| Cupid, son of Venus | Allecto, a Fury |
| Sea Nymphs | Iris, messenger goddess |
| Vulcan, blacksmith god | Juturna, sister of Turnus |

**END OF AP LATIN: VERGIL
PRACTICE EXAM 2**

# PRACTICE EXAM 2

## AP Latin: Vergil

## Answer Key

## List of Authors and Passages Appearing on This Exam

### Multiple-Choice[1]

#### Required Author Passage

"Aeneas confronts Turnus" (*Aeneid* 12.938-49)

#### Sight Passages

"Romulus reacts to the news of his brother's death" (Ovid, *Fasti* 4.845–55)

"Pliny congratulates a friend" (Pliny, *Epistulae* 6.34)

A festival celebrates the blessings of the farm" (Tibullus, *Elegies* 2.1.5–16)

### Free-Response

Translation 1: *Aeneid* 4.45–51

Translation 2: *Aeneid* 12.913–18

Long Essay: *Aeneid* 2.486-92, 665–71

Short Essay: *Aeneid* 1.456-65, 483–87

Identification: Allecto, Cupid, Sea Nymphs, and Vulcan; Allecto, Iris, and Juturna

---

[1] Translations of all multiple-choice passages are provided below.

## Answers to the Multiple-Choice Questions:
## Vergil, Practice Exam 2

| "Aeneas" | "Romulus" | "Pliny" | "Festival" |
|----------|-----------|---------|------------|
| 1. (C) | 14. (B) | 26. (D) | 39. (A) |
| 2. (D) | 15. (A) | 27. (B) | 40. (B) |
| 3. (A) | 16. (D) | 28. (A) | 41. (D) |
| 4. (B) | 17. (A) | 29. (D) | 42. (C) |
| 5. (B) | 18. (B) | 30. (B) | 43. (D) |
| 6. (B) | 19. (A) | 31. (A) | 44. (B) |
| 7. (C) | 20. (B) | 32. (C) | 45. (C) |
| 8. (C) | 21. (C) | 33. (C) | 46. (B) |
| 9. (D) | 22. (B) | 34. (C) | 47. (D) |
| 10. (A) | 23. (B) | 35. (A) | 48. (A) |
| 11. (D) | 24. (A) | 36. (D) | 49. (C) |
| 12. (D) | 25. (D) | 37. (B) | 50. (C) |
| 13. (D) | | 38. (D) | |

# PRACTICE EXAM 2

## AP Latin: Vergil

## Detailed Explanations of Answers to Multiple-Choice Questions

### "Aeneas confronts Turnus"

1. **(C)**
   Lines 1–2 translate "Aeneas stood fierce in arms, shifting his eyes, and he restrained his weapon-hand." Thus, the correct answer is (C) "vigilant but non-combative."

2. **(D)**
   **Cunctantem** is a present participle (note the **–nt-** in the form) modifying **eum** (Aeneas), understood. Answer (A) noun is incorrect, as **cunctantem** would not make sense in this context as a substantive. In Answer (B) the active periphrastic would be **cunctaturum est** and in Answer (C), the gerundive **cunctandum**. For participles, see Chapter 16A.

3. **(A)**
   From your familiarity with the story of Book 12, you should know that Turnus' speech (**sermo**) of resignation and defeat in the lines previous to the multiple-choice passage had given Aeneas pause.

4. **(B)**
   Lines 3–4 read, "And now, and now (Turnus') words had begun to sway him more (**magis . . . flectere**) as he hesitated (**cunctantem**)," so Answer (B) "change his mind" is correct. Note the emphatic use of anaphora in **iam iamque** (line 3).

5. **(B)**
   These lines contain an example of hyperbaton because the adjective **infelix** is widely separated from the noun it modifies, **balteus**, in order to emphasize the swordbelt's ill-fortune. The words **infelix . . . balteus** also "wrap around" Turnus' shoulder!

6.  **(B)**

In line 6, the pronoun **quem** introduces a relative clause describing **Pallantis pueri**. **Quem** serves as the object of **Turnus straverat** (lines 6–7) and is modified by the perfect passive participle **victum**. For relative pronouns, see Chapter 13B.

7.  **(C)**

**Straverat** is the pluperfect tense of **sterno, sternere, stravi, stratum**, to throw down, lay someone low. Therefore, Answer (C) "he had thrown down" is correct. For the forms and meanings of indicative verbs, see Chapter 14A.

8.  **(C)**

Lines 4–7 translate, "when the luckless swordbelt (**infelix ... balteus**) high on his (Turnus') shoulder (**umero cum ... alto**) came into his (Aeneas') view (**apparuit**) and the belt (**cingula**) of the youth Pallas (**Pallantis pueri**) shone (**fulserunt**) with its familiar studs (**notis ... bullis**), (the youth) whom Turnus had thrown down (**straverat**), overcome by a wound (**victum ... vulnere**), and (Turnus) was wearing it on his shoulders (**umeris ... gerebat**) as the token of a foe (**inimicum insigne**)." The correct answer is, therefore, (C) "(Aeneas) noticed Turnus wearing Pallas' swordbelt."

9.  **(D)**

Answer (D) dactyl-dactyl-dactyl-spondee is correct. Be sure to include the two elisions, **atque umeris** and **inimicum insigne**, in your scansion. The –**que** in **atque** is short and the second elision is long by position, i.e., it is followed by two consonants, **ns**-. For scansion, see Chapter 11.

10. **(A)**

In lines 8–9, note that Aeneas really does not see both "the reminder of cruel grief" (**saevi monimenta doloris**) and the swordbelt (**exuviasque**). As required by the sense, **saevi monimenta dolori** is really in apposition to **exuvias**. Therefore, this is an example of hendiadys and Answer (A) is correct. For figures of speech, see Chapter 10.

11. **(D)**

**Indute** is a perfect passive participle with a vocative ending, modifying **Tu** (=Turnus). For participles, see Chapter 16A.

12. **(D)**

Lines 10–11 are translated, "Are you, adorned with the plunder of one of mine (**meorum**), to be snatched away from me?" **Eripiare** is a form of the present subjunctive passive of the verb **eripio, eripere** in a deliberative question. The form **eripiare** is condensed from **eripiaris**. For deliberative questions, see Chapter 16D, Section 2; for alternative verb forms, see Chapter 11.

13. **(D)**
     In lines 11–12, Aeneas pathetically invokes the name of Pallas (note the anaphora), in whose name he is striking the fatal blow. "Pallas (is the one who) makes a death-sacrifice of you (**immolat**) with this wound, Pallas (is the one who) exacts retribution (**poenam . . . sumit**) from your villainous blood."

## "Romulus reacts to news of his brother's death"

14. **(B)**
     In lines 1–2, the relevant words **lacrimas . . . habet** translate, "he (Romulus) chokes back the tears having welled up inside and keeps the wound closed away in his heart." The correct answer is therefore (B) "suppressed his grief."

15. **(A)**
     Although the **–as** ending of **obortas** could lead you to Answer (B) a present subjunctive (see Chapter 16D, Section 1), or (D) a main verb (first conjugation, present tense indicative), the verb **oborior, oboriri, obortus sum** is deponent, that is, it is passive in form and active in meaning. Therefore, **obortas** is a perfect passive (past) participle modifying **lacrimas**. For deponent verbs, see Chapter 14B; for past participles of deponent verbs, see Chapter 16A.

16. **(D)**
     Line 3 answers the question by translating "He does not wish to weep openly and maintains (= wishes to maintain) strength as an example." Therefore, Answer (D) "grieved privately" is correct.

17. **(A)**
     The verb of this famous saying is a jussive subjunctive, which required the meaning of "let." The verb form required by Answer (B) is present tense, **transit**, and Answer (C) future tense, **transibit**. **Hostis** is a nominative subject and cannot serve as the direct object of **transeat**, therefore Answer (D) "he may overtake the enemy" is incorrect. The entire sentence translates, "Let the enemy cross over my walls and this (**sic**) will happen," i.e., the enemy will die, just as Remus did. For the forms and uses of the independent subjunctive, see Chapters 16D, Sections 1 and 2.

18. **(B)**
     **Nec iam**, "no longer," is an idiomatic phrase commonly found throughout Latin literature.

19. **(A)**
     Lines 5–6 say, "However, he conducts the funeral rites (and) no longer able to hold back the tears, his hidden devotion is disclosed and he presses final kisses (on the body) placed on the bier." The finality implied in Answers (B) and (D) is not present or suggested in these words. The sequence of the Latin in this sentence implies that Romulus had "broken down" during the funeral rites, which presumably took place before transport to the grave on the bier.

20. **(B)**

The words that interlock are **osculaque** with **suprema** (accusative plural, neuter) and **posito** with **feretro** (ablative singular, neuter), giving **osculaque ... posito suprema feretro** as the synchysis. For figures of speech, see Chapter 10.

21. **(C)**

Ovid takes this famous line directly from Catullus, Poem 101, on the death of the poet's brother. It reads, "Brother, taken away from me against your will, farewell." The words **invito** and **adempte** imply an early/unexpected death, giving (C) "his brother had died prematurely" as the correct answer. **Ademptus** is the perfect passive participle of **adimo, adimere, ademi, ademptus** and has a vocative ending, modifying **frater.**

22. **(B)**

This sentence requires careful reading, as the sense requires that the future active participle **arsuros** be translated with a passive meaning: Romulus annointed (**unxit**) the body (**artus**, accusative plural) about to be cremated (**arsuros**, modifying **artus**, a fourth declension noun). The correct sequence is reversed in Answer (A); Answer (B) mistakes **artus**, "limbs," for a form of **ars, artis**, "skill"; and Answer (D) mistranslates **unxit** (for **iunxit**?) The use of **artus** for body is an example of synecdoche. For the future active participle, see Chapter 16A.

23. **(B)**

**Fecere** is a poetic condensation of **fecerunt**, which is third person plural, perfect active indicative = "they made" or "they did." It cannot be a form of the future tense (Answer A), a present infinitive (Answer C), or a present imperative (Answer D) because the stem **fec-** is in the perfect tense. For alternative verb forms, see Chapter 11.

24. **(A)**

In line 10, the ending of the adjective **maestas** requires that it modify the noun **comas**, but it is not the hair that is sad, but Acca herself. Therefore, the meaning of **maestas** may be transferred to **Acca** from **comas** (note also the juxtaposition of **maestas** with **Acca**). For figures of speech, see Chapter 10.

25. **(D)**

Break down this sentence by noticing the interlocking of **ultima ... flamma** with **plorato ... rogo** and the separation of the elements of the main verb, which is **subdita ... est**. The adjective **ultima** may be translated adverbially, as Answer (D) "at last." The verb **subdo, subdere, subdidi, subditum** means *to place under*. **Plorato ... rogo** is an ablative absolute meaning "the funeral pyre having been lamented, or, "after the funeral pyre was lamented." Hence, the correct answer is (D) "At last the fire has been placed under the pyre after it was lamented, i.e., the lamentable pyre."

## "Pliny congratulates a friend"

26. **(D)**

Answer (D) "has pledged to present games in Verona" is correct because Line 1 reads, "You have done well, Valerius, because you have sponsored gladiatorial games for our fellow Veronese."

27. **(B)**

The listing of three verbs in a row without punctuation – **amaris suspiceris ornaris** – is asyndeton. Normally, you would find **amaris et suspiceris et ornaris**. See Chapter 10 for figures of speech.

28. **(A)**

That Valerius' wife was deceased is surmised from the past tense of the verb, i.e., **uxorem . . . habuisti**, the use of the words **memoriae** (line 3) and **funeri** (line 4), and Pliny's comment here that gladiatorial combats are particularly suitable for funeral tributes (their original function). The sentence in lines 2–4 reads, "From there (Verona) you had a wife very dear and most acceptable to you, to whose memory you owe either some public work (**opus**) or show (**spectaculum**), and this is very much the kind of show that is especially appropriate (**hoc potissimum quod maxime**) for a funeral."

29. **(D)**

The case of the noun **memoriae**, dative, depends upon the verb **debebatur** (line 4): "to the memory of whom (**cuius**, i.e., the wife) . . . there was owed." Avoid taking both **memoriae** and **cuius** as genitive. For the dative case, see Chapter 13A.

30. **(B)**

This is a tricky sentence. The key to the meaning is the observation of **negare** as a subjective infinitive, i.e., **negare** serves as the subject of the result clause **ut . . . videretur**. Subjective infinitives serve as neuter nouns, therefore **constans** and **durum** modify **negare**. For this use of infinitive, see Chapter 16C.

31. **(A)**

In lines 1–5, Pliny congratulates Valerius for having done well (**recte fecisti**) in proposing the games. Thereafter, he concentrates on talking about the games themselves. Therefore, **illud quoque egregie** correctly follows after **fecisti**, understood: "You did that admirably, too, the fact that (**quod**) . . . ." Thus, the correct answer is (A) **fecisti** (understood from line 1).

32. **(C)**

The correct translation of the gerund **edendo** is Answer (C) "sponsoring." The ablative case is used after the preposition **in**. Answer (A) is a red herring, designed to get you to think about the distinction between a gerund and a passive periphrastic. The perfect active participle in Answer (B) "having sponsored," cannot be expressed directly in Latin, as **edo, edere** is not a deponent verb. The meaning given in Answer (D) "about to be sponsored" requires a future passive participle or gerundive, which is an adjective; **edendo** functions as a noun here. For more on gerunds and gerundives, see Chapter 16B.

33. **(C)**

Answer (C) is correct because Pliny characterizes Valerius in line 5 as **tam facilis tam liberalis**, "so efficient (and) so lavish" (in giving the games). Note the asyndeton.

34. **(C)**

**Vellem** is imperfect subjunctive, first person singular. The subjunctive appears here because Pliny is expressing a wish (optative), which is a non-fact. For independent subjunctives, see Chapter 16D, Section 2.

35. **(A)**

As given, the sentence reads "If only (**Vellem**) the panthers (**Africanae**) . . . had arrived (**occurrissent**) on the appointed day (**ad praefinitum die**)." Vellem is optative subjunctive, for which, see Chapter 16D, Section 2. For the form of occurrissent, see Chapter 16D, Section 1. Answer (A) is correct because the renderings of the verb tenses in Answers (B) "will arrive," (C) "would arrive," and (D) "had wished," are incorrect.

36. **(D)**

The relevant Latin in line 7 reads, "but it is granted (**licet**) that they (**illae**, the panthers), having been delayed by a storm (**tempestate detentae**) were late (**cessaverint**)." **Cessaverint** is perfect subjunctive after **licet** (for impersonal verbs, see Chapter 14D). Thus, Answer (D) "did not arrive on time because of a storm" is correct.

37. **(D)**

The words **quo minus** (sometimes spelled **quominus**) introduce the subjunctive clause **quo minus ... exhiberes**. **Quo minus** is found with the subjunctive when hindering or preventing is stated or implied, as it is here. Answer (A) **licet** governs **cessaverint**; Answer (B) **ut** introduces a clause with **fieret**; Answer (C) **quod** introduces a causal clause with **stetit**. For subjunctive clauses, see Chapter 16D, Section 6.

38. **(B)**

The Latin says, "you nonetheless deserved that the credit (**acceptum**, a financial term referring to something entered into the credit column) should go (**fieret**) to you, because (**quod**) it was not your fault (**non per se stetit**, an idiomatic use of **stetit**) that you could not show them (**quo minus exhiberes**)." Therefore, Answer (C) "Valerius deserves credit for his intentions" is correct.

## "A festival celebrates the blessings of the farm"

39. **(A)**

The required lines (1–2) tell us "the earth and the ploughman should have a day of rest on festival day (**luce sacra**) and that, with the plough lifted (**suspenso vomere**), the heavy work should cease." "The plough lifted" refers to the removal of the ploughshare from the earth. Answer (A) "a day of rest for all" is the correct answer. Note the metonymy of light (**Luce**) for day.

40. **(B)**

With **suspenso**, **vomere** completes the ablative absolute. For this construction, see Appendix 9.

41. **(D)**

Lines 3–4 are translated, "Now the oxen, with garlanded heads, should stand at feeding troughs that are full," leading to Answer (D) "the cattle should be fed well." The other answers exploit, but confuse, the wording of this sentence. **Solvite vincla iugis** refers to loosening the harnesses from the yokes.

42. **(C)**

Answer (C) "Let all things be done for the god" correctly translates **Omnia sint operata deo** (line 5). **Sint** is a jussive subjunctive, the subject of which is the substantive **omnia**, modified by the adjective **operata**. **Deo** refers, presumably, to Bacchus, Ceres, or some other divinity associated with fertility or the farm. At the beginning of the poem, which is not provided here, both of these deities are invoked in celebration of the festival. For independent subjunctives, see Chapter 16D, Section 2.

43. **(D)**

In line 6, the dative case of **pensis** depends upon the compound verb **imposuisse**. This portion of the sentence reads, "let no one (**nec . . . ulla**) dare to have applied (**imposuisse**) her spinner's hand (**lanificam . . . manum**) to the **pensum** (the day's work)." For the dative case, see Chapter 13A.

44. **(B)**

The translation of lines 7–8 leads to the meaning, "I bid you all be far away; let him depart from the altar to whom Venus (love) brought pleasure last night (**hesterna gaudia nocte**)." Thus, Answer (B) "must stay away from the festival" is correct. Use scansion to determine whether **hesterna** is accusative modifying **gaudia** or ablative with **nocte**. (It is the latter.)

45. **(C)**

The substitution of **Venus** for love or passion is metonymy. For figures of speech, see Chapter 10.

46. **(B)**

The possible answers require careful reading! Answer (B) "draw the spring's water with pure hands" is correct. Answer (A) "wash their garments in pure spring water" incorrectly translates **pura cum veste venite** ("arrive with purified garments") and Answer (C) "make chaste offerings to the gods with pure garments" incorrectly interprets **casta placent superis** ("purity is pleasing to the gods)." Answer (D) "draw purified water by hand from the spring" is incorrect because **puris** modifies **manibus** and not **aquam**.

47. **(D)**

Answer (D), "Observe how the sacred lamb goes to the shining altars," is correct. Answer (A) reverses **fulgentes** (shining) and **sacer** (sacred); Answer (B) incorrectly renders **fulgentes** as vocative; and Answer (C) incorrectly translates **eat** as future tense. **Eat** is present subjunctive of the verb **eo, ire** in an indirect question introduced by **ut**. For irregular verbs, see Chapter 14C; for present participles, see Chapter 16A; for subjunctive clauses with **ut**, see Chapter 16D, Section 4.

48. **(A)**

The word **fulgentes** is pulled away from the prepositional phrase **ad aras** and placed in an emphatic position, framing the activity anticipated to take place at the altar: fulgentes ut eat sacer agnus ad aras. For anastrophe and hyperbaton, see Chapter 10.

49. **(C)**

Scansion of this pentameter line (the second line of an elegiac couplet, for which, see Chapter 11) helps you to determine that the –a of olea is long and that therefore olea is ablative (of means).

50. **(C)**

Answer (A) sacrificial procession refers to the preceding line. Answer (B) exploits the appearance of the word **olea** (olive tree) as a distractor and Answer (D) exploits the context of the poem, which is about farming. This difficult final line is rendered "behind it (referring to the procession taking the sacrificial lamb to the altar) a throng (garbed) in white (cf. line 9), their hair bound up (literally, bound up as to their hair or with regard to their hair) with olive branches (**vinctaque olea ... comas**)." The past participle **vinctaque** (from **vincio,** not **vinco**) modifies **candida turba**.

# Translations of the Multiple-Choice Passages

## "Aeneas confronts Turnus"

Aeneas stood fierce in arms, shifting his eyes, and he restrained his weapon hand; and now, and now (Turnus') words had begun to sway him more as he hesitated, when the luckless sword-belt high on his (Turnus') shoulder came into his view and the belt of the youthful Pallas shone with familiar studs, (Pallas the youth) whom Turnus had thrown down, overcome by a wound, and he (Turnus) was wearing it on his shoulders as a token of the foe. He (Aeneas), after he caught sight of the swordbelt, testament to cruel grief, inflamed with madness and frightful with anger, proclaimed "Are you, adorned with the plunder of one of mine, to be snatched away from me? Pallas (is the one who) makes a sacrifice of you with this death-blow, Pallas (is the one who) exacts retribution from your villainous blood."

## "Romulus reacts to news of his brother's death"

When the king (Romulus) learned this (that his brother had been killed), he chokes back the tears having welled up inside and keeps the wound closed away in his heart.[1] He does not wish to weep openly and he maintains strength as an example. "Let it be the same for (any) enemy who should cross my walls," he says. Nonetheless, he conducts the funeral rites (and), no longer able to hold back the tears, his hidden devotion is disclosed and he presses final kisses (on the body) placed on the bier, and says, "O brother, taken from me before your time, farewell!" (Romulus) annointed the body about to be cremated. Both Faustulus and Acca, having loosened her hair in grief, did what he had done. Then the not-yet-citizen Quirites wept for the youth. At last the fire has been placed under the pyre after it was lamented, i.e., the lamentable pyre.

## "Pliny congratulates a friend"

You have done well, Valerius, because you have sponsored gladiatorial games for our fellow citizens of Verona, by whom for a long time now you are loved, respected, and honored. You had a wife, also from there (Verona) who was very dear to and most compatible with you, to/in whose memory you owe either some public work or show, and this is very much the kind of show that is especially appropriate for a funeral. Moreover, you were asked by so many people, that to refuse would seem not stubborn, but rude. You did that admirably too, the fact that you were so efficient and lavish in producing (the games); for even through things like this, the

---

[1] The verbs in the present tense in this passage may be translated as past.

523

true spirit (of generosity) is shown. If only the panthers, which you had purchased in quantity, had arrived on the appointed day: but granted that they, having been delayed by a storm, were late, you nonetheless deserved that the credit should go to you, because it was not your fault that you could not show them. Farewell.

## "A festival celebrates the blessings of the farm"

On (this sacred day) let the earth rest, let the ploughman rest and, with the plough lifted (from the soil), the heavy work should cease. Loosen the harness from the yokes; now the oxen with garlanded heads should stand at feeding troughs that are full. Let all things be done for the god; let no one dare to have applied her spinner's hand to the day's work. Also, I bid that you be far away, let him depart from the altar to whom love brought pleasure last night. Purity is pleasing to the gods: come with pure garments and draw the spring's water with pure hands. Look how the sacred lamb proceeds to the shining altar and behind (it) the white-robed throng, their hair bound up with olive leaves.

# Answers to Free-Response Section

## Question 1

### Translation

"Indeed, I think that, with the guidance of the gods and with Juno favorable, the Trojan ships have held their course here on the wind. What a city you will see here, sister, what a kingdom you will see rise up by way of such a marriage! To what heights will Punic glory rise with Trojan arms accompanying (us)! Only ask the gods for pardon and, sacrifices having been offered, be generous with (your) hospitality and weave together reasons for him to stay."

### Grading

*9 pts. total, one-half point for each segment. Round up your score.*

1. dis equidem auspicibus
2. reor Iliacas carinas . . . tenuisse
3. et Iunone secunda
4. hunc cursum
5. vento
6. quam tu . . . hanc urbem . . . cernes

7. quae . . . regna

8. coniugio tali

9. Teucrum

10. comitantibus armis

11. Punica . . . gloria

12. quantis rebus

13. attollet

14. tu modo posce deos veniam

15. sacris litatis

16. indulge hospitio

17. causasque innecte

18. morandi

## Acceptable Translations for Question 1, Vergil: Practice Exam 2

For instructional purposes, more grammatical and syntactical information is provided here than is usually found in the grading reports on the translation question.

1. **dis:** [= **deis**]

   **equidem**: indeed/surely/truly

   **auspicibus**: favor/auspices/patronage/guide [**auspex, auspicis**, is a noun; **dis auspicibus** is an ablative absolute without a participle]

2. **reor**: (I) think/suppose/reckon/be of the opinion [deponent verb]

   **Iliacas**: Trojan/Ilian [must modify **carinas**]

   **carinas**: keels; synecdoche for ships/boats [the subject of **tenuisse** in indirect statement after **reor**]

   **tenuisse**: hold/keep/preserve/maintain [perfect active infinitive in indirect statement after **reor**]

3. **et**: [joins the two ablatives absolute, **dis . . . auspicibus** and **Iunone secunda**]

   **Iunone**: Juno **secunda**: favorable/following/propitious/aiding [take with **Iunone**; another ablative absolute lacking a participle]

4. **hunc cursum**: this course/journey/direction/way [**hunc cursum**, the direct object of **tenuisse**, may also be rendered "to this place" or "to here" = **huc**]

5. **vento**: wind [ablative of means]

6. **quam**: What/How great

   **tu**: [refers to Dido]

**hanc urbem**: this city [note that, as above with **hunc**, **hanc** may also be rendered as "here, in this place" = **hic**]

**cernes**: (you) will see/observe/witness/perceive/regard [future tense]

7. **quae**: what [take with **regna**; parallels **quam**]

   **regna**: kingdom/realm/dominion/sovereignty [may be singular; parallels **quam . . . cernes**, so the verb **cernes** is understood here]

8. **coniugio**: marriage/wedlock/wedding/union [ablative of cause, "because of "]

   **tali**: such/of such a kind [modifies **coniugio**]

9. **Teucrum**: Trojan/Teucrian/Teucri [genitive plural = **Teucrorum**, completes **armis**]

10. **comitantibus**: accompany/join/escort/attend/follow [present participle of deponent verb, with **armis** in an ablative absolute]

    **armis**: arms/weapons

11. **Punica**: Punic/Carthaginian

    **gloria**: glory/renown/fame/pride/achievement [subject of **attollet**]

12. **quantis**: [dative of reference, "(with reference) to"; paralleling **quam . . .cernes** and **quae regna (cernes)** above]

    **rebus**: the meaning here is equivalent to **gloria**: heights/honor/acclaim/esteem/prestige

13. **attollet**: (it) will rise/elevate/climb/raise or lift up/soar [future tense]

14. **modo**: only/just now

    **tu . . . posce**: ask for/seek from/request of or from/inquire of/call upon/demand [imperative]

    **deos**: the gods [one of two direct objects of the verb **posco**, **poscere**, to ask something of/from someone]

    **veniam**: pardon/favor/grace/indulgence/good will [the other of the two direct objects of **posce**]

15. **sacris**: sacred or holy things/sacrifices [substantive]

    **litatis**: to make a favorable sacrifice/appease/pacify/placate [must be taken with **sacris** to complete the ablative absolute]

16. **indulge**: be generous/be kind/favor/indulge [imperative]

    **hospitio**: hospitality/welcome/reception [dative after **indulge**]

17. **causas**: reason/cause/pretext/inducement/excuse [direct object of **innecte**; must complete **morandi**]

    **innecte**: weave/connect/fasten/tie or bind together [imperative]

18. **morandi**: of/for staying/remaining/delaying/lingering [gerund; genitive with **causas**]

# Question 2

## Translation

And so to Turnus, with whatever courage he sought a way (to win), the dread goddess denies success. Then different imaginings spin around in his mind; he observes the Rutulians and his city and hesitates through fear and trembles that death is imminent, neither does he see to where he might escape, nor in what way he might attack the enemy, nor (does he see) his chariot anywhere, or his sister, the charioteer.

## Grading

### *9 pts. total, one-half point for each segment. Round up your score.*

1. sic Turno
2. quacumque
3. viam . . . petivit
4. virtute
5. successum . . . negat
6. dira dea
7. tum pectore
8. sensus . . . varii
9. vertuntur
10. Rutulos aspectat et urbem
11. cunctaturque
12. metu
13. letumque instare
14. tremescit
15. nec quo se eripiat
16. nec qua vi tendat in hostem
17. nec currus usquam videt
18. aurigamve sororem (videt)

## Acceptable Translations for Question 2, Vergil: Practice Exam 2

For instructional purposes, more grammatical and syntactical information is provided here than is usually found in the grading reports on the translation question.

1. **sic**: thus/and so/therefore

   **Turno**: Turnus [dative with **negat**]

2. **quacumque**: whatever or wherever [acceptable either as an indefinite adjective in the ablative case modifying **virtute** and meaning "with whatever courage," or as an adverb, "wherever"]

3. **viam**: way/path/means/method **petivit**: (he) sought/looked for/determined/strove after/endeavored to obtain

4. **virtute**: courage/bravery/fortitude/fearlessness/valor/boldness [ablative of means]

5. **successum**: success/accomplishment/fulfilment/attainment

   **negat**: (she) denies/refuses/rejects/turns down

6. **dira**: dread/terrible/horrible or horrifying/fearful/cruel/deadly

   **dea**: goddess

7. **tum**: then/thereupon/at that time

   **pectore**: mind or heart [the context here suggests **pectus** is the seat of consciousness, or mind; the preposition **in** is understood = ablative of place where]

8. **sensus**: imaginings/visions/perceptions/feelings [must be nominative plural, the subject of **vertuntur**]

   **varii**: different/diverse/various/manifold/variant/dissimilar [modifies **sensus**]

9. **vertuntur**: spin/turn/turn around/whirl/wheel/fly about/roll around [may be translated as active]

10. **Rutulos**: Rutuli/Rutulians/people of Turnus [one of the two direct objects of **aspectat**]

    **aspectat**: (he) observes/sees/gazes on/looks at [the first of a series of three verbs, including **cunctaturque** and **tremescit**]

    **et**: [must connect **Rutulos** and **urbem**]

    **urbem**: [the other direct object of **aspectat**]

11. **cunctaturque**: (he) hestitates/delays/stays/remains/lingers/bides time [deponent verb]

    **-que**: [connects **cunctatur** with **aspectat**]

12. **metu**: fear/dread/apprehension/fright/terror [ablative of cause]

13. **letumque**: death/ruin/annihilation [accusative subject of infinitive **instare** in indirect statement]

    **-que** [must connect **cunctatur** with **tremescit**]

    **instare**: be imminent/threaten/press upon/be close/pursue [infinitive in indirect statement after **tremescit**]

14. **tremescit**: (he) dreads/fears/trembles at

15. **nec**: neither/and . . . not/nor [negates **videt**; may be taken with **quo** to mean "not anywhere," i.e., nowhere, = **nusquam**]

    **quo**: anywhere [place where to]

    **se eripiat**: (he) may or might escape/rescue himself/snatch himself from [present tense of the subjunctive in the indirect question introduced by **quo**]

16. **nec**: same as in #15.

    **qua vi**: in what or which way/with what force/by what means [ablative of means]

    **tendat**: (he) may or might strive after/make for/contend with [with **in hostem**, attack the enemy; present subjunctive in indirect question introduced by **qua**]

17. **nec**: same as in #15 [**nec** can be taken with **usquam** to mean nowhere, = **nusquam**]

    **currus**: chariot [accusative plural, direct object of **videt**; may be singular]

    **usquam**: anywhere/in any place

    **videt**: (he) sees/notices/heeds/takes note of/regards

18. **aurigam**: charioteer/chariot driver [in apposition to **sororem**]

    **-ve**: = **vel**, or [connects **aurigam sororem** with **currus**; may be translated as "nor," in correlation with **nec**, = "neither (the chariot) . . . nor (his sister, the charioteer)"]

    **sororem**: sister

# Question 3

## Long Essay

For the grading scale used for evaluating essays, see Chapter 7. Here are some high points of each description to consider in your comparative analysis, followed by a sample essay. Such observations, which will set up your formal essay, may be made in writing during the 15–minute reading period. The sample essays may seem overly thorough, but the author is attempting to accommodate the wide range of answers that will be given by users of this book.

(A) The Greeks are sacking Troy and Pyrrhus is breaking into the interior of the palace.

- The inner house is full of shrieks (gemitu), uproar (misero tumultu), and confusion (miscetur).

- The vaulted halls echo (ululant) with women's cries (pangoribus . . . femineis); the noise reaches to the very stars. The diction creates an atmosphere of noise and confusion; the interlocking of cavae plangoribus aedes femineis) through synchysis causes the women's wailing to "echo" against the valuted halls; ad sidera is hyperbole and ululant onomatopoeia.

- The panic-stricken women (<u>pavidae . . . matres</u>) roam through the immense quarters, clasp and hold tight to the door-posts (<u>amplexaeque tenent postes</u>) and plant kisses on them (<u>oscula figunt</u>). The interlocking of fear, halls, and women in <u>pavidae tectis matres ingentibus</u> (4) accentuates the interrelationship of all three. The chiasmus of <u>tenent postes atque oscula figunt</u> (5) gives the impression that the women are actually embracing and kissing the door-posts.

- Pyrrhus appears suddenly, with <u>instat</u> in prime position in the line. The juxtaposition and alliteration of <u>vi patria Pyrrhus</u> adds to the intensity of his dramatic entrance. Neither the bolts nor the guards are strong enough to withstand him. The hard <u>c</u> of <u>nec claustra nec</u> . . . <u>custodes</u> suggests the sounds of hacking or knocking at the interior doors.

(B)   Carthage reacts to the news that Queen Dido has killed herself.

- This passage also begins with noise (a single shriek?) raised to the heights (<u>ad alta atria</u>; cf. Passage A, line 3). Note the hyperbaton <u>concussam</u> . . . <u>urbem</u> that frames <u>bacchatur Fama</u>, which runs riot inside the shaken city. <u>Bacchatur</u> is a metaphor that suggests the wild uncontrolled behavior of the worshippers of Bacchus.

- The halls resonate with the sobbing (<u>lamentis</u>), groaning (<u>gemitu</u>), and wailing of women (<u>femineo ululatu</u>). Cf. <u>gemitu</u>, Passage A, line 1, and <u>femineis ululant</u>, line 3.

- The heavens echo (<u>resonat</u> . . . . <u>aether</u>) with loud laments (<u>magnis plangoribus</u>). Next comes a simile comparing the noise and confusion with that of a city, such as Carthage or Tyre, falling to the enemy (<u>immissis</u> . . . <u>hostibus</u>). Note the hyperbole of <u>resonat</u> . . . <u>aether</u> (cf. Passage A, line 3) and the whoosh of s's in line 5, which suggest the onrush of the enemy. The enjambment of <u>Karthago aut antiqua Tyros</u> adds drama.

- Further description of a sacked city describes the raging flames (<u>flammaeque furentes</u>) rolling over the rooftops (<u>culmina</u>) of the houses of men and gods.

## Sample Long Essay

These two passages, which describe the downfalls of two households at two different times and places, are remarkable similar in setting, tone, diction, and imagery. Death and destruction are common elements. Passage (A) depicts the noise and confusion in the inner palace of Priam during the sack of Troy. Passage (B) describes the noise and confusion in the inner palace of Dido (and in the city of Carthage) after the news has been received that Dido has killed herself.

As mentioned, both narratives describe their respective scenes as noisy, confused, and filled with grief. The same words are sometimes used: Passage (A) <u>plangoribus</u>, <u>ululant</u>, <u>clamor</u>; Passage (B) <u>clamor</u>, <u>ululatu</u>, <u>plangoribus</u>. In Passage (A), words expressing disorientation and despair include <u>gemitu</u>, <u>tumultu</u>, <u>pavidae</u>, and <u>amplexaeque</u> . . . <u>figunt</u> (line 5); in Passage (B), <u>concussam</u>, <u>bacchatur</u>, <u>immissis</u>

ruat hostibus (line 5), and <u>furentes</u>, all onomatopoetic, or nearly so. There is a pre-occupation with the structure of both households or cities as if they were almost living beings and participants in the commotion: Passage (A) <u>domus interior</u> (line 1), <u>cavae</u> . . . <u>aedes</u> (line 2), <u>tectis</u>. . . <u>ingentibus</u> (line 4), <u>tenent postes</u> (line 5), and <u>nec</u> . . . <u>claustra</u> . . . <u>valent</u> (lines 6–7); Passage (B) <u>ad alta atria</u> (1–2), <u>tecta</u> (line 4) and <u>culmina</u> (line 5). All this adds to the reader's sense of mayhem and chaos and to the sense that both buildings and people are vulnerable during a crisis. Also in both instances, women are depicted as the true victims of what has happened, at least with regard to their reactions: Passage (A) <u>plangoribus</u>. . . . <u>femineis ululant</u> (lines 2–3) and <u>pavidae matres</u> (line 4), etc.; Passage (B) <u>femineo ululatu</u> (line 3), and perhaps <u>bacchatur</u> (line 2). Vergil uses exaggeration (hyperbole) in both scenes to pump up the action: Passage (A) <u>ferit aurea sidera clamor</u> (line 3), "the noise reaches the golden stars," and (B) <u>resonat magnis plangoribus aether</u> (line 4), "the high heavens resound with great shrieks."

Word order also contributes to the reader's appreciation of what is happening: interlocking is used effectively in Passage (A) where the wailing of the women seems to "echo" from the vaulted halls (<u>cavae plangoribus aedes femineis</u>, lines 2–3). The interlocking of fearful, halls, and women in <u>pavidae tectis matres ingentibus</u> (line 4) accentuates the interrelationship of all three. Word-pictures also contribute to the description of the uproar. In Passage (A), line 5, <u>tenent</u> . . . <u>figunt</u> depicts the women actually "embracing" (<u>amplexaeque</u>) the door-posts; in Passage (B), the hyperbaton of <u>concussam</u> . . . <u>urbem</u> in line 2 frames <u>bacchatur Fama</u>, which literally "runs riot" inside the shaken city.

The differences between these two passages are few but significant. In Passage (A), all the action seems to funnel down into the dramatic arrival of a single individual, Pyrrhus, who becomes a catalyzing element in the destruction of the royal family and of Troy by killing King Priam. The prime position of <u>instat</u> and the juxtaposition and alliteration of <u>vi patria Pyrrhus</u> in line 6, add to the dramatic intensity of the warrior's entrance. In Passage (B), the final three lines employ a simile which compares the downfall of Carthage, which is implied by the death of Dido, to the sack of a great city by an enemy. Note that the houses of the gods are destroyed in the simile in Passage B, which perhaps suggests purification by fire for the pollution brought upon Carthage by Dido's broken vow. Did Vergil have in his files a stock description for depicting the downfall of a household?

# Question 4

## Short Essay

For the grading scale used for evaluating essays, see Chapter 7. Here are some high points of the passage to consider in your comparative analysis.

- Aeneas and Achates, hidden from view by a mist, inspect the murals in the Temple of Juno at Carthage. The first reaction of Aeneas is weeping (<u>lacrimans</u>). He asks Achates, in a tone of despair, what region of the earth has not heard of their tragedy? Note the ellipsis of <u>est</u>; abbreviated sentence structure is a feature of expressions of high emotion.

- Aeneas spots the dead Priam and makes the ironical observation that these are the rewards of virtue. He also speaks of compassion (lacrimae) for suffering (rerum) and mortal woes (mortalia) touching the human heart (mentem). Note the compressed sentence structure of En Priamum and the emphatic repetition of sunt (3–4). The words lacrimae and mortalia contribute to the development of pathos.

- Aeneas then does an "about face" by reverting to a condensed version of his previous "O socii" speech. He advises Achates (whose presence allows Aeneas to vocalize his thoughts and thus heighten our sympathy for both) not to fear: "the struggle you witness here (i.e., our fama or reputation) will bring us salvation." Metus is another charged word; note the poetic plural, which multiplies the fear.

- Aeneas then does another "about face" and relapses into despair as he studies "the empty picture" (pictura . . . inane). He groans and his face becomes wet with a flood of tears. Note the evocative words gemens, umectat, and largo . . . flumine, the metaphorical use of pascit, and the solemn m-sounds throughout the passage.

- The final five lines describe significant events of the war and Aeneas' reaction upon seeing them portrayed on the mural. The postponement of the subject Achilles in the sentence of lines 8–9 is notable in developing anticipation, as if Aeneas was hoping to defer his grief over such painful memories. There are many significant words and phrases used in these lines: exanimum . . . corpus, corpus amici, tendentem manus Priamum . . . inermes. Aeneas' reaction to all this is a tremendous groan (ingentem gemitum dat pectore ab imo). Note the sound play of ingentem gemitum, which suggests the groans themselves. The anaphora of ut, the asyndeton, and the enjambment of inermes are all emphatic and therefore contribute to developing in the reader a sense of compassion for Aeneas and the Trojans.

## Sample Short Essay

In this passage, Vergil provides the reader with many opportunities to develop and heighten a sense of pathos or compassion. Word selection, the sounds of words, the use of altered sentence structure through abbreviation and repetition, the use of imagery, and the interplay of dialogue and narrative description all contribute. The subject of Aeneas' attention in this passage, i.e., events of the Trojan War as portrayed on the murals of the Temple of Juno at Carthage, certainly warrants an emotional reaction on the part of Aeneas, as he himself was a participant in those tragic events.

This passage teems with words that communicate or suggest the grief and pain suffered by Aeneas and Achates while viewing the murals. Words such as lacrimans (line 1), lacrimae (line 4), largoque umectet flumine vultum (line 7), and ingentem gemitum . . . pectore ab imo (line 10) all denote the tearful pain and suffering experienced by Aeneas. Additional words are suggestive: mortalia (line 4), metus (line 5), inani (line 6), exanimum . . . corpus (line 9), corpus amici (line 11), and tendentem manus Priamum . . . inermes (line 12).

Vergil also uses words whose sounds evoke the solemnity of remembering trauma and death. Consonance of m sounds is found throughout the passages, especially in lines 4, 7, 10, and 12. Also, the interplay of ingentem and gemitum suggests the sounds made by Aeneas when he groans and moans. Events or speeches of high emotion usually contain some alteration in sentence structure, as events speed up or slow down. Vergil's "craft" here includes the use of short sentences, such as En Priamum (line 3), examples of ellipsis (est in line 5), the use of anaphora (sunt . . . sunt, lines 3–4, and ut, line 11), and asyndeton (line 11).

Because the use of elaborate imagery in this passage would detract from the simplicity of the emotions portrayed here, figurative speech contributes little to developing pathos in the reader. Exaggeration (hyperbole) appears in flumine (line 7), exaggerating the amount of weeping, and pectore ab imo (line 10), amplifies the expressiveness of the groan. Animum . . . pascit (line 6) expresses the image that Aeneas is "grazing" as he looks at the pictures.

The use of dialogue between Aeneas and Achates, including a rhetorical question (lines 1–2), spliced into the descriptive narrative, personalizes the emotions and allows Aeneas to make observations that heighten his own feelings (lines 6–7).

When we first meet Aeneas in the Aeneid, he is lamenting the fact that he did not die at Troy. We learned at that time that it was acceptable in a warrior culture, even for heroes, to break down and cry. In the passage here, Vergil is masterful in portraying the humanity of Aeneas without sacrificing our appreciation of his sense of himself as a man.

# Question 5

Because it is difficult to do justice to this question in the space provided here (there are nine possible combinations of characters that can be discussed), you are given below some information about each "lesser deity." Compare the content of your own answer with those provided. On the actual AP Vergil Exam, a short analytical essay is expected.

## Group A

**Cupid**: The son of Venus appears in the latter stages of Book 1 and precipitates the action in the next three books. Upon being invited by Queen Dido to a banquet, Aeneas sends back to the ships for his son Ascanius. Venus, fearful of Juno's continuing interference, disguises her son Cupid as Ascanius. At the banquet, Dido embraces Ascanius/Cupid and then falls passionately in love with Aeneas. This scene leads in Book 2 to Aeneas' narration of the Trojan War and in Book 3 to his account of his travels, which then lead to the subsequent relationship between Dido and Aeneas described at length in Book 4. Though acting in a minor role, Cupid precipitates momentous events in the Aeneid.

**Sea Nymphs**: In Book 9, Jupiter, at the behest of his mother Cybele, changed the Trojan ships, which had been torched by Turnus and the Rutulians, into sea nymphs, who swam away unharmed. They return to the Latin coast as Aeneas arrives with Evander's fleet, which had sailed down the Tiber. Cymodocea, one of the sea nymphs, tells Aeneas of the transformation of the Trojan fleet and promises help in the rescue of Ascanius and the Trojans beleaguered by Turnus.

**Vulcan**: Vulcan, who is the blacksmith of the gods and husband of Venus, has a small but significant role in the drama of the Aeneid. In Book 8, Venus asks Vulcan to forge weapons and armor for her son, which with the help of the Cyclopes, he does. These weapons preserve Aeneas' life in the fighting that lies ahead, especially during his duel with Turnus in Book 12. In a magnificent ecphrasis that rivals Jupiter's speech to Venus in Book 1, Vergil uses the engraving on the shield to portray the future history of Rome. The center of the shield depicts the Battle of Actium, in which Octavian defeated Antony and Cleopatra, paving the way for Octavian to become Augustus, Vergil's literary patron. Without Vulcan's participation in the story of the Aeneid, Aeneas himself, although a demigod, would have risked death.

## Group B

**Allecto**: One of three Furies who drove their victims insane (furor). Allecto serves as Juno's henchwoman in Book 7, first stirring up trouble by alienating both Amata and Turnus to the idea of a Trojan presence in Italy, then by causing Ascanius to wound a pet stag of the Latins while hunting. She appears both disguised as an old woman and in her real role as a terrible Fury.

**Iris**: Iris, a messenger goddess, plays a minor role in each of her several appearances in the Aeneid. In each, the goddess acts a handmaid to Juno and therefore implicitly is an adversary of Aeneas. Prompted by Juno, Iris cuts a lock of Dido's hair, which frees Dido's spirit to go to the Underworld, bringing closure to the story in Book 4. In Book 5, she is sent by Juno to stir up discontent among the Trojan women, which leads to the torching of the Trojan ships. Finally, in Book 9, Iris is sent by Juno to advise Turnus and the Rutulians to attack the Trojans in the absence of Aeneas, who has gone to seek help from Evander.

**Juturna**: Juturna, Turnus' sister, is active in the story of Book 12. She is manipulated by Juno to protect her brother, and thus interferes with the success of Aeneas and the Trojans in Italy. She assumes the guise of Turnus' charioteer and saves him more than once on the battlefield. Her resolute, almost obsessive, concern for her brother does not lead to her destruction, as she is a water nymph. Juturna jumps into a river and disappears from the story.

# PRACTICE EXAMS

## AP Latin Literature

# PRACTICE EXAM 1

**This exam is also on CD-ROM in our special interactive AP Latin TEST*ware*®**

## AP Latin Literature

### Multiple-Choice Section

**TIME:** 60 Minutes
50 Questions

**DIRECTIONS:** Each reading passage is followed by a series of questions and incomplete statements that are related to the passage. Select the best answer or completion and fill in the appropriate oval on your answer sheet.

### Catullus is grief-stricken

Etsi me assiduo confectum cura dolore
   sevocat a doctis, Hortale, virginibus,
nec potis est dulces Musarum expromere fetus
*Line*   mens animi, tantis fluctuat ipsa malis --
5  namque mei nuper Lethaeo in gurgite fratris
   pallidulum manans alluit unda pedem,
Troia Rhoeteo quem subter litore tellus
   ereptum nostris obterit ex oculis.

      . . . . . . . . . *

10    numquam ego te, vita frater amabilior,
aspiciam posthac?

\* This line is missing from the original manuscript.

1.   The words <u>me assiduo confectum cura dolore</u> / <u>sevocat</u> (lines 1–2) are translated

   (A)  Weary with concern for my continual grief, he calls me away

   (B)  Grief continually calls me away from completing my task

   (C)  Sorrow calls me away, worn out from continual grief

   (D)  Since my grief has continued, my sorrow has consumed me

2.	What figure of speech occurs in line 1?

(A)	hendiadys

(B)	oxymoron

(C)	ellipsis

(D)	interlocked word order (synchysis)

3.	In lines 1–2, Catullus is telling us that

(A)	he has been too depressed to think about poetry

(B)	his sorrow has kept him from falling in love

(C)	writing about women has helped to distract him

(D)	the Muses have helped him deal with his sorrow

4.	Line 3, <u>dulces</u> . . . <u>fetus</u> refers to

(A)	words of comfort

(B)	children

(C)	poetry

(D)	fruit

5.	The metrical pattern of the first four feet of line 3 is

(A)	dactyl-spondee-dactyl-spondee

(B)	dactyl-spondee-spondee-spondee

(C)	spondee-dactyl-spondee-spondee

(D)	spondee-spondee-dactyl-dactyl

6.	The pronoun <u>ipsa</u> (line 4) refers to

(A)	<u>cura</u> (line 1)

(B)	<u>fetus</u> (line 3)

(C)	<u>mens</u> (line 4)

(D)	<u>unda</u> (line 6)

7.	The case of <u>fratris</u> (line 5) is determined by

(A)	<u>mei</u> (line 5)

(B)	<u>gurgite</u> (line 5)

(C)	<u>unda</u> (line 6)

(D)	<u>pedem</u> (line 6)

8.	In lines 5–6 (<u>namque</u> . . . <u>pedem</u>), Catullus is describing

(A)	how his brother died

(B)	how he and his brother used to wash their feet in the river

(C)	his brother's presence in the Underworld

(D)	the fact that he hopes to remember his brother

9.	Which of the following figures of speech is found in line 7 (<u>Troia</u> . . . <u>tellus</u>)?

(A)	transferred epithet

(B)	chiasmus

(C)	metaphor

(D)	asyndeton

10. The pronoun <u>quem</u> (line 7) refers to

   (A) <u>fratris</u> (line 5)        (C) <u>Troia</u> (line 7)

   (B) <u>pedem</u> (line 6)        (D) <u>tellus</u> (line 7)

11. The words <u>Troia</u> . . . <u>oculis</u> (lines 7–8) tell us that Catullus' brother

   (A) died at Troy

   (B) is buried at Troy

   (C) was abducted from Troy

   (D) lived at Troy

12. The words <u>vita frater amabilior</u> (line 10) are translated

   (A) My brother loved life

   (B) Brother, more worthy of love than life

   (C) Life was a loving brother

   (D) The life of my brother was loving

13. Catullus also wrote about his brother's death in which of the following poems?

   (A) Lugete, O Veneres Cupidinesque (Poem 3)

   (B) Miser Catulle, desinas ineptire (Poem 8)

   (C) Si quicquam mutis gratum acceptumve sepulcris (Poem 96)

   (D) Multas per gentes et multa per aequora vectus (Poem 101)

### The Sabine women prevent war

Iam stabant acies ferro mortique paratae
   iam lituus[1] pugnae signa daturus erat,
cum raptae veniunt inter patresque virosque
*Line*   inque sinu natos, pignora[2] cara, tenent.
  5   Ut medium campi scissis tetigere capillis,
   in terram posito procubuere genu,
et quasi sentirent, blando clamore nepotes
   tendebant ad avos[3] bracchia parva suos.
Tela viris animique cadunt, gladiisque remotis
  10   dant soceri[4] generis accipiuntque manus,
laudatasque tenent natas, scutoque[5] nepotem
   fert avus: hic scuti dulcior usus erat.

1 <u>lituus</u>, -<u>i</u>, m.: bugle, war trumpet
2 <u>pignus</u>, <u>pignora</u>, n.: pledge, token
3 <u>avus</u>, -<u>i</u>, m.: grandfather
4 <u>soccer</u>, <u>soceri</u>, m.: father-in-law
5 <u>scutum</u>, -<u>i</u>, n.: shield

14. In lines 1–2 (<u>Iam</u> ... <u>erat</u>), we learn that
    (A) everything was ready for battle
    (B) the signal for battle had been given
    (C) the fighting was just under way
    (D) the fighting was fierce and to the death

15. Which of the following figures of speech occurs in line 1 (<u>Iam</u> ... <u>paratae</u>)?
    (A) transferred epithet      (C) prolepsis
    (B) synecdoche               (D) polysyndeton

16. In line 3, <u>raptae</u> is translated
    (A) having captured
    (B) while capturing
    (C) about to capture
    (D) having been captured

17. In line 4, the subject of <u>tenent</u> is
    (A) <u>raptae</u> (line 3)
    (B) <u>patresque virosque</u> (line 3)
    (C) <u>natos</u> (line 4)
    (D) <u>pignora</u> (line 4)

18. In line 5, <u>tetigere</u> is translated
    (A) touch                (C) to have touched
    (B) they touched         (D) to touch

19. In lines 5–8 (<u>Ut</u> ... <u>suos</u>), we learn that
    (A) the women improved their appearance
    (B) the women embraced their husbands around the knees
    (C) the young children held out their arms to their grandfathers
    (D) the older folk wept and grieved for their misfortune

20. In line 7, <u>quasi sentirent</u> is translated
    - (A) as if they understood
    - (B) which they understood
    - (C) so that they might understand
    - (D) since they understand

21. In line 8, <u>ad avos</u> ... <u>suos</u> means
    - (A) to his own grandfather
    - (B) to someone else's grandfathers
    - (C) to the grandfathers themselves
    - (D) to their own grandfathers

22. Which of the following figures of speech occurs in lines 9–10 (<u>Tela</u> ... <u>manus</u>)?
    - (A) metaphor
    - (C) zeugma
    - (B) chiasmus
    - (D) polyptoton

23. In line 9, <u>gladiis remotis</u> is translated
    - (A) while putting away their swords
    - (B) after they had put away their swords
    - (C) when their swords were being put away
    - (D) as they were about to put away their swords

24. In lines 11–12 (<u>laudatasque</u> ... <u>usus erat</u>), we learn that
    - (A) gifts were exchanged by the adversaries
    - (B) grandfathers carried their grandsons on their shields
    - (C) sons praised and embraced their fathers
    - (D) children were returned to their parents

25. In line 12, <u>dulcior</u> means
    - (A) sweeter
    - (B) very sweet
    - (C) rather sweetly
    - (D) much sweeter

**Why Fabricius recommended an enemy for the consulship**

Fabricius Luscinus magnā glōriā vir magnisque rebus gestis fuit.
P. Cornelius Rufinus manu quidem strenuus et bellator bonus
militarisque disciplinae peritus admodum fuit, sed furax homo[1] et
avaritiā acri erat. Hunc Fabricius non probabat neque amico utebatur
osusque eum morum causā fuit. Sed cum in temporibus rei publicae
difficillimis consules creandi forent ēt is Rufinus peteret consulatum
competitoresque eius essent inbelles quidam et futtiles, [2] summa ope
adnixus est Fabricius uti Rufino consulatus deferretur. Eam rem plerisque
admirantibus, quod hominem avarum cui esset inimicissimus, creari
consulem vellet, "Malo," inquit, "civis me compilet, [3] quam hostis vendat."

*Line* appears at line 4, *5* at line 5, *10* at line 10.

   1 osus, -a, -um, adj: having hated
   2 futtilis, -is, -e, adj.: good for nothing, worthless
   3 compilo, -are, -avi, -atus: to rob

26.  In lines 2–3 (P. Cornelius ... fuit), we learn that Rufinus was

   (A)  antagonistic and vengeful

   (B)  skilled in matters of war

   (C)  inexperienced as a leader

   (D)  tough but undisciplined

27.  The case of disciplinae (line 3) depends on

   (A)  bellator (line 2)          (C)  peritus (line 3)

   (B)  militarisque (line 3)       (D)  fuit (line 3)

28.  Lines 3–4 (sed ... erat) tell us that Rufinus was also

   (A)  cruel          (C)  ambitious

   (B)  clever         (D)  greedy

29.  In lines 4–5 (Hunc ... fuit), we are told that Fabricius

   (A)  respected Rufinus, but did not like him

   (B)  thoroughly disliked Rufinus because of his character

   (C)  considered Rufinus a friend, despite his shortcomings

   (D)  disapproved of Rufinus, but did not hate him

30.  In lines 5–6 (Sed ... forent), we learn that, during the Republic, consuls

   (A)  were elected in troubled times

   (B)  made the times more difficult

   (C)  could be appointed rather than elected

   (D)  sometimes failed to deal with a crisis

31.  In line 6, <u>forent</u> is an alternative to the more traditional form

    (A)  fuerunt           (C)  essent

    (B)  futurum esse       (D)  fuisse

32.  In lines 6–7 (<u>et</u> ... <u>futtiles</u>), we learn that

    (A)  the enemies of Rufinus were seeking the consulship

    (B)  Rufinus intended to make war on the consuls, who were his enemies

    (C)  His rivals for the consulship planned to kill Rufinus

    (D)  Rufinus' political adversaries were weak

33.  In line 6, <u>peteret</u> is subjunctive because it completes

    (A)  a causal clause (since)

    (B)  an indirect statement

    (C)  a concessive clause (although)

    (D)  a purpose clause

34.  The –<u>que</u> (line 7) connects

    (A)  <u>Rufinus</u> and <u>competitores</u> (lines 6–7)

    (B)  <u>peteret</u> and <u>essent</u> (lines 6–7)

    (C)  <u>consulatum</u> and <u>competitores</u> (lines 6–7)

    (D)  <u>competitores</u> and <u>inbelles</u> (line 7)

35.  In lines 7–8 (<u>summa</u> ... <u>deferretur</u>), we learn that Fabricius

    (A)  worked hard to defeat Rufinus

    (B)  requested that Rufinus postpone his bid for office

    (C)  used all his resources to support Rufinus' candidacy

    (D)  purchased the consulship for himself

36.  The case of <u>plerisque admirantibus</u> (lines 8–9) depends upon

    (A)  <u>Eam rem</u> (line 8)

    (B)  <u>esset inimicissimus</u> (line 9)

    (C)  <u>creari consulem vellet</u> (lines 9–10)

    (D)  <u>inquit</u> (line 10)

37.  Lines 8–10 (<u>Eam</u> ... <u>vellet</u>) tell us that many people were wondering

    (A)  why Fabricius wanted a personal enemy to become consul

    (B)  if Fabricius himself wanted to become consul

    (C)  whether a greedy man could become consul

    (D)  why Rufinus wanted to become consul

38. Line 10 (<u>Malo</u> . . . <u>vendat</u>) are translated

    (A) The citizen who robs me and then sells me to the enemy is wicked.

    (B) I prefer that a citizen rob me than an enemy sell me.

    (C) The citizen who sells me to an enemy, robs me.

    (D) I would rather have a citizen rob me than an enemy.

### Martial describes an acquaintance

Vicinus meus est manuque tangi
de nostris Novius potest fenestris.
Quis non invideat mihi putetque
*Line*  horis omnibus esse me beatum,
  5   iuncto cui liceat frui sodale?[1]
Tam longe est mihi quam Terentianus,
qui nunc Niliacam regit Syenen. [2]
Non convivere, nec videre saltem, [3]
non audire licet, nec urbe tota
  10   quisquam est tam prope tam proculque nobis.
Migrandum est mihi longius vel illi.
Vicinus Novio vel inquilinus [4]
sit, si quis Novium videre non vult.

1 <u>sodalis</u>, -<u>is</u>, m.: close friend
2 <u>Niliacam</u> . . . <u>Syenen</u>: Syene, located on the Nile River
3 <u>nec</u> . . . <u>saltem</u>: "not even"
4 <u>inquilinus</u>, -<u>i</u>, m.: fellow tenant

39. In lines 1–2 (<u>Vicinus</u> . . . <u>fenestris</u>), we learn that Martial and Novius

    (A) use the same window

    (B) like to leave windows open

    (C) are close neighbors

    (D) share a room

40. In line 3, <u>Quis non invideat mihi</u> is translated

    (A) Who does not envy me

    (B) Who would not envy me

    (C) Whom would I not envy

    (D) He who does not envy me

41. As he expresses in line 5 (<u>iuncto</u> . . . <u>sodale</u>), why does Martial think most people would consider him fortunate?

    (A) his friends envy him

    (B) he has a friend close by

    (C) his friends enjoy getting together with him

    (D) he makes his friends happy

42. The noun-adjective combination <u>iuncto</u> . . . <u>sodale</u> (line 5) takes its case from

    (A) the pronoun <u>cui</u>

    (B) the verb <u>liceat</u>

    (C) the verb <u>frui</u>

    (D) the general sense of the context

43. In line 6, the words <u>Tam</u> . . . <u>quam</u> mean

    (A) Now . . . then

    (C) As . . . as

    (B) So . . . than

    (D) So . . . that

44. Martial's point in lines 6–7 (<u>Tam</u> . . . <u>Syenen</u>) is that

    (A) Terentianus is as far from him as the Nile is from Syene.

    (B) Rome is a less friendly place than Africa.

    (C) Novius has a friend in Africa named Terentianus.

    (D) Novius might as well be in Africa.

45. The case of <u>Syenen</u> (line 7) is

    (A) nominative

    (C) accusative

    (B) genitive

    (D) vocative

46. In lines 8–10 (<u>Non</u> . . . <u>nobis</u>), Martial declares that

    (A) no one is farther away from him than his neighbor

    (B) he enjoys the company of his neighbors

    (C) there is no one in the entire city, near or far, who is not his friend

    (D) people in a large city should avoid each other

47. Which of the following figures of speech occurs in lines 8–10 (<u>Non</u> . . . <u>nobis</u>)?

    (A) prolepsis

    (C) zeugma

    (B) anaphora

    (D) chiasmus

48. Line 11 (<u>Migrandum</u> ... <u>illi</u>) is translated

    (A) He and I ought to move away together.

    (B) I should move closer to him.

    (C) He intends to move farther away from me.

    (D) I must move farther away or he must.

49. In line 13, <u>sit</u> is translated

    (A) he is           (C) I wish that he were

    (B) let him be      (D) Be!

50. The figure of speech that appears in lines 12–13 (<u>Vicinus</u> ... <u>vult</u>) is

    (A) alliteration       (C) chiasmus

    (B) polyptoton       (D) ellipsis

## STOP

**This is the end of the Multiple-Choice Section of the AP Latin Literature
Exam. If time remains, you may check your work only in this section.
Do not begin the Free-Response Section until instructed to do so.**

# PRACTICE EXAM 1

## AP Latin Literature

## Free-Response Section

**TIME:** 2 hours (including a 15-minute reading period)

---

**DIRECTIONS:** Answer SIX of the questions in this Section, following directions carefully. You are required to answer all of the Catullus questions in Part A and then choose the additional three questions from any one of the choice authors, Cicero, Horace, or Ovid, in Part B.

---

## Part A

### Question 1 – Catullus (15 percent)

#### (Suggested time – 10 minutes)

> Alfene immemor atque unanimis false sodalibus,
> iam te nil miseret, dure, tui dulcis amiculi?
> Iam me prodere, iam non dubitas fallere, perfide?
> *Line* nec facta impia fallacum hominum caelicolis placent.
> 5 Quae tu neglegis ac me miserum deseris in malis.
> Eheu, quid faciant, dic, homines, cuive habeant fidem?
>
> **Catullus 30.1–6**

Give a literal translation of the passage above.

## Question 2 – Catullus (20 percent)

### (Suggested time – 30 minutes)

Begin your answer to this question on a fresh page.

> Phaselus ille, quem videtis, hospites,
> ait fuisse navium celerrimus,
> neque ullius natantis impetum trabis
> *Line* nequisse praeterire, sive palmulis
> 5 opus foret volare sive linteo.
> Et hoc negat minacis Hadriatici
> negare litus insulasve Cycladas
> Rhodumque nobilem horridamque Thraciam
> Propontida trucemve Ponticum sinum,
> 10 ubi iste post phaselus antea fuit
> comata silva; nam Cytorio in iugo
> loquente saepe sibilum edidit coma.
> Amastri Pontica et Cytore buxifer,
> tibi haec fuisse et esse cognitissima
> 15 ait phaselus: ultima ex origine
> tuo stetisse dicit in cacumine,
> tuo imbuisse palmulas in aequore,
> et inde tot per impotentia freta
> erum tulisse, laeva sive dextera
> 20 vocaret aura, sive utrumque Iuppiter
> simul secundus incidisset in pedem;
> neque ulla vota litoralibus deis
> sibi esse facta, cum veniret a mari
> novissime hunc ad usque limpidum lacum.
> 25 Sed haec prius fuere: nunc recondita
> senet quiete seque dedicat tibi,
> gemelle Castor et gemelle Castoris.

**Catullus 4**

In Poem 4, Catullus uses the technique of personification to express his feelings about his bean-shaped boat. In a well-developed essay, discuss the manner in which he does this throughout the poem.

(Remember to support what you say by making direct reference to the Latin **throughout** the text. Cite and translate or closely paraphrase the relevant Latin. Do <u>not</u> simply summarize or paraphrase what the poem says.)

# Question 3 – Catullus (15 percent)

## (Suggested time – 20 minutes)

Begin your answer to this question on a fresh page.

> "Certe ego te in medio versantem turbine leti
> eripui, et potius germanum amittere crevi
> quam tibi fallaci supremo in tempore dessem.
> *Line* Pro quo dilaceranda feris dabor alitibusque
> 5 praeda, neque iniecta tumulabor mortua terra.
> Quaenam te genuit sola sub rupe leaena?
> Quod mare conceptum spumantibus exspuit undis,
> quae Syrtes, quae Scylla rapax, quae vasta Charybdis,
> talia qui reddis pro dulci praemia vita?"

**Catullus 64.149–57**

In the passage above, Ariadne expresses her feelings to Theseus. In a **short** essay, discuss the manner in which she communicates to the reader how she feels.

(Remember to support your observations from the **entire text** of each poem and be sure to cite and translate or closely paraphrase directly from the Latin text.)

**PROCEED TO THE APPROPRIATE
AUTHOR IN PART B**

# Part B

IF YOU HAVE CHOSEN **CICERO**, ANSWER THE FOLLOWING THREE QUESTIONS. IF YOU HAVE CHOSEN ANOTHER AUTHOR, MOVE TO THE APPROPRIATE SECTION.

## Question 4 – Cicero (20 percent)
### (Suggested time – 20 minutes)

Begin your answer to this question on a fresh page.

Cicero justifies study of the liberal arts.

> Quod si non hic tantus fructus ostenderetur et si ex his studiis delectatio
> sola peteretur, tamen, ut opinor, hanc animi adversionem humanissimam
> ac liberalissimam iudicaretis. Nam ceterae neque temporum sunt neque
> *Line* aetatum omnium neque locorum: haec studia adolescentia acuunt,
> 5 senectutem oblectant, secundas res ornant, adversis perfugium ac solacium
> praebent, delectant domi, non impediunt foris, pernoctant nobiscum,
> peregrinantur, rusticantur.
>
> *Pro Archia Poeta* 16

In his speech, Cicero presents arguments in favor of study of the liberal arts. In a **short** essay, discuss the advantages of pursuing liberal studies as presented in this passage.

(Remember to support your observations from the **entire text** of the passage and be sure to cite and translate or closely paraphrase directly from the Latin text.)

## Question 5 – Cicero (15 percent)

### (Suggested time – 10 minutes)

Begin your answer to this question on a fresh page.

Cicero discusses the nature of friendship.

> Est enim amicitia nihil aliud nisi omnium divinarum humanarumque
> rerum cum benevolentia et caritate consensio, qua quidem haud scio an
> excepta sapientia nil quicquam melius homini sit a dis immortalibus
> *Line* datum. Divitias alii praeponunt, bonam alii valetudinem, alii potentiam,
> 5 alii honores, multi etiam voluptates.
>
> ***De Amicitia*** 20

Give a literal translation of the passage above.

# Question 6 – Cicero (15 percent)

## (Suggested time – 10 minutes)

Begin your answer to this question on a fresh page.

Cicero appeals to the judges to consider the importance of poets.

> Quare suo iure noster ille Ennius sanctos appellat poetas, quod quasi
> deorum aliquo dono atque munere commendati nobis esse videantur.
> Sit igitur, iudices, sanctum apud vos, humanissimos homines, hoc poetae
> Line  nomen, quod nulla umquam barbaria violavit. Saxa et solitudines voci
> 5    respondent, bestiae saepe immanes cantu flectuntur atque consistunt: nos
> instituti rebus optimis non poetarum voce moveamur?

*Pro Archia Poeta* 18–19

1. (a) In line 1, how does Ennius characterize poets?

   (b) How does Cicero clarify this characterization in lines 1–2 (quod ...
   videantur)?

2. (a) Translate Sit ... violavit (lines 3–4).

   (b) What Latin words contrast in this sentence?

3. Name a figure of speech that occurs in lines 4–5 (Saxa ... respondent) and
   write out the Latin that illustrates it.

4. Explain the allusion in bestiae ... consistunt (line 5) and its relevance to
   Cicero's argument.

5. How does Cicero follow up in lines 5–6 (nos ... moveamur) on his point in
   line 4 (quod ... violavit)?

6. Explain why the subjunctive mood is required in the verb moveamur (line 6).

## END OF AP LATIN LITERATURE
## PRACTICE EXAM 1

IF YOU HAVE CHOSEN **HORACE**, ANSWER THE FOLLOWING THREE QUESTIONS. IF YOU HAVE CHOSEN ANOTHER AUTHOR, MOVE TO THE APPROPRIATE SECTION.

## Question 7 – Horace (20 percent)

### (Suggested time – 20 minutes)

Begin your answer to this question on a fresh page.

> Diffugere nives, redeunt iam gramina campis
>     arboribus comae;
> mutat terra vices, et decrescentia ripas
>     flumina praetereunt;
> *Line*
>   5   Gratia cum Nymphis geminisque sororibus audet
>     ducere nuda choros.
> Immortalia ne speres, monet annus et almum
>     quae rapit hora diem:
>
> Frigora mitescunt Zephyris, ver proterit aestas
>   10   interitura simul
> pomifer Autumnus fruges effuderit, et mox
>     bruma recurrit iners.
>
> Damna tamen celeres reparant caelestia lunae:
>     nos ubi decidimus
>   15   quo pater Aeneas, quo Tullus dives et Ancus,
>     pulvis et umbra sumus.

> *Odes* 4.7.1–16

In a **short** essay, discuss how Horace uses nature to illustrate his theme in the poem above. In your discussion, comment on how the poem is organized.

(Remember to support your observations from the **entire text** of the passage and be sure to cite and translate or closely paraphrase directly from the Latin text.)

# Question 8 – Horace (15 percent)

## (Suggested time – 15 minutes)

Begin your answer to this question on a fresh page.

> Multos castra iuvant et lituo tubae
> permixtus sonitus bellaque matribus
> detestata. Manet sub Iove frigido
*Line* venator tenerae coniugis immemor,
> 5 seu visa est catulis cerva fidelibus,
> seu rupit teretes Marsus aper plagas.
> Me doctarum hederae praemia frontium
> dis miscent superis.

**Odes 1.1.23–30**

Give a literal translation of the passage above.

# Question 9 – Horace (15 percent)

## (Suggested time – 10 minutes)

Begin your answer to this question on a fresh page.

> Est ut viro vir latius ordinet
> arbusta sulcis, hic generosior
>    descendat in Campum petitor,
>      moribus hic meliorque fama
>
> *Line*
> 5  contendat, illi turba clientium
>   sit maior: aequa lege Necessitas
>    sortitur insignes et imos;
>     omne capax movet urna nomen.

**Odes 3.1.9–16**

1. (a) What two general types of roles are describes in lines 1–6 (<u>Est</u> ... <u>maior</u>)?

   (b) Comment on the aspects of Roman politics described or alluded to in lines 1–6 (<u>Est</u> ... <u>maior</u>).

2. In what case is the pronoun <u>illi</u> (line 5) found and why?

3. Translate lines 6–7 (<u>aequa</u> ... <u>imos</u>).

4. What English word, besides "Necessity," could you use to indicate better the true meaning of <u>Necessitas</u> (line 6)?

5. (a) To what Roman belief about life and death does Horace allude in line 8 (<u>omne</u> ... <u>nomen</u>)?

   (b) Name a figure of speech that occurs in line 8 (<u>omne</u> ... <u>nomen</u>) and write out the Latin that illustrates it.

   (c) Write out and scan line 8 (<u>omne</u> ... <u>nomen</u>) and indicate how the rhythm of this line reflects its meaning.

## END OF AP LATIN LITERATURE
## PRACTICE EXAM 1

IF YOU HAVE CHOSEN **OVID**, ANSWER THE FOLLOWING THREE
QUESTIONS. IF YOU HAVE CHOSEN ANOTHER AUTHOR, MOVE
TO THE APPROPRIATE SECTION.

## Question 10 – Ovid (20 percent)

### (Suggested time – 20 minutes)

Begin your answer to this question on a fresh page.

> Proiectae triviis iaceatis, inutile lignum,
>   vosque rotae frangat praetereuntis onus.
> Illum etiam, qui vos ex arbore vertit in usum,
> *Line*   convincam puras non habuisse manus;
>   5   praebuit illa arbor misero suspendia collo,
>   carnifici diras praebuit illa cruces;
> illa dedit turpes raucis bubonibus umbras,
>   vulturis in ramis et strigis ova tulit.

*Amores* **1.12.13–20**

Prior to the passage above, Ovid has received an unwelcome message for which he
blames his writing tablets. In a **short** essay, discuss the various ways in which he
"takes out his anger" on the unfortunate tablets.

(Remember to support your observations from the **entire text** of the passage and
be sure to cite and translate or closely paraphrase directly from the Latin text.)

## Question 11 – Ovid (15 percent)

### (Suggested time – 15 minutes)

Begin your answer to this question on a fresh page.

> Mille domos adiere locum requiemque petentes,
> mille domos clausere serae. Tamen una recepit,
> parva quidem, stipulis et canna tecta palustri,
> *Line*   sed pia; Baucis anus parilique aetate Philemon
>   5   illa sunt annis iuncti iuvenalibus, illa
> consenuere casa paupertatemque fatendo
> effecere levem nec iniqua mente ferendo.

*Metamorphoses* **8.628–34**

Give a literal translation of the passage above.

# Question 12 – Ovid (15 percent)

## (Suggested time – 10 minutes)

Begin your answer to this question on a fresh page.

> "Fer, pater," inquit, "opem, si flumina numen habetis!
> Qua nimium placui, mutando perde figuram!"
> Vix prece finita, torpor gravis occupat artus;
> *Line*  mollia cinguntur tenui praecordia libro,
> 5  in frondem crines, in ramos bracchia crescunt;
> pes modo tam velox pigris radicibus haeret,
> ora cacumen habet; remanet nitor unus in illa.
>
> ***Metamorphoses*** 1.545–52

1.  (a)  Translate Daphne's plea for help in lines 1–2 (<u>Fer</u> . . . <u>figuram</u>).

    (b)  To whom or what does <u>Qua</u> (line 2) refer?

2.  Identify the grammatical construction <u>prece finita</u> (line 3).

3.  Lines 3–7 (<u>Vix</u> . . . <u>illa</u>) describe the six stages in Daphne's transformation:

    (a)  Write out and translate the Latin for each of the first **four** stages, in the sequence given in the passage.

    (b)  Write out and scan line 6 (<u>pes</u> . . . <u>haeret</u>) and tell how the rhythm contributes to the sense.

    (c)  Name a figure of speech that occurs in lines 6–7 (<u>pes</u> . . . <u>illa</u>) and write out the Latin that illustrates it.

4.  What single aspect of the original Daphne remained?

### END OF AP LATIN LITERATURE
### PRACTICE EXAM 1

# PRACTICE EXAM 1

## AP Latin Literature

## Answer Key

## List of Authors and Passages Appearing on This Exam

### Multiple-Choice[1]

#### *Required Author Passage*

"Catullus is grief-stricken" (Poem 65.1–11)

#### *Sight Passages*

"The Sabine women prevent war" (Ovid, *Fasti* 3.215–22, 225–28)

"Why Fabricius recommended an enemy for the consulship" (Aulus Gellius, *Noctes Atticae* 4.8)

"Martial describes an acquaintance" (Martial, *Epigrams* 1.86)

### Free-Response

#### *Required Author*

Translation: Catullus, Poem 30.1–6

Long Essay: Catullus, Poem 4

Short Essay: Catullus, Poem 64.149–57

#### *Choice Author: Cicero*

Short Essay: *Pro Archia Poeta* 16

Translation: *De Amicitia* 20

Short Answer: *Pro Archia Poeta* 18–19

---

[1] Translations of all multiple-choice passages are provided below.

### Choice Author: Horace

Short Essay: *Odes* 4.7.1–16

Translation: *Odes* 1.1.23–30

Short Answer: *Odes* 3.1.9–16

### Choice Author: Ovid

Short Essay: *Amores* 1.12.13–20

Translation: *Metamorphoses* 8.628–34 (Baucis and Philemon)

Short Answer: *Metamorphoses* 1.545–52 (Daphne and Apollo)

## Answers to the Multiple-Choice Questions: Latin Literature, Practice Exam 1

| "Catullus" | "Sabine women" | "Fabricius" | "Martial" |
|---|---|---|---|
| 1. (C) | 14. (A) | 26. (B) | 39. (C) |
| 2. (D) | 15. (B) | 27. (C) | 40. (B) |
| 3. (A) | 16. (D) | 28. (D) | 41. (B) |
| 4. (C) | 17. (A) | 29. (B) | 42. (C) |
| 5. (B) | 18. (B) | 30. (A) | 43. (C) |
| 6. (C) | 19. (C) | 31. (C) | 44. (D) |
| 7. (D) | 20. (A) | 32. (D) | 45. (C) |
| 8. (C) | 21. (D) | 33. (A) | 46. (A) |
| 9. (B) | 22. (C) | 34. (B) | 47. (B) |
| 10. (A) | 23. (B) | 35. (C) | 48. (D) |
| 11. (B) | 24. (B) | 36. (D) | 49. (B) |
| 12. (B) | 25. (A) | 37. (A) | 50. (A) |
| 13. (D) | | 38. (B) | |

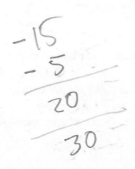

# PRACTICE EXAM 1

## AP Latin Literature

## Detailed Explanations of Answers to Multiple-Choice Questions

### "Catullus is grief-stricken"

1.   **(C)**
Recognition of the synchysis of **me ... confectum** and **assiduo ... dolore** leads to the correct translation in Answer (C) "Sorrow calls me away, worn out from continual grief." In Answer (A), "weary" (**assiduo**) does not modify "he" in the translation provided; in Answers (B) and (C), "grief" and "sorrow" (**dolore**) cannot be the subjects. **Me** is modified by the past participle **confectum**. In English word order, this line would read **cura sevocat me confectum assiduo dolore.**

2.   **(D)**
As mentioned, there is an example of interlocked word order (synchysis) found in line 1: **me ... confectum** interlocks with **assiduo ... dolore**. Thus, Answer (D) is correct. For figures of speech, see Chapter 10.

3.   **(A)**
In line 2, Catullus is being called away from the "learned maidens," presumed to be the Muses from what follows in line 3 (although **doctis ... virginibus** could also refer to Catullus' lovers!). In line 2, the Muses are used as a metonymy for poetry or poetic inspiration here, as often. The words **cura** and **dolore** in line 1 make it clear that the poet is sad, so Answer (A) "he has been too depressed to think about poetry" is correct.

4.   **(C)**
In line 3, **dulces ... fetus** means "sweet offspring," where **fetus** is used as a metaphor for the product of imagination or thought (**mens animi**, line 4), i.e., poetry. Lines 3–4 read, "nor is the disposition of my mind (or heart, **mens animi**) able to produce the sweet offspring (i.e., verses) of the Muses." **Fetus** is the accusative plural direct object of **expromere**.

5.  **(B)**
    The correct answer is (B), dactyl-spondee-spondee-spondee:

    $$\text{–} \quad \text{u u} \quad \text{–} \quad \text{– –} \quad \text{– –} \quad \text{u} \quad \text{u} \quad \text{– –}$$
    nec potis est dulces Musarum expromere fetus.

Be mindful of the elision between **Musarum** and **expromere**. For scansion, see Chapter 11.

6.  **(C)**
    The intensive pronoun **ipsa** refers back to **mens**, "the mind itself," which is nominative singular and feminine and is used as the subject of **fluctuat** in line 4. This part of the sentence reads, "(My) mind tosses about on (waves of) great troubles." For pronouns, see Chapter 13B.

7.  **(D)**
    The case of the genitive forms **(mei) . . . fratris** depends upon **pedem**, the direct object of **alluit** in line 6. For the genitive case, see Chapter 13A.

8.  **(C)**
    Because of the allusion to Lethe (**Lethaeo in gurgite**, line 5), the River of Forgetfulness, Catullus is referring to the Underworld, so Answer (C) "his brother's presence in the Underworld" is correct. He waxes poetic in these lines, which describe his brother's death. Lines 5–6 read, "for the liquid wave (**manans . . . unda**) of Lethe's flood (**Lethaeo in gurgite**) has recently washed over (**alluit**) the pale foot (**pallidulum . . . pedem**) of my brother," i.e., he has died recently. Note the difficulty of translating **pallidulum** as a diminutive.

9.  **(B)**
    The criss-crossing of adjective-noun combinations **Troia . . . tellus** and **Rhoeteo . . . litore** create a chiasmus. The brother, **quem**, in effect, is "buried" beneath (**subter**) the Rhoetean coast (**Rhoeteo . . . litore**) and the soil of Troy (**Troia . . . tellus**).

10. **(A)**
    As indicated in the previous answer, **quem** in line 7 refers to Catullus' brother (line 5); therefore Answer (A) **fratris** is correct. For relative pronouns, see Chapter 13B.

11. **(B)**
    The meaning of lines 7–8 tells us that the brother died at Troy. These lines read, "(my brother) upon whom (**quem**), snatched away (**ereptum**) from my eyes (**nostris . . . ex oculis**), the Trojan earth (**Troia . . . tellus**) below the Rhoetean shore (**Rhoeteo . . . subter litore**) lies heavy (**obterit**)." The exact meaning of these lines is difficult to express literally – Catullus means to say something like his brother is buried in the Trojan soil beneath the Rhoetean coast. For the earth not to lie heavy on the buried dead is a formulaic phrase (= S.T.T.L., **Sit terra tibi**

**levis**, "May the earth rest gently upon you.") Also, note the poetic plural in the use of **nostris** (line 8).

12. **(B)**

In line 10, the words **vita frater amabilior** are an apostrophe to Catullus' brother. **Frater** is in the vocative case of direct address (note the punctuation). The comparative adjective **amabilior** can modify either **vita** or **frater**. The omission of **quam** with the comparative **amabilior** suggests that an ablative of comparison appears here, which must be **vita** (scansion confirms that the –a in **vita** is long). Therefore, **vita frater amabilior** reads, "(O) brother, more worthy of love than life," which is Answer (B). Note the juxtaposition of **ego** and **te** and of **vita** and **frater** in line 10. For the use of the ablative with comparatives, see Chapter 13A and 13C.

13. **(D)**

All of the options are poems about death, literally or metaphorically, but Answer (D) Poem 101 is the only poem addressed to Catullus' brother. This is a background question! The theme of Poem 3 in Answer (A) is Lesbia's dead sparrow; in Answer (B) Poem 8, Catullus argues with himself about whether or not he still loves Lesbia; Poem 96 in Answer (C) is a consolation to Quintilius on the death of his wife.

## "The Sabine women prevent war"

14. **(A)**

Answer (A) is correct, because the Latin of lines 1–2 does not give any indication that the battle (between the Romans and the Sabine men) was already under way. These lines are translated, "Now the battle lines (**acies**) were standing fast (**stabant**), prepared for the sword and for death (**ferro mortique paratae**), now the bugle (**lituus**) was ready to give the signal (**signa daturus erat**) for attack (**pugnae**)."

15. **(B)**

The word **ferro**, iron or steel, the material of which the weapon is made, substitutes in line 1 for the weapon itself. This is an example of synecdoche. For figures of speech, see Chapter 10.

16. **(D)**

**Raptae** is a perfect passive participle of **rapio, rapere, rapui, raptus**, serving here as a substantive, i.e., "those women (note the feminine ending) having been abducted," "the abducted women" (hence, the "rape" of the Sabine women). For more on participles, see Chapter 16A.

17. **(A)**

The subject of **tenent**, as it is of **veniunt**, previously, is **raptae** (line 3). See the previous answer for the use of a participle as a noun. This part of the sentence translates, "when the abducted women (**raptae**) came between (**veniunt inter**) the fathers and husbands (not simply "men" for **virosque**) and held to their bosoms (**in sinu . . . tenent**) their sons, dear pledges (of love) (**pignora cara**)".

18. **(B)**

**Tetigere** is a poetic alternative for **tetigerunt**, the third person plural of the perfect active indicative = "they touched." Thus, Answer (B) is correct. For alternative verb forms, see Chapter 11.

19. **(C)**

This sentence says, "When they reached (**tetigere**) the middle of the field, their hair shorn (in grief) (**scissis . . . capillis**) they sank (**procubuere**) to the ground on bended knee (**posito . . . genu**) and, as if they understood, with a persuasive call (**blando clamore**), the grandsons reached out their tiny arms to their grandfathers." Thus, Answer (C) "the younger children held out their arms to their grandfathers" is correct.

20. **(A)**

**Quasi sentirent** is a present contrary to fact conditional clause. The verb is imperfect subjunctive, because the idea that the children understood what was happening is imaginary or could not possibly happen, which emphasizes the importance of what was actually happening, i.e., that they were being encouraged to make contact with their grandfathers (**tendebant ad avos bracchia parva suos**). Thus, Answer (A) "as if they understood (but they did not)" is the correct answer. For conditionals, see Chapter 16D, Section 3.

21. **(D)**

Answers (A) and (C) are incorrect because each child was calling (**avum** is accusative). Answer (B) is incorrect because the child was seen by the grandfather, rather than vice versa (**visum [est]** is passive). Thus, Answer (D) "to their own grandfathers" is correct.

22. **(C)**

In line 11 we find a "one for two," an example of zeugma. The subjects of the single verb cadunt are both tela, "weapons," and animi, "their hostility," i.e., how they felt. Thus, the men are dropping both an object and a feeling. For more on figures of speech, see Chapter 10.

23. **(B)**

**Gladiisque remotis** is an ablative absolute, "after they had put away their swords." The key to the correct answer is the word "after," since **remotis** is a past participle. Answer (A) "while . . . " indicates an action contemporary with that of the main verb, i.e., a present participle. Answer (C) "were being" is an ongoing or continuous action, whereas in a past participle such as **remotis**, the action has been completed. In Answer (D) "were about to," the meaning is in the future tense. The translation in Answer (A) is acceptable in the active voice because the identity of those putting away their swords is made clear by the context. Technically, **gladiis remotis** means "(their) swords having been put away," with no understanding of who it was that had put them away. For the ablative absolute, see Chapter 16A.

24. **(B)**

Answer (C) is tempting, but **natas** means daughters, not sons (gotcha!). Nothing was exchanged or returned, so Answers (A) and (D) are incorrect. The Latin that leads to the correct answer (B) translates, "(each) grandfather carried his grandson on his shield: this was a sweeter use of the shield."

25. **(A)**

**Dulcior** is a comparative adjective modifying **usus**. The correct answer is therefore (A) "sweeter." Answer (B) "very sweet" is in the superlative degree (**dulcissimus**), Answer (C) "rather sweetly" is a comparative adverb (**dulcius**), and Answer (D) "much sweeter" (**multo dulcior**) is an example of the ablative of degree of difference, for which, see Chapter 13A. For forms of adjectives and adverbs, see Chapter 13C.

## "Why Fabricius recommended an enemy for the consulship"

26. **(B)**

Lines 1–2 tell us that Rufinus was skilled in hand-to-hand combat (**manu . . . strenuus**) and a fine warrior (**bellator bonus**), who was thoroughly experienced in military training (**militarisque disciplinae peritus**). Thus, Rufinus may be said to have been "skilled in matters of war" (Answer A).

27. **(C)**

**Disciplinae** is genitive because this case is required by the meaning of the adjective **peritus, -a, -um**, "experienced in" (literally "experienced of"). The genitive case usually establishes a connection between two nouns or between a noun and certain adjectives. See Chapter 13A.

28. **(D)**

The answer is (D) greedy, because we are told in lines 2–3 that Rufinus was thievish (furax) and fiercely greedy (avaritia acri).

29. **(B)**

**Hunc Fabricius non probabat** tells us that "Fabricius did not approve of him (**Hunc** =Rufinus)," **neque amico utebatur**, that "he did not accept him as a friend ," and **osusque eum morum causa fuit**, that "he (Fabricius) hated him because of his character (**morum causa**)." Thus, Answer (B) is correct. Answers (A), (C), and (D) all require some degree of acceptability of Rufinus by Fabricius, which is not indicated in the Latin.

30. **(A)**

The grammar of the clause **cum . . . creandi forent** (line 4) makes this sentence tricky. **Forent** is a substitute for the more common form of the imperfect subjunctive, which is **essent.** In its more fmiliar form, **creandi essent** is a passive periphrastic whose subject is **consules**, giving the meaning "the consuls must be or had to be elected." The subjunctive mood is required in the form **essent** because **creandi essent** completes a **cum** causal clause, according to the best sense of the context. Thus, this part of the sentence reads, "But since in the very troubled times (**in temporibus . . . difficillimis**) of the Republic (or state, **rei publicae**), consuls had to be elected . . . . " For the passive periphrastic construction, see Chapter 16B; for **cum** clauses with the subjunctive, see Chapter 16D, Section 6.

31. **(C)**

See the answer to the previous question.

32. **(D)**

In line 5, the subjunctive clause **is Rufinus peteret consulatum** and is the second clause introduced by **cum,** which is found at the beginning of the sentence. This clause tells us that Rufinus was seeking the consulship. A third subjunctive clause, also dependent upon **cum,** is **competitoresque . . . futtiles**, which tells us that Rufinus' (**eius**) adversaries for the consulship were **inbelles** (also spelled **imbelles**). . . **et futtiles** (also spelled **futiles**), meaning "unwarlike and ineffective." Thus, Answer (D) "Rufinus' political adversaries were weak" is correct.

33. **(A)**

As indicated previously, the sense of the sentence in lines 4–6 (**Sed . . . deferretur**) requires that **cum . . . forent . . . peteret . . . essent** be translated as causal clauses, "Since . . . . " Answer (B) is impossible because there is no infinitive in this sentence; the **cum** concessive clause in Answer (C) is usually found with **tamen**; and, although an **ut** purpose clause does appear in this sentence (**uti . . . deferretur**), it is separate and grammatically distinct from the **cum** clauses found in the earlier part of the sentence. Thus, Answer (A) causal clause is correct. For **ut** clauses, see Chapter 16D, Section 4; for **cum** clauses, see Chapter 16D, Section 6.

34. **(B)**

The enclitic **–que** connects the two clauses **is Rufinus peteret consulatum** and **competitoresque eius essent inbelles quidam et futtiles,** hence Answer (B) **peteret** and **essent** is correct. When connecting clauses, **-que** is usually attached to the first word of the connected clause. The conjunction does not always connect the word to which it is attached with the word or those words immediately preceding it, but may be separated by intervening words.

35. **(C)**
In lines 5–6, **summa ope ādnixus est Fabricius** tells us that Fabricius labored with great resources so that the consulship would be given to Rufinus (**uti Rufino consulatus deferretur**). Thus, Answer (C) "used all his resources to support Rufinus' candidacy" is correct. There is no indication in this passage that Fabricius himself had political ambitions (Answer D), or that he had interfered in any other way with Rufinus' candidacy (Answers A and B).

36. **(D)**
**Plerisque admirantibus** is in the dative case after **inquit** in the next line. This has the meaning, "To many wondering . . . , he said . . . . " The adjective **inimicus**, "unfriendly to" (Answer B) is found with the dative case, but it is not to be considered in the context of the participial phrase **plerisque admirantibus**.

For the dative case, see Chapter 13A.

37. **(A)**
Lines 6–7 (**Eam . . . vellet**) tell us that "To many (people) wondering at the state of affairs wherein he (Fabricius) wanted a greedy man, to whom he was most unfriendly, to be elected consul." Thus, Answer (A) "why Fabricius wanted a personal enemy to become consul" is correct. The Latin does not support the other interpretations.

38. **(B)**
Fabricius' punchline says, "I prefer that a citizen rob me than (that) an enemy sell (me)." The other answers do not do justice to the Latin as it stands.

## "Martial describes an acquaintance"

39. **(C)**
In lines 1–2, Martial indicates that he and Novius are close neighbors by saying, "Novius is my neighbor and can be reached (by hand) from my window." **Nostris**, incidentally, is an example of the use of poetic plural (= **meis**). Answers (A) and (B) use the word **fenestris** as a distractor. Answer (D) goes too far past the meaning of **vicinus**.

40. **(B)**
This is a deliberative question with the subjunctive, "Who would not envy me?" Answer (B), as a statement of fact, requires the indicative mood, but **invideat** is subjunctive. Answer (C) swaps **Quis** with mihi, which is the dative object of invideat, making the sentence in Latin, Cui ego non invideam? Answer (D) is not a question. For this use of the independent subjunctive, see Chapter 16D, Section 2.

41. **(B)**
Lines 3–4 set up the answer to this question. "Who would not envy me and (who would not) think that I am happy all the time, I who (**cui**) am allowed (**licet**)

to enjoy (**frui**) close companionship (**iuncto sodale**)?" Martial is saying that a neighbor who lives as close as Novius does to him, and the companionship that this implies, is ordinarily cause for feelings of satisfaction.

42. **(C)**

The deponent verb **fruor, frui, fructus sum**, to enjoy, takes the ablative case, therefore Answer (C) the verb **frui** is correct. **Cui** itself is the dative object of **liceat** (Answers A and B). For special deponent verbs, see Chapter 14B.

43. **(C)**

**Tam** and **quam** are correlatives, which requires that they take their meaning as a pair. The sentence in which these words are found (line 6) reads, "(He) is <u>as</u> far away from me <u>as</u> Terentianus." Answer (C) is therefore correct. For correlatives, see Chapter 16E.

44. **(D)**

The sentence in lines 6–7 reads, "(He) is as far away from me as Terentianus, who now governs Syene, on the Nile." This implies that Novius might as well be in Africa with Terentianus, which is Answer (D).

45. **(C)**

**Syenen** (line 7) is an example of a Greek accusative (the name of the city is Greek). The Greek ending **–n** becomes the Latin ending **–m**; both are accusative singular. See Chapter 10.

46. **(A)**

In lines 8–9, the series of instances in which Martial may not rely upon his neighbor Novius (neither enjoying his company nor seeing nor hearing him) leads to the conclusion in lines 9–10 that "there is no one in the entire city so near and yet so far from me." Answer (A) "no one is farther away from him than his neighbor" is therefore correct; the other answers give inaccurate meanings. Note the reappearance of the poetic plural, **nobis**.

47. **(B)**

The repetitions of **non**, **nec**, and **tam** in lines 8–10 are all examples of anaphora, which creates a cumulative effect. For figures of speech, see Chapter 10.

48. **(D)**

The passive periphrastic **Migrandum est** is impersonal, requiring the subject "it", literally, "It must be moved." **Mihi**, a dative of agent, is the one who "must be moved." To create better sense, the passive is turned around to become active, i.e., "It must be moved by me" becomes "I must move." **Illi**, which refers to Novius, also serves as a dative of agent with **Migrandum est**. Thus, the correct answer is (D) "I must move farther away or he must (move farther away)." For the use of a gerund/ive in a passive periphrastic, see Chapter 16A.

49.  **(B)**

In lines 12–13, Martial explains what he meant in the previous line. **Sit** is the jussive use of the present subjunctive, requiring the translation "let," e.g., "Let the one who does not want to see Novius be his neighbor or his roommate." Answer (A) requires the Latin word **est**, (C) **(velim) esset**, and (D) **esto.**

50.  **(A)**

Note the emphatic use of the letter **v** in the final two lines: **Vicinus Novio vel . . . Novium videre . . . vult**. For alliteration and other figures of speech, see Chapter 10.

# Translations of the Multiple-Choice Passages

## "Catullus is touched by his brother's death"

And yet sorrow calls me, worn out from continual grief, away from the learned maidens, Hortalus, and the disposition of my heart is unable to produce the sweet offspring of the Muses, (since) my mind tosses about on great troubles -- for the liquid wave of Lethe's flood has recently washed over the pale foot of my brother, upon whom, snatched away from my eyes, the Trojan earth beneath the Rhoetean shore lies heavy. Brother more worthy of love than life, will I never see you again?

## "The Sabine women prevent war"

Now the battle lines were standing fast, prepared for the sword and for death, now the bugle was ready to give the signal for attack, when the abducted women came between the fathers and husbands and held to their bosoms their sons, dear pledges of love. When they reached the middle of the field, their hair shorn (in grief), they sank to the ground on bended knee and, with a persuasive call, the grandsons, as if they understood, reached out their tiny arms to their grandfathers. The weapons and hostility dropped away from the men and, their swords having been put away, the fathers-in-law gave and received the hands (i.e., shook the hands) of their family (members) [or, the fathers-in-law of the family gave and received hands, i.e., shook hands], and praised their daughters and held onto them, and (each) grandfather carried his grandson on his shield: this was a sweeter use of the shield.

## "Why Fabricius recommended an enemy for the consulship"

Fabricius Luscinus was a man of great reputation and great deeds. P. Cornelius Rufinus, indeed was skillful in hand-to-hand (combat) and a fine warrior and completely experienced in military matters, but a man thievish and fiercely greedy. Fabricius did not approve of him nor associated with him as a friend, and hated him because of his character. But since there was need of electing consuls during the trying times of the Republic, and Rufinus sought the consulship and his political opponents were unwarlike and feeble, Fabricius strove with great resources in order that the consulship should be given to Rufinus. To many wondering at this state of affairs, the fact that he wanted a greedy man to whom he was a sworn enemy to be elected consul, Fabricius said, "I would prefer that a citizen rob me, than an enemy sell me."

## "Martial describes an acquaintance"

Novius is my neighbor and can be touched by hand from my window. Who would not envy me and think me happy all the time, I who am permitted the joy of close companionship? He is as far away from me as Terentianus, who now governs Syene on the Nile. I may not enjoy his company, nor even see or hear him, who is so near and yet so far from me. Either I must move away or he must. If anyone does not want to see Novius, let him be his neighbor or his roommate.

## Answers to Free-Response Section

### REQUIRED AUTHOR

## Question 1 (Catullus)

### Translation

Alfenus, forgetful of and misleading to your like-minded comrades, do you have no pity now, cruel one, for your dear friend? Do you not refrain from betraying me now, from deceiving me now, traitor? The unholy deeds of dishonest men are not pleasing to the gods above. All of which you disregard and you ignore downhearted me in my time of trouble. Oh, what should men do, tell me, whom should they trust?

## Grading

*9 pts. total, one-half point for each segment. Round up your score.*

1. Alfene immemor atque . . . false
2. unanimis . . . sodalibus
3. iam te nil miseret
4. dure
5. tui dulcis amiculi
6. iam me prodere . . . dubitas
7. iam non dubitas fallere
8. perfide
9. facta impia
10. fallacum hominum
11. nec . . . caelicolis placent
12. quae
13. tu neglegis
14. ac me miserum deseris
15. in malis
16. eheu . . . dic
17. quid faciant . . . homines
18. cuive habeant fidem

## Acceptable Translations for Question 1

For instructional purposes, more grammatical and syntactical information is provided here than is usually found in the grading reports on the translation question.

1. **Alfene**: Alfenus [addressee of the poem, vocative]

   **immemor**: forgetful/unmindful/ignorant/heedless/inattentive [vocative, modifies **Alfene**]

   **atque**: and/and also [connects **immemor** and **false**]

   **false**: misleading/false/deceitful/lying/cheating [vocative, modifies **Alfene**]

2. **unanimis**: like-minded/feeling the same/agreeable [with **sodalibus**, "soul mates"]

   **sodalibus**: comrade/friend/companion [dative of reference]

3. **iam**: now/at this time

   **te**: you (Alfenus) [one of two objects of the impersonal verb **miseret**]

   **nil**: nothing/not at all [negates **miseret**]

**miseret**: **miseret** means to make someone (accusative) feel pity for something (genitive) [**te nil miseret . . . amiculi** means, literally, "does it make you (**te,** acc.) feel pity not at all (**nil**) for your friend (**amiculi,** genitive); more idiomatic English is acceptable, i.e., "Do you feel no pity for your dear friend?]

4. **dure**: cruel/harsh/hard-hearted/shameless/"cold" [vocative, refers to Alfenus]

5. **tui**: your [referring to Alfenus]

   **dulcis**: dear/sweet/beloved/delightful [modifies **amiculi**]

   **amiculi**: friend/little friend/close or dear friend [genitive, the second object of **miseret**; see above]

6. **iam**: now/at this time **me**: me, referring to Catullus [direct object of **prodere**]

   **prodere**: betray/hand over/give up/forsake/deliver [infinitive after **dubitas**]

   **dubitas**: you refrain from/hesitate/be in doubt/shrink from/waver in

7. **iam non dubitas**: [see above]

   **fallere**: deceive/betray/lie to/break faith with/sell out/double-cross [infinitive after **dubitas**]

8. **perfide**: traitor/deceitful one/betrayer/"back-stabber"/turncoat [vocative, refers to Alfenus]

9. **facta**: deeds/acts/actions [subject of **placent**]

   **impia**: unholy/sacrilegious/disloyal/impious/undutiful/wicked [modifies **facta**]

10. **fallacum**: dishonest/betraying/deceitful/faithless [modifies **hominum**]

    **hominum**: men/people/souls [genitive plural with **facta**; with **fallacum** can mean "deceiver"]

11. **nec**: not/and not/nor [negates **placent**]

    **caelicolis**: god/divinity/deity/sky-one/heavenly one [dative after **placent**]

    **placent**: they are pleasing to/please/placate/be aggreable or acceptable to [the subject is **facta**]

12. **quae**: all of which/which things [connecting relative pronoun, relating to **facta** in the previous line]

13. **tu**: you [emphatic subject of **neglegis**]

    **neglegis**: you disregard/ignore/neglect/be indifferent to

14. **ac**: and/and also [= **atque,** line 1]

    **me**: me, referring to Catullus [direct object of **deseris**]

    **miserum**: downhearted/miserable/unhappy/despondent/"blue"/"bummed out" [modifies **me**]

>    **deseris**: you ignore/abandon/desert/foresake/leave

15.  **in malis**: in time of trouble/in trouble or distress/crisis [substantive; may be singular]

16.  **Eheu**: Oh! Alas! Woe! **dic**: tell/say/indicate [singular imperative of **dico**]

17.  **quid**: what [introduces deliberative question **quid faciant?**]

>    **faciant**: [present tense; **quid faciant ... homines** = What should men do? What are men to do?]

18.  **cui**: to whom/whom [dative after **fidem habere**]

>    **-ve**: = **vel**, or [connects deliberative questions **quid faciant** with **cui habeant fidem**]

>    **habeant**: have [present tense; with **fidem** may be translated as "trust"]

>    **fidem**: trust/faith/belief/honesty [direct object of **habeant**]

# Question 2 (Catullus)

## Long Essay

For the grading scale used for evaluating essays, see Chapter 7. Here are some high points of each speech to consider in your comparative analysis, followed by a sample essay. Such observations, which will set up your formal essay, may be made in writing during the 15-minute reading period. The sample essays may seem overly thorough, but the author is attempting to accommodate the wide range of answers that will be given by users of this book.

Catullus, Poem 4: the poet apostrophizes his bean-boat that carries him from Bithynia to Sirmio.

Examples of personification or animation:

- (phaselus) ait (line 2)
- natantis ... trabis (line 3): animation; metaphor/metonymy
- nequisse, palmulis (line 4)
- volare (line 5): animation; metaphor
- (litus) ...negat (line 6)
- negare (line 7): the places where the boat has been do the speaking here, not the boat itself
- comata silva (line 11)
- loquente ... coma (line 12)
- the boat's "genealogy" (lines 10–17)
- Amastri Pontica et Cytore buxifer: these places are addressed in an apostrophe; cf. lines 16–17
- ait phaselus (line 15)
- (phaselus) dicit (line 16)

- erum (line 19)
- pedem (line 21): metaphor?
- (phaselus) senet (16)
- (phaselus) seque dedicat (line 26)

## Sample Long Essay

A close reading of Catullus Poem 4 suggests that the poet thought of his bean-boat (phasellus) not so much as a conveyance, but as a trusted friend. Various words, phrases, and techniques vivify and animate the boat, which, in this lengthy apostrophe, takes Catullus from boring Bithynia back home to his "gem," Sirmio. In this poem, some scholars believe that Catullus is celebrating life's journey or that the poem has some other allegorical significance. But a literal understanding of the poem does not detract from the success of the poet's use of the technique of personification in expressing his feelings about the boat.

The phaselus is described throughout as having the faculty of speech—ait (lines 2 and 15), nequisse (line 4), loquente (line 12), dicit (line 16), dedicat (line 26)—all of which humanizes the boat. Even the leaves of the trees which supplied its wood could speak (loquente . . . coma, line 12). Although perhaps not personification in the strict sense, this boat can also swim (natantis, line 3) and fly (volare, line 5). It has human body parts, such as little hands (palmulis, lines 4 and 17, a metaphor/diminutive for oars), hair (comata, line 11, and coma, 12, metaphors for leaves), and "feet" (pedem, line 21, the nautical term for sheet or sail-rigging).

Central to the poem, both literally and figuratively, is the boat's description of its early "childhood" ultima ex origine (line 15), which may be seen as its "genealogy." The boat was at first a stand of trees (comata silva, line 11) on the heights (cacumine) of Mt. Cytorus, where the trees rustled with leaves that "spoke" (loquente . . . coma). Later, it "grew" into a mature boat, leaving the womb of Pontic Amastrus, from where it was launched (tuo imbuisse palmulis in aequore), ready to strike out for more challenging places (lines 6–9 and 18–19).

The idea of the boat having a master (erum, line 19) also suggests that Catullus is deliberately attempting to humanize the boat, although this word is perhaps antithetical to the notion that Catullus thinks of the boat as a friend, rather than as a slave or subordinate. The places that Catullus and the boat have been, the Adriatic, the Cyclades, Rhodes, Thrace, and the Pontic Gulf (lines 6–9), are also personified through apostrophe. These places "do not deny" (negat . . . negare, lines 6–7) the achievements of the phaselus, and Pontic Amastrus and box-bearing Mt. Cytorus (the place names in line 13 are vocative) bear witness to the seasoning of the boat into a sea-worthy craft. These additional examples of personification contribute to the overall tone that the poet develops throughout Poem 4.

Finally, the bean-boat is put into drydock (nunc recondita, line 25), where it "grows old" (senet, line 26) and "dedicates itself" (seque dedicat, line 26) to the twin gods of the sea, the Gemini (Castor and Pollux). At the end of the poem, we are left with the same impression with which we begin: that Catullus respects, admires, and even loves his phaselus, the celerrimus navium.

# Question 3 (Catullus)

## Short Essay

For the grading scale used for evaluating essays, see Chapter 7. Here are some high points of Ariadne's speech to consider in your analysis.

In Poem 64, Ariadne expresses her anger and despair to Theseus, who has abandoned her on an island.

- In an apostrophe to Theseus, Ariadne attempts to make him feel guilty by reminding him of how she saved him from the whirlwind of death (i.e., the Minotaur) (lines 1–2); how she chose to lose her brother (germanum, the Minotaur) rather than forsake Theseus when he needed her (lines 2–3); the fact that she, now abandoned, will die a horrible death (lines 4–5); and the fact that she will not be buried after she dies (line 5).

- Ariadne, now angry, insults Theseus by casting aspersions on his mother in a series of rhetorical questions. She uses the stock epic images of a lioness, the Syrtes, Scylla, and Charybdis, plus the appealing notion that he was vomited up (exspuit) from the sea.

- The passage ends with a return to the "guilt trip" at the beginning: is this the reward I deserve for the promise of such a sweet life, she asks?

- Relevant analysis:

  —apostrophe: Theseus (1)

  —juxtaposition: ego te (1)

  —hyperbaton and word play: iniecta tumulabor mortua terra (5); quaenam
    . . . leaena (6)

  —alliteration and onomatopoeia (7)

  —anaphora: quae (8)

  —tricolon crescens (8)

  —use of stock monster imagery (cf. Catullus Poem 60)

  —words with overtones: fallaci (line 3); supremo in tempore (3); dilaceranda
    . . . praeda (4–5)

  —sibilation/onomatopoeia in line 7 suggest hissing, spitting (exspuit) by
    Ariadne

  —use of rhetorical questions

## Sample Short Essay

Catullus creates a powerful emotional scene in this passage, which is reminiscent of other great "rejection scenes" in ancient literature, such as those of Dido in the Aeneid and Medea in Euripides. These lines are full of passion and passionate words and images, which one imagines Ariadne literally spitting out at the now-departed Theseus. Examples include turbine leti (line 1), fallaci (line 3), dilaceranda (line 4), neque iniecta tumulabor mortua terra (line 5), spumantibus exspuit undis ( line 7), and quae Syrtis, quae Scylla rapax, (line 8).

Ariadne is portrayed as a woman scorned, a woman full of despair and dashed hopes, and a woman full of feelings of rejection and revenge. (The juxtaposition of ego and te in line 1 is ironical!) Ariadne first attacks Theseus in hopes of causing him to feel guilty because she: has lost her brother (line 2), will suffer a horrible and torturous death (lines 4–5), will die without burial (line 5), and has suffered un-requited love, line 9). (Note, however, that Ariadne is indeed "buried" in the line: neque iniecta [tumulabor mortua] terra.) The emotion in each set of lines increases in intensity until she moves from the horror of imagining herself torn to pieces by wild beasts (lines 4–5) to Theseus' own bestial origins. Using a series of stock epic images within rhetorical questions, Ariadne casts aspersions on Theseus' mother. Was Theseus born of a lioness at the foot of a cliff? Was he conceived at sea and vomited forth from the foaming waves (line 7)? Ariadne must have literally spit out these words at Theseus (note the alliteration and onomatopoeia in the sibilation of spumantibus exspuit undis, line 7). What about the the tricolon in line 8, with its increasingly terrible monsters having cacophonous names -- the Syrtes, Scylla, and Charybdis – all punctuated by the emotive anaphora of quae, quae, quae?

All of Ariadne's anger and frustration, vented in lines 1–8, end with this sin-gle ironical line: "Do you (Theseus) give back such rewards (talia . . . praemia) for a life so sweet (pro dulci . . . vita)"?

# CHOICE AUTHOR

# Question 4 (Cicero)

## Short Essay

For the grading scale used for evaluating essays, see Chapter 7. Here are some points to consider in your analysis.

Cicero justifies the study of liberal arts.

- Cicero, for the sake of argument, proposes that intellectual enjoyment (delectatio) is the sole purpose of liberal studies (lines 1–2) and further proposes that mental stimulation (animi adversionem) is very civilizing and enlightening.

- Other pursuits do not belong to all times, all ages, all places (nam . . . locorum)

- These pursuits (i.e., liberal studies) sharpen the senses of the young (<u>adolescentia acuunt</u>, 4) and entertain the elderly (<u>senectutem oblectant</u>); they embellish success (<u>secundas res ornant</u>); they provide refuge and consolation in difficult times (<u>adversis . . . praebent</u>); they give pleasure at home (<u>delectant domi</u>) and don't get in the way out in the world (<u>non impediunt foris</u>); they spend the night (<u>pernoctant nobis</u>), travel abroad (<u>peregrinantur</u>), and visit the country with us (<u>rusticantur</u>).

## Sample Short Essay

In his speech of defense <u>Pro Archia Poeta</u>, Cicero "digresses" in order to present arguments in favor of the pursuit of liberal studies, since Archias was both a poet and Cicero's former teacher. His attitude in the passage here about intellectual pursuits (<u>studiis</u>) is decidedly upbeat.

Cicero finds that there is enjoyment (<u>delectatio</u>, line 1) in the pursuit of liberal studies, which are civilizing (<u>humanissimam</u>, line 2), and enlightening (<u>liberalissimam</u>, line 3). He repeats this benefit by using the words <u>oblectant</u> in line 5 and <u>delectant</u> in line 6. By implication, with respect to what he says in lines 3–4 (<u>Nam</u> . . . <u>locorum</u>), Cicero believes that intellectual pursuits are beneficial for all times, ages, and places. In lines 4–7, using the technique of asyndeton (lack of conjunctions), he goes on to give examples of times, ages, and places in which <u>studia</u> provide advantage, e.g., they sharpen the senses of the young (<u>adolescentia acuunt</u>), entertain the elderly (<u>senectutem oblectant</u>), embellish success (<u>secundas res ornant</u>), provide refuge and consolation (<u>perfugium ac solacium praebent</u>), give pleasure both at home (<u>delectant domi</u>) and out in the world (<u>foris</u>), and are our companions at night (<u>pernoctant</u>), when traveling abroad (<u>peregrinantur</u>), or when we are in the country (<u>rusticantur</u>).

Thus, Cicero believes that intellectual pursuits are essential for us whether we succeed or fail, whether we're young or old, and whether we're at home or out in the world. The enjoyment of liberal studies is the <u>sine qua non</u> of a civilized and enlightened person.

# Question 5 (Cicero)

## Translation

For friendship is nothing other than when there are good will and common affection in all things human and divine, than which indeed it is uncertain whether anything better, with the exception of wisdom, has been given to man by the immortal gods. Some prefer wealth, others good health, some prefer power, others public recognition, and many even prefer physical pleasures.

## Grading

### *9 pts. total, one-half point for each segment. Round your score up.*

1. est enim amicitia
2. nihil aliud nisi
3. omnium divinarum humanarumque rerum
4. cum benevolentia et caritate
5. consensio
6. qua quidem
7. haud scio an
8. excepta sapientia
9. nil quicquam melius
10. homini
11. sit . . . datum
12. a dis immortalibus
13. divitias alii praeponunt
14. bonam alii valetudinem
15. alii potentiam
16. alii honores
17. multi etiam voluptates

## Acceptable Translations for Question 5

For instructional purposes, more grammatical and syntactical information is provided here than is usually found in the grading reports on the translation question.

1. **est**: (it) is

    **enim**: for/indeed/truly/certainly

    **amicitia**: friendship [subject of **est**]

2. **nihil aliud nisi**: phrase "nothing other than," "nothing else but," "nothing else than" "nothing else except," "no other thing but/except"

3. **omnium**: all

    **rerum**: in or of things/affairs/matters [genitives following **benevolentia et . . . consensio**, below]

    **divinarum**: divine

    **humanarumque**: human

    **-que**: [combines **divinarum** with **humanarum**, both modifying **rerum**]

4. **cum benevolentia et caritate benevolentia**: good will/friendly disposition/kindness [subject of **sunt**, understood]

   **caritate**: affection/warmth/devotion/esteem [ablative of respect or specification = "with respect to"]

   **et** [connects **benevolentia** with **caritate**]

5. **consensio**: harmony/agreement/consent

6. **qua**: which [ablative of comparison after **melius**; **qua** refers to **consensio**]

   **quidem**: indeed

7. **haud scio an**: formulaic, "it is uncertain," "I do not know whether" [governs **sit . . . datum** in indirect question, line 3]

8. **excepta**: (having been) excepted/taken out/omitted/excluded/passed over [past participle in ablative absolute]

   **sapientia**: wisdom/good sense/prudence/good judgment

9. **nil quicquam**: "not anything," "no other thing"

   **melius**: better [modifies **nil quicquam**]

10. **homini**: man/mankind/humanity/people [dative after **sit . . . datum**]

11. **sit . . . datum**: give/grant/bestow [perfect passive subjunctive in indirect question after **an**, line 2; the subject is **nil quicquam**]

12. **a dis**: by the gods [= **a deis**]

    **immortalibus**: immortal/eternal/deathless/unperishable

13. **divitias**: wealth/riches/material possessions [direct object of **praeponunt**]

    **alii**: some [**alii . . . alii**: some . . . others]

    **praeponunt**: they prefer/favor/choose/select/pick/opt for [this verb governs this phrase and all those following]

14. **bonam**: good

    **alii**: some/others **valetudinem**: health/well-being

15. **potentiam**: power/ability/talent/physical strength/political influence

16. **honores**: public honor or award/acclaim/honor/respect/distinction [singular or plural]

17. **multi**: many (people) [substantive]

    **etiam**: even/besides

    **voluptates**: physical or sensual pleasure/delight/enjoyment

# Question 6 (Cicero)

## Short Answer

There are eight points possible for this question. Latin support is provided below for your convenience, but is not required in your answer, unless stated in the question.

1(a) **1 point**

Ennius characterizes poets as holy or sacred (<u>sanctos</u>).

1(b) **1 point**

They seem to have been given to us (or bestowed upon us) as a gift of the gods.

2(a) **1 point**

Therefore, judges, let this name of poet be sacred among you, most compassionate (or sympathetic or understanding, etc.) men, a name which no lack of culture (or barbarism, lack of civilization or cultivation) has ever dishonored (or disrespected, desecrated, defamed, profaned, etc.)

2(b) **1 point**

<u>Humanissimos homines</u> contrasts with <u>barbaria</u> (lines 3–4); <u>humanissimos</u> is acceptable.

3. **1 point**

<u>Saxa et solitudines</u> . . . <u>respondent</u> is an example of hendiadys (the rocks and wilderness reply = the rocky wilderness replies or the solitary or deserted rocks reply)

OR

personification, i.e., the rocks and wilderness speak.

4. **1 point**

The allusion in line 5 (<u>bestiae</u> . . . <u>consistunt</u>) is to the famed musician Orpheus' ability to charm the savage beasts with song. Cicero offers this as an example of the importance of poetry/song.

5. **1 point**

In line 5, he says that even the uncultured and "barbaric" can appreciate poetry, so it is even more incumbent upon us who are well-educated (<u>instituti rebus optimis</u>) to appreciate its appeal.

6. **1 point**

<u>Moveamur</u> is present subjunctive in a deliberative question (Should we be moved?), which is a use of the independent subjunctive.

# Question 7 (Horace)

## Short Essay

For the grading scale used for evaluating essays, see Chapter 7. Here are some points to consider in your analysis.

In *Odes* 4.7, Horace uses nature to make the point that, although nature continues in a cycle of life, man's life is fleeting and impermanent.

- This passage can be seen as two two-stanza units, each of which reflects the other. In the first unit, lines 1–6, the poet uses examples of the passing of the seasons to illustrate the changes in nature. In lines 7–8, his "punchline," Immortalia . . . diem, verbalizes his theme of carpe diem (rapit hora diem). The second stanza is organized in the same fashion, devoting five lines to examples of the changes in seasons (Frigora . . . lunae), followed by the reminder that when we die, we are only dust and shadow (pulvis et umbra).

- Use of nature:
  - Stanzas 1 and 2: transition from winter to spring – snows melt and grasses and leaves return, rivers subside, and the Graces and nymphs dance in celebration.

  - Stanza 3: transition from winter to spring to summer to autumn to winter – winter is described as listless or lifeless (iners), spring through the metonymy of gentle breezes (Zephyris), and autumn as fruitful (pomifer and fruges effuderit). Note the suggestive participle interitura, which could be also mean "die" in relation to human mortality, especially if the abundance of the autumn harvest is considered a life image. Also, the paradox (oxymoron) of recurrit iners (12).

  - Stanza 4: summary statement that, for nature, time passes but is a cycle, which is represented by the monthly phases of the moon (damna . . . lunae). The word decidimus (14), a euphemism for dying, may also be seen as a metaphor of nature for the setting of the sun (cf. Catullus 5), fall (the loss of leaves and foliage by trees), etc.

## Short Essay

As often in his Odes, Horace uses nature to illustrate his enduring message about human life: that we should not spend our lives worrying about death (immortalia ne speres, line 7), which comes to all, but that we should enjoy the fleeting time that we have (monet . . . diem, lines 7–8).

In this passage, the organization of the stanzas reflects the balance of theme between nature and life. The poet uses his familiar technique of citing examples (lines 1–6 and 9–13) and then drawing a generalized (philosophical) conclusion from them (lines 7–8 and 14–16). The first six lines describe the cycle of nature as the passing of winter (diffugere nives) into spring, when the leaves return to the trees (redeunt . . . comae), the rivers subside (et . . . praetereunt), and the deities of spring celebrate (Graces and Nymphs, lines 5–6). These examples lead to the general conclusion in lines 7–8 that we should take advantage of the time we have (immortalia . . . diem). Nature teaches us this (monet annus, 7). The same lesson is taught in the next two stanzas, using the same imagery but in a bit different way. Winter (frigora) turns into spring (the metonymy Zephyris), summer is hard on the heels (proterit) of spring, summer itself is about to pass on (interitura) into fruit-bearing autumn (pomifer Autumnus) and then back full circle to lifeless winter (iners bruma). This is all summed up in line 13, which employs the monthly phases of the moon to illustrate that nature is a cycle (damna . . . reparant) and not a terminal point. Once again, we are reminded that there is no return from death (decidimus . . . sumus). Horace "personalizes" death, again by using examples of naming individuals familiar to the Roman reader (Aeneas, Tullus Hostilius, and Ancus Marcius, the latter two legendary kings of Rome) and completes the message by using the image of "dust to dust" (pulvis et umbra sumus, line 16).

Within these lines there appear individual words that personify nature, thereby connecting nature more closely with human life, e.g., comae (hair for foliage, line 2), interitura (pass on or be lost, in the context of summer = euphemism for die, line 10), and decidimus (fall down, in the context of leaves from trees, sun from the sky, etc. = euphemism for die, line 14). Consider that pulvis et umbra (dust and shadow, line 16), are metaphors for death drawn from nature.

Horace's message mutat terra vices (line 3) but nos ubi decidimus . . . pulvis et umbra sumus (lines 14, 16) also appears in Poem 5 of Catullus, where we again find the eternal cycle of nature (sunrise and sunset). Although the use of nature to comment on man's life was common even in Roman times, Horace, a "good ole country boy," perhaps understood and conveyed this lesson better than most.

# Question 8 (Horace)

## Translation

Military camps delight many, and the sound of the war-horn mixed with the bugle, and wars despised by mothers. The hunter stays beneath the cold sky, forgetful of his loving wife, whether the deer has been detected by the faithful hounds or whether the Marsian boar bursts apart the billowing hunting nets. Me, the ivy, reward of the learned brow, mixes with the gods above.

## Grading

### 9 pts. total, one-half point for each segment. Round your score up.

1. multos
2. castra iuvant
3. et . . . tubae . . . sonitus
4. permixtus lituo
5. bellaque . . . detestata
6. matribus

7. manet . . . venator

8. sub Iove frigido

9. tenerae coniugis immemor

10. seu . . . seu

11. visa est . . . cerva

12. catulis . . . fidelibus

13. rupit . . . Marsus aper

14. teretes . . . plagas

15. me . . . miscent

16. hederae praemia

17. doctarum . . . frontium

18. dis . . . superis

## Acceptable Translations for Question 8

For instructional purposes, more grammatical and syntactical information is provided here than is usually found in the grading reports on the translation question.

1. **multos**: many/many people [substantive; object of **iuvant**]

2. **castra**: military camp/camp/encampment [neuter, nominative plural; first subject of **iuvant**]

   **iuvant**: delight/please/gratify/bring pleasure to [present tense; understood as the main verb of the following two clauses, lines 1–3]

3. **et**: [connects **castra iuvant** and **sonitus (iuvant)**]

   **tubae**: war-horn/trumpet/bugle [genitive with **sonitus**; the meanings of **lituo** and **tubae** are interchangeable here]

   **sonitus**: sound/noise/call [nominative singular; second subject of **iuvant** (understood); acceptable as plural, despite **permixtus**, because of **iuvant**]

4. **permixtus**: (having been) mixed with/mingled with **lituo**: bugle/war-horn/trumpet/curved bugle [dative or ablative with **permixtus**]

5. **bella**: war/strife/conflict/fighting [neuter, nominative plural, third subject of **iuvant**]

   **-que**: [joins **et . . . sonitus permixtus (iuvant)**, 1–2, with **bella . . . detestata (iuvant)**, 2–3]

   **detestata**: (having been) despised/detested/hated/loathed/abhorred [take with **bella**]

6. **matribus**: mothers [dative of agent, after **detestata**]

7. **manet**: remain/stay/linger [present tense]

**venator**: hunter

8.  **sub Iove**: beneath/under and sky [the metonymy of Jove for sky must be recognized]

    **frigido**: cold/chilly/frozen/frigid/wintry

9.  **tenerae**: loving/gentle/tender/young/dear **coniugis**: wife/spouse/partner [genitive after **immemor**]

    **immemor**: forgetful of/unmindful of/heedless of [modifies **venator**]

10. **seu . . . seu**: whether . . . or

11. **visa est**: (has been or was) detected/seen/spotted/spied/glimpsed **cerva**: deer/doe/female deer/hind [subject of **visa est**]

12. **catulis**: hound/dog/young hound

    **fidelibus**: faithful/loyal/trusty/reliable/steadfast

13. **rupit**: (it) has burst/broken/broken apart or open [perfect tense]

    **Marsus**: Marsian, from the Marsian mountains

    **aper**: boar/wild boar or pig

14. **teretes**: billowy/billowing/curved/swollen [modifies **plagas**; the cables of the hunting nets were fastened to trees, causing the net to billow out when the animal attempted to flee]

    **plagas**: hunting net [object of **rupit**]

15. **me**: [object of **miscent**]

    **miscent**: mingle/mix/join/unite/combine, all including "with" (ablative of accompaniment) or "to" (dative of reference) [present tense]

16. **hederae**: ivy/ivy leaves or vines [subject of **miscent**; poetic plural; singular is acceptable]

    **praemia**: reward/honor/award/recognition [in apposition to **hederae**; poetic plural, singular is acceptable]

17. **doctarum**: learned/well-informed/educated [but wasn't it Catullus who was the **doctus poeta**!]

    **frontium**: brow/forehead [genitive plural with **praemia**; acceptable as "head" through synecdoche]

18. **dis** [= **deis**, dative or ablative after **miscent**]

    **superis**: above/heavenly/high/upper

# Question 9 (Horace)

## Short Answer

There are eight points possible for this question. Latin support is provided below for your convenience, but is not required in your answer unless stated in the question.

1(a) **1 point**

Farmers (<u>viro</u> . . . <u>sulcis</u>) and political candidates or politicians (<u>hic</u> . . . <u>maior</u>).

1(b) **1 point**

These lines refer specifically to candidates seeking public office (<u>hic</u> . . . <u>petitor</u> . . . <u>hic</u> . . . <u>contendat</u>). <u>Descendat in Campum</u> refers to members of the nobility coming down from their homes on the Palatine and elsewhere to the Campus Martius and the Forum, where public gatherings were held. Each candidate has different qualities to offer: noble birth (<u>generosior</u>), reputation and character (<u>moribus</u> . . . <u>meliorque</u> <u>fama</u>), or number of clients (<u>turba clientium</u> . . . <u>maior</u>).

2. **1 point**

Dative of possession, <u>illi turba clientium sit maior</u>, "there is to him (i.e., he has) a larger crowd of clients."

3. **1 point**

"On equal terms (or impartially) Necessity determines by lot (the fates of) the high and the low." There are many acceptable variations of the translation for <u>insignes et imos</u>: well-born and base-born, significant and simple, noble and plebeian, etc., all referring to relative status in the social order of Rome.

4. **1 point**

Fate, Destiny, The Future, Fortune, Providence or Death, Doom, Final Day, etc., all referring to man's mortality and the inevitability of death.

5(a) **1 point**

This line develops the image raised by <u>sortitur</u> (7), which is the casting of lots to determine one's fate. When your "number" (<u>nomen</u>) comes up, you die. The Fates shook the lots (<u>sortes</u>) in an urn (<u>capax</u> . . . <u>urna</u>, 8).

5(b) **1 point**

Hyperbaton: <u>omne</u> . . . <u>nomen</u> frames <u>capax movet urna</u>,

OR

chiasmus: <u>omne</u> . . . <u>nomen</u> and <u>capax</u> . . . <u>urna</u>.

Note: the following techniques are technically not found on The College Board's list of figures of speech; however, in the opinion of the author, they are valid for the purpose of literary analysis:

Word play: the word order of <u>omne</u> . . . <u>nomen</u> and <u>capax</u> . . . <u>urna</u>, with <u>movet</u> in the center, blends form and function,

OR

Sound play: the entire line consists of disyllabic words, which contribute to the sense of rhythm of the dice tossing about in the container,

OR

The *Scrabble*-like play of the words <u>omne</u> and <u>nomen</u>.

5c. **1 point**

The final line of the Alcaic stanza contains dactyls:

$$\bar{}\ \ u\ u\ \bar{}\ \ \ u\ u\ \bar{}\ \ u\ \bar{}\ \ \bar{}$$
omne capax movet urna nomen.

This cadence suggests the back-and-forth tossing about of the lots when shaken in the urn.

# Question 10 (Ovid)

## Short Essay

For the grading scale used for evaluating essays, see Chapter 7. Here are some points to consider in your analysis.

Ovid blames his writing tablets for bringing back the answer "No" from his girlfriend.

Organization

- one self-contained thought in each couplet

Words and phrases

- associates the tablets with hanging (<u>suspendia</u>, 5), executioners (<u>carnifici</u>, 6), and crucifixion (<u>cruces</u>, 6)
- associates the tablets with unlucky omens, such as owls (<u>raucis bubonibus</u>, 7, <u>strigis</u>, 8), vultures (<u>vulturis</u>, 8), and darkness (<u>umbras</u>, 7).

Relevant imagery and figures

- apostrophe (<u>inutile lignum</u>, 1)
- anaphora (<u>praebuit illa</u> . . . <u>praebuit illa</u> . . . <u>illa</u>, 5–7)
- framing, word picture (<u>turpes raucis bubonibus umbras</u>, 7; noisy owls are in the shadows)

Mood and tone

- angry, sarcastic, cursing (use of hortatory subjunctive <u>iaceatis</u>, 1, <u>frangat</u>, 2)
- hopes that the tablets meet the unfortunate fate of being run over and broken in the street by a passing cart (1–2)
- condemns the man who made the tablets as villainous (<u>puras non habuisse manus</u>) and their wood as coming from a hangman's tree (5)

Sounds

- onomatopoeia of <u>raucis</u> and harsh-sounding words <u>carnifici</u>, <u>cruces</u>, <u>raucis</u> (6–7)

- onomatopoeia of <u>bubonis</u> (7), suggesting the hooting cry of the owl

## Sample Short Essay

Ovid takes out his feelings of rejection by his girlfriend on his unfortunate writing tablets (<u>tabellae</u>). He decides to "kill the messenger." Each couplet, nay every line, in this passage is chock-full of curses, invective, and bile, all designed to help the poet vent his frustration.

He begins by hoping that the tablets meet a worthy end by lying in the road (<u>proiectae</u> . . . <u>iaceatis</u>) and being crushed by a passing cart (<u>vosque</u> . . . <u>onus</u>, lines 1–2). Note the appearance of the hortatory subjunctives <u>iaceatis</u> (line 1) and <u>frangat</u> (line 2), which express something that Ovid hopes might happen. He then curses both the craftsman who made the tablets, calling him an impious rogue in <u>puras non</u> . . . <u>manus</u>, line 3, and the very wood from which the tablets were made (from a hangman's tree, <u>misero suspendia collo</u>, line 5, or an executioner's cross, <u>carnifici</u> . . . <u>cruces</u>, line 6). The final couplet administers the <u>coup de gras</u> by claiming that the tree from which the wood came was the nesting site for all sorts of ill-omened birds: noisy hoot- and screech-owls (<u>raucis bubonibus</u> and <u>strigis</u>, line 8) and vultures (<u>vulturis</u>, line 8).

The poet provides some additional choice zings. He addresses the tablets directly through apostrophe in <u>inutile lignum</u> (useless wood, line 1), which also contains examples of personification and synecdoche (<u>lignum</u> = <u>tabellae</u>). The anaphora and positions of (<u>praebuit</u>) <u>illa</u> (lines 5–7) emphasize the points Ovid is making about the wood of which the tablets were made. And the final couplet uses word order and onomatopoeia to draw attention and to punctuate. The words <u>turpes</u> . . . <u>umbras</u> frame the noisy owls (<u>raucis bubonibus</u>, line 7), suggesting that the birds are in the foul (fowl?) shadows. The onomatopoeia of <u>raucis</u> and <u>bubonibus</u> (note the owl-sounds of "hoo, hoo"), the harsh sounds of <u>carnifici</u>, <u>cruces</u> (line 8), and <u>raucis</u> (line 7), and the end-rhyme sibilation of the words in line 7 all add to the effect of the invective. Ovid has "successfully" vented his frustration.

# Question 11 (Ovid)

## Translation

They came to a thousand homes seeking a place of rest (but) door-latches closed up the (same) thousand homes. However, one received them, indeed a small but humble one, covered with straw and marsh reed. The old woman Baucis and Philemon, equal in age, were married in that (hut) in the years of their youth and in that hut grew old together, and they made their poverty bearable by admitting (to it) and by enduring (it) with a not resentful (agreeable) disposition.

## Grading

### *9 pts. total, one-half point for each segment. Round up!*

1. mille domos . . . mille domos:
2. adiere
3. locum requiemque petentes
4. clausere serae
5. tamen una recepit
6. parva quidem . . . sed pia
7. stipulis et canna . . . palustri
8. tecta
9. Baucis anus . . . Philemon
10. aetate parilique
11. illa . . . illa . . . casa
12. sunt . . . iuncti
13. annis . . . iuvenalibus
14. consenuere
15. paupertatemque fatendo
16. effecere levem
17. nec iniqua mente
18. ferendo

## Acceptable Translations for Question 11

For instructional purposes, more grammatical and syntactical information is provided here than is usually found in the grading reports on the translation question.

1.  **mille**: one/a thousand [modifies **domos** in both cases]

    **domos**: home/house/household/dwelling/abode

2.  **adiere**: (they) came to/approached/arrived at/reached [alternative third person plural, perfect tense = **adierunt**; the subject "they" refers to the gods Jupiter and Mercury, acceptable with or without a name]

3.  **locum:** place/location/site

    **requiemque**: rest/peace [with **locum**, may be rendered as "place and rest" or as hendiadys, "place of rest"]

    **petentes**: (while) seeking/looking for/striving after/requesting/asking for [present active participle modifying "they" in the main verb **adiere**]

4.  **clausere**: they closed/shut [alternative third person plural, perfect tense = **clauserunt**]

**serae**: door-latch/bar/bolt/fastener [with **clausere**, **serae** may be translated "the bolts latched (or bolted or locked)"]

5. **tamen**: however/yet/nevertheless

    **una**: one [modifies **domus**, understood]

    **recepit**: (it) received/took in/accepted/welcomed/admitted/greeted

6. **parva**: small/tiny

    **sed:** but

    **pia**: humble/kind/upright/god-fearing [**parva** and **pia**, as **una** above and **tecta** below, modify **domus** or perhaps **casa** (line 6) understood]

    **quidem**: indeed

7. **stipulis**: straw/ reeds/stubble [ablative of means]

    **et**: [connects **stipulis** and **canna**] **canna**: reed [ablative of means]

    **palustri**: marsh-/marshy/swamp-/of or from a marsh or swamp [modifies **canna**]

8. **tecta**: (having been) covered/roofed/protected [perfect passive participle, modifying **domus**, understood]

9. **Baucis**: Baucis (wife)

    **anus**: old/aged woman/lady

    **Philemon**: Philemon (husband)

10. **aetate**: age/lifetime/time of life [ablative of description]

    **parili**: equal/same/similar [modifies **aetate**]

11. **illa . . . illa . . . casa**: that [**illa**, line 5, modifies **casa**, line 6; ablatives of place where, with the preposition understood = "in that hut"]

12. **sunt . . . iuncti**: (they have been) married/joined/wedded/united [perfect passive verb; subject is **Baucis . . . Philemon**, line 4)

13. **annis**: year/time [ablative of time when]

    **iuvenalibus**: youthful/young/early

14. **consenuere**: (they) grew old/reached old age/aged (translation must contain some sense of the word "together" (**con-**); alternative perfect tense = **consenuerunt**; cf. lines 1 and 2]

15. **paupertatemque**: poverty/humble circumstance [may be translated as the object of **fatendo** or **effecere**]

    **-que**: and [connects **consenuere** with **effecere**]

    **fatendo**: by admitting to/confessing to/acknowledging/conceding/ granting [gerund, ablative of means]

    **levem**: bearable/light/endurable/tolerable [modifies **paupertatem**]

16. **effecere**: (they) made [alternative perfect tense = **effecerunt**]

17. **nec**: and not/nor [connects two gerunds, **fatendo** and **ferendo**]

**iniqua**: resentful/uneven/unequal/disagreeable/unbalanced/perverse [with **nec**, may be translated as litotes = **aequae**, agreeable, contented]

**mente**: disposition/attitude/outlook/temperament/frame of mind [ablative of means]

18. **ferendo**: by enduring/bearing/tolerating/suffering [gerund; ablative of means; cf. **fatendo**, line 6]]\

# Question 12 (Ovid)

## Short Answer

There are eight points possible for this question. Latin support is provided below for your convenience, but is not required in your answer unless stated in the question.

1(a) **1 point**

"Bring (me) help, father" she said, "if you rivers have any divine power! Destroy the beauty with which I was too-pleasing by changing it!"

1(b) **One-half point**

Qua refers to figuram at the end of the line. In poetry, and particularly in Ovid, the antecedent often comes after its relative pronoun.

2. **One-half point**

Ablative absolute.

3(a) **2 points (one-half point for each of the four stages)**

1. torpor gravis occupat artus, "a heavy sluggishness seizes/seized her limbs"

2. mollia cinguntur tenui praecordia libro, "her soft breasts are/were surrounded with (or by) inner bark"

3. in frondem crines . . . (crescunt), "her hair grows/grew into leaves"

4. in ramos bracchia crescunt, "her arms grow/grew into branches"

3(b) **2 points**

```
 -   u u -   - -   - - -   - u u   - -
```
Pes modo tam velox pigris radicibus haeret,

a hexameter line. The rhythm of the line slows as the feet of the once-swift girl change into roots.

3(c) **1 point**

Contrast (antithesis) and juxtaposition: velox (swift) with pigris (sluggish) OR

chiasmus: pes . . . velox pigris radicibus, interlocking the feet with the roots as they change.

4. **1 point**

Her radiance, nitor (or splendor, brightness, glow, beauty, elegance, etc.)

# PRACTICE EXAM 2
## AP Latin Literature

### Multiple-Choice Section

**TIME:** 60 Minutes
50 Questions

**DIRECTIONS:** Each reading passage is followed by a series of questions and incomplete statements that are related to the passage. Select the best answer or completion and fill in the appropriate oval on your answer sheet.

### Catullus critiques another poet

Suffenus iste, Vare, quem probe nosti,
homo est venustus et dicax et urbanus,
idemque longe plurimos facit versus.
*Line* Puto esse ego illi milia aut decem aut plura
5 perscripta, nec sic ut fit in palimpsesto
relata: cartae regiae, novi libri,
novi umbilici, lora rubra, membranae,
derecta plumbo, et pumice omnia aequata.
Haec cum legas tu, bellus ille et urbanus
10 Suffenus unus caprimulgus aut fossor
rursus videtur: tantum abhorret ac mutat.

1. The more common form of <u>nosti</u> (1) is

   (A) <u>novi</u>              (C) <u>nosci</u>

   (B) <u>noscis</u>            (D) <u>novisti</u>

2. In lines 1–2 (<u>Suffenus</u> . . . <u>urbanus</u>), Suffenus is described as
   (A) arrogant        (C) charming
   (B) impersonal      (D) truthful

3. The pronoun <u>idemque</u> (line 3) refers to
   (A) Suffenus
   (B) Varus
   (C) the information in line 2
   (D) an unnamed writer

4. How many elisions are found in line 4 (<u>Puto</u> . . . <u>plura</u>)?
   (A) five        (C) one
   (B) three       (D) none

5. The words <u>esse</u> . . . <u>perscripta</u> (lines 4–5) are translated
   (A) are being written
   (B) are about to be written
   (C) had been written
   (D) have been written

6. Which figure of speech is found in lines 4–5 (<u>Puto</u> . . . <u>perscripta</u>)?
   (A) chiasmus        (C) ellipsis
   (B) hyperbole       (D) litotes

7. The phrase <u>sic ut fit</u> (line 5) is translated
   (A) in order that it might happen in this way
   (B) so that it might become
   (C) as usually happens
   (D) to make it so

8. The word <u>palimpsesto</u> (line 5) refers to
   (A) a secretary who takes dictation
   (B) the process of editing something written
   (C) scraped or re-used parchment
   (D) a type of stylus or pen

9. In lines 6–8 (cartae . . . aequata), we learn about
   (A) the writings materials used by Suffenus
   (B) the topics about which Suffenus writes
   (C) books that Suffenus has read
   (D) different types of Roman books

10. The figure of speech found in lines 6–8 (cartae. . . aequata) is
    (A) polyptoton
    (B) anaphora
    (C) interlocked word order (synchysis)
    (D) asyndeton

11. In line 8, the form derecta is a
    (A) perfect passive infinitive lacking esse
    (B) neuter noun
    (C) perfect passive participle
    (D) main verb in the passive voice

12. Haec cum legas tu (line 9) is translated
    (A) Although you have read these
    (B) When you read these
    (C) After having read these
    (D) You will read these things when you . . .

13. Lines 9–11 (bellus . . . videtur) tell us that Suffenus is
    (A) would rather be seen as a person of the city, rather than of the country
    (B) someone who snubs country folk
    (C) a city person who writes about country folk
    (D) someone who appears to be sophisticated, but is in fact rustic

### Romulus reacts to news of his brother's death

Haec ubi rex didicit,[1] lacrimas introrsus obortas
    devorat et clausum pectore vulnus habet.
Flere palam non vult exemplaque fortia servat,
*Line*    "Sic"que "meos muros transeat hostis," ait.
5    Dat tamen exsequias[2] nec iam suspendere fletum
    sustinet, et pietas dissimulata patet,
osculaque applicuit posito suprema feretro[3]
    atque ait, "Invito frater adempte, vale!"
Arsurosque artus unxit. Fecere, quod ille,
10    Faustulus et maestas Acca soluta comas.
Tum iuvenem nondum facti flevere Quirites.
    Ultima plorato subdita flamma rogo[4] est.

1 <u>Haec ubi rex didicit</u>: in this version of the story, Remus had been killed by Celer, who had been put in charge of building Rome's walls.
2 <u>exsequiae</u>, -<u>arum</u>, f.pl.: funeral rites
3 <u>feretrum</u>, -<u>i</u>, n.: bier to carry the body to the grave
4 <u>rogus</u>, -<u>i</u>, n.: funeral pyre

14. In lines 1–2 (<u>Haec</u> . . . <u>habet</u>), we learn that Romulus

    (A) could not contain his grief

    (B) suppressed his grief

    (C) postponed his grief

    (D) felt no grief

15. In line 1, the verb form <u>obortas</u> is

    (A) a deponent          (C) a gerund

    (B) a present subjunctive    (D) a main verb

16. As indicated in line 3 (<u>Flere</u> . . . <u>servat</u>), it appears that Romulus

    (A) wept openly

    (B) was pleased at the news

    (C) did what everyone expected

    (D) grieved privately

17. In line 4, <u>transeat hostis</u> is translated

    (A) let the enemy go across

    (B) the enemy is passing over

    (C) the enemy will go over

    (D) he may overtake the enemy

18. In line 5, the phrase <u>nec iam</u> means
    (A) not only now      (C) and yet not
    (B) no longer      (D) never again

19. In lines 5–8 (<u>Dat</u> . . . <u>vale</u>), we learn that Romulus was unable to conceal his grief
    (A) during the funeral rites
    (B) after he had buried his brother
    (C) when he kissed the funeral bier
    (D) after he had bid his brother farewell

20. Which of the following figures of speech appears in lines 7–8 (<u>osculaque</u> . . . <u>vale</u>)?
    (A) hendiadys
    (B) interlocked word order (synchysis)
    (C) hyperbole
    (D) polysyndeton

21. In line 8 (<u>Invito</u> . . . <u>vale</u>), Romulus' final words to his brother imply that
    (A) his brother had welcomed death
    (B) his brother's body had been stolen
    (C) his brother had died prematurely
    (D) he had wanted his brother to die

22. <u>Arsurosque artus unxit</u> (line 9) is translated
    (A) He cremated the body and then annointed it.
    (B) He annointed the body about to be cremated.
    (C) With great skill, he prepared the body to be cremated.
    (D) He embraced the body before cremation.

23. In line 9, the form <u>Fecere</u> is
    (A) future indicative      (C) present infinitive
    (B) perfect indicative      (D) present imperative

24. Which of the following figures of speech is found in line 10 (<u>Faustulus</u> . . . <u>comas</u>)?
    (A) transferred epithet      (C) litotes
    (B) metonymy      (D) aposiopesis

25. Line 12 (<u>Ultima</u> . . . <u>est</u>) is translated
    (A) The final lament is given over the burning pyre.
    (B) Romulus, as a final act of grief, ignited the pyre.
    (C) After the pyre was arranged, the wretched fire was finally lit.
    (D) At last the fire has been placed beneath the lamentable pyre.

### Pliny congratulates a friend

Recte fecisti, Valeri, quod gladiatorum munus Veronensibus nostris promisisti, a quibus olim amaris suspiceris ornaris. Inde etiam uxorem carissimam tibi et probatissimam habuisti, cuius memoriae aut opus *Line* aliquod aut spectaculum atque hoc potissimum, quod maxime funeri, 5 debebatur. Praeterea tanto consensu rogabaris, ut negare non constans, sed durum videretur. Illud quoque egregie, quod tam facilis tam liberalis in edendo fuisti; nam per haec etiam magnus animus ostenditur. Vellem Africanae,[1] quae coemeras plurimas, ad praefinitum diem occurrissent: sed licet cessaverint[2] illae tempestate detentae, tu tamen meruisti ut 10 acceptum tibi fieret, quod quo minus exhiberes, non per te stetit. Vale.

1 <u>Africanae</u>, -<u>arum</u>, f.pl.: = <u>Africanae ferae</u>, panthers
2 <u>licet cessaverint</u>: "granted that they were late"

26. In lines 1–2 (<u>Recte</u> . . . <u>ornaris</u>), we learn that Valerius
    (A) is a well-known gladiator in Verona
    (B) wants to win votes by sponsoring games
    (C) is being honored by gladiatorial games
    (D) has pledged to present games in Verona

27. The figure of speech that occurs in lines 1–2 (<u>Recte</u> . . . <u>ornaris</u>) is
    (A) alliteration     (C) hyperbole
    (B) asyndeton     (D) ellipsis

28. In lines 2–5 (<u>Inde</u> . . . <u>debebatur</u>), we learn that Valerius' wife
    (A) was deceased
    (B) was a wealthy and powerful woman
    (C) was not loved or respected by her husband
    (D) cared little for the games

29. The case of the noun <u>memoriae</u> (line 3) depends upon

    (A) <u>uxorem</u> (line 2)     (C) <u>funeri</u> (line 4)

    (B) <u>cuius</u> (line 3)     (D) <u>debebatur</u> (line 5)

30. Complete the following translation of lines 5–6 (<u>Praeterea</u> . . . <u>videretur</u>): "Moreover, you were asked by so many people . . ."

    (A) that to deny that you were not strong-minded would seem shameless

    (B) that to say no would seem not resolute, but rude

    (C) that those who did not seem to agree with you were considered harsh, rather than steadfast

    (D) that no one appeared to deny your determination and toughness

31. In line 6, <u>Illud</u> is the direct object of

    (A) <u>fecisti</u> (understood from line 1)

    (B) <u>edendo</u> (line 7)

    (C) <u>fuisti</u> (line 7)

    (D) the verb <u>est</u> (understood)

32. In the context of line 7, <u>edendo</u> is translated

    (A) must sponsor     (C) sponsoring

    (B) having sponsored     (D) about to be sponsored

33. In lines 6–7 (<u>Illud</u> . . . <u>ostenditur</u>), Pliny characterizes Valerius as generous because

    (A) Verona had never had gladiatorial games before

    (B) he had honored his wife with the show

    (C) he was efficient and lavish in giving the games

    (D) public games were usually financed by the state

34. The form <u>Vellem</u> (line 7) is

    (A) present infinitive     (C) imperfect subjunctive

    (B) present indicative     (D) present subjunctive

35. The words <u>Vellem Africanae . . . ad praefinitum die occurrissent</u> (lines 7–8), are translated

    (A) I wish that the panthers had arrived on the appointed day.

    (B) I want you to know the panthers will arrive as scheduled.

(C)   I wished I knew on what day the panthers would arrive.

(D)   If only the panthers had arrived on the day I wished.

36.   In line 9 (<u>sed</u> . . . <u>detentae</u>), we learn that the panthers

(A)   arrived on time despite a storm

(B)   did not arrive at all

(C)   were unwilling to travel because of the weather

(D)   did not arrive on time because of a storm

37.   In lines 9–10 (<u>tu</u> . . . <u>stetit</u>), Pliny assures Valerius that

(A)   Pliny will take responsibility for what happened

(B)   Valerius can display the panthers at another time

(C)   Valerius deserves credit for his intentions

(D)   No one will blame him

38.   The clause that ends with the subjunctive verb <u>exhiberes</u> (line 10) is introduced by

(A)   <u>licet</u> (line 9)          (C)   <u>quod</u> (line 10)

(B)   <u>ut</u> (line 9)             (D)   <u>quo minus</u> (line 10)

### A festival celebrates the blessings of the farm

Luce sacra requiescat humus, requiescat arator,
    et grave suspenso vomere[1] cesset opus.
Solvite vincla iugis; nunc ad praesepia[2] debent
*Line*     plena coronato stare boves capite.
5   Omnia sint operata deo;[3] non audeat ulla
    lanificam pensis[4] imposuisse manum.
Vos quoque abesse procul iubeo, discedat ab aris,
    cui tulit hesterna gaudia nocte Venus.
Casta placent superis: pura cum veste venite
10   et manibus puris sumite fontis aquam.
Cernite, fulgentes ut eat sacer agnus ad aras
    vinctaque post olea[5] candida turba comas.

1  <u>vomer</u>, <u>vomeris</u>, m.: ploughshare
2  <u>praesepium</u>, -<u>i</u>, n.: manger; corn crib
3  <u>deo</u>: Bacchus or Ceres
4  <u>pensum</u>, -<u>i</u>, n.: a portion of wool weighed out to a spinner as a day's task; "a day's work"
5  <u>olea</u>, -<u>ae</u>, f.: the olive tree or fruit

39. As we learn from lines 1–2 (<u>Luce</u> . . . <u>opus</u>), the poet asks that the festival include
    (A) a day of rest for all
    (B) more rigorous work than usual
    (C) postponement of all work but the ploughing
    (D) only light chores

40. In line 2 (<u>et</u> . . . <u>opus</u>), the noun <u>vomere</u> is ablative
    (A) of means or instrument
    (B) in an ablative absolute
    (C) with a special verb
    (D) of manner 42. In lines 3–4 (<u>Solvite</u> . . . <u>capite</u>), we learn that

41. In lines 3–4 (Solvite . . . . capite), we learn that
    (A) the farm equipment should be cleaned
    (B) corn cribs should be decked with wreaths
    (C) oxen are to be prepared for sacrifice
    (D) the cattle should be fed well

42. In line 5, <u>Omnia sint operata deo</u> is translated
    (A) All things have been done for the god
    (B) Let the god do all things
    (C) Let all things be done for the god
    (D) All things are being done by the god

43. In line 6, the case of <u>pensis</u> depends upon
    (A) <u>Omnia</u> . . . <u>deo</u> (line 5)
    (B) <u>audeat</u> (line 5)
    (C) <u>lanificam</u> . . . <u>manum</u> (line 6)
    (D) <u>imposuisse</u> (line 6)

44. In lines 7–8 (<u>Vos</u> . . . <u>Venus</u>), we learn that those who have been recent lovers
    (A) are especially welcome at the festival
    (B) must stay away from the festival
    (C) may be present, but not at the altars
    (D) may be together only the night of the festival

45. In line 8, <u>Venus</u> is an example of which figure of speech?
    - (A) transferred epithet
    - (C) metonymy
    - (B) hendiadys
    - (D) onomatopoeia

46. In lines 9–10 (<u>Casta</u> . . . <u>aquam</u>), we learn that festival celebrants are to
    - (A) wash their garments in the pure spring water
    - (B) draw the spring's water with pure hands
    - (C) make chaste offerings to the gods
    - (D) purify themselves after they arrive

47. Line 11 (<u>Cernite</u> . . . <u>aras</u>) is translated
    - (A) See how the shining lamb goes to the sacred altars
    - (B) O shining ones, tell us when the sacred lamb will go to the altars
    - (C) Determine whether the sacred lamb will go to the shining altars
    - (D) Observe how the sacred lamb goes to the shining altars

48. In line 11 (<u>Cernite</u> . . . <u>aras</u>), which figure of speech occurs?
    - (A) hyperbaton
    - (C) anaphora
    - (B) hyperbole
    - (D) polysyndeton

49. The case and number of <u>olea</u> (line 12) are
    - (A) nominative singular
    - (B) nominative plural
    - (C) ablative singular
    - (D) accusative plural

50. Line 12 (<u>vinctaque</u> . . . <u>comas</u>) describes the
    - (A) sacrifice of the lamb
    - (B) harvesting of olive branches
    - (C) celebrants in festival attire
    - (D) honoring of the farm's crops

## STOP

**This is the end of the Multiple-Choice Section of the AP Latin Literature Exam. If time remains, you may check your work only in this section. Do not begin the Free-Response Section until instructed to do so.**

# PRACTICE EXAM 2

## AP Latin Literature

## Free-Response Section

**TIME:** 2 hours (including a 15-minute reading period)

**DIRECTIONS:** Answer SIX of the questions in this Section, following directions carefully. You are required to answer all of the Catullus questions in Part A and may choose the additional three questions from any one of the choice authors, Cicero, Horace, or Ovid, in Part B.

# Part A

## Question 1 – Catullus (15 percent)
### (Suggested time – 10 minutes)

> Dicebas quondam solum te nosse Catullum,
>     Lesbia, nec prae me velle tenere Iovem.
> Dilexi tum te non tantum ut vulgus amicam,
> *Line*     sed pater et gnatos diligit et generos.
>     5 Nunc te cognovi: quare etsi impensius uror,
>         multo mi tamen es vilior et levior.
>     Qui potis est? inquis. Quod amantem iniuria talis
>         cogit amare magis, sed bene velle minus.
>
> **Catullus 72**

Give a literal translation of the passage above.

# Question 2 – Catullus (20 percent)

## (Suggested time – 30 minutes)

Begin your answer to this question on a fresh page.

(A)

Ille mi par esse videtur,
ille, si fas est, superare divos,
qui sedens adversus identidem te

*Line*       spectat et audit
  5  dulce ridentem, misero quod omnes
eripit sensus mihi: nam simul te,
Lesbia, aspexi, nihil est super mi
      . . . . . .\*
lingua sed torpet, tenuis sub artus
  10  flamma demanat, sonitu suopte
tintinant aures, gemina teguntur
      lumina nocte.

**Catullus 51.1–12**

\* This line is missing from the original manuscript.

(B)

Non prius ex illo flagrantia declinavit
lumina, quam cuncto concepit corpore flammam
funditus atque imis exarsit tota medullis.
*Line*  Heu misere exagitans immiti corde furores
  5  sancte puer, curis hominum qui gaudia misces . . .
qualibus incensam iactastis mente puellam
fluctibus in flavo saepe hospite suspirantem!

**Catullus 64. 91–95, 97–98**

In each of the two passages above, Catullus describes someone falling in love. In a well-developed essay, compare and contrast the two passages by discussing their similarities and differences.

(Remember to support what you say by making direct reference to the Latin **throughout** the passages. Cite and translate or closely paraphrase the relevant Latin. Do <u>not</u> simply summarize or paraphrase what the poem says.)

# Question 3 – Catullus (15 percent)

## (Suggested time – 20 minutes)

Begin your answer to this question on a fresh page.

> Annales Volusi, cacata carta,
> votum solvite pro mea puella:
> nam sanctae Veneri Cupidinique
*Line*   vovit, si sibi restitutus essem
>   5   desissemque truces vibrare iambos,
> electissima pessimi poetae
> scripta tardipedi deo daturam
> infelicibus ustulanda lignis.
> Et haec pessima se puella vidit
>  10   iocosis lepide vovere divis.
> Nunc, O caeruleo creata ponto, . . .
> acceptum face redditumque votum,
> si non illepidum neque invenustum est.
> At vos interea venite in ignem,
>  15   pleni ruris et infacetiarum
> annales Volusi, cacata carta.

**Catullus 36.1–11, 16–20**

In the poem above, Catullus describes a "joke" that he has played on Lesbia. In a **short** essay, discuss the nature and circumstances of the joke, making clear what was at stake for each party and who was the real recipient of the joke.

(Remember to support your observations from the **entire text** of the poem and be sure to cite and translate or closely paraphrase directly from the Latin text.)

## PROCEED TO THE APPROPRIATE AUTHOR IN PART B

# Part B

IF YOU HAVE CHOSEN **CICERO**, ANSWER THE FOLLOWING THREE QUESTIONS. IF YOU HAVE CHOSEN ANOTHER AUTHOR, MOVE TO THE APPROPRIATE SECTION.

## Question 4 – Cicero (20 percent)

### (Suggested time – 20 minutes)

Begin your answer on a fresh page.

### Cicero considers the merits of friendship.

Cumque plurimas et maximas commoditates amicitia contineat, tum illa nimirum praestat omnibus, quod bonam spem praelucet in posterum, nec debilitari animos aut cadere patitur. Verum etiam amicum qui intuetur,
*Line* tamquam exemplar aliquod intuetur sui. Quocirca et absentes adsunt
5 egentes abundant et imbecilli valent, et, quod difficilius dictu est, mortui vivunt; tantus eos honos, memoria, desiderium prosequitur amicorum, ex quo illorum beata mors videtur, horum vita laudabilis.

**Cicero,** *De Amicitia* 23

In his treatise on the subject, Cicero considers the value of friendship. In a **short essay**, identify the advantages of true friendship that are presented by Cicero in this passage.

(Remember to support your observations from the **entire text** of each passsage and be sure to cite and translate or closely paraphrase directly from the Latin text.)

## Question 5 – Cicero (15 percent)

### (Suggested time – 10 minutes)

Begin your answer to this question on a fresh page.

**Cicero prefers literature to more popular pursuits.**

Quare quis tandem me reprehendat aut quis mihi iure suscenseat, si,
quantum ceteris ad suas res obeundas, quantum ad festos dies ludorum
celebrandos, quantum ad alias voluptates et ad ipsam requiem animi et
*Line*  corporis conceditur temporum, quantum alii tribuunt tempestivis con-
5  viviis, quantum denique alveolo, quantum pilae, tantum mihi egomet
ad haec studia recolenda sumpsero?

*Pro Archia Poeta* 13

Give a literal translation of the passage above.

## Question 6 – Cicero (15 percent)

### (Suggested time – 10 minutes)

**Cicero comments on the place of amibition in life.**

Neque enim est hoc dissimulandum, quod obscurari non potest, sed prae
nobis ferendum, trahimur omnes studio laudis et optimus quisque
maxime gloriā ducitur. Ipsi illi philosophi etiam illis libellis, quos de
*Line*  contemnendā gloriā scribunt, nomen suum inscribunt: in eo ipso, in quo
5  praedicationem nobilitatemque despiciunt, praedicari de se ac nominari
volunt.

*Pro Archia Poeta* 26

1.  (a)  To what does <u>hoc</u> (line 1) refer?

   (b)  In <u>Neque</u> . . . <u>ferendum</u> (lines 1–2), what does Cicero say that we must
        do?

2.  What do you notice about the organization or structure of lines 2–3 (<u>tra-
    himur</u> . . . <u>ducitur</u>)?

3.  Translate <u>trahimur</u> . . . <u>ducitur</u> (lines 2–3).

4. (a) What evidence does Cicero present in lines 3–4 (Ipsi . . . inscribunt) to make his point that the desire for recognition is universal?

   (b) Is <u>contemnenda</u> a gerund or a gerundive in the context of <u>quos</u> . . . <u>scribunt</u> (lines 3–4)? Explain your answer.

5. Translate lines 4–6 (<u>in</u> . . . <u>volunt</u>).

6. Find an example of word play in the final sentence (<u>Ipsi</u> . . . <u>volunt</u>, lines 3–6) and explain its effect on the meaning.

**END OF AP LATIN LITERATURE
PRACTICE EXAM 2**

IF YOU HAVE CHOSEN **HORACE**, ANSWER THE FOLLOWING THREE QUESTIONS. IF YOU HAVE CHOSEN ANOTHER AUTHOR, MOVE TO THE APPROPRIATE SECTION.

## Question 7 – Horace (20 percent)

(Suggested time – 20 minutes)

Begin your answer to this question on a fresh page.

> O fons Bandusiae splendidior vitro,
> dulce digne mero non sine floribus,
>    cras donaberis haedo,
> *Line*     cui frons turgida cornibus
>
> 5  primis et Venerem et proelia destinat;
> frustra: nam gelidos inficiet tibi
>    rubro sanguine rivos
>     lascivi suboles gregis.
>
> Te flagrantis atrox hora Caniculae
> 10  nescit tangere, tu frigus amabile
>    fessis vomere tauris
>     praebes et pecori vago.
>
> Fies nobilium tu quoque fontium,
> me dicente cavis impositam ilicem
> 15   saxis, unde loquaces
>     lymphae desiliunt tuae.

*Odes* 3.13

*Fons Bandusiae* is a hymn in celebration of the spring on the Horace's farm. In a **short** essay, identify and discuss the ways in which the poet uses the technique of contrast to express his theme.

(Remember to support your observations from the **entire text** of the poem and be sure to cite and translate or closely paraphrase directly from the Latin text.)

# Question 8 – Horace (15 percent)
## (Suggested time – 15 minutes)

Begin your answer to this question on a fresh page.

> Tu ne quaesieris, scire nefas, quem mihi, quem tibi
> finem di dederint, Leuconoe, nec Babylonios
> temptaris numeros. Ut melius, quidquid erit, pati,
> *Line*   seu plures hiemes seu tribuit Iuppiter ultimam,
>   5   quae nunc oppositis debilitat pumicibus mare
> Tyrrhenum: sapias, vini liques, et spatio brevi
> spem longam reseces. Dum loquimur, fugerit invida
> aetas: carpe diem, quam minimum credula postero.
>
> **Odes 1.11**

Give a literal translation of the passage above.

# Question 9 – Horace (15 percent)
## (Suggested time – 10 minutes)

Begin your answer to this question on a fresh page.

> Ibam forte via Sacra, sicut meus est mos,
> nescio quid meditans nugarum, totus in illis.
> Accurrit quidam notus mihi nomine tantum,
> *Line*   arreptaque manu, "Quid agis, dulcissime rerum?"
>   5   "Suaviter, ut nunc est," inquam, "et cupio omnia quae vis."
> Cum adsectaretur, "Num quid vis?" occupo. At ille
> "Noris nos," inquit; "docti sumus." Hic ego, "Pluris
> hoc," inquam, "mihi eris." Misere discedere quaerens,
> ire modo ocius, interdum consistere, in aurem
>   10   dicere nescio quid puero, cum sudor ad imos
> manaret talos.
>
> **Satires 1.9.1–11**

1.  In lines 1–2 (Ibam . . . illis), the poet describes two things that he is doing. What are they?

2.  How well-known to Horace is his acquaintance? Cite and translate the relevant Latin in line 3 to support your answer.

3. Translate <u>Quid</u> . . . <u>vis</u> (lines 4–5).

4. Lines 4–8 contain a highly colloquial conversation between the poet and the pest. In your answers to the following questions, express the relevant Latin in standard English, but preserve the meaning of the Latin.

   (a) What does the poet ask in line 6? (<u>Num quid vis</u>?)

   (b) What is the pest's reply in line 7? (<u>Noris</u> . . . <u>docti sumus</u>).

   (c) What does the poet say in lines 7–8, in return? (<u>Pluris</u> . . . <u>eris</u>).

5. Translate the historical infinitive <u>ire</u> (line 9) as appropriate to context.

6. In lines 8–11, how does the narrator react to the pest's words and behavior? Cite and translate <u>two</u> Latin words or phrases in support of your answer.

**END OF AP LATIN LITERATURE
PRACTICE EXAM 2**

> IF YOU HAVE CHOSEN **OVID**, ANSWER THE FOLLOWING THREE QUESTIONS. IF YOU HAVE CHOSEN ANOTHER AUTHOR, MOVE TO THE APPROPRIATE SECTION.

## Question 10 – *Ovid* (20 percent)

### (Suggested time – 20 minutes)

Begin your answer to this question on a fresh page.

> Inter opus monitusque genae maduere seniles,
> et patriae tremuere manus; dedit oscula nato
> non iterum repetenda suo, pennisque levatus
> *Line* ante volat comitique timet, velut ales ab alto
> 5 quae teneram prolem produxit in aera nido,
> hortaturque sequi, damnosasque erudit artes,
> et movet ipse suas et nati respicit alas.
>
> *Metamorphoses* 8.210–16

In the passage above, Ovid describes the preparations of Daedalus and Icarus for flight. In a **short** essay, discuss the ways in which the poet creates a sense of anticipation in the reader with regard to the flight and its consequences.

(Remember to support your observations from the **entire text** of the passage and be sure to cite and translate or closely paraphrase directly from the Latin text.)

## Question 11 – *Ovid* (15 percent)

### (Suggested time – 15 minutes)

Begin your answer to this question on a fresh page.

> Me miserum! Certas habuit puer ille sagittas:
> uror, et in vacuo pectore regnat Amor.
> Sex mihi surgat opus numeris, in quinque residat;
> *Line* ferrea cum vestris bella, valete, modis.
> 5 Cingere litorea flaventia tempora myrto,
> Musa per undenos emodulanda pedes!
>
> *Amores* 1.1.25–30

Give a literal translation of the passage above.

# Question 12 – Ovid (15 percent)

## (Suggested time – 10 minutes)

Begin your answer to this question on a fresh page.

> "Ecce, metu nondum posito, ne fallat amantem,
> illa redit, iuvenemque oculis animoque requirit,
> quantaque vitarit narrare pericula gestit.
> *Line* Utque locum et visa cognoscit in arbore formam,
> 5 sic facit incertam pomi color; haeret an haec sit.
> Dum dubitat, tremebunda videt pulsare cruentum
> membra solum, retroque pedem tulit, oraque buxo
> pallidiora gerens exhorruit aequoris instar,
> quod tremit, exigua cum summum stringitur aura.

*Metamorphoses* **4.128–36**

1. For what two reasons, given in lines 1–3 (Ecce . . . gestit), did Thisbe return to the place of the rendezvous?

2. With regard to the verb form <u>vitarit</u> (line 3):

   (a) identify the tense and mood;

   (b) briefly explain why this form is required, given the grammatical context in which it is found;

   (c) give the prose equivalent.

3. What is the cause of Thisbe's uncertainty as expressed in lines 4–5 (Utque . . . <u>sit</u>)?

4. Name a figure of speech that occurs in lines 6–7 (<u>sic</u> . . . <u>solum</u>) and write out the Latin that illustrates it.

5. Write out and scan line 6 (<u>Dum</u> . . . <u>cruentum</u>).

6. In lines 7–9 (<u>oraque</u> . . . <u>aura</u>), what two images does the poet use to express the fear and anguish on Thisbe's face? Write out and translate or accurately paraphrase the Latin that illustrates each.

## END OF AP LATIN LITERATURE
## PRACTICE EXAM 2

# PRACTICE EXAM 2
## AP Latin Literature

## Answer Key

## List of Authors and Passages Appearing on This Exam

### Multiple-Choice[1]
#### Required Author Passage
"Catullus critiques another poet" (Poem 22.1–11)

#### Sight Passages
"Romulus reacts to the news of his brother's death" (Ovid, *Fasti* 4.845–55)

"Pliny congratulates a friend" (Pliny, *Epistulae* 6.34)

"A festival celebrates the blessings of the farm" (Tibullus, *Elegies* 2.1.5–16)

### Free-Response
#### Required Author
Translation: Catullus 72

Long Essay: Catullus, Poem 51.1–12 , 64.86–87, 91–95, 97–98

Short Essay: Catullus, Poem 36.1–11 and 16–20

#### Choice Author: Cicero
Short Essay: *De Amicitia* 23

Translation: *Pro Archia Poeta* 13

Short Answer: *Pro Archia Poeta* 26

---

[1] Translations of all multiple-choice passages are provided below.

### Choice Author: Horace

Short Essay: *Odes* 3.13
Translation: *Odes* 1.11
Short Answer: *Satires* 1.9.1–11

### Choice Author: Ovid

Short Essay: *Metamorphoses* 8.210–16 (Daedalus and Icarus)
Translation: *Amores* 1.1.25–30
Short Answer: *Metamorphoses* 4.128–36 (Pyramus and Thisbe)

## Answers to the Multiple-Choice Questions: Latin Literature, Practice Exam 2

| "Catullus" | "Romulus" | "Pliny" | "Festival" |
|---|---|---|---|
| 1. (D) | 14. (B) | 26. (D) | 39. (A) |
| 2. (C) | 15. (A) | 27. (B) | 40. (B) |
| 3. (A) | 16. (D) | 28. (A) | 41. (D) |
| 4. (A) | 17. (A) | 29. (D) | 42. (C) |
| 5. (D) | 18. (B) | 30. (B) | 43. (D) |
| 6. (B) | 19. (A) | 31. (A) | 44. (B) |
| 7. (C) | 20. (B) | 32. (C) | 45. (C) |
| 8. (C) | 21. (C) | 33. (C) | 46. (B) |
| 9. (A) | 22. (B) | 34. (C) | 47. (D) |
| 10. (D) | 23. (B) | 35. (A) | 48. (A) |
| 11. (C) | 24. (A) | 36. (D) | 49. (C) |
| 12. (B) | 25. (D) | 37. (C) | 50. (C) |
| 13. (D) | | 38. (D) | |

# PRACTICE EXAM 2

## AP Latin Literature

## Detailed Explanations of Answers to Multiple-Choice Questions

## "Catullus critiques another poet"

1. **(D)**

    **Nosti** is a syncopated or contracted form of **novisti**. Answer (A) is first person singular, perfect tense; Answer (B) second person singular, present tense; and Answer (C) present passive infinitive. For syncope, see Chapter 11.

2. **(C)**

    The correct Answer is (C) "charming" because line 2 tells us that he is charming (**venustus**), witty (**dicax**), and sophisticated (**urbanus**).

3. **(A)**

    The pronoun **idemque** (line 3) refers to Suffenus, Answer (A): "that same fellow writes scads of verses, by far." For pronouns, see Chapter 13B.

4. **(A)**

    This line contains five elisions: Put<u>o esse ego</u> illi mili<u>a a</u>ut dece<u>m a</u>ut plura, perhaps emphasizing the accumulation of Suffenus' lines of verse. For elisions, see Chapter 11.

5. **(D)**

    **Perscripta esse** is a perfect passive infinitive in an indirect statement after **puto** (line 4), so Answer (D) "have been written" is correct. Answers (A) would be **perscribi**, (B) **perscriptura esse**, and (C) "had been written" is not possible when the main verb is other than a past tense. For infinitives, see Chapter 16C.

6. **(B)**

    **Milia aut decem aut plura** (line 4) tells us that Suffenus has written "tens of thousands (of verses) or more," which is an example of hyperbole. For figures of speech, see Chapter 10.

7.   **(C)**
    **Sic ut fit** (line 5) translates "as usually happens," Answer (C). **Ut** when followed by the indicative mood (**fit**) usually means "as" or "when." This line reads, "(written, **relata**) not on palimpsest, as usually happens," "as is usual," "as is usually the case."

8.   **(C)**
    A palimpsest was a sheet of parchment with the ink scraped off so that it could be re-used, i.e., recycled paper. Catullus is saying here that Suffenus used fresh, new paper every time he wrote something. Papyrus was the more usual writing material for everyday use.

9.   **(A)**
    Lines 6–8 list the various items that Suffenus used in his writing, all top-drawer: high-grade paper (**cartae regiae**), new rolls (**novi libri**), new ornamental knobs (**novi umbilici**), red straps (**lora rubra**), parchment wrappers (**membranae**), the paper all ruled with lead (**derecta plumbo**) and smoothed with pumicestone (**pumice omnia aequata**).

10.  **(D)**
    The lack of conjunctions in the list of materials in lines 6–8 is asyndeton, Answer (D). For figures, see Chapter 10.

11.  **(C)**
    **Derecta** (line 8) is a perfect passive participle, Answer (C). The grammatical context does not call for an elliptical infinitive (Answer A) or main verb (Answer D) and **derecta** is not a substantive here. For participles, see Chapter 16A.

12.  **(B)**
    **Haec cum legas** means, "When you read these (writings or verses)," which is Answer (B). The **cum** clause is circumstantial, and **legas** is a present subjunctive. Note the postposition of **cum**. For subjunctive forms, see Chapter 16D, Section 1, and for **cum** clauses, see Chapter 16D, Section 6.

13.  **(D)**
    Lines 9–11 read, "(When you read these poems), that suave and sophisticated Suffenus seems at the same time a goat-milker or a ditch-digger." Thus, Answer (D) "someone who appears to be sophisticated but is in fact rustic" is correct.

## "Romulus reacts to news of his brother's death"

14.  **(B)**
    In lines 1–2, the relevant words **lacrimas . . . habet** translate, "he (Romulus) chokes back the tears having welled up inside and keeps the wound closed away in his heart." The correct answer is therefore (B) "suppressed his grief."

15. **(A)**

Although the –**as** ending of **obortas** could lead you to Answer (B) a present subjunctive (see Chapter 16D, Section 1), or (D) a main verb (first conjugation, present tense indicative), the verb **oborior, oboriri, obortus sum** is deponent, that is, it is passive in form and active in meaning. Therefore, **obortas** is a perfect passive (past) participle modifying **lacrimas**. For deponent verbs, see Chapter 14B; for past participles of deponent verbs, see Chapter 16A.

16. **(D)**

Line 3 answers the question by translating "He does not wish to weep openly and maintains (= wishes to maintain) strength as an example." Therefore, Answer (D) "grieved privately" is correct.

17. **(A)**

The verb of this famous saying is a jussive subjunctive, which required the meaning of "let." The verb form required by Answer (B) is present tense, **transit**, and Answer (C) future tense, **transibit. Hostis** is a nominative subject and cannot serve as the direct object of **transeat**, therefore Answer (D) "he may overtake the enemy" is incorrect. The entire sentence translates, "Let the enemy cross over my walls and this (**sic**) will happen," i.e., the enemy will die, just as Remus did. For the forms and uses of the independent subjunctive, see Chapters 16D, Sections 1 and 2.

18. **(B)**

**Nec iam**, "no longer," is an idiomatic phrase commonly found throughout Latin literature.

19. **(A)**

Lines 5–6 say, "However, he conducts the funeral rites (and) no longer able to hold back the tears, his hidden devotion is disclosed and he presses final kisses (on the body) placed on the bier." The finality implied in Answers (B) and (D) is not present or suggested in these words. The sequence of the Latin in this sentence implies that Romulus had "broken down" during the funeral rites, which presumably took place before transport to the grave on the bier.

20. **(B)**

The words that interlock are **osculaque** with **suprema** (accusative plural, neuter) and **posito** with **feretro** (ablative singular, neuter), giving **osculaque . . . posito suprema feretro** as the synchysis. For figures of speech, see Chapter 10.

21. **(C)**

Ovid takes this famous line directly from Catullus, Poem 101, on the death of the poet's brother. It reads, "Brother, taken away from me against your will, farewell." The words **invito** and **adempte** imply an early/unexpected death, giving (C) "his brother had died prematurely" as the correct answer. **Ademptus** is the perfect passive participle of **adimo, adimere, ademi, ademptus** and has a vocative ending, modifying **frater.**

22. **(B)**

This sentence requires careful reading, as the sense requires that the future active participle **arsuros** be translated with a passive meaning: Romulus annointed (**unxit**) the body (**artus**, accusative plural) about to be cremated (**arsuros**, modifying **artus**, a fourth declension noun). The correct sequence is reversed in Answer (A); Answer (B) mistakes **artus**, "limbs," for a form of **ars, artis**, "skill"; and Answer (D) mistranslates **unxit** (for **iunxit**?) The use of **artus** for body is an example of synecdoche. For the future active participle, see Chapter 16A.

23. **(B)**

**Fecere** is a poetic condensation of **fecerunt**, which is third person plural, perfect active indicative = "they made" or "they did." It cannot be a present infinitive (Answer C) or a present imperative (Answer D) because the stem **fec-** is in the perfect tense. The perfect stem also precludes **fecere** as an alternative to the second person singular form of the present passive indicative, **faceris.** For alternative verb forms, see Chapter 11.

24. **(A)**

In line 10, the ending of the adjective **maestas** requires that it modify the noun **comas**, but it is not the hair that is sad, but Acca herself. Therefore, the meaning of **maestas** may be transferred to **Acca** from **comas** (note also the juxtaposition of **maestas** with **Acca**). For figures of speech, see Chapter 10.

25. **(D)**

Break down this sentence by noticing the interlocking of **ultima . . . flamma** with **plorato . . . rogo** and the separation of the elements of the main verb, which is **subdita . . . est**. The adjective **Ultima** may be translated adverbially, as Answer (D) "at last." The verb **subdo, subdere, subdidi, subditum** means to place under. **Plorato . . . rogo** is an ablative absolute meaning "the funeral pyre having been lamented, or, "after the funeral pyre was lamented." Hence, the correct answer is (A) "At last the fire has been placed under the pyre after it was lamented, i.e., the lamentable pyre."

## "Pliny congratulates a friend"

26. **(D)**

Answer (D) "has pledged to present games in Verona" is correct because Line 1 reads, "You have done well, Valerius, because you have sponsored gladiatorial games for our fellow Veronese."

27. **(B)**

The listing of three verbs in a row without punctuation – **amaris suspiceris ornaris** – is asyndeton. Normally, you would find **amaris et suspiceris et ornaris**. See Chapter 10 for figures of speech.

28. **(A)**

That Valerius' wife was deceased is surmised from the past tense of the verb, i.e., **uxorem . . . habuisti**, the use of the words **memoriae** (line 3) and **funeri** (line 4), and Pliny's comment here that gladiatorial combats are particularly suitable for funeral tributes (their original function). The sentence in lines 2–4 reads, "From there (Verona) you had a wife very dear and most acceptable to you, to whose memory you owe either some public work (**opus**) or show (**spectaculum**), and this is very much the kind of show that is especially appropriate (**hoc potissimum quod maxime**) for a funeral."

29. **(D)**

The case of the noun **memoriae**, dative, depends upon the verb **debebatur** (line 4): "to the memory of whom (**cuius**, i.e., the wife) . . . there was owed." Avoid taking both **memoriae** and **cuius** as genitive. For the dative case, see Chapter 13A.

30. **(B)**

This is a tricky sentence. The key to the meaning is the observation of **negare** as a subjective infinitive, i.e., **negare** serves as the subject of the result clause **ut . . . videretur**. Subjective infinitives serve as neuter nouns, therefore **constans** and **durum** modify **negare**. For this use of infinitive, see Chapter 16C.

31. **(A)**

In lines 1–5, Pliny congratulates Valerius for having done well (**Recte fecisti**) in proposing the games. Thereafter, he concentrates on talking about the games themselves. Therefore, **Illud quoque egregie** correctly follows after **fecisti**, understood: "You did that admirably, too, the fact that (**quod**) . . . ." Thus, the correct answer is (A) **fecisti** (understood from line 1).

32. **(C)**

The correct translation of the gerund **edendo** is Answer (C) "sponsoring." The ablative case is used after the preposition **in**. Answer (A) is a red herring, designed to get you to think about the distinction between a gerund and a passive periphrastic. The perfect active participle in Answer (B) "having sponsored," cannot be expressed directly in Latin, as **edo, edere** is not a deponent verb. The meaning given in Answer (D) "about to be sponsored" requires a future passive participle or gerundive, which is an adjective; **edendo** functions as a noun here. For more on gerunds and gerundives, see Chapter 16B.

33. **(C)**

Answer (C) is correct because Pliny characterizes Valerius in line 5 as **tam facilis tam liberalis**, "so efficient (and) so lavish" (in giving the games). Note the asyndeton.

34. **(C)**
**Vellem** is imperfect subjunctive, first person singular. The subjunctive appears here because Pliny is expressing a wish (optative), which is a non-fact. For independent subjunctives, see Chapter 16D, Section 2.

35. **(A)**
As given, the sentence reads "If only (Vellem) the panthers (Africanae) . . . had arrived (occurrissent) on the appointed day (ad praefinitum die)." Vellem is optative subjunctive, for which, see Chapter 16D, Section 2. For the form of occurrissent, see Chapter 16D, Section 1. Answer (A) is correct because the renderings of the verb tenses in Answers (B) "will arrive," (C) "would arrive," and (D) "had wished," are incorrect.

36. **(D)**
The relevant Latin in line 7 reads, "but it is granted (**licet**) that they (**illae**, the panthers), having been delayed by a storm (**tempestate detentae**) were late (**cessaverint**). **Cessaverint** is perfect subjunctive after **licet** (for impersonal verbs, see Chapter 14D). Thus, Answer (D) "did not arrive on time because of a storm" is correct.

37. **(C)**
The Latin says, "you nonetheless deserved that the credit (**acceptum**, a financial term referring to something entered into the credit column) should go (**fieret**) to you, because (**quod**) it was not your fault (**non per se stetit**, an idiomatic use of **stetit**) that you could not show them (**quo minus exhiberes**)." Therefore, Answer (C) "Valerius deserves credit for his intentions" is correct.

38. **(D)**
The words **quo minus** (sometimes spelled **quominus**) introduce the subjunctive clause **quo minus . . . exhiberes**. **Quo minus** is found with the subjunctive when hindering or preventing is stated or implied, as it is here. Answer (A) **licet** governs **cessaverint**; Answer (B) **ut** introduces a clause with **fieret**; Answer (C) **quod** introduces a causal clause with **stetit**. For subjunctive clauses, see Chapter 16D, Section 6.

## "A festival celebrates the blessings of the farm"

39. **(A)**
The required lines (1–2) tell us "the earth and the ploughman should have a day of rest on festival day (**Luce sacra**) and that, with the plough lifted (**suspenso vomere**), the heavy work should cease." "The plough lifted" refers to the removal of the ploughshare from the earth. Answer (A) "a day of rest for all" is the correct answer. Note the metonymy of light (**Luce**) for day.

40. **(B)**

With **suspenso, vomere** completes the ablative absolute. For this construction, see Appendix 9.

41. **(D)**

Lines 3–4 are translated, "Now the oxen, with garlanded heads, should stand at feeding troughs that are full," leading to Answer (D) "the cattle should be fed well." The other answers exploit, but confuse, the wording of this sentence. **Solvite vincla iugis** refers to loosening the harnesses from the yokes.

42. **(C)**

Answer (C) "Let all things be done for the god" correctly translates **Omnia sint operata deo** (line 5). **Sint** is a jussive subjunctive, the subject of which is the substantive **Omnia**, modified by the adjective **operata**. **Deo** refers, presumably, to Bacchus, Ceres, or some other divinity associated with fertility or the farm. At the beginning of the poem, which is not provided here, both of these deities are invoked in celebration of the festival. For independent subjunctives, see Chapter 16D, Section 2.

43. **(D)**

In line 6, the dative case of **pensis** depends upon the compound verb **imposuisse**. This portion of the sentence reads, "let no one (**nec . . . ulla**) dare to have applied (**imposuisse**) her spinner's hand (**lanificam . . . manum**) to the **pensum** (the day's work). For the dative case, see Chapter 13A.

44. **(B)**

The translation of lines 7–8 leads to the meaning, "I bid you all be far away; let him depart from the altar to whom Venus (love) brought pleasure last night (**hesterna gaudia nocte**)." Thus, Answer (B) "must stay away from the festival" is correct. Use scansion to determine whether **hesterna** is accusative modifying **gaudia** or ablative with **nocte**. (It is the latter.)

45. **(C)**

The substitution of **Venus** for love or passion is metonymy. For figures of speech, see Chapter 10.

46. **(B)**

The possible answers require careful reading! Answer (B) "draw the spring's water with pure hands" is correct. Answer (A) "wash their garments in pure spring water" incorrectly translates **pura cum veste venite** ("arrive with purified garments") and Answer (C) "make chaste offerings to the gods with pure garments" incorrectly interprets **Casta placent superis** ("Purity is pleasing to the gods")." Answer (D) "draw purified water by hand from the spring" is incorrect because **puris** modifies **manibus** and not **aquam**.

47.  **(D)**

Answer (D), "Observe how the sacred lamb goes to the shining altars," is correct. Answer (A) reverses **fulgentes** (shining) and **sacer** (sacred); Answer (B) incorrectly renders **fulgentes** as vocative; and Answer (C) incorrectly translates **eat** as future tense. **Eat** is present subjunctive of the verb **eo, ire** in an indirect question introduced by **ut**. For irregular verbs, see Chapter 14C; for present participles, see Chapter 16A; for subjunctive clauses with **ut**, see Chapter 16D, Section 4.

48.  **(A)**

The word **fulgentes** is pulled away from the prepositional phrase **ad aras** and placed in an emphatic position, framing the activity anticipated to take place at the altar: **fulgentes ut eat sacer agnus ad aras**. For anastrophe and hyperbaton, see Chapter 10.

49.  **(C)**

Scansion of this pentameter line (the second line of an elegiac couplet, for which, see Chapter 11) helps you to determine that the **–a** of **olea** is long and that therefore **olea** is ablative (of means).

50.  **(C)**

Answer (A) sacrificial procession refers to the preceding line. Answer (B) exploits the appearance of the word **olea** (olive tree) as a distractor and Answer (D) exploits the context of the poem, which is about farming. This difficult final line is rendered "behind it (referring to the procession taking the sacrificial lamb to the altar) a throng (garbed) in white (cf. line 9), their hair bound up (literally, bound up as to their hair or with regard to their hair) with olive branches (**vinctaque olea ... comas**)." The past participle **vinctaque** (from **vincio**, not **vinco**) modifies **candida turba**.

## Translations of the Multiple-Choice Passages

### "Catullus critiques another poet"

That Suffenus, Varus, whom you know well, is a man charming, witty, and sophisticated, and that very same man writes multitudes of verses, by far. I think that thousands or tens of thousands or more verses have been written by him, not, as usually happens, composed on palimpsest, (but) top-grade paper, new rolls, new ornamental knobs, red straps, parchment wrappers, having been ruled with lead, and all made even with pumice-stone. When you read these (verses), that charming and sophisticated Suffenus seems at the same time a goat-milker and ditch-digger: so much is he unlike himself and is he transformed.

### "Romulus reacts to news of his brother's death"

When the king (Romulus) learned this (that his brother had been killed), he chokes back the tears having welled up inside and keeps the wound closed away in his heart. He does not wish to weep openly and he maintains strength as an example.[1] "Let it be the same for (any) enemy who should cross my walls," he says. Nonetheless, he conducts the funeral rites (and), no longer able to hold back the tears, his hidden devotion is disclosed and he presses final kisses (on the body) placed on the bier, and says, "O brother, taken from me before your time, farewell!" (Romulus) annointed the body about to be cremated. Both Faustulus and Acca, having loosened her hair in grief, did what he had done. Then the not-yet-citizen Quirites wept for the youth. At last the fire has been placed under the pyre after it was lamented, i.e., the lamentable pyre.

### "Pliny congratulates a friend"

You have done well, Valerius, because you have sponsored gladiatorial games for our fellow citizens of Verona, by whom for a long time now you are loved, respected, and honored. You had a wife, also from there (Verona) who was very dear to and most compatible with you, to/in whose memory you owe either some public work or show, and this is very much the kind of show that is especially appropriate for a funeral. Moreover, you were asked by so many people, that to refuse would seem not resolute, but rude. You did that admirably too, the fact that you were so efficient and lavish in producing (the games); for even through things like this, the true spirit (of generosity) is shown. If only the panthers, which you had purchased in quantity, had arrived on the appointed day: but

---

[1] The verbs in the present tense in this passage may be translated as past.

granted that they, having been delayed by a storm, were late, you nonetheless deserved that the credit should go to you, because it was not your fault that you could not show them. Farewell.

## "A festival celebrates the blessings of the farm"

On (this sacred day) let the earth rest, let the ploughman rest and, with the plough lifted (from the soil), the heavy work should cease. Loosen the harness from the yokes; now the oxen with garlanded heads should stand at feeding troughs that are full. Let all things be done for the god; let no one dare to have applied her spinner's hand to the day's work. Also, I bid that you be far away, let him depart from the altar to whom love brought pleasure last night. Purity is pleasing to the gods: come with pure garments and draw the spring's water with pure hands. Look how the sacred lamb proceeds to the shining altar and behind (it) the white-robed throng, their hair bound up with olive leaves.

# Answers to Free-Response Section

## REQUIRED AUTHOR

## Question 1 (Catullus)

### Translation

You once said that you knew only Catullus (or that Catullus alone knew you), Lesbia, and that you did not wish to possess Juppiter in preference to me. I cherished you then, not so much as a common man his mistress, but as a father cherishes his sons and sons-in-law. Now I know you: therefore, even though I burn more passionately (for you), you are nevertheless much cheaper and more fickle to me. How is this possible? you ask. Because such an indignity obliges a lover to love more, but to like less.

## Grading

### *9 pts. total, one-half point for each segment. Round your score up!*

1. dicebas quondam
2. solum te nosse Catullum
3. nec (te) . . . velle
4. prae me. . . tenere Iovem
5. dilexi tum te
6. non tantum . . . sed
7. ut vulgus amicam (diligit)
8. sed (ut) pater et gnatos diligit et generos
9. nunc te cognovi
10. quare etsi
11. impensius uror
12. multo . . . vilior et levior
13. mi tamen es
14. Qui potis est? inquis
15. quod . . . iniuria talis
16. cogit amantem
17. amare magis
18. sed bene velle minus

## Acceptable Translations for Question 1

For instructional purposes, more grammatical and syntactical information is provided here than is usually found in the grading reports on the translation question.

1. **dicebas**: (you) said/were saying/maintaining/asserting/stating/declaring

   **quondam**: once/formerly/once upon a time/previously

2. **solum**: alone/only [must modify **Catullum** because **solum** is masculine]

   **te**: you [ambiguous: can be the subject or object of **nosse**, but refers to Lesbia]

   **nosse**: knew/became acquainted with/got to know [acceptable in either past or present tense; **nosco** in the perfect tense means "know." Note: although this word has sexual overtones, it is best not to express these in your answer, as what might be considered "offensive language" by a Reader can disadvantage you.]

   **Catullum**: [serves as either the subject or object of **nosse** in the indirect statement after **dicebas**; see above]

3. **nec**: and not/nor [connects **nosse**, line 1, with **tenere**, line 2]

   **velle**: wished/wanted/was willing [present infinitive translated in the past tense because of **dicebas**, line 1. The subject is **te** (Lesbia) carried over from line 1]

4. **prae me**: in preference to me/before me/instead of me/in place of me

   **tenere**: possessed/kept/held [when taken with **prae**, may be translated "prefer"; past tense after **dicebas**]

5. **dilexi**: I cherished/loved/adored/idolized

   **tum**: then/at that time

   **te**: you (Lesbia)

6. **non tantum . . . sed**: idiomatic, "not only . . . but " or "so much . . . but"

7. **ut**: as [the indicative verb **diligit**, line 4, is understood]

   **vulgus**: common, ordinary, everyday man, man-on-the-street

   **amicam**: mistress/girlfriend/female friend/girl/friend/lover

8. **sed**: but [connects line 3 with line 4]

   **pater**: father

   **et . . . et**: both . . . and [may be rendered simply as "(sons) and (sons-in-law)"]

   **gnatos**: son/child

   **diligit**: (he) cherishes/loves/takes delight in

   **generos**: son-in-law

9. **nunc**: now/at present/at this moment

   **te**: you [= Lesbia]

   **cognovi**: I have recognized/gotten to know/become acquainted with [may be translated in present tense, just as **nosse** in line 1]

10. **quare**: therefore/wherefore/on which account [referring to **nunc te cognovi**]

    **etsi**: although/even if

11. **impensius**: passionately/intensely [comparative adverb, must be taken with **uror**]

    **uror**: I burn/am on fire [may be translated in the active voice, i.e., "I myself am burning (emotionally)"]

12. **multo**: much/by much [ablative degree of difference]

    **vilior**: cheap/worthless/vile/despicable/sordid/vulgar/tacky

    **levior**: fickle/trifling/unimportant/"light"

13. **mi**: to me [with **es**, "you are to me," "you seem to me," "you are in my view or sight "]

    **tamen**: nevertheless/however

    **es**: (you) are

14. **qui**: how/in what way

    **potis est**: be possible/be able/can [= **potest**]

    **inquis**: (you) say/declare/state [the subject, if expressed specifically, may be either "you (Lesbia)," or "you (the reader)"]

15. **quod**: because/since

    **iniuria**: indignity/insult/injury/affront/abuse/humiliation/embarrassment

    **talis**: such/of such a kind or type [modifies **iniuria**]

16. **cogit**: (it, the **iniuria**) obliges/requires/necessitates/compels/forces

    **amantem**: lover [substantive use of the present participle; object of **cogit**]

17. **amare**: to love **magis**: more

18. **sed**: but/however

    **bene velle**: to like/be fond of [literally, "to wish well"; the contrast between **amare magis** and **bene velle minus** may be expressed in several ways, i.e., "to be more of a lover and less of a friend" or "to be more loving and less obliging or well-disposed"]

    **minus**: less [must contrast with **magis**]

# Question 2 (Catullus)

## Long Essay

For the grading scale used for evaluating essays, see Chapter 7. Here are some high points of each speech to consider in your comparative analysis, followed by a sample essay. Such observations, which will set up your formal essay, may be made in writing during the 15-minute reading period. The sample essays may seem overly thorough, but the author is attempting to accommodate the wide range of answers that will be given by users of this book.

(A) Catullus falls in love with Lesbia at first sight.

- Catullus describes himself as jealous of the man she's with and praises her implicitly as a goddess (1–2)

- Catullus is unhappy (misero) because Lesbia is enjoying herself with this man (dulce ridentem, 5)

- The poet "loses his senses" (omnes eripit sensus): his tongue grows swollen, his limbs tingle, his ears ring from the inside, and he seems to be dizzy (9–12)

The visual is emphasized in Poem 51, as is appropriate for love at first sight: <u>videtur</u>, <u>spectat</u>, <u>aspexi</u>, <u>lumina</u>. In a general sense, both <u>misero</u> (A, 5) and <u>misere</u> (B, 6) refer to the lovesickness that the would-be lovers are feeling. However, in another, more specific way, the word <u>misere</u> in the Ariadne passage (B) introduces <u>exagitans immiti corde furores</u> (4) and <u>qualibus . . . iactasti . . . . fluctibus</u> (6–7), which strongly foreshadow Ariadne's subsequent pain and suffering.

(B) Ariadne falls in love with Theseus, who has just arrived in Crete

- she cannot turn away her passionate gaze (<u>non . . . flagrantia declinavit lumina</u>, 1)

- she is completely on fire inside (<u>cuncto . . . funditus</u>, 2–3)

- she is entirely aflame in her innermost marrow (<u>imis exarsit tota medullis</u>, 3)

An anguished (<u>heu</u>, <u>misere</u>, 4) apostrophe to Cupid, who with ruthless heart (<u>immiti corde</u>) stirs up passion (<u>furores</u>) and mingles joys (of love) with troubles (5)

The apostrophe continues in 6–7 by describing Ariadne (still on fire, <u>incensam . . . mente</u>, 6) as tossed on the waves and as often sighing (<u>saepe suspirantem</u>) for her blonde-haired visitor.

Standard language and images for falling/being in love: falling in love at first sight (<u>non . . . lumina</u>, 1–2, esp. <u>flagrantia</u>), being completely on fire (<u>cuncto . . . funditus</u>, esp. <u>flammam</u>, 2–3), and burning deep inside her marrow (<u>imis . . . medullis</u>, esp. <u>exarsit</u>, 3). More fire in line 6 (<u>incensam</u>), which is "doused with water" in line 7 (<u>fluctibus</u>)! The emotions are accented by the metaphors (fire for passion) and by the alliteration of <u>cuncto concepit corpore</u> in line 2.

## Sample Long Essay

Each passage describes someone falling in love at first sight: in Passage (A), Catullus describes his feelings upon seeing Lesbia for the first time and in Passage (B), the feelings of Ariadne are described after she first met Theseus.

Catullus is obviously in the presence of Lesbia, at least within ear- and eyeshot, whereas it is unclear whether Ariadne has done anything more than look upon Theseus. The tone of Passage (A) seems somehow upbeat, despite Catullus' claim that he is "blue" (<u>misero</u>, line 5), because of the enthusiasm and anticipation implicit in his description of the physical consequences of seeing Lesbia (albeit stolen from Sappho). He is lovesick: his tongue swells (<u>lingua sed torpet</u>), his limbs tingle (<u>tenuis . . . demanat</u>; note the appearance of <u>flamma</u>, a metaphor for love), his ears ring from inside (<u>sonitu . . . aures</u>), and he grows dizzy (<u>gemina . . . nocte</u>). In Passage (A), Catullus is preoccupied with the visual, which is appropriate for love at first sight: <u>videtur</u> (line 1), <u>spectat</u> (line 4), <u>aspexi</u> (line 7), and <u>lumina</u> (line 12). Passage (A), which begins with an intriguing and blasphemous pronouncement about Lesbia, ends with a dazzling display of poetic wit, including the double-sounds of ringing in the ears (<u>sonitu</u>

suopte and tintinant, lines 10–11) and, in lines 11–12, contrast (lumina nocte), metaphor (lumina), transferred epithet (gemina), and sound play (gemina . . . lumina), all used to describe the poet's lovesickness.

Although we know that Catullus later has difficulties (cf. curis, Passage B, line 5) in his relationship with Lesbia, we do not feel the foreboding in Passage (A) that we do in (B). Ariadne also feels physically lovesick – as soon as she sees him, she cannot help staring (non . . . lumina, 1–2), and her body catches on fire with passion (flammam, line 2, and imis exarsit . . . medullis, line 3). But, there seems to be a darker side to love here. Although the image of fire continues (incensam, line 6), it is "doused" by troubled waters (qualibus . . . fluctibus, lines 6–7). The apostrophe to Cupid (lines 4–7) sets a melancholy tone (heu misere, line 4) which implies that the consequences of love for Ariadne may not be what she had hoped. Cupid has a cruel heart (immiti corde, line 4) and he stirs up madness (exagitans . . . . furores), mingles difficulties (curis) with the joys (gaudia) of love, and tosses Ariadne about on the ever-changing but redundant waves of the sea (lines 6–7). The apostrophe to Cupid provides "chorus-like" commentary on the price of falling in love. A quick-scan of a random line (line 8) shows a preponderance of spondees, which slows down the pace and adds to the more solemn tone of the apostrophe. The onomatopoeia of suspirantem (with saepe!) in line 9 also perhaps contributes the suggestion of a sigh of depression, as well as infatuation.

## Question 3 (Catullus)

### Short Essay

For the grading scale used for evaluating essays, see Chapter 7. Here are some highlights of Poem 36 to consider in your analysis.

Catullus asks the Annals of Volusius to pay up, since Lesbia has fulfilled her vow to the gods of love.

Poem 36 begins and ends at the same place (1–2 and 14–16). The poet, in an apostrophe, orders the Annals of Volusius to "come into the fire" (venite in ignem, 14) in order to pay off Lesbia's vow (3–4, 12–13).

Lesbia has vowed that she would sacrifice to the love gods (Veneri Cupidinique, 3) the "choicest writings of the worst poet" (electissima pessimi poetae scripta) if Catullus did not cease writing invectives about her (desissemque truces vibrare iambos, 5) and come back to her arms (si sibi restitutus essem, 4). At this point, we presume that, by pessimi poetae, Lesbia means Catullus himself. The fashionable words of the novi poetae used in lines 10 (iocosis and lepide) and 13 (illepidum and invenustum) suggest that this is all in good fun (Lesbia, too, is characterized as "wicked," pessima . . . puella, 9).

Catullus appropriately asks Venus, the goddess of love, to accept the fact that the terms of the vow have been fulfilled (nunc . . . invenustum est, 11–13), i.e., that Catullus and Lesbia have reconciled.

The "joke" is that Catullus has substituted the writing of Volusius, apparently a notoriously bad writer about whom Catullus complains elsewhere, for his own. It is Volusius who is the <u>pessimus poeta</u>. The fun begins and ends with name-calling, i.e., Volusius' <u>Annals</u> are only good for use as toilet paper! Catullus distinguishes between his own poems of invective, or "wicked verses," (<u>truces . . . iambos</u>) and Volusius' simply bad writing (<u>pleni ruris et infactiarum</u>).

## Sample Short Essay

Poem 36 begins and ends at the same place (lines 1–2 and 14–16). The poet, in an apostrophe, orders the <u>Annals</u> of Volusius to "come into the fire" (<u>venite in ignem</u>, 14) in order to pay off the vow of his girlfriend Lesbia (lines 3–4, 12–13). Lesbia has vowed that she would sacrifice to the love gods (<u>Veneri Cupidinique</u>, line 3) the "choicest writings of the worst poet" (<u>electissima pessimi poetae scripta</u>) if Catullus did not cease writing invectives about her (<u>desissemque truces vibrare . . . iambos</u>, line 5) and come back to her (<u>si sibi restitutus essem</u>, line 4).

At this point, we presume that, by <u>pessimi poetae</u>, Lesbia means Catullus himself. (She would only call him this if they were not getting along!) The fashionable words of the <u>novi poetae</u> used in lines 10 (<u>iocosis</u> and <u>lepide</u>) and 13 (<u>illepidum</u> and <u>invenustum</u>) suggest that this is all in good fun (Lesbia, too, is characterized as wicked, <u>pessima . . . puella</u>, line 9). The poet uses mock-epic or hyper-poetic phrases, e.g., <u>tardipedi deo</u> (= Vulcan = fire, line 7), <u>infelicibus . . . lignis</u> ("unlucky" because the wood is used to burn bad poetry, line 8), and <u>caeruleo creata ponto</u> (= Venus, line 11), to exaggerate the whole situation. He also employs sound play by selecting sibilant words (to hiss at Lesbia? Volusius?): <u>essem</u>, <u>desissem</u>, <u>electissima</u>, <u>pessimi</u>, and <u>pessima</u> (lines 4–9).

Catullus appropriately asks Venus, the goddess of love, to accept the fact that the terms of the vow have been fulfilled (<u>nunc . . . invenustum est</u>, 11–13), i.e., that Catullus and Lesbia have reconciled. The "joke" is that Catullus has substituted the writing of Volusius, apparently a notoriously bad writer and about whom Catullus complains elsewhere, for his own. It is Volusius who is the <u>pessimus poeta</u>. The fun begins and ends with name-calling, i.e., Volusius' <u>Annals</u> are only good for use as toilet paper! Catullus distinguishes between his own poems of invective, or "wicked verses," <u>truces . . . iambos</u>) and Volusius' simply bad writing (<u>pleni ruris et infactiarum</u>). So . . . Catullus and Lesbia get back together at the cost of a little teasing and both have fun at Volusius' expense.

## CHOICE AUTHOR

# Question 4 (Cicero)

## Short Essay

For the grading scale used for evaluating essays, see Chapter 7. Here are some points to consider in your discussion of Cicero's thoughts about friendship.

Cicero considers the merits of friendship.

- friendship (<u>amicitia</u>) creates hope for the future (<u>quod</u> . . . <u>posterum</u>, 2) and fosters strength of spirit (<u>nec</u> . . . <u>patitur</u>, 2–3)

- a true friend (<u>verum</u> . . . <u>amicum</u>, 3) is seen as an image of oneself (<u>tamquam</u> . . . <u>sui</u>, 3–4)

- friends, although absent, are still at hand (<u>absentes adsunt</u>, 4)

- when there is "a friend in need, there is a friend indeed" (<u>egentes</u> . . . <u>valent</u>, 4)

- in times of weakness, friends are strong (<u>imbecilli valent</u>, 4)

- although dead, friends can yet be alive (<u>mortui vivunt</u>, 5)

Respect, reminiscence, and longing (<u>honos</u>, <u>memoria</u>, <u>desiderium</u>, 5) provide the living friend with fond memories. The dead seem fortunate (<u>beata mors videtur</u>, 6) because they have had friends, and the living seem to have lives worthy of praise (<u>vita laudabilis</u>, 6), because they remember their departed friends.

## Sample Short Essay

In his treatise <u>De Amicitia</u>, Cicero explores the nature of friendship (<u>amicitia</u>). In this passage, he discusses some of the advantages that come to and from friends.

An introductory statement that friendship has many advantages (<u>plurimas et maximas commoditates</u>) leads to the general observation that friendship exceeds all things in the respect that it creates hope for the future (<u>bonam spem praelucet in posterum</u>, line 2) and fosters strength of spirit (<u>nec debilitari</u> . . . <u>patitur</u>, lines 2–3).

The metaphorical use here of <u>praelucet</u>, meaning to shine a light upon someone or something, and the medical associations of the words <u>debilitari</u> . . . <u>aut cadere</u>, suggest that the importance of friendship is something greater than the literal meanings of the words. Cicero goes on to declare that when someone looks at a true friend, he looks at a sort of image of himself (<u>exemplar sui</u>, lines 3–4). The redundancy of <u>intuetur</u> in this sentence perhaps suggests the "double image" of a friend being like another self. He continues by virtually listing the advantages of friendship in a series of four hard-hitting, antithetical, two-word combinations. Friends, although absent, are still at hand (<u>absen-</u>

tes adsunt, line 4); when there is "a friend in need, there is a friend indeed" (egentes . . . valent, line 4); in times of weakness, friends are strong (imbecilli valent, line 4); and, although they may be dead, friends are yet alive (mortui vivunt, line 5). At the end of the passage, Cicero expands upon this last observation, by claiming that respect, recollection, and reminiscence (note the forceful asyndeton of honos, memoria, and desiderium, line 5) can keep friends "alive." He ends with the statement that, dead or alive, one need friends. The dead seem fortunate (beata mors videtur, line 6) because they have had friendships and the living seem worthy of praise (vita laudabilis, line 6) because they cherish the memory of their friends.

# Question 5 (Cicero)

## Translation

Finally, in what way can anyone blame me or can anyone rightly censure me, if, as much time as is given to others to dealing with their own affairs (or) to celebrating festivals during holidays, (as much time as is given) to other pleasures and to the very rest of the mind and body, as (much time as) some devote to convenient dinner parties, and finally to the game-board or ball-playing, I will have devoted as much (time) in cultivating these intellectual pursuits for myself?

## Grading

### *9 pts. total, one-half point for each segment. Round up your score!*

1. quare
2. quis . . . me reprehendat
3. aut quis mihi . . . suscenseat
4. iure
5. si . . . (sumpsero)
6. quantum . . . ceteris (temporum conceditur)
7. ad suas res obeundas
8. quantum (temporum conceditur)
9. ad festos dies ludorum celebrandos
10. quantum ad alias voluptates (temporum conceditur)
11. ad ipsam requiem animi et corporis
12. (quantum) conceditur temporum
13. quantum alii tribuunt tempestivis conviviis
14. quantum (alii tribuunt) denique alveolo
15. quantum (alii tribuunt) pilae
16. (quantum) . . . tantum

17. (si) . . . mihi egomet . . . sumpsero

18. ad haec studia recolenda

## Acceptable Translations for Question 5

For instructional purposes, more grammatical and syntactical information is provided here than is usually found in the grading reports on the translation question.

1. **quare**: in what way/how

2. **quis**: who **me**: me (= Cicero)

   **reprehendat**: would blame/scold/reprimand/condemn/find fault with [deliberative subjunctive]

3. **aut**: or

   **quis**: who

   **mihi**: me [dative object after compound **suscenseo**]

   **suscenseat**: would censure/be angry at/bear a grudge with respect to

4. **iure**: rightly/with good reason/according to the law [modifies **suscenseat**]

5. **si**: if [introduces **sumpsero**, line 6, in protasis of a condition; brackets a series of **quantum** clauses which correlate with **tantum** . . . **sumpsero**, 5–6]

6. **quantum**: as much [all examples of **quantum** to follow correlate with **tantum**, 5; the first three are subjects of **conceditur**, 6]

   **ceteris**: others/some (people)/the rest/the remaining [dative after **conceditur**]

7. **ad**: to/for the purpose of **suas res**: their own affairs/matters/interests/possessions and property ["their own" may be rendered as "their"]

   **obeundas**: dealing with/attending to/taking on/undertaking [gerundive of purpose after **ad**; **ad** . . . **obeundas** may be translated "to deal with," etc.]

8. **quantum**: see above, #6

9. **ad**: to/for

   **festos dies**: festivals/festal or festive days/(public) holidays **ludorum**: holiday/game/show [may be combined with **festos dies** to mean "festivals" or "holidays"]

   **celebrandos**: celebrating/attending [gerudive of purpose with **ad**; may be translated "to celebrate"]

10. **quantum**: see above, #6 **ad**: to/for

    **alias**: other/different/various

    **voluptates**: pleasure/delight/enjoyment/amusement [singular or plural]

11. **ad**: to/for

    **ipsam**: very/itself [emphasizes **requiem**]

    **requiem**: rest/quiet/peace/relaxation/repose

    **animi**: mind/soul/spirit

    **corporis**: body/flesh

12. **quantum**: see above, #6

    **conceditur**: is given/granted/used

    **temporum**: time [partitive genitive with **quantum**, throughout lines 2 and 3; may be translated as singular]

13. **quantum**: as much [this and succeeding appearances of **quantum (temporum)** are objects of **alii tribuunt**, 4]

    **alii**: some/other

    **tempestivis**: convenient/timely [could refer to early or late]

    **conviviis**: dinner party/banquet/feast/entertainment [dative after **tribuunt**]

14. **quantum**: see above, #13

    **denique**: finally/at last

    **alveolo**: game or gaming board [dative after **tribuunt**]

15. **quantum**: see above, #13

    **pilae**: ball playing/ball-game/ball [dative after **tribuunt**]

16. **tantum**: as much/also much [correlates with **quantum** throughout]

17. **mihi**: for me [indirect object of **sumpsero**]

    **egomet**: I myself [emphatic form of **ego**]

    **sumpsero**: (I) will have devoted/given/spent [completes the condition introduced by **si**, line 1]

18. **ad**: to/for the purpose of

    **haec studia**: these intellectual pursuits/studies/pursuits [must be plural]

    **recolenda**: for cultivating/nurturing [gerundive of purpose after **ad**; may be rendered "to cultivate," etc.]

# Question 6 (Cicero)

## Short Answer

There are eight points possible for this question. Latin support is provided below for your convenience, but is not required in your answer, unless stated in the question.

1(a) **1 point**

Hoc refers to everyone's desire for praise (trahimur ... ducitur, 2–3), which serves as the antecedent of the quod-clause in line 1.

1(b) **1 point**

We must not pretend with regard to what is obvious to all, but we must abide (the fact that we are all influenced by the desire for praise).

2. **1 point**

This segment in lines 2–3 consists of two independent clauses (trahimur omnes studio laudis and optimus quisque maxime gloria ducitur) bracketed by the "bookend" arrangement of trahimur and ducitur. This arrangement is chiastic, where trahimur and ducitur are a pair, then omnes and optimus quisque, then the ablatives studio and gloria. (Either or both of these observations earns the point.)

3. **1 point**

We are all influenced (trahimur) by the desire for praise (studio laudis) and the best of any of us (optimus quisque) is greatly impressed (maxime ducitur) with public reputation (gloria).

4(a) **1 point**

Even philosophers write their names on the very books in which they scorn ambition and pride.

4(b) **1 point**

Contemnenda is a gerundive because it modifies gloria.

5. **1 point**

In (the book) itself (in eo ipso) in which they disdain (despiciunt) public recognition (praedicationem) and celebrity (nobilitatemque), they desire to be recognized (praedicari) and called by name (nominari).

6. **1 point**

With the virtual polyptoton of the noun praedicationem and the verb praedicari (and the noun nobilitatem and the verb nominari), Cicero mocks the philosophers for what is an unacceptable hypocrisy. Comments about scribunt and inscribunt (line 4) are also acceptable.

# Question 7 (Horace)

## Short Essay

For the grading scale used for evaluating essays, see Chapter 7. Here are some points to consider in your analysis of *Odes* 3.13.

Horace celebrates the spring on his Sabine farm. Examples of the use of contrast (antithesis):

- the waters of the spring are clearer than crystal (<u>splendidior vitro</u>, 1)
- the sacrificial death of the kid-goat (3–6) vs. the offspring of the "frisky flock" (<u>lascivi suboles gregis</u>, 8); <u>lascivi</u> (8) also contrasts with <u>fessis</u> (11), describing the goat and the cattle, respectively
- love (<u>Venerem</u>, 5) and war (<u>proelia</u>, 5)
- cold waters (<u>gelidos . . . rivos</u>, 6–7) and (hot) blood (<u>rubro sanguine</u>, 7); the red blood contrasts in color and temperature with the crystal-clear water, although both are life fluids
- the hot season of summer (<u>flagrantis . . . Caniculae</u>, 9) contrasts with the cool refreshment of the water (<u>frigus amabile</u>, 10)
- The static images of the oak and the rocks (<u>ilicem saxis</u>, 14–15) contrast with the dynamic images of the "babbling waters leaping down" (<u>loquaces lymphae desiliunt</u>, 15–16)

## Sample Short Essay

Horace's <u>fons Bandusia</u>, while seemingly a simple poem in its message, is highly complex in the ways in which the poet conveys his message of life and death. The spring, which the poet is celebrating during the annual festival of the Fontinalia, is the source of life for his farm. And the life of the farm is perpetuated by sacrificial death, in this case that of a kid-goat (<u>haedo . . . primis</u>, 3–5). One of the poetic means by which Horace communicates his message is that of antithesis, or contrast, which brings not only narrative interest to the poem, but a sense of familiarity to the reader.

The death of the young goat, expired before its horns had grown enough for it to fight and mate (<u>Venerem et proelia</u>, 5, themselves contrast), is distinguished from its life as the "offspring of the frisky flock" (<u>lascivi suboles gregis</u>, 8). Note, too, that the goats are lively while the cattle are weary (<u>fessis</u>, 11). The imagery of color and temperature also contributes to the contrast of life and death in this poem. The waters of Bandusia are crystal-clear and (<u>splendidior vitro</u>, 1) and offer cool refreshment (<u>gelidos . . . rivos</u>, 6–7, and <u>frigus amabile</u>, 10). These images contrast with those connected to the sacrificial death of the goat: redness of the blood (<u>rubro sanguine</u>, 7) and the hot life-blood of the just-killed goat (note the effective juxtaposition and framing of <u>rubro sanguine</u>, the dying goat, which is "immersed in" the <u>gelidos . . . rivos</u>, the cool spring-waters, in Stanza 2). The contrast between hot and cold extends into Stanza 3, where the dog days of summer (<u>flagrantis atrox hora Caniculae</u>, 9) are compared with the cool sustenance of the spring's water (<u>frigus amabile</u>, 10). In the final stanza, the message is maintained by the correlation of static images, the oak (<u>ilicem</u>, 14) and the rocks (<u>saxis</u>, 15) with the "babbling waters leaping down" (<u>loquaces lymphae desiliunt</u>, 15–16). Although foliage often appears as a life-image in Horace's poems, here it serves the second purpose of emphasizing, through its fixture in the rock, the liveliness of the spring. What have become stock images are sometimes mixed elsewhere in the poem, where warmth is usually equated with life and cold with death, but it is the appearance of such paradoxes that makes poems interesting and successful.

Ode 3.13 is a memorable poem because of its vivid imagery, an important part of which is the effective use of contrast. Hot and cold, light and dark, fast and slow, dynamic and static, all help the reader to experience the welcome coolness of the spring, which is the lifeblood of Horace's Sabine farm.

# Question 8 (Horace)

## Translation

Do not ask, it is forbidden to know, what end the gods have given to me (or) to you, Leuconoe, and do not test Babylonian astrologers. How much better (it is) to accept whatever will be, whether Jupiter allots (us) more winters or the final (one), which now wears out the Tyrrhenian Sea with its opposing rocks: you should be wise, strain your wine, and cut back lengthy hope within (our) brief time (of life). While we are speaking, envious time flees: seize today, trusting as little as possible in tomorrow.

## Grading

*9 pts. total, one-half point for each segment. Round your score up!*

1. tu ne quaesieris
2. scire nefas
3. quem mihi (finem), quem tibi finem
4. di dederint
5. nec Babylonios temptaris numeros
6. ut melius . . . pati
7. quidquid erit
8. seu plures hiemes (tribuit Iuppiter)
9. seu tribuit Iuppiter ultimam
10. quae nunc . . . debilitat
11. mare Tyrrhenum
12. oppositis . . . pumicibus

13.  sapias, vina liques

14.  et spatio brevi spem longam reseces

15.  dum loquimur

16.  fugerit invida aetas

17.  carpe diem

18.  quam minimum

19.  credula postero

## Acceptable Translations for Question 8

For instructional purposes, more grammatical and syntactical information is provided here than is usually found in the grading reports on the translation question.

1.  **tu**: you [refers to Leuconoe]

    **ne quaesieris**: do not ask/inquire/seek/desire to know [**ne** + perfect subjunctive = poetic alternative to prose imperative **noli quaerere**]

2.  **scire**: to know/understand/comprehend/realize/fathom

    **nefas**: forbidden/impious/not allowed by the gods [understand **est**, used impersonally with "it" as subject]

3.  **quem**: what [modifies **finem**, object of **dederint**]

    **mihi . . . tibi**: to/for me, to/for you [indirect objects of **dederint**; may use "and/or" i.e., "you and/or me"; may apply the English courtesy of placing the other person first, or retain the Latin, i.e., "you and me" or "me and you"]

    **finem**: end/limit/boundary/death [= end of life]

4.  **di**: [= **dei**]

    **dederint**: (they) have given/allotted/assigned/allocated [perfect subjunctive in indirect question dependent upon **quem finem**]

5.  **nec**: and . . . not [= **ne . . . (temptaris)**; cf. line 1]

    **Babylonios**: Babylonian/Chaldean/Mesopotamian/Eastern

    **temptaris**: (you) test/make trial of/probe/question/inspect [= **temptaveris**, perfect subjunctive in alternative command, parallel to (**ne**) **. . . quaesieris**, line 1]

    **numeros**: astrologer/number/calculation/star/(astrological) tables

6.  **ut**: how **melius**: better

    **pati**: to accept/endure/allow/stand for/submit to

7.  **quidquid**: whatever [object of **pati**]

    **erit**: will be/occur/happen

8. **seu**: whether

   **plures**: more/added/manifold/

   **hiemes**: winter [metonymy for "year" or "time," which is acceptable]

9. **seu**: or [**seu . . . seu** = "whether . . . or"]

   **tribuit**: (he) allots/assigns/allocate [may be translated as present or perfect tense]

   **Iuppiter**: Jupiter/Jove **ultimam**: final/last [modifies **hieme**, understood; note the condensation and parallelism, **seu plures hiemes (tribuit Iuppiter) seu tribuit Iuppiter ultimam (hiemem)**, in this line]

10. **quae**: which [refers to **ultimam (hiemem)**]

    **nunc**: nunc: now/at this time

    **debilitat**: (it) wears out, away, or down/weaken/diminish

11. **mare**: sea/ocean [accusative singular object of **debilitat**]

    **Tyrrhenum**: Tyrrhenian/Tuscan/Etruscan

12. **oppositis**: opposing/facing/placed against/hostile

    **pumicibus**: rock/pumice or pumice-stone [may be translated as "cliff" via synecdoche; ablative of means]

13. **sapias**: (you, Leuconoe) should be wise/sensible/intelligent [the verbs in this sentence are jussive subjunctives]

    **vina**: wine [may be taken as singular]

    **liques**: (you) should strain/purify/remove the sediment from [jussive subjunctive]

14. **et**: [connects **liques** with **reseces**]

    **spatio**: time/limit/space or period (of time) [may be taken as a metaphor for "lifetime" = **aetate**; ablative of cause]

    **brevi**: brief/short/fleeting/short-term/swift/short-lived

    **spem**: hope [may be translated as plural]

    **longam**: lengthy/long/extended

    **reseces**: (you) should cut back/prune/restrain/limit/restrict/contain [jussive subjunctive]

15. **dum**: while

    **loquimur**: (we) are speaking/talking/holding forth

16. **fugerit**: (it) will have fled/will have run away [may be translated as present tense, "flees"]

    **invida**: envious/jealous/grudging/unfavorable/hostile

    **aetas**: time/age/time or period of life

17. **carpe**: seize/pick/pluck [properly means "pick the flower" or "reap the harvest"; this meaning is acceptable in translation]

    **diem**: (to)day [may be taken as a metaphor for "opportunity" or "moment"]

18. **quam minimum**: "as little as possible" (**quam** + superlative = "as . . . as possible"]

19. **credula**: trusting/believing/relying on/depending upon [adjective modifying **Leuconoe**, line 2]

    **postero**: tomorrow/next/later/future/coming after [**diei**, dative after **credula**, is understood with

    **postero** = "the next day," "tomorrow"]

# Question 9 (Horace)

## Short Answer

There are eight points possible for this question. Latin support is provided below for your convenience, but is not required in your answer, unless stated in the question.

1. **1 point**

   Horace is walking along the Sacred Way (Ibam forte via Sacra, 1), absorbed in thinking about little or nothing at all (nescio quid meditans nugarum, totus in illis, 2)

2. **1 point**

   Notus mihi nomine tantum (3), "known to me only by name."

3. **1 point**

   "How are you doing, most delightful fellow in all the world?" "Okay (i.e., agreebly, satisfactorily), as things stand now," I say, "and I desire everything that you wish" (i.e., I hope things are turning out the way you want).

4(a) **1 point** "You don't want anything, do you?"

4(b) **1 point**

   "(I wish that) you would get to know me; I am a learned person." (Nos and sumus (7) are poetic plurals.)

4(c) **1 point**

   "You will be (worth) more to me because of this."

5. **1 point**

   "I was going (or preceeding or moving)."

6. **1 point**

1. He tries desperately to get away (<u>Misere discedere quaerens</u>, 8)

OR

2. He walked a little faster (<u>ire modo ocius</u>, 9)

OR

3. He stopped perdiocially (<u>interdum consistere</u>, 9)

OR

4. He said something o his slave (<u>in aurem discere nescio quid puero</u>, 9–10)

OR

5. He began to sweat all the way to his feet (<u>cum sudor ad imos manaret talos</u>, 10–11)

# Question 10 (Ovid)

## Short Essay

For the grading scale used for evaluating essays, see Chapter 7. Here are some points to consider in your analysis of "Daedalus and Icarus."

Daedalus instructs his son Icarus in the skill of flying. Examples of foreshadowing:

- <u>genae maduere seniles</u> (1)
- <u>patriae tremuere manus</u> (2) Note the chiasmus of <u>genae maduere (seniles)</u> . . . <u>(patriae) tremuere manus</u> (1–2)
- <u>dedit oscula nato non iterum repetenda suo</u> (2–3)
- <u>damnosasque</u> (6)
- words that suggest fear or anxiety (<u>monitus</u>, 1; <u>ante volat</u> and <u>timet</u>, 4; <u>respicit</u>, 7)
- simile of the young bird (4–5) "protected" in the center of the nest (<u>ab alto</u> . . . <u>teneram prolem</u> . . . <u>nido</u>). The words <u>alto</u>, 4 (the nest is high) and <u>teneram</u>, 5 (the bird is young) contribute to the overall sense of anticipation.

## Sample Short Essay

Daedalus' sollicitous concern for his son Icarus as they plan to make good their flight from King Minos speaks to all fathers and sons. He plans for the worst by making the best preparations (<u>monitusque</u>, 1 and <u>hortaturque</u>, 6) and by expressing love for his son (<u>dedit oscula nato</u>, 2).

The father's anxiety is revealed through description of his tear-stained cheeks (<u>genae maduere seniles</u>, 1) and trembling hands (<u>patriae tremuere manus</u>, 2). Something more than a hint is given in the foreboding words <u>dedit</u>

oscula nato non iterum repetenda suo (2–3), "he gave his son kisses not to be given again." He teaches his son the "destructive or ruinous" skills (damnosasque erudit artes, 6) Daedalus is a doting and sollicitous parent throughout the passage (monitusque, 1, ante volat, 4, timet, 4, respicit, 7). The simile of the young bird (velut . . . nido, 4–5), which places the birdlet (teneram prolem) protectively in the middle of the high (alto) nest, adds touching imagery to the contrast between young (teneram) and old (seniles, 1), and therefore between impulsive and careful. Despite his craftsmanship and instruction (inter opus monitusque, 1), Daedalus seems to sense impending disaster.

The words and images of precognition in this passage hint at the approaching doom of Icarus, hints that develop into a full-blown sense of dread on the part of the reader. The chiastic interplay of words in lines 1–2, genae maduere seniles et patriae tremuere manus, brings an ironic balance to unbalanced premonition and emphasizes the tone of the entire passage.

# Question 11 (Ovid)

## Translation

Poor me! Accurate were the arrows that boy had: I am on fire, Love rules in my empty heart. Let my work rise up in six measures and let it fall back in five; farewell, iron wars with your (six) measures. Bind your golden locks, with myrtle from the seashore, Muse, to be measured out in eleven feet!

## Grading

### *9 pts. total, one-half point for each segment. Round your score up!*

1. me miserum
2. certas . . . sagittas
3. habuit puer ille
4. uror
5. et in vacuo pectore
6. regnat Amor
7. sex . . . numeris
8. mihi surgat opus
9. in quinque (numeris) residat
10. ferrea . . . bella
11. cum vestris . . . modis
12. valete
13. cingere
14. flaventia . . . tempora
15. litorea . . . myrto

16. Musa

17. per undenos . . . pedes

18. emodulanda

## Acceptable Translations for Question 11

For instructional purposes, more grammatical and syntactical information is provided here than is usually found in the grading reports on the translation question.

1. **me**: me [= Ovid; exclamatory accusative]

   **miserum**: poor/unhappy/unfortunate/wretched

2. **certas**: accurate/sure/certain/sure-fire

   **sagittas**: arrow/shaft/dart/missile

3. **habuit**: (he) had

   **puer ille**: that boy [= Cupid]

4. **uror**: (I) am on fire/burning/aflame/I burn

5. **et**: [connects **uror** and **regnat**]

   **vacuo**: empty/vacant/desolate

   **in . . . pectore**: in (my) heart ["chest" is overly literal, but permissible]

6. **regnat**: (he) rules/reigns/holds sway/is in power

   **Amor**: Love/Cupid

7. **sex**: six

   **numeris**: measure/number/foot/metrical unit [the preposition **in** later in the line is brought back to here as an ablative of place where]

8. **mihi**: my [dative of reference, "with reference or respect to me"]

   **surgat**: let (it) rise up/arise/stand up [jussive subjunctive]

   **opus**: work/labor/effort [neuter, nominative singular; serves as the subject of both **surgat** and **residat**: [the translation of "writing" or "poetry" for "Ovid's "work" is acceptable]

9. **in**: in [ablative of place where]

   **quinque**: five **residat**: let (it) fall back/settle back/sit down [jussive subjunctive; Ovid is acknowledging that elegiac meter has a line of six feet, followed by one of five]

10. **ferrea**: iron [by synecdoche, may be translated "cruel, vicious, violent"]
    **bella**: wars [may be translated as singular]

11. **cum . . . modis**: with (your six) measures [ablative of accompaniment]
    **vestris**: your [refers to **bella**]

12. **valete**: farewell/goodbye [directed at **bella**, which is personified]

13. **cingere**: bind/gird/tie up/fasten/secure/wrap [passive imperative with active meaning]

14. **flaventia**: golden/yellow/blonde

    **tempora**: temple = side of the head [not "time"!]

15. **litorea**: from or of the seashore

    **myrto**: myrtle/ivy [note how the **litorea . . . myrto** "binds up" the **flaventia tempora**!]

16. **Musa**: Muse/Erato [vocative]

17. **per . . . pedes**: in/through feet/measures

    **undenos**: eleven or eleven at a time or each [= a line of six plus a line of five feet]

18. **emodulanda**: to be measured [also acceptable is "to be sung to the lyre," which includes the entire meaning of **emodulor**]

# Question 12 (Ovid)

## Short Answer

There are eight points possible for this question. Latin support is provided below for your convenience, but is not required in your answer, unless stated in the question.

1. **1 point**

    Thisbe didn't want to deceive her lover (ne fallat amantem, 1)

    AND

    She did want to tell him about her dangerous adventure (quantaque vitarit narrare pericula gestit, 2).

2(a) **1 point**

    Vitarit is perfect subjunctive.

2(b) **1 point**

    Vitarit is a perfect subjunctive in an indirect question clause of indirect question, quantaque vitarit, 2.

2(c) **1 point**

    Vitaverit.

3. **1 point**

    She thought that she had returned to the agreed-upon tree of their rendezvous, but was uncertain because the color was different (sic facit pomi color, 5), since Pyramus' blood had stained the fruit red.

4. **1 point**

    Interlocked word order (synchysis), tremebunda . . . cruentum membra solum.

5. **1 point**

<pre>
  -    u u -   u  u -   u u -   - - u  u-  -
</pre>
Dum dubitat tremebunda videt pulsare cruentum;

this is a hexameter line. The cadence suggests the death throes of Pyramus' body.

6. **1 point**

Simile 1: <u>oraque buxo pallidiora gerens</u>, "displaying a face paler (or more pale) than boxwood"

Simile 2: <u>exhorruit aequoris instar, quod tremit, exigua cum summum stringitur aura</u>, "she shuddered (or trembled) like the sea, which ripples when struck on the surface by a slight breeze."

# ANSWER SHEETS

## AP Latin

# PRACTICE EXAM 1

## AP Latin: Vergil

## Multiple-Choice Section

### Answer Sheet

1. Ⓐ Ⓑ Ⓒ Ⓓ
2. Ⓐ Ⓑ Ⓒ Ⓓ
3. Ⓐ Ⓑ Ⓒ Ⓓ
4. Ⓐ Ⓑ Ⓒ Ⓓ
5. Ⓐ Ⓑ Ⓒ Ⓓ
6. Ⓐ Ⓑ Ⓒ Ⓓ
7. Ⓐ Ⓑ Ⓒ Ⓓ
8. Ⓐ Ⓑ Ⓒ Ⓓ
9. Ⓐ Ⓑ Ⓒ Ⓓ
10. Ⓐ Ⓑ Ⓒ Ⓓ
11. Ⓐ Ⓑ Ⓒ Ⓓ
12. Ⓐ Ⓑ Ⓒ Ⓓ
13. Ⓐ Ⓑ Ⓒ Ⓓ
14. Ⓐ Ⓑ Ⓒ Ⓓ
15. Ⓐ Ⓑ Ⓒ Ⓓ
16. Ⓐ Ⓑ Ⓒ Ⓓ
17. Ⓐ Ⓑ Ⓒ Ⓓ

18. Ⓐ Ⓑ Ⓒ Ⓓ
19. Ⓐ Ⓑ Ⓒ Ⓓ
20. Ⓐ Ⓑ Ⓒ Ⓓ
21. Ⓐ Ⓑ Ⓒ Ⓓ
22. Ⓐ Ⓑ Ⓒ Ⓓ
23. Ⓐ Ⓑ Ⓒ Ⓓ
24. Ⓐ Ⓑ Ⓒ Ⓓ
25. Ⓐ Ⓑ Ⓒ Ⓓ
26. Ⓐ Ⓑ Ⓒ Ⓓ
27. Ⓐ Ⓑ Ⓒ Ⓓ
28. Ⓐ Ⓑ Ⓒ Ⓓ
29. Ⓐ Ⓑ Ⓒ Ⓓ
30. Ⓐ Ⓑ Ⓒ Ⓓ
31. Ⓐ Ⓑ Ⓒ Ⓓ
32. Ⓐ Ⓑ Ⓒ Ⓓ
33. Ⓐ Ⓑ Ⓒ Ⓓ
34. Ⓐ Ⓑ Ⓒ Ⓓ

35. Ⓐ Ⓑ Ⓒ Ⓓ
36. Ⓐ Ⓑ Ⓒ Ⓓ
37. Ⓐ Ⓑ Ⓒ Ⓓ
38. Ⓐ Ⓑ Ⓒ Ⓓ
39. Ⓐ Ⓑ Ⓒ Ⓓ
40. Ⓐ Ⓑ Ⓒ Ⓓ
41. Ⓐ Ⓑ Ⓒ Ⓓ
42. Ⓐ Ⓑ Ⓒ Ⓓ
43. Ⓐ Ⓑ Ⓒ Ⓓ
44. Ⓐ Ⓑ Ⓒ Ⓓ
45. Ⓐ Ⓑ Ⓒ Ⓓ
46. Ⓐ Ⓑ Ⓒ Ⓓ
47. Ⓐ Ⓑ Ⓒ Ⓓ
48. Ⓐ Ⓑ Ⓒ Ⓓ
49. Ⓐ Ⓑ Ⓒ Ⓓ
50. Ⓐ Ⓑ Ⓒ Ⓓ

# Free-Response Section

Use the following pages to prepare your essays.

# **Free-Response Section** *(Continued)*

# PRACTICE EXAM 2

## AP Latin: Vergil

## Multiple-Choice Section

### Answer Sheet

1. Ⓐ Ⓑ Ⓒ Ⓓ
2. Ⓐ Ⓑ Ⓒ Ⓓ
3. Ⓐ Ⓑ Ⓒ Ⓓ
4. Ⓐ Ⓑ Ⓒ Ⓓ
5. Ⓐ Ⓑ Ⓒ Ⓓ
6. Ⓐ Ⓑ Ⓒ Ⓓ
7. Ⓐ Ⓑ Ⓒ Ⓓ
8. Ⓐ Ⓑ Ⓒ Ⓓ
9. Ⓐ Ⓑ Ⓒ Ⓓ
10. Ⓐ Ⓑ Ⓒ Ⓓ
11. Ⓐ Ⓑ Ⓒ Ⓓ
12. Ⓐ Ⓑ Ⓒ Ⓓ
13. Ⓐ Ⓑ Ⓒ Ⓓ
14. Ⓐ Ⓑ Ⓒ Ⓓ
15. Ⓐ Ⓑ Ⓒ Ⓓ
16. Ⓐ Ⓑ Ⓒ Ⓓ
17. Ⓐ Ⓑ Ⓒ Ⓓ

18. Ⓐ Ⓑ Ⓒ Ⓓ
19. Ⓐ Ⓑ Ⓒ Ⓓ
20. Ⓐ Ⓑ Ⓒ Ⓓ
21. Ⓐ Ⓑ Ⓒ Ⓓ
22. Ⓐ Ⓑ Ⓒ Ⓓ
23. Ⓐ Ⓑ Ⓒ Ⓓ
24. Ⓐ Ⓑ Ⓒ Ⓓ
25. Ⓐ Ⓑ Ⓒ Ⓓ
26. Ⓐ Ⓑ Ⓒ Ⓓ
27. Ⓐ Ⓑ Ⓒ Ⓓ
28. Ⓐ Ⓑ Ⓒ Ⓓ
29. Ⓐ Ⓑ Ⓒ Ⓓ
30. Ⓐ Ⓑ Ⓒ Ⓓ
31. Ⓐ Ⓑ Ⓒ Ⓓ
32. Ⓐ Ⓑ Ⓒ Ⓓ
33. Ⓐ Ⓑ Ⓒ Ⓓ
34. Ⓐ Ⓑ Ⓒ Ⓓ

35. Ⓐ Ⓑ Ⓒ Ⓓ
36. Ⓐ Ⓑ Ⓒ Ⓓ
37. Ⓐ Ⓑ Ⓒ Ⓓ
38. Ⓐ Ⓑ Ⓒ Ⓓ
39. Ⓐ Ⓑ Ⓒ Ⓓ
40. Ⓐ Ⓑ Ⓒ Ⓓ
41. Ⓐ Ⓑ Ⓒ Ⓓ
42. Ⓐ Ⓑ Ⓒ Ⓓ
43. Ⓐ Ⓑ Ⓒ Ⓓ
44. Ⓐ Ⓑ Ⓒ Ⓓ
45. Ⓐ Ⓑ Ⓒ Ⓓ
46. Ⓐ Ⓑ Ⓒ Ⓓ
47. Ⓐ Ⓑ Ⓒ Ⓓ
48. Ⓐ Ⓑ Ⓒ Ⓓ
49. Ⓐ Ⓑ Ⓒ Ⓓ
50. Ⓐ Ⓑ Ⓒ Ⓓ

# Free-Response Section

Use the following pages to prepare your essays.

# Free-Response Section *(Continued)*

# PRACTICE EXAM 1

## AP Latin Literature

### Multiple-Choice Section

## Answer Sheet

1. Ⓐ Ⓑ Ⓒ Ⓓ
2. Ⓐ Ⓑ Ⓒ Ⓓ
3. Ⓐ Ⓑ Ⓒ Ⓓ
4. Ⓐ Ⓑ Ⓒ Ⓓ
5. Ⓐ Ⓑ Ⓒ Ⓓ
6. Ⓐ Ⓑ Ⓒ Ⓓ
7. Ⓐ Ⓑ Ⓒ Ⓓ
8. Ⓐ Ⓑ Ⓒ Ⓓ
9. Ⓐ Ⓑ Ⓒ Ⓓ
10. Ⓐ Ⓑ Ⓒ Ⓓ
11. Ⓐ Ⓑ Ⓒ Ⓓ
12. Ⓐ Ⓑ Ⓒ Ⓓ
13. Ⓐ Ⓑ Ⓒ Ⓓ
14. Ⓐ Ⓑ Ⓒ Ⓓ
15. Ⓐ Ⓑ Ⓒ Ⓓ
16. Ⓐ Ⓑ Ⓒ Ⓓ
17. Ⓐ Ⓑ Ⓒ Ⓓ

18. Ⓐ Ⓑ Ⓒ Ⓓ
19. Ⓐ Ⓑ Ⓒ Ⓓ
20. Ⓐ Ⓑ Ⓒ Ⓓ
21. Ⓐ Ⓑ Ⓒ Ⓓ
22. Ⓐ Ⓑ Ⓒ Ⓓ
23. Ⓐ Ⓑ Ⓒ Ⓓ
24. Ⓐ Ⓑ Ⓒ Ⓓ
25. Ⓐ Ⓑ Ⓒ Ⓓ
26. Ⓐ Ⓑ Ⓒ Ⓓ
27. Ⓐ Ⓑ Ⓒ Ⓓ
28. Ⓐ Ⓑ Ⓒ Ⓓ
29. Ⓐ Ⓑ Ⓒ Ⓓ
30. Ⓐ Ⓑ Ⓒ Ⓓ
31. Ⓐ Ⓑ Ⓒ Ⓓ
32. Ⓐ Ⓑ Ⓒ Ⓓ
33. Ⓐ Ⓑ Ⓒ Ⓓ
34. Ⓐ Ⓑ Ⓒ Ⓓ

35. Ⓐ Ⓑ Ⓒ Ⓓ
36. Ⓐ Ⓑ Ⓒ Ⓓ
37. Ⓐ Ⓑ Ⓒ Ⓓ
38. Ⓐ Ⓑ Ⓒ Ⓓ
39. Ⓐ Ⓑ Ⓒ Ⓓ
40. Ⓐ Ⓑ Ⓒ Ⓓ
41. Ⓐ Ⓑ Ⓒ Ⓓ
42. Ⓐ Ⓑ Ⓒ Ⓓ
43. Ⓐ Ⓑ Ⓒ Ⓓ
44. Ⓐ Ⓑ Ⓒ Ⓓ
45. Ⓐ Ⓑ Ⓒ Ⓓ
46. Ⓐ Ⓑ Ⓒ Ⓓ
47. Ⓐ Ⓑ Ⓒ Ⓓ
48. Ⓐ Ⓑ Ⓒ Ⓓ
49. Ⓐ Ⓑ Ⓒ Ⓓ
50. Ⓐ Ⓑ Ⓒ Ⓓ

# Free-Response Section

Use the following pages to prepare your essays.

# Free-Response Section (Continued)

# PRACTICE EXAM 2

## AP Latin Literature

### Multiple-Choice Section

## Answer Sheet

1. Ⓐ Ⓑ Ⓒ Ⓓ
2. Ⓐ Ⓑ Ⓒ Ⓓ
3. Ⓐ Ⓑ Ⓒ Ⓓ
4. Ⓐ Ⓑ Ⓒ Ⓓ
5. Ⓐ Ⓑ Ⓒ Ⓓ
6. Ⓐ Ⓑ Ⓒ Ⓓ
7. Ⓐ Ⓑ Ⓒ Ⓓ
8. Ⓐ Ⓑ Ⓒ Ⓓ
9. Ⓐ Ⓑ Ⓒ Ⓓ
10. Ⓐ Ⓑ Ⓒ Ⓓ
11. Ⓐ Ⓑ Ⓒ Ⓓ
12. Ⓐ Ⓑ Ⓒ Ⓓ
13. Ⓐ Ⓑ Ⓒ Ⓓ
14. Ⓐ Ⓑ Ⓒ Ⓓ
15. Ⓐ Ⓑ Ⓒ Ⓓ
16. Ⓐ Ⓑ Ⓒ Ⓓ
17. Ⓐ Ⓑ Ⓒ Ⓓ

18. Ⓐ Ⓑ Ⓒ Ⓓ
19. Ⓐ Ⓑ Ⓒ Ⓓ
20. Ⓐ Ⓑ Ⓒ Ⓓ
21. Ⓐ Ⓑ Ⓒ Ⓓ
22. Ⓐ Ⓑ Ⓒ Ⓓ
23. Ⓐ Ⓑ Ⓒ Ⓓ
24. Ⓐ Ⓑ Ⓒ Ⓓ
25. Ⓐ Ⓑ Ⓒ Ⓓ
26. Ⓐ Ⓑ Ⓒ Ⓓ
27. Ⓐ Ⓑ Ⓒ Ⓓ
28. Ⓐ Ⓑ Ⓒ Ⓓ
29. Ⓐ Ⓑ Ⓒ Ⓓ
30. Ⓐ Ⓑ Ⓒ Ⓓ
31. Ⓐ Ⓑ Ⓒ Ⓓ
32. Ⓐ Ⓑ Ⓒ Ⓓ
33. Ⓐ Ⓑ Ⓒ Ⓓ
34. Ⓐ Ⓑ Ⓒ Ⓓ

35. Ⓐ Ⓑ Ⓒ Ⓓ
36. Ⓐ Ⓑ Ⓒ Ⓓ
37. Ⓐ Ⓑ Ⓒ Ⓓ
38. Ⓐ Ⓑ Ⓒ Ⓓ
39. Ⓐ Ⓑ Ⓒ Ⓓ
40. Ⓐ Ⓑ Ⓒ Ⓓ
41. Ⓐ Ⓑ Ⓒ Ⓓ
42. Ⓐ Ⓑ Ⓒ Ⓓ
43. Ⓐ Ⓑ Ⓒ Ⓓ
44. Ⓐ Ⓑ Ⓒ Ⓓ
45. Ⓐ Ⓑ Ⓒ Ⓓ
46. Ⓐ Ⓑ Ⓒ Ⓓ
47. Ⓐ Ⓑ Ⓒ Ⓓ
48. Ⓐ Ⓑ Ⓒ Ⓓ
49. Ⓐ Ⓑ Ⓒ Ⓓ
50. Ⓐ Ⓑ Ⓒ Ⓓ

# Free-Response Section

Use the following pages to prepare your essays.

# Free-Response Section *(Continued)*

# AP LATIN

## Appendices

# Guide to Electronic Resources

## AP Latin Resources of the College Board[1]

### Bibliography of Publications Useful for Exam Preparation

- *Latest edition of the AP Latin Course Description* (published annually or biennially, last published for the 2006 and 2007 exams) (Item # 727247) *2005 AP Latin Literature and Latin: Vergil Released Exams*, complete multiple-choice and free-response sections of both the Vergil and Literature exams (Item #05008172)
- *1999 AP Latin Literature and Latin: Vergil Released Exams* (Item #255180)
- *1994 AP Latin Free-Response Guide with Multiple-Choice Section* (Item #255154)
- *Teacher's Guide (for AP Latin)*, by Jeff S. Greenberger, n.d. (Item #989390)
- Relevant issues of *The Classical Outlook* (The Journal of the American Classical League).

Note:

> Each year in *The Classical Outlook (CO)*, an analytical report on each of the two AP Latin Exams is given by the Chief Reader. This report provides valuable feedback on how the expectations of the teachers who designed the exams were met by the students who took the exams. This report, which also includes scoring guidelines, and sample student and Reader responses, is especially useful because it provides insight into the grading of literal translations required on the free-response sections. See, for example, John Sarkissian, "The Grading of the 2005 Advanced Placement Examinations in Latin: Vergil," *CO*, Fall 2005, Vol. 83, No. 1, pp. 1–12.

The materials listed above are available from the CBO (College Board Online) Web site **http://apcentral.collegeboard.com** (click on "The Exams," then "Exam Questions Index" then "Latin Literature" or "Latin: Vergil"). Additional resources are available from

> College Board Publications
> Dept. CBO
> PO Box 869010
> Plano, TX 75074
> (212) 713–8165

---

[1] As of this writing, scoring information and data about the 2006 AP Latin Exam were not available.

## Webliography of online sites useful for exam preparation

- The Official College Board AP Latin website:
  http://apcentral.collegeboard.com

  For the AP Latin: Vergil Course Home Page, go to
  http://apcentral.collegeboard.com/latinvergil

  For the AP Latin Literature Course Home Page, go to

  http://apcentral.collegeboard.com/latinlit

- Note:
  Within these Web pages, you may may download the *AP Latin Course Description* "Acorn Book" and gain access to specific course and exam information, e.g., sample teacher-made multiple-choice questions. These pages provide much information about the exams, including the complete free-response sections for recent years of the Exam and the scoring rubrics for each, plus sample student and Reader responses.

- An Unofficial Website for AP Latin (Ginny Lindzey and the Texas Classical Association)

  http://txclassics.org/aplatin.htm

- "Useful Internet Links for AP Latin" (Barbara McManus and Marianthe Colakis, VRoma = Virtual Rome, Miami University, Oxford, OH)

  http://www.vroma.org/-bmcmanus/aplinks.html

# Online Latin Texts of All AP Latin Authors

- Bibliotheca Augustana (Ulrich Harsch, Augsburg University, Germany)
  http://www.fh-augsburg.de/-harsch/Chronologia/Lsante01/Vergilius/ver_intr.html
  Unannotated texts, plus additional resources in Latin.

- The Latin Library at Ad Fontes Academy
  http://thelatinlibrary.com
  Unannotated texts.

- The Perseus Digital Library (click on Classics, then scroll down to "P. Vergilius Maro")
  http://www.perseus.tufts.edu
  Latin hypertexts and online parsers.

# Webliography for Vergil

The Web sites provided in this book have been chosen for their utility and "user-friendliness" in helping you to prepare for the AP Latin Exam. All sites are active as of 2006. For the best current textbooks and translations, consult your teacher, and see also the following book, which has been well-received by AP Latin students: Christine G. Perkell, ed., *Reading Vergil's* Aeneid: *An Interpretive Guide*, Oklahoma Series in Classical Culture, University of Oklahoma Press, 1999.

## The Life and Works of Vergil

- Aelius Donatus, Life of Vergil (David Wilson-Okamura, virgil.org)
  http://virgil.org/vitae/
  Fourth-century CE biographer of Vergil, translated by Wilson-Okamura.

- The Secret Life of a Very Private Poet (William Harris, Middlebury College)
  http://community.middlebury.edu/~harris/Classics/Vergil-TheSecretLife.html

- Suetonius, Life of Vergil (Fordham University)
  http://www.fordham.edu/halsall/pwh/suet-vergil.html
  Loeb translation, 1913.

- Wikipedia hypertext article on Vergil
  http://en.wikipedia.org/wiki/Virgil

## Useful General Resources for Vergil and the *Aeneid*

- AP Vergil site (Tim Abney, Marquette High School)
  http://abney.homestead.com/aeneid.html

  Teacher website chock full o' goodies for AP Latin, including helpful writing tips and grammar review materials; updated regularly.

- Article on the *Aeneid* (Classics Technology Center, Ablemedia)
  http://ablemedia.com/ctcweb/netshots/vergil.htm
  Hypertext discussion of literary epic, historical background for Vergil; reading the *Aeneid*; questions on comprehension and interpretation.

- Electronic Resources for the *Aeneid* (The Evolution of the Female Image in the Epic Tradition, Zina B. Lewis, Monmouth College)
  http://personal.monm.edu/lewis_zinab/webpages/epicpoetlinks/vergilwebsites.htm
  Links to current websites on Vergil and the *Aeneid*. See also Jim O'Hara, UNC-Chapel Hill, http://www.unc.edu/~oharaj/VergilLinks.html.

- Mr. J's Vergil Page (Bruce M. Johnson, Park View High School)
  http://www.hoocher.com/vergil.htm
  Includes useful teacher-produced articles on the Augustan Age, the epic hero, and the mythological background of the Trojan War.

- The Story of Aeneas (Instructor Resources, The Nature of Roman Mythology, support website for Mark P.O. Morford and Robert J. Lenardon, *Classical Mythology*, 7ᵗʰ edition, Oxford Univ. Press)

  http://www.us.oup.com/us/companion.websites/0195153448/instructorresources/?view=usa

  Outline of book content: legends of the founding of Rome, the tradition before Vergil, Vergil's *Aeneid*, Aeneas as a new epic hero, etc.

- The Vergil Project (The Legend of Aeneas and the Foundation of Rome, Vergil's *Aeneid*: Commentary, Univ. Pennsylvania)

  http://vergil.classics.upenn.edu/comm2/legend/legend.html

  Hypertext article bridging the time of Trojan Aeneas with that of the Alban Kings and Romulus and Remus.

- The Virgil Home Page (Steven Hale, DeKalb College)

  http://www.gpc.edu/~shale/humanities/literature/world_literature/virgil.html

  Links to online texts and translations, background readings, Internet resources on the *Aeneid*, Vergil websites.

- Virgil.org (David Scott Wilson-Okamura)

  http://virgil.org

  Thorough collection of information about Vergil's life and works, including information about the commentator Servius, the Latin text of "The Thirteenth Book of the *Aeneid*," etc., plus a search engine for the *Aeneid*.

For a sample description of a college course on Vergil's *Aeneid* (David Cramer, Univ. Texas), go to http://ccwf.cc.utexas.edu/~dcramer/312k/. See also, "The Epic Tradition" (Rob S. Rice, Univ. Pennsylvania), http://ccat.sas.upenn.edu/rrice/clas160.html.

## Translations of the *Aeneid*

- Romans Online

  http://www.romansonline.com/sources/vrg/Indx01.asp

  Hypertext English translation by Theodore H. White (1910) with facing Latin text.

- Anthony (Tony) S. Kline (2002)

  http://www.tkline.freeserve.co.uk/Virgilhome.htm

- Andrew Wilson (The Classics Pages, 2003)

  http://www.users.globalnet.co.uk/%7Eloxias/oldindex.htm

  Translations of Books 1 (2005), 2, 4, and 6; Books 2 and 6 are hypertexts, with or without frames. Book 6 is incomplete.

# Webliography for Latin Literature

The Web sites provided in this book have been chosen for their utility and "user-friendliness" in helping you to prepare for the AP Latin Exam. All sites are active as of 2006. For the best current textbooks and translations, consult your teacher. A book useful for its simple but cogent analyses of the poems but, alas, now out of print, is Stuart G.P. Small's, *Catullus, a Reader's Guide to the Poems,* Roman and Little-field, 1983. See also the resources listed in Chapter 8.

## Catullus

### *Useful General Resources for Catullus*

- AP Catullus Page (Tim Abney, Marquette High School)
  http://abney.homestead.com/catullus.html
  See activities for scansion and figures of speech under "Working with Individual Poems."

- C. Valerius Catullus (John Porter, Univ. Saskatchewan)
  http://duke.usask.ca/-porterj/CourseNotes/CatullusNotes.html
  The poems and life of Catullus: Catullus as *Eques*; Catullus as Neoteric Poet; Catullus and Lesbia (cross-linked with English translations of relevant Catullan poems).

- Catullus' Social Set: His Friends, Lovers, Rivals (Henry Walker, Bates College, VRoma)
  http://www.vroma.org/-hwalker/VRomaCatullus/Friends.html

- Catullus Web Sites (Useful Internet Links for AP Latin, Barbara McManus and Marianthe Colakis, VRoma),
  http://www.vroma.org/-bmcmanus/aplinks.html
  Three useful sites on background, and five on texts, all annotated.

- The Life of Catullus (Derek Adams, Sol Magazine)
  http://www.solpubs.freeserve.co.uk/catullus.htm
  Reconstruction of the life of Catullus, using translated excerpts from his poems as resources.

- Mr. J's Catullus Page (Bruce M. Johnson, Park View High School),
  http://www.hoocher.com/catullus.htm
  Links to teacher-produced biography of Catullus, many links to other common-used Catullan web sites

- Links for the Study of Catullus (Alison W. Barker, VRoma)
  http://www.vroma.org/-abarker/catulluslinks.html
  Eighteen links to texts, history and culture, and language and meter.

- The Modern Student's Guide to Catullus (Raymond M. Koehler, Brunswick School, Ablemedia, Classics Technology Center),
  http://ablemedia.com/ctcweb/consortium/catullusguideintro.html
  Fictional scenario in Catullan Room of Museum of Lyric; Latin texts of Poems 1, 51, 8, 85, 7; 2, 85, 4, 8 read/sung aloud. Cross-linked to Walker's VRoma texts and translations.

### Latin Texts and Translations of Catullus

- The Gaius Valerius Catullus Society [**Latin texts**]
  http://www.informalmusic.com/Catullus/
  Includes Latin texts of all poems, numbered every five lines, and links useful for Catullan meters.

- Anthony (Tony) S.Kline (2001) [**translations**]
  http://www.adkline.freeuk.com/Catullus.htm
  Best translations online; with titles.

- Rudy Negenborn (Utrecht, Netherlands) [**Latin texts with translations**]
  http://www.negenborn.net/catullus/
  Translations in many languages, Latin texts, sample scansions.

- Shocked Catullus (Robert Larson, Kent State University) [**Latin hypertexts**]
  http://www.personal.kent.edu/~rlarson/catullus/
  Needs Shockwave plug-in. Does not include syllabus poems added in 2005, but excellent for reading practice.

- VRoma Catullus web site (Henry Walker, Bates College) [**Latin texts with translations**]
  http://www.vroma.org/~hwalker/VRomaCatullus/
  Latin text with side-by-side/facing line-by-line translation. Linked to Merrill's Perseus text. Includes many support resources.

- Wikipedia hypertext article on Catullus [**select Latin texts and translations**]
  http://en.wikipedia.org/wiki/Catullus
  Latin texts of 24 poems, with translations of the 18 that appear on the AP syllabus. Poem 1 is scanned in hendecasyllabic meter. Cross-linked with Walker's VRoma site.

For a sample AP Catullus-Ovid high school reading schedule (Tim Abney, Marquette High School), see http://www.tabney.com/files/catullus/ap-catullus-ovid-syllabus.htm (Term 1– Catullus, Term 2– Ovid; Catullus read in sequence of corpus numbers). See also Tom Sears, Univ. North Carolina, AP Catullus-Horace course online at http://www.learnnc.org/courses/AP_Latin_Literature.

# The Choice Authors

## Cicero

### *Useful General Resources for Cicero*

- AP Cicero Web site (Bruce M. Johnson, Park View High School)
  http://www.hoocher.com/cicero.htm
  Good source of links.

- The Cicero Homepage (Andrew M. Riggsby, Univ. Texas-Austin)
  http://www.utexas.edu/depts/classics/documents/Cic.html
  Links to major Latin texts of Cicero, chronology of life, bibliography.

- Cicero Web Sites (Useful Internet Links for AP Latin, Barbara McManus
  and Marianthe Colakis, VRoma)
  http://www.vroma.org/-bmcmanus/aplinks.html
  Six sites usful for background (not updated for *Pro Archia Poeta* and *De
  Amicitia*).

- Home and Forum: Cicero between "Public" and "Private" (Susan Treggiari,
  Stanford Univ.)
  http://www.apaclassics.org/Publications/PresTalks/TREGGIARI97.html
  Cicero's personal values in his public life.

- Wikipedia hypertext article on Cicero
  http://en.wikipedia.org/wiki/Cicero

### *Texts and Translations of* Pro Archia Poeta

- Cicero's Orations (Southwest Missouri State Univ.) [**Latin texts with
  translations**]
  http://cicero.missouristate.edu/-cicero/Orationes/default.htm
  Latin text, plus English translation.

- J.B. Greenough (via Nicholas Koenig, Univ. Texas) [**Latin text**]
  http://www.utexas.edu/depts/classics/documents/archia.html

- Claude Pavur (Saint Louis Univ.) [**Latin text**]
  http://www.slu.edu/colleges/AS/languages/classical/latin/tchmat/readers/
  accreaders/cicero/archia.htm
  The Latin text is laid out in what the College Board would consider sense
  units or "segments."

- Joseph T. Richardson (The Society for Ancient Languages) [**Latin text
  with translation**]
  http://www.uah.edu/student_life/organizations/SAL/texts/latin/classical/
  cicero/proarchia.html
  With introduction, Latin text, English translation, translation notes.

- Wikipedia: Marcus Tullius Cicero – *Orationes* – *Pro A. Licinio Archia poeta* [**Latin texts**]
  http://la.wikisource.org/wiki/Marcus_Tullius_Cicero
  This site includes the Latin texts of all orations.

### Texts and Translations of De Amicitia

- Andrew P. Peabody [**translation**]
  http://ancienthistory.about.com/library/bl/bl_text_cic_friendship.htm
  Includes introduction and a one-sentence synopsis of the complete work, section-by-section.

- Joseph T. Richardson (The Society for Ancient Languages) [**Latin text with translation**]
  http://www.uah.edu/student_life/organizations/SAL/texts/latin/classical/cicero/deamicitia.html
  Latin text, English translation, and text with facing translation.

- Wikipedia: Marcus Tullius Cicero – Operae Philosophae – *Laelius De Amicitia* [**Latin text**]
  http://la.wikisource.org/wiki/Laelius_de_Amicitia

For a typical syllabus of a college course on Cicero (Ann R. Raia, College of New Rochelle), see http://www.cnr.edu/home/araia/cicero2.htm.

## Horace

### Useful General Resources for Horace

- Analysis of the Roman *Odes* (P. Balmforth, ancienthistory.about.com)
  http://ancienthistory.about.com/gi/dynamic/offsite.htm?zi=1/XJ&sdn=ancienthistory&zu=http%3A%2F%2Fwww.angelfire.com%2Fart%2Farchictecture%2Farticles%2F046.htm
  Book 3, *Odes* 1–6 (Ode 3.1 on syllabus).

- Horace (Joan Jahnige, Kentucky Educational Television)
  http://www.dl.ket.org/latinlit/carmina/index.htm
  Biography (life, works, philosophy), people of Horace, mythical references in *Ode* 2.14, hypertext of *Satires* 1.9.

- Horace Web Sites (Useful Internet Links for AP Latin, Barbara McManus and Marianthe Colakis, VRoma)
  http://www.vroma.org/-bmcmanus/aplinks.html
  Five useful sites on background, and four on texts, all annotated.

- Links for the Study of Horace's *Odes* (Alison Barker, VRoma)
  http://www.vroma.org/-abarker/horaceodes.html
  Twelve links to texts and translations, mythology, archaeology, meter, et al., including Stoicism and Epicureanism.

- Quotations from Horace http://www.brainyquote.com/quotes/authors/h/horace.html (BrainyQuote.com)
  A convenient quick study of Horace's view of the world. See also http://www.quotationspage.com/quotes/Horace (The Quotations Page)

- Wikipedia hypertext article on Horace
  http://en.wikipedia.org/wiki/Horace
  Horace's life, works, later influence, English translators, links.

## *Texts and Translations of Horace*

## Odes

- A New Interpretation of the Pyrrha Ode (1.5) (Shirley Werner's Rutgers students, VRoma)
  http://www.vroma.org/~bmcmanus/werner_pyrrha.html
  Contrasts *Ode* 1.5 with Catullus 8.

- Anthony (Tony) S. Kline (2005) [**translations**]
  http://www.tkline.freeserve.co.uk/Horacehome.htm

- Diotima site (Steven Willett, stoa.org) [**select translations**]
  http://www.stoa.org/diotima/anthology/horawill.shtml
  Translations of *Odes* 1.5, 1.11, 1.13, 1.23, 1,25, 1.37; linked to Perseus Latin text of Horace.

- Project Gutenberg (C. Smart, Pembroke College, Cambridge, 2004) [**translations**]
  http://www.gutenberg.org/catalog/world/readfile?fk_files=106758&pageno=2

- Horace's Villa Page (Bernard Frischer) [**select Latin texts with translations**]
  http://www.humnet.ucla.edu/horaces-villa/poetry/Ode1.22.html
  Fourteen Latin texts and facing translations of poems (only two from syllabus, 3.1 and 3.3), some read aloud. Good for sight reading practice.

- Intratext [**Latin texts**]
  http://www.intratext.com/Catalogo/Autori/Aut186.HTM
  *Odes* and *Satires* 1.9. Linked to concordance.

- *Odes* (Joseph Richardson, The Society for Ancient Languages) [**Latin texts**]
  http://www.uah.edu/student_life/organizations/SAL/texts/latin/classical/horace/carmina.html
  Includes an introduction to the *Odes*.

- *Odes* of Horace (Michael Gilleland) [**select Latin texts with translations**]
  http://www.merriampark.com/horace.htm
  Latin text, translation, notes for syllabus poems 1.9, 1.11, 1.22, 1.38; 2.3, 2.14; 3.13; 4.7; includes Latin prose paraphrases of the above poems and other resources.

- Poet Seers [**select translations**]
  http://www.poetseers.org/the_great_poets/the_classics/horace/poems_horace
  Seven translated poems from the syllabus: 1.9, 1.11, 1.38, 2.3, 2.10, 2.14, 4.7.

- Shocked Horace (Robert Larson, Kent State University) [**Latin hypertexts**]
  http://www.personal.kent.edu/~rlarson/horace/
  All AP Horace poems, save *Satires* 1.9. Excellent for reading practice!

## Satires 1.9

- Kentucy Educational Television (Joan Jahnige) [**Latin hypertext**]
  http://www.dl.ket.org/latinlit/carmina/index.htm
  Wonderful color-coded Latin hypertext of *Satires* 1.9, with pop-up windows.

- The Society for Ancient Languages (Joseph J. Richardson) [**Latin hypertexts and translations**]
  http://www.uah.edu/student_life/organizations/SAL/texts/latin/classical/horace/sermones.html
  Includes introduction, hypertext, and translation notes available as a frame below the Latin text.

- Wikipedia, *Satires* 1.9 [**Latin text**]
  http://la.wikisource.org/wiki/Sermones_%28Horatius%29_-_Liber_prior_-_Sermo_IX_-_Ibam_forte_via_sacra%2C_sicut_meus_est_mos
  Numbered every five lines.

## Ovid
### *Useful General Resources for Ovid*

- AP Ovid (Tim Abney, Marquette High School)
  http://abney.homestead.com/ovid1.html
  Valuable site for interactive exercises on scansion and figures of speech for both *Metamorphoses* and *Amores*.

- Ovid Web Sites (Useful Internet Links for AP Latin, Barbara McManus and Marianthe Colakis, VRoma)
  http://www.vroma.org/~bmcmanus/aplinks.html
  Four useful links to background Web sites, and four to those on texts, all annotated.

- FAQs about Ovid (Sean Redmond)
  http://www.jiffycomp.com/smr/rob/faq/ovid_faq.php3
  Who was Ovid?, What did Ovid write? Why was Ovid exiled?, etc. Answers to questions include links to other resources.

- Wikipedia hypertext article on Ovid
  http://en.wikipedia.org/wiki/Ovid
  Works and artists inspired by Ovid, links, et al.

### Texts and Translations of the Metamorphoses

- Intratext [**Latin text**]
  http://www.intratext.com/IXT/LAT0537/_P48.HTM

- The Ovid Collection (Electronic Text Center, Univ. Virginia Library) [**Latin text**]
  http://etext.lib.virginia.edu/toc/modeng/public/OviLMet.html

- Anthony (Tony) S. Kline [**translation**]
  http://www.tkline.freeserve.co.uk/Ovhome.htm
  Recent (2000) prose paragraph translation, hyper-linked to the mythology index. Also available at http://etext.lib.virginia.edu/latin/ovid/trans/Ovhome.htm (Electronic Text Center, Univ. Virginia) and http://www.mythology.us/ovid_metamorphoses_book_1.htm

- *Metamorphoses* by Ovid [**translation**]
  http://www.mythology.us

### Texts and Translations of the Amores

- Intratext [**Latin texts**]
  http://www.intratext.com/X/LAT0086.htm

- Anthony (Tony) S. Kline (2001) [**translations**]
  http://www.adkline.freeuk.com/Amoreshome.htm

For a description of a typical college course on Ovid (Timothy Moore, Univ. Texas), see http://www.utexas.edu/depts/classics/faculty/Moore.

### Content and Analysis of the Metamorphoses

- Bookrags: *Metamorphoses*
  http://www.bookrags.com/notes/met/
  Bio, one-page plot summary, character descriptions, object/place descriptions, theme tracker (revenge, violence, women), book-by-book summaries of the mythological stories.

- Ovid's *Metamorphoses* (Larry A. Brown)
  http://larryavisbrown.homestead.com/files/xeno.ovid1.htm
  An intro and commentary, with discussion of myths and links to sources and influences in art and literature. Some analysis and thematic cross-linked summaries.

- The Structure of the *Metamorphoses* (Joseph Farrell, Univ. Pennsylvania)
  http://ccat.sas.upenn.edu/~jfarrell/courses/spring96/myth/metstruc.html
  A detailed outline of the entire work.

- Wikipedia: *Metamorphoses*
  http://en.wikipedia.org/wiki/Metamorphoses_%28poem%29

### Content and Analysis of the Amores

- Diotima article on the *Amores* (John Svarlien and Diane Arnson Svarlien, stoa.org)
  http://www.stoa.org/diotima/anthology/amores_index.shtml
  Good background information by William W. Batstone.

- Wikipedia: *Amores*
  http://en.wikipedia.org/wiki/Amores

# Online Resources for Background Questions
## Vergil
### Homer's Iliad and Odyssey, and the Story of Troy

- The Aftermath: post-*Iliad* through the *Odyssey* (Donna Patrick, et al., Ablemedia, Classics Technology Center)
  http://ablemedia.com/ctcweb/consortium/aftermathpath.html
  Multi-resource exercise takes students from the death of Patroclus in the *Iliad* to Odysseus' arrival in Ithaca.

- Classical Epic (Eugene Cotter, Seton Hall University)
  http://pirate.shu.edu/~cottereu/aeneid.htm
  Resources for a college course in classical epic (outlines of topics and questions on *Iliad, Odyssey*, and *Aeneid*).

- The Epic Cycle (Vergil's *Aeneid*: Commentary, The Vergil Project, Univ. Pennsylvania)
  http://vergil.classics.upenn.edu/comm2/sources/cycle/
  Description and discussion of post-Homeric Greek epic poems that complete the story of Homer's epics.

- The Epic Hero: Common Elements in Most Cultures (Bruce M. Johnson, Park View High School)
  http://www.hoocher.com/theepichero.htm

- Homer in the Roman Tradition (William Harris, Middlebury College)
  http://community.middlebury.edu/-harris/Humanities/homer.html
  Part of the article "Homer in a Changing Tradition."

- The Legend of the Trojan War (Ian Johnston, Malaspina University-College, BC)
  http://www.mala.bc.ca/-johnstoi/clas101/troy.htm
  Prose outline of the events of the Trojan War up to the escape of Aeneas; includes "The Cultural Influence of the Legend of the Trojan War."

- Outline of the Trojan War (Artzia.com)
  http://artzia.com/History/Ideas/Mythology/Troy/
  Summary of the events of the Trojan War up to the escape of Aeneas, with lists of participants on each side.

- Pages on the Trojan War and on Troy (Greek Mythology Link, Carlos Parada)
  http://homepage.mac.com/cparada/GML/Troy.html; see also,
  http://homepage.mac.com/cparada/GML/TrojanWar.html

- ThinkQuest website on Homer's *Iliad* and *Odyssey* (Tony Arkwright, et al.)
  http://library.thinkquest.org/19300/data/homer.htm
  Includes interactive "Virtual *Iliad*" and "Virtual *Odyssey*"; useful background information on Homer.

- The Trojan War: Mythological Background (Bruce M. Johnson, Park View High School)
  http://www.hoocher.com/trojanwar.htm
  Outline of major episodes of the Homeric poems involving gods and goddesses.

- The Underworld (Joan Jahnige, Kentucky Educational Television)
  http://www.dl.ket.org/latin1/mythology/1deities/underworld/intro.htm
  Includes links to characters and places, with some illustrations.

- "The Underworld Adventure of Aeneas in the *Aeneid*" and "*Aeneid* VI: Hades' Realm" (about.com)
  http://ancienthistory.about.com/library/weekly/aa082200a.htm
  With glossary entries, links to related subjects, and information on the corresponding passages in the *Odyssey*

- Wikipedia hypertext article on Homer
  http://en.wikipedia.org/wiki/Homer; for the Trojan War, see
  http://en.wikipedia.org/wiki/Trojan_War

- Yahoo/Geocities site on Homer and Troy
  http://www.geocities.com/Pentagon/Quarters/2471/Troy.html#Troy
  Hypertext archaeological and literary history of Troy, glossaries of gods and goddesses and Greeks and Trojans, images.

## The Augustan Age

- Augustan Sites on the Web (Resources for Augustan Studies, Eric Kondratieff, Forum Antiquum)
  http://www.sas.upenn.edu/~ekondrat/Augustus.html#Augsites
  Links to resources for the Augustan period, incl. link with The Latin Library text of the *Aeneid*.

- Augustus- Images of Power (Mark Morford, Univ. Virginia)
  http://etext.virginia.edu/users/morford/augimage.html
  Pictures and brief discussions of the visual symbols of Augustan propaganda.

- "Caesar Augustus, An Annotated Guide to Online Resources" (David Wilson-Okamura, virgil.org)
  http://virgil.org/augustus

- The Emergence of the Augustan Age (Bruce M. Johnson, Park View High School)
  http://www.hoocher.com/theemergenceoftheaugustanage.htm
  Convenient chronological outline of events in Roman history from the death of Caesar to 29 BCE.

- A Literary History of the Augustan Age (Bruce M. Johnson, Park View High School)
  http://www.hoocher.com/literaryhistory.htm

- Patron Augustus-Client Rome (Sondra Steinbrenner, ancienthistory.about.com)
  http://ancienthistory.about.com/gi/dynamic/offsite.htm?site=http://roman%2Dempire.net/articles/article%2D010.html
  Excellent exploration of the symbols of Augustan *auctoritas*.

- Princeps: The Life of Augustus Caesar (Suzanne Cross)
  http://augustus.fws1.com/
  Recent online appreciation of Octavian/Augustus.

- Rome: Republic to Empire ("Augustus and Tiberius," Barbara F. McManus, VRoma)
  http://www.vroma.org/~bmcmanus/romanpages.html
  Illustrated synopsis of the historical background of Augustan rule.

# Online Resources for Spot Questions
## Catullus
### *Clodia/Lesbia*

- Feminae Romanae: The Women of Ancient Rome (Suzanne Cross)
  http://dominae.fws1.com/Influence/Clodia/Index.html

- Resources for a college course "Women in the Roman World" (David Noy, Univ. Wales)
  http://www.lamp.ac.uk/-noy/roman4.htm
  Clodia and Cicero's *Pro Caelio*.

- VRoma (Henry Walker, Bates College)
  http://www.vroma.org/-hwalker/VRomaCatullus/Clodia.html
  One classicist's outline of the "Lesbia Cycle," cross-linked to his texts and translations.

- Wikipedia hypertext article on Clodia
  http://en.wikipedia.org/wiki/Clodia

## Cicero
### *Roman Oratory*

- Cicero on the Genres of Rhetoric (translated by John F. Tinkler, Towson State Univ.)
  http://www.towson.edu/-tinkler/reader/cicero.html
  Relevant excerpts on the nature of Roman oratory, translated from Cicero's oratorical works.

- Cicero's *Pro Archia Poeta*: Literature and the Foundations of a Legal Education (Kevin Patrick, Univ. Georgia)
  http://www.uga.edu/juro/2004/patrick2.htm
  Political and literary context of the speech, with notes and bibliography.

- Corax: The Crow's Nest (Thomas J. Kinney, Univ. Arizona)
  http://www.u.arizona.edu/-tkinney/resources/rhetoric.html#history
  A Web site devoted to ancient rhetoric, including elements, theory, and history.

- Roman Orator (Smith's *A Dictionary of Greek and Roman Antiquities* in Bill Thayer's Lacus Curtius Web site)
  http://penelope.uchicago.edu/Thayer/E/Roman/Texts/secondary/SMIG-RA*/Orator.html
  The making and function of a good orator; the status of oratory as a profession.

- Roman Oratory (Joseph T. Richardson, The Society for Ancient Languages)
  http://www.uah.edu/student_life/organizations/SAL/texts/misc/romanora.html
  Roman oratory to the time of Cicero; discussion of the five canons for the preparation for and delivery of a good speech in Latin.

- Roman Oratory (Kelly A. MacFarlane, Univ. Alberta)
  http://www.ualberta.ca/~kmacfarl/CLASS_104/10.Oratory.html
  Includes methods of oratory: *controversiae* and *suasoriae*.

- Wikipedia: Rhetoric-Roman Rhetoricians
  http://en.wikipedia.org/wiki/Rhetoric

### Cicero's Philosophical Writings

- Cicero (The Internet Encyclopedia of Philosophy, Edward Clayton, Central Michigan Univ.)
  http://www.utm.edu/research/iep/c/cicero.htm
  On Cicero's philosophical works, his relationship to various schools of ancient philosophy, plus a brief synopsis of *De Amicitia*.

## Horace

See "The Augustan Age," above.

## Ovid

### *Myth in the* Metamorphoses

- Encyclopedia Mythica
  http://www.pantheon.org/mythica.html
  Compendium of articles on various subjects pertaining to ancient myth.

- Gods, Heroes, and Myth (Nikki Burke)
  http://www.gods-heros-myth.com/godpages/atlas.html
  Well-organized quick-studies of Greek, Roman, and Norse deities

- Greek Mythology Link (Carlos Parada)
  http://homepage.mac.com/cparada/GML/
  Wonderful resources for a variety of topics on Greek myth. See especially
  http://homepage.mac.com/cparada/GML/METAMORPHOSES.html
  Page from Greek Mythology Link, tracking changes that are described in ancient literature "character or thing turned into" plus a brief description and literary source.

- Mythology in Western Art (Project Mythmedia, Ora Zehavi and Sonia Klinger, Univ. Haifa)
  http://lib.haifa.ac.il/www/art/mythology_westart.html
  Collection of art images relating to classical myth.

- The Olympian Gods (Classical Myth: The Ancient Sources, Laurel Bowman)
  http://web.uvic.ca/grs/bowman/myth/gods.html
  Images and text sources for the Olympian gods.

# Webliography on Figures of Speech

## General Web Sites

- Figures of Speech (T. Abney, teacher's web site)
  http://abney.homestead.com/files/aeneid/tropedefinitioncards.htm
  Clickable exercise asking for definitions of 22 figures.

- Figures of Speech (Bruce M. Johnson, teacher's web site)
  http://www.hoocher.com/figuresofspeech.htm
  Definitions of required figures, with examples from Catullus and the *Aeneid.*

- A Glossary of Rhetorical Terms with Examples (Ross Scaife, Univ. Kentucky)
  http://www.uky.edu/AS/Classics/rhetoric.html
  Twenty-six of the 34 figures required by the College Board are found here, with English and Latin examples.

- Interpreting Poetry (Joan Johnige, Kentucky Educational Television)
  http://www.dl.ket.org/latinlit/carmina/index.htm
  Definitions with examples of figures from Catullus and Horace.

- Literary Devices (Jerard White, teacher's web site)
  http://www.fralibrary.com/teachers/white/literary_devices.htm
  Figures are designated as AP or non-AP; includes the 34 for AP, plus anastrophe, caesura, elision, framing, the golden line, hiatus, and rhetorical question.

- Mr. Prueter's Literary Devices (teacher's web site)
  http://www.prueter.org/bill/literarydevices.html
  English and Latin examples.

- *Quia* java games (Ruth Sameth)
  http://www.quia.com/jg/11339.html
  Concentration, flashcards, matching, word search on figures of speech. See also http://www.quia.com/hm/80390.html

- Silvae Rhetoricae (Gideon O. Burton, Brigham Young University)
  http://humanities.byu.edu/rhetoric/Figures/Figures-Overview.htm
  Contains a useful search engine (Search the Forest); English and Latin examples.

## The following sites are by and for English students, but are also useful to the Latin student.

- Literary Terms (maintained by students in Ted Nellen's high school Cyber English class)
  http://www.tnellen.com/cybereng/lit_terms/

- Mrs. Dowling's Literature Terms
  http://www.kidskonnect.com/FigurativeLanguage/FigurativeLanguage-Home.html

- Virtual Salt: A Handbook of Rhetorical Devices (Robert A. Harris)
  http://www.virtualsalt.com/rhetoric.htm
  Thoroughgoing list, with numerous examples in English and a self-test. Produced by a writer.

## Web Sites for Figures of Speech in AP Latin

### Vergil

- AP Vergil's *Aeneid* (Tim Abney, teacher's web site)
  http://abney.homestead.com/aeneid.html
  Click-and-drag matching exercises for many figures found in the required Books of the *Aeneid*; a valuable resource! See also,
  http://abney.homestead.com/files/aeneid/aeneid2tropes6b1flashcards.htm
  Flashcards for figures in the *Aeneid*; 50 items drawn from entire *Aeneid*.

### Catullus

- Figures of Speech (T. Abney, teacher's web site)
  http://abney.homestead.com/files/catullus/catullustropeflashcards1.htm
  Flashcards for figures in Poems 64, 65, 68, 69, 76, 77, 85, 109, 116.

### Cicero

- Test: Figures of Speech in Cicero (Robert Patrick)
  http://www.quia.com/quiz/259156.html
  Twenty-five clickable multiple-choice questions on Cicero's favorites (you will receive a score, but not the correct answers).

### Horace

- The World of Horace's *Odes* (Ortwin Knorr)
  http://www.willamette.edu/cla/classics/faculty/knorr/horace/Horace_c.1.1.html
  This promises to be a useful site, but it is still under construction. Good for *Odes* 1.1.

### Ovid

- Ovid (Tim Abney, teacher's web site)
  http://abney.homestead.com/ovid1.html
  Click-and-drag matching activities on figures from the *Amores* and from each of the five required myths of the *Metamorphoses*.

# Webliography for Meter and Scansion

- Examples of Greek and Latin Meters in English Verse (Rosemary Wright)
  http://www.cornellcollege.edu/classical_studies/meters.shtml
  An example of dactylic hexameter from English verse.

- *Hexametrica*: An Introduction to Latin Hexameter Verse (Dan Curley, Skidmore College)
  http://www.skidmore.edu/academics/classics/courses/metrica/scansion.html
  Thorough-going presentation of all aspects of the hexameter line, geared toward students of Vergil.

- Latin Poetic Meter (Ben Johnson, Hampden Academy, Hampden, ME)
  http://www.ha.sad22.us/BenJohnson/scansion.html
  A one-page quick-study of hexameter and elegiac.

- Meter and Scansion (Iona College)
  http://www.iona.edu/latin/meter.html
  Hexameter, elegiac, and Sapphic as background for the Catullus poems on the Web site.

- Scansion (Kentucky Educational Television)
  http://www.dl.ket.org/latinlit/carmina/scansion/index.htm
  Good for rules about elision and for poetic terms.

- Scansion of Latin Poetry (Marc Moskowitz, via N.S.Gill)
  http://ancienthistory.about.com/od/scansion1
  The basic rules for scansion.

- Tutor.BestLatin.net (Laura Gibbs, under construction)
  http://tutor.bestlatin.net/about/meter_dachex.htm
  Includes audio examples of hexameter from Aesop's fables and from Theobaldus, Avianus, and others, in Latin. Also, elegiac couplet and Sapphic stanza. A fun site, including *Bestiaria Latina* with a Legend of the Day, *Mythologiae* (Ritchie's *Fabulae Faciles*), *Biblia Vulgata*, and *Legenda Aurea* (the Lives of the Saints).

- *Viva Voce* – Roman Poetry Recited (V. Nedeljkovic, University of Belgrade)
  http://dekart.f.bg.ac.yu/~vnedeljk/VV
  Several passages of hexameters from Vergil and Juvenal read aloud.

# Latin Passages
# Used in this Book

Locations are cited by chapter or Practice Exam. Practice Exam passages are in boldface.

**VMC 1** = Vergil Multiple-Choice Section, Practice Test 1; **VFR 1** = Vergil Free-Response Section, Practice Test 1, **LFR** = Literature Free Response Section, etc.

## Vergil
### Book 1
> lines 50–57 (Chapter 6: Translation)
>
> 81–91 (Chapter 10: Figures of Speech)
>
> 102–7 (Chapter 10: Figures of Speech)
>
> **276–82 (Free Response, Practice Test 1, = VFR 1)**
>
> **459–65 and 483–87 (VFR 2)**

### Book 2
> 13–17 (Chapter 6: Translation)
>
> 209–11 (Chapter 10: Figures of Speech)
>
> **486–92 (VFR 2)**
>
> **776–84 (VFR 1)**

### Book 4
> **23–29 (VFR 1)**
>
> **45–51 (VFR 2)**
>
> 381–87 (Chapter 6: Translation)
>
> **665–71 (VFR 2)**

### Book 6
> 83–94 (VFR 1)
>
> 469–74 (VFR 1)
>
> 868–74 and 882–86 (VMC 1)

**Book 10**

> **466–72 (VFR 1)**
>
> 501–9 (Chapter 6: Translation)

**Book 12**

> 791–99 (Chapter 10: Figures of Speech)
>
> 818–28 (Chapter 4: Multiple-Choice)
>
> **913–18 (VFR 2)**
>
> **938–49 (VMC 2)**

## Catullus

**Poem 4 (LFR 1)**

Poem 14a.12–23 (Chapter 4: Multiple-Choice)

**Poem 22.1–11 (LMC 2)**

**Poem 30.1–6 (LFR 1)**

**Poem 36.1–11, 16–20 (LFR 2)**

Poem 44 (Chapter 6: Translation)

Poem 49 (Chapter 7: Essays)

**Poem 51.1–12 (LFR 2)**

**Poem 64.91–95 and 97–98 (LFR 2)**

**Poem 64. 149–57 (LFR 1)**

**Poem 65.1–11 (LMC 1)**

Poem 68.20–24 (Chapter 10: Figures of Speech)

Poem 70 (Chapter 6: Translation)

**Poem 72 (LFR 2)**

Poem 76.17–22, 25–26 (Chapter 6: Translation)

Poem 85 (Chapter 11: Meter and Scansion)

Poem 87 (Chapter 11: Meter and Scansion)

Poem 96 (Chapter 11: Meter and Scansion)

Poem 109 (Chapter 6: Translation)

## Cicero

*Pro Archia* 1 (Nam quoad . . . ferre debemus) (Chapter 6: Translation)

*Pro Archia* 8 (Si nihil aliud . . .Heracleae esse dicunt) (Chapter 8: Background0

*Pro Archia* 12 (Quaeres a nobis . . . relaxemus) (Chapter 6: Translation)

***Pro Archia* 13 (Quare quis . . . sumpsero) (LFR 2)**

***Pro Archia* 16 (Quod si . . . rusticantur) (LFR 1)**

*Pro Archia* 18–19 (**Quare . . . moveamur**) (**LFR 1**)

*Pro Archia* 26 (**Neque . . . nominari volunt**) (**LFR 2**)

*Pro Archia* 31 (quae cum ita sint . . . esse videatur) (Chapter 8: Background)

*De Amicitia* 20 (**Est enim amicitia . . . voluptates**) (**LFR 1**)

*De Amicitia* 23 (**Cumque . . . laudabilis**) (**LFR 2**)

*De Amicitia* 100 (Virtus inquam C. Fanni . . . quaesita) (Chapter 8: Background)

*De Amicitia* 102 (Sed quoniam . . .exstincta non est) (Chapter 6: Translation)

## Horace

*Odes* **1.1.23–30 (LFR 1)**

*Odes* 1.9.17–20 (Chapter 11: Meter and Scansion)

*Odes* **1.11 (LFR 2)**

*Odes* 1.37.12–21 (Chapter 8: Background)

*Odes* 2.3.21–28 (Chapter 6: Translation)

*Odes* 2.10.1–4 (Chapter 11: Meter and Scansion)

*Odes* **3.1.9–16 (LFR 1)**

*Odes* 3.1.16 (Chapter 11: Meter and Scansion)

*Odes* 3.9.17–24 (Chapter 8: Background)

*Odes* **3.13 (LFR 2)**

*Odes* 3.13.9–16 (Chapter 10: Figures of Speech)

*Odes* 3.30–1–7 (Chapter 6: Translation)

*Odes* **4.7.1–16 (LFR 1)**

*Satires* **1.9**

> **lines 1–11 (LFR 2)**
>
> lines 60–66 (Chapter 6: Translation)
>
> lines 72–78 (Chapter 8: Background)

## Ovid

*Metamorphoses*

**Daphne and Apollo (Book 1, lines 452–567)**

> lines 466–69 (Chapter 10: Figures of Speech)
>
> lines 481–87 (Chapter 7: Essays)
>
> lines 474–80 (Chapter 6: Translation)
>
> lines 545, 547 (Chapter 11: Meter and Scansion)
>
> **lines 545–52 (LFR 1)**

**Pyramus and Thisbe (Book 4, lines 55–166)**

      lines 73–80 (Chapter 8: Background)

      **lines 128–36 (LFR 2)**

**Daedalus and Icarus (Book 8, lines 183–235)**

      **lines 210–16 (LFR 2)**

**Baucis and Philemon (Book 8, lines 616–724)**

      **lines 628–34 (LFR 1)**

      lines 684–91 (Chapter 8: Background)

**Pygmalion (Book 10, lines 238–97)**

      lines 238–46 (Chapter 6: Translation)

      lines 259–66 (Chapter 10: Figures of Speech)

*Amores*

**Book 1**

      Poem 1, lines 1–6 (Chapter 8: Background)

      **Poem 1, lines 25–30 (LFR 2)**

      Poem 9, lines 17–20 (Chapter 11: Meter and Scansion)

      Poem 12, lines 7–14 (Chapter 6: Translation)

      Poem 12, lines 7–8, 11–14, 19–28 (Chapter 10: Figures of Speech)

      **Poem 12, lines 13–20 (LFR 1)**

## Appendix III

# Latin Passages Appearing on AP Latin Exams, 2001–2006

**Vergil**

**Book 1**

lines 37–49 (long essay, 2001, cf. 12.818–28)

lines 92–101 (long essay, 2005; cf. 198–209)

lines 124–41 (long essay, 2004; cf. 4.74–89)

lines 198–209 (long essay, 2005; cf. 92–101)

lines 291–96 (short essay, 2002)

lines 378–85 (translation, 2006)

lines 450–65 (short essay, 2003)

**Book 2**

lines 10–16 (translation, 2004)

lines 201–207 (translation, 2005)

lines 237–43 (translation, 2001)

lines 289–94 (translation, 2002)

lines 560–66 (translation, 2006)

lines 768–93 (long essay, 2003)

**Book 4**

lines 20–29 (long essay, 2002; cf. 320–30)

Lines 74–89 (long essay, 2004; cf. 1.124–41)

lines 160–66 (translation, 2003)

lines 320–30 (long essay, 2002; cf. 20–29)

lines 675–85 (short essay, 2001)

**Book 6**

lines 83–94 (short essay, 2005)

lines 868–86 (long essay, 2006)

lines 893–99 (translation, 2004)

**Book 10**

> lines 450 and 453–56 (translation, 2001)
>
> lines 457–65 (short essay, 2004)
>
> lines 491–96 and 500–505 (short essay, 2006; cf. 500–505)

**Book 12**

> lines 803–809 (translation, 2003)
>
> lines 818–28 (long essay, 2001; cf. 1.37–49)
>
> lines 908–14 (translation, 2002)
>
> lines 930–36 (translation, 2005)

## Catullus

Poem 1 (long essay, 2004)

Poem 3 (long essay, 2002)

Poem 5 (short essay, 2003)

Poem 10.1–7, 14–34 (long essay, 2003)

Poem 14a.12–23 (long essay, 2005; cf. Poem 30)

Poem 30 (long essay, 2005; cf. Poem 14a.12–23)

Poem 31.7–14 (translation, 2005)

Poem 35.1–10 (translation, 2006)

Poem 40 (long essay, 2006; cf. 116)

Poem 44.6–12 (translation, 2003)

Poem 46 (translation, 2001)

Poem 51.1–12 (short essay, 2005)

Poem 69 (short essay, 2006)

Poem 70 (translation, 2004; cf. 87)

Poem 72.5–8 (short essay, 2004; cf. 85)

Poem 77 (long essay, 2001; cf. 84)

Poem 83 (short essay, 2002)

Poem 84 (long essay, 2001; cf. 77)

Poem 85 (short essay, 2004; cf. 72.5–8)

Poem 86 (short essay, 2001)

Poem 87 (translation, 2004; cf. 70)

Poem 116 (long essay, 2006; cf. 40)

## Horace

### *Odes*

#### Book 1

Ode 1, lines 3–10 (spot, 2006)

Ode 9, lines 1–9 (translation, 2005)

Ode 11 (short essay, 2001)

Ode 13.1–8 (translation, 2004)

Ode 22, lines 17–24 (translation, 2003)

Ode 23 (spot, 2005)

Ode 24, lines 3–10 (spot, 2002)

#### Book 2

Ode 3, lines 13–20 (translation, 2001)

Ode 7, line 1–12 (spot, 2004)

Ode 10, lines 1–8 and 21–24 (short essay, 2002)

#### Book 3

Ode 1, lines 5–16 (short essay, 2005)

Ode 1, lines 37–46 (translation, 2006)

Ode 9, lines 9–24 (short essay, 2003)

Ode 13, lines 9–16 (translation, 2002)

#### Book 4

Ode 7, lines 17–28 (spot, 2001)

### *Satires* 1.9

lines 35–41 (spot, 2003)

lines 48–60 (short essay, 2004)

lines 60–68 (short essay, 2006)

## Ovid

### Metamorphoses

#### Daphne and Apollo (Book 1, lines 452–567)

lines 481–89 (spot, 2004)

lines 553–67 (short essay, 2001)

#### Pyramus and Thisbe (Book 4, lines 55–166)

lines 55–62 (translation, 2005)

lines 71–80 (short essay, 2002)

lines 147–57 (short essay, 2006)

**Daedalus and Icarus (Book 8, lines 183–235)**

       lines 183–89 (translation, 2003)

       lines 203–13 (short essay, 2005)

       lines 223–28 (translation, 2002)

**Baucis and Philemon (Book 8, lines 616–724)**

       lines 631–36 (short essay, 2004; cf. 712–30)

       lines 681–86 (translation, 2001)

       lines 712–30 (short essay, 2004; cf. 631–36)

**Pygmalion (Book 10, lines 238–97)**

       lines 238–46 (spot, 2003)

*Amores*

**Book 1**

       Poem 1, lines 5–6 and 19–27 (short essay, 2003)

       Poem 3, lines 5–12 (spot, 2001)

       Poem 9, lines 17–24 (spot, 2002)

       Poem 9, lines 25–32 (translation, 2006)

       Poem 11, lines 11–15 (translation, 2004)

       Poem 12, lines 1–7 (spot, 2006)

**Book 3**

       Poem 15, lines 1–7 (spot, 2005)

# AP LATIN

## Index

# Index

# REA's Test Preps
# The Best in Test Preparation

- REA "Test Preps" are **far more** comprehensive than any other test preparation series
- Each book contains up to **eight** full-length practice tests based on the most recent exams
- **Every** type of question likely to be given on the exams is included
- Answers are accompanied by **full** and **detailed** explanations

*REA publishes over 70 Test Preparation volumes in several series. They include:*

**Advanced Placement Exams (APs)**
Biology
Calculus AB & Calculus BC
Chemistry
Economics
English Language & Composition
English Literature & Composition
European History
French
Government & Politics
Physics B & C
Psychology
Spanish Language
Statistics
United States History
World History

**College-Level Examination Program (CLEP)**
Analyzing and Interpreting Literature
College Algebra
Freshman College Composition
General Examinations
General Examinations Review
History of the United States I
History of the United States II
Human Growth and Development
Introductory Sociology
Principles of Marketing
Spanish

**SAT Subject Tests**
Biology E/M
Chemistry
English Language Proficiency Test
French
German

**SAT Subject Tests (cont'd)**
Literature
Mathematics Level 1, 2
Physics
Spanish
United States History

**Graduate Record Exams (GREs)**
Biology
Chemistry
Computer Science
General
Literature in English
Mathematics
Physics
Psychology

**ACT** - ACT Assessment

**ASVAB** - Armed Services Vocational Aptitude Battery

**CBEST** - California Basic Educational Skills Test

**CDL** - Commercial Driver License Exam

**CLAST** - College Level Academic Skills Test

**COOP & HSPT** - Catholic High School Admission Tests

**ELM** - California State University Entry Level Mathematics Exam

**FE (EIT)** - Fundamentals of Engineering Exams - For both AM & PM Exams

**FTCE** - Florida Teacher Certification Exam

**GED** - High School Equivalency Diploma Exam (U.S. & Canadian editions)

**GMAT** - Graduate Management Admission Test

**LSAT** - Law School Admission Test

**MAT** - Miller Analogies Test

**MCAT** - Medical College Admission Test

**MTEL** - Massachusetts Tests for Educator Licensure

**NJ HSPA** - New Jersey High School Proficiency Assessment

**NYSTCE: LAST & ATS-W** - New York State Teacher Certification

**PLT** - Principles of Learning & Teaching Tests

**PPST** - Pre-Professional Skills Tests

**PSAT / NMSQT**

**SAT**

**TExES** - Texas Examinations of Educator Standards

**THEA** - Texas Higher Education Assessment

**TOEFL** - Test of English as a Foreign Language

**TOEIC** - Test of English for International Communication

**USMLE Steps 1,2,3** - U.S. Medical Licensing Exams

**U.S. Postal Exams 460 & 470**

---

## *Research & Education Association*
61 Ethel Road W., Piscataway, NJ 08854
Phone: (732) 819-8880    **website: www.rea.com**

**Please send me more information about your Test Prep books.**

Name _____

Address _____

City _____ State _____ Zip _____

# REA's Test Prep Books Are The Best!
## (a sample of the <u>hundreds of letters</u> REA receives each year)

*(more on front page)*